FØR: 158,-
NÅ°: 85,-

FØR: 158,-
NÅ°: 85,-

The Marshall Cavendish Illustrated Encyclopedia of
HOW THE BODY WORKS

The Marshall Cavendish Illustrated Encyclopedia of
HOW THE BODY WORKS

Marshall Cavendish London & New York

Academic Advisors:
Professor Ian MacDonald, M.D., D.Sc., F.L., Biol.,
Professor of Applied Physiology,
Guy's Hospital Medical School,
London.

Dr. F.A. Chandra, B.Sc., M.B., B.S., Ph.D.,
Advisor in Clinical Physiology.

Editors:
Michael Bisacre
Richard Carlisle
Deborah Robertson
John Ruck

Published by Marshall Cavendish Books Ltd.,
58 Old Compton Street, London W1V 5PA.

© Marshall Cavendish Limited 1975, 1976, 1977, 1979

First printing: 1979

Printed in Great Britain by Severn Valley Press Limited

ISBN 0 85685 742 4

Introduction

The Illustrated Encyclopedia of How the Body Works
gives a clear picture of the structure of the human anatomy
as well as supplying information on the multiple aspects
of modern medical science.
Part I examines human physiology in detail, beginning with
the five senses through which we experience the world, and
moving on to the more complex workings of the nervous
system and the brain. All the major body systems – circulation,
respiration, digestion, excretion, reproduction are looked at closely,
together with the associated organs.
In Part II this knowledge is related to the stages of
human development, from foetus to adult, explaining how and when
the various senses, skills and body functions develop.
A variety of topics relating to the health of body and mind are
examined. How do different kinds of food or exercise affect
the body? What do we know about dream activity
and biorhythms? How should drugs be used? There are entries on
the science of psychology, its methods of analysis, and discoveries
concerning the human mind.
In addition there are many original illustrations
and diagrams which help to make this vast range of information
more readily accessible. The articles, researched from every
branch of medical science, work in partnership with these
pictures to present a really comprehensive account of human
biology and medical science.

Contents

Part I The Human Machine

Part II Development and Behaviour

Part I

The Human Machine

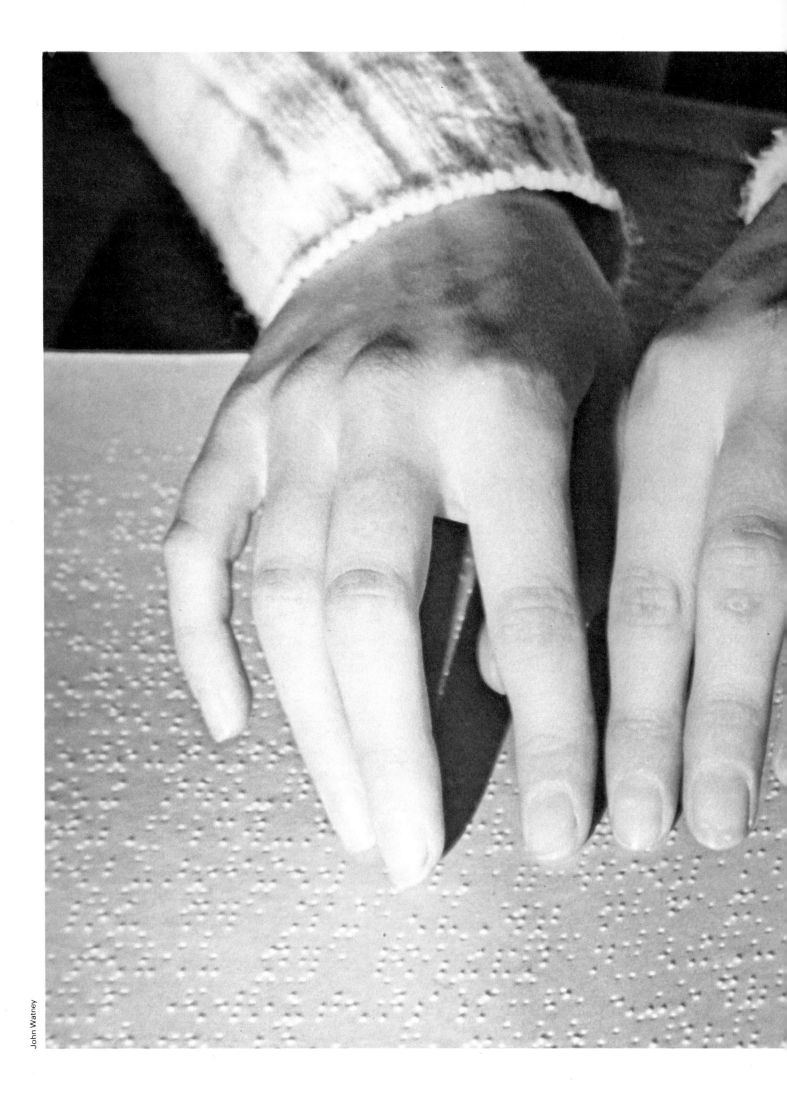

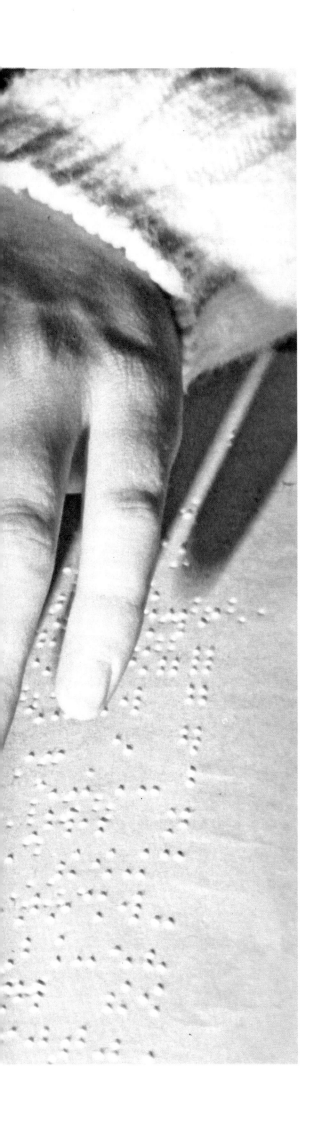

Chapter 1
The Senses

As one sense is lost others develop new
finesse to compensate. Awareness
through the fingertips enables many
blind readers to interpret up to 100
words a minute.

Sight

Man depends on sight more than upon any other sense to supply information about his environment. His upright posture, the mobility of his eyes and head and stereoscopic vision—vision from the two slightly different angles of the eyes—give man a panoramic view of the world, containing information on depth, distance, dimension and movement. Further, the adaptability of the eye and its sensitivity to colours and contours enables man to perform close and detailed tasks.

The eye has a highly complex structure. The *cornea,* the bulge at the front, is a transparent window that lets light rays into the eye and bends, or refracts, them. A flat, circular coloured membrane, the *iris,* lies behind the cornea and gives the eyes their characteristic colours. Between the cornea and the iris is a small compartment containing a clear fluid, the *aqueous humour,* which nourishes the cornea.

The iris governs the size of the *pupil,* a small hole in its centre that regulates the amount of light entering the eye. The *crystalline lens,* lying behind the pupil, further refracts the light to focus a sharp image on the *retina.* This thin, nerve-laden screen lining the back of the eye, transforms light energy into electrical messages that are transmitted to the brain by the *optic nerve* which runs from the back of the eye. A large compartment, containing a viscous fluid called the *vitreous humour,* lies between the lens and the retina and makes up most of the volume of the eyeball.

The case of the eyeball, apart from the transparent cornea at the front, is made from tough, white fibrous tissue called the *sclera.* The sclera contains fine blood vessels and when the eye is irritated, say by dust or disease, the blood vessels become enlarged and the 'white' of the eye appears pink or bloodshot.

Light and sight
Some light is always necessary for seeing. The human eye cannot perceive the image of an object unless it is carried by light rays. A luminous source, such as a candle, may either send light directly to the eye, or the rays may bounce off the surface of an object before reaching the eye.

Light rays, which normally travel in straight lines through air, are refracted or change direction slightly when they enter a denser medium such as water or glass. The eye uses refraction to focus the light rays it receives from the object on to the retina.

Light first passes through the cornea and, as this is denser than air, the rays are refracted. This begins the process of focussing an image on to the retina. Since the cornea bends the light rays more than any other part of the eye, it is referred to as the coarse focus.

The aqueous humour has hardly any effect on the light rays as it is of a similar density to the cornea. It is renewed every four hours but may occasionally have small impurities in it which cast shadows on the retina, creating 'spots before the eyes'. Pressure on the eyeball has a similar effect of causing 12 coloured patterns. These arise because

Left: A light ray passing from air into a denser medium such as glass is bent or refracted. A light ray entering the eye is refracted slightly by the cornea. This starts the process of focussing the image on to the retina. The aqueous humour lying behind the cornea continues the process, which is completed by the lens.

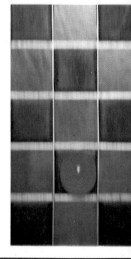

Right: Astigmatism is a common visual defect caused by an imperfectly curved cornea. It results in blurred vision. Light rays entering the eye are refracted to a greater degree in either the horizontal or vertical plane. Astigmatism is corrected by lenses that compress the image in the direction opposite to that of the distortion.

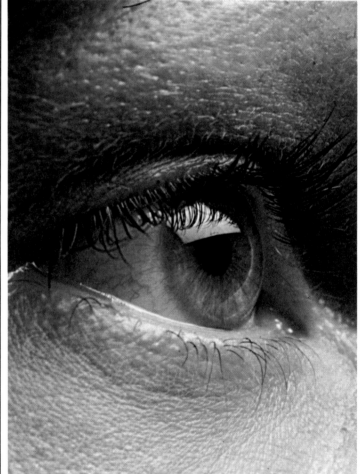

Left: Several features protect the eye.

Eyebrows prevent sweat running into the eye.

Eyelashes keep the eye clean and protect it from glare. Each eye has about 200 lashes and each lasts between three and five months.

Eyelids sweep dirt from the surface of the eye, protect it from injury and help distribute tear fluid.

Tears are sterile and constantly bathe the front of the eye and its thin, protective covering membrane, the *conjunctiva.* Though tear flow is continual, only about $\frac{1}{2}$ to $\frac{3}{4}$ of a gram of fluid is produced per day. This is drained off through a small duct leading from the inner corner of the lower eyelid and into the nose. Sometimes mucus and dust collect as 'sleep' in the inner corner of the eye.

The *eyeball,* together with the muscles that control eye movement, blood vessels, nerves and the lacrimal gland are lodged in a bony socket in the skull. The socket is lined with fat and has a volume five times as great as that of the eyeball.

Right: The structure of the eye.

NEAR SIGHT

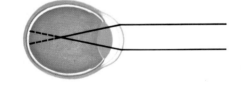
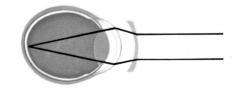

Top left and right: Short-sightedness or *myopia* occurs when the light rays from a distant object are focussed in front of the retina. If the eyeball is too long from front to back, or if the lens provides too great a degree of refraction, the focussed image falls short of the retina. Adolescents sometimes suffer from short-sightedness, as the eyeball becomes excessively long during uneven body growth.

Bottom left: Spectacles with concave glass lenses are worn to correct short sight. The lenses diverge the rays slightly so that they have to travel further through the eyeball and are focussed exactly on the retina.

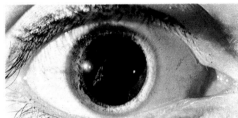

the eye can only interpret stimulation in terms of 'visual' signals.

Normally the aqueous humour is secreted behind the iris, circulates through the pupil and filters out between the iris and the cornea. If, however, the fluid is secreted faster than it can be reabsorbed into the veins, pressure rises and a condition known as *glaucoma* develops. If untreated, this will cause damage to the optic nerve fibres, and a gradual restriction of visual field.

Where the cause of this condition can be found, it is usually obstruction to the outlet of fluid, rather than excessive production of the aqueous humour. As a result, drugs can often be used to reduce the pressure—for example, by constricting the pupil and so relieving congestion of the fluid outlets.

Control of the amount of light entering the eye is essential if the retinal image is not to be blurred. The pupil determines the amount of light let in as a result of the contraction and expansion of the muscles of the iris. This control is particularly important for detailed work in which a special sharpness or *acuity* of vision is vital. In close work, such as reading, the pupil shrinks in order to sharpen the focus by limiting the access of light rays from a single point on the object. People who spend much of their time doing intricate work, such as artists, often look at their work through half-closed eyes to 'distance' it. Again, this cuts down the amount of light entering the eyes so that they see the shape and perspective more clearly.

Accommodation

The process of adjustment for near and distant vision is called *accommodation* and is controlled by the movement of the crystalline lens. The lens of the eye, although it resembles a piece of curved glass, differs from glass in that it does not have a uniform structure, but consists of 2,000 thin layers of tissue. As the light rays pass through each layer they are refracted to a minute degree.

The lens of the eye differs from a glass lens in another important way—it is more flexible. Whereas the lens of a camera, for example, has to be moved backwards and forwards until the correct focus is found, the lens of the eye simply changes shape.

The lens is supported by a sheath of transparent material, called the *suspensory ligament*. The eye adjusts its focus by changing the curvature or thickness of the lens. *Ciliary muscles* control the tension in the suspensory ligament which pulls the lens into different shapes. To focus on near objects, for example, the ciliary muscles contract, allowing the suspensory ligament to relax. This causes the pliable lens to become more spherical, decreasing its focal length and increasing its refractive power. Thus it is able to focus a clear image of a near object on to the retina. The pupil decreases in diameter at the same time to concentrate the light on to the central part of the lens where the accommodation changes are most marked.

For focussing on a distant object, the lens becomes flatter. Light rays from such an object are almost parallel by the time they reach the eye so there is no need for such a large degree of refraction as for the divergent rays from a near object. The lens therefore has less adjustment to

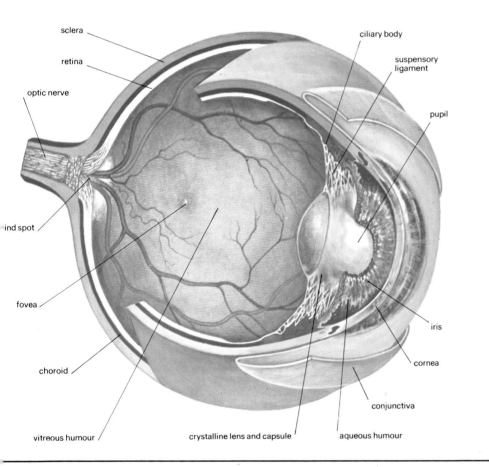

sclera
retina
optic nerve
ind spot
fovea
choroid
vitreous humour
crystalline lens and capsule
ciliary body
suspensory ligament
pupil
iris
cornea
conjunctiva
aqueous humour

FAR SIGHT

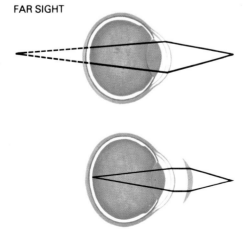

13

Left: The camera obscura, a dark room with a small hole in one wall, is like an eye. Light travelling in straight lines from a point on an object through the hole or pupil casts a sharp, inverted image on the far wall or retina. The image is upside down because the light rays cross at the aperture. The brain turns it up the right way.

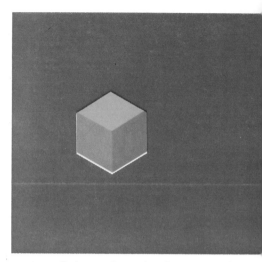

Right: To find the blind spot, hold the page at arms' length. Close the left eye and focus the right eye on the left hand object. Bring the page slowly towards you until the object on the right vanishes. Its image has fallen on the point where the optic nerve leads from the back of the eye. There are no rods or cones here.

make when the rays have passed through the cornea.

The focussing power of the lens is influenced by the eye's rate of growth and age. An eye which has reached normal maturity can focus clear images of near and distant objects. Ageing makes the lens less pliant, however, and consequently less able to adjust its shape quickly for close and distant focus. Bifocal spectacles help to correct this condition—the upper half of the lens aids distant vision, and the lower half, near vision—and compensate for the overall rigidity of the lens.

The elderly are also far more prone to *cataract,* a condition causing opacity of the lens, than the young. This often results in complete or partial blindness. Sometimes this can be alleviated by removing the damaged lens and replacing it with thick-lensed spectacles. This operation is relatively simple but the effect, restoration of sight, is dramatic.

The cavity containing the vitreous humour lies behind the lens. The fluid keeps the retina in position and maintains the spherical shape of the eyeball. The density of the vitreous humour is similar to that of the lens so it does not interfere with light passing through it.

Rods and cones

The retina, the screen on which light rays are projected, is a network of more than 130 million tightly packed fibres, covering the transparent innermost layer of the eyeball. The nerve fibres are composed of two types of light sensitive receptors, *rods* and *cones.* There are two types because man exists in two visual worlds— day and night, light and dark. The clarity of an image depends on light intensity and the angle of perception. The seven million cones operate for the detailed examination of an object in bright light; the rods are used for seeing in dim light.

The cones contain the chemical, *iodopsin,* and are sensitive to coloured light. Rods respond only to shades of black and white. They contain a chemical, *rhodopsin* or *visual purple,* allowing them to function in dim light only, when colours are much subdued and often lost completely. Bright light bleaches the chemical, reducing the sensitivity of the visual system to light. Consequently, when a person walks into a dark room from a sunny garden he is temporarily 'blinded' until the visual purple is formed again.

A mixture of cones and rods are distributed unevenly in the retina. In the centre of the retina, the *fovea* contains only cones and is used for accurate vision in bright light. This is why it is so difficult to read, for example, in a poorly lit room when the cones are not functioning efficiently.

The fovea has a limited field of view so the eyeball moves continuously to keep the image within this. There are also cones on the periphery of the retina but too few for sharp focus—they serve to alert man to movement and the eyeball shifts so that a sharp image falls on the fovea. Again this explains why it is impossible to read this page or do any detailed work out of the corner of an eye. Either the head or the eyes or both must be moved to face the object of interest before its image falls on the fovea and it comes into clear focus.

The fovea, because it contains only cones, is useless in dim light. To see an object in such light, the light rays have to fall outside the fovea and on to the area of rods. So instead of looking directly at the object under these conditions, a person tends to look to one side of it. Although this peripheral vision does not give as much clear detail about the object it does provide enough information to discern its basic outline.

Left and below: Stereo vision is vision from two slightly different angles. It is one of the means by which man perceives depth and distance. The stereoscope, a popular Victorian device, allows the viewer to see two pictures of the same scene taken from different angles, the difference corresponding to the distance between the eyes, which are set some 65mm or 2½ in. apart. Viewed through a stereoscope the picture of the couple turns from a flat photograph into a three dimensional scene. Stereo vision can be demonstrated by opening and closing each eye alternately. Near objects will seem to shift in relation to distant objects.

Right: Double vision, or *diplopia,* is usually caused by paralysis or weakness of one or more of the six muscles that control the movement of each eye. With normal vision the eyes, when viewing an object, move to such a position that the two slightly different images received fall on corresponding parts of the retina and are therefore exactly superimposed. Failure of the muscles of one eye creates an imbalance which results in one clear image overlaid with a 'ghost' image. Double vision is also a symptom of several nervous diseases and of diphtheria. A temporary state is sometimes induced by an excess of alcohol.

Colour vision

The way in which the eye distinguishes between the colours of the spectrum is not fully understood and there are several theories of the mechanism of colour vision. Currently, the most widely accepted theory that explains most of the facts is the Young-Helmholtz theory, the basis of which was laid in 1801 by the English physician and physicist, Thomas Young. It was developed in the mid-nineteenth century by the German scientist, Hermann von Helmholtz.

According to this theory, there are three types of cones, each of which is sensitive to either red, green or blue light, the three primary colours. Each type of cone has its own visual pigment, equivalent to the visual purple of the rods. Coloured light excites various proportions of the three types of cones and in this way, intermediate colours, combinations of the primary colours—are detected. Green light, for example, stimulates only green-sensitive cones, while yellow light stimulates both red and green units in equal amounts, producing the effect of yellow.

A similar process occurs in a colour television receiver. Pictures on a colour television screen are composed of thous-

Above and below: In the seventeenth century Sir Isaac Newton discovered that white light was composed of colours. Passing a narrow beam of light through a prism produced a spectrum of colours at the other side —starting with red at one end and going through orange, yellow, green, blue and indigo to violet at the other.

Light is the only source of colour and objects assume their colour because they absorb some of the colours of the spectrum and reflect others. A red rose chiefly reflects red rays and it is these which enter the eye and give the concept of redness. White surfaces reflect all the colours of the spectrum.

ands of minute dots, colour coded to appear in the correct patterns. In a similar way, the mosaic of cones on the retina sorts out the colour distribution in the image by reacting in differing degrees of sensitivity to light rays.

The German physiologist, Ewald Hering, challenged the Young-Helmholtz theory. His opponent-process theory holds that there are three pairs of sensory reaction—black-white, red-green and yellow-blue. No part of the last two pairs can be active at the same time though black and white can operate together, to allow perception of grey shades. Recent research suggests that both main theories of colour vision have validity.

Colour blindness, the inability to distinguish between certain colours, is a congenital abnormality which affects about six per cent of males and one per cent of females. In red-green colour blindness, which is the most common defect, a person is unable to tell the difference between red and green. It is not that red looks green or green looks red but that both look grey, blue or yellowish depending on the amount of the blue and yellow in the light. Exactly what goes wrong in the colour vision mechanism to make someone colour blind is not clear.

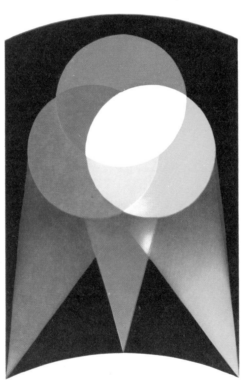

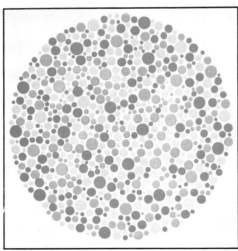

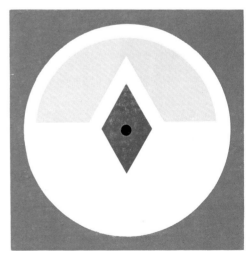

Left: What number do you see? People with normal colour vision perceive three basic colours—red, green and blue—and see the number 74. Individuals with red-green colour blindness, the most common type, cannot tell red from green and see the number 21. Totally colour blind people see no number.

Above: Focus on the dot for 20 seconds and then look at a white surface. Because red and green and blue and yellow share the same colour coding mechanism, and the removal of one stimulus temporarily triggers the other, an after image will appear, showing the other of the paired colours.

Taste and Smell

Ever since man first stood up on his hind legs and lifted his nose from the ground his sense of smell and the associated sense of taste have become relatively less important to his survival than they are to other animals. Increasingly he has come to rely on his sight, hearing and touch to provide information about his surroundings. Consequently taste and smell tend to be the least developed and most neglected of the human senses, reserved almost exclusively for the selection and appreciation of food and drink.

Taste and smell are both chemical senses. Unlike the eyes that are stimulated by light or the hearing mechanism that is excited by sound waves, the senses of taste and smell are triggered by the chemical content of substances in the environment. Chemical particles are picked up by receptor sites in the mouth and nose respectively and converted into nerve impulses for conduction to the brain.

Exciting the taste buds

The sense of taste is the least versatile of the five human senses, being strictly limited in the range and potential of its discoveries. In fact the tongue is able to detect only four 'basic' tastes. It can tell the difference between the sourness of lemon juice, the sweetness of syrup, the bitterness of coffee and the saltiness of bacon. There is no taste category for 'savoury' as such, for example, which is used to describe a multitude of different foods. Basically the impression of 'savoury' depends on the relative proportions and combinations of the four 'basic' tastes.

The sense of taste depends on the stimulation of taste receptors on the tongue. In order to be tasted the chemicals of the food must be in liquid form. Put a dry piece of food into a dry mouth and there is very little sensation of taste. Particles of dry food have to be dissolved in saliva before they can be detected by the taste buds, the organs of taste. Salt is picked up very quickly because it is highly soluble in water and rapidly dissolves in the saliva. More complex substances take slightly longer to dissolve and are therefore not picked up as quickly.

Taste buds are buried in shallow pits on the tip, sides and back of the upper surface of the tongue. Children usually have more taste buds than adults and consequently have a more highly developed sense of taste. Some of their taste buds are also distributed in the lining and roof of the mouth, cheeks and throat.

Although a particular food probably tastes roughly the same to most people, there are a few who suffer from taste 'blindness' to certain substances. A simple test with a chemical called phenylthiocarbimide (PTC) distinguishes between 'tasters', who detect a bitter taste, and 'non-tasters', for whom the liquid is tasteless. This ability or inability to detect PTC seems to run in families and therefore appears to be inherited. Such differences in the personal experience of tastes may well exist for other substances.

The combination of all the information received by the brain from the mouth about the nature of the food influences the way in which the brain interprets its chemical taste. Hot foods often taste different when they are cold and tough meat seems to have less taste than a tender cut. This is not because the taste buds react any differently to the chemicals in the food but because other sensory receptors in the mouth for temperature and touch are stimulated in different ways.

Confusion often arises between the detection of taste by the taste buds and the stimulation of temperature, pressure and pain receptors in the mouth. Peppermint, for example, 'tastes' cool because it excites temperature receptors on the tongue. In the same way, certain spices like curry and ginger 'taste' hot because they cause a burning sensation by stimulating the pain nerve endings. Curry paste has a similar effect if it is applied to soft skin on other sensitive parts of the body.

Touch and pressure receptors provide information about the texture of a food, whether it is crisp or creamy, hard or soft. The ears detect what sound it makes as it is chewed in the mouth. The jaw muscles used for chewing report on how much chewing it needs. The eyes report on the food's colour and presentation.

Colour and appearance of the food are two very important components of taste appreciation. Most people find it impossible, for example, to tell the difference between grapefruit and orange juice if they are blindfolded before the test and unable to see the different colours of the two liquids.

By far the greatest influence on the sense of taste is the sense of smell itself. What

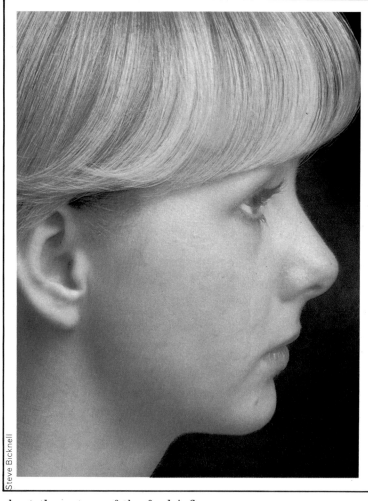

Steve Bicknell

Air flows up the nostrils into two chambers, the nasal cavities, behind the nose. The nasal cavities are lined with a thick mucous membrane which is richly supplied with blood vessels, nerves and glands. This nerve-laden lining is extremely sensitive to pain. The blood vessels of the nose can become dilated during menstruation and pregnancy, causing the distortion of the sense of smell and the craving for unusual foods that sometimes develops during pregnancy. It is also one of these blood vessels that ruptures during a nose bleed. Glands in the mucous membrane secrete the mucus that keeps the lining of the nasal cavities moist. Over-activity of these glands results in excessive mucus production that can block the nose. The smell-detecting part of the lining of the nose is called the olfactory area. Tucked away in two small pits or olfactory clefts towards the roof of the nasal cavities, each patch covers about 2.5 sq cm (1 sq in) on either side. As air passes up the nose and into the nasal cavities it is warmed and moistened. Some of it is then deflected up over the olfactory area by the three bony turbinate plates on the walls of the chamber. Before an odour can be smelled it must be dissolved in the fluids coating the lining of the nasal cavity.

Right: The tongue is covered with tiny taste detectors, taste buds, which are buried in its surface. Food placed in the mouth dissolves in saliva and then washes over the taste buds, each of which is sensitive to one of the four basic tastes — bitter, sweet, salt and sour. Although taste buds sensitive to each are scattered all over the tongue, those sensitive to one particular taste tend to be concentrated in separate regions which can be mapped.

Bitter: The bitterness of black coffee, beer or the quinine in tonic water is chiefly detected at the back of the tongue. These liquids only really taste bitter when they hit the back of the throat as they are swallowed. Sweet: Sweetness is largely picked up by the tip of the tongue. Sipping sherry or licking a lollipop effectively concentrates their sugary sweetness on the tip of the tongue. A sugar lump placed in the centre of the tongue tastes far less sweet than if it is tested with the tip. Salt: Sensitivity to the saltiness of salted peanuts or bacon is greatest on the tip of the tongue. Salt dissolves quickly on the tongue and is almost instantly recognizable. Sour: Sourness is a characteristic of all acids such as the citric acid in grapefruit or acetic acid in vinegar and is mostly picked up by the sides of the tongue.

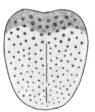

bitter

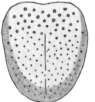

sweet

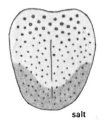

salt

sour

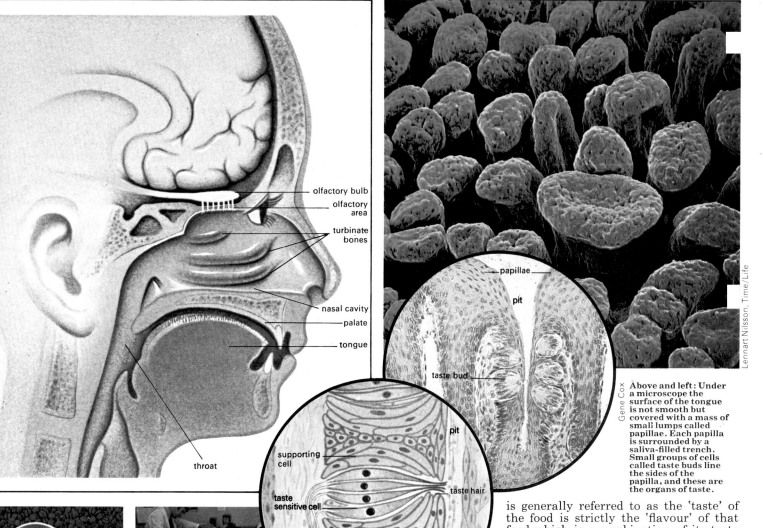

olfactory bulb

olfactory area

turbinate bones

nasal cavity

palate

tongue

throat

papillae

pit

taste bud

supporting cell

taste sensitive cell

nerve fibre

pit

taste hair

Above and left: Under a microscope the surface of the tongue is not smooth but covered with a mass of small lumps called papillae. Each papilla is surrounded by a saliva-filled trench. Small groups of cells called taste buds line the sides of the papilla, and these are the organs of taste.

Gene Cox

Lennart Nilsson, Time/Life

Above: Each taste-sensitive cell in the taste bud ends in a hair-like microvillus. These project through a tiny pore into the saliva-filled trench. The microvilli may be pierced with tiny holes, each plugged with protein. This reacts with the taste chemical and triggers a message to the brain.

Syndication International

Above: Using his highly-developed senses of taste and smell a professional tea taster can distinguish between many subtle blends of teas.

Right: Smells reach the smell-sensitive regions of the nose by two routes. During normal breathing most air passes straight through the nose into the wind pipe. Sniffing helps to break up the airflow, sending eddies of smell-laden air over the olfactory region, thus increasing the sense of smell. Vapours from food in the mouth can also escape via the throat into the nasal cavities. Smell is thus an important element in the appreciation of the flavour of food.

Gordon Roberton

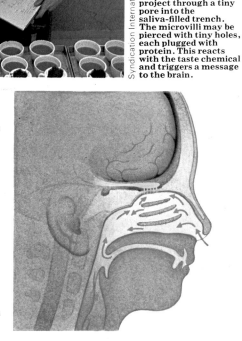

is generally referred to as the 'taste' of the food is strictly the 'flavour' of that food which is a combination of its taste and smell. The sense of taste provides the basic background information about the food while the sense of smell adds all the subtle elaborations. In practice it is very rare to taste something without smelling it as well, because the mouth and nose are positioned so close together on the face and linked by an air passage up the back of the throat.

Taste or smell?

The relationship between the senses of taste and smell is dramatically highlighted during a heavy cold when the nose becomes blocked. Food tends to lose much of its taste at such times because vapours from the food are unable to travel up the nose to the smell-sensitive regions of the nasal cavities. In the same way it is almost impossible to tell the difference between finely-grated apple, potato or onion on the tongue without chewing it, if your eyes are closed and your nose is blocked. Chewing the food would agitate some vapours up the back passage to the nose and hence to the olfactory region where they would be recognized as onion, potato or apple. On the tongue all taste slightly sweet.

A simple game with food mixtures illustrates how many different clues are used to identify a food. Three or four different foods are mixed together. Then someone is blindfolded, given a spoonful of the mixture and asked to name its constituents. The right answers are usually only reached after the food has been thoroughly tested and played with in the mouth.

Mixtures of foods also raise the question of the influence of one food's taste on that of another food. Sweet foods, for example, often tend to taste less sweet if eaten after some other sweet food. It appears that the taste buds get used to tasting sweetness and need a short break before they are able to pick it up again at full power.

To be smelly a substance must give off particles of the chemical of which it is made. In other words it must be volatile. A saucepan of chicken soup boiling on the stove smells more strongly of chicken than a plate of cold chicken because many more 'chicken' particles are escaping from the broth than they are from the cold meat. For the same reason a smell gets stronger closer to its source because the cloud of vapour gets denser.

The particles of a smelly substance must remain in the air so that they can be swept up into the nose where the sense of smell is located in the lining of the nasal cavities. Just like the sense of taste, the smelly substance must be soluble in water before it can reach its receptors. Travelling over the olfactory membrane some of the odour particles dissolve in the mucus layer and come into contact with the smell-sensitive surface of the mucous membrane.

Wetness also generally heightens smells. By definition a smelly substance is soluble in water. As the water evaporates from the wet surface of an object it carries some particles of the substance with it. A wet dog is smellier than a dry dog and wet earth smells more 'earthy' than when dry because of the water vapour rising from their surfaces.

Loss of smell

The sense of smell wanes rapidly with exposure to the odour. Someone working in a coffee shop would be oblivious to the strong smell of freshly-roasted coffee beans that greets the customers as they enter the shop. Similarly, it becomes possible to tolerate an unpleasant smell when one has got used to it. A person entering a crowded, stuffy room is often repulsed by the mixture of body odours and stale smoke. Yet after a comparatively short time he will probably become as unaware of these smells as the people already in the room.

This apparent change in a person's sensitivity to a smell arises because of the phenomenon of *adaptation* in which the odour receptors quickly become occupied by odour particles. The detection of a smell depends on the interaction between the chemical units of the smelly substance and their receptor sites in the nose. When all the receptor sites are filled, such an interaction can no longer take place. Consequently the olfactory region stops signalling to the brain that the smell exists.

Water is an exception to the rules of solubility and volatility of smelly substance. For although water is both soluble and volatile it is quite odourless. One theory suggests that the mucous membrane of the olfactory region is permanently adapted to the presence of water since it is bathed in the fluid all the time. Therefore it stops signalling the presence of water which is consequently odourless.

As with taste, other factors influence the way in which the brain interprets messages about a smell. The characteristic smells of ammonia or chlorine, for

18

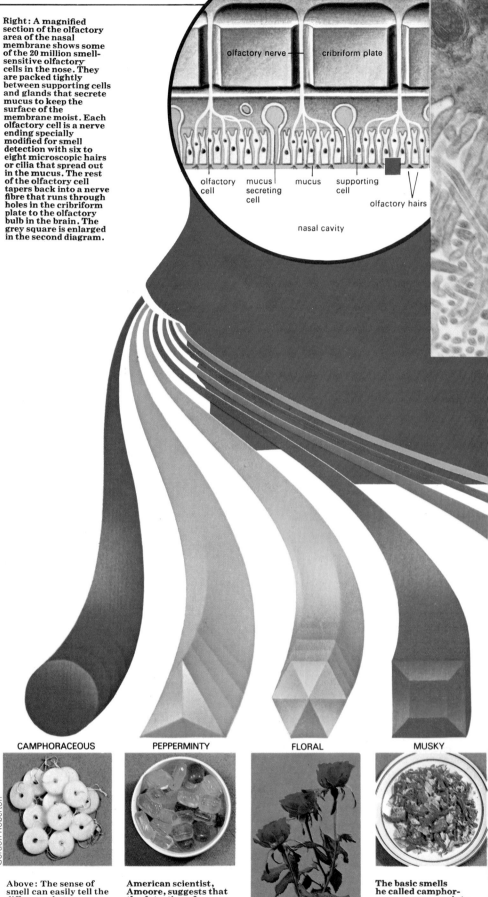

Right: A magnified section of the olfactory area of the nasal membrane shows some of the 20 million smell-sensitive olfactory cells in the nose. They are packed tightly between supporting cells and glands that secrete mucus to keep the surface of the membrane moist. Each olfactory cell is a nerve ending specially modified for smell detection with six to eight microscopic hairs or cilia that spread out in the mucus. The rest of the olfactory cell tapers back into a nerve fibre that runs through holes in the cribriform plate to the olfactory bulb in the brain. The grey square is enlarged in the second diagram.

olfactory bulb

olfactory nerve — cribriform plate

olfactory cell — mucus secreting cell — mucus — supporting cell

olfactory hairs

nasal cavity

Gordon Roberton

CAMPHORACEOUS

PEPPERMINTY

FLORAL

MUSKY

Above: The sense of smell can easily tell the difference between a rose and bad eggs but it is not yet clear how it does so. Despite many tests it is not known exactly how odour chemicals are recognized nor how the chemical signal is converted into an electrical nerve impulse for conduction to the brain.

American scientist, Amoore, suggests that the detection of different smells depends on the shape and size or electric charge of the chemical particles of seven 'basic' odours. Examples of these basic smells are (above from left to right): mothballs, peppermints, roses, dried angelica root and paraffin.

The basic smells he called camphoraceous, pepperminty, floral, musky and ethereal. According to this theory, each is distinguished at specific receptor sites on the olfactory hairs by its unique shape. Different mixtures of the basic odours produce the huge variety of smells that man can distinguish.

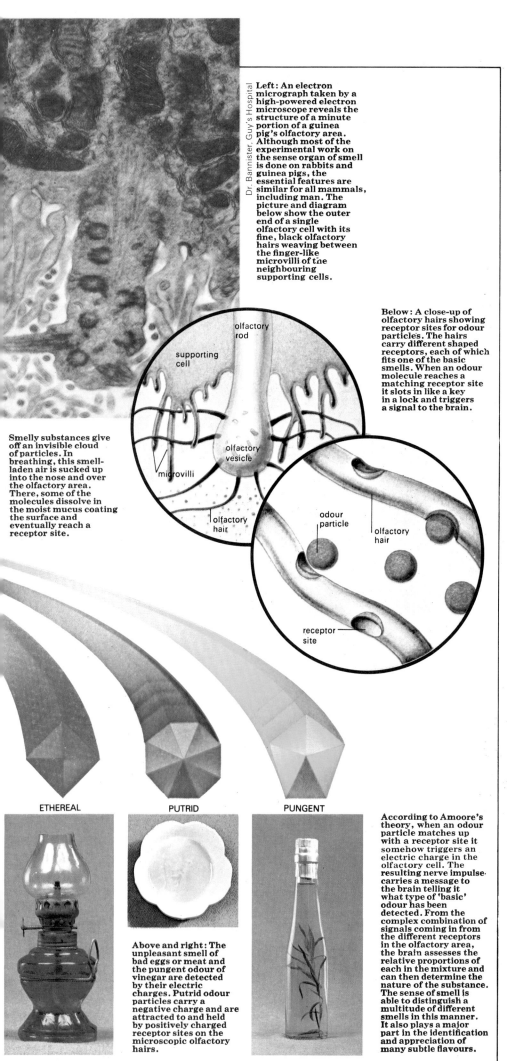

Left: An electron micrograph taken by a high-powered electron microscope reveals the structure of a minute portion of a guinea pig's olfactory area. Although most of the experimental work on the sense organ of smell is done on rabbits and guinea pigs, the essential features are similar for all mammals, including man. The picture and diagram below show the outer end of a single olfactory cell with its fine, black olfactory hairs weaving between the finger-like microvilli of the neighbouring supporting cells.

Below: A close-up of olfactory hairs showing receptor sites for odour particles. The hairs carry different shaped receptors, each of which fits one of the basic smells. When an odour molecule reaches a matching receptor site it slots in like a key in a lock and triggers a signal to the brain.

olfactory rod

supporting cell

olfactory vesicle

microvilli

olfactory hair

odour particle

olfactory hair

receptor site

Smelly substances give off an invisible cloud of particles. In breathing, this smell-laden air is sucked up into the nose and over the olfactory area. There, some of the molecules dissolve in the moist mucus coating the surface and eventually reach a receptor site.

ETHEREAL

PUTRID

PUNGENT

Above and right: The unpleasant smell of bad eggs or meat and the pungent odour of vinegar are detected by their electric charges. Putrid odour particles carry a negative charge and are attracted to and held by positively charged receptor sites on the microscopic olfactory hairs.

According to Amoore's theory, when an odour particle matches up with a receptor site it somehow triggers an electric charge in the olfactory cell. The resulting nerve impulse carries a message to the brain telling it what type of 'basic' odour has been detected. From the complex combination of signals coming in from the different receptors in the olfactory area, the brain assesses the relative proportions of each in the mixture and can then determine the nature of the substance. The sense of smell is able to distinguish a multitude of different smells in this manner. It also plays a major part in the identification and appreciation of many subtle flavours.

example, in cleaning fluids or at a swimming pool, are partly due to their caustic attack on the lining of the nose that stimulates pain receptors in the nasal cavity. Peppermints and the camphor in moth balls can also induce a feeling of coldness.

The senses of taste and smell are more than mere sensory decoration. They serve as valuable early warning·systems in situations where there are no auditory or visual clues. It is possible, for example, to smell the smoke of the fire before the flames appear. A smell had to be added to odourless natural gas when it was introduced for domestic use because people were unable to see or smell the potentially dangerous gas leaks.

At a more primitive level, taste and smell are used for choosing food and avoiding poisonous substances. Most people are naturally repulsed by the smell and taste of bad eggs or rotting meat and will therefore not eat large quantities that might be harmful.

The message in smells

Throughout the animal world smells play an important part as a means of communication between individuals and as a way of influencing one another's behaviour. Such chemical signals are referred to as *pheromones*. Humans, too, use artificial smells like perfumes to express their sexuality. Certain scents are associated with women while others are considered more masculine. There may also be a primitive hidden language of odours between humans which they react to unconsciously but which nevertheless plays a part in exciting responses of fear, hostility or friendliness. Chemical compatability or incompatability may be an important aspect of a relationship.

Each person has his or her own distinctive natural smell. Body odour arises largely from the action of bacteria on the chemicals in sweat, producing a rank odour. There are basically two kinds of sweat glands on the body, those associated with cooling and temperature regulation that excrete mostly water and mineral salts. The others differ between the sexes and produce a fatty substance which the bacteria attack. Masking these natural body odours with deodorants and anti-perspirants may also smother the communication of fear, hostility, nervousness or sexual excitement to another person.

It is possible to identify and isolate the chemicals responsible for the characteristic tastes and smells of many different substances. These chemicals can be reproduced in the laboratory and substituted for the natural substance. Taste and smells are rapidly becoming an important branch of the chemical industry as the demand for artificial flavours and odours is growing all the time. There are pleasant smells to mask unpleasant smells, marketed as air fresheners, and 'old car' smells to spray in new cars to give them extra 'character'.

On the whole, tastes and smells are very memorable. The smell of a place or a person and the taste of a particular food are often evocative. They add an extra dimension to a scene, one that it is impossible to capture on film or in words. They tend to be very personal memories, experiences that cannot be shared with anyone else who has not experienced them for himself.

Hearing

A human being's sense of hearing involves a natural mechanism with awe-inspiring powers of sensitivity and range. In the hearing process an intricate chain of events operates in which sound waves are conducted through the ear and translated into electrical impulses. These impulses are then routed to the brain for decoding. Almost instantly the hearer can distinguish the meaning of these signals. A clackety-clack is recognized as a typewriter, a click of metal on metal is understood as the sound of a key in the lock, and the vibrations of human vocal chords are heard as a familiar voice.

Equally remarkable is man's ability, within limits, to select the focus of his listening attention. Many clearly audible sounds may scarcely be noticed while other slight sounds may alert the hearer's attention immediately. This selective process is important because life would be a nightmare if every sound in the environment forced itself into one's consciousness.

Sound itself is both a physical and psychological phenomenon. Waves of sound caused by a vibrating object are basically minute changes in air pressure. The waves have no meaning, no message until they reach the ear. There they are translated into nerve impulses for interpretation by the brain.

The three compartments of the ear

The ear is divided into three sections: the outer, middle and inner ear. The outer ear consists of the *auricle,* which is the visible shell of the ear, and the *ear canal* which leads to the eardrum. The functions of the outer ear are limited to concentrating and directing sound waves into the auditory canal where they are condensed, increasing the pressure of the higher frequency sounds, and conveyed to the eardrum.

The middle ear begins at the *tympanic membrane,* or eardrum. This cavity is air-filled, and the internal air pressure is maintained at the same level as the external atmosphere by means of the *Eustachian tube.* The tube leads from the ear to the throat and opens whenever a person swallows or yawns, to protect the most delicate parts of the ear from abrupt changes in the air pressure. Another protection of the hearing mechanism is operated by the muscles of the middle ear. These react automatically to extremely loud sounds, cutting down the volume by tightening the eardrum and pulling the bones of the middle ear back from the delicate inner ear.

The middle ear contains the *ossicles,* three tiny bones named for their distinctive shapes: the *malleus* (meaning hammer), *incus* (anvil) and *stapes* (stirrup). When a sound wave reaches the tympanic membrane it causes the tightly-stretched membrane to vibrate; this vibration is magnified in force by the action of the ossicles. It is picked up by the malleus and pushed on through the incus and stapes. From the ossicles the amplified vibrations of sound pressure are transmitted via a tiny membrane called the *oval window* to the fluid-filled inner ear.

The inner ear cavity houses the *cochlea,* a minute, coiled tube of two canals

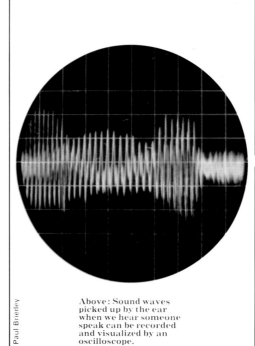

Paul Brierley

Above: Sound waves picked up by the ear when we hear someone speak can be recorded and visualized by an oscilloscope.

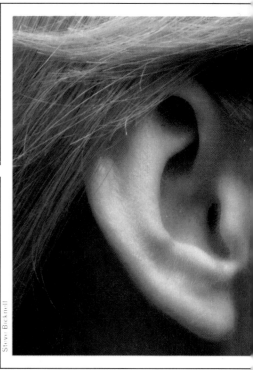

Steve Bicknell

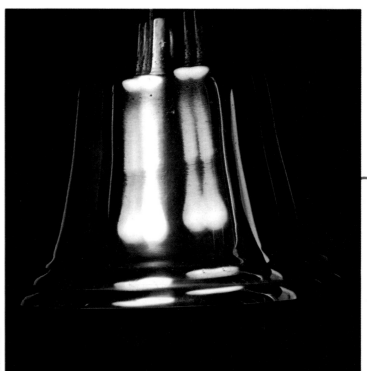

David Levin

Left: As the clapper hits the sides of the bell it sets up tiny vibrations in the metal. The movements compress and separate surrounding air particles, causing a sound wave that is detected by the ear. The loudness and pitch of the bell's ringing are determined by the size and rapidity of the vibrations.

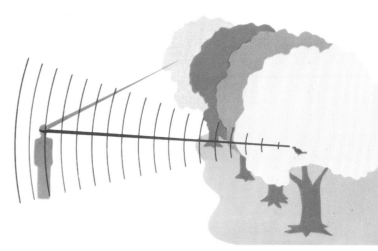

Right: It can be very difficult to pinpoint the source of a sound. The bird's song coming from behind reaches the man's ear a split second before the left ear picks it up. Sound waves coming from the tree ahead would reach the right and left ears with exactly the same time gap. Since his brain uses any minute time gap to assess where a sound is coming from, the man cannot distinguish between the two possible sources of sound. He has to move his head so that the relative positions of the real and imagined birds are changed. While the true source remains in the same place the shadow sound moves, indicating that the bird is indeed singing in the tree behind him.

20

Outer ear

The auricle, the visible ear flap, helps to direct sound into the ear canal, which is lined at its entrance with fine hairs and wax-secreting cells to protect the ear from dirt and dust. The canal leads down to the eardrum, the tympanic membrane, stretched across the mouth of the middle ear cavity.

Middle ear

This air-filled space is spanned by the ear ossicles, the malleus, incus and stapes (hammer, anvil and stirrup). These small hinged bones convey vibrations of the eardrum to the oval window of the inner ear. The Eustachian tube, connected to the back of the nose, balances air pressure with that of the middle ear. When ears 'pop' the tube has opened to equalize pressure inside and outside the ear.

Inner ear

This consists of the fluid-filled cochlea, the coil that houses the delicate hearing mechanism.

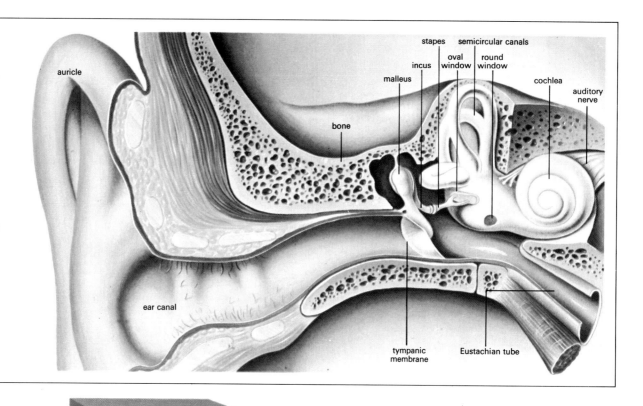

Right: The three tiny bones of the middle ear, the ossicles, serve as connecting links from the eardrum to the wall of the inner ear. The ossicles are connected to each other by hinges and act as mechanical levers to carry and push the vibrations of the ear drum forward to the flexible membrane of the oval window.

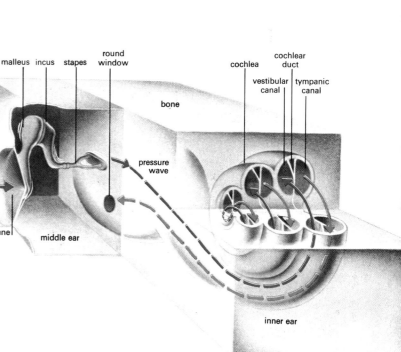

Above: The process of hearing really starts when the sound wave enters the ear canal. The wave motion sets the eardrum vibrating. The higher the pitch of the sound, the faster the membrane vibrates. The louder the sound, the greater the vibrations. These movements are then transmitted via the ossicles to the inner ear. The knocking of the stapes on the membrane of the oval window causes pressure waves in the fluid that travels through the cochlear coil. After their passage through the cochlea the waves are finally dispersed when they reach the membrane of the round window.

Below: An important characteristic of sound is its amplitude. This is the degree of a sound's loudness, and is measured in decibels (db). The hearing threshold—the point at which the average young adult can just detect sound from silence—is 0 db. 115-120 db is the threshold of pain.

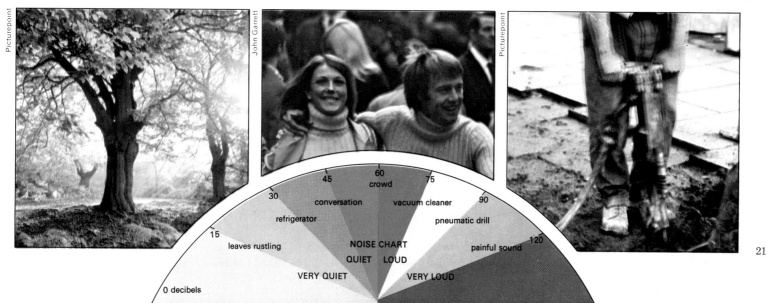

Picturepoint

John Garrett

Picturepoint

NOISE CHART

QUIET · LOUD

VERY QUIET · VERY LOUD

0 decibels · 15 · 30 · 45 · 60 · 75 · 90 · 120

leaves rustling · refrigerator · conversation · crowd · vacuum cleaner · pneumatic drill · painful sound

21

and a duct subdivided by a thin elastic membrane partition. Sound vibrations reaching the inner ear become waves of pressure which are transmitted through the fluid of the cochlear canals — the *vestibular canal* and the *tympanic canal* — and around the *cochlear duct* which separates them.

As the pressure of the waves flows over the *basilar membrane,* which is the vibrating wall of the cochlear duct, fluid inside the duct is agitated. This agitation in turn stimulates the incredibly sensitive and highly-developed *organ of Corti* where pressure is converted into electrical impulses. After circuiting the cochlear route the pressure waves reach the *round window,* a membrane just below the oval window, where they are dissipated.

Research now seems to show that sounds of different frequencies produce maximal displacement at different points on the cochlear partition, and it is this factor which plays an important role in man's ability to discriminate pitch. Scientists, however, have not reached a complete understanding of how the complex and precise translation of information operates.

Sound also reaches the inner ear by bone conduction. If a tuning fork is struck and placed on the forehead its vibrations travel not only through the air passage to the inner ear, but also through the bones of the skull. When a person speaks he hears his voice simultaneously through these two routes of air and bone conduction. When a person hears his own voice from a tape recorder he often fails to recognize it, because he is hearing himself through air conduction alone.

Learning to distinguish sounds
The newborn baby can certainly hear, but he has not yet acquired the selective process of listening. Any loud noise will startle him, causing him to fling up his arms and legs. Gradually, as he begins to recognize the sounds around him, this reflex is inhibited.

By six weeks of age the sound of his mother's voice is familiar enough to give him pleasure on recognition, and by 20 weeks he can distinguish between speech sounds as similar as 'p' and 't'. As the child grows older he becomes able to recognize any one of hundreds of voices. His developing interests will cause him to concentrate on some occupation so hard that the sounds of a radio, passing cars or insistent calls from his mother will fail to disturb him. He will be able to choose which conversation he 'tunes into' in a crowd and switch from one to another, according to his interest.

Normal hearing plays a vital role in developing and maintaining communications with others through language. The young child with a hearing loss will attempt to match his own speech with the distorted utterances he hears from others, and he will need special training if his speech is to be intelligible.

In conversation a person needs to be able to hear his companion's words, although these alone do not convey understanding. Understanding of what one hears is aided by visual clues of expression and gesture, anticipation of what one is expecting to hear and, most importantly, experience of language. The use of telephones for communication relies on this

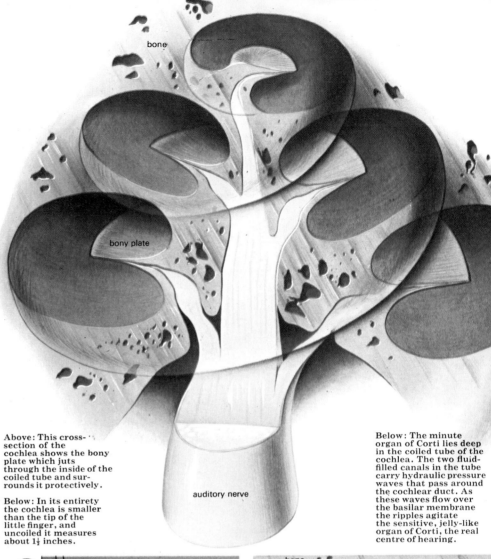

Above: This cross-section of the cochlea shows the bony plate which juts through the inside of the coiled tube and surrounds it protectively.

Below: In its entirety the cochlea is smaller than the tip of the little finger, and uncoiled it measures about 1½ inches.

Below: The minute organ of Corti lies deep in the coiled tube of the cochlea. The two fluid-filled canals in the tube carry hydraulic pressure waves that pass around the cochlear duct. As these waves flow over the basilar membrane the ripples agitate the sensitive, jelly-like organ of Corti, the real centre of hearing.

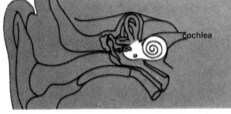

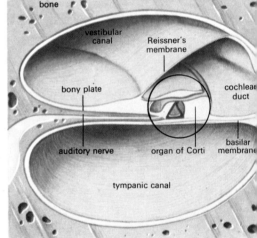

hearing experience because the frequency response of the telephone is limited. For example, the words 'socks' and 'fox' would be indistinguishable out of conversational context over the telephone. Hearing further relates to spoken language in that it enables the speaker to hear himself in order to monitor his own speech, in particular its inflection volume.

Conductive deafness is a failure of the sound waves to be conducted to the inner ear. For example, childhood middle ear infections can cause secretions which hamper the movement of the ossicles and prevent the Eustachian tube from acting as an airway. This is also often experienced with a heavy cold.

In middle and old age the ossicles may become progressively less mobile in a condition known as otosclerosis. The effect of these conditions is to dampen the subject's reception for sounds at all frequencies. He may speak quietly because he hears his own voice loudly and clearly by bone conduction but fails to hear sounds in the environment. Conductive deafness is treatable and amplification from a hearing aid also helps.

There is no cure for perceptive deafness, however, where there is damage to the sound-receiving centres of the inner ear. Most congenital deafness is of this type. Usually the reception of high frequency sounds is more affected than the reception of low frequency sounds, such as vowels in speech, until the sufferer's speech develops poorly, lacking the high frequency consonants that he is failing to hear.

In modern, industrial societies an increasing amount of hearing loss seems to be caused by noise from the automated, urban environment, and such a loss is irreversible. The ingenious protective mechanism of the ear cannot cope with sudden or repeated sounds of very high intensity.

A British study in 1971 of the incidence of hearing loss among workers in a drop forge — one of the noisiest industries — found approximately half the sample of 2,900 men tested had a mild hearing loss and 10 per cent were suffering from occupational deafness of a severe degree. In the US in 1969 Rupp and Koch were two of many researchers to point out the potential danger of rock music amplified to the borders of pain. They found significant hearing loss for high frequencies among group members tested, although other researchers who have tested rock musicians and fans consider that the case against loud music as a specific cause of hearing loss is inconclusive.

In Western countries it is accepted that a deterioration in hearing may occur as a normal part of the ageing process. But recent studies of hearing among members of primitive tribes living in quiet isolation show no loss of hearing in elder tribesmen. A test of 500 African Mabaans revealed that nearly all of them, regardless of age, could hear a whisper over a distance as great as the length of a football field, an ability few Westerners could match. Such surveys indicate that the potential human range of hearing is far greater than that perceived in people who live against a background of constant noise from radios, traffic, typewriters, machinery and the babble of conversation.

Another cause for concern is that the sounds of an increasingly noisy environment may adversely affect a person's psychological state. It seems that noise may reduce work performance, disrupt sleep and cause annoyance and irritability, but sensitivity to noise varies considerably among individuals.

The selective listening process

Linguists have isolated the levels at which we analyze the sounds of language, and some ingenious experiments have been devised by psycho-linguists to show their psychological reality. In one study, for example, a brief click was superimposed on a tape recorded sentence. Subjects hearing the message were asked at which point the click occurred. There was a significant tendency for the subjects to report that they had heard the click at a grammatical juncture (the end of a phrase), although they were often sounds and even words off the correct spot.

Such experiments give some information about the way in which people manage to understand each other. Psychologists have also looked at the ability to select the focus of attention in what is called 'the cocktail party phenomenon'. How is it that loud voices all around do not significantly mask the interesting gossip one may be listening to over one's shoulder? In one experiment subjects had different messages played to each ear through headphones. It was found that with no prior instructions a subject's attention would be caught involuntarily by the loudest message. When instructed to pay attention to one particular message the subjects successfully reproduced the substance of the quieter message indicated, ignoring a louder one. However certain words — in particular the subject's own name — if embedded at equal volume in the rejected message, will cause him to switch his attention away from the task of following a selected message.

It seems that it is the fact that a human has two ears which enables him to localize different sound sources and to choose the message he will hear. For a microphone at a cocktail party acts as a single ear, and on listening to a tape recording of the conversations it becomes impossible to select one focus of attention. It is this natural human ability to pick up sounds from different directions that inspired the development of stereophonic equipment to reproduce a fuller, more natural effect in sound recording. Binaural, or two-eared, hearing is perhaps the most vital factor in the way in which a person perceives the world around him.

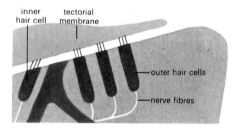

tectorial membrane   inner hair cell   arch of Corti   hairs   cells of Hensen

nerve fibres

basilar membrane

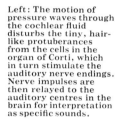

inner hair cell   tectorial membrane

outer hair cells

nerve fibres

Left: The motion of pressure waves through the cochlear fluid disturbs the tiny, hair-like protuberances from the cells in the organ of Corti, which in turn stimulate the auditory nerve endings. Nerve impulses are then relayed to the auditory centres in the brain for interpretation as specific sounds.

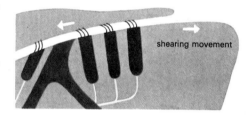

shearing movement

Left and below: Hair tips projecting from the organ of Corti brush against the tectorial membrane. As the organ of Corti bends with the pressure of waves the tectorial membrane bends in the opposite direction, creating a shearing motion against the hair tips which activates the hair cells.

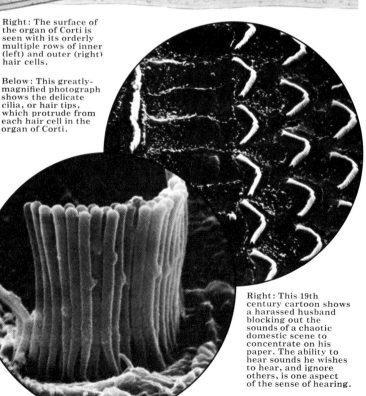

Right: The surface of the organ of Corti is seen with its orderly multiple rows of inner (left) and outer (right) hair cells.

Below: This greatly-magnified photograph shows the delicate cilia, or hair tips, which protrude from each hair cell in the organ of Corti.

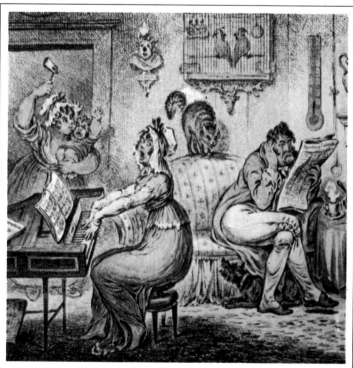

Right: This 19th century cartoon shows a harassed husband blocking out the sounds of a chaotic domestic scene to concentrate on his paper. The ability to hear sounds he wishes to hear, and ignore others, is one aspect of the sense of hearing.

Touch

The sense of touch is the most basic means by which a person makes contact with the world around him. The ability to feel shapes and textures provides the brain with more precise information about the environment than is perceived through sight and hearing. The sensations of temperature and pain inform the brain of dangers to the body—often before the individual is consciously aware of such sensations—so that the body can immediately react to protect itself. Personal communication is also heightened by touch, which may be used to express a whole range of emotions.

In many ways a human being's sense of touch is the sense in which he places the greatest faith. Often it is not until an object can actually be touched that a person is finally convinced of its existence. But why should the information from our touch receptors be more 'real' than from our other sensory systems? If touch were the first of our senses to evolve in infancy our dependence on it might be explained. However, recent research has shown that the infant's world is far from the 'buzzing, booming confusion' that early psychologists, such as William James, thought it was. Young babies have in fact quite sophisticated visual and auditory abilities.

The reality sense
There are two likely reasons why touch tends to be considered as the 'reality' sense. Unlike the other four senses— sight, hearing, taste and smell—touch responds to more than one type of energy stimulus: it is responsive to both temperature and pressure. Secondly, each of the other senses is localized in a particular organ of the body (eyes, ears, mouth and nose), whereas the sense 'organs' for touch are distributed all over the body. The sense of touch is in this way more than a single sense. Early experimenters tried to classify the sense of touch into various sensory modalities, or channels, of sensation. The 19th century German physiologist, Hermann von Helmholtz, for example, classified four such modalities—touch, heat, cold and pain— all of which can be experienced by simply bringing an object into contact with an area of skin.

The first theories to explain this complex mechanism were based upon the microscopic examination of nerve endings in the skin. These nerve endings were found to be of several types, differing in appearance and each type was thought to be responsive to a particular stimulus.

According to one theory, five different types of nerve ending, said to respond to the stimuli of different sensory modalities, were differentiated as: pain—free nerve endings; pressure—Pacinian corpuscles; cold—Krausse end bulbs; heat—Ruffini endings; and touch—Merckels discs and Meissner corpuscles. Pressure was defined as the sensation of feeling the 'weight' of an object pressed on the skin or the 'hardness' of something against the skin. Whereas touch proper was identified as the perception of a touch or stroke against the skin and the size and shape of objects felt.

24   However, this 'classical' approach to

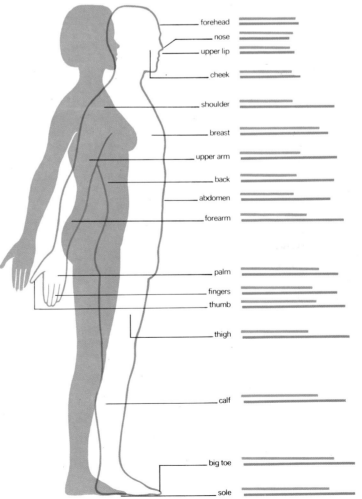

forehead
nose
upper lip
cheek
shoulder
breast
upper arm
back
abdomen
forearm
palm
fingers
thumb
thigh
calf
big toe
sole

Left: The Pacinian corpuscles, the end-organs most receptive to pressure, not only form different patterns of distribution throughout the body but vary between men and women. Men are generally more tolerant of pressure sensations, indicated by the longer blue lines. The chart also shows the relative tolerance levels of various parts of the body. The back, for example, has fewer receptors and is capable of enduring more intense pressure than the forehead.

Above: Shaking hands with someone is a positive way of making contact which allows us to express our pleasure in getting to know them or renewing old friendship.

Right and below: The form of greeting expressed by different races is often a reflection of social attitudes towards physical contact. The degree of intimacy permitted is subject to both the relationship and to the conventions of the society. Initial contact may be as distant as the Japanese bow (right) or as intimate as the embrace of the two Arabs (top right).

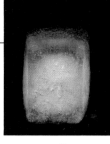

pain   cold   heat

Meissner corpuscle

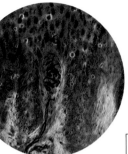

Pacinian corpuscle

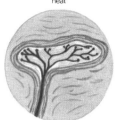

free nerve endings   Krausse end bulbs   Ruffini corpuscle

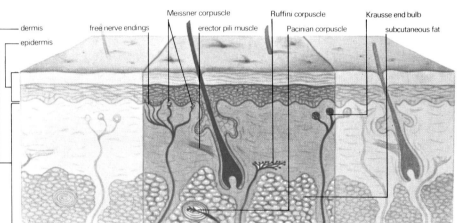

dermis — free nerve endings — Meissner corpuscle — Ruffini corpuscle — Krausse end bulb — epidermis — erector pili muscle — Pacinian corpuscle — subcutaneous fat

Left: The human skin
contains receptors
which are sensitive to
outside stimuli. By
reporting the nature,
intensity and direction
of the stimuli, the
sense receptors enable
the brain to make
decisions about
adapting the internal
environment. Although
there is a large
spectrum of sensations,
to which the sensory
apparatus responds,
some receptors are
known to be particularly
sensitive to certain
types of stimuli.

A cross-section of the
skin (bottom left)
reveals that most of
these specialized
receptors are found
in the dermis or
innermost layer, and
that they have a
variety of forms.
Free nerve endings,
which are sensitive to
pain, (above left) are
the commonest form
and have no special
shape. The nerve
endings most sensitive
to cold and heat are
fewer and less
discriminating, so that
heat and cold may
be sensed
simultaneously.

Far left: Pacinian
corpuscles, which
respond to pressure
are highly concentrated
in the fingertips,
although they are
widely distributed
throughout the body.
Meissner corpuscles,
also more concentrated
in the hands, are quite
numerous in young
babies but gradually
decrease with age.

Keystone

Rene Burri, Magnum

the explanation of the sense of touch soon ran into difficulties. It was found that some of these sense organs in the skin respond to more than one type of stimulation. It also became apparent that the different end organs that early researchers had identified are not really completely distinct and that the sensations identified were but a few from the wide spectrum of stimuli which the end organs were capable of receiving.

Associated with each nerve ending is a 'receptive field', which is the area of the skin that can be stimulated to produce activity in that nerve. The receptive fields of sensory fibres overlap, so that by putting pressure on a particular point on the skin surface, several sensory nerves will be stimulated at the same time. Any particular sensory nerve may also be activated by both pressure and temperature changes in its receptive field.

Investigations have shown that nerve fibres respond continually to a variety of stimuli, but only those relating to temperature and pressure are intense enough to be detected. This is due to the fact that these particular stimuli cause a greater degree of excitation in the nerve fibre and the impulses are therefore conducted to the central nervous system at a greater rate. It has been suggested that it is the frequency rate of the firing of these nerves, that is, the rate at which impulses are conducted, which constitutes the message carried to the brain to tell it what type of stimulus is present.

The receptive fields vary around the body in degrees of sensitivity, depending on the concentration of nerve endings in different parts of the skin. The fine distinctions between these receptive fields of the skin do, strangely enough, change over a period of time. If the receptive fields for a certain area of skin are established, and then tested at a later date, it has been found that some of the receptive fields have disappeared and others have been created. It seems that the areas of skin over which a certain nerve can be stimulated are constantly changing, although it is not yet clear how or why this mysterious process happens.

The transmission process

The next stage in the process of transmitting touch information to the brain is accomplished when the individual nerve fibres leading from the end organs, which are actually receiving the stimuli, pass through somatic nerves—those nerves which carry sensory stimuli to the central nervous system. The fibres in these nerves are known to be of different thicknesses, which directly affects the speed with which messages can pass along them.

Experiments have been carried out to establish whether these different types of fibre carry messages about different kinds of stimuli. Various researchers have found that particular fibres transmit messages only when the skin is damaged, heated, pinched, and so on. Furthermore, a disease of the spinal cord called *syringomyelia* causes lesions which interrupt the nerve fibres carrying pain and temperature stimuli. People suffering from this disease may accidently handle objects which burn them or cut them without being aware of it. But they do not lose their actual sense of touch and still experience other tactile sensations.

These discoveries appear to verify those 25

Right: Information on the texture, shape and size of objects is vital in relating to and moving around in our environment.

Below: Sensitivity varies throughout the parts of the hand. Colour 5 represents the least sensitive part and Colour 1 the most sensitive.

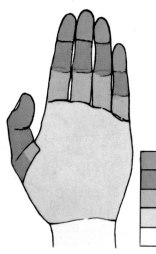

1
2
3
4
5

Right: In the ancient art of massage, both therapist and patient experience a variety of tactile sensations. Through techniques such as stroking, pressing, kneading and rubbing, the masseur can detect and treat discomfort from over-tensed muscles and stimulate blood flow to improve circulation.

Below: Most blind people rely on a developed secondary sense to compensate for loss of vision. Through his highly sensitive fingertips, a good braille reader can feel and interpret the small raised dots, set 2½ to 3mm apart, at the rate of 2,000 to 2,500 a minute, the equivalent of 100 words a minute.

theories which attributed the role of responding to particular stimuli to specific end organs. However, it is not the end organ itself that responds in this way, but the nerve fibres later in the chain of the nervous system. The final stages of the touch transmission process carry the information from the somatic nerves into the spinal cord and from there to the brain.

It is no longer possible to explain the different sensations experienced by saying that they result from the stimulation of different sense organs found in the skin. Although there may be some types of nerve endings that are more responsive to certain kinds of external pressure, current theories assume that it is the firing rates and the distribution of impulses among the small and large nerve fibres which form a pattern which is then recognized as a particular sensation.

Besides providing information about the temperature, texture or weight of an object, the sense of touch also performs other functions. One of the most important sources of tactile stimulation is other human beings. The way in which a person is touched by others tells him a great deal about them, whether through a kiss, a pat on the back or a blow on the jaw. Even the feel of an initial handshake will colour one's attitude towards a stranger.

Equally, social psychologists have suggested that there is a definite 'hierarchy' of touch that defines human personal relationships. The minimal distance man tolerates between himself and another person depends on both the person's familiarity and the formality of the occasion.

A more serious example of the role of touch in communication between people has been studied recently in the USA. Mothers whose premature babies were placed in an incubator immediately after birth were found to have problems in their attachment to their children later on. In comparison, mothers of normal babies who experienced periods of mutual touching in the first few days of the infant's life were later found to have more satisfactory relationships with their children.

There are other aspects of the sense of touch that are susceptible to social and cultural influences. Pain in particular is an area of touch sensation that seems to be dramatically modified by cultural factors. In certain cultures, for example, childbirth is accompanied by extremes of painful sensation, while in other societies childbirth appears to be of only minor inconvenience to the women concerned.

Phantom limbs

The sensitivity of the sense of touch has more directly applicable advantages. The system of braille, for example, enables the blind to read through their fingertips. However, this sensitivity does have some consequences that can be unpleasant. After amputation of a limb a phenomenon known as a 'phantom limb' often occurs which can cause great distress and discomfort to a patient. This phantom limb feels to the person just like the one he has lost and although the physical limb is gone, the pain remains where it was, and is real to the sufferer. Eventually this exact replica fades; sometimes the 'limb' will disappear leaving only the sensation of the extremity, the hand or the foot, as a persistent phantom reminder.

The sense of touch responds to several stimulae. The potter's skill depends on a delicate response to pressure and texture. Sensory messages are carried to the central nervous system through *somatic* nerves.

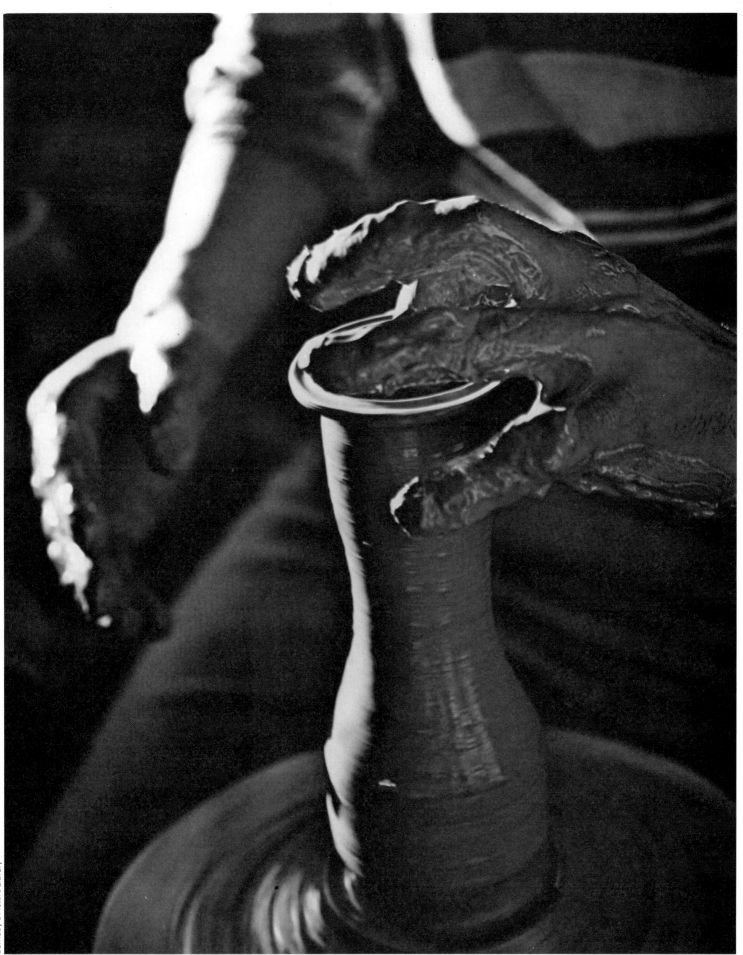

The Nervous System

The nervous system is the most highly developed, and perhaps the most important, communication system of the human body. It receives information about the outside world and relays it to the organs, tissues and cells, so enabling them to adapt to external events.

Without this highly complex mechanism, man would be unable to relate or respond to the outer world and keep the cells and tissues of his inner world functioning healthily. If, for example, the body were unable to adapt to extremes of heat or cold, the welfare and development of the body as a whole would be threatened. The nervous system, therefore, maintains the delicate balance between the two environments.

The nervous system is made up of two parts: an outer system, sometimes referred to as the *somatic* system and an inner or *visceral* system. The somatic system consists of the sense organs—sight, hearing, taste, touch and smell—and the organs of motion, the muscles, bones and joints. The visceral system controls the internal organs such as the heart, glands, blood vessels and intestines. The activities of both are co-ordinated by the central nervous system, formed by the brain and spinal cord.

From the base of the brain 12 pairs of cranial nerves emerge, and 31 pairs of spinal nerves originate from either side of the spinal column. These are known as the *peripheral nerves* or the peripheral nervous system. They are made up of bundles of nerve fibres bound together with sheaths of connective tissue. A peripheral nerve may contain fibres which convey messages from the brain and spinal cord to the muscles in the head, neck, trunk and the limbs, known as *motor* or efferent fibres. Similarly, a peripheral nerve may contain *sensory* or afferent nerve fibres which convey information from the skin and the sense organs to the brain and spinal cord. Many peripheral nerves, however, contain both motor and sensory fibres.

The transmission of the electrical impulses from the skin and sense organs to the central nervous system is controlled by the parent cells of the nerve or *neurone*. Those which control the activity of the sensory nerve fibres are located just outside the spinal cord, buried in the bones of the vertebral column, while the parent cells of the motor nerves are situated within the matter of the brain and spinal cord. Neurones are of a variety of sizes and shapes—they may be spherical, star- or pyramid-shaped, or look like baskets of ferns. Each neurone has a cell-body, a central nucleus which controls the activities of the cell. This is covered with a fine membrane. Projecting from the cell-bodies of the neurones are one or more *axons*, the main conducting fibres. They may be as short as a fraction of a millimetre or as long as a metre: an axon projecting from its parent cell in the base of the spine may extend to a muscle in the foot. Extensive, thread-like branches (called *dendrites*) also project from the cell-body.

Michael Boys/Susan Griggs Agency

The intricate relay network

Neurones may be connected to each other in several different ways. A neurone may send its axon and dendrites to only one other neurone and receive the axon and dendrites of that particular neurone. But a neurone generally forms connections with hundreds of other neurones from which it also receives connecting axons and dendrites. The interconnections between an estimated 10 billion neurones, therefore, forms an extremely complex relay network.

Nerve cells are accompanied by other types of cells which supply them with food and energy. Those found in the brain and spinal cord are known as *neuroglia* while the cells which accompany the peripheral nerve fibres are called *Schwann cells*, after the researcher who first discovered them. Since neurones are the largest cells of the body—the longest stretching from the tip of the toes to the brain—they are dependent on the supporting cells for their survival. A neurone which loses contact with its supporting cell rapidly dies: neurones are so specialized that they are incapable of reproducing themselves.

The nerve fibre has to be insulated to ensure that the messages are conducted without interference and to protect it from damage. Each fibre is enclosed in a myelin sheath—a tube made of a fatty substance formed · of Schwann cells—except at intervals known as nodes of Ramvier. Damaged nerve fibres have the ability to heal themselves, provided the myelin sheath is intact. If the myelin sheath is cut or otherwise unable to restore itself, regeneration of nerve fibres cannot take place and they cease to function.

Nerve fibres have been likened to a telegraph system in that the function of both is to convey messages over long distances at great speed. For example, when we hold an object such as a pencil, the specialized touch receptors in our fingers respond to the size, weight, length, temperature and texture of the pencil and send this information, translated into electrical impulses, along the sensory nerve fibres to the central nervous system—spinal cord and the brain.

The number of impulses and the speed at which they are conveyed along the sensory nerves—which may be up to 100 metres per second, depending on the diameter of the sensory fibre—in a given time enables the brain, the most complex part of the nervous system, to

Left: Our ability to relate to the world around us is dependent on information received through the senses. Stimuli from the outside world are converted into pulses of electro-chemical energy by specialized receptors in the eyes, ears, nose, mouth and skin. These impulses are relayed to the brain for interpretation at a rate of a hundred million per second.

Far right: The central nervous system is made up of nerve cells or neurones specialized to transmit impulses. These neurones are grouped together into the brain and spinal cord, protected by the skull and the vertebrae. The cell-bodies of the neurones are housed within the brain and spinal cord. The axons, the main conducting fibres and their terminals, the dendrites, are spread throughout the body. Together they form the bundles of nerve fibres known as the peripheral nerves, containing sensory nerve fibres (which conduct impulses to the central nervous system) and motor fibres (which conduct impulses from the central nervous system to the internal organs).

Right and below: The tissue of the spinal cord. The H-shaped grey matter contains motor nerves which carry impulses from the brain, while the surrounding white matter contains sensory nerves which convey impulses to the brain.

SPINAL COLUMN

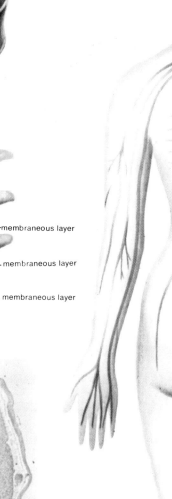

spinal cord — white matter — grey matter — membrane — nerve trunk

grey matter — white matter — central canal — sensory nerve root — motor nerve root — membraneous layer — membraneous layer — membraneous layer

Left: The spinal cord is protected by three layers of membranes and the vertebrae, the spinal bones. The spinal nerves emerge in pairs from each side of the vertebrae.

CENTRAL AND PERIPHERAL NERVOUS SYSTEM

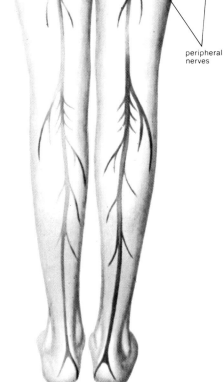

cerebrum — cerebellum — brain stem — spinal cord — peripheral nerves

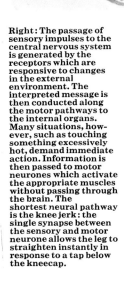

V-DIA

Right: The passage of sensory impulses to the central nervous system is generated by the receptors which are responsive to changes in the external environment. The interpreted message is then conducted along the motor pathways to the internal organs. Many situations, however, such as touching something excessively hot, demand immediate action. Information is then passed to motor neurones which activate the appropriate muscles without passing through the brain. The shortest neural pathway is the knee jerk: the single synapse between the sensory and motor neurone allows the leg to straighten instantly in response to a tap below the kneecap.

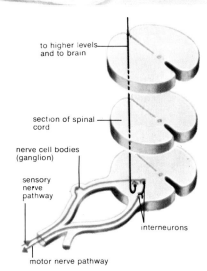

to higher levels and to brain — section of spinal cord — nerve cell bodies (ganglion) — sensory nerve pathway — interneurons — motor nerve pathway

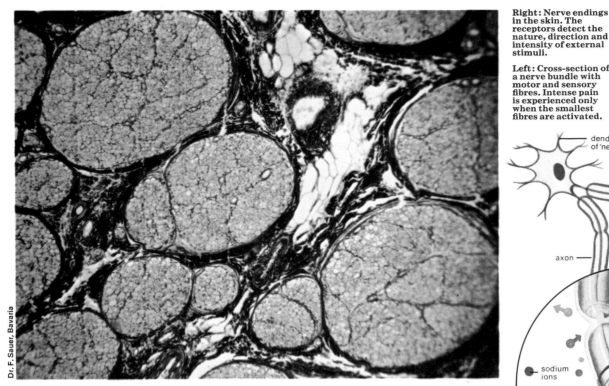

Dr. F. Sauer, Bavaria

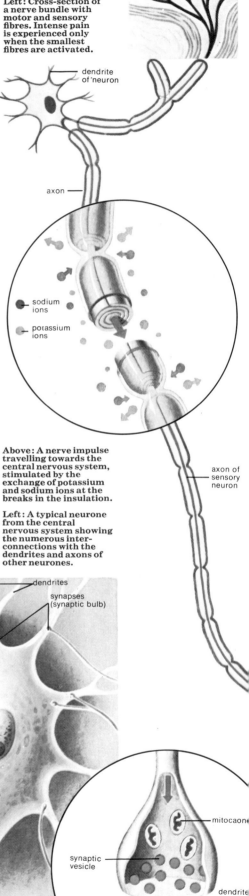

skin receptors

dendrite of neuron

axon

sodium ions

potassium ions

axon of sensory neuron

dendrites

synapses (synaptic bulb)

nucleus

axon

mitocaone

synaptic vesicle

synaptic cleft

dendrite

determine the nature of the events taking place in the world outside. These nerve inputs are interpreted by the brain with the aid of memory—impressions of sights, sounds, smells, textures and temperatures stored from past events.

Receptors—the vital link

The impulses conveyed to the central nervous system may be received through receptors (specialized cells connected to sensory nerve fibres) or through nerve fibres embedded in the skin or deeper tissues of the body.

Receptors are generally classified into various groups depending on the type of stimuli to which they respond. They give us information about changes in our external environment through sensation of different temperatures and atmospheres, by direct contact through touching external objects or from the specially adapted organs of sight, hearing, taste and smell. These receptors are highly sensitive to particular types of events—the receptors in the ear do not respond to changes in light intensity, nor do the retinal receptors in the eye respond to changes in temperature.

Receptors situated in the deeper tissues of the body supply information about the internal system of the body itself. Through them, the body is constantly monitoring changes such as the pressure within the blood vessels, bladder and gut and the temperature and chemistry of the blood and body fluids. Changes in the position and movements in the head and limbs are also monitored, enabling the body to relate to gravity and the space around it.

The transmission process

Unlike a telegraph system, which has electricity supplied to it and transmitted along it, the nerve fibre has to generate its own electrical current to enable the impulses to pass along it.

All animal and plant tissues contain fluids both inside each cell (*intracellular fluid*) and in the small spaces between the cells (*extracellular fluid*). In the neurone,

these two fluids are separated by a membrane composed of lipid (fats) and protein. The intracellular fluid contains a high concentration of potassium ions (electrically charged particles) and a low concentration of sodium ions; whereas the opposite concentrations are present in the extracellular fluid.

The differing concentrations of ions on opposite sides of the cell membrane imparts a negative electrical charge to the inside of the cell and a positive electrical charge to the outside. The potential difference between the outside and the inside of the cell is called the *membrane potential*. When the nerve fibre is in a resting state, this potential remains steady at about 70 millivolts (less than 1/20th of the voltage of a torch battery) and the cell membrane is said to be *polarized*.

However, when the nerve is conducting an impulse, a small region of the neurone's membrane temporarily changes its properties, acting as though the membrane had suddenly been punctured. The two fluids previously separated by the membrane begin to pass across it. These movements of electrically charged ions from one side of the membrane to the other alter the size of the membrane potential. For a short period of time (less than one millisecond) the inside of the cell becomes positively charged and the outside negatively charged. This brief reversal of the membrane potential is called an *action potential*.

When a small region of the nerve cell is made to generate an action potential an electrical current flows between this active region and the resting region immediately next to it. The process is

Below: The end plates connecting motor nerve fibres to the muscles direct them to contract or relax depending on the instruction they receive from the impulses. This is an all-or-nothing response, and to keep a muscle contracted a continual stream of impulses is required.

Cable & Wireless

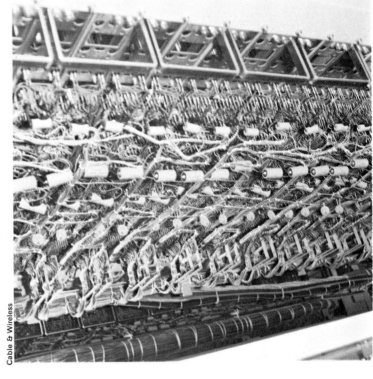

Above: A telephone exchange is a simple example of a communications network. The body's nervous system, however, involves billions of interconnections.

motor neuron axis

Right: All nerve fibres are insulated against damage to prevent interruption of the neural transmission. The insulating material contains Schwann cells which supply the nerves with food and energy. Without these supporting cells, the neurones would die since they are too specialized to reproduce themselves.

interneuron

Schwann cell (nucleus)

node of Ranvier

myelin sheath

neurilemma

nerve cell bodies (ganglion)

sensory neuron axis

Above: Nerve impulses arriving at the spinal cord are routed by the interneurones to the brain or motor neurones.

Right: This diagram shows the pathway of a typical spinal reflex – known as the reflex arc. This is the shortest neural pathway.

motor neuron axis

interneurons

similar to the chain reaction caused by lighting one end of a gunpowder trail, with the essential difference that the nerve cell membrane can be reactivated after a very short time.

This electrical charge from a nerve cell will allow an impulse, from a sense receptor, for example, to travel freely along its nerve fibre. The speed at which the impulse travels along the fibre depends on its thickness. The thickest fibres may conduct an impulse, such as the stimulus from touching something excessively hot, at 100 metres per second, while a sensation of actual pain may follow at one metre per second.

The Synapse

The electrical impulse travelling along the nerve fibre stops abruptly when it reaches the *synapse* at the end of the axon. The synapses are the junction points between individual neurones and each neurone is separated from its neighbours by a small gap, the *synaptic cleft*. The continuation of the nerve impulse requires a special mechanism to generate it across this gap. The terminals from the axon secrete particular chemicals—some of which are still unknown—which deliver a certain excitation to the cell membrane of the next neurone. The excitatory state induced by an impulse travelling along the fibre lasts only a short time. Since the cell membrane of the postsynaptic neurone is unable to maintain this charge for very long as it is a poor conductor, the current delivered leaks away as it spreads. The number of nerve impulses arriving at a neurone therefore, determines the degree to which it responds.

The number of impulses and the speed at which they eventually arrive by this process at the neurones in the central nervous system form the frequency code containing information about particular events. When the brain receives this coded message, it is able to begin its vital function of maintaining the balance between the external and internal environments.

Nerve reflexes and responses

Throughout the body changes in both our external and internal environments are constantly being monitored by *receptors*, specialized nerve endings in our sense organs and skin. These receptors convert the light, sound, mechanical and chemical energy in the environment into pulses of electrochemical energy, which are passed along the sensory nerves by an electrochemical process to the central nervous system—the brain and spinal cord. It has been estimated that as many as 100 million nerve impulses reach our central nervous system every second. From this data we have to construct our impressions of the world and instruct our muscles, glands and organs to adapt their functions accordingly.

This mass of information would be totally overwhelming if we had to respond to each item. The nervous system has therefore evolved a 'filter' system which enables it to select only a fraction of the information to process at any one time. Only a small proportion of the information from the environment is allowed to reach our central nervous system via our receptors and peripheral nerves, and an even smaller proportion reaches those parts of the brain which we call 'consciousness'.

Pathways in the nervous system
A nerve impulse travelling along a sensory nerve fibre to the central nervous system enters a network of at least 10,000 million interconnecting neurones, The synaptic connection between neurones is comparable to a simple 'on-off' switch in an electrical circuit, either allowing or preventing the passage of electrical messages. Indeed the central nervous system can be likened to a digital computer with 10,000 million on-off switches, able to select and process data with which it is provided.

Nerve impulses will cross the synaptic clefts between the neurones by means of a stimulus from transmitter chemicals released from the nerve terminals. However, there are also neurones which may stop an impulse going any further. In practice they release 'inhibitory' chemical transmitters that make it harder for the receiving neurone to fire off another impulse. Many of the neurones in the central nervous system may, therefore, be influenced both by neurones which excite it to generate nerve impulses and others which inhibit it. Depending on the balance of these conflicting influences, the neurone is either excited to conduct impulses or prevented from doing so.

Inside the central nervous system
Inside the central nervous system the branches of a sensory nerve fibre have numerous synaptic connections. There are, consequently, numerous routes which the sensory nerve impulses may take before triggering responses in the motor nerve supply to the muscles or glands. In this way the central nervous system is able to 'switch' or direct nerve impulses along the most appropriate pathways.

The most direct, and therefore, the shortest route that a sensory nerve im-

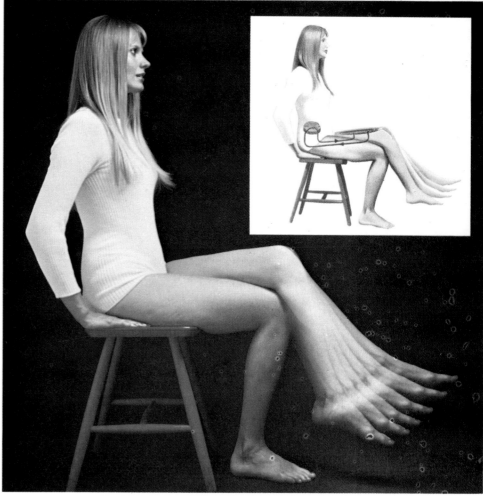

Dave Kelly

pulse may take is known as a *reflex arc*. The sensory nerve synapses directly with the cell body or dendrites (branch-like projections) of a motor neurone which, in turn, synapses with and regulates the activity of a muscle or gland. The synapse between sensory and motor neurone usually occurs in the spinal cord or base of the brain. These are activities of which we are not normally consciously aware, and over which we are unable to exercise voluntary control.

Reflex action
The reflex arc is, perhaps, best illustrated by a test often used by physicians; it is known as the reflex response. The patient is instructed to sit with one leg hanging limply over the other. The physician gives the patient's pendulous leg a sharp tap just below the knee at the tendon joining muscle on the upper surface of the thigh to the shin bones. The blow on the tendon briefly stretches the upper thigh muscle; the receptors embedded in the muscle generate a signal which is transmitted to the endings of a sensory nerve. The impulse is conducted along that nerve to enter the spinal cord at its lower end. Within the spinal cord the sensory nerve impulse is transmitted directly to the motor nerve supplying the same upper thigh muscle. Activating the motor nerve causes the muscle to contract briefly and the muscle exerts a lever action on the lower leg, causing it to shoot out.

In reflexes such as the knee jerk, the only synapses involved within the central nervous system are located in the spinal cord and are called spinal reflexes. These reflexes provide a simple method of checking whether or not the various

Above: The knee jerk, the simplest type of reflex, provides a means of detecting spinal damage. The tendon below the left knee has been tapped lightly. A volley of impulses (see inset) is sent along the sensory fibres to the spinal cord and down the motor fibres to the muscles, causing the leg to shoot out.

Below: An illustration from Descartes' 16th-century book Traite de l'Homme showing how a reflex action might work. The fire causes a thread in the nerve (B) to be pulled, this opens a pore (D) in the brain. Fluid flows from the ventricle reservoir (F) to the foot muscles, causing it to be withdrawn.

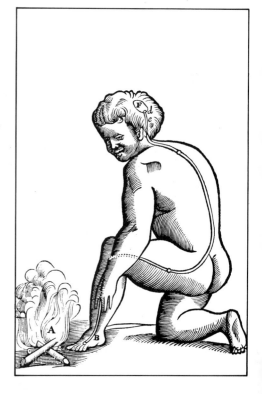

Below: The spinal nerves which convey impulses to the main muscle groups causing reflex actions emerge in pairs from either side of the vertebrae. The group Cervical nerves emerging from the first vertebrae at the top of the spinal column send impulses to the throat, chest shoulders, arms and hands; the 12 Thoracic nerves send impulses to the area from the top of the breastbone to the bottom of the rib cage; the four Lumbar nerves are connected to the muscles of the solar plexus and abdomen, while the Sacral nerves supply the area from the lower abdomen to the toes. The front and back views of the body (right) are colour coded to show the complete network.

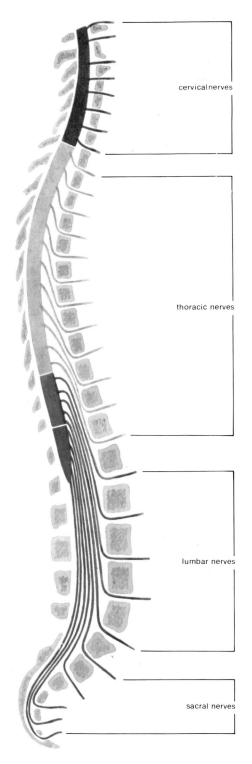

cervical nerves

thoracic nerves

lumbar nerves

sacral nerves

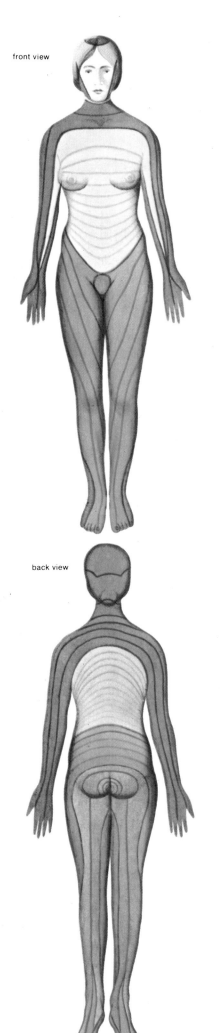

front view

back view

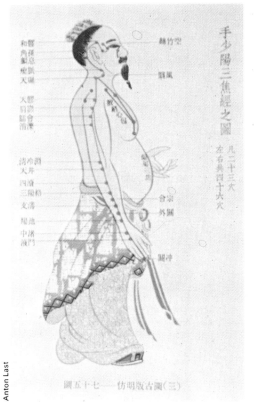

Anton Last

Above: Acupuncture is an ancient form of healing which has been used in China and parts of the East for 5,000 years. Although the meridians, or energy channels, do not directly correspond with the network of the nervous system, it has been found that needles placed superficially in the skin on certain meridians have the effect of stimulating nerve impulses to travel to the brain and back to the diseased organ, so clearing the nerve channels and restoring normal functioning. Acupuncture is also used as an anaesthetic. Needles placed on certain meridians have the effect of blocking the nerve channels.

Below: The brain, spinal cord and peripheral nerves as seen in 1824.

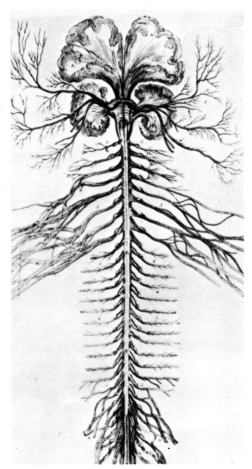

parts of the nervous system are in working order. Reflex mechanisms of this kind generally have a protective function. A particle of dust in the eye, for example, triggers blinking; coughing results from food or liquid which finds its way into the larynx, and sneezing when receptors in the nose are stimulated by irritation. Reflex actions also enable us to recover our balance and save us from falling when we stumble.

Many branches of sensory nerve fibres not only synapse with motor neurones to trigger spinal reflexes but also travel on up the spinal cord before synapsing in the brain. They may also synapse in the spinal cord with other neurones which ascend the cord to the brain.

If you touch a hot object, for example, sensory nerve endings in the skin send messages which initiate a spinal reflex causing you to quickly withdraw your hand. Branches of the sensory fibres also carry nerve impulses to centres in the brain. These impulses will be interpreted as conscious impressions of heat and pain. And yet you are not actually aware of the heat and pain until after you have withdrawn your hand. This shows that the conscious perception of the heat and pain are associated with, but do not motivate, the reflex action.

The autonomic nervous system
In situations of stress, anger or danger another part of the nervous system is stimulated. This is called the *autonomic* system and it controls the inner organs of the body. Its most important and constant activity is to maintain a state of equilibrium by regulating the heart rate, respiration, organs of blood circulation, bladder and certain endocrine glands.

Yet when danger threatens, many changes will take place inside the body, and these are geared to extraordinary circumstances: the pupils of the eyes may dilate, the hair may stand on end, the heart-rate may increase, glucose may be released from the liver to be available to the muscles. All these things may take place unnecessarily as the danger may pass, but what is happening is that the body is preparing itself in every way possible for action.

There are two divisions of the autonomic system, known as the *sympathetic* and *parasympathetic* systems. The activities of the two systems are complementary: the sympathetic system has an excitatory or accelerating effect on the various organs and glands under its influence, while the parasympathetic depresses or inhibits action. This second system, in effect, calms you down.

In its working the sympathetic nervous system differs from ordinary motor or efferent fibres (supplying the blood vessels, sweat glands and smooth muscle of the limbs) because it makes connections with two sets of neurones—one inside the spinal cord, and another set outside. This second set is composed of groups of neurones known as ganglia which form 'swellings' in front of the vertebral column. Impulses in the sympathetic system pass along the axons which emerge from either side of 16 vertebrae and enter these swellings to synapse with the neurones. The impulses then pass on from the ganglia to organs and muscles where they excite or accelerate in preparation for physical action. Parasympathetic nerve fibres, on the other hand, emerge from five cell

bodies lying at the base of the brain and three at the base of the spinal cord.

Both the sympathetic and parasympathetic systems are active all the time and are harmoniously balanced according to the demands being made on them by circumstances. When the body responds to danger, for instance, the sympathetic nerve endings secrete a chemical transmitter into the adrenal glands. This has the effect of stimulating them to secrete adrenalin into the bloodstream. The presence of this hormone speeds up the heart rate, which diverts blood flow from the skin and intestines to the muscles, supplying them with extra oxygen and glucose from the liver, so preparing the body for tremendous physical effort. Meanwhile the parasympathetic division inhibits the activity of the colon and rectum, so that their action cannot interfere with the body's state of preparation if a violent encounter should take place.

The autonomic nervous system is not entirely involuntary as its name suggests, but has aspects of its behaviour organized by the hypothalamus and medulla centres in the brain. Yet the more basic and essential a function is to man's survival, the more completely it can be organized by the neurones at the lower levels of the spinal cord. The higher centres of the brain, however, co-ordinate the various responses to external events. For example, whec the autonomic nervous system initiates a response to a threatening situation, such as running away, the hypothalamus alters the basic rhythm, depth and rate of breathing, so ensuring that the two systems function harmoniously.

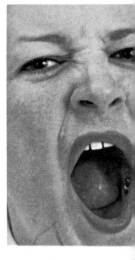

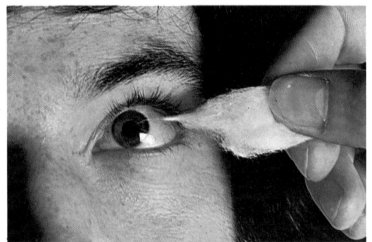

Reflex actions are basically survival mechanisms. Sneezing is a reflex response to irritation inside the nose and yawning to lack of oxygen.

Below left: a wisp of cotton wool drawn across the eyeball elicits a blinking response.

Below right: receptors in the skin react to intense heat, stimulating nerve impulses to travel along the sensory nerve fibres to the cell bodies in the spinal column. With the aid of chemicals, the impulses are passed across the synaptic junctions between neurones to the cell-bodies of the motor neurones and travel down the motor fibres to the muscles, which withdraw the hand.

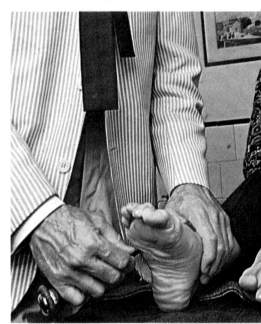

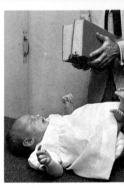

Above: Many reflexes operate even in sleep. The plantar reflex, for example, which is tested by drawing a sharp instrument along the sole of the foot, responds to situations such as touching a hot water bottle filled with boiling water, by automatically withdrawing the foot.

Right: A young baby will cry and fling its limbs wildly outwards in response to all loud noises since the parts of the brain which inhibit nervous response have not yet developed.

Below and right: The autonomic nervous system is one of the body's most basic survival mechanisms. The functions of the two divisions are antagonistic: the sympathetic system has an accelerating effect on the organs, glands and muscles to which it supplies

motor fibres, and the parasympathetic has an inhibiting effect. The sympathetic system is responsible for energy expenditure while the parasympathetic conserves energy and maintains the normal functioning of organs.

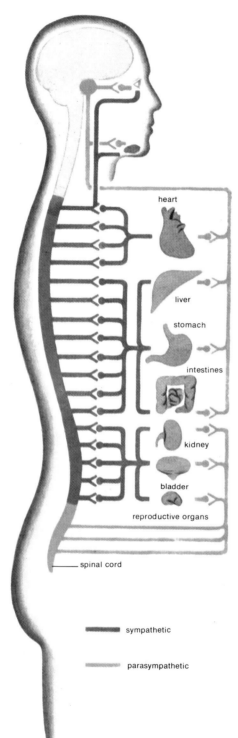

heart

liver

stomach

intestines

kidney

bladder

reproductive organs

spinal cord

━━━ sympathetic

━━━ parasympathetic

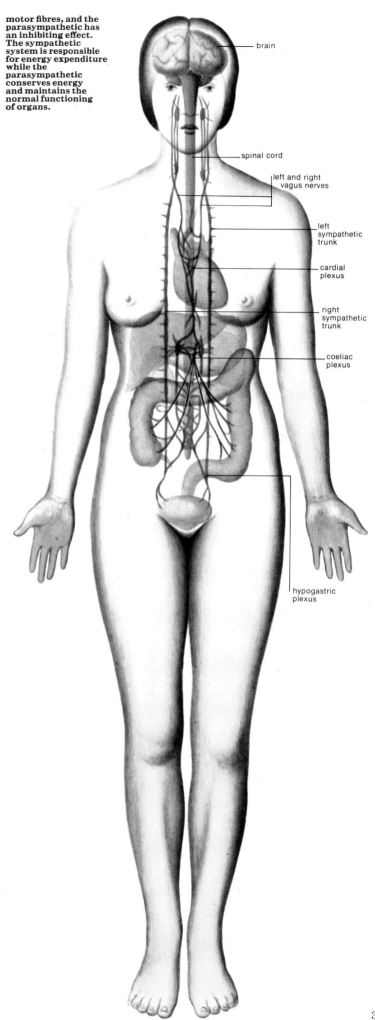

brain

spinal cord

left and right vagus nerves

left sympathetic trunk

cardial plexus

right sympathetic trunk

coeliac plexus

hypogastric plexus

Left: The autonomic system performs an emergency function in stress or fear situations. The victim's sympathetic nervous system immediately reacts to the prospect of being shot: nerve impulses are sent along the thoracic nerve fibres causing him to raise his arms involuntarily, and to his adrenal glands which secrete adrenalin into the blood-

stream. This hormone speeds up his heart, increasing blood flow and feeding extra oxygen and glucose to his muscles for extra energy. The realization that he has been the victim of a practical joke activates his parasympathetic nervous system which dampens down the heart and respiratory systems, 'relieving' him from overstimulation

35

A photographic montage showing the human skull (red), brain (blue) and its vastly inferior technological rival, the computer circuit board.

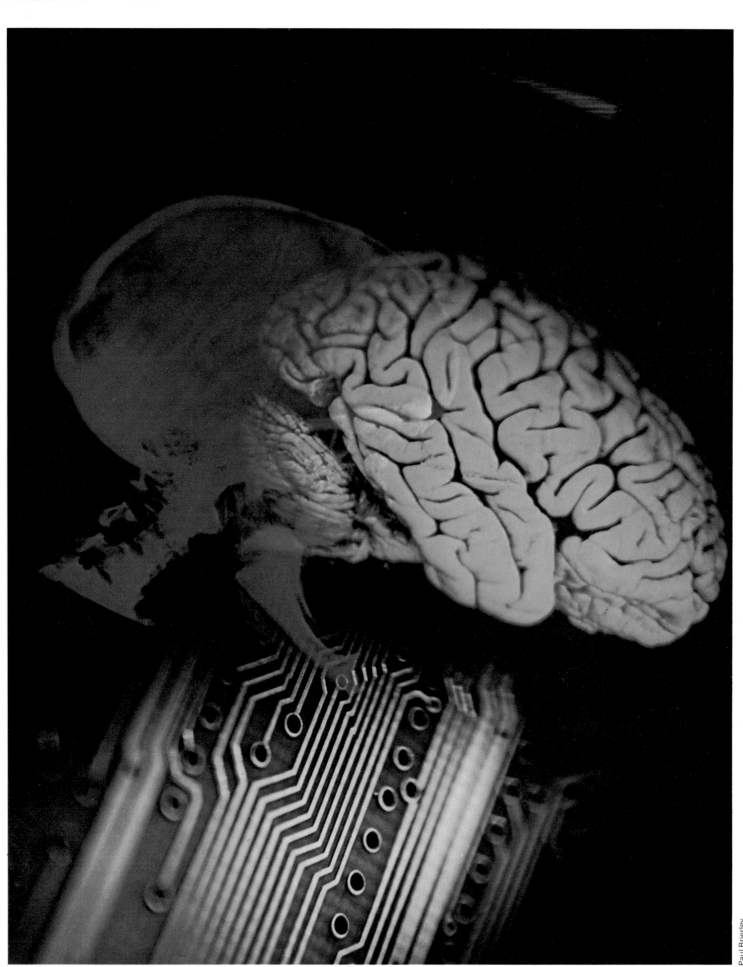

36

Paul Brierley

The Biological Computer

The human brain has been likened to a delicate flower perched on top of a slender stalk. The top three inches of the stalk, known as the brain stem, lie entirely within the skull, and are surrounded by the two bulging halves, or hemispheres of the brain. The spinal cord is the continuation of the brain stem outside of the skull.

The brain itself is a moist, pinkish-grey mass about the size of a grapefruit, and weighs less than three pounds. A shock-absorbing fluid cushions it against bumps and blows and its extra-tough outer envelope assists in its protection. Surrounding this is a crate of bone, called the cranium.

Although the human brain has often been compared to a computer, the comparison is a weak one, for the brain of an adult human being far outstrips any computer yet built by man. A computer can perform more than 4,000,000 additions of 36 figures in a single second, but the human brain, sometimes referred to as a biocomputer (biological computer), is still more versatile than the computers it builds.

An interesting fact about the brain is that its size is not related to intelligence. The French philospher Anatole France had a brain much smaller than average, but it in no way impaired his ability as a thinker. The largest brain ever weighed turned out to be that of a congenital idiot.

Electrical brain activity

Today, physiologists and neurologists have a considerable knowledge of the brain, yet the details of what actually happens in the brain when we think, remember, dream or imagine are still vague. It has been shown, for instance, that even when asleep, 50,000,000 'nerve messages' are being relayed back and forth between the brain and different parts of the body every second, but experiments have failed to isolate or identify the mechanism (or mechanisms) by which this balance is controlled and maintained.

Brain activity is mainly electrical. The brain sends and receives electrical currents from its own nerve cells to and from the many millions of nerves cells in various parts of the body. The basic nerve cell units which make up both the brain and the nervous system are called 'neurones'. Neurones differ in shape and size. They can be oval, round or spindle-shaped. Each neurone, which measures as little as 0.025mm (approximately 0.001 ins) across, has a tiny electrical charge even when it is not in use. This electrical charge is produced by the chemical difference between the interior of the nerve cell and the tissue which surrounds it. Touching and tasting, and other stimuli, alter this chemical balance and cause an electrical change which can be recorded. Physiologists refer to this as an electrochemical change.

An electrochemical change in a single neurone brings about a whole series of similar changes along the length of a

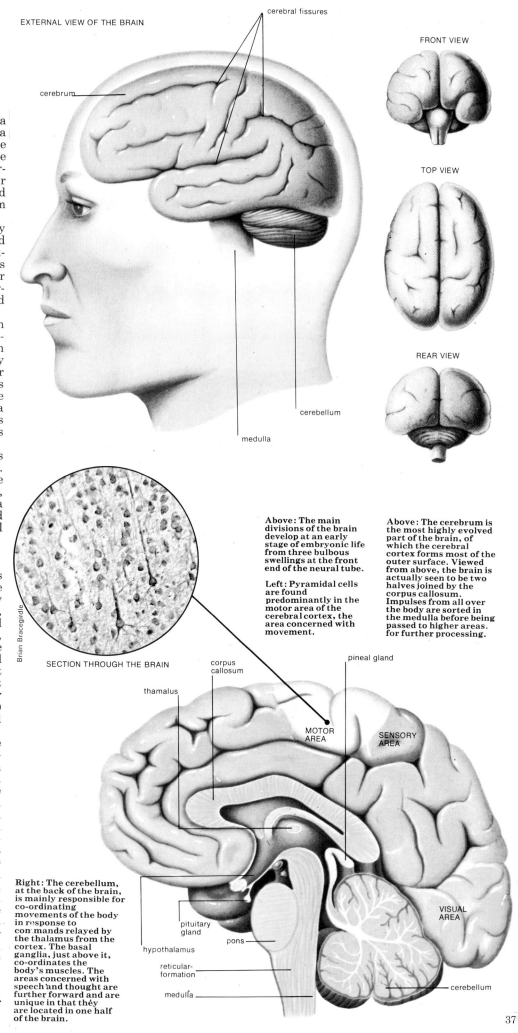

EXTERNAL VIEW OF THE BRAIN

cerebral fissures

cerebrum

FRONT VIEW

TOP VIEW

REAR VIEW

cerebellum

medulla

Brian Bracegirdle

SECTION THROUGH THE BRAIN

Above: The main divisions of the brain develop at an early stage of embryonic life from three bulbous swellings at the front end of the neural tube.

Left: Pyramidal cells are found predominantly in the motor area of the cerebral cortex, the area concerned with movement.

Above: The cerebrum is the most highly evolved part of the brain, of which the cerebral cortex forms most of the outer surface. Viewed from above, the brain is actually seen to be two halves joined by the corpus callosum. Impulses from all over the body are sorted in the medulla before being passed to higher areas. for further processing.

thamalus

corpus callosum

pineal gland

MOTOR AREA

SENSORY AREA

Right: The cerebellum, at the back of the brain, is mainly responsible for co-ordinating movements of the body in response to commands relayed by the thalamus from the cortex. The basal ganglia, just above it, co-ordinates the body's muscles. The areas concerned with speech and thought are further forward and are unique in that they are located in one half of the brain.

pituitary gland

pons

hypothalamus

reticular-formation

medulla

VISUAL AREA

cerebellum

nerve fibre, so causing an electrical impulse to flow like a spark along a fuse. When an electrical impulse is produced in this way, it is described as the *firing of a neurone*. The current initiated in one neurone often causes neighbouring neurones to undergo electrochemical changes, and they in turn fire to assist in the operation required. Millions of neurones are firing every second of our lives. The electrical impulses caused by this firing quickly find their way to the brain as 'coded messages', although many of them may be rejected as not belonging to 'priority categories'. For example, if message A is that the hand is in contact with something very hot, and message B is that a bird is singing, then the brain will select message A as the more important.

Seen under a microscope, a single brain cell may resemble the crown of a tree and a thin section of brain tissue looks remarkably like a collection of garden weeds. The communication system between neurones is composed of delicate fibres called 'dendrites'. But there is also another fibre attached to each neurone called the 'axon', and these link the brain with the whole of the body. A nerve fibre is made up of some thousands of axons. The overall communication system of the body is composed of over 13,000,000,000 neurones, yet such is the complexity of the brain that it alone contains 10,000,000,000 of these. The skin has some 4,000,000 special neurones which can detect pain, heat and cold. Other neurones throughout the muscles and organs of the body respond to leg and arm positions, stomach ache, the colour of a flower or the pitch of a note of music.

Interior and exterior control

The astounding versatility of the brain comes into focus when one considers that it is in charge of an interior environment as well as an exterior one. It keeps us alive by balancing the processes of growth and decay. Apart from the priority example given above, the brain is also deeply involved in the balance of itself as a mechanism. Because of this, it has to survey all the functions of the body simultaneously to ensure that each of its operations is co-ordinated. For example, sugar is one of the body's main energy-providing substances, and as human beings we must have just the right amount. It has been said that we walk a biological tight-rope between coma and convulsion, for only a slight change out of the ordinary in our blood-sugar level can send us in one direction or the other.

However, with the advance warning system of coded messages flooding into our brains every second, adjustments can be effectively made to ensure our survival. This leads us to the incomprehensible fact that our brains must 'know' that our required sugar level is about a 1/60th of an ounce for every pint of blood. Similar standards of control and regulation apply to breathing (we inhale and exhale 18 to 20 times per minute), to heartbeat rate (about 70 times per minute), and to body temperature (98.4° Fahrenheit).

When triggering impulses reach the brain from the sense organs, the brain adjusts to the outside world by dividing its operation into three parts: first it takes in the sense-impression messages, then organizes each input on the basis of past experience, present events and future

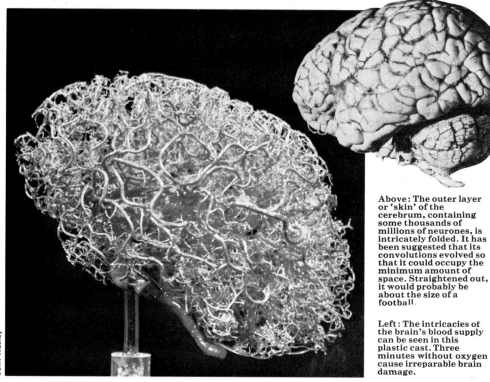

Above: The outer layer or 'skin' of the cerebrum, containing some thousands of millions of neurones, is intricately folded. It has been suggested that its convolutions evolved so that it could occupy the minimum amount of space. Straightened out, it would probably be about the size of a football.

Left: The intricacies of the brain's blood supply can be seen in this plastic cast. Three minutes without oxygen cause irreparable brain damage.

John Watney

Right: Transverse section of the brain. (See diagram below). The spaces or ventricles formed by the folds of the cerebrum are filled with cerebro-spinal fluid, which protects the delicate tissue from shock or damage, resulting, for example, from a blow to the skull.

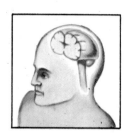

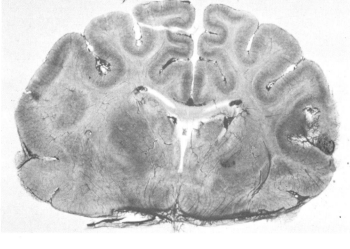

Brian Bracegirdle

plans, and lastly selects and produces appropriate output as action or actions. The brain does relax in sleep (due to the reduction of sensory impressions) but as long as it is alive, it finds no actual rest.

The main mass of the brain rests snugly on a bony shelf inside the skull. The brain stem is connected to the brain through a hole in this shelf. At the direct centre of the brain stem reside many millions of neurones. This complex of neurones is called the *reticular formation*, which means 'like a net'. One of the most important recent discoveries has been that it is in this dense neurone-fibre centre that the brain's most important decisions are made. The many millions of messages which arrive at the brain are decoded by the reticular formation and put into order of importance. It is now also thought that this neurone-centre controls consciousness and awareness.

At the rear of the brain stem lies an elaborately folded area known as the *cerebellum*. It is from here that orders are sent down from the brain's higher levels to the muscles. For example, if someone is told to write the word 'man' with a pen, then the cerebellum co-ordinates the movements of the fingers.

The largest part of the brain, however, is the *cerebrum*, or fore-brain. The cerebrum is divided into two main halves or hemispheres and, like the cerebellum, is intricately folded. It has been suggested that the folds have evolved so that the entire mass can occupy as small a place as possible.

Two bands of neurones, separated by a deep cleft, run up, across, and down the cerebrum just above the ears. The band of neurones at the front controls the action of the muscles, and is called the *motor area*, while the band at the back receives messages from the skin, and is called the *sensory area*. In the motor area muscular reactions to stimuli are initiated and in the sensory area we sense the difference between warm and cold, the prick of a pin or the cut of a knife. Curiously enough, although the cerebrum can register pain or feeling within itself, it does not register pain or feeling when touched or cut during an operation.

Seeing is governed by the back part of the cerebrum. Messages arrive from the eyes via the retinas and optic nerves. The prime function of the eyes is to change light into a series of complex electrical impulses. The neurones at the

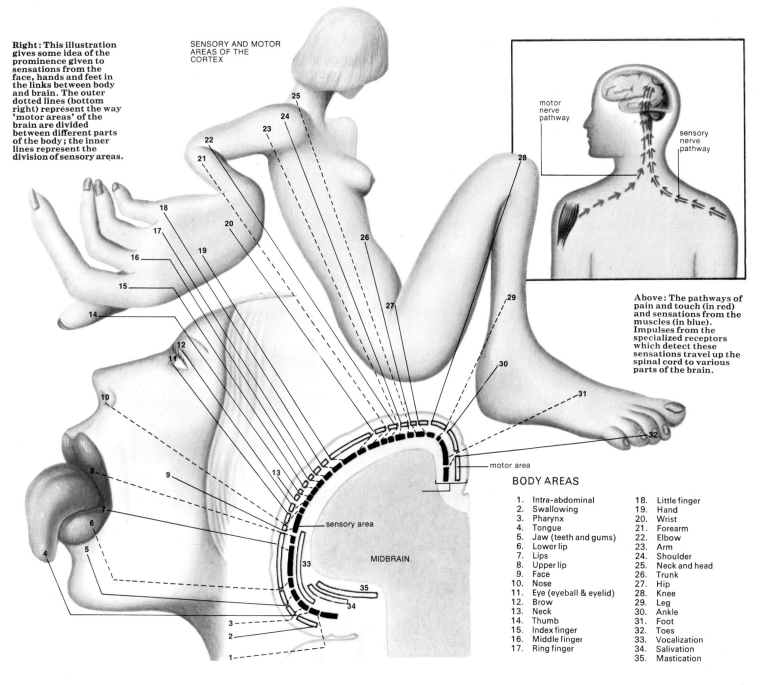

Right: This illustration gives some idea of the prominence given to sensations from the face, hands and feet in the links between body and brain. The outer dotted lines (bottom right) represent the way 'motor areas' of the brain are divided between different parts of the body; the inner lines represent the division of sensory areas.

SENSORY AND MOTOR AREAS OF THE CORTEX

motor nerve pathway

sensory nerve pathway

Above: The pathways of pain and touch (in red) and sensations from the muscles (in blue). Impulses from the specialized receptors which detect these sensations travel up the spinal cord to various parts of the brain.

motor area

sensory area

MIDBRAIN

BODY AREAS

1.	Intra-abdominal	18.	Little finger
2.	Swallowing	19.	Hand
3.	Pharynx	20.	Wrist
4.	Tongue	21.	Forearm
5.	Jaw (teeth and gums)	22.	Elbow
6.	Lower lip	23.	Arm
7.	Lips	24.	Shoulder
8.	Upper lip	25.	Neck and head
9.	Face	26.	Trunk
10.	Nose	27.	Hip
11.	Eye (eyeball & eyelid)	28.	Knee
12.	Brow	29.	Leg
13.	Neck	30.	Ankle
14.	Thumb	31.	Foot
15.	Index finger	32.	Toes
16.	Middle finger	33.	Vocalization
17.	Ring finger	34.	Salivation
		35.	Mastication

back of the cerebrum translate this jumble of signals into meaningful patterns of light and dark, colour and shape.

One of the odd things about the cerebrum's functioning is that the neurones on its left side control muscle movements on the right side of the body, and vice versa. Why this is so is not yet known. The frontal area of the cerebrum, along with certain sections of the back and sides, show no electrical activity, and have been termed the 'silent areas'. Some researchers have suggested that it is in these silent areas that we 'know ourselves'. If, however, some of the neurones in these areas are destroyed, a person can quite often suffer from loss of judgement and initiative.

The human brain has evolved gradually, over many millions of years. The earliest forerunner of the brain in primitive creatures consisted of a slim, hollow tube of nerve tissue. A relic of this early brain can still be found in modern man, buried deeply in four hollow spaces at the base of the cerebrum. Just below these spaces is a small mass of brain divided into two lobes. This is the *thalamus*, or 'preliminary sorting office' for messages going to the cerebrum.

Although termed a sorting office, the thalamus can only tell us, for example, that something 'warm' is touching part of the body, but it is the cerebrum which must decide which part of the body, and the nature of the object. It is thought by physiologists that the thalamus is responsible for the general feeling of well-being.

Just below the thalamus is the *hypothalamus*, a tiny mass of nerve tissue which controls the functioning of the pituitary gland. The pituitary hangs down from the hypothalamus on a small stalk. As the 'master gland' of the body, the pituitary governs, in turn, the thyroid and other glands through the secretion of hormones. This includes the secretion of sex hormones. The hypothalamus is involved in the way our bodies react to situations; it exerts control over the pituary, adjusting the quantities of hormones which are secreted by this gland. When we have a dry mouth, sweaty hands or a pounding heart, it is the hypothalamus which is directing these body activities.

The brain's complexity can be approached through an understanding of how computers work. The computer's memory is based on the two-number

system. As with the brain, a computer is a highly complex mechanism, parts of which are either transmitting an electrical current or not. Two wires in a computer's circuit can transmit four different messages in code: off-off; off-on; on-off, and on-on. This corresponds to the firing of two neurones in the nervous system. If, however, we consider a computer circuit with three wires (or neurones), then we are faced by an operation of eight coded messages: off-off-off; off-off-on; off-on-off; off-on-on; on-off-off; on-off-on; on-on-off and on-on-on. The permutation of 'off' and 'on' doubles each time the circuit of wires or neurones is increased by one. As the human brain and nervous system contain over 13,000,000,000 neurones, or computer wires, then the number of possible 'on' and 'off' permutations becomes staggering.

This information, however, does not help us to understand how the brain decodes the messages it receives in meaningful terms, nor how it makes 'decisions'. Dreaming, feeling, emotion, reasoning and thinking creatively are also puzzles which have not yet been unravelled, although there are indications that a breakthrough is imminent.

Activities of the Brain

Early anatomists spent years carefully mapping the numerous folds and fissures of the cerebral cortex of the human brain, hoping to isolate functional sites. Unfortunately there is wide variation in the actual positions of the smaller fissures in individual human brains, and it was only when different anatomists decided to compare drawings that they began to realize that perhaps the brain was not such a simple uniform structure. They did, however, concentrate on the cortex, the thin surface layer of the brain, which seems to be mainly concerned with the so-called higher functions of brain activity.

More recently investigators have concerned themselves more with the effects of electrical stimulation by inserting *electrodes* (fine conducting needles) into the cortex, also with removing various parts of animal and, occasionally, human brains. In this way scientists have progressed from the early brain maps showing centres for such mental faculties as writing, prudence, reserve and patriotism, to the present idea of the organization of the brain into systems of zones, each of which performs a role in the total functioning of the system.

The effects of damage to or electrical stimulation of specific areas of the cortex indicate that these areas are involved in certain aspects of brain function, but we cannot conclude from this that these are the *only* areas responsible for these functions. In some types of brain injury only a certain aspect of a particular function will be impaired. For instance, damage to parts of the *frontal lobes* will cause difficulty in speech comprehension because the person is unable to sort out the sounds which make up speech into meaningful units. A phrase 'which sounds to us like this' might 'so undt ohi mli keth is'. Difficulty in speech comprehension can also be caused by damage to the *temporo-parieto-occipital* area (a lower region of the cerebrum far removed from the frontal lobes). In this case the difficulty is due to loss of ability to attend to several words at once, resulting in fragmentation of speech.

Human and animal brains often show a certain adaptability of function in that some areas can take over the function of other damaged parts. This is more noticeable in infants, where the brain has not matured into the more specialized adult organ. To some extent it is still setting up neural pathways in response to experiences.

Our superficial impression of the brain as a grey folded mass is greatly misleading. We know that this grey matter contains more than 13 billion neurones and that these generally work together in units with radically differing functions. Since we are dealing with such an incredibly complex structure it is easier to divide the brain into three functional units, and look at each of these in turn.

The first unit

The first functional unit is located at the base of the brain and consists of the

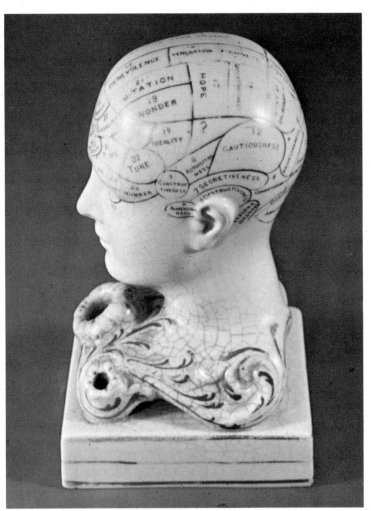

reticular formation, the *mid brain*, the *thalamus* and the *hypothalamus*. It is the first area encountered by inputs from the sense organs and information stemming from the metabolic functions within the body. This unit plays a role in the regulation of activity in the cortex and maintains the alertness of the higher areas of the brain. It does this not by single isolated nerve impulses, but by waves of electrical activity spreading throughout the unit and travelling up to the cortex. It is similar to a power source, which feeds the higher areas and which, if removed, causes a state of drowsiness.

The second unit

The second major functional unit of the brain is found in the rear halves of the *cerebral hemispheres*. It is a system for receiving, processing and storing information received via the sense organs from the outside world.

We are constantly bombarded with masses of stimuli from our environment which we interpret as sounds, colours, shapes, patterns and so on. It is within this unit that neurones of extremely high specificity have been found which respond only to very specialized properties of visual stimuli such as shades of colour, the character of lines, the direction of movement. Here we have a processing system which is capable of translating the confusion of the outside world into meaningful patterns and shapes. This unit is also capable of correlating all the information from all the different sense organs, thereby building up a complete picture of the environment.

Visual stimuli received by the eyes are translated into electrical pulses by the

C. M. Dixon

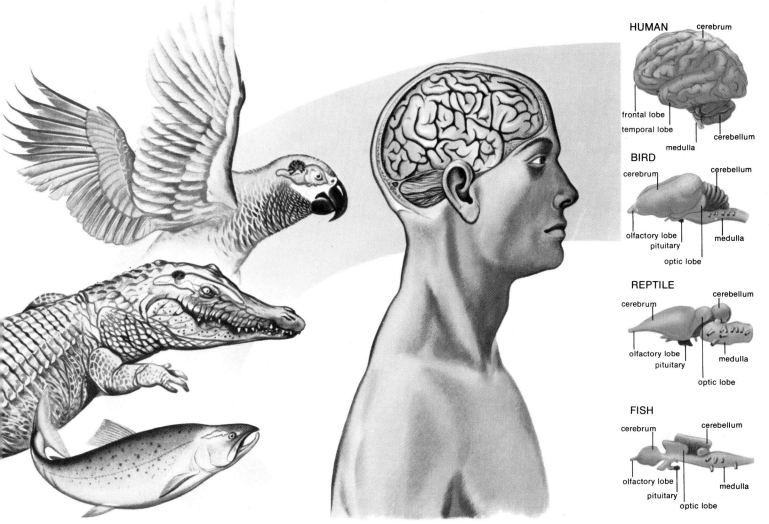

HUMAN
cerebrum
frontal lobe
temporal lobe
medulla
cerebellum

BIRD
cerebrum
cerebellum
olfactory lobe
pituitary
medulla
optic lobe

REPTILE
cerebrum
cerebellum
olfactory lobe
pituitary
medulla
optic lobe

FISH
cerebrum
cerebellum
olfactory lobe
pituitary
optic lobe
medulla

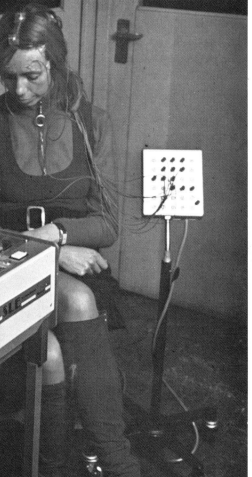

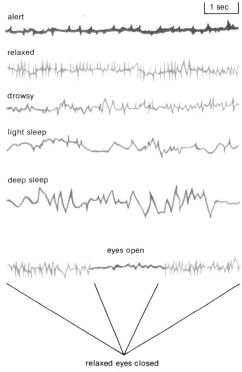

1 sec

alert

relaxed

drowsy

light sleep

deep sleep

eyes open

relaxed eyes closed

Left: Brain activity
can be studied in
action by using an
electroencephalograph
(EEG) machine.
Recording electrodes
placed on the head
pick up minute
electrical changes
in the brain. The
recorder on the left
can show simultaneous
activity in different
parts of the brain.

Above: These are
actual EEG recordings
taken from a human
brain showing the
transition from the
alert state to deep
sleep. Opening the eyes
can be seen to change
the normal resting
rhythm. Research is
still being undertaken
to match the readings
with higher mental
functions.

retinal cells, and transmitted by very fine
nerve fibres to the visual area of the
cortex. Here the visual image is broken
down into millions of component features
by highly specialized nerve cells which
respond only to particular parts of the
visual image. These cells are visual
analysers which register independently
such aspects as the different gradations
of colour, smooth, angular or round
lines, the movement from a peripheral
point to a centre, or from a centre to
a periphery. This section of the cortex
is known as the *primary visual cortex*.
Adjacent to it is the *secondary visual
cortex* which consists of star-shaped cells
whose function is to combine stimuli
transmitted to them from the primary
visual cortex into complete structures.

If electrodes are inserted into the
primary visual cortex (this can be done
during a brain operation and is entirely
painless) and a tiny current is passed
through them, the patient will report
seeing glowing points, circles or fiery
tips before the eyes. If electrodes are
inserted into the secondary visual cortex,
the patient sees complex patterns or at
times complete objects—trees swaying, a
squirrel leaping, a friend approaching and
waving.

These secondary areas seem to act as
part of the visual memory system since
stimulation here can provoke graphic
recollections of the past, such as images
of objects once seen. Damage to this part
of the brain has a bewildering effect on
the person's vision. He can still distinguish individual parts of an object, for
instance the two circles, crossbar and
cane-like attachments which make up a
pair of spectacles, but can no longer 41

synthesize them into a complete image. The world is transformed from an easily recognizable language into an alien confusion of symbols.

To obtain a complete picture of the outside world requires much more than the simple perception of objects. We must be able to gauge the complex relationships and correspondences between them. The organs of balance (the *vestibular mechanism*) in the inner ears give us a concept of our bodily position in relation to our environment; eye movements help us gauge the distance and position of objects and their interrelationships; limb position, touch and sound all help us to reconstitute the outside world. One quarter of this second functional unit is taken up by the section which deals with these spatial relationships. It is known as the *tertiary zone*, and it combines the visual, tactile-motor and auditory-vestibular sections of the cortex. The tertiary zone was the last part of the brain to develop in the course of evolution, and is really only active in humans. It is not even fully developed in infants, but matures gradually and becomes effective around about the ages four to seven.

The tertiary zone goes beyond the integration of the visual system and into the functional area dealing with word meanings and complex grammatical structures, systems of numbers and abstract relationships. All of these play an essential role in the conversion of concrete perception into abstract thinking, forming the basis for intentions, plans and actions.

The third unit

This brings us to consider the third functional unit of the human brain: the parts responsible for programming our courses of action, making sure that the behaviour corresponds to these programmes, comparing the effects of these actions with the original programmes, and correcting any mistakes.

The structures of this third unit are located in the front half of the cerebral hemispheres. They include the frontal lobes and the *motor cortex*. The motor cortex is the outlet channel for the plans

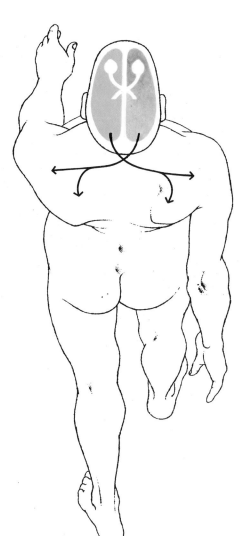

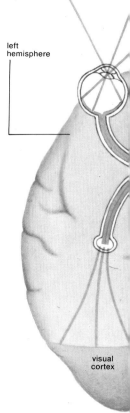

Right: If we fix our eyes on a point, the information from the left of the point goes to the right hemisphere of the brain, and information from the right goes to the left hemisphere. The corpus callosum joins the two hemispheres. When this is cut the patient cannot verbally describe objects placed in the left visual field because information can no longer pass over to the speech centre, which is in the left hemisphere.

Left: Control of the muscles which enable movement stems from the opposite side of the brain. When we move our right hand it is the left hemisphere which is giving the instructions. It is this hemisphere which is dominant in right-handed people, allowing greater control and hence better manipulation with the right hand.

left hemisphere

visual cortex

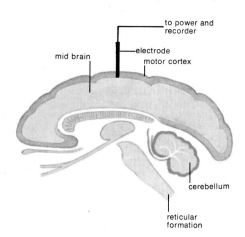

to power and recorder

electrode

motor cortex

mid brain

cerebellum

reticular formation

Above and right: By performing experiments on animals, researchers have discovered much about brain function applicable to humans. Here we see the site and equipment involved in placing electrodes in the motor cortex of a monkey. Passing a tiny current into specific areas will cause either whole limb movement or the twitching of single muscles. From this it is possible to isolate the type of cells which co-ordinate groups of muscles, and those controlling single ones. The complex equipment regulates and records from various electrodes placed in the different cells of the cortex.

Matt Herron, Transworld

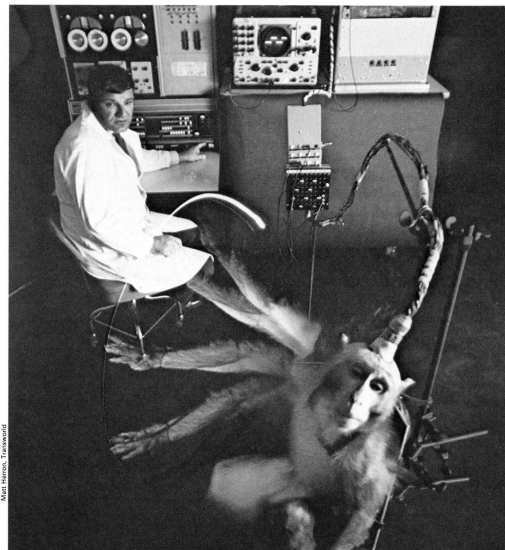

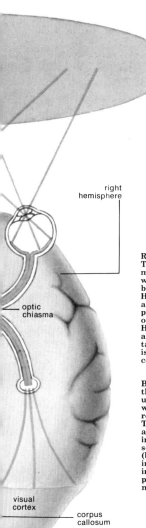

right
hemisphere

optic
chiasma

visual
cortex

corpus
callosum

Right: Robot ARFA.
This is one of the
most sophisticated
working models of
behaviour available.
He can sense objects
and make very simple
plans with the aid
of a computer link.
Here he is executing
a simple handling
task. The human brain
is infinitely more
complex than this.

Below: The regions of
the brain. The first
unit (top) regulates
wakefulness and
response to stimuli.
The second unit codes,
analyses and stores
information from the
senses. The third unit
(bottom) is involved
in the formation of
intentions and
programmes—the higher
mental activities.

S.R.C. Tactile Robot Project

FIRST UNIT (green)

thalamus

hypothalamus

cerebellum

reticular
formation

SECOND UNIT (red)

cerebral
hemisphere

cerebellum

THIRD UNIT (blue)

motor cortex

frontal
lobe

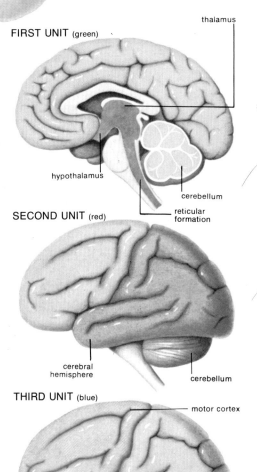

produced in the frontal lobes; it gives
rise to the nerve fibres leading to the
limbs, torso, face, lips and tongue.
Impulses are sent along these nerve fibres
to the periphery of the body in order to
cause movements appropriate to the
devised programmes.

The main distinguishing feature of
human conscious behaviour is the great
part language and speech play in the
thought processes. Even the simplest
kinds of human behaviour require their
aid; it is the frontal lobes which give rise
to linguistic ability and speech and hence
to complex behaviour patterns. A rich
system of interconnections can be found
between the frontal lobes and the other
two functional units of the brain. The
first unit maintains the necessary energy
tone of the cortex by sending up powerful
streams of impulses, the second unit
analyses and processes the sensory information, and the third unit provides plans
of action and the corresponding motor
control.

The split brain

The brain of man and the higher mammals
has the appearance of a double organ
consisting of the right and left hemispheres
of the cerebrum connected by a band of
nervous tissue known as the *corpus
callosum*. An operation to cut the corpus
callosum, hence separating the two halves
of the cerebrum, has proved to be remarkably successful in the control of *epilepsy*
without impairing the general intelligence
or noticeably changing the temperament
or personality of the patient. However,
after conducting more sophisticated tests
on these patients, it has been found that
the two halves of the brain can act to
some extent independently, and even have
separate thoughts and emotions. (It must
be emphasized, however, that this operation is only used as a last resort to control
certain severe forms of epilepsy and where
the fits involve the entire brain. Modern
drugs are quite successful in dealing with
most forms of the disease and this
operation to split the brain has very
rarely been used.)

Sensory information from the right
hand is sent to the left hemisphere of the
brain, and vice versa. In the same way,
visual information from the right half of
our visual field is sent to the left hemisphere and that from the left half of the
visual field is sent to the right hemisphere.
There is, however, some overlap of control
between the two halves of the brain: the
left hemisphere, for example, exercises
normal control over the right hand, but
less than full control over the left hand;
similarly with the right hemisphere.

In right-handed persons the left hemisphere has become dominant to a great
extent. It is this hemisphere which has
become responsible for speech functions
and hence is more active in conscious
thought processes. It has been found, for
instance, that split-brain patients are
able to deal quite well, both orally and in
writing, with information presented to
the dominant left hemisphere. But when
the same information is presented to the
right hemisphere, the response is confused
or incomprehensible. Thus, this means
that if a pencil is placed in the right hand
of a split-brain patient he will describe it
readily as a pencil. Place the same pencil
in the left hand and he might call it a can
opener or a cigarette lighter, or he might
not even attempt to describe it.

Yet the right hemisphere is not subordinate in all higher functions. It is, for
example, more successful than the left in
recognizing patterns (while still less able
to verbally identify them) and in perception of three-dimensional space. The right
hemisphere can also independently
generate emotional reactions and in split-
brain patients this has been successfully
demonstrated. The patient, however, may
still be unable to verbally explain the
emotion.

The above evidence points towards the
astonishing conclusion that the human
brain can be regarded as two brains, each
capable of advanced, although often quite
separate, mental functions. In this respect
it is interesting to note that split-brain
patients can actually carry out two tasks
as fast as the normal person can do one.

43

Chapter 2
Co-ordination

To produce the skilled movements a
juggler needs to maintain balance
simultaneously, the cerebellum receives
mental 'models' from the cerebral
cortex (see p.54). When the movements
are as complex as this, the 'model'
undergoes many rapid variations.

Muscle, contractile tissue making up between 35 and 45 per cent of the body's weight, powers all its actions from the flicker of an eyelid to the tremendous effort needed to lift great weights.

Muscles

The muscles of a fully developed adult male can produce sufficient power to lift a weight of about 25 tonnes. This muscular power-house is totally contained in 42 per cent of a man's body weight. (In a woman, muscles make up 36 per cent of body weight.) It consists of 620 muscles working together to move the 206 bones of the human skeleton. A further 30 or so muscles are needed to ensure the passage of food through the intestines, to circulate the blood round the body and operate certain internal organs.

In man, three different types of muscle can be found: *skeletal* (or *striated*) muscle which is used for locomotion, *smooth* muscle which lines the various organs and intestine, and *heart* (*cardiac*) muscle. They all operate in the same general way —they contract and they relax. This action is possible because the fibres which make up the muscles are able to shorten their length by 30 to 40 per cent.

With very few exceptions (such as the blinking of the eye) single muscles never contract by themselves: rather, whole sets of muscles contract together or in sequence. To produce the complex movements necessary for even the simplest handling task there must be a correspondingly subtle control mechanism. This is the job of the nervous system: it neutralizes the actions of the muscles that are not required, and causes the contraction of muscles which are required. The brain and spinal cord exercise this control through the motor nerve fibres.

Each muscle, however, does not have a 'private line' from the central nervous system (CNS). Impulses travel down the nerve axon from the CNS, branching off to supply a group of muscles which contract together. In order to co-ordinate movement, the CNS must be supplied with information about the length of the muscle and the tension of the *tendons* which attach it to the skeleton.

For example, if we wish to pick up an object our CNS must know the present tension, length and position of the arm muscles in order to cause the correct amount of contraction to move the arm. The CNS must stop increasing the contractions when the arm reaches the object, maintain sufficient contraction to hold the object, and then cause the muscle contractions required to move the arm away. This information is provided by special sense organs called *muscle spindles*, which measure the strain in the muscles, and can be used to pre-set the tension of the muscles.

The control of muscles

Skeletal muscles must contract rapidly in response to messages from the CNS and they must develop tension at the same time to produce an effective mechanical force. Examination of skeletal muscle reveals a junction between the nerve fibre and the muscle surface. This gap (the *end plate*) acts as a kind of amplifier, increasing the effect of the tiny current coming down the nerve fibre to stimulate the much larger muscle fibre.

On the arrival of the nerve impulse, a chemical (known as *acetylcholine*) is released from the motor nerve ending and passes across the gap to stimulate the

Below: This illustration shows the operation of pairs of opposed muscles in the arm. It is the biceps of the upper arm that contract to raise the arm. When the triceps contract and the biceps relax, the arm is lowered. During the contraction, a muscle can shorten its length by up to 40%.

FLEXION

triceps

biceps

EXTENSIONS

triceps

biceps

Right: The major skeletal muscles of the body, seen from the front. Posture and movement are the result of the combined action of these muscles and the skeleton. Muscles work together in groups contracting and relaxing to produce the fine control needed to do even simple tasks like writing one's name.

Below: These remarkable anatomical drawings were published in 1543 by Vesalius. Unlike his contemporaries he made his own detailed examinations rather than rely on already established dogma, so setting new standards in biological studies. These pictures show muscle distribution in the body.

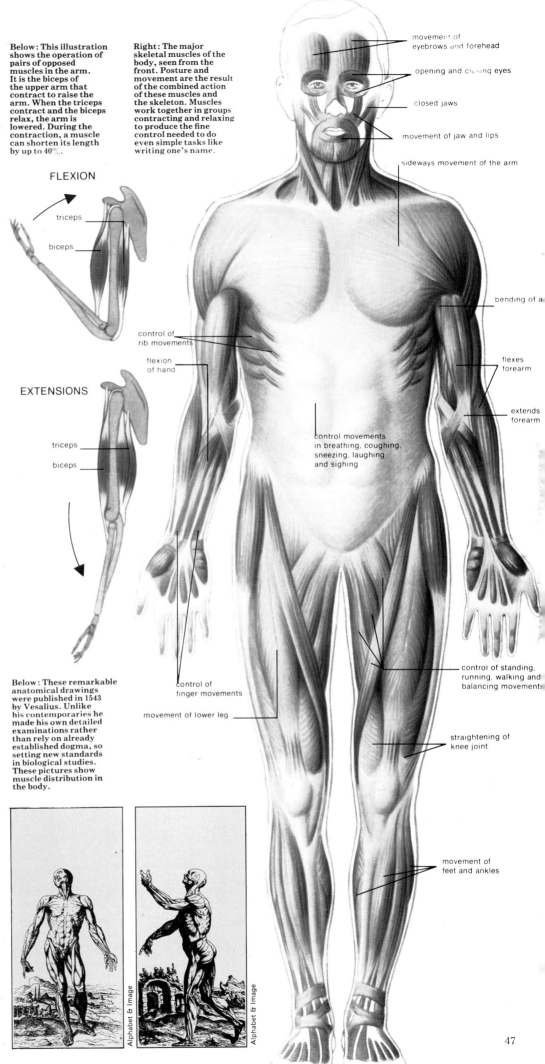

movement of eyebrows and forehead

opening and closing eyes

closed jaws

movement of jaw and lips

sideways movement of the arm

bending of a

flexes forearm

extends forearm

control of rib movements

flexion of hand

control movements in breathing, coughing, sneezing, laughing and sighing

control of finger movements

movement of lower leg

control of standing, running, walking and balancing movements

straightening of knee joint

movement of feet and ankles

Alphabet & Image

Alphabet & Image

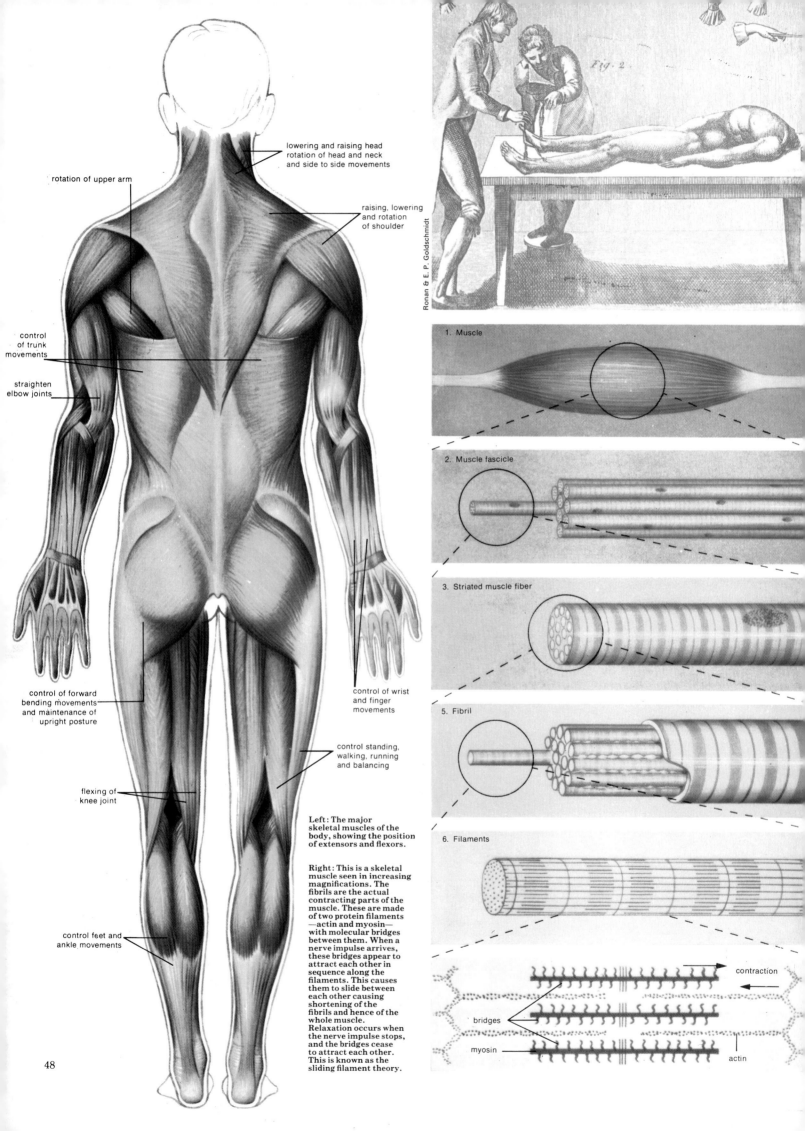

rotation of upper arm

lowering and raising head
rotation of head and neck
and side to side movements

raising, lowering
and rotation
of shoulder

control
of trunk
movements

straighten
elbow joints

control of forward
bending movements
and maintenance of
upright posture

flexing of
knee joint

control feet and
ankle movements

control of wrist
and finger
movements

control standing,
walking, running
and balancing

Ronan & E. P. Goldschmidt

1. Muscle

2. Muscle fascicle

3. Striated muscle fiber

5. Fibril

6. Filaments

contraction

bridges

myosin

actin

Left: The major
skeletal muscles of the
body, showing the position
of extensors and flexors.

Right: This is a skeletal
muscle seen in increasing
magnifications. The
fibrils are the actual
contracting parts of the
muscle. These are made
of two protein filaments
—actin and myosin—
with molecular bridges
between them. When a
nerve impulse arrives,
these bridges appear to
attract each other in
sequence along the
filaments. This causes
them to slide between
each other causing
shortening of the
fibrils and hence of the
whole muscle.
Relaxation occurs when
the nerve impulse stops,
and the bridges cease
to attract each other.
This is known as the
sliding filament theory.

48

Left: The conduction of electricity through a corpse making the muscle of a frog's leg (inserted in the corpse's leg nerve) twitch. Galvani in 1771 first discovered the connection between electricity and muscle contraction.

Below: The Jivaro tribe in Ecuador uses curare tipped darts to paralyse their prey. Curare blocks the chemical nerve transmitter acetylcholine, so stopping impulses from reaching the muscles. Curare is made by boiling certain vines. The picture shows the darts and the gourd in which curare is carried.

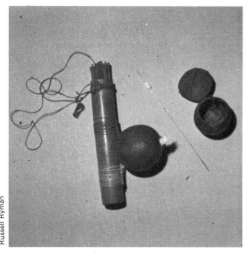

Below: The pictures are photographs taken through a microscope of the different types of muscles found in the body. Both skeletal and heart muscle are striated, meaning they are regularly divided into bands of protein filaments which slide over each other to cause contraction. Smooth muscle is made of small cells which do not have the protein filaments. It is not yet understood how these contract. Heart and smooth muscle have their own internal pacemakers and contract without needing instructions from nerve impulses. Experiments have shown that heart muscle removed from the body and kept alive will continue to beat for a short period of time.

membrane of the muscle fibre. This stimulation is in the form of an electric current which passes along the surface of the muscle, causing it to contract. It takes one millisecond (1/1000th of a second) for the current to pass along the surface of the muscle fibre, the contraction being an all-or-nothing response. Then the fibre relaxes unless another impulse arrives. (If this chemical mechanism is blocked, the result would be paralysis.) And indeed many South American Indian hunters use a poison which effectively does just that and paralyses their prey. The poison, which is called *curare*, is smeared on arrows and spears, and when it enters an animal's bloodstream it instantly blocks the action of acetylcholine.

Heart muscle differs slightly from skeletal muscle because it has a built-in mechanism to maintain the necessary rhythmical contraction quite independently of any nervous connections. A turtle's heart, for instance, entirely removed from its body, can keep on beating for a long time; even small pieces of human heart muscle, kept alive in special solutions, may continue to contract rhythmically.

Smooth muscles react much more slowly to stimulation than skeletal muscles. The nerves, when present, alter the activity of the muscle rather than initiating it. This is in some respects similar to the heart muscle. Contraction takes place rhythmically without direct control from the CNS, and the impulses for contraction come from within the muscle itself.

The mechanics of contraction

To the unaided eye, skeletal muscles have a grainy appearance because they are made up of small fibres. Examination of the fibres through a microscope shows them to be cylinders, which may be several centimetres long, with regular bands (*striations*) dividing them into sections, rather like coins stacked in a pile. The fibres themselves are made up of many cylindrical subunits, the *fibrils*, and these are the structures that actually contract.

Further examination of the fibrils has revealed that they are made of two types of protein—*actin* and *myosin*—which are in the form of long *filaments*, thick ones consisting of myosin and thin ones made of actin. These filaments interlock and are able to slide over each other, so that when the muscle is stretched the filaments tend to be pulled apart like two pieces of a telescope. During shortening they slide into one another. During this contraction

it appears that cross-links are made between the actin and myosin filaments. These are almost instantaneously broken and new links set up slightly further along the filaments. So, by a process of making and breaking these cross-links, the two filaments move towards one another and the whole muscle shortens. This process, of course, takes place very rapidly.

Heart muscle has a similar appearance to skeletal muscle; it has striations and is thought to contract in the same way as skeletal muscle. Smooth muscle has no striations and is composed of small spindle-shaped cells totally lacking in filaments. The mechanism of contraction in smooth muscle still remains a mystery.

The chemistry of contraction

The muscles are biological machines which convert chemical energy into force and mechanical work. The energy for contraction, as for all the other life processes, comes from the chemical reaction between the foodstuffs that we eat and the oxygen that we breathe. Muscles therefore need a good blood supply to bring the essential food and oxygen, and to remove waste products. The actual chemical process involves the breakdown of *glucose* to carbon dioxide and water, thereby releasing energy which is used by the muscle proteins to cause contraction. This chemical reaction requires a very liberal supply of oxygen which is often not available; even during fairly moderate exercise the blood supply is often insufficient to carry enough oxygen to the muscles. To overcome this problem the muscles are able to convert the glucose into a substance called *lactic acid*, without the use of oxygen, which still gives the necessary release of energy.

There is, of course, a limit to the intensity with which we can exercise our muscles. Beyond this limit movement becomes painful and finally impossible. This is due to the accumulation of lactic acid which eventually fatigues the muscles and causes cramps. Removal of the lactic acid requires oxygen; this causes the familiar panting after exercise which brings in oxygen as rapidly as possible to pay off the *oxygen debt*.

Muscles are in fact able to store glucose in the form of *glycogen* (a *carbohydrate*) granules and it is this store which is used during exercise. It has in fact been worked out that if the total amount of fat on the average adult male (about one gallon) were to be converted into muscular energy, this would be enough to cycle 2,000 miles.

Cardiac

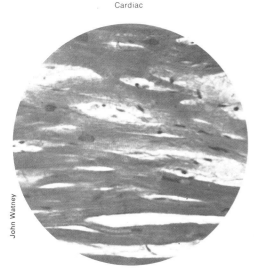

Striated

Smooth

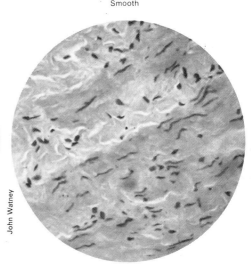

The Skeleton

The skeleton is a masterpiece of architectural and mechanical design. It is the structural support system for the body, enabling us to run, jump and contort ourselves with a freedom unknown amongst our mechanical creations. The 206 bones of the average adult work together with the muscles and connective tissues to move, support and protect the vital organs making up the human body. The individual bones are carefully contoured to fulfil their role in this system, ranging in size from the powerful thigh bone or *femur*—about 500 mm (20 inches) long and more than 25 mm (1 inch) across at mid-shaft—to the *pisiform*, the smallest of the wrist bones, found at the base of the little finger and shaped like a split pea.

The skeleton as a whole consists of *bone*, *cartilage*, *tendons* and *ligaments* having a remarkable external and internal design. The femur, for example, must withstand great weight and pressure—at times up to 1200 pounds per square inch (83 bar) during walking. Its shaft is shaped like a hollow cylinder to give maximum strength with minimum bulk; internally it is filled with cross-hatching of bone combining great resistance to pressure with very light weight. Another example of functionalism appears in the *vertebrae* of the spinal column. To help bear the weight of the body they are formed as solid cylinders with a bony ring at the back to provide a protected passage for the nerve cord. Behind the ring three spurs protrude, to join with the ribs and anchor the muscles of the back.

The rib cage provides an excellent example of the versatility of joints and the protective function of the skeleton. It must protect the delicate tissues of the lungs and heart, whilst being able to expand and contract to bring in fresh supplies of air. Cartilage joins the ribs to the breastbone in the front, providing a movable elastic connection. At the back, the ribs are fitted onto the vertebrae by tiny gliding, rotating joints permitting individual movement and allowing the rib cage to adopt different rhythms of breathing. In contrast to these tiny joints is the large ball-and-socket joint of the hip, which holds the rounded end of the femur in a self-lubricating socket. The flexibility of this joint can be seen in the movements of a ballerina, or the contortions of a gymnast.

Movement is restricted to certain planes by the action of other joints. For example, the knee joint makes certain that the leg only bends in one way like a simple hinge; the shoulder has a shallow ball-and-socket joint restricting its movement (as anyone who has suffered from a dislocated shoulder will testify). The head rotates on the two top vertebrae in the neck. These are known as the *atlas* (named after the Greek god who carried the world on his shoulders) and the *axis*, which pivots the head and the atlas. The movements of these joints enables us to shake, nod and turn our heads.

The composition of bone

Bones have a complex internal structure. The structure of the femur, for example, varies from the thick-walled middle sections of the shaft, to the thin, expanded

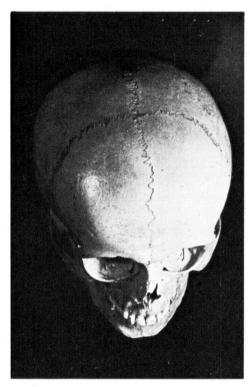

end parts. Here, the surface is contoured to accommodate the many insertions of ligaments and muscles concerned with joint action. Underneath the expanded ends is a delicate tracery of small bone filaments which have the appearance of foam. Although they look delicate, they are orientated to take the forces which act on the end of the bone giving the strength and lightness which is characteristic of the skeleton. The spaces in the centre of the bone are filled with *marrow* which supplies most of the blood components and aids the bone's nutrition.

Closer examination of bone reveals a basic structure of fibrous protein (*collagen*) twisted like a rope, surrounded and impregnated with needle-like crystals of *apatite* (a phosphate of calcium). In the embryo these fibrils of collagen are tangled up more or less at random, whilst in older bones they are arranged in very thin sheets. This difference is due to the quick build-up of bone during the embryonic stage, and the later erosion of these tangled fibres to expand the size of the bone when a child is born and begins to move about. Transferring the fibrous protein from the centre to the outside, and laying it down in sheets, gives the bone its characteristic hard cylindrical structure. Any growth or change of shape takes place either by the laying down of new bone on an already existing surface, or by the erosion of pre-formed bone and its transference to the outside of the bone.

By this method of eroding and laying down of new bone, a complex system of canals is formed, known as the *Haversian canals*, which contain the blood vessels and nerves. Bone is, in fact, well supplied with blood. If we strip away the outermost layer blood oozes out of the minute pores on the surface.

Unlike the shells of animals like snails, bone is very much alive. It is full of bone cells called *osteocytes*, which live entombed in tiny caverns called *lacunae*, and actually form the hard parts of the bone. These cells can communicate with each other through small tubes containing slender extensions of the cells. Blood

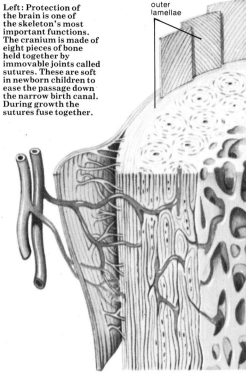

Left: Protection of the brain is one of the skeleton's most important functions. The cranium is made of eight pieces of bone held together by immovable joints called sutures. These are soft in newborn children to ease the passage down the narrow birth canal. During growth the sutures fuse together.

outer lamellae

Right: This microscopic photograph shows the growth area of bone. Cartilage (shown here in blue) is formed first by the cartilage cells; this attracts a deposit of calcium which covers the protein fibres. The cartilage cells are now known as osteoblasts (bone-formers) and cause apatite crystals to be deposited around the calcium, thereby forming hard bone (shown here in white). Cartilage can be seen changing to hard bone at the centre of the photograph. Hundreds of cartilage and bone-forming cells can be seen clustered around this area—the epiphyseal plate—between the end of the bone and its shaft, the major site of bone expansion.

Picturepoint

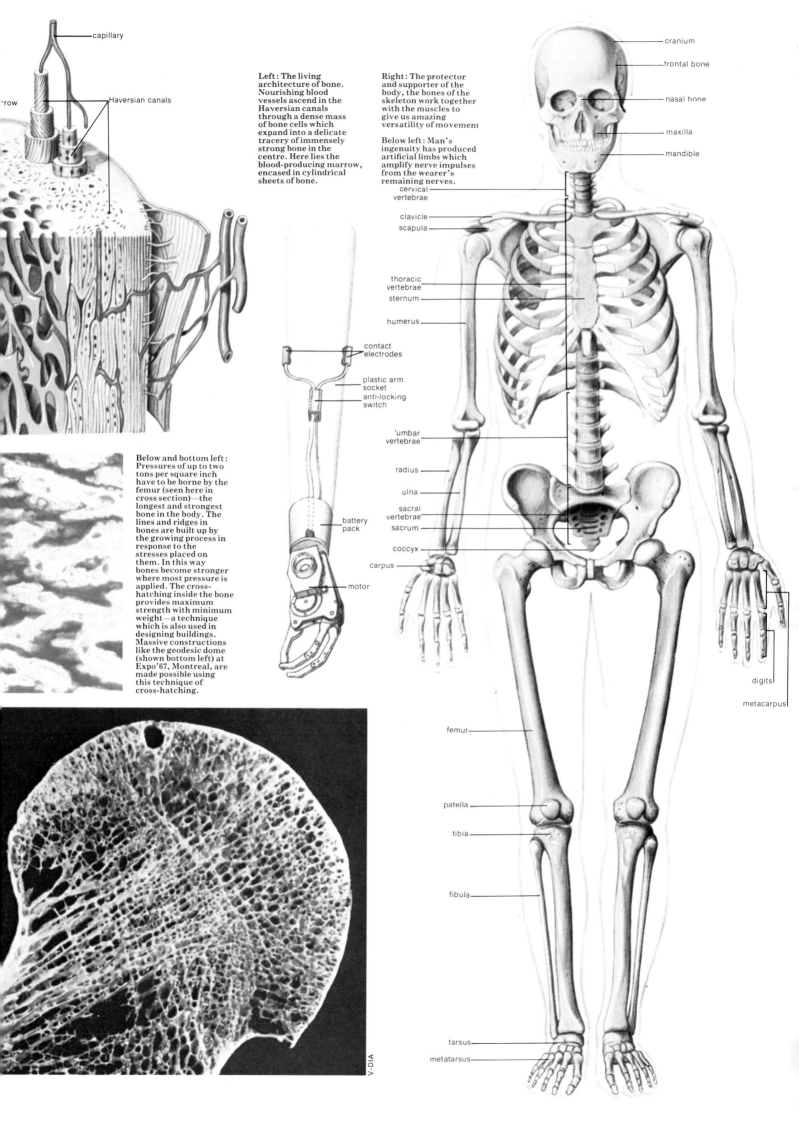

capillary

Haversian canals

row

Left: The living
architecture of bone.
Nourishing blood
vessels ascend in the
Haversian canals
through a dense mass
of bone cells which
expand into a delicate
tracery of immensely
strong bone in the
centre. Here lies the
blood-producing marrow,
encased in cylindrical
sheets of bone.

Right: The protector
and supporter of the
body, the bones of the
skeleton work together
with the muscles to
give us amazing
versatility of movement

Below left: Man's
ingenuity has produced
artificial limbs which
amplify nerve impulses
from the wearer's
remaining nerves.

Below and bottom left:
Pressures of up to two
tons per square inch
have to be borne by the
femur (seen here in
cross section)—the
longest and strongest
bone in the body. The
lines and ridges in
bones are built up by
the growing process in
response to the
stresses placed on
them. In this way
bones become stronger
where most pressure is
applied. The cross-
hatching inside the bone
provides maximum
strength with minimum
weight—a technique
which is also used in
designing buildings.
Massive constructions
like the geodesic dome
(shown bottom left) at
Expo'67, Montreal, are
made possible using
this technique of
cross-hatching.

contact
electrodes

plastic arm
socket
anti-locking
switch

battery
pack

motor

cranium
frontal bone
nasal bone
maxilla
mandible

cervical
vertebrae
clavicle
scapula

thoracic
vertebrae
sternum
humerus

'umbar
vertebrae

radius

ulna

sacral
vertebrae
sacrum

coccyx

carpus

digits

metacarpus

femur

patella

tibia

fibula

tarsus
metatarsus

V·DIA

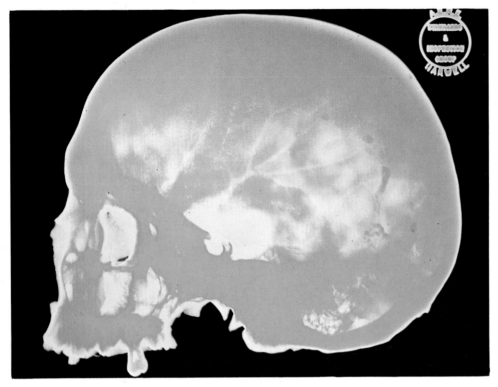

The structure of joints

Cartilage is found mainly in the joints. For example, its rubbery nature makes it an ideal protective padding between the vertebrae of the spinal column. It eases the movement of the small bones and helps to absorb the shocks being transmitted along the spine every time we take a step forward. The ends of the bones making up joints, like the ball-and-socket of the hip and the hinge of the knee, are also covered by a smooth, protective layer of cartilage which persists for life. Our joints work so smoothly and effortlessly that only when there is some malfunction do we notice them. Inflammation and swelling, or wear and tear on the cartilage of the weight-bearing joints in particular, often causes crippling pain. A slipped-disc, another painful malfunction, is the result of one of the thick pads of cartilage separating the vertebrae becoming dislodged and protruding onto a nerve.

The space between the bones in a joint is filled with a small amount of lubricating fluid, known as *synovial fluid*. Like the oil in a car engine, it reduces the friction between the moving parts. The whole joint is enclosed in a protective bag and prevented from moving too far by the *ligaments* which are strong bands of collagen connecting the two bones at the joint, so preventing dislocation.

In both the male and female pelvis, the bones are tightly bound together by joints made entirely of cartilage, but in the female, during the last stage of pregnancy, these joints loosen and separate slightly to enable the large head of the child to emerge more easily. The bone plates making up the skull of a new-born child are soft and able to move over each other slightly. This too makes it easier for the child's head to negotiate the narrow birth canal. The skull plates actually fix together as the child grows, to form a strong protective helmet for the delicate tissues of the brain.

Fractures and the growth of bone

Although the femur is able to withstand pressures up to 20,000 pounds per square inch during the landing from pole-vaulting, if a fraction of that pressure is applied at right angles to the shaft of the bone it will break. The cylindrical shape and hard, brittle material are designed to withstand great pressures applied to the ends, not to the sides. This makes bones vulnerable to fractures, especially through a blow or fall. (The healing process, however, can soon make these undetectable.)

The healing process begins immediately with the formation of a large blood clot between the broken ends of the bone. After a few days the minerals from the sharp ends of the bone are completely absorbed into the bloodstream leaving only the rubbery collagen fibres. Meanwhile a fibrous network of connective tissue grows through the blood clot holding the fragments together. Osteocytes migrate from inside the bone and begin to produce new hard bone at the fracture site. In two to three weeks this soft, calcium-rich bone has formed a callous, bridging the gap between the bone ends. The callous hardens and the bone is ready to perform its supportive functions. Over a number of years remodelling removes all trace of the callous.

Above: An X-ray photograph (radiogram) of a 300 year old skull. The photograph has been artificially coloured to show the different densities. Information about the diet, conditions and physique of past humanity can be found from the study of skeletal remains, some of which are over 2 million years old.

Below: The knee joint, the largest joint in the body, is shown here in cross-section. It is held together by muscles and ligaments, and enclosed in a capsule containing fluid which lubricates the joint. The patella (knee-cap) protects the joint and anchors the tendons coming from the powerful leg muscles.

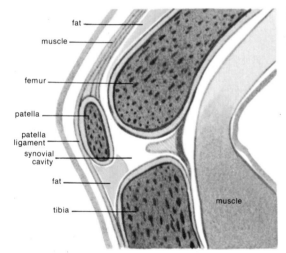

fat
muscle
femur
patella
patella ligament
synovial cavity
fat
tibia
muscle

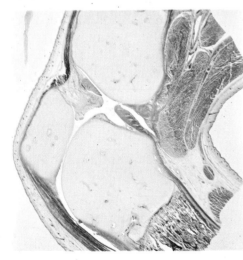

Brian Bracegirdle

vessels, which permeate the bone, provide nutrients for the cells and a means by which the 'metabolized' products can be expelled. Even so, osteocytes in patches of bone may die, leaving empty lacunae which fill with mineral deposits. These act as a storehouse for the body's mineral reserves.

Throughout the body's life bone is being continually laid down and removed in response to stresses placed upon it. This results in the building up of bone where it is under pressure around the joints, and the removal of unnecessary bumps. Should, for example, a child break a femur which is then wrongly aligned, the healing will look initially unsightly due to the formation of a large *callous*. This will be removed in a couple of years by remodelling of the bone.

Both the volume and density of bone can be made to increase by doing extra work and subjecting the skeleton to increased loads. Cavalrymen have been known to acquire bones in their buttocks and thighs, for example, quite distinct from the normal hip and femur bones. These have arisen entirely as a result of the cavalrymen's continual work on horses. Conversely, by leading a sedentary life bone is lost, so people kept in bed for long periods suffer from thin, weakened bones. Astronauts on prolonged flights have similar problems due to the lack of gravity which reduces stress on the skeleton. The sudden return to normal gravity, and the rigorous effort of moving again in a world of normal weight, causes new strains on the weakened skeleton.

All the parts of the skeleton are made of collagen fibres, except that in bone the collagen is surrounded and impregnated with mineral deposits which give it its strength. By dissolving away most of these mineral components, the remaining collagen resembles a dog's rubber bone; in fact a long bone like the femur can be tied in a knot. If the collagen part of the bone is removed by burning or decay, the result will be a dry, brittle, hard object with the strength of reinforced concrete.

Protection of the brain is one of the skeleton's most important functions. The cranium is made up of eight pieces of bone. In the foetus these are soft, with gaps between them called *fontanelles* to allow for moulding of the head during pregnancy.

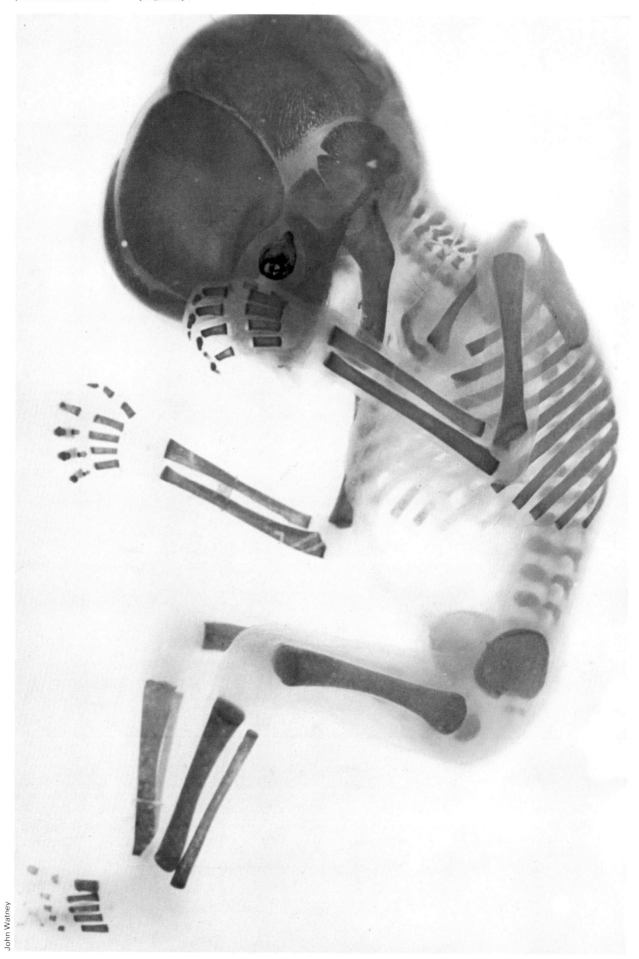

Co-ordination and Control

The whole gamut of human behaviour depends upon the integrated actions of the skeleton, muscles and nervous system. Together they provide us with the marvellously sophisticated co-ordination and control necessary for even the simplest of actions. Walking, for example, requires the orderly contraction and relaxation of the muscles of the legs, trunk and arms acting on the bones and joints of the skeleton.

This _all_ happens without a conscious effort having to be made, but the skill of walking, although taken very much for granted once acquired, has to be learnt. A young baby rolls over, crawls and sits before finally standing; the feet are then placed widely apart to give a stable base, and the first steps are attempted. The baby quickly learns to balance more efficiently and progresses to even more complex co-ordinated tasks such as running, jumping and avoiding objects, and

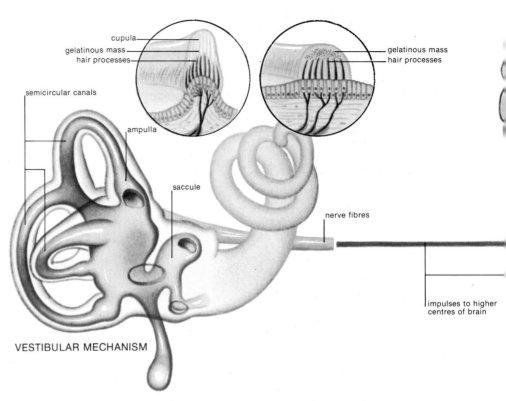

cupula
gelatinous mass
hair processes

gelatinous mass
hair processes

semicircular canals

ampulla

saccule

nerve fibres

impulses to higher centres of brain

VESTIBULAR MECHANISM

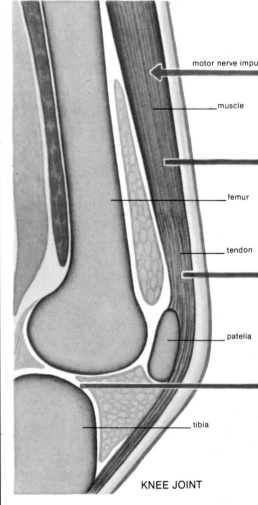

motor nerve impu

muscle

femur

tendon

patella

tibia

KNEE JOINT

Above: Information about the inner world of the body is sent to the CNS by sense organs called proprioceptors. The vestibular apparatus in the inner ear tell us our position in space by movement of the fluid as we tilt our head. The joint receptors respond to changes in angle of the joint. The muscle spindles record the amount of stretching in the muscle, and the Golgi tendon organs prevent overstretching by inhibiting motor impulses reaching the muscles.

Left: Joints, muscle and bone team together to give the marvellous versatility of the hand, seen here in a triple exposed X-ray photograph.

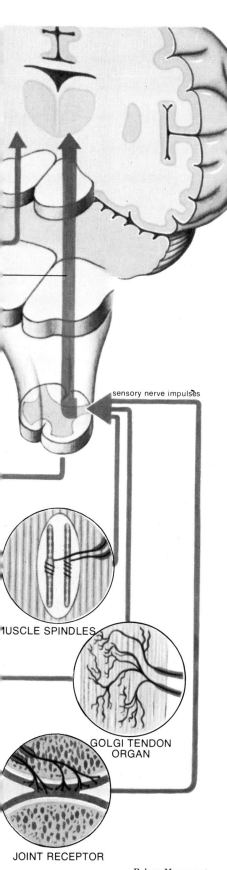

sensory nerve impulses

MUSCLE SPINDLES

GOLGI TENDON
ORGAN

JOINT RECEPTOR

Below: Movement as
seen by the camera of
Eadweard Muybridge
(1830-1904).

throughout life goes on acquiring more and more modifications of the basic walking pattern. This is only one example of co-ordinated physical activity, but the same applies to intellectual, perceptual and emotional responses.

In order to carry out any co-ordinated movement we must first know the positions and relationships in space of the parts of the body. This information is obtained from the eyes, the balance mechanism in the inner ear, the muscles, the joints and the skin. Information about the conditions in the interior of the body is known as proprioceptive information and the sense organs involved are called *proprioceptors*.

We can get some idea of the sensitivity of the proprioceptors by trying a simple test: with the eyes closed, hold your right hand out in front of you. Move your left hand as far out to the side as possible, and slowly move it towards the front so that the index fingers of both hands come into contact. Although the contact might not be absolutely accurate, it will be very close.

An appreciation of the position of the limbs and bodily parts comes mainly from information supplied to the central nervous system by the proprioceptors in the joints. These are found inside the fibrous joint capsules and are basically of two types: one responds to the increase in the bending (flexing) of the joint, and the other type responds to the straightening extension of the joint. Most of the receptors are active over a limited range of movement, which gives the central nervous system accurate information about the position of the joint whilst both stationary and in motion.

Muscle receptors
Very complex proprioceptors lie within the muscles themselves acting as microscopic strain gauges, sending nerve messages to the central nervous system about the length and rate of movement of the muscle fibres. These are the *muscle spindles*. Their information is used to keep a constant check on the action of the motor nerves on the muscles: monitoring and regulating the streams of impulses travelling to the muscle fibres.

The muscle spindles are very important in the maintenance of posture. They can be pre-set to a particular muscle tension, so that variations in the stretching of the muscle will cause contraction of that muscle in order to maintain the pre-set tension. For example, if a soldier standing to attention sways forward slightly, the muscle spindles will be stimulated and the information will be sent along the stretch reflex pathway to the central nervous system (CNS) and to the muscles. This causes contraction of the back muscles, so pulling the body back to its original position. This is the basis of all the stretch reflex actions (which includes the knee-jerk reflex) and is not under conscious control.

In the junction between the muscle and tendons lie the *Golgi tendon organs*. They only respond to larger stretching of the muscle, bearing some weight. They are not concerned with the stretch reflex, which is activated by only minute stretches. Although their function is still something of a mystery, it is thought that they protect the muscle from damage by stopping motor impulses from the CNS to the muscle when it is becoming over-stretched. This stops contraction in the muscle and hence prevents damage.

Co-ordinated muscle action
Individual muscles do not act in isolation. Movement requires the co-ordinated actions of groups of muscles. Almost all the limb muscles run over two or more joints, so that when they contract several quite different movements may be produced in several joints. It is the job of the nervous system to co-ordinate the actions of the muscles. To take a relatively simple example, the biceps muscle is attached at its upper end to the outer tip of the shoulder blade and at its lower end to the ulna, one of the bones of the forearm. When the biceps contracts, three movements tend to occur: the elbow flexes, the forearm rotates so that the palm becomes uppermost, and the upper arm rises away from the side of the chest. If we wish to drive in a screw, for example, it is necessary to rotate the forearm and to neutralize the flexing of the elbow. This is accomplished by a powerful contraction of the triceps (the muscle on the back of the upper arm). In fact, this kind of movement is still more complex since numerous other muscles participate.

The control of these contracting muscles is a very complicated task, and is brought about by the motor nerve fibres from the brain and spinal cord. Each nerve fibre has branches which supply a group of muscle fibres, and when impulses travel down the nerve fibre all the members of this group (the *motor unit*) contract together. The number of muscle fibres in a motor unit varies according to the precision required. In the muscles which move the eyeballs, for example, only about ten muscle fibres are linked together in each motor unit, while in the biceps each motor unit contains more than a thousand muscle fibres: the eyeballs need much finer control mechanisms than the arms.

Skilled movements
Adult human beings are able to execute an astonishing number of skilled movements acquired mainly in the first few years of life. They require a complex feed-back of information from the senses to maintain the sequence of events which makes up the movement. Unlike simple reflex actions which continue through to their conclusion after the stimulus has been applied, requiring no further information, complex movements require constant monitoring.

The importance of this feed-back of

information can be seen when we look at the formation of speech. As we talk, our words are constantly being monitored by our ears. If the speaker is prevented from hearing his own words as he says them, but is allowed to do so after a brief delay, his speech becomes totally incoherent, with jumbled words and widely changing frequencies. He is trying to monitor feedback of sounds which are no longer appropriate to the sentence and the words being spoken. Equally, if a person is asked to write but, instead of seeing his hand directly, sees it projected on a television screen, there is no disturbance in his performance so long as the angle of the camera corresponds with that of his own eyes. But if the camera position is altered so that the picture no longer appears at the normal angle, his performance becomes confused and writing becomes very difficult.

The cerebellum seems to play an important part in the production of skilled movements. Proprioceptive information arrives at the cerebellum, and appears to be compared with a mental 'model' of the movement received from the cerebral cortex. Muscular movements are then modified to correspond with this 'model'. If the skilled movements are very complex

Above and right: Walking is more difficult than it appears. Widely spaced legs provide a stable base for this child learning man's upright posture. Many mistakes are made before the CNS is able to co-ordinate the mass of information received each second from the sense organs, and exert the fine control necessary for movement.

Sport stretches our powers of co-ordination to the limit. Constant monitoring and feed-back of information takes place at a phenomenal rate unknown to the conscious mind. To construct a machine with the skills of an athlete is inconceivable.

Below: Muybridge pictures.

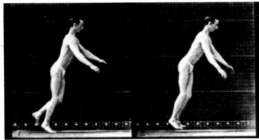
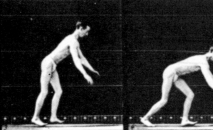

(playing the piano for example) the 'model' produced by the cerebral cortex must undergo many rapid changes in response to the variations required by the movement. Models, and the ability to change them, have to be learned, and it is this learning process which makes necessary the long hours of practice to acquire skills like piano-playing.

Posture

The maintenance of posture is one of the most fundamental tasks of co-ordination and control, yet it requires the whole range of mechanisms so far described. The most important point to remember when considering posture, or indeed any control system, is that accurate control is impossible if accurate information is absent. For postural control we must have certain information. We must know the body position. Is the body lying, standing, sitting or falling? This information is provided by the eyes, by the balance mechanism and by the skin receptors. We must know the position of the limbs. The eyes coupled with the joint receptors provide this information. Finally we must know the state of contraction of the muscles. The spindles and the Golgi tendon organs tell us this. The central nervous system receives all such information and uses it to direct muscular contraction in the appropriate way.

Fatigue

Muscle is living tissue and depends on an intact nerve and blood supply, bringing oxygen and nutrients for tissue metabolism into the area, and removing the products of this process. During exercise, a muscle requires about fifty times more oxygen per minute than when at rest. Thus the oxidation process is speeded up and many more breakdown products accumulate in the tissues. This causes the muscle to be stiff and painful—particularly if the muscle is only fully exercised occasionally. Continued use causes channels to be opened which aid the removal of these excess products, and so the muscle gets used to vigorous exercise.

Muscle fatigue, however, will occur after repetitive action of a particular muscle, and contraction of the muscle may become impossible for a short time afterwards. This is not due to malfunction of the muscle tissue itself or the nerve supplying it, but is caused by blockage at the junction between these two—the *neuromuscular junction*. Transmission from neurone to neurone, and neurone to muscle, is by a chemical transmitter substance and when this is blocked in some way conduction across the synapse ceases. This can be seen happening on repeated stimulation of the knee-jerk reflex. At first the response is brisk but continued taps on the patellar tendon result in an increasingly sluggish response and eventually no response at all. Fatigue has occurred in the synapses of this reflex pathway.

Tension and anxiety also affect alertness and efficiency of muscle action. A little tension, such as that experienced by an athlete before a race, may serve to enhance performance, but prolonged stress will eventually lead to a deterioration. In the neuromuscular system, this manifests itself as muscle weakness, and in severe cases as muscle tremor.

Normally, we carry out complex co-ordinated activities without ever having to think how we are going to do them or what changes are taking place in the body in order to perform them. Even simple tasks are surprisingly complicated when we examine all the components needed to produce movement. We have built in reactions which cope with all the changes necessary and the resulting movement is smooth, co-ordinated and controlled.

Photri

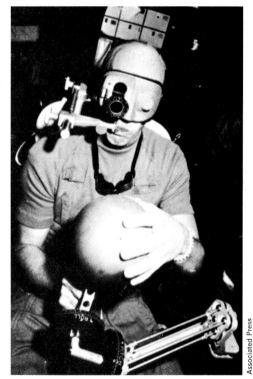

Associated Press

Left and above: Space flights cause new problems in co-ordination. Astronauts in weightless conditions have to learn to orientate themselves without normal functioning of the balance mechanism. Space walkers must use great caution. The photograph (left) shows Edward White hovering near the Gemini 4 space-ship. Rigorous testing procedures are undertaken to check the ability of astronauts to orientate themselves without gravitational clues. The equipment above is used to test visual and tactile orientation without gravity. Astronauts perform quite successfully on these tests.

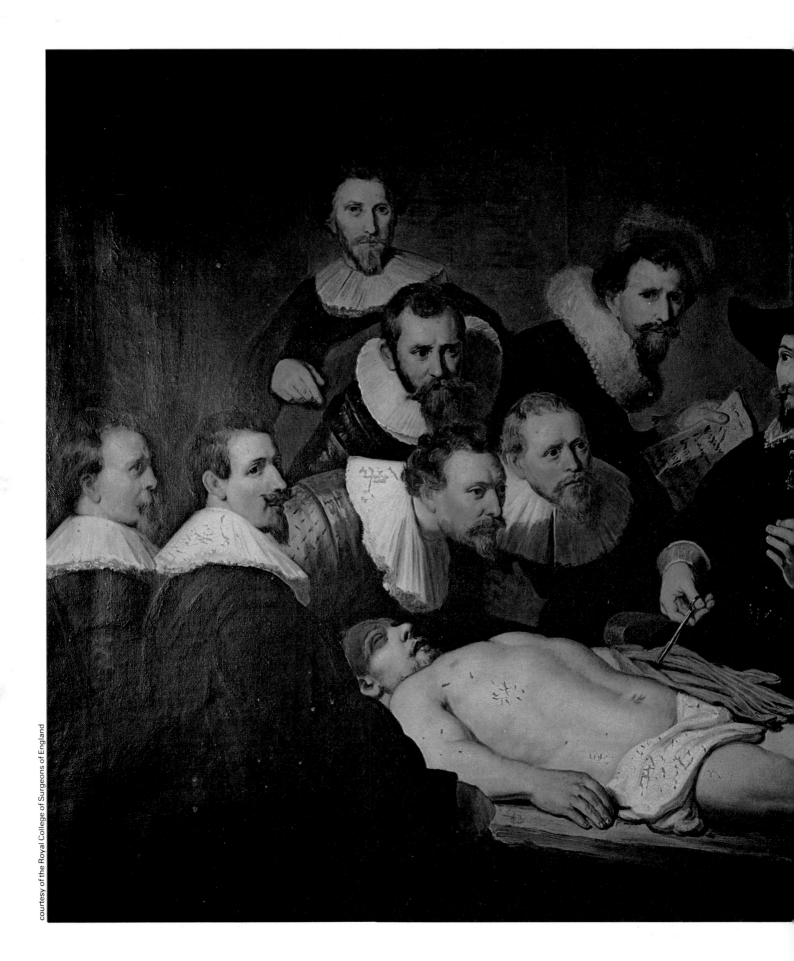

Chapter 3
Circulation

The circulation of the blood was
discovered by William Harvey, who
published his treatise on the subject
in 1628. The main purpose of circulation
is to carry oxygen and nutrients to the
tissues, and to disperse carbon dioxide
and waste products.

The Essence of Blood

Blood is truly 'the essence of life' for this vital fluid carries to every living cell in the body the nutrients necessary for providing energy and the raw materials needed for tissue growth, maintenance and repair.

It is vital, too, in clearing away from the cells all the waste products of their various activities, particularly the carbon dioxide produced when food is burned with oxygen for energy.

And blood has a third essential role: it acts as the body's policeman, destroying or neutralizing any potentially-dangerous foreign invaders like bacteria or other germs.

The average man has some five litres (10 pints) of blood in his body; women have about 15 per cent less. Blood makes up about 1/14th of the total weight of the human body. Around 45 per cent of the blood volume is composed of various types of specialized cells each adapted for its particular task. These cells—the most important are called *red cells* or *red corpuscles*, and *white cells* or *white corpuscles*—are suspended in a pale yellow liquid called *plasma*. They are so small that just one drop of blood will contain as many as 250,000,000 red cells and 400,000 white ones.

The transporting medium

The body contains slightly more than three litres of plasma, much of which is water. Its main task is to transport round the body a variety of substances in solution, some of which are salt, proteins and glucose.

Most nutrients in food are absorbed into the blood through the walls of the small intestine; some of them can be taken directly to cells; others first have to be processed into more useful compounds by

Mansell

John Watney

Mary Evans

Left: Blood-letting was a popular method of treatment until the last century (and is still used in some parts of the world). Ill health was believed to be caused by an imbalance of the body humours due to a surfeit of blood. Some heart conditions are still treated by reducing the amount of blood to relieve strain on the circulation.

Above and top: Haemophilia, a disease which prevents blood from clotting, was common amongst European royal families —10 princes descended from Queen Victoria were affected. The normal clotting process is shown above—the thread-like fibrins mesh around the blood cells and eventually form a solid clot.

the specialized 'chemical factories' of the body—that is the liver and other glands. Some of these chemicals, called *hormones*, regulate body processes, while others, such as *enzymes*, act as catalysts for various chemical reactions in the cells.

The capillaries, the smallest branches of the blood vessels allow water, sugars for energy, amino-acids (the constituents of proteins which are themselves the building blocks of living matter) and various other chemicals to seep through their walls. Big molecules like the plasma proteins, however, cannot readily squeeze through the capillary walls. At the beginning of the return journey to the heart, the pressure in the capillaries has dropped and the waste products of the cells' activities are drawn in. Blood is continually being 'washed' by the kid-

neys: they extract the waste products which are finally disposed of in the urine.

The plasma proteins are called *albumin*, *globulin* and *fibrinogen*. The main task of the most abundant one, albumin, is in maintaining the blood's *osmotic pressure*. It is this pressure—acting in the opposite direction to that exerted by the heart—which pulls in water and the cells' waste products as the blood begins its journey back through the veins. Antibodies, special compounds which neutralize foreign invaders such as germs, are made of gamma-globulin proteins. They are formed in the spleen or lymph nodes in response to specific infections and they continue to circulate in the blood after the initial infection has been conquered, so providing *immunity* against further attack. Fibrinogen is responsible for blood clotting and like albumin, is manufactured in the liver.

The oxygen carriers

Red blood cells get their colour from a special pigment called *haemoglobin*—formed from a protein and an iron compound. Each cell is very small, about .008 cm (three-thousandths of an inch) in diameter and is shaped like a round cushion, with a hollow on each side. The haemoglobin picks up oxygen from the lungs and transports it to every cell in the body. On releasing its oxygen cargo—and changing from bright red to a dark red or purplish colour in the process—the red cell picks up carbon dioxide which is deposited on the next circuit through the lungs.

Red cells are manufactured in the bone marrow and have a life span of some 120 days. When they wear out—and it is a staggering fact that something like five million red cells are being destroyed in our bodies every second—they are broken down into their constituent parts, some of which can be used again in the manu-

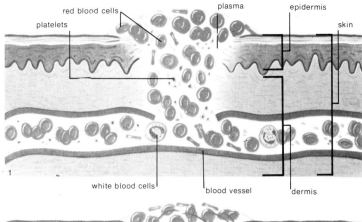

red blood cells
platelets
plasma
epidermis
skin

1

white blood cells
blood vessel
dermis

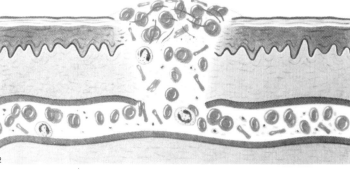

2

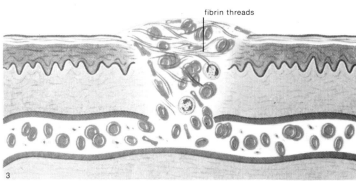

fibrin threads

3

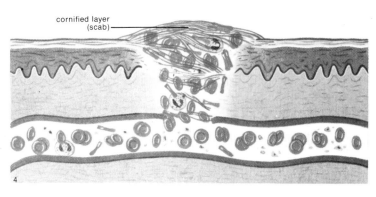

cornified layer
(scab)

4

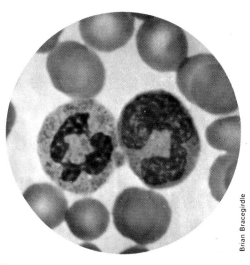

Brian Bracegirdle

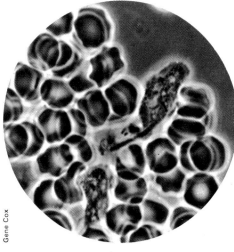

Gene Cox

PER LITRE OF NORMAL ADULT BLOOD

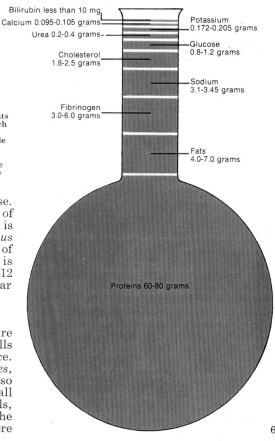

Bilirubin less than 10 mg
Calcium 0.095-0.105 grams
Urea 0.2-0.4 grams
Cholesterol 1.8-2.5 grams
Fibrinogen 3.0-6.0 grams

Potassium 0.172-0.205 grams
Glucose 0.8-1.2 grams
Sodium 3.1-3.45 grams
Fats 4.0-7.0 grams

Proteins 60-80 grams

Right: A litre of blood taken from a normal, healthy adult should contain all of the ingredients in the quantities listed in the table. Excessive amounts of some substances, such as cholesterols, cause heart problems in middle and later years, while deficiencies (of calcium for instance) impede the growth of bones and the clotting process.

facture of new red cells.

There are many diseases due to deficiencies of red cells and they are collectively known as *anaemia*. *Haemolytic anaemia*, for example, is due to excessive destruction of red cells, which may be caused by poisoning, by a disease like malaria, or by an inherited condition. There is also a special type of haemolytic anaemia which sometimes occurs in newborn babies.

Iron is essential for the manufacture of haemoglobin and although the body usually has good stores, a slow but steady loss of blood—as, say, from an ulcer—can cause anaemia. Women seem to be more vulnerable than men, and excessively heavy periods can make the problem worse. In pregnancy, too, when the mother is supplying iron to her baby,

she may not have enough for her own use. Anaemia is sometimes a symptom of malnutrition, especially if the diet is lacking in iron and folic acid. *Pernicious anaemia*, in which large numbers of abnormally large red cells are made, is due to a lack of proper absorption of B12 but is now easily controlled by regular injections of the vitamin.

The disease fighters

White cells, known as *leukocytes*, are spherical, slightly bigger than red cells and form the body's disease fighting force. There are two main types: *granulocytes*, also formed in bone marrow and so called because they contain many small granules scattered throughout their cells, and *lymphocytes* which are formed in the lymphatic system and in the spleen. There

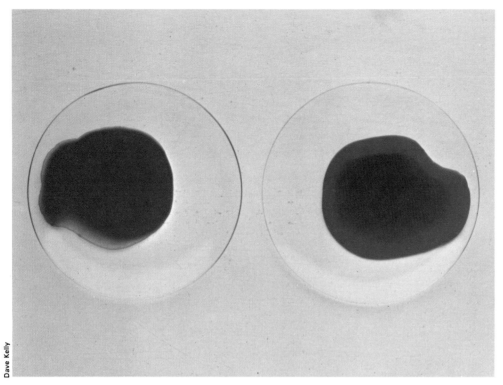

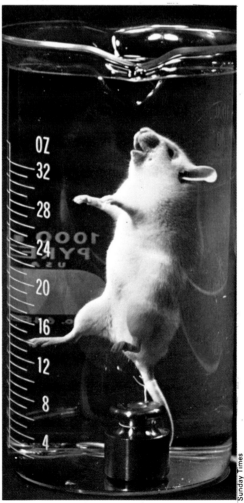

are about three times as many granulocytes as lymphocytes.

Granulocytes attack invaders such as bacteria by engulfing and consuming them. They are geared for instant action and congregate quickly at the appearance of an infection or injury. Lymphocytes act more slowly and are involved in the production of antibodies. There are actually more lymphocytes outside the blood than in it, living in all tissue. In fact, white cells seem to use blood only as a means of transport and unlike red cells they can seep out of blood vessels into surrounding tissue.

There is a considerable increase in white cell production when the body is invaded. Bacterial infection, for example, may cause them to multiply their numbers by three or four times. A *blood count*, in which a small quantity of blood is examined to find out the numbers and types of cell present, can therefore be a valuable aid to diagnosis. For example, in a patient suffering from an ill-defined stomach ache, large numbers of white cells might indicate appendicitis rather than indigestion. Haemoglobin levels can be checked in blood counts, too, and powerful modern microscopes make possible visual examination of any physical abnormalities in the cells.

Sometimes white cells proliferate needlessly, producing a cancer-like condition called *leukaemia* and chronic overproduction of granulocytes leads to a similar condition called chronic leukaemia.

Bone marrow is sensitive to various poisons and to radiation, which can hinder the production of both red and white cells, leading to a dangerous but rare condition called *aplastic anaemia*.

The *pus* which may arise from inflammation is a mixture of dead white cells and the micro-organisms they have engulfed. White cells may also break down and dispose of inanimate invaders, even something as large as a wood splinter or a thorn. They also carry away clotted blood and dead tissue after wounds have healed.

Above: The blood sample on the left is arterial blood. It is bright red when it has just left the lungs, where the haemoglobin particles absorb oxygen, forming oxyhaemoglobin, but as it passes through the tissues, giving up the oxygen, it returns to the dark red colour of the sample of blood on the right.

Below: An experiment to test the viability of a form of artificial blood for emergency purposes. The mouse was suspended in the oxygen-carrying liquid to determine the amount of oxygen in it. When removed from the liquid after a few hours the mouse continued to breathe normally and suffered no ill effects.

The clotting process

Obviously so essential a fluid as the blood must be guarded against losses. Although we can lose up to 15 per cent without any ill-effects, a greater loss can be serious and often fatal.

Loss of blood from the circulation—either internally or externally—is called *haemorrhage*. Slow sustained bleeding leads to anaemia and rapid bleeding causes *shock*, resulting from a fall in pressure to a level inadequate to maintain blood flow to the heart. While most body organs can function for a time with reduced blood supply, the brain cannot and this is the lethal factor following serious injury or acute illness.

The body has a built-in system to prevent blood loss: the *clotting mechanism*, and specialized cells called *platelets* play a vital role in the process. Platelets, also made in the bone marrow, are much smaller than red cells. There are some 15 million of them in each drop of blood. When a blood vessel is damaged, platelets congregate and stick to the site of the injury and to each other, forming a plug. As they stick together platelets release substances essential to set the clotting mechanism going (the injured tissue itself also releases similar substances).

Clotting is fundamentally a change in that soluble plasma protein fibrinogen to an insoluble, thread-like protein, *fibrin*—more than a dozen factors are involved in this conversion, but they cannot come into operation until those substances are released by the platelets. The fibrin strands mesh around blood cells and then contract, squeezing a clear yellowish fluid called *serum*, and forming a solid clot.

The platelets help to control blood loss in yet another way. They release a hormone called serotonin which stimulates blood vessels to contract, thus reducing the flow.

Abnormal bleeding is a characteristic of a number of diseases, scurvy, epidemic meningitis (spotted fever) and the Black Death (bubonic plague) among them. Poisoning or radiation may affect the bone marrow and interfere with platelet production. Sometimes the number of platelets falls for no apparent reason. Surgical removal of the spleen often cures the trouble, but it is not yet certain why this is successful.

Vitamin K is essential for the formation of some of those dozen or so clotting factors but it cannot be absorbed into the bloodstream unless there is bile in the intestine. In some types of jaundice, when the bile flow is obstructed, clotting is affected.

The best-known of all clotting diseases, however, is *haemophilia*, an inherited disease from which only men suffer, although women may be carriers and pass it on to their sons. Its notoriety is due to its effects on members of Queen Victoria's family, notably the last Tsarevitch of Russia, but it is a relatively rare disease, affecting about one boy in 10,000.

It is caused by the absence of one of the clotting factors, a plasma protein known as anti-haemophiliac globulin or Factor VIII. The slightest injury can lead to uncontrolled bleeding and, in the past, few haemophiliacs survived childhood. Blood transfusions and now, injections of the vital factor, which can be extracted from plasma, can, however, give haemophiliacs some semblance of normal life.

Blood Circulation

The main functions of the circulatory system are to carry oxygen and nutriments, particularly glucose, to the tissues and to carry away carbon dioxide and other waste products produced by metabolic processes in the cells.

The most important unit in the circulatory system is the heart. The heart is a muscular pump which propels oxygenated blood to the tissues of the body through thick-walled vessels called arteries. The arteries branch into smaller vessels called arterioles through which much of the control of the circulation is achieved —the muscle cells in their walls can contract and thus alter the flow of blood. The arterioles further sub-divide and the blood eventually passes into the capillaries, the finest of the vessels, which have a diameter of only 0.006 mm.

The total surface area of capillary walls in the body is over 6,000 square metres; it is through this enormous area that the exchange of nutriments and oxygen for waste products takes place between the blood and the cells of the tissues. The blood becomes darker in colour as it gives up its oxygen. This deoxygenated or venous blood then flows into slightly larger vessels called venules which, in turn, drain into the veins which take the blood back to the heart. The lining of the walls of the veins is folded at intervals to form one-way venous valves which prevent the backflow of blood to the tissues.

The returned blood is then pumped by the heart through the pulmonary arteries to the capillaries of the lungs. The acquired carbon dioxide is given up, to be breathed out, and as fresh oxygen is taken in the newly oxygenated blood returns via the pulmonary veins to the heart ready for another trip round this double circuit.

The circulatory system does a prodigious amount of work. At rest, blood is pumped round the body at a rate of five litres per minute, but during violent exercise the amount pumped can increase to over 25 litres per minute. It has been calculated that during a man's lifetime a total of 500,000,000 litres of blood is pumped round the body.

The distribution of blood throughout the body is neither even nor fixed, since the basic requirements of different tissues vary. Under normal conditions the liver receives 28% of the total cardiac output; the kidneys receive 24%, the skeletal muscles 15%, the brain 14% and the heart 5%. However, these are only average figures and nervous control of the size of the arterioles allows extra blood to be diverted to particular areas in times of need. During exercise, for example, the increased cardiac output is directed mainly to the skeletal muscles to provide them with fuel. At the same time, the blood flow to the skin is increased so that the extra heat generated by the body can be radiated to the atmosphere—the effect responsible for the familiar reddening of the face during exertion—particularly when running, or playing energetic games such as squash.

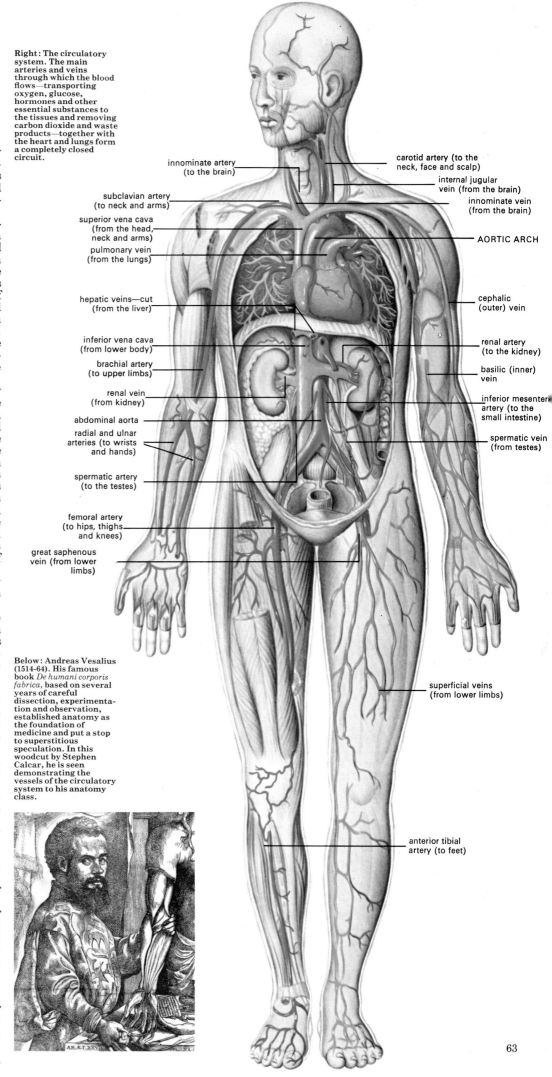

Right: The circulatory system. The main arteries and veins through which the blood flows—transporting oxygen, glucose, hormones and other essential substances to the tissues and removing carbon dioxide and waste products—together with the heart and lungs form a completely closed circuit.

Below: Andreas Vesalius (1514-64). His famous book *De humani corporis fabrica*, based on several years of careful dissection, experimentation and observation, established anatomy as the foundation of medicine and put a stop to superstitious speculation. In this woodcut by Stephen Calcar, he is seen demonstrating the vessels of the circulatory system to his anatomy class.

innominate artery (to the brain)

subclavian artery (to neck and arms)

superior vena cava (from the head, neck and arms)

pulmonary vein (from the lungs)

hepatic veins—cut (from the liver)

inferior vena cava (from lower body)

brachial artery (to upper limbs)

renal vein (from kidney)

abdominal aorta

radial and ulnar arteries (to wrists and hands)

spermatic artery (to the testes)

femoral artery (to hips, thighs and knees)

great saphenous vein (from lower limbs)

carotid artery (to the neck, face and scalp)

internal jugular vein (from the brain)

innominate vein (from the brain)

AORTIC ARCH

cephalic (outer) vein

renal artery (to the kidney)

basilic (inner) vein

inferior mesenteric artery (to the small intestine)

spermatic vein (from testes)

superficial veins (from lower limbs)

anterior tibial artery (to feet)

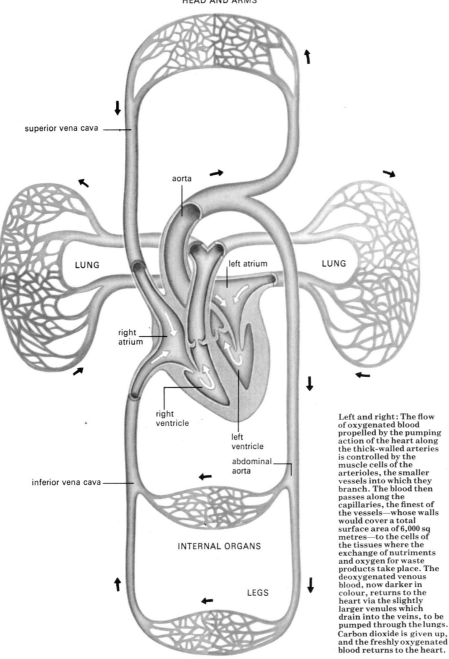

superior vena cava

aorta

left atrium

LUNG

LUNG

right atrium

right ventricle

left ventricle

abdominal aorta

inferior vena cava

INTERNAL ORGANS

LEGS

Right: Resin is injected into the circulatory network of a foetus to demonstrate the complexity of veins, arteries and capillaries.

Below: Skylab, the orbiting laboratory, where astronauts spend up to 84 days in training. Blood pressure and heart functioning are checked for signs of stress.

Artery

Arteriole

Transworld

Capillary

Venule

Vein

Right: The eye photographed with an ophthalmoscope, showing the retinal blood vessels through which we see the world and the blind spot where the vessels and nerves leave the eyeball.

Below: Thermographic pictures demonstrate how smoking constricts blood vessels and so reduces the amount of heat radiated. Black, at the extreme left of the colour code, represents the lowest temperature, white the highest and the colours in between a rising scale each representing 0.5°C. The picture on the left shows the normal amount of heat radiated before smoking. The picture on the right, taken after smoking, shows the drop in temperature in several parts of the hand.

Left and right: The flow of oxygenated blood propelled by the pumping action of the heart along the thick-walled arteries is controlled by the muscle cells of the arterioles, the smaller vessels into which they branch. The blood then passes along the capillaries, the finest of the vessels—whose walls would cover a total surface area of 6,000 sq metres—to the cells of the tissues where the exchange of nutriments and oxygen for waste products take place. The deoxygenated venous blood, now darker in colour, returns to the heart via the slightly larger venules which drain into the veins, to be pumped through the lungs. Carbon dioxide is given up, and the freshly oxygenated blood returns to the heart.

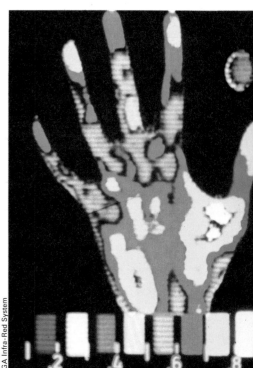

AGA Infra-Red System

Control of the circulation

The flow of any fluid through a tube is determined by the diameter of the tube and the force behind the fluid. The flow rate in the circulatory system is governed by the alteration of the diameter of the arterioles and by control of the force and rate of the heartbeat. The muscle in the arteriolar walls is acted upon by a chemical, *noradrenaline*, released from the endings of their nerves, to produce constriction of the arteriole. Similarly, the heart rate is increased by noradrenaline released from the endings of the cardiac nerves. Thus, it is the nervous system which is largely responsible for the control of the circulation.

Since the brain is more sensitive to a lack of oxygen than any other organ in the body, and its function is so vital to life, its blood flow must be maintained at all costs. For this reason, the body has developed a system called 'autoregulation' by which various nerves act to maintain the flow to the brain even if the flow to the rest of the body falls dramatically, as in the case of a severe haemorrhage.

At a more general level, the autonomic nervous system is constantly receiving messages from the brain and spinal cord to adjust the flow to the various organs. For example, when a person stands up quickly this system operates immediately to counteract the effect of gravity which would retain the blood in the lower parts of the body. Occasionally, the system may be a little slow: the result is the type of giddiness or fainting that may be experienced after a hot bath.

There is also a mechanism for maintaining blood flow through the kidneys. If the blood flow falls, a substance called *renin* is released from the kidney. This causes the formation of another chemical called *angiotensin* in the blood. Angiotensin acts directly on the muscles of the arterioles. It also stimulates the release of the hormone, *aldosterone*, from the adrenal glands, which acts to increase the blood volume and hence raise the blood flow to the kidney. The increased flow then shuts off the secretion of renin. This system is an example of what engineers call a negative feedback loop and serves to maintain the status quo.

Another hormone, *adrenaline*, is produced by the adrenal gland in response to the emotion of fear. Adrenaline causes the redistribution of blood pressure, as a preparation for either fighting or fleeing. The sensations of a thumping heart and

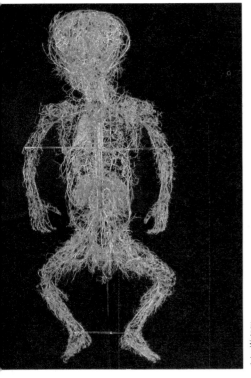

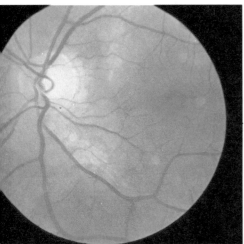

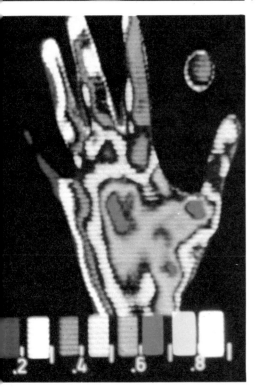

John Watney

Transworld

cold, clammy skin are the well-known results of an unpleasant fright.

Blood clotting

Blood is a complex mixture of cells and dissolved proteins. The clotting or coagulation system serves to minimize blood loss through any damaged vessel. It begins when exposure of blood cells to the air, or tissue damage, causes the release of substances which initiate a chain of reactions which result in the solidifying of the blood as a clot to block the wound. Under normal circumstances, clotting of the blood does not occur, first because the initiators of clotting are not available and secondly because some blood cells contain *heparin*, an acid, which prevents accidental clotting.

Very occasionally, a clot does form in the circulation—the accidental process called *thrombosis*. However, when a vessel is blocked by a clot, blood can often bypass the blockage by using alternative vessels which are, in this situation, called a *collateral circulation*. Clots can also be dissolved by the fibrinolytic system, continually in operation inside the vessels.

Blood pressure

The pressure of the blood in arteries and arterioles reaches a peak, called the *systolic* pressure, with each contraction of the heart and then gradually decreases to a minimum, the *diastolic* pressure, before the next contraction. Blood pressure is always expressed as two figures, for example, 120/80 in healthy young adults, representing respectively the systolic and diastolic pressures in millimetres of mercury.

Blood pressure may be increased for short periods by anxiety or exercise; it is also increased by a number of diseases and increases gradually with age. An individual is regarded as having high blood pressure if the systolic pressure consistently exceeds 100 + his age, or if the diastolic is greater than 100. The lower limit of normal adult blood pressure is 80/40. However, there is actually no such thing as a 'norm'. Blood pressure is a continuum in which the higher it goes, especially the diastolic, the more harmful the effects are likely to be.

Abnormally low blood pressure will occur, for example, after the loss of a large amount of blood, after a heart attack and in the terminal stages of many diseases. When the blood pressure is very low insufficient blood, and hence oxygen, reaches the brain and other vital organs and death is imminent. Drugs which contract the muscular walls of blood vessels and thus raise blood pressure are an effective short-term treatment until the cause of the low pressure can be treated directly, by such methods as transfusion to compensate for blood loss.

Abnormally high blood pressure may be due to an excess of adrenaline, the hormone which causes constriction of arterioles, and is produced by a tumour of the adrenal gland called a *phaeochromocytoma*. It may also be due to damage to one or both kidneys, causing them to release too much renin—this raises blood pressure by forming angiotensin which constricts blood vessels. In the vast majority of cases, however, no obvious cause for the high blood pressure can be found; this condition is referred to as idiopathic hypertension.

Yet whatever the reasons for high blood pressure, if the condition is not treated it leads to an early death. The pressure damages the walls of arteries which during healing, scar and narrow, thus raising the pressure still further and reducing the flow of blood to the body tissues. The kidney may be damaged and so contribute to a further rise in pressure by releasing renin. This may result in heart failure—as the pressure puts an excessive strain on the heart which will be unable to pump blood out of the lungs to the body. The pressure may also burst a blood vessel in the eye or the brain and cause blindness or a stroke.

Effective treatment can greatly reduce the risk of these complications. Surgical removal of an adrenal tumour or a single diseased kidney will return the blood pressure to normal. Idiopathic hypertension can be treated with drugs which prevent the action of the noradrenaline released by the sympathetic nervous system which, in health, maintains blood pressure by controlled contraction of the muscle in arteriolar walls. Different drugs decrease the production, release or effectiveness of noradrenaline so that in each case the blood vessels can release and dilate, thereby increasing blood flow and decreasing blood pressure.

The affluent disease

In Western civilization the most common disease of the arteries is *atherosclerosis* or hardening of the arteries. The process starts with the deposition and accumulation of fat on the inside of the vessel walls. Small blood cells, called platelets, then stick to the irregular accumulation within the vessels. These changes cause scarring, and by continuing platelet and fat accumulation the vessel walls become thick so the internal diameter of the arteriole is reduced. The whole process contributes to the rise of blood pressure with age and can itself be partly caused by high blood pressure. No single cause for atherosclerosis can be given but it seems to be inherited and to occur most frequently in those who are overweight, take too little exercise, are under stress or smoke cigarettes.

The most serious effect of atherosclerosis is that it eventually blocks arteries and therefore prevents sufficient blood being pumped to various parts of the body. For example, if the arteries supplying the heart are narrowed by atherosclerosis, it may not be able to get enough blood to fulfil its oxygen requirements during exercise. In this case, pain in the chest, angina pectoris, will result because the heart muscle, like other muscles, can only survive on very low oxygen for a while. It does this by using glucose in a way that produces lactic acid, and this is what causes pain. On stopping exercise, the heart then receives sufficient oxygen, the lactic acid is destroyed and the pain is relieved. Indeed the blockage of any artery is dangerous, since without an adequate blood supply tissue will die.

Poor circulation can have other consequences. For example, if the valves in the superficial veins of the legs are defective the blood cannot flow efficiently back to the heart. Instead it remains in the veins causing them to swell and occasionally burst. This condition is known as *varicose veins*. Treatment involves support of the swollen veins with elastic stockings which have a gentle, squeezing effect or, in severe cases, their surgical removal.

Cardiovascular System

The second century AD blessed the scientific world with the 'divine' teachings of Galen, the last of the great biologists of antiquity. His observations, right and wrong, halted scientific progress for 1,500 years. He did, however, recognize the structural differences between the arteries and veins, and successfully demonstrated that the arteries contain blood not air—a belief which had been held for 400 years. Galen taught that blood was made in the liver and reached the various parts of the body in a manner rather like the tidal movements of the sea: ebbing and flowing.

It was not until the seventeenth century when an Englishman, William Harvey, looked into the mechanics of circulation that any further progress in biology began to be made. He discovered that the blood flows in one direction only, controlled by the valves in the veins and the pumping of the heart. Unfortunately he never managed to pin-point the place where the blood ceased moving away from the heart and began moving towards it. This was left to the Italian physiologist Marcello Malpighi who discovered the tiny network of capillaries linking the veins and arteries in the lungs of a frog, finally establishing the circulation of the blood.

The heart of the average adult pumps something like 9,000 litres (2,000 gallons) of blood along almost 100,000 km (60,000

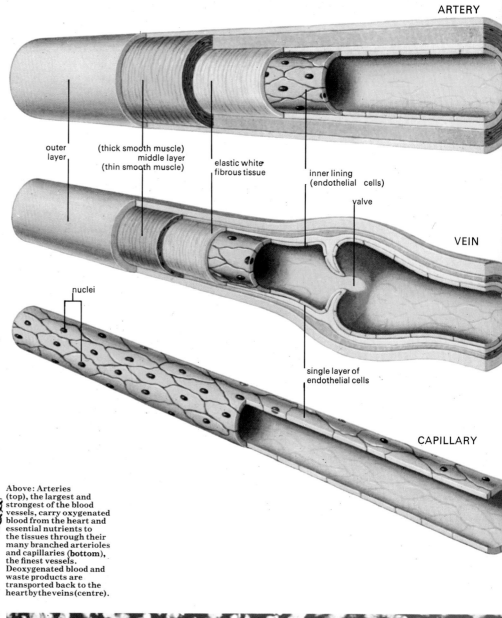

ARTERY

outer layer

(thick smooth muscle) middle layer (thin smooth muscle)

elastic white fibrous tissue

inner lining (endothelial cells)

valve

VEIN

nuclei

single layer of endothelial cells

CAPILLARY

Above: Arteries (top), the largest and strongest of the blood vessels, carry oxygenated blood from the heart and essential nutrients to the tissues through their many branched arterioles and capillaries (bottom), the finest vessels. Deoxygenated blood and waste products are transported back to the heart by the veins (centre).

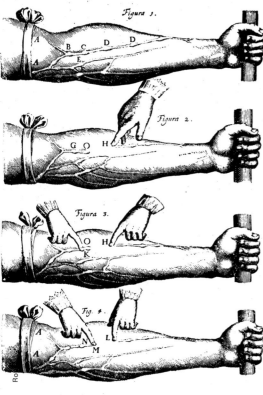

Figura 1.

Figura 2.

Figura 3.

Fig. 4.

Above: Illustrations from *De Motu Cordis*, written by the 17th century biologist, William Harvey, who discovered how the blood circulates round the body. The figures demonstrate by pressing on the veins how the direction of the blood flowing towards the heart is maintained by the valves.

Right: Transverse section of the liver showing the complexity of the capillary network, the finest vessels in the circulatory system. Efficient blood flow to the liver is particularly important since it is the only organ apart from the brain which stores glucose for energy.

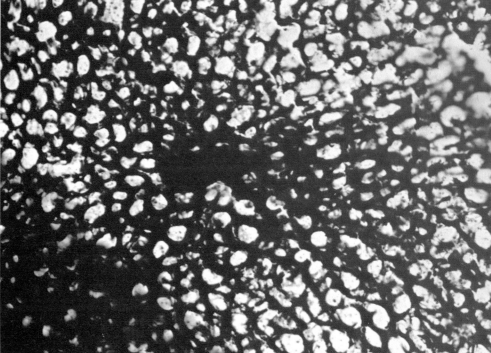

John Watney

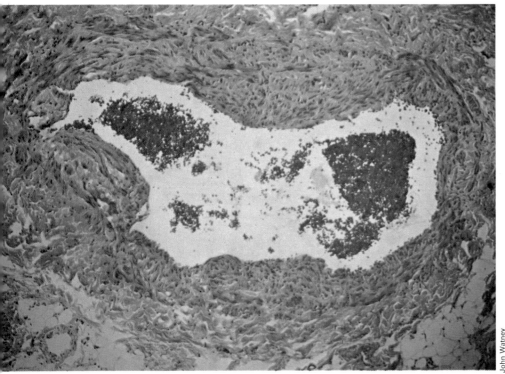

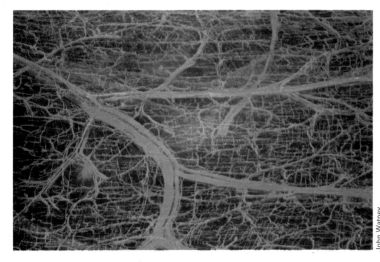

Above: A transverse
section of an artery
shows how the red cells
have clotted together.
Since a constant supply
of blood is essential
to the body's
functioning, especially
the brain, a clot which
cannot be dispersed by
the fibrolinytic system
may deprive the
surrounding tissues of
oxygen, resulting in a
stroke, or death if the
brain is deprived of
oxygen for more than
three minutes.

Right: The capillary
network permeates every
tissue of the body. The
capillaries are only
.0018cm in diameter, but
the action of the heart
allows the body's 5
litres of blood to be
pumped through their
100,000 km in a few
minutes.

John Watney

John Watney

miles) of tubing in the circulatory system every day. This ceaseless activity takes place without our conscious knowledge, controlled by the central nervous system and the body's chemical co-ordinators.

The heart, veins, arteries and capillaries are collectively known as the cardiovascular system. All the blood vessels except the tiny capillaries have the same basic structure. They are made of three types of tissue: the endothelium—an inner lining made up of a single layer of flat cells resembling irregular stones fitted together in a smooth pavement—sheathed in a layer of muscle cells, interwoven with a layer of fibrous tissue. The muscle cells give the vessel a certain amount of elasticity, which allows the expansion and contraction of the vessels following the surge of blood from the pumping of the heart. The wall of the tube is so thin that it is only visible as a thin line when magnified 1,000 times. In fact it is less than .3025 cm (.0001 inch) thick.

The arteries leaving the left side of the heart branch off into smaller vessels, the arterioles, losing some of the elastic content of their walls as they do so. The arterioles play the major role in regulating the blood flow and pressure through the capillaries. Contraction of the thick muscular wall of the arterioles causes them to close up, reducing the blood flow through them (*vasoconstriction*); relaxation of the wall opens the arterioles, allowing the blood to flow easily through them (*vasodilatation*).

It is essential that at all times the heart and brain receive an adequate blood supply in order to carry out their vital functions; lack of blood to these organs will result in death in a matter of minutes. Skin cells, however, are able to survive short periods without blood, so that during periods of exertion blood can be diverted away from the skin to the gut or other areas of most need. This is carried out by alteration of the size of arterioles in different areas of the body which consequently alters the blood flow to these areas.

The microcirculation
The real purpose of the cardiovascular system is to carry to the cells of the body the substances needed for their metabolism and regulation, and to take away synthesized and waste products. The heart, veins and arteries are really only assistants in this task; it is the capillaries which permeate the tissues of the body

maintaining a suitable environment for the cells.

Some capillaries perform the sole function of joining up the arterial system with the venous system. These are more numerous in the skin. They help to regulate the body temperature by vasodilatation when the body is too hot—this increases the volume of blood available to be cooled by the air. Other capillaries deliver nutrients to the body cells through their thin walls which act as *semipermeable membranes*, allowing some, but not all, substances to pass through them.

Two processes, *diffusion* and *osmosis*, allow the passage of materials through the capillary walls. When two gases of different composition come into contact they intermingle. The air we breathe out, for example, has more carbon dioxide and less oxygen than the air we breathe in. However, this expired air does not float around the room as a separate portion of air, it diffuses into the rest of the air so that eventually the whole room contains less oxygen and more carbon dioxide. This same process of diffusion takes place between the blood inside the capillary walls and the tissue fluid outside them. It is also responsible for the exchange of oxygen, carbon dioxide, glucose and other nutrients. Osmosis is the passage of water from a weak solution to a stronger one through a semi-permeable membrane, a process which eventually makes the two solutions of equal strength. The two processes of diffusion and osmosis together enable the body cells to take what they need from the blood, and to deliver wastes and synthesized products to the blood for removal.

The veins
The blood, now deoxygenated and dark red, begins its journey back from the tissues to the heart. The blood from the capillaries flows into the venules, slightly larger vessels, then into the larger veins.

The walls of the veins are much thinner than those of the arteries: they do not contract to any noticeable extent and are not involved in adjusting the blood flow through the body tissues. They do, however, possess their own pumping mechanism which is really a by-product of the action of the muscles working in close proximity to the veins. These muscles squeeze the veins, forcing the blood through the vessels towards the heart. The direction of flow is maintained by pocket-shaped valves, formed from the endothelium and strengthened by connective tissue, which only allow the blood to travel in one direction. The venous system has, in fact, quite a lot of work to do, returning blood from the lower parts of the body where gravity drags the blood away from the heart. The driving pressure caused by the heart beat is very low after having passed through the intricacies of the microcirculation, so the pumping mechanism of the venous system is essential in the return process.

Cardiovascular control
Any bodily system with a job as important as the supply of oxygen and nutrients to body tissues must be able to work at a fairly constant rate, despite changing internal and external conditions.

Total blood flow will be affected by two factors: cardiac output and arterial vessel resistance. The latter is determined by size and both are controlled by a variety 67

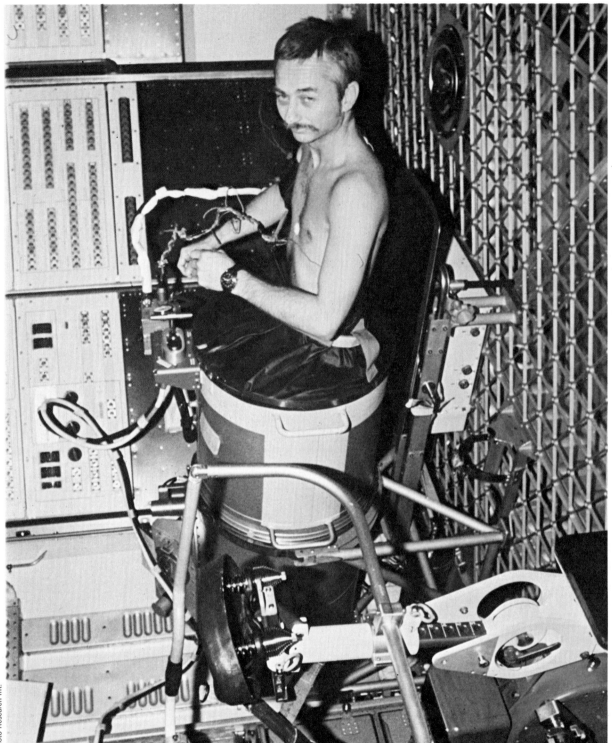

blood
flow

valve
open

muscle
action

valve
closed

Above: Blood is returned through the veins to the heart by squeezing action of the muscles which acts as a pump. If the flow of blood is restricted, the heart has insufficient blood to pump to the brain and fainting or loss of consciousness occurs, forcing the person to become horizontal to improve the blood flow.

Left: An astronaut undergoes rigorous tests on Skylab 3 Orbital Workshop. These tests not only provide information on the time and nature of the adaptation of the cardiovascular system during a space flight, but indicate the degree of impairment or reduced capacity to be expected on his return to earth.

Above right: Decompression sickness, 'the bends', is common amongst divers. A sudden return to normal atmospheric pressure releases excess nitrogen dissolved in the blood, it forms bubbles in the vessels and obstructs the flow. To correct this, divers are returned to high pressure areas and brought up gradually.

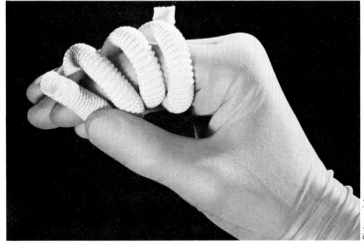

Left: The science of prosthetics or 'spare-part' surgery is still at a primitive stage; new non-allergic, synthetic materials, however, such as the Dacron from which this artery is made, has made the replacement of damaged vessels easier and saved many limbs from gangrene and a consequent amputation.

Right: The 'Circle of Willis', the arterial circuit at the base of the brain, named after the 17th century English anatomist, Thomas Willis. The left and right internal carotid arteries and the basilar artery join to form a ring whose function it is to balance the pressure of the blood reaching the brain.

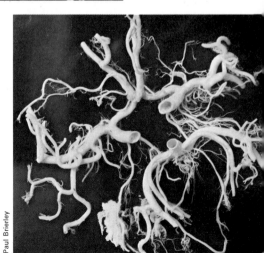

Photo Research Int.

Picturepoint

Paul Brierley

Barnaby's

of mechanisms, both neural and hormonal. For example, nerves of the autonomic branch of the nervous system travel from the medulla, an area at the back of the brain, to both veins and arteries. The function of these nerves is to maintain the blood pressure in the arteries and distribute blood according to the functions and needs of the different organs.

Different areas of the body contain different concentrations of the nerve endings leading to the medulla. Regional blood flow may therefore be controlled and altered by central mechanisms. But local mechanisms also operate. Local nerve reflexes, hormones such as histamine and angiotensin, the concentration of metabolic products in nearby tissues and the amount of blood gases, such as oxygen and carbon dioxide, affect regional blood flow by causing local vasodilatation or vasoconstriction.

However efficiently these control systems of regional blood supply operated, they would be of little use without some system which ensured that the overall arterial pressure within the cardiovascular system remained constant. For this purpose the main arteries contain within their walls specialized nerve endings which are highly sensitive to changes in pressure. These nerve endings, known as *pressoreceptors* or *baroreceptors*, are most numerous in the arteries running up the sides of the neck. They convey information concerning changes in pressure up to the medulla.

In the medulla there is a complex neuronal system which collects all the information relating to the cardiovascular system, somehow assesses the relative importance of this information, and sets into operation various processes which will keep the system stable. Exactly how this is done, or even which parts of the medulla are most active, is not yet known.

It has been discovered that the stimulation of arterial baroreceptors resulting from a rise in blood pressure causes the medulla to alter cardiac output and peripheral resistance through the autonomic nervous system, so that blood pressure falls again. Young ladies of the Victorian era were expected to show their good breeding by fainting if anything distressing or embarrassing occurred. Those who were not naturally so delicate were taught to induce the faint by clasping their hands to their necks. By pressing on the blood vessels at the side of the neck, the arterial baroreceptors are stimulated, and the consequent reductions in cardiac output and blood pressure result in a faint.

Changes in external conditions may also have profound effects on the functioning of the body, and man has had to find ways of adapting to such changes. For example, when the Spaniards conquered the Incas, mountain dwellers of South America, both they and their horses suffered a variety of ills caused by the reduced atmospheric pressure which accompanies increased altitude. Symptoms ranged from mild irritability and lassitude to violent nausea, vomiting and headaches. Yet the Incas showed no such reactions since they had lived at those heights for generations and had therefore become well acclimatized.

Most of the symptoms of mountain sickness fade over a period of several weeks. Breathing becomes faster so that more oxygen can enter the blood stream, there is an increase in the number of red blood cells, the circulation increases and the way in which oxygen is actually used by the tissues becomes more efficient. But full acclimatization takes a long time and the Spanish living among the Incas suffered a low birth rate for many years.

Obviously there are limits to the natural adaptations that are possible, and if man wishes to survive under still more extreme conditions he must resort to artificial protective devices. For example, sudden or extreme drops in atmospheric pressure may be encountered both by deep sea divers who return to the surface very quickly, and by airmen who make rapid ascents. In each case the falling pressure may cause gases dissolved in the blood, especially nitrogen, to come out of solution and form bubbles. The victim may suffer from intolerable pain in the joints and limbs and feel forced to keep his arms and legs bent. Hence the condition is called 'the bends'. It can be fatal if vital vessels in the brain or heart are obstructed by the bubbles, unless treatment is given immediately. Airmen must return to normal altitudes and divers must be put in compressed air chambers with a pressure as high as that existing at the depth to which they descended. The air pressure must then be very gradually reduced, so that the gas in the blood can escape slowly and harmlessly.

Space flights present human physiology with particularly difficult problems. Oxygen must be supplied and maintained at a steady pressure despite enormous changes outside the space capsule. In attempting to leave the earth the spaceship must accelerate rapidly enough to break free of gravitational forces. The astronaut's body is thus exposed to very high G forces. If his head points towards the top of the rocket, the blood will pool in his feet and he will lose consciousness (blackout). With his head pointing the other way, the blood will pool in his head and although the vessels supplying the brain will be unaffected because the skull and cerebrospinal fluid protect them, the vessels in the eyes may rupture (redout). So the astronaut must lie transversely (cross-wise) to the line of flight. Even so his body will be made much heavier by the acceleration, prohibiting him from performing any delicate tasks.

Having left the atmosphere he is faced by the opposite problem—weightlessness. Future travellers may need vigorous exercise to avoid total breakdown with the subsequent return to earth gravity.

Blood Groups

Thirty years ago, hundreds of women in Britain alone died each year from haemorrhage (loss of blood) in childbirth. Because of transfusions such deaths have now been reduced to a mere dozen or so.

The discovery of blood groups in the early twentieth century has meant that hundreds of thousands of lives have been saved by transfusions. Highly sophisticated surgical operations, which are now carried out almost routinely, could not even have been contemplated if blood was not available—open heart operations, for example, can use 10 to 20 pints of blood. Transfusions also help sufferers from leukaemia, haemophilia and certain types of anaemia. They save the lives of those with severe burns. The fact that blood comes in different types or groups has proved to be of the greatest practical significance, for only with this knowledge can blood transfusions be carried out safely.

The ABO system

The main constituents of the blood are the fluid plasma and the billions of red and white cells suspended in it. In identifying blood groups we are concerned only with the red cells and the plasma.

The fundamental discoveries about blood groups were made by a Viennese scientist, Karl Landsteiner, who found that when the red cells from one person were mixed with serum from another there was sometimes, although not always, a reaction: the red cells clumped together. Serum is the clear liquid which is left when the blood clots. In other words it is plasma without the chemicals which cause clotting. The reason for this clumping (known as *agglutination*) is the presence of certain chemicals on the surfaces of red cells and in the plasma which react together.

Every red blood cell has a thin shell and the chemicals in this shell vary from person to person. Two of the most important of them are known as the A and B *antigens*. We inherit the presence or absence of these substances from our parents. People who have the A antigen only belong to blood group A; those with just the B antigen are group B. A small number of people have both antigens, so they are categorized as belonging to group AB. A much larger proportion of people have neither: they are classified as group O.

Blood groups are identified by checking the reaction of a sample of blood with known types of plasma or serum. The antibodies circulating in the plasma, ready to attack and neutralize any foreign invaders such as disease-carrying germs, are also geared to recognize and attack any substance entering the blood which is made of some foreign protein. It is this reaction which causes the rejection of transplanted organs. The body regards the transplant as a 'foreign invader' and attacks.

Circulating in plasma are specific antibodies which will react with those antigens on the red cells. These substances are known as the *Anti-A* and *Anti-B antibodies*. Obviously no one is going to have antibodies against his own blood, since the antigen-antibody reaction not

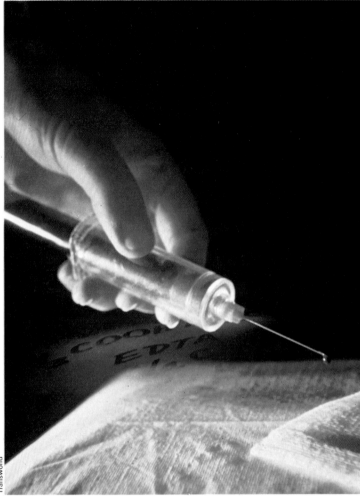

Transworld

National Blood Transfusion Service

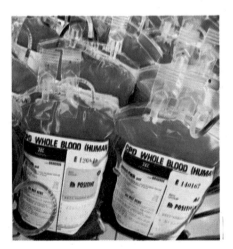

National Blood Transfusion Service

Above: Before blood from a donor can be used, a sample must be taken for typing according to ABO grouping and RH-factor to determine with which groups it will be compatible. To do this cells are mixed with anti-sera containing known antibodies—produced by repeated inoculation of blood with a known antigen into volunteers —and the agglutination pattern identified from the reactions (right). Group O serum contains anti-A and anti-B antibodies and will agglutinate (clump together) groups A, B and AB. However, it has no antigen sites on the red cells and is not changed itself by mixing with any serum. Serum from group A will agglutinate group B blood and vice versa. Both will agglutinate group AB. Group AB serum has no antibodies.

Above left: Automatic analysis of blood samples. Plasma and red cell samples are selected by probes from the tray in the foreground, then separated by a cleansing saline solution. Samples showing agglutination are recorded as a positive result on filterpaper on which they are absorbed.

Left: The 'shelf-life' of blood is about three weeks, during which it is stored in a blood bank at a temperature of 4-6 °C. The plasma can then be separated from the other constituents by high-speed spinning on a centrifuge and stored for much longer periods.

BLOOD GROUP ANALYSIS AND REACTIONS

GROUP A BLOOD

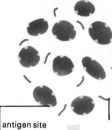

antigen site on corpuscle

AGGLUTINATION

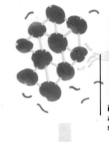

GROUP AB BLOOD

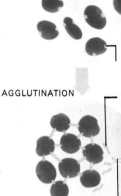

AGGLUTINATION

AGGLUTINATION

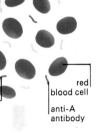

GROUP O BLOOD

red blood cell

anti-A antibody

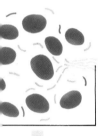

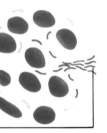

GROUP B BLOOD

dy

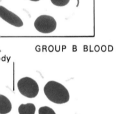

red blood cell

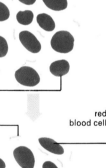

AGGLUTINATION

only causes red cells to clump together but may also destroy them completely. So people in blood group A have circulating in their plasma just the Anti-B antibody. Similarly, those in group B have only Anti-A antibody while those in group AB have neither of the antibodies circulating in their plasma. The group O, on the other hand, have both Anti-A and Anti-B antibodies.

The ABO system, as it is called, was discovered and described by Karl Landsteiner between 1900 and 1902. It is vital in transfusions—if someone is given blood of the wrong group the antigen-antibody reaction may be powerful enough to destroy large numbers of red cells and may lead to death. It can be seen that people in group AB can *receive* blood from anyone without any antibodies attacking the transfused red cells but may only *give* blood to another AB person. Someone in group O can *receive* blood only from another O without clumping the transfused red cells because his plasma contains Anti-A and Anti-B antibodies, but he can *give* blood to anyone. If the recipient's blood is not known, group O is given.

The Rhesus system

The Rhesus system was also discovered by Landsteiner, in 1940, during experiments with Rhesus monkeys. It too involves the presence or absence of substances, or *factors*, in the red cells. There are in fact half a dozen Rhesus factors but one, coded factor D, is especially important. In the majority of people this factor is present and they are known as *Rhesus positive* or *Rh+*. About 15 per cent of the population, however, inherit blood lacking this Rhesus factor. They are *Rhesus negative* or *Rh—*. There is no naturally-occurring anti-Rh antibody but if Rh+ blood gets into a Rh— person's system, it can stimulate production of an antibody against the 'foreign' D factor and this antibody may eventually destroy the donated red cells.

The reaction, however, is very slow and one transfusion of Rh+ blood into an Rh— person does not usually cause much trouble. But if another transfusion of Rh+ blood is given later then a fierce reaction, in which the foreign red cells are destroyed by anti-Rh antibodies, can take place.

The Rhesus factor is especially important in pregnancy. Some, or all, of the children of an Rh negative woman and an Rh positive man may inherit the factor from the father. Although during pregnancy the baby's Rh+ blood does not mix with the mother's blood, during delivery there may be bleeding and some of the baby's blood can get into the mother's system. Her blood may then form antibodies against the Rhesus factor. Although these antibodies disappear after a few months the mother is *sensitized*: she will immediately start producing anti-Rh antibodies whenever Rh positive cells again appear in her circulation.

The result of this is more marked in second or subsequent pregnancies. If the babies are Rh+, the mother may respond to the baby's presence in the womb by more antibody production which can pass into the baby and attack its red cells. This can cause the child to be still born, or it may die at birth with heart failure due to severe anaemia (such babies seldom live more than a few months) or

possible phenotypes ■   impossible phenotypes ▨

A × A	A × B	A × AB	A × O	B × B
A or O	A,B,O or AB	A,B or AB	A or O	B or O
B and AB	none	O	B and AB	A and AB

B × AB	B × O	AB × AB	AB × O	O × O
A,B or AB	B or O	A,B or AB	A or B	O
O	A and B	O	AB and O	A,B and AB

RH—   RH+

RH+

Above: The ABO system of blood typing discovered in 1900 by Karl Landsteiner. Blood groups are classified according to the variants of the chemical components, present in the thin shell of the red blood cells, that act as antigens. A child's blood group is determined by those of his parents. The table shows both the group a child is likely to inherit, and those that cannot be.

Right: The Rh system, the second main system, determined by the dominant and recessive genes, discovered by Landsteiner in 1940. Eight different genotypes are possible, classified as Rh+ and Rh—.

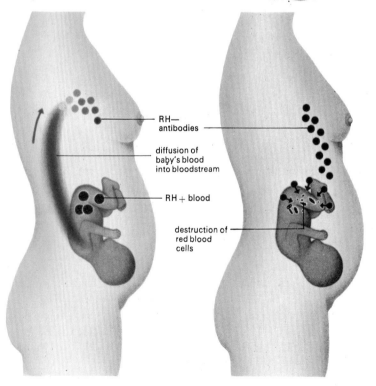

RH— antibodies

diffusion of baby's blood into bloodstream

RH+ blood

destruction of red blood cells

Above: The Rhesus factors are particularly important during pregnancy, especially when a Rh— mother conceives a Rh+ baby. If the blood supplies of the mother and baby—separated during pregnancy by membranes in the placenta—mix during delivery and some of the baby's blood gets into the mother's system, her blood may form antibodies against the Rhesus factor. The mother is therefore sensitized: in subsequent pregnancies she may produce anti-Rh bodies which attack the baby's red cells. The highly poisonous pigment released as they break down can attack the baby's nervous system causing permanent brain damage, or the baby may be still-born or die at birth of heart failure due to severe anaemia. However, slow exchange transfusions—a few millilitres at a time—can save some 95 per cent of affected babies and the mother can now be desensitized with massive doses of anti D gamma globulin, if injected within 72 hours after each birth.

Above: The second transfusion performed by Jean Baptiste Denys, the 17th-century French physician, resulted in the death of his patient, in spite of one previous success. These early attempts were only made possible by Harvey's discovery that the blood was not free-flowing, but travels round the body in vessels.

Below: Blood is injected into a vein—a primitive transfusion technique. Real progress was not achieved until the early 20th century, when the classification and typing of blood groups by Karl Landstein made transfusion safe. (Bottom) Direct donor to patient transfusions are now rare. Blood must be tested for compatibility.

jaundice. As the red cells are broken down they release a yellowish pigment which is highly poisonous to a young baby's nervous system. Untreated it can cause permanent brain damage.

It is possible to overcome the problem with an *exchange transfusion*, the gradual removal of the baby's blood, a few millilitres at a time, and its replacement with Rh negative blood. In this way some 95 per cent of affected babies can be saved.

The condition brought about by Rhesus incompatibility is known as haemolytic disease of the newborn. Although 85 per cent of men are Rhesus positive and 15 per cent of their wives Rhesus negative, only about one baby in 200 is ever affected. This is because Rh— babies run no risk, because women often do not form antibodies (or do so only after two or three successful pregnancies), or because the antibody reaction may be mild.

The risk has recently been lessened even further by the development of a vaccine made from the anti-Rh antibody (which is actually a protein known as Rh immune globulin). If this is given to the mother within 24 hours of the birth of an Rh+ baby, it removes from her blood any Rh+ cells which may have seeped in, so she does not become sensitized.

The vaccine is now given as a preventative measure to Rh— mothers and it is repeated at each pregnancy. Because of all these factors the number of deaths from haemolytic disease of the newborn is falling rapidly.

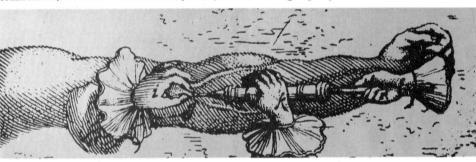

There are many other blood-typing systems all based on the presence or absence of other substances in the red cells. As with the Rhesus factors, there are no naturally-occurring antibodies, even transfusion of incompatible groups seldom stimulates a fierce antibody reaction, and often there is no antibody production at all. So they are of little or no significance. Sometimes, however, a patient who has had a large number of transfusions may form antibodies against all the commoner groups and he will need a transfusion of blood of exactly the right type. To meet needs like this, most countries have panels of donors of rare blood types. There is also an international panel, which includes even rarer groups from people all over the world.

Distribution of blood groups
There are wide variations in the geographical distribution of the ABO blood groups. The most common is O, with A the next most frequent. But while B is rare in Europe, it exceeds A in Asia. Australian aborigines, however, have only O and A blood.

Within Britain, too, there are interesting regional variations. Overall about 46 per cent of the British population are Group A while eight per cent are Bs and only two per cent ABs. The other 44 per

cent are group O. The original pre-Roman inhabitants of Britain, the Celts, were largely Os, and they survived in the remote corners of Scotland and Wales, where the proportion of Os is much higher than average today—51 per cent in the far north. The invaders from the continent were largely As and they predominate in the east and south of the country.

It also seems that people in Group A may be more prone to heart attacks than those in the other groups. Studies have shown that they have higher levels of serum cholesterol, a substance implicated in hardening of the arteries.

There is a definite though complicated pattern of inheritance of blood groups, a fact which was proved useful in paternity suits. Although it is not possible to prove a man *is* a child's father, one may be able to demonstrate conclusively that he is not.

Blood transfusion
Although it is likely that transfusion was tried earlier, the first recorded successful attempt was in 1665 when Dr. Richard Lower at Oxford transferred blood from one dog to another. The first animal-to-man transfusion took place in 1667, on a boy of 15 in Paris. This practice continued for some years until it caused so many deaths that in 1678 the Pope forbade it. It was not until 1818 that Dr. James Blundell working in London invented an apparatus for transferring blood from one person to another and suggested that only human blood should be used. But of course lack of knowledge about blood groups meant there were many deaths when incompatible blood was used.

The First World War stimulated the demand for blood transfusion. This was usually done directly, the donor lying next to the patient. Techniques of refrigeration, however, now enable blood to be stored and in most countries hospitals or regions have their own 'blood banks'. This means that instead of person-to-person transfusion the blood is dripped into a vein from a bottle. But even when it is chilled to four degrees C, the usual temperature in blood banks, blood will not keep for ever. After 21 days it begins to deteriorate.

Happily blood coming to the end of its 'shelf life' is not wasted; for by high speed spinning in a centrifuge the constituents of the blood can be separated— the heavy constituents sink to the bottom of the container. Plasma itself can be used instead of whole blood for patients whose basic problem is lack of blood *volume*, where loss of blood has reduced the amount in the body to a dangerously low level. The advantage of plasma is that it can be stored for several months, without refrigeration, before it deteriorates. The platelets, too, can be separated and given to patients with clotting problems.

Further, high speed spinning of the plasma enables isolation of plasma proteins such as anti-haemophilic globulin, Rh immune globulin and gamma globulin. Injections of anti-haemophilic globulin are given to haemophiliacs after an injury to enable clotting to take place. For some who suffer severely, routine injections may be given as a protective measure. Gamma globulin contains disease-fighting antibodies and can be useful in combatting diseases like polio, infectious hepatitis and mumps.

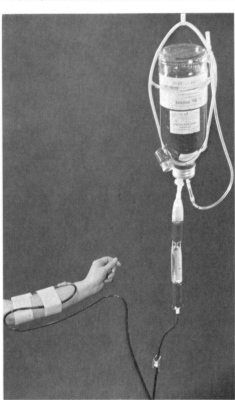

Alphabet and Image

The Lymphatic System

In very simple animals such as the jellyfish there is really very little difference between the internal and external environments. All the cells of the jellyfish are bathed in seawater and can take up nutrients and give out waste products directly by diffusion from their surroundings. As animals move up the evolutionary ladder, however, cells and groups of cells become more specialized, so more sophisticated systems for ensuring nutrition and waste removal are necessary. In man, as in other mammals, these systems have become very sophisticated indeed.

The cells of the human body, like the cells of the jellyfish, are surrounded by fluid, known as *interstitial* fluid, which is the direct source of nutrition. The composition of this interstitial fluid varies under different conditions and in different parts of the body; it is quite similar to blood plasma although its protein content is very small. In fact most of the interstitial fluid originates from the blood in the capillaries, and may diffuse back into it.

Other materials have diffused from the cells bathed by the fluid, and these too may diffuse into the blood in the capillaries. Some substances, particularly those composed of large molecules such as proteins, can leave the blood capillaries and enter the interstitial fluid, but cannot return because the pressure difference between blood vessels and extracellular fluid is too great. An extra drainage system is required to collect up these proteins and other substances and return them to the bloodstream. This drainage is provided by the lymphatic system.

Secondary transportation

Most parts of the body contain a set of lymphatic capillaries, which are completely separate from the network through which the blood flows.

They are somewhat similar to blood capillaries in that their walls are composed of similar kinds of cells, and they form a dense network of vessels to provide maximum contact with body tissues. But they differ in several aspects: for example, lymph vessels form a closed system and their terminal branches end blindly with rounded or swollen ends; they are irregular in shape, and very difficult to follow in their course through the body. The flow of lymph within them is very slow because there is no pumping force such as that provided in the blood system by the heart.

Indeed, it appears that lymph flow depends almost entirely on forces external to the system, such as the mechanical squeezing of the lymphatics by contraction of the muscles through which they course. The one-way flow is assured by the presence of valves like those found in larger veins. Directly above each pair of valves the vessel may show prominent layers of smooth muscle cells, which probably contract and help to propel the lymph onwards.

The lymph is collected from all over the body into progressively larger lymphatic vessels formed by the union of smaller

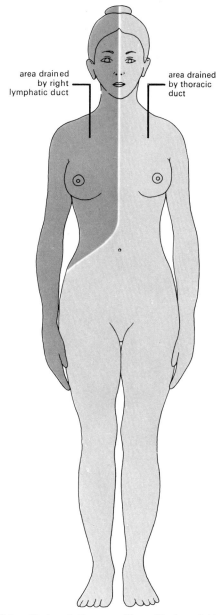

area drained by right lymphatic duct

area drained by thoracic duct

Below: The lymphatic system performs the vital function of acting as a secondary transport system. It supports and complements the circulatory system—which operates within a closed circuit—by collecting from the tissues all over the body the fluid squeezed out of the blood capillaries, recycling it and returning it to the circulation.

Above: The tissue fluid collected by the lymph vessels is emptied into two main ducts. The right lymphatic duct collects from the upper half of the right side of the body while the thoracic duct drains the remaining body area. Both ducts enter the large veins at the root of the neck by which the lymph is returned to the circulatory system.

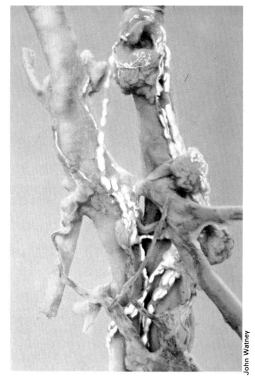

John Watney

Above: Blood vessels at the root of the neck where lymph is returned to the circulation. The white 'sausage' shapes are the lymphatic vessels and the spaces are the valves.

Below: Diagram showing how the lymphatic system works. The tissue fluid squeezed out of the capillaries contains some large molecules which cannot re-enter the capillaries because of the different pressures inside and outside the blood vessels. This fluid passes through the lymph nodes where masses of lymphocytes engulf and destroy bacteria and toxins and large particles are broken down. The clear lymph fluid is drawn back into the capillary by osmosis.

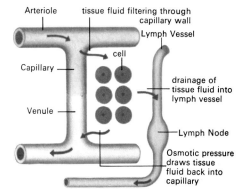

Arteriole

tissue fluid filtering through capillary wall

Lymph Vessel

Capillary

cell

Venule

drainage of tissue fluid into lymph vessel

Lymph Node

Osmotic pressure draws tissue fluid back into capillary

Erich Lessing/Magnum

ones. Most eventually empties into the thoracic duct which enters the large veins at the root of the neck on the left side. Lymph collected from the right upper half of the body enters the great veins via the right lymphatic duct. Back flow of venous blood into the lymphatic system is prevented by valves at the openings of the ducts.

It is unclear why the two main drainage points between the lymphatic and venous systems should serve such different size areas, but the thoracic duct alone empties from 4 to 10 mls of lymph into the veins every minute. If this lymph is drained away instead of being allowed to reach the blood, plasma protein begins to fall and blood volume decreases. In the course of a day 60 per cent of plasma volume and 50 per cent of the total amount of protein circulating in the blood is lost from the capillaries and returned to the bloodstream by the lymphatic system.

As is predictable from its relationship to both blood and interstitial fluid, lymph is similar in composition to plasma although not identical. In general it contains less protein than plasma, although regional differences in protein content are marked so that lymph from the liver contains similar amounts to plasma, far more than that from the skin. It also contains a variety of substances derived from cell metabolism and cell secretion, including enzymes, hormones and metabolites. Most importantly, however, the lymphatic system picks up bacteria and other foreign bodies which escape from the capillaries, playing a vital role in keeping the body free from disease.

The fight against disease
Lymphocytes, a type of white cell found in large numbers in the lymphatic system, aid in the manufacture of antibodies and the destruction of invading organisms. Although these white cells are rather large, they seem to be able to move quite freely in and out of both blood and lymphatic capillaries, by actually wriggling between the cells of the vessel walls with an amoeba-like movement.

Lymph is also involved, perhaps surprisingly, in one aspect of food transport: it picks up small globules of fat from the intestines and delivers them to the blood via the thoracic duct. Shortly after a meal, the lymph changes from its ordinary yellowish transparent colour to a milky colour due to the presence of the fat globules. The inner structure of the intestines contains a rich supply of lymphatic vessels which become quite visible as very fine white lines after digesting food. These lymphatics are called *lacteals* and their contents are known as *chyle*.

Certain other substances which have large molecules such as cholesterol, hormones and enzymes, may be transported directly from their sites of origin to the blood stream via lymphatic tissues. Others, which are found in much smaller concentrations, are probably returned to the bloodstream, having leaked out of capillary walls. Lymph can be seen as a clear yellowish fluid seeping from damaged tissues, especially near a pimple.

At points along the larger lymph vessels are lumpy enlargements of tissue which form the lymph nodes; all the lymph passes through at least one lymph node before it reaches the bloodstream. Several

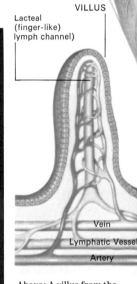

Right and below: The lymph nodes or glands are collected in specific groups at the sides of the neck, in the armpits and groin, at the root of the lungs and near the large veins of the abdomen and pelvis. They may become inflamed as a result of containing bacterial infection and preventing it from spreading.

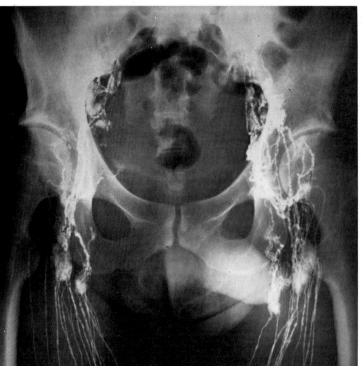

Above: A villus from the small intestine. It absorbs soluble food products of digestion, and sugars and amino acids are passed into the blood. The lacteals, the finger-like lymph channels, absorb fats, giving them a milky appearance. The fats are then conducted through the lymphatic vessels to the thoracic duct.

VILLUS

Lacteal (finger-like) lymph channel)

Vein
Lymphatic Vessel
Artery

vessels will enter into a small cavity (sinus) around the node and valves at the entrances prevent backflow of the lymph. Within the node, the lymph passes through cell-lined sinusoids which filter out solid particles. By this process white cells in the node can ingest and destroy foreign particles, bacteria and dead tissue cells.

Lymphocyte production
The nodes are centres for the production and storage of the lymphocytes and other antibody-manufacturing cells. When the lymph has slowly percolated through the tissues of the node, and has been cleansed of impurities, it leaves the node through a single lymphatic vessel. The lymph nodes near the lungs of city dwellers are often black with soot and dust particles carried there by macrophage cells. This gradual clogging up of the nodes may help to explain why people who are constantly exposed to atmospheric pollution by smoke and industrial waste find it harder to resist lung and chest infections.

During any kind of infection the lymphatic nodes may become swollen and sore as they attempt to deal with both invading organisms and white cells destroyed by the infection. Those just beneath the ear, under the jaw, and in the armpits and groin, are most obvious when enlarged.

The number of lymphocytes in the body normally remains fairly constant, but may rise (lymphocytosis) or fall (lymphopenia) under certain conditions. For example, in the disease known as glandular fever the body produces many times the number of white cells, including lymphocytes, in an effort to combat the

infection. Lymphopenia is only likely to occur in response to stresses such as starvation or debilitating conditions.

The body's drainage system
The lymphatic system has several functions which complement the functions of the blood circulatory system in many important ways. It returns body fluid and protein to the blood, it transports substances with large molecules such as fats, hormones and enzymes from their manufacturing sites to the bloodstream, it filters out foreign particles and it helps to combat infection. Although animals with much simpler body structures seem to manage without a separate drainage and defensive system, its importance in the higher animals is easily demonstrated by the widespread problems which accompany its malfunction.

In some people the system fails to develop properly at birth, causing gradual swelling of the affected part, as water and proteins accumulate in the tissues. This swelling, known as *oedema,* is characteristic of lymphatic malfunction. It may be temporary, such as the swelling of the ankles experienced by people on very long coach rides which quickly subsides when they begin to move about again and the action of the muscles squeezes the lymph into movement. The oedema can be permanent and crippling if the lymphatic vessels themselves become blocked or destroyed.

The evolutionary puzzle
In evolutionary terms the lymphatic system is a fairly new one and, since biologists tend to study the smaller and

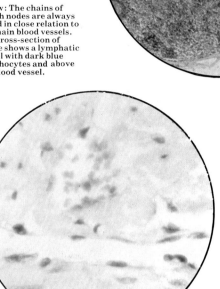

simpler animals in preference to the larger and more complex ones, its functioning was very poorly understood until comparatively recently.

For many years it was thought a great puzzle that nature had bothered to evolve this other circulatory system. But consideration of the nature of the blood supply in mammals demonstrated its necessity.

The cardiovascular system in those animals, including man, is a closed system operating under very high pressures. The pressure ensures that all organs and tissues are completely perfused with blood, but it also means the system is prone to leaks. It was formerly thought that substances of high molecular weight such as proteins could only escape from blood capillaries with great difficulty, or if the vessels had been damaged in some way. As we have seen this assumption was quite wrong, and plasma protein levels and total blood volume can only be maintained for as long as this drainage system collects up substances leaked from the blood capillaries.

Modern research indicates it may play an important regulatory role in a number of conditions in which no lymphatic involvement was previously suspected. For example, it seems that lymphatic drainage of the kidneys is vital in maintaining their ability to balance the water content of the body. This may explain why patients who have undergone kidney operations pass very dilute urine. Surgery may have damaged local lymph vessels, reducing their capacity for drainage and interfering with the reabsorption of water by the kidneys.

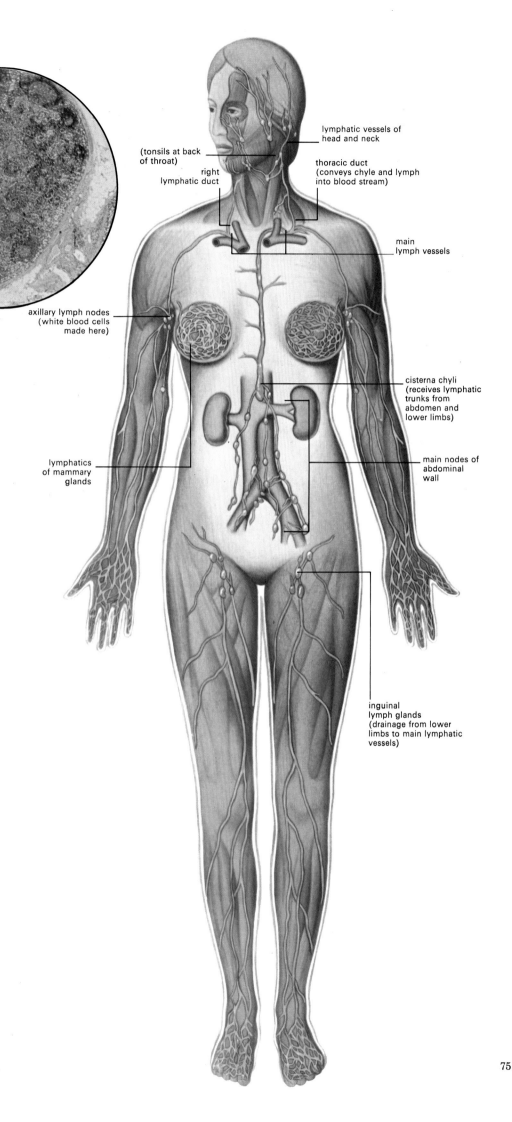

lymphatic vessels of head and neck

(tonsils at back of throat)

right lymphatic duct

thoracic duct (conveys chyle and lymph into blood stream)

main lymph vessels

axillary lymph nodes (white blood cells made here)

cisterna chyli (receives lymphatic trunks from abdomen and lower limbs)

lymphatics of mammary glands

main nodes of abdominal wall

inguinal lymph glands (drainage from lower limbs to main lymphatic vessels)

Defence Mechanisms

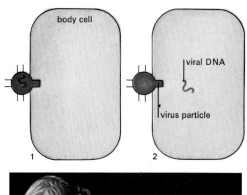

The balance which the body maintains between illness and health is a somewhat delicate one because of its relationship with the single-celled micro-organisms known as bacteria. Louis Pasteur, often thought of as the father of modern bacteriology, discovered in the nineteenth century that bacteria are one of the major causes of infectious disease. However, it has also been discovered that many bacteria, so tiny that they can hardly be seen with a normal laboratory microscope, are also useful to man.

Most of the 15,000 or so known species of bacteria do not cause disease. Many are essential for the breakdown and disappearance of waste animal and vegetable matter into simple molecules which can re-enter the earth's natural cycles. Bacteria gain energy from these breakdown reactions, but the products of their activity provide some useful food sources: for example, the fermentation of milk by an organism called *Lactobacillus bulgaricus* to produce yoghurt.

Some bacteria depend on the breakdown of simple molecules such as ammonia for energy, but far more common are those which obtain energy from the breakdown of complex organic molecules like sugars. Included in this group are disease-causing bacteria which use the human body as a source of nutrients during infection. A few may be present in the body even when it is healthy; for example pneumococci, which live in the nasal and respiratory passages, can cause pneumonia when the body is weakened.

Bacterial invasion

When bacteria invade the body, they can cause disease in a variety of ways. In some infections they simply overwhelm the body's defences by virtue of their cell structures which resist normal defence mechanisms. In others, the bacteria produce poisons, or toxins, which interfere with the normal processes of the host. The lethal food poisoning called botulism is caused by a bacterial toxin. It has been calculated that a little more than 1,000 grams of this toxin would be, in theory, enough to wipe out the entire human population of the world.

Laboratory experiments have shown that some bacteria can divide once every 20 minutes. At this rate, given unlimited food supplies, a single bacterium would produce an offspring mass greater than that of the world within a few days. Luckily, there are limiting factors which prevent this happening, and in the body bacterial growth is much slower, particularly in the initial stages of infection.

In the human body, proteins called antibodies are produced that can counter the effects of the toxins or disrupt the workings of the bacterial cells. But invasion by bacteria is not the only cause of infection. The other main group of disease-causing agents that attack humans are known as viruses.

Viruses have three important characteristics: they are very small—as many as 20,000 viruses can fit inside a small bacterial cell—and some non-pathogenic

Above: Edward Jenner, the 18th-century English physician, vaccinating a child. He invented the practice of vaccination after observing that people who had contracted cowpox, a a cattle-disease which can cause a mild infection in humans, had an immunity to smallpox and resisted inoculation with the smallpox virus.

Right: The French chemist Louis Pasteur was the first of the great biologists of the 19th century to discover the relationship between germs and putrefaction and fermentation. His method of heating milk to 65 C (149 F) then rapidly cooling it, now known as pasteurization, prevents the transmission of diseases.

Above: With frightening efficiency a virus invades and ultimately destroys a cell. (1) The virus attaches itself to the membrane of a host cell. (2) It pierces the cell with its tail, injecting the nucleic acid (its DNA or RNA which contains all necessary instructions for the synthesis of new viruses within a host) in its head into the cell. (3) Inside the cell, the virus DNA or RNA reproduces very quickly, effectively taking over the cell's own reproductive mechanism. (4) New viruses are now assembled inside the host cell. (5) The dead cell ruptures, releasing the multiplied viruses which can each go on to attack and destroy other host cells.

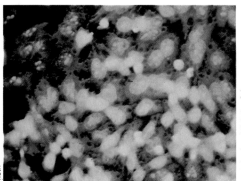

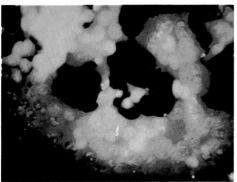

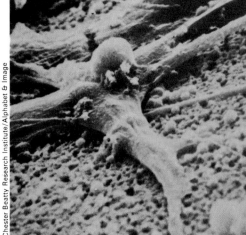

Above left: Normal cells of the amnion, the fibrous membrane which lines the cavity of the womb during pregnancy. The same cells are shown (left) infected with measles, one of the most widespread and contagious viruses, transmitted by air-borne droplets. After 6 days of infection the nuclei have clumped together.

Above: A cancer cell. Some forms of cancer are believed to be caused by infection with viruses, transmitted in some cases by mosquitoes. Although no virus can yet be positively identified, it is possible that infection causes acceleration of the normal cell-division process by which tissue is replaced or repaired, resulting in tumours.

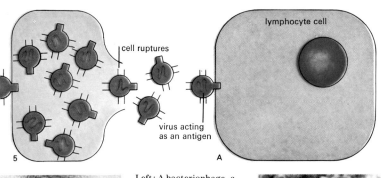

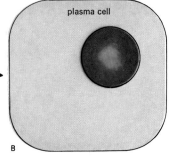

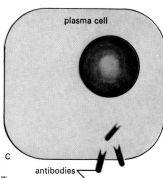

5 — cell ruptures — virus acting as an antigen

lymphocyte cell — A

plasma cell — B

plasma cell — C

antibodies

antibodies attaching to antigen

Left: A bacteriophage, a species of virus which has the ability of breaking up and destroying bacteria as it grows. Most viruses are inert until they attach themselves to a bacterium. Since they do not have the chemical components to sustain life they must become parasitical and take over a cell in order to replicate themselves.

Right: An epithelial cell from the lining of the mouth. The surface of the cell is covered with dozens of bacteria (visible here as tiny white spots). The different varieties can usually be recognized by the way they are affected by different dyes. Most species of bacteria are static, although some are able to 'swim'.

Alphabet & Image

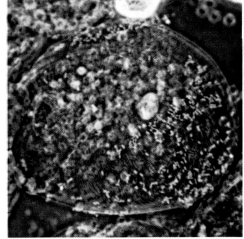

Gordon Leedale

Above: Diagrams to show how the body's immune reaction works. A virus particle is enabled by its molecular composition to act as an antigen. It contacts a lymphocyte and stimulates it to change into a plasma cell, or plasmacyte. The plasma cell produces antibodies which attach themselves to the antigen (in this case the virus, although it could be any foreign body) thereby preventing it from destroying the tissue cells and reproducing itself using the mechanisms of the host cells.

Below: A diagram representing a longitudinal section of tissue showing the viral attack on the lymphocyte and the counter attack by its antigens.

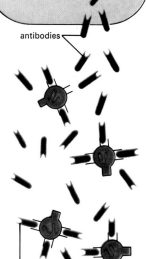

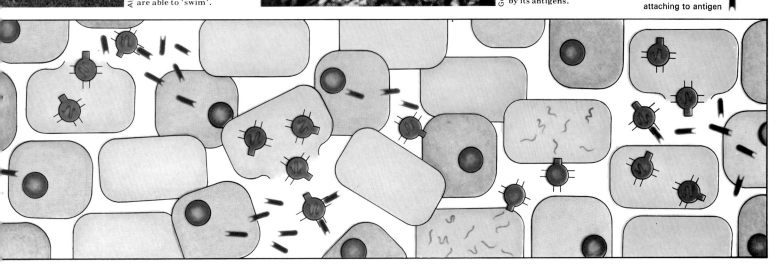

(non disease-causing) viruses, known as *phages*, are parasitic upon bacteria; they are structurally simple—most viruses consist of a core of one of the nucleic acids, RNA or DNA, covered by a protein sheath. (Some viruses in the pure form can crystallize in the same way as pure protein). Viruses cannot reproduce outside living cells.

When a virus is free it is inert, but in animals and plants viruses invade living cells and take over the internal chemical processes, directing the formation of new virus particles. Biologists regard viruses as a unique biological phenomenon—neither living nor non-living, but a bridge between the two categories.

Compared with the complexities of bacterial cells, viruses are very simple. They can be regarded as tiny packages of genetic information ready to be injected into the host cells. The protein outer coat of the virus serves two functions. It protects the nucleic acid core from attack by other substances within the body and demonstrates a specific affinity for the outer membranes of certain types of other cells. This is thought to be the reason why influenza viruses attack the lining of the nasal passages, hepatitis viruses infect the cells of the liver and those that cause

gut diseases such as gastro-enteritis attack the cells lining the gut wall. Affinity is shown only for those types of cell where the virus can reproduce.

Viruses exist in a wide range of shapes and sizes. One of the smallest is the polio virus (0.01μ, where μ = one millionth of a metre) which has a diameter approximately equal to the thickness of the outer membrane covering most cells, while closely related micro-organisms such as the *rickettsia* are much bigger (0.45μ, or almost half a millionth of a metre). Many viruses are spherical, but some are brick-shaped and others rod-like in appearance. Cells of nearly every type of organism from bacteria to complex animals are vulnerable to attack by some type of virus.

Viruses produce a wide range of diseases in humans. They are responsible for the common cold, influenza, smallpox, some forms of hepatitis and for many of the so-called childhood infections such as chickenpox, mumps and measles. The antibodies produced during childhood diseases usually confer life-long immunity from further infection. But there are so many strains of some viruses, such as those causing the common cold, that protection against one strain will not give protection against others.

Bacterial mutants

It has been noticed that from time to time new strains of the influenza virus arise. These new types of virus are caused by a genetic change known as mutation.

The mutant strain is often so different from those the body has met before that previous exposure to other strains provides no protection against it. Thus the new strains can be extremely virulent, causing pandemics, world-wide epidemics.

After the First World War an influenza pandemic swept the world killing more people than the previous four years of hostilities. But the new strains do not always kill the host and as natural immunity is built up the pandemic slows and dies out.

Many viral infections can be prevented by vaccination. Vaccination against smallpox was practised in the East long before it became common practice in Western medicine. The methods employed by the Chinese involved infecting a person with a little material taken from someone recovering from the disease. This produced a mild form of the disease in most people, conferring immunity to a second and more serious infection. But it by no means provided certain protection and people often died as a result.

Edward Jenner, an eighteenth-century physician, improved the method when he noticed that people who had suffered from cowpox never caught smallpox. Cowpox, caused by a virus similar to the smallpox virus, does not do serious damage in the human body. But it does stimulate the production of antibodies which are also effective against the smallpox virus.

However, in dealing with most microbial diseases, scientists have not been able to find a closely related, comparatively harmless micro-organism which can be used as a natural vaccine. Instead they have been forced to produce vaccines of dead organisms, by treating cultures with heat or chemicals, or vaccines of living strains which have a reduced virulence. This is possible either by selection or under artificial conditions.

The virulent diseases

Although vaccines have been produced for a wide range of human diseases, not all of them are very effective. New strains of influenza, for example, arise suddenly and the disease is usually well under way before the strain, from which a vaccine can be made, is isolated.

Most foreign substances and organisms cause the body to produce antibodies to neutralize them and the body is then said to be immune to that particular foreign particle. Occasionally animals produce antibodies against their own proteins. When this happens, the result is auto-immune disease. This can be seen in humans in some forms of anaemia.

Antibodies are proteins produced in the body in response to invasion by specific bacteria or viruses. The antibodies, produced in the lymphatic system, can act in

Above: Edward Jenner's enterprising attempt at perfecting a vaccine (derived from the cowpox virus) to resist smallpox had its opponents. This cartoon appeared in June 1802 in the journal of the Anti-Vaccine Society.

Right: A model of an influenza virus. Influenza is one of the most indefatigable forms of viral infection, for although an attack provides immunity to that particular strain, each successive wave of influenza which appears every few years breeds a modified form of the virus. Each time, therefore, a new vaccine must be prepared in order to block the entry of the virus into the cell. Vaccines have considerably improved in recent years, but influenza still causes thousands of deaths.

Below right: The body's disease-fighting agents at work. Cells called plasmacytes are stimulated to produce anti-bodies by the entry of a virus into a cell. The anti-bodies attack the virus in the process of replicating and contribute to its destruction before it can destroy the host cell.

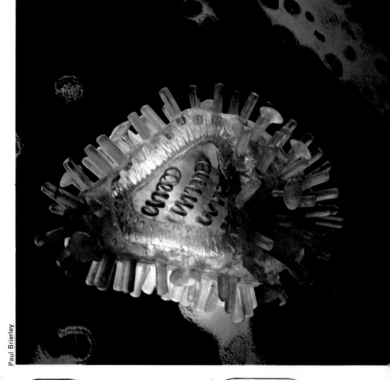

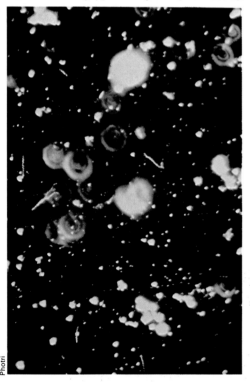

Above: The spirochaete or spiral bacteria of syphilis, one of the most serious of the venereal diseases. It can only be transmitted by close contact, nearly always sexual, and is particularly dangerous to unborn children, since it is one of the few micro-organisms which can pass through the placenta in the mother's womb to infect the child.

Right: A virus can be prevented from entering a host cell by a vaccine containing a substance which prevents it from adhering to the outside of the cell. It is then vulnerable to attack by the plasmacytes which it still stimulates. Immunity to many virulent diseases is assured if vaccination is boosted at intervals.

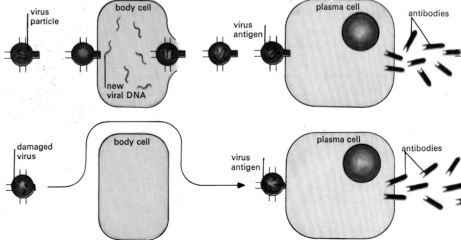

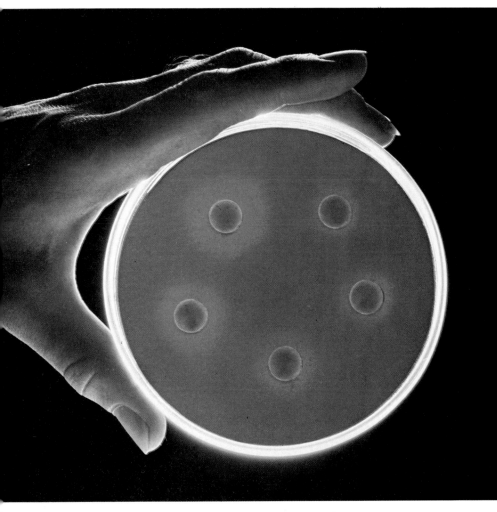

a variety of ways. Some combine chemically with the protein coatings of bacteria and viruses, rendering them harmless, while others have an anti-toxic effect by neutralizing the poisons produced by the invading organism.

This is the basis of natural immunity. Antibodies are thought to be so specific because they 'fit' the molecular shape of the antigen or toxin just as a key fits a lock. An antibody 'key' which does not closely conform to the 'lock' of the antigen or toxin will generally not be effective against it.

The antibody proteins found in the blood belong to a group of proteins called globulins. During the course of an infectious disease the concentration of these globulins rises and consequently the level of the specific antibody also increases. When the infection has passed, the antibody level in the blood falls, but on subsequent re-infection the presence of the antigen immediately stimulates massive antibody production.

Certain forms of immunity can also be responsible for the rejection of tissue grafts made in surgery. Drugs are used to suppress the immune response after a major transplant, but this leaves the patient open to bacterial infection. It is therefore essential to adopt sterile conditions until the graft has taken.

Passive and active immunity

Active immunization against disease is obtained by injecting suitable preparations of killed or weakened (attenuated) bacteria, viruses or toxins. These preparations cause no ill effects in themselves but stimulate the production of antibodies. For example, the Sabin strain of polio virus can produce infection in a person taking the vaccine orally without any danger of the paralytic symptoms developing. The BCG vaccine promotes immunity against tuberculosis following local infection.

Passive immunity against infection is obtained by injecting serum containing the required antibody. These antisera are usually obtained from animals artificially immunized with the antigen or from humans who have recently recovered from the disease. Passive immunity is conferred only as long as the antiserum is present in the blood stream. However, this treatment is rarely used today because of the great risk of serum shock.

The stamping out of childhood diseases such as diphtheria has been one of the major achievements of medical science in this century. Paradoxically, however, the reduction in child mortality has contributed to the population explosion which, in some countries, threatens famine. Nevertheless the discovery of antibacterial drugs—or antibiotics—has given the fight against disease a powerful boost.

About 1905 Paul Ehrlich, the German scientist and bacteriologist, used the term 'chemotherapy' to describe the use of synthetic chemical substances which were specifically effective against disease-causing micro-organisms. The development of modern chemotherapy began with the synthesis of sulphanilamide in Germany and the discovery by Sir Alexander Fleming of the antibiotic penicillin which is produced from the fungal mould, penicillium. The discovery of such chemotherapeutic agents is one of the most important landmarks in the history of medicine.

Above: The effects of antibiotics on bacteria can be tested by suspending the bacteria on blood agar (blood mixed with a gelatinous substance made from seaweed) and incubating the culture at blood heat for 18 hours. The degree of effectiveness of the five different antibiotics is shown in the rate and amount of diffusion round each patch.

Left: Mass smallpox vaccination in Ghana. The World Health Organization is near to realizing its hope of eradicating smallpox in many countries.

Below: Thousands in Calcutta are still prey to diseases like cholera. It is contracted from contaminated food or drinking water.

79

The Heart

Blood is the major transportation system within the vast complex of the human body. Its flow is maintained by a series of pumping mechanisms throughout the cardiovascular system; the most important of which is the heart, whose ceaseless rhythm pushes our blood through more than 1,000 complete circuits every day of our lives.

The work done by the heart seems out of all proportion to its size. Even while we are asleep the heart steadily pumps about two ounces of blood with every beat—341 litres (75 gallons) every hour, enough blood, in fact, to fill an average petrol tank nine times every hour. Moderate exercise doubles this output, and during strenuous activity, such as running a race, the heart may pump up to 2,273 litres (75 gallons) per hour. All this from an organ no bigger than a fist.

The fact that the blood actually circulated in a closed system was not realized in the West until William Harvey the 17th century English physician calculated that the heart must act as a pump which recycles the same blood again and again, knowledge which was available to the Chinese some 3,000 years earlier. A medical treatise of that time reported that 'the heart regulates all the blood of the body . . . . The blood current flows continuously in a circle and never stops', but this discovery was unfortunately overlooked by later peoples, until Harvey rediscovered it.

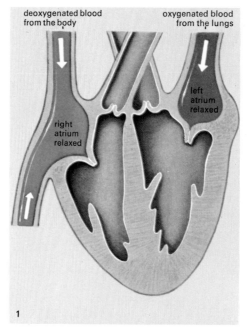

deoxygenated blood from the body

oxygenated blood from the lungs

left atrium relaxed

right atrium relaxed

1

The design

The heart is really two separate pumps, placed side by side, welded together by the *septum*, a thick dividing wall. The reason for this oddity lies in the course of evolution. Our double heart evolved by the gradual separation of a single heart: the right heart pumps blood to the lungs via the *pulmonary artery*, and the left heart pumps the refreshed blood out through the *aorta*, the main artery, to the body tissues.

Each side of the heart consists of an ante-chamber, the *atrium*, and a larger chamber, the *ventricle*. Dark red blood from the body—low in oxygen and high in carbon dioxide—first enters the right atrium which serves as a reservoir for the larger and stronger ventricle below it. Relaxation of the ventricle (an action known as *diastole*) causes blood from the atrium to surge into it, and contraction of the atrium completes this transfer.

The thick muscular wall of the right ventricle performs systolic action—it contracts rapidly—which pumps the blood upwards out of the heart and into the

Below: A 13th-century English manuscript showing some of the Greek physician Galen's ideas of how the internal organs worked. Despite gross errors in his observations, most of his theories were unchallenged until 1,500 years after his death when the English physician William Harvey calculated that the heart must act as a pump, recycling the same blood over and over again—a fact which the Chinese had established some 3,000 years earlier.

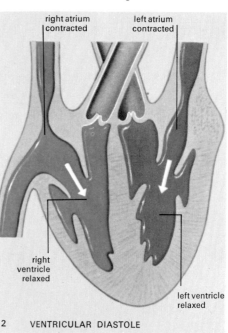

right atrium contracted

left atrium contracted

right ventricle relaxed

left ventricle relaxed

2   VENTRICULAR DIASTOLE

Above left: The beginning of the cardiac cycle which takes place during a single heartbeat. The atria fill with blood from the lungs (through the pulmonary veins) and from the head, neck, arms and chest (through the inferior venae cavae). The valves to the ventricles are forced open by the pressure and they fill with blood. (Left) The atria contract pushing the remaining blood into the ventricles whose walls become distended. A wave of muscular contraction sweeps over them and (below) the valves are snapped shut by the difference in the pressure between the ventricles and the atria. As the valves are closing, blood is forced out of the ventricles into the aorta or the pulmonary artery from which it travels to all parts of the body except the lungs. (Right) The pressure in the ventricles falls and they relax. The period during which the atria and ventricles fill is known as the diastole, and the contraction period as the systole.

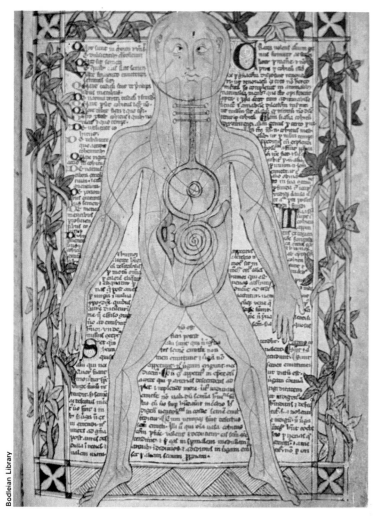

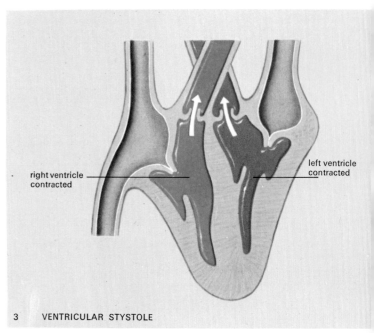

right ventricle contracted

left ventricle contracted

3   VENTRICULAR STYSTOLE

large pulmonary artery. The blood is forced through the capillaries of the lungs where carbon dioxide is unloaded, and oxygen is taken up, turning the dark red blood bright red. The return to the left heart is made via the *pulmonary vein*. The oxygen-rich blood is conducted into the left atrium, by the relaxation of the left ventricle, and is ready to be thrust out into the aorta and round the body.

The wall of the left ventricle is much thicker than that of the right: it has to pump harder to distribute the blood throughout the fine network of vessels in the body. The blood is not simply pushed out of the ventricles, it is wrung out of them by the action of the spiral muscles circling around them. The muscles are arranged in several layers of spiral and circular bands enclosing the ventricles in a common envelope.

The two ventricles pump almost simultaneously ensuring that each side of the heart ejects an equal volume of blood. This is necessary to prevent congestion or depletion of one side of the heart by the other side pumping too much or too little blood. The septum helps the effectiveness of the pumping action by becoming rigid just before contraction, acting as a fixed point for muscle band contraction.

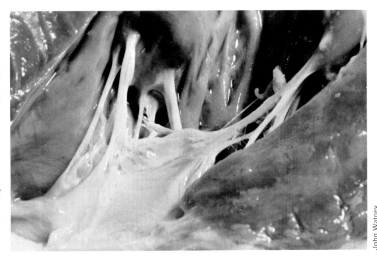

Left: The heart of a sheep showing the tendons known as chordae tendineae. These are responsible for preventing the ventricular valves from being forced back into the atria by the pressure of blood filling up the ventricles. The chordae tendineae are anchored to the papillary muscles in the ventricle walls.

Below: Longitudinal section of the heart, centre of the blood circulation system that combines the vital functions of central heating, drainage, air conditioning, water main and food supply. Basically a muscular tube, the heart has slowly developed into a four-chambered organ as evolutionary survival demanded greater complexity and efficiency.

John Watney

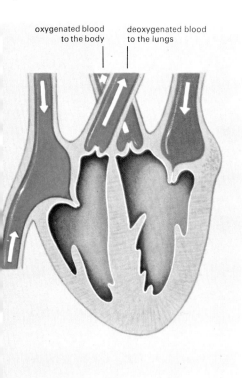

oxygenated blood to the body   deoxygenated blood to the lungs

Before birth, an opening known as the *foramen ovale* in the septum allows blood enriched with oxygen from the mother to flow directly from the right to the left atrium, bypassing the lungs which do not function until the moment of birth. The *foramen ovale* normally closes at birth, but very occasionally it remains open, resulting in poor circulation through the lungs where it fails to take up enough oxygen, causing the skin of the new-born child to turn blue (an indication of serious oxygen starvation). This condition is known as a hole in the heart, and can quite often be repaired by surgery. Especially small holes may remain undetected for years.

The blood is prevented from rushing back into the atrium by the flaplike valves between the atrium and ventricle which

Camera Press

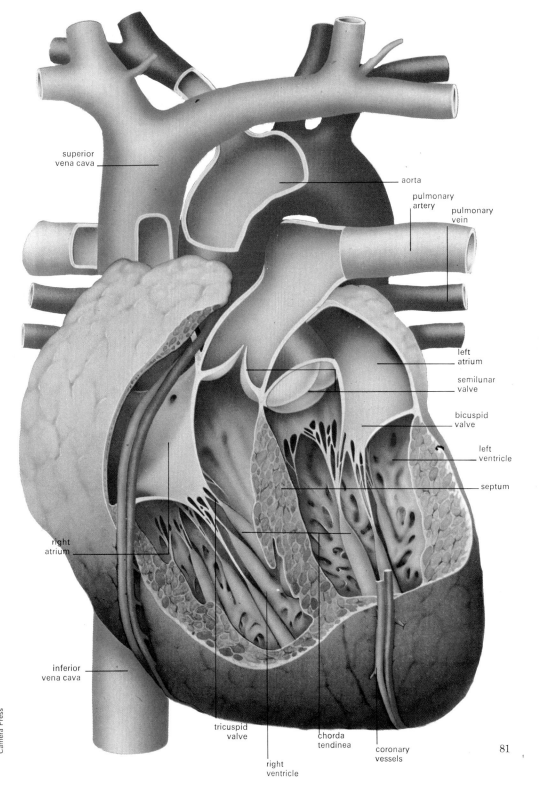

superior vena cava

aorta

pulmonary artery

pulmonary vein

left atrium

semilunar valve

bicuspid valve

left ventricle

septum

right atrium

inferior vena cava

tricuspid valve

right ventricle

chorda tendinea

coronary vessels

81

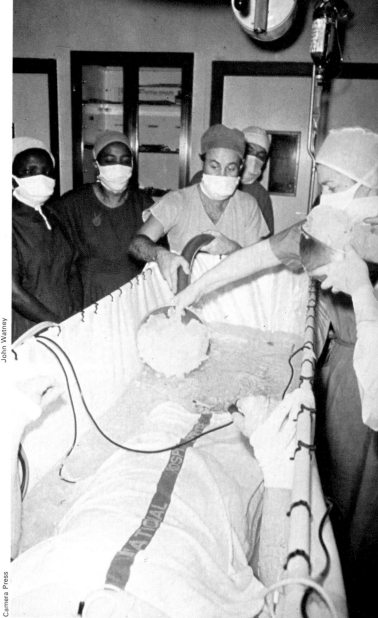

Left: Anterior view of a model showing the vessels which carry the blood supply to and from the heart. The heart removes 75% of the oxygen in the blood supplied to it, unlike other muscles which only use 25%. The coronary arteries are of immense importance, since their blockage by disease and the resulting loss of oxygen leads to heart failure.

are forced shut by the pressure as the ventricle begins to contract. The slamming shut of the valves can be heard through a doctor's stethoscope as a dull 'boom'. Shortly afterwards, three smaller, crescent-shaped valves open to allow the blood to flow into the main arteries leaving the heart. Then, as the muscles relax, the pressure in the chambers falls, and the outlet valves close preventing the expelled blood from returning to the heart. As they close, these valves make a shorter, higher, almost clicking sound which is distinctly audible with a stethoscope.

Safety factors of the heart

The presence of the atria in the heart appears on first examination to contradict the usual biological rule of maximum efficiency and utilization of all the parts. The atria seem to unnecessarily complicate the cardiac pump, since the ventricles are capable of performing the pumping task by themselves. However, they do provide a safety factor, necessary in this vital organ. Under normal circumstances the atria play a relatively minor role in the filling of the ventricles, but when disease narrows the valve openings between the atria and the ventricles, their pumping action is then essential to drive the blood through the restricted openings.

A heart completely deprived by disease of the use of the right ventricle has the amazing ability to continue pumping blood through the lungs to the left ventricle. It is even possible to divert the blood flow so that it bypasses the right heart, and still maintain an efficient circulation.

As for the left ventricle, this has such large margins of safety that it can function as a good pump when as much as half of its muscle mass is dead. These kinds of safety factors are indispensable to organs such as the heart on which immense strains are placed, particularly through stress in urban societies.

There are also inbuilt safety factors in the valves, whose function is to maintain

Right: The time needed for some of the simpler heart operations can now be extended by cooling the patient to slow his metabolism and reduce the oxygen requirement. The patient is immersed in water to which ice is added until he reaches 28°C. When the operation is completed warm water is pumped into the bath until normal temperature is restored.

Below: The removal of the heart from the body, so that more intricate operations, such as the replacement of valves, can be performed, was only made possible by the invention of the heart-lung machine. It takes over the activity of pumping blood to the tissues which would otherwise suffer from oxygen starvation.

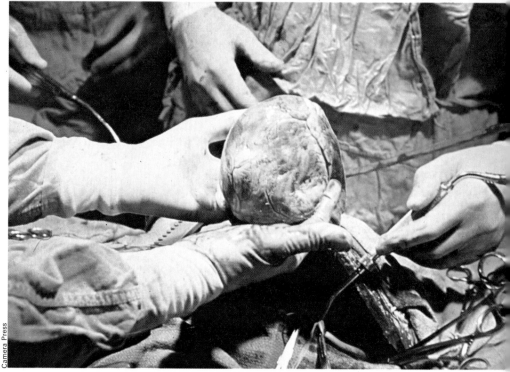

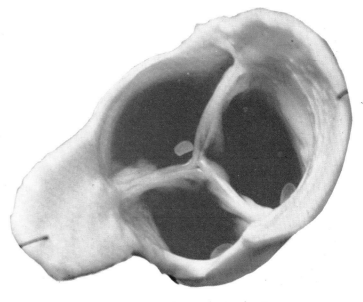

Camera Press

John Launois/Transworld

Above right: A heart valve taken from a dead person, freeze-dried and stored in a sterile 'organ bank'. This valve has been selected for its size (there are 13 sizes from 2cm to 4cm in diameter), revived in warm water and penicillin for about 20 minutes, trimmed to fit and made leakproof with a few drops of antibiotic solution. Valves are absolutely vital in the heart to ensure blood flow only in one direction.

Left: The valve is joined to the wall of the aorta by about 50 stitches and begins work instantly.

Below left: An artificial valve being stitched into a patient. Now widely used in heart surgery, they have a longer life than transplanted ones.

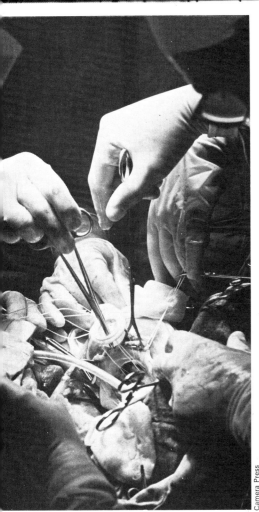

Camera Press

the forward movement of the blood through the chambers. Doctors have long known that patients with serious leaks in the heart valves are able to maintain a good circulation simply by harder pumping of the heart. There are two main safety factors involved in this compensatory pumping: one is known as 'Starlings Law' which, in brief, says that the more a heart muscle is stretched, the more vigorously it responds, within its own limits, so that when the inlet or outlet valves of the ventricles leak, they fill with an excess of blood. This stretches the heart muscle, causing it to pump harder, and compensate for the loss of blood backward through the valves. The other safety factor is provided by the spiral arrangement of the deep bands of muscle around the ventricles which tend to direct the flow of blood forward rather than backward through the leaky valves.

Unfavourable circumstances sometimes conspire to reduce the force of the heart's contraction, but fortunately drugs like *digitalis* can often restore a failing heart by heightening muscle contractions.

The sounds produced by the slamming shut of the heart valves and the turbulence in the blood as it flows into the chambers give doctors valuable information about the working of the valves. When a valve leaks, the distinct thud as the valve shuts is accompanied by a 'murmur' like the sigh of a gust of wind coming through a leaking window-pane. The timing, quality and position of the murmur indicate the type of heart complaint. Constriction of the valve openings, for example, will cause a characteristic hissing sound similar to the noise made by water coming out of the constricted nozzle of a hosepipe.

The heart's blood supply

Surprisingly, the heart has a very low margin of safety in one particular aspect —its oxygen supply. The coronary arteries supply oxygen to the heart, and are of immense importance since blockage of one of these vessels results in death. Unlike other body tissues, which use as little as one fourth of the oxygen supplied to them, the heart removes over 75 per cent of the oxygen from the blood brought to it. The blood supply is therefore of critical importance to the heart, especially when its workload is increased by exercise of various types.

Two large coronary arteries pipe oxygen-rich blood to the heart muscles. They curl around the surface of the heart, dividing almost immediately into two branches supplying different sections of heart muscle. The surface vessels divide repeatedly until they penetrate deep into the walls of the heart, surrounding the muscle elements with very fine capillaries which give up their oxygen to the muscle cells. Eventually three systems of veins return the blood to the right heart to be pumped back to the lungs.

Sudden blockage of any one of the coronary arteries will result in complete lack of blood to the area served by that artery. The muscles, deprived of blood, will soon stop contracting, die and be replaced by non-functional scar tissue, considerably weakening the pumping power of the heart. It has been noticed that, particularly in young people, the block of a main coronary artery over a number of years does not always result in death of the muscle it serves. It appears that vessels from other arteries can take over the area of supply, growing into the muscle tissue to form a collateral circulation. This, however, can only occur over a long period, although experiments indicate that the development of a collateral circulation takes place faster if exercise is taken regularly.

Heart muscle is able to survive without oxygen for periods up to ten minutes, whilst brain cells have a survival limit of about three minutes without oxygen. This involves doctors in an important moral problem when they are involved in cases of drowning or heart failure. It is often possible to restart the heart even after considerable brain damage has occurred, so that after the heart has stopped beating for three minutes the doctor has to decide whether or not to revive the patient who may then no longer be a human being in the normal sense.

Cardiac Control

The heart of a mammal can be completely separated from all its nerve connections, and yet it will continue to beat for hours, its only requirement being blood. This must have been well known to many ancient peoples who cut out the hearts of animals in their sacrificial rites, holding the still-beating heart aloft.

The reason why the heart differs from other muscles is because it has its own in-built mechanism which maintains the rhythmic beat independently of its nerve connections. This mechanism is known appropriately as the 'pacemaker' and its existence eluded biologists until comparatively recent times: William Harvey (1578-1657) rather despairingly concluded that 'the motion of the heart was to be comprehended only by God'. We are now so close to understanding the heart's functioning and control that doctors can replace pieces of the heart with completely artificial parts, maintaining the circulation of the blood almost as efficiently as the natural heart.

The pacemaker mechanism

Close examination of the rear wall of the heart's right atrium reveals a barely visible knot of tissue known as the *sino-atrial* or *S-A node*. This tiny area is the seat of the elusive pacemaker mechanism, generating a brief electrical impulse of low intensity approximately 72 times every minute in a resting adult. From this point the impulse spreads out over the sheets of tissue which make up the two atria, exciting the muscle fibres as it does so. This causes contraction of the two atria, the reservoirs of the heart, thereby thrusting the blood into the empty ventricles. The impulse quickly reaches another small specialized knot of tissue known as the *atrioventricular* or *A-V node*, located between the atria and the ventricles, which delays it for about 0.07 seconds (seven-hundredths of a second),

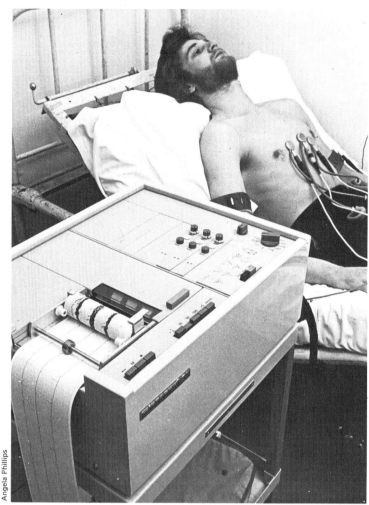

Angela Phillips

Transworld

Above: Computers provide rapid diagnoses of heart complaints.

Left: A modern ECG, attached to the chest, arms and legs may be monitored on an oscilloscope or traced by a pen recorder which shows both normal activity and that of the patient's own heart.

Right: An X-ray picture of a battery-powered pacemaker, surgically implanted under the left arm. The batteries can be replaced about every three years without removing the electrode.

Below: One of the first electrocardiograph (ECG) machines made in the 1900s. Wires attached to metal containers in which the patient's hands and left leg are immersed, picked up through the skin the electrical changes that accompany the cardiac cycle and transmitted them to a recording needle which traced out the activity.

Right: A nuclear powered artificial pacemaker. A radioactive isotope produces a tiny electric current at regular intervals stimulating the heart to maintain a steady pumping action of 72 times a minute. Although still being tested these pacemakers are expected to last up to 10 years, 4 years longer than the battery type.

Radio Times Hulton Picture Library

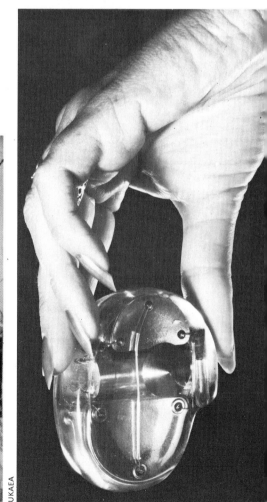

UKAEA

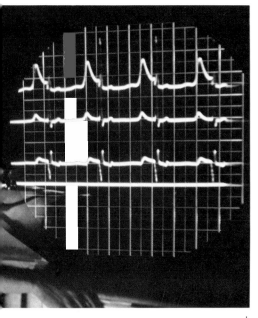

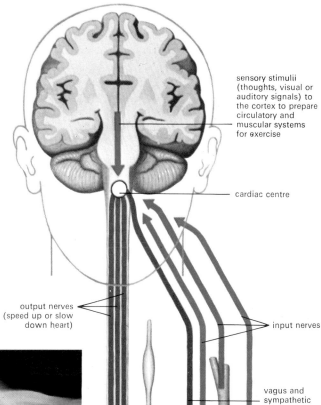

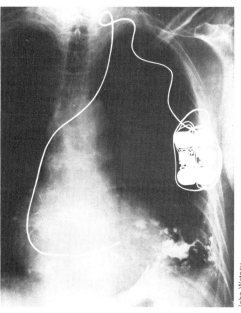

Right: The heart's natural pacemaker is a lump of small nerve fibres, the sino-atrial node, near the top of the heart. The body's demands alter the activity of the pacemaker through a reflex arc. Cardiac receptors send messages to cardiac centres in the brain, which send back instructions to the pace-maker via the autonomic nerves. Stimulation by the parasympathetic fibres slows down the cardiac cycle; the sympa-thetic fibres speed it up.

Below: An X-ray confirms that a catheter tube inserted into a vein in the arm has arrived at the heart. Pressure transducers at this end of the tube measure changes in the blood. The other end is attached to an oscilloscope (an electronic instrument which analyzes frequency patterns). Readings from this indicate the efficiency of the heart valves in coping with tidal backflow of the blood.

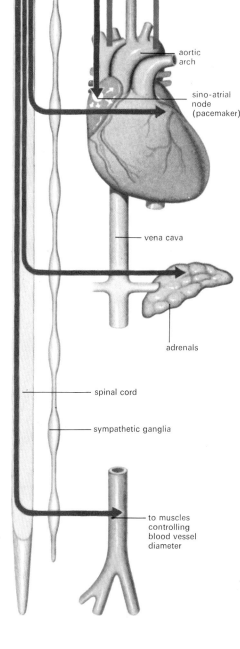

sensory stimulii (thoughts, visual or auditory signals) to the cortex to prepare circulatory and muscular systems for exercise

cardiac centre

output nerves (speed up or slow down heart)

input nerves

vagus and sympathetic nerve

aortic arch

sino-atrial node (pacemaker)

vena cava

adrenals

spinal cord

sympathetic ganglia

to muscles controlling blood vessel diameter

exactly enough time to allow the atria to complete their contractions.

The electrical current races across the surface of the two ventricles through a specialized system of conducting fibres which carry the impulse to every muscle cell of the ventricles within 0.06 seconds (six-hundredths of a second), causing the squeezing, thrusting motion of these powerful pumping chambers. Even at this speed precise synchronization does not occur; some muscle fibres contract very slightly before others, giving the heart its characteristic motion as the ventricles contract, wringing the blood out into the arteries.

Here in the pacemaker mechanism there are in-built safety factors: the A-V node, in an emergency situation, can take over the functions of the S-A node by becoming the generator of the impulses. It is not so efficient—it can only produce a maximum rate of forty or fifty beats per minute, and its output excites both the atria and ventricles simultaneously—but when the S-A node is destroyed by disease it becomes the only link between life and death. Patients have been known to survive for up to twenty years with a damaged S-A node, which is quite a feat even for this versatile organ.

Science, however, has come to the aid of heart sufferers by developing artificial pacemakers. Taking over the functioning of the heart's own mechanisms, these provide the necessary electrical impulses to cause the rhythmical contractions of the heart muscle. Powered by nuclear batteries they can be inserted in conveni-ent parts of the body (under the arm, for example) and have lives of six years or more.

Sometimes the heart sequence becomes disturbed, resulting in chaotic, unco-ordinated contractions. This is known as *fibrillation* and can be rectified by the application of a sudden strong electric current.

Control of the pacemaker

Anatomists have traced two sets of nerves to the heart which, although they are not important in originating the heart beat, play a vital role in controlling its rate. These are the *vagus* and *sympathetic* nerves which act like the brake and accelerator in a car. The vagus nerves continually check the tempo of the heart beat induced by the pacemaker, slowing it down and preventing over-exertion of the heart muscles. This implies that when the vagus nerves are cut the heart rate

As the heart rate increases, the pressure of the blood pounding against the walls of the aorta increases. When this reaches a certain level these nerves transmit impulses up to the medulla stimulating the inhibitory reflex whereby more impulses are sent down to the pacemaker mechanism. The overall effect is like applying the brake in a car running downhill: it decreases the rate and force of the heart beat, thus reducing the pressure of the blood forced into the aorta. The fall in pressure cuts down the number of impulses sent to the medulla and consequently the depression of the heart's activity is diminished.

Stimuli from outside the body detected by the eyes, ears and nose operate in a similar way to the blood-pressure receptors in the aorta, increasing or decreasing the heart rate. In this way the body can prepare itself for necessary action; the sight of an enemy, for example will cause accelerating impulses to be sent to the heart, speeding up the heart rate and increasing the oxygen supply to the muscles ready for fight or flight. Equally, purely internal stimuli in the form of ideas and emotions arising in the brain can act on the accelerating or inhibiting centres in the medulla. Everyone is familiar with the pounding of the heart before an examination, or the feeling of faintness following sudden emotional or physical shock—both results of a rapid decrease in the heart rate and dilatation of the blood vessels.

The effect of the nerves on the heart rate is immediate and of short duration, very necessary for survival in a world of suddenly changing situations. There is, however, a slower and longer lasting means of control over the heart rate, brought about by the action of the hormone *adrenaline*. The sympathetic nerves which increase the heart rate also cause the *adrenal glands* situated near each kidney to pour adrenaline into the bloodstream. Adrenaline has a similar action to the sympathetic nerve endings on the pacemaker mechanism, increasing its rate. In fact the sympathetic nerve endings themselves have been shown to release adrenaline which is rapidly destroyed, preventing its accumulation and a break-down in the regulatory system.

The heart is thus much more than just a pump. It is a subtle control mechanism which, through its control of the circulatory system, influences the ability of the body to respond to external and internal situations rapidly and efficiently. It is embodied with such efficient safety factors that the heart of a normal, healthy, adult cannot be taxed beyond its reserve powers of contraction.

During strenuous exercise the muscles themselves will fatigue or reach their limits of contraction well before the heart is injured. On the other hand, a person with damaged valves, coronary blood vessels or other heart diseases is likely to exceed the reserve capacities of the heart by even minor activities. Becoming emotionally upset whilst sitting in an office, for example, will increase the heart rate, placing much more strain on the heart than playing golf where the pumping of the blood is assisted by the skeletal muscles. More people suffer from heart attacks during emotional upsets than in any other times—the price we pay for civilization.

will rapidly increase—which is exactly what happens.

The sympathetic nerves accelerate the beat during strenuous activity and excitement, and their removal or a blockage of their impulses causes the rate of beating to slow down. The function of the heart is thus to a great extent determined by the balance between these two sets of antagonistic nerves—both acting to control the in-built pacemaker mechanism.

The ceaseless rhythm of the pacemaker is influenced and modified by several different factors. Messages from receptors in the circulatory system are processed in the medulla of the brain which sends appropriate impulses via the vagus or sympathetic nerves to slow down or speed up the pacemaker's rhythm. During exercise, the movement of the muscles against the veins forces more blood back to the heart and into the right atrium, stretching the muscular walls. This stretching causes nerve impulses to be transmitted through the central nervous system to the medulla which, in turn, accelerates the heart rate to increase the blood-flow to the working muscles.

The muscle cells now using more energy increase their take-up of oxygen from the blood, consequently releasing an increased amount of carbon dioxide. Special sense organs in the carotid artery and aorta detect the increased carbon dioxide content of the blood and this information is relayed to the accelerating centres in the medulla. Again these speed up the heart rate, increase the circulation through the lungs, thereby removing the carbon dioxide faster, and supply more oxygen to the working muscles: a fast and direct response to the extra requirements of the body.

The safety mechanism
To prohibit the heart from beating so fast that it damages itself there must be a mechanism to slow it down and prevent the rate increasing beyond a certain limit. The aorta leaving the left heart has nerve endings which detect the pressure of the blood pumped into it from the ventricle.

Above: An astronaut undergoes a simulation take off on a rocket sled to test the affects of acceleration on his heart. The body can tolerate up to 35 g (35 x earth's gravity) providing the acceleration is at 90° to the direction of the spine but various disturbances from nose bleeds to blackouts can occur. Even at 7 g, the level at which these tests are conducted, the blood has an equivalent weight to liquid iron which increases blood pressure.

Below: The sagging eyes, cheeks and lower lip of this astronaut are the results of being spun on a centrifuge at 7 g pressure. The ECG reading shows the irregular heart activity.

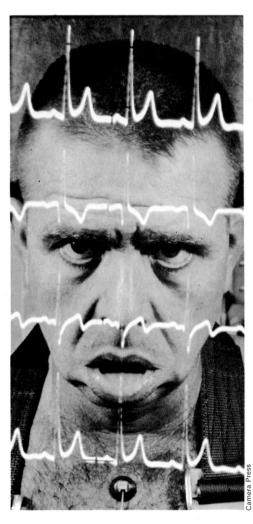

Coronary arteries, showing blocked vessels. The healthy heart is a highly efficient machine, capable of pumping up to 2,273 litres (75 gallons) of blood per hour during strenuous exercise.

The Hormone System

The specialized organs and cells of the human body which both control the conditions and generate the materials essential to our continued well-being have to be controlled and balanced. Any deviation from 'normality' has to be immediately remedied, otherwise life itself can be endangered. To do this, both the nervous system and the chemical 'messenger service' known as the hormone system, work together.

The hormone system at its simplest works like the thermostat in any heating system. Just as room temperature may fall, the body temperature may also fall and make adjustment necessary. The thermostat may instruct the central heating to switch on and, when the temperature rises, the thermostat again comes into operation and switches the system off. In this sense the temperature controls the thermostat as much as the thermostat controls temperature. And in the same way the hormone system controls conditions in the human body as much as it is itself controlled by them. This analogy, however, is over simple. The body's hormone system controls numerous positive-negative systems which keep the 'weather' inside the body stable whatever outside conditions or circumstances prevail.

It is this constant fine control that makes the hormone system so elegant. The hormone that controls the excretion of water, for example, is itself controlled by the amount of water in the body. If that were constant, the output of the hormone would be constant and the water excretion constant. In fact, all three vary a little during every 24 hours and in extreme conditions they can vary widely —whether during a long evening drinking in a bar or a march across a dry desert. It is a rare emergency when the hormone system cannot cope, restoring the delicate balance of conditions inside the body. If, for example, too little water is present in your body several mechanisms come into action and among the hormones that are released is one that helps to stimulate you to drink. Or if danger threatens, as part of the general 'fight or flight' mechanism ordered by the brain, the hormone *adrenaline* will be released to prepare the skeletal muscles for violent action.

The endocrines

The many hormones present in the body and the glands that produce them, are collectively known as the *endocrine* system. The vital fact about an endocrine gland is that it releases its secretion, the hormone, into general circulation to act where it can; other glands, which direct their secretion down some path to a particular place, are called *exocrine*. The sex glands, for example, are endocrine because they secrete sex hormones into the blood to be carried all over the body to produce a variety of effects. The same is true of the *thyroid*, the *adrenals*, and several other glands. Indeed, even when the target of the hormone is quite small and near the gland, the hormone may

Below: The endocrine system. The human body is controlled by two types of activity, electrical and chemical. The nervous system, which exerts electrical control, is integrated with the chemical control of the endocrine system to maintain the body in a balanced state. The endocrine system has glands which release chemical messengers, called hormones, which are carried by the blood to specific 'targets' in the body. The target organs are provoked into releasing substances essential to the development and maintenance of life.

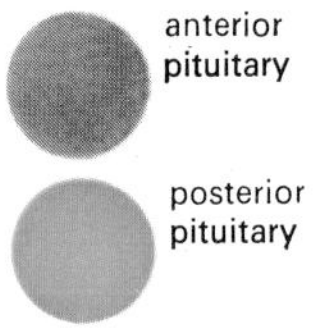

Many glands which control these activities are themselves controlled by the pituitary (Fig.1 and inset) which is, in turn, regulated by the hypothalamus at the base of the brain. The pituitary, known as the master gland (Fig.2), is attached to the hypothalamus by the pituitary stalk. The anterior lobe secretes hormones when stimulated by the hypothalamus. The posterior lobe stores hormones from the hypothalamus.

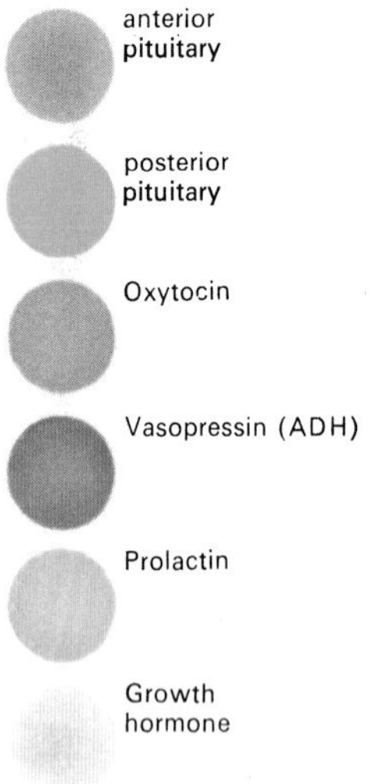

anterior pituitary

posterior pituitary

anterior pituitary

posterior pituitary

Oxytocin

Vasopressin (ADH)

Prolactin

Growth hormone

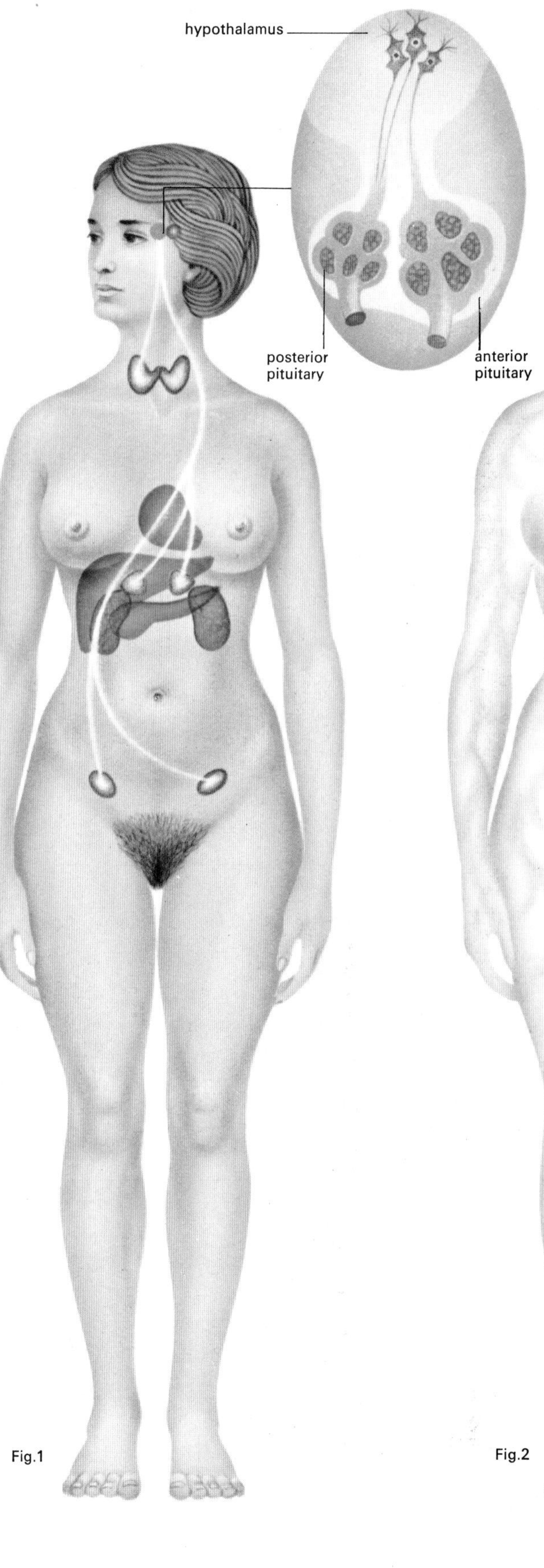

hypothalamus

posterior pituitary

anterior pituitary

Fig.1

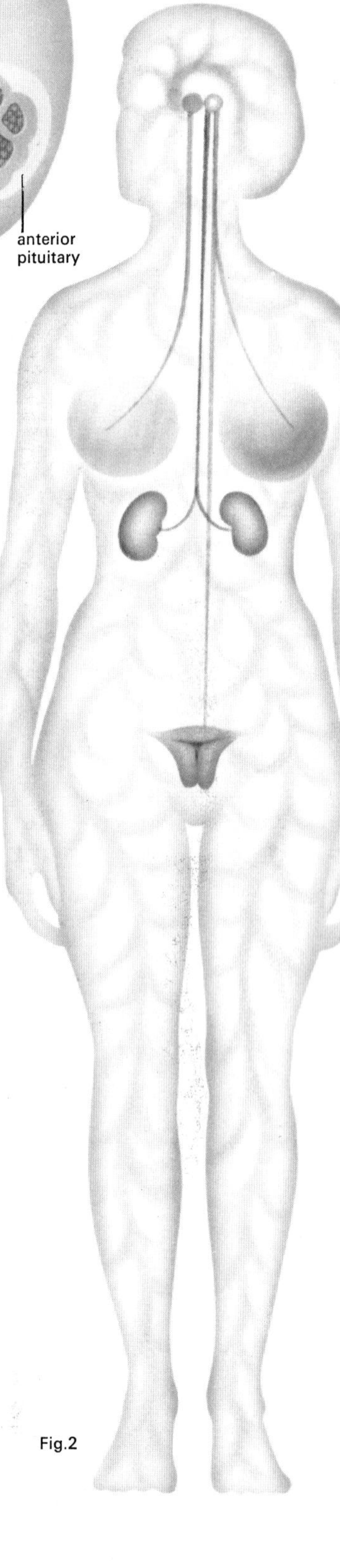

Fig.2

88

The release of the hormones is either stimulated or inhibited by the hypothalamus, depending on the information it receives about body needs. The hypothalamus itself produces only two hormones, vasopressin and oxytocin (Fig.2) which are sent to the posterior pituitary to be stored until the body requires them. Vasopressin (or ADH) is released when receptors in the hypothalamus sensitive to changes in the water level, inform it that the blood has too much or too little water. ADH stimulates the tubules of the kidney to absorb more or less water so that the balance is restored.

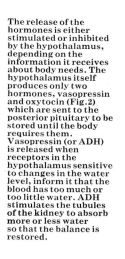

Thyroxine

Insulin

Glucagon

The action of oxytocin, which causes contraction of the uterus during labour and expulsion of milk from the breasts after birth, is triggered by nerve impulses from the uterus to the brain via the spinal cord. The anterior pituitary produces six hormones which, with the exception of growth hormone, stimulates particular endocrines. The adrenals (Fig.4) secrete adrenaline which stimulates the heart and the whole body (shown only in the right adrenal) and other hormones which act on the kidneys and also on the whole body to maintain salt levels (shown only in the left adrenal).

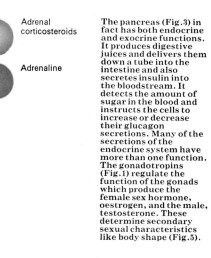
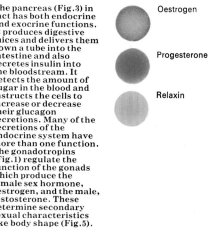

Adrenal corticosteroids

Adrenaline

The pancreas (Fig.3) in fact has both endocrine and exocrine functions. It produces digestive juices and delivers them down a tube into the intestine and also secretes insulin into the bloodstream. It detects the amount of sugar in the blood and instructs the cells to increase or decrease their glucagon secretions. Many of the secretions of the endocrine system have more than one function. The gonadotropins (Fig.1) regulate the function of the gonads which produce the female sex hormone, oestrogen, and the male, testosterone. These determine secondary sexual characteristics like body shape (Fig.5).

Oestrogen

Progesterone

Relaxin

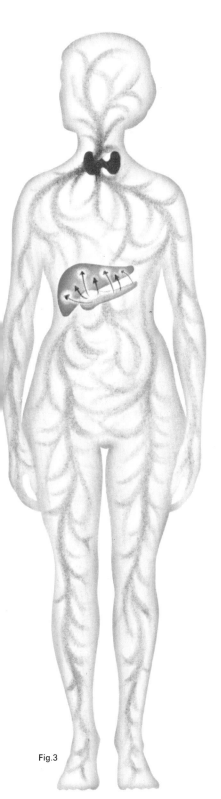

Fig.3

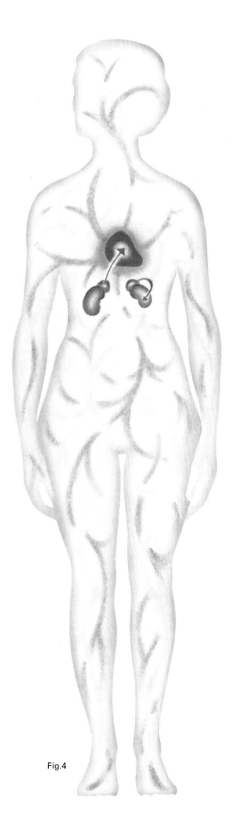

Fig.4

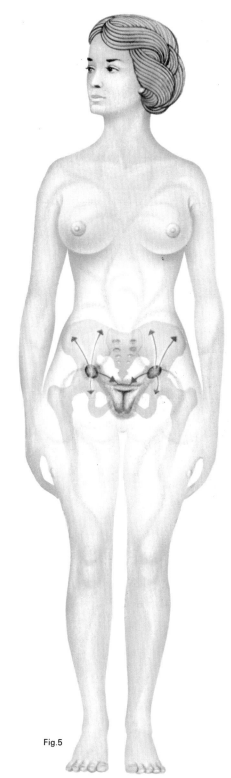

Fig.5

still travel right round the bloodstream—as, for example, do hormones produced in the stomach to act in another part of the stomach.

An exocrine gland, in contrast, is a simple and crude local worker. Saliva comes straight from the (exocrine) *salivary* glands into the mouth; wax from the (exocrine) *sebaceous* glands of the skin go on to its surface; and tears from the (exocrine) *lachrymal* glands go directly into the eye.

Some glands, however, may be both exocrine and endocrine. The cells of the *pancreas*, one of whose jobs is to produce digestive juices, do so in a simple exocrine fashion; they produce the juices and deliver them down a tube into the intestine. But the pancreatic cells responsible for controlling the amount of sugar in the blood have a more complicated job. They need to influence cells in many other parts of the body, increasing or decreasing their rate of sugar use or conservation. So they produce a hormone called *insulin* and secrete it into the bloodstream. Then when they detect an excess of sugar in the blood they can produce more, instantly signalling to all relevant tissues the need to take sugar out of circulation.

A number of classic techniques have been evolved to investigate the nature of a gland and determine whether or not it is endocrine. First, the gland is removed to determine the effects of stopping the gland's secretions. (Most of the experiments described are performed on animals, but there are also occasions when the same effect can be observed in man.) An extract of a fresh gland can then be prepared and injected into the animal to see whether the ill-effects, if any, disappear.

This initial test, however, will only establish that the gland is in fact a gland. It does not prove that the gland is endocrine. To do that, the gland from one animal is removed and, when it shows symptoms of abnormality, its blood circulation is connected to that of another animal which has not had the gland removed. If the gland-less animal recovers from its symptoms the blood of the other animal must have been responsible. Therefore, we can assume that the gland removed was an endocrine gland which secreted hormones throughout the body. Alternatively, the gland can be transplanted within the same animal from one place to another. In the new site it will soon build up a blood supply but will lack all other former connections: if the whole body system does not suffer, its secretion must, therefore, be endocrine.

But experiments on a gland like the pancreas, which is both endocrine and exocrine, have to be more sophisticated and such techniques are available today. Modern methods of analysis can, for example, measure hormones in quantities too small to be imagined: down to one part in a million million. The chemical identification of hormones, complex as they are, has also largely been achieved. This has opened the door to experimentation with pure molecules, as well as to powerful hormone replacement drugs, in larger quantities and at cheaper cost than is possible with the use of animal extracts.

To understand how the endocrine system works, we must first of all look at the *pituitary* and at the part of the brain called the hypothalamus which controls it. These two must come first because they

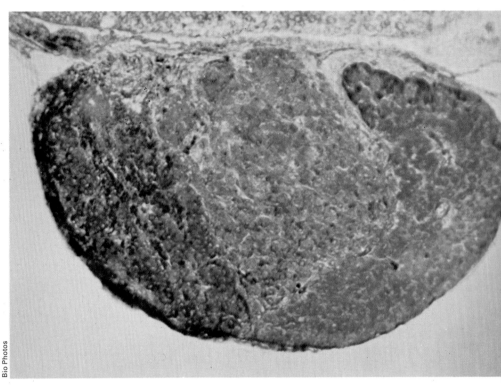

Bio Photos

not only produce hormones, but also release substances to control production of hormones from the other endocrine glands.

The master gland

The pituitary, a small gland situated at the base of the brain, is traditionally called 'the conductor of the endocrine orchestra'. If that analogy applies, however, then an even grander one must be found for the hypothalamus since this part of the brain controls the pituitary. It is here that the nervous system and the endocrine system are co-ordinated.

The anterior part of the pituitary produces no fewer than six different hormones and is controlled by hormone-like 'releasing factors' which come via a special blood vessel link from the hypothalamus. The posterior pituitary, producing just two hormones, is controlled by nerves, rather than chemical secretions, but their source is again the hypothalamus.

Four of the six hormones produced by the anterior pituitary are tropic (or trophic) hormones, that is, they regulate the action of other endocrine glands. *Thyroid-stimulating hormone* (TSH) stimulates the thyroid to produce its hormones. *Adrenocorticotropic hormone* (ACTH) does the same for the part of the adrenal gland that produces aldosterone, which regulates electrolyte metabolism (salt balance). *Follicle-stimulating hormone* (FSH) and *luteinising hormone* (LH) are both gonadotropins—hormones that stimulate development and hormone synthesis in the reproductive system. FSH promotes the development of the spermatazoa in the male and the ova in the female. LH stimulates the secretion of the male sex hormones, testosterone and one of the female sex hormones, oestradiol. Another anterior pituitary hormone, *prolactin*, stimulates the secretion of milk from the breasts. The sixth and final anterior hormone is growth hormone.

The hypothalamus receives inputs from all parts of the body including the emotional centres of the brain. If, for example, it detects that there is a need

Above: A pituitary gland. The fluorescent dye staining the gland is absorbed by the cells which produce the gonadotropic hormones, FSH and LH. The first is responsible for maturing spermatazoa in the testes and ova in the ovaries; LH stimulates secretion of progesterone.

Top right: Electromicrograph of a secretory cell of the pituitary. The large granular body in the centre is the nucleus which controls the cell's activities. The black spots, globules of gonadotropic hormone, diffuse through the outer membrane (white) and are carried into the bloodstream.

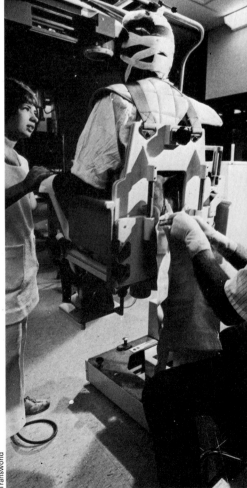

Transworld

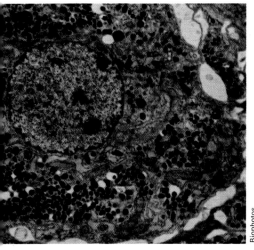

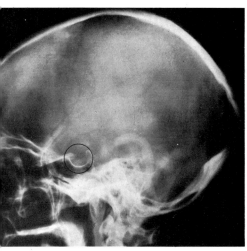

Left, above and below: A unique new method of speeding up the diagnosis of brain disorders which in this case has outlined the pituitary gland. The patient is strapped into a rotating chair (left) and air is injected into the spine. The chair is then rotated in a full circle (below) to regulate the movement of air up the spine into the brain.

The air distributes itself in the brain (above) filling up the ventricles (spaces) and outlining parts of the brain, (here, spaces around the pituitary show up clearly) allowing the medical team to view any abnormal growth of tissue, or lesions, more clearly. TV monitoring and videotape also make examination easier.

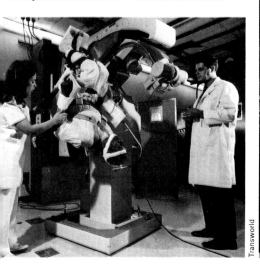

Above right and right: One of the methods of detecting glandular malfunction of the thyroid. Radioactive iodine (iodine which gives off radiation) is injected into the patient's bloodstream. It accumulates in the thyroid, where iodine is a natural component of its hormone, thyroxin. The radiation levels from

the radioactive iodine can be picked up by a gamma ray detector and the resulting pattern of accumulation screened to show its distribution (right). The scanner plots the iodine content of the thyroid in colours according to local concentration. Radiation treatment can sometimes be used to control over-production.

for more cortisol, it produces corticotropin releasing factor; this stimulates the pituitary to release some of its store of corticotropin (ACTH), which in turn stimulates the release of cortisol from the adrenal glands down by the kidneys. There is a releasing factor for each of the anterior pituitary hormones. In some cases, especially prolactin and growth hormone, there is also an inhibiting factor which the hypothalamus releases when it requires the pituitary to stimulate the system less.

Three of these pituitary hormones—growth hormone (anterior), antidiuretic (water retaining) hormone and oxytocin (posterior)—are slightly more important than the rest since their effects are more direct than the tropic hormones.

Growth hormone is still rather a mystery. Its job is to stimulate growth, therefore it plays its most important role in the growing years. But it works on many systems of the body and its effects do not stop after adolescence. Only recently have some of its actions been partially understood.

Growth hormone encourages the growth of cartilage at the ends of bones—the cartilage that forms the matrix for new bone to be laid down. It increases the rate of protein production by the body's growing cells and it increases the amount of energy-giving sugar and fat in the bloodstream.

In many of its effects growth hormone interacts with other hormones such as insulin, which regulates blood sugar by instructing body cells to increase or decrease their secretion of glucagon. At various times of life the thyroid hormones

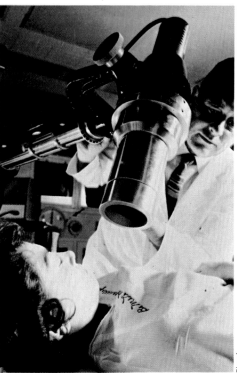

and the sex hormones share a growth-promoting role. But the overall influence of growth hormone is shown when its secretion is abnormal. Too little is occasionally a cause of dwarfism—today preventable by treatment with growth hormone—while too much causes a person to grow to an unusual height and to have an abnormal bone structure.

The functions of the two posterior pituitary hormones are more specific. *Antidiuretic hormone* (ADH), sometimes called *vasopressin* because in artificial conditions it can cause constriction of blood vessels and hence a rise in blood pressure, is responsible for the regulation of water loss from the kidneys. (Diuresis means the production of a flow of urine; antidiuresis means the prevention of water loss into urine.) So it is clear from the hormone's name that it exerts a braking effect.

In the first stage of urine production in the kidneys, a large amount of water is skimmed off the blood along with all the waste products for excretion. If that first mixture were to flow out as urine, too much water would usually be lost. Therefore at a second stage a different part of the kidney reabsorbs some of the water, leaving the eventual urine less dilute. Under the influence of antidiuretic hormone the kidney will reabsorb a lot of water. If, on the other hand, the body contains too much water this situation will be assessed by the hypothalamus which will signal to the pituitary to release less ADH. With its reabsorbing system receiving less stimulus, the kidney will allow more water through into the urine.

ADH secretion is influenced by other factors than the quantity of body water: for example, alcohol depresses it, so the drinker tends to lose even more fluid than he takes in. Dehydration may be one of the contributary causes of the hang-over.

The other posterior pituitary hormone, *oxytocin*, is most important during childbirth and breast feeding although it may exert minor effects on the reproductive system at other times.

During labour, oxytocin production increases, causing the uterus to contract. It is interesting that at the same time the uterine muscle becomes abnormally sensitive to the hormone. Many women have their labour induced or helped by oxytocin which they receive intravenously.

In breast feeding, oxytocin encourages the expulsion of milk from the nipple. A baby does not suck milk out of the nipple by its own power, as it has to from a bottle. The sucking of the child's mouth stimulates nerves in the breast which are linked to the hypothalamus. The hypothalamus sends a nerve message to the pituitary, which releases oxytocin into the bloodstream. When it reaches the breast, oxytocin, causes the milk within it to be carried along the ducts towards the nipple then forcibly ejected.

Hormones, rivalled only by the nervous system to which they are wedded, are one of the best examples of the genius of nature's design. They make up the 'weather' inside our bodies but, unlike the weather outside, they are reliable. They keep our internal machine neither too wet nor too dry, neither too warm nor too cold and function smoothly through the many complex stages of our lives from birth to death.

Hormone Activity

The endocrine system is made up of endocrine glands which secrete substances called hormones into the bloodstream to exert their effect somewhere else in the body. The endocrine glands are often under the influence of the pituitary gland, which is itself controlled by a part of the brain called the hypothalamus.

The role of the thyroid gland, situated in the neck, is to set the rate at which the metabolic combustion of food into energy takes place. The gland produces its hormones, mainly *thyroxine* and smaller amounts of *triiodothyronine* and one or two others, and stores them in the form of *colloid* (minute particles suspended in liquid) within the tiny sacs called follicles. When, under the influence of the hypothalamus which is continually monitoring the body's metabolism, the pituitary gland releases more TSH (*thyroid stimulating hormone*), the thyroid releases thyroxine from the colloid into the blood circulation. The TSH also stimulates it to produce and store more thyroxine.

The hypothalamus is likely to initiate this chain of events under a number of circumstances: when potential energy, in the form of food, has entered the body; when it wants to create body heat; or whenever else it detects that the living machine needs to run a little faster.

The role of thyroid hormones lies in growth and development. Its absence is demonstrated by the cretinism—mental retardation and dwarfism—of hypothyroid children. But provided this condition is noted early enough, it can today be prevented by administration of thyroid hormone.

The thyroid hormones contain in their structure minute quantities of the element iodine, which is otherwise of virtually no significance to man. Although the amounts are tiny, people living in areas where the food and water contain little iodine have enlarged thyroids.

As well as metabolic hormones, the thyroid also produces a hormone called *calcitonin* which affects bone growth. The effect of calcitonin, however, is more easily understood in relation to the parathyroid glands whose hormone is also concerned with bone and calcium metabolism.

Calcium is essential for teeth and bones. Almost all of the one kilo (2.2 lb) of calcium in the adult body is in bone, while a little circulates in the blood and other body fluids. This small circulating amount is, however, vital to many normal body processes and it must be kept within strict limits. The bones can therefore act as a kind of reservoir; if the body fluids need more calcium they can take it from bones, and if they need less they can lose some to the bones.

This balance of calcium in the body fluids, made relatively easy to control by the fact that bone is constantly being broken down and re-formed, is under the control of the parathyroid hormones.

The parathyroids are formed of four small structures, which lie close to the thyroid. (It is an occasional problem that a patient whose thyroid has to be removed also loses his parathyroids.) The hormone known as *parathormone* which is produced here increases the movement of calcium from bone to blood and the amount secreted depends on the need for such movement. Thus, when the blood calcium is low, the parathyroids are stimulated to produce more of their hormone. Conversely, parathormone secretion is depressed by a high level of calcium in body fluids.

The circulation of calcium is important because its level is influential in blood clotting, contraction of muscles, and the action of nerves. A deficiency of calcium in the blood, for example makes muscles contract uncontrollably, resulting in the potentially fatal condition called *tetany*. The thyroid hormone *calcitonin*, on the

Radio Times Hulton Picture Library

other hand, has the opposite effect to parathormone. It encourages the movement of calcium from the blood into the bones. However, the importance of this effect in normal people is uncertain.

The *catecholamines*, as adrenaline and noradrenaline are collectively known, are released from the inner layer of the adrenal glands in response to pain, emotional disturbance, fear, muscular effort, and other challenging experiences. They increase the rate of the heartbeat, and allow more blood to go to the muscles at the expense of the skin and the gut. They produce an increase in the level of blood sugar to provide the muscles with fuel, increase the depth and rate of breathing, and act on tiny muscles in the skin to make the hair stand on end. They also slow the movement of food through the gut.

The *glucocorticoid* hormones, including *cortisol*, are secreted from the cortex, or outer layer, of the adrenals in response to ACTH (*Adrenocorticotrophic hormone*) released from the pituitary. These hormones are influential in many ways, not least in permitting the action of other hormones; it has been shown that their absence results in the malfunction of a range of metabolic activities.

The *mineralocorticoid* hormone, *aldosterone*, which also comes from the adrenal cortex, regulates the amount of

MEN

Gonadotrophin

Testosterone

Growth Hormone

WOMEN

Gonadotrophin

Oestrogen

Growth Hormone

AGE

ARBITARY SCALE

Above and right: Growth and change of the human body is governed by hormonal activity. Some hormones are active on a daily cycle, known as 'circadian rhythm', some monthly, while others are influential in specific stages of development (see graph above). Growth hormone, particularly active during the first few years of life continues to contribute to the processes of anabolism (building) and catabolism (chemical synthesis for the release of energy). The sex hormones, which dictate male and female shapes and prepare both for reproduction, are less active in later years.

Left: Chang, the Chinese giant photographed in 1880. His height of nearly 8 ft was due to an overproduction of growth hormone.

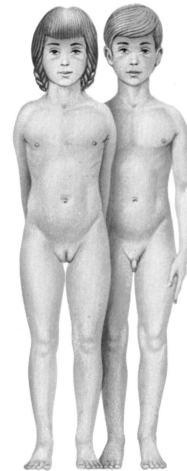

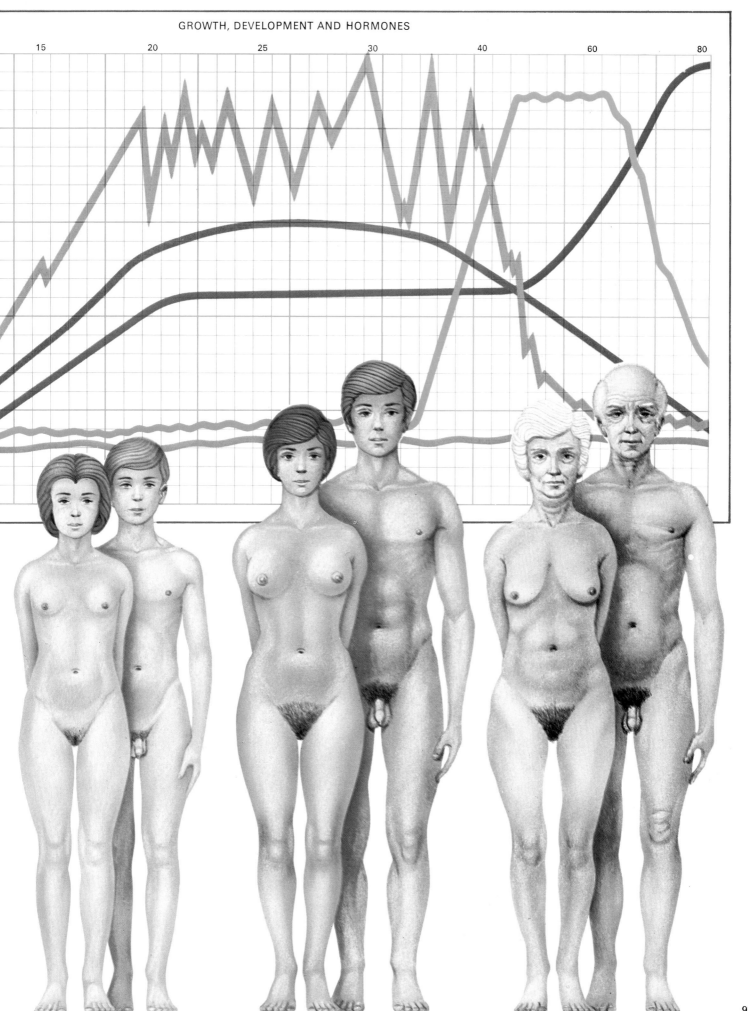

sodium and potassium in the blood. Although this control, like that of calcium, may seem esoteric, it is in fact vitally important to the maintenance of blood pressure, of metabolism and of the proper working of the nervous system. The kidney is also involved in salt balance by the production of *renin* which stimulates production of *angiotensin* in the blood. Angiotensin, as well as possessing properties of its own, stimulates the production of aldosterone by the adrenals.

The adrenal glands have another function, and this is to produce sex hormones. But their production here is much less important than their production by the sex organs themselves, although it can be significant in certain rare cases.

Probably one of the best-known success stories in medical history has been the control of the condition called diabetes which arises from an imbalance in *insulin* produced by the pancreas. Insulin is produced in response to an increase in blood sugar. Like so many other normal components of the body fluids, sugar (glucose) is essential but must be kept within limits—neither too low nor too high. In that task, insulin—and to a lesser extent a related but opposite-acting hormone called *glucagon*—are pre-eminent.

An increase in the quantity of insulin released by the pancreas results in an immediate movement of sugar into muscle cells and a number of other metabolic changes. The diabetic who either cannot

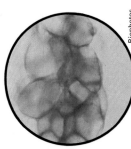

Right: The thyroid gland showing the ring-like follicles in which its hormones are produced.

Below: The exact function of iodine in thyroxin production is not yet understood, but it is well known that a deficiency results in goitre, in which the thyroid gland becomes grossly enlarged. These Paraguayans lack the minute amount of iodine required in their drinking water.

WHO/Paul Almasy

produce insulin or (in some older diabetics) cannot properly release it from the pancreas, suffers the potentially catastrophic effects of a toxic blood glucose level.

Hormones and the life cycle

Although the endocrine glands are present from birth to death, and are active for most of that time, the extent of their influence on the body varies greatly in different periods of life and even during each 24 hour day.

The growth and changes the body undergoes are, indeed, largely under hormonal control. So also is the variation in our internal environment that repeats its cycle regularly every day—the so-called 'circadian rhythm'.

From before birth several hormone systems are active—for example those controlling excretion and metabolism. Others, like growth hormone and thyroid are not only present but are especially influential in this period of rapid growth and development. On the other hand, the activity of the sex hormones is insignificant before puberty and their influence wanes again when reproductive life is over.

The events of puberty, like most others orchestrated by the hormones, are given their signal by the hypothalamus. Under its control, increased secretion of sex hormones from the adrenals causes the dramatic rise in speed of growth, while *gonadotropins* from the pituitary gland stimulate the major producers of sex hormones—the ovaries and the testes—to grow and begin to secrete.

The effect is well-known, and dramatic. In boys the voice breaks, hair grows on the face and elsewhere, and the muscles begin to strengthen. In girls the breasts develop, menstruation begins, and the storage of fat beneath the skin assumes its typical adult female pattern. And along with these 'secondary' sexual characteristics comes the primary one—that both sexes are capable of reproduction, a biological necessity reflected in the adolescent's new and powerful awareness of sexuality and physical attraction.

The most obvious hormonal changes occurring later in life again concern the sex hormones. Today many women demand *oestrogen* tablets to relieve many of the uncomfortable symptoms experienced in the menopause, when the body's secretion of oestrogen ceases.

Most hormones exhibit a daily cycle, and not just because man is socially conditioned to wake during the day and sleep at night. The endocrine rhythm is inbuilt. Perhaps the most striking example, however, of the cyclical nature of hormones is the 28-day pattern of the menstruation cycle. For the first few days after a period the levels of sex hormones are fairly steady. Then, just before the egg is released in mid-cycle there is a massive rise and an equally sharp fall in the amount of oestrogen in the blood. After ovulation, both oestrogen and *progesterone*, which stimulates development of the uterus, exhibit a long, slow rise and fall.

In the maintenance of *homoeostasis*—the balance within the body—hormones are vital. Although investigation has produced cures for many endocrine disorders, science cannot hope to mimic the fine control exercised naturally in the healthy individual by this intricate and powerful band of circulating chemicals.

HORMONE	SECRETED BY	PRINCIPAL EFFECTS
Growth hormone	Pituitary (anterior)	Stimulates hard and soft tissue growth ; helps regulate metabolism
Thyroid stimulating hormone (TSH)	Pituitary (anterior)	Stimulates secretion of the thyroid
Adrenocorticotrophic hormone (ACTH)	Pituitary (anterior)	Stimulates secretion of the adrenal cortex
Follicle stimulating hormone (FSH)	Pituitary (anterior)	Stimulates egg production and oestrogen secretion by the ovaries ; testosterone secretion and sperm development in the testes
Leuteinising hormone (LH)	Pituitary (anterior)	Stimulates progesterone secretion by the ovaries ; preparation of the uterus for fertilized egg ; mammary gland development
Prolactin	Pituitary (anterior)	Stimulates milk secretion by the mammary glands
Oxytocin	Pituitary (posterior)	Stimulates uterine contraction during birth ; milk ejection
Vasopressin (ADH)	Pituitary (posterior)	Causes arteriole constriction ; regulates water absorption by the kidneys
Thyroxin	Thyroid	Increases metabolic rate
Parathyroid hormone (PTH)	Parathyroids	Increases blood calcium level ; decreases blood phosphate level
Aldosterone	Adrenal cortex	Regulates blood mineral levels ; increases body fluid
Hydrocortisone	Adrenal cortex	Regulates carbohydrate, protein and fat metabolism ; anti-inflammatory
Gonadocorticoids (sex hormones)	Adrenal cortex	See specific sex hormones
Glucagon	Pancreas	Increases blood sugar level ; conversion of proteins and fats to glucose ; increases blood potassium and phosphate levels
Insulin	Pancreas	Decreases blood sugar level ; promotes glucose storage ; decreases blood potassium and phosphate levels
Thymus hormone	Thymus	Stimulates antibody production in the lymphoid tissue and liver
Oestrogen	Ovaries	Development of feminine characteristics ; maturation of female sex organs
Progesterone	Ovaries	Mammary gland development ; prepares the uterus for egg implantation
Testosterone	Testes	Development of masculine characteristics ; maturation of male sex organs

The blood supply to the adrenal gland (top L.) and the venous drainage from it. Adrenal glands release adrenalin, noradrenalin and cortisol, as well as some sex hormones.

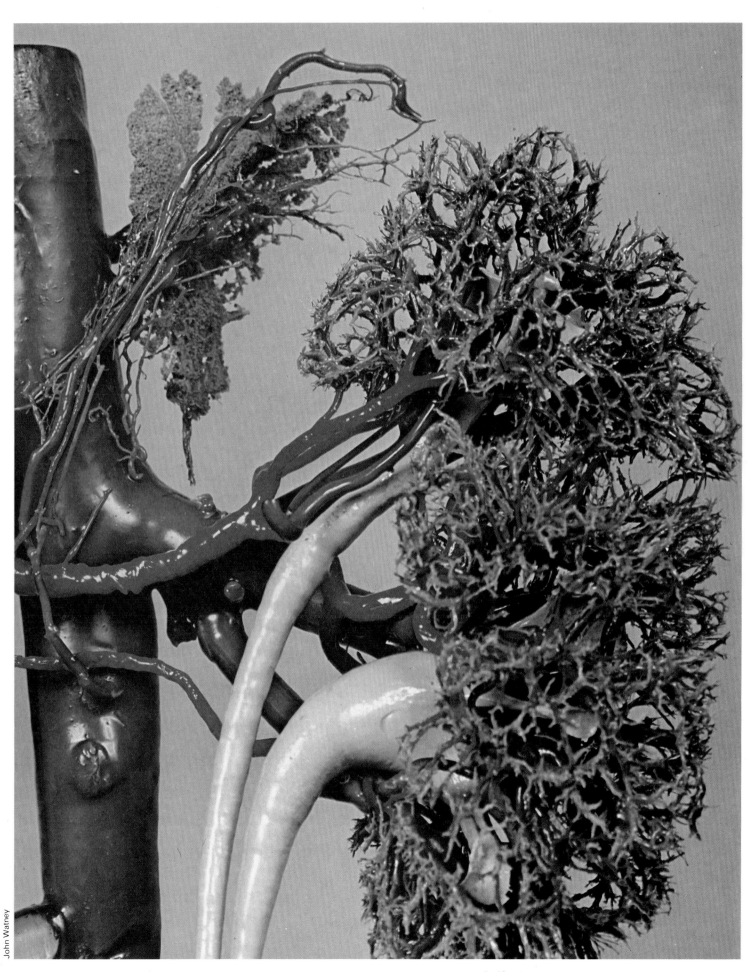

Chapter 4
Respiration

The playing of brass and wind
instruments requires a close control
of breathing. The *respiratory centre* in
the *medulla oblongata* of the brain sends
messages to the respiratory muscles,
causing them to expand and contract.

Respiration

Respiration does not simply mean 'breathing'—it is used to describe all the processes associated with the release of energy in the body. Oxygen is supplied via the blood to the cells of all tissues. Cells need oxygen to break down such substances as carbohydrates and fats to obtain energy, at a rate which varies according to the activity involved. During normal quiet breathing an adult uses about 8,000 ml (15 pints) of air per minute, but sprinting to catch a bus would use much more—because the body muscles are working harder and more fuel is being oxidized to provide the necessary energy.

Breathing has to convey oxygen from the atmosphere to the haemoglobin inside the red blood cells, and carry the unwanted carbon dioxide from the plasma to the atmosphere, in such a way that the gas concentrations in the blood remain within the narrow range vital to health.

As the required amount of gas exchange ranges from just enough to keep the body quietly ticking over to providing extra supplies for energetic activity, a large reserve capacity is essential. Furthermore, a balance has to be constantly maintained between the rate and depth of breathing and the flow of blood through the lungs. These requirements have resulted in *alveoli* which provide a large surface area, to bring air and blood into contact, and a very sensitive system of sensory and motor nerves to control ventilation of the lungs and blood flow.

The respiratory organs

The respiratory system includes the upper respiratory passages in the head and neck, the two lungs with their air passages, arterial, venous, lymphatic and nervous systems, and the thoracic cage with its bones and muscles, of which the diaphragm is especially important.

The nose and mouth form the upper respiratory passages. They join at the back where the soft palate acts like a swinging door to shut off one or the other. Lining the nose are hairs, ciliated cells and a mucous membrane, each of which remove irritants and contamination from the air. The cilia are small whip-like 'hairs' which protrude from the cell surfaces. They beat in unison in a liquid medium, wafting mucus and captured particles into the throat to be swallowed. The spaces, or *sinuses*, in the bases of the cheeks and forehead, also lined with a mucous membrane and ciliated cells, open into the nasal passages. The mouth also has a mucous lining, so air passing through the nose or mouth is moistened to trap dust and other particles, as well as being warmed in preparation for entering the lungs.

Just beyond the junction of the oral and nasal passages, the air passage branches forward into a short passageway known as the *larynx*, or voicebox, while the *oesophagus*, or food passage, continues downwards behind it. The top of the larynx is closed off when swallowing by a cartilage plate, the *epiglottis*, which prevents food and liquid from going down the wrong way. Extending beyond the larnyx is the *trachea*, or windpipe, a wide, single tube which divides into the right and left main *bronchi* at the

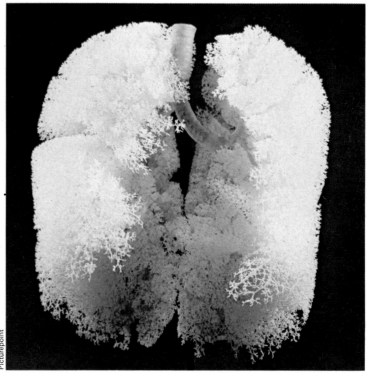

Picturepoint

level of the upper angle of the breastbone, or *sternum*. The main bronchi, accompanied by the left and right pulmonary arteries, enter the lungs. Soon after they divide into smaller secondary bronchi, one for each lobe of the lung; the left lung has two, the right lung has three. Branching continues, the airways becoming smaller and smaller as they pass from *bronchioles* to terminal bronchioles.

This bronchial 'tree' divides the air into about 30,000 separate jets in the gas exchange zone. Any air still contained in the airways at the end of a breath cannot take part in gas exchange and is regarded as 'dead space', air which just has to be exhaled again. It amounts to about 100 to 200 ml (between 0.2 and 0.4 pints). Approximately the first five divisions of the bronchi are held open by cartilage and are lined with a mucous membrane.

In the gas exchange part of the lung the bronchioles begin to have small sacs of *alveoli* in their walls. As the divisions continue more alveoli appear, until eventually there are so many that they form clusters. A mature pair of lungs contains about 300 million alveoli, presenting a total surface area up to about 50 times that of the body surface.

Each bronchus and bronchiole is accompanied by a pulmonary arterial branch which breaks up into capillaries when it reaches the alveoli. These capillaries form a network within the alveolar wall with air on each side. The blood is then separated from the air by only two layers of cells—one of which lines the capillary, the other lining the alveolus—and a variable amount of connective tissue in between. This amounts to a distance of about 0.01 mm across which oxygen and carbon dioxide have to diffuse.

The pulmonary arteries carry oxygen-depleted or venous blood from the right side of the heart to the lungs to be replenished. After picking up the oxygen, the blood passes through the tributaries of the pulmonary veins back to the left side of the heart to be pumped to the body's organs (including the lungs themselves

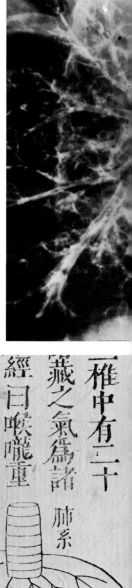

Left: These lungs were injected with plastic under pressure and then placed in a chemical to dissolve the tissue, leaving a model of the airways. Part of the trachea, or windpipe, can be seen branching into the two main bronchi. The coral-like mass consists of bronchioles terminating in 300 million alveoli.

Right: Bronchograms are used to locate blockages in the bronchial tree in the lungs. A small quantity of very mildly radioactive particles is inhaled into the lungs, and then filmed.

Below: A diagram of the lungs from a Chinese book of 1607. Although the windpipe was a good guess, the six lobes of the lung, looking like leaves, were sadly inadequate.

Below right: This machine measures the carbon dioxide exhaled during respiration so that the amount of oxygen used can be calculated. Strenuous activity burns up more fuel, so extra supplies of oxygen must reach the body's cells.

Alphabet & Image

稚中有二十

藏之氣爲諸

肺系

經曰喉嚨重

十二兩

廣二寸

一尺二寸九

半至

九節

胃篇但高曰

兩耳

六葉

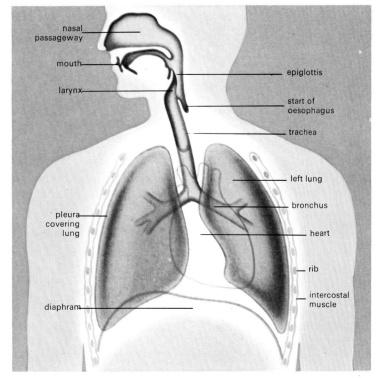

- nasal passageway
- mouth
- larynx
- epiglottis
- start of oesophagus
- trachea
- left lung
- bronchus
- heart
- rib
- intercostal muscle
- pleura covering lung
- diaphram

which are supplied by a separate set of bronchial arteries). There is also a turnover of tissue fluids which drain through lymphatic channels from the lungs to the lymph glands near the origins of the main bronchi.

Each lung is enclosed and protected by a shiny membrane, the *pleura*, which also lines the inner surface of the chest wall. Between each pleural membrane is a narrow space, the pleural cavity, which contains a small amount of fluid. This acts as a lubricant, preventing the lung and chest wall surfaces from sticking together during breathing. In pleurisy, a painful illness, the membranes become so inflamed that they rub against each other during breathing.

Even with this well-planned system, without the necessary muscular action we would be unable to breathe. The muscles concerned with breathing lie between the ribs (the intercostal muscles) and between the thorax and abdomen (the diaphragm). The job of these muscles is to assist breathing in, or *inspiration*, and breathing out, or *expiration*.

For air to flow into the lungs, the pressure inside the lungs must be less than atmospheric pressure. This is achieved by increasing the volume of the lungs. In

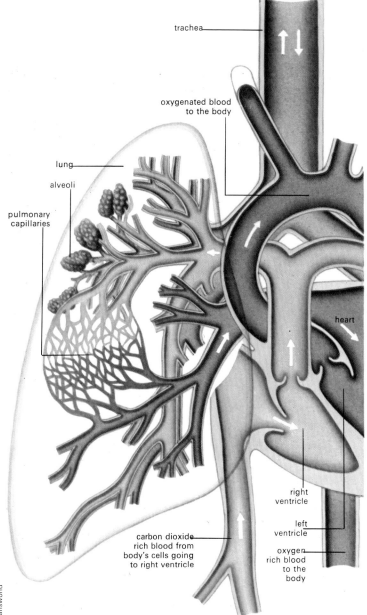

- trachea
- oxygenated blood to the body
- lung
- alveoli
- pulmonary capillaries
- heart
- right ventricle
- left ventricle
- carbon dioxide rich blood from body's cells going to right ventricle
- oxygen rich blood to the body

Transworld

99

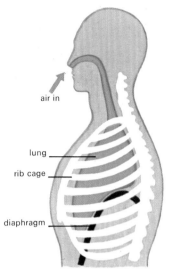

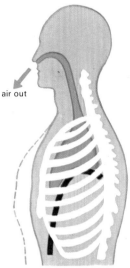

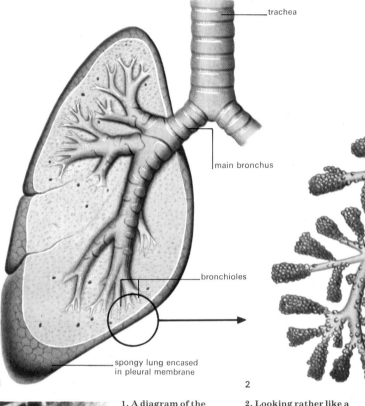

air in

air out

lung

rib cage

diaphragm

trachea

main bronchus

bronchioles

spongy lung encased
in pleural membrane

order to do this the muscles must work to create a negative pressure, or partial vacuum, between the chest wall pleura and the pleura covering the lung. The diaphragm contracts, flattening its dome-shaped protrusion into the thorax, and the intercostal muscles lift the ribs forwards and upwards. This increases the size of the thoracic cavity, the pressure falls and the lungs are sucked out by the partial vacuum. Air now flows in through the nose or mouth and down into the 300 million alveoli, flowing into the upper parts of the lung first.

At the end of inspiration the muscles relax and the elasticity of the pulmonary tissue allows the alveoli to close, so in quiet expiration the air flows out passively. However, there are also muscles to assist expiration during violent respiration or when parts of the body are diseased.

Central control

Breathing is controlled by centres in the brain, the main one being the *respiratory centre* which is found in the *medulla oblongata*. From here the nerve impulses are sent to the respiratory muscles, causing them to expand or contract. Information about oxygen and carbon dioxide levels is obtained directly from the concentrations in the blood. If, for example, the concentration of carbon dioxide rises, the centre increases both ventilation (in other words we breathe deeper and faster) and pulmonary blood flow so that the carbon dioxide is blown off. However, if too much carbon dioxide is removed, the centre causes ventilation to decrease.

The respiratory centre and other vital centres in the brain actually depend on carbon dioxide for their own stimulation. It is possible to overbreathe deliberately—sustained rapid breathing blows off carbon dioxide so that these vital centres switch off and the person falls unconscious. This curtails the voluntary over-breathing and, after a short period without taking a breath (known as *apnoea*) the carbon dioxide content rises again and the vital centres restart.

It is because the respiratory centre has connections with the cerebral cortex that man can voluntarily alter his breathing pattern and perform such feats as holding his breath while swimming underwater. However, when the level of carbon dioxide reaches a critical point, no amount of effort can stop the involuntary control centres taking over and breathing starting again.

100

Above: Breathing in and out. Muscular action increases the size of the chest cavity and the air pressure inside the chest falls. This causes air from outside to enter the lungs to equalize external and internal air pressures. The muscles relax, the cavity grows smaller, and the carbon dioxide-rich air is forced out.

1

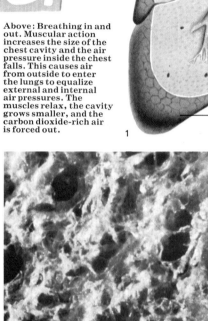

Brian Bracegirdle

Above: A transverse section cut from a piece of dried lung and magnified x50. The lung was dried out under vacuum, leaving it rather like a bath sponge. The section shows the air spaces in the alveoli and a reticulum created by groups of alveoli. This tissue normally is very elastic.

1. A diagram of the lung showing the trachea encircled by a series of cartilage rings, the main bronchus passing into the lung, and part of the bronchioles. As these airways become smaller the cartilage rings are replaced by cartilage plates until finally in the bronchioles the walls are only muscle.

2. Looking rather like a bunch of grapes, the bronchioles terminate in numerous alveoli or air sacs.

3. A greatly enlarged diagram showing the terminal bronchioles proliferating into alveoli which are covered with a network of blood capillaries. These come from the pulmonary artery and

2

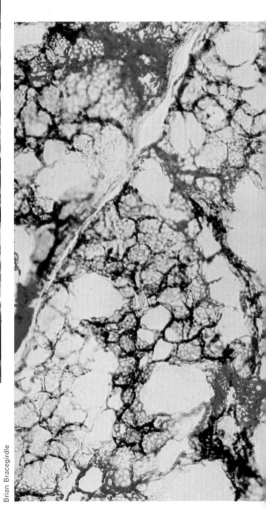

Brian Bracegirdle

Right: In this section, cut from a piece of fresh lung, the areas stained red are the arterial capillaries containing carbon dioxide rich blood. The green areas are the venous capillaries which carry oxygenated blood back to the heart. The gaps are air spaces in the alveoli, and the red 'canal' is an arteriole.

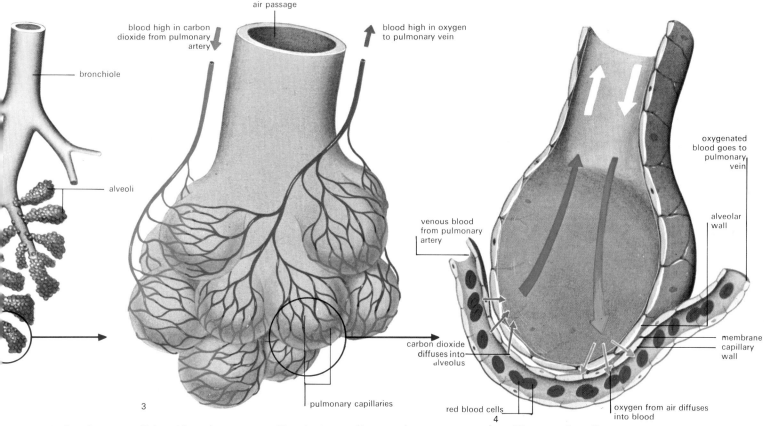

bronchiole

alveoli

air passage

blood high in carbon dioxide from pulmonary artery

blood high in oxygen to pulmonary vein

oxygenated blood goes to pulmonary vein

venous blood from pulmonary artery

alveolar wall

membrane capillary wall

carbon dioxide diffuses into alveolus

pulmonary capillaries

red blood cells

oxygen from air diffuses into blood

3

4

return to the pulmonary vein. Laid end to end, these capillaries would stretch for miles.
4. Oxygen in the air in the alveolus diffuses swiftly through the alveolar tissue, the basement membrane and the capillary tissue, to enter red blood cells, while carbon dioxide moves into the alveolus to be expired.

Below: A bronchoscope, here held outside the body with a narrow sucker for clearing mucus, is used to examine the interior of the lungs. It consists of a telescope and a light guide of glass fibres to allow a strong outside light source to be used.

Bottom right: A view of the bronchial region.

Respiratory disease in some people produces prolonged high carbon dioxide levels and low oxygen concentrations in the blood. In this case the oxygen level may take over as the driving force, instead of carbon dioxide. Thus, if the oxygen concentration was suddenly raised by breathing higher concentrations than the 20% found in air, the respiratory centre would switch off, with fatal results.

Information about the degree of expansion in the lungs reaches the brain from the *stretch receptors* in the alveolar walls and others in the respiratory muscles. The muscles themselves are activated by motor nerves which are partly under voluntary control and partly under involuntary control. There are also smooth muscle fibres in the walls of the larger bronchi and bronchioles which can alter the size of these airways. It is the contraction of these muscles, causing the airways to close off, that gives asthmatics their attacks of breathlessness. There are also muscle fibres in the arterial walls, allowing blood flow to be altered. However, they are not under voluntary control.

The cough reflex
The brain also responds to irritating stimuli. Immediately something gets stuck in the windpipe it stimulates the cough reflex. It forces a deep breath followed by the vocal cords coming together to close the larynx. Forced breathing out then builds up pressure in the bronchi until it is suddenly released by relaxing the vocal cords. The sudden expulsion of air, the cough, is often enough to dislodge the irritant.

Minor stimuli, such as small particles of dust or irritant gases, are dealt with by the mucus. The cilia sweep the mucus steadily up towards the oesophagus, where it is swallowed. Extra mucus is secreted if there is serious irritation or inflammation in the upper or lower air passages, in the case of a heavy cold, for example. But only particles smaller than 0.05mm ever reach the gas exchange part of the lung, and they are captured by scavenger cells within the alveoli.

Irritation in the nasal passages often causes sneezing—a spasmodic contraction of muscles, forcing air from the lungs.

How a baby starts breathing
The respiratory system develops early during the growth of a foetus in the womb. By the sixteenth week after fertilization, the branching pattern of the airways and arteries is complete. The gas exchange part of the lungs, however, develops much more slowly and is only completed in childhood, by the age of about eight. It remains filled with fluid until the baby is born.

At about 28 weeks, cells which secrete a wetting agent, or *surfactant*, start to appear in the alveolar walls. This is essential for when breathing starts. The surfactant prevents the alveolar walls from sticking together by surface tension. Otherwise the new-born baby, lacking the strength, would be unable to separate them to fill the alveoli with air. This is, in fact, one of the major difficulties with premature babies since an inadequate supply of surfactant results in poor ventilation and thus poor oxygenation.

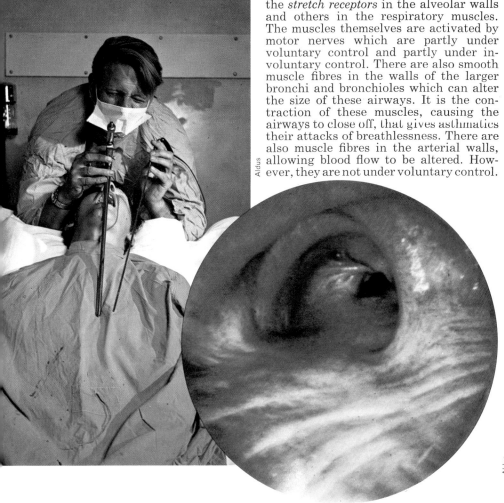

Breathing Conditions

The delicate and complex mechanisms of our breathing apparatus—from the nasal passages to the cells of the tissues—not only have to cope with all sorts of gases, organic and inorganic particles, but also with bacteria, viruses, and fungi.

Only the smallest particles can reach the part of the lung where exchange of gases takes place, but such particles, less than half a micron (half a thousandth of a millimetre) in diameter, do exist in urban atmospheres. These minute particles, which include carbon particles from smoking factory chimneys, vehicle exhaust and tobacco smoke are inhaled with the air, often in droplets of water. They tend to stick to the mucus of the upper airways and irritate the epithelial lining which reacts by becoming inflamed. Specialized cells, whose function it is to defend the body against foreign invaders rush in to engulf the germs, the blood supply is increased, the tissues become swollen, and extra mucus is produced. The lining feels uncomfortable and sore and the swelling and mucus obstruct the passages. Eventually the invaders are overcome and normal respiration is again possible.

Inanimate invaders

The same process occurs if the invaders are merely inanimate particles to which the individual is sensitive, such as pollen, dust or feathers. Unfortunately the sufferer is more likely to have recurring doses of 'hay fever' than of cold virus, to which he is likely to develop immunity.

Some germs and particles penetrate further down the conducting airways before being trapped. If the lining of these airways becomes inflamed the symptoms are those of bronchitis with a sore chest and productive cough. Both infections and allergies also make the bronchial muscle contract. This produces the wheezing, obstructed expiration of *asthma*, the infectious part of which can usually be overcome but the allergic reaction is likely to return to plague the sufferer.

Some fibres, particularly asbestos, can also penetrate the defences of the conducting airways. These particles are engulfed by motile, scavenging cells which move out of the alveolar walls into the alveolar air spaces. Most particles are digested and removed, or at any rate neutralized, by these cells. But some particles resist and kill the cells. This condition is known as *fibrosis*.

Particles containing silica obstruct respiration when they stimulate the production of substances which encourage the growth of fibrous tissue in the alveolar walls. This impairs the diffusion of oxygen from the air to the blood more than the carbon dioxide from the blood to the air because carbon dioxide diffuses 20 times more readily. The fibrosis also makes the lungs stiffer so that inspiration becomes harder.

Severe damage by silica particles is a gradual process which particularly affects people in such occupations as mining, quarrying and tunnelling of siliceous

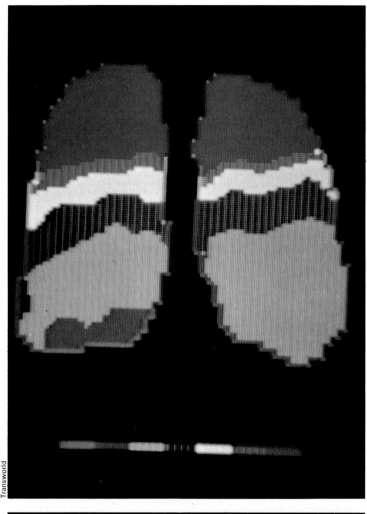

Transworld

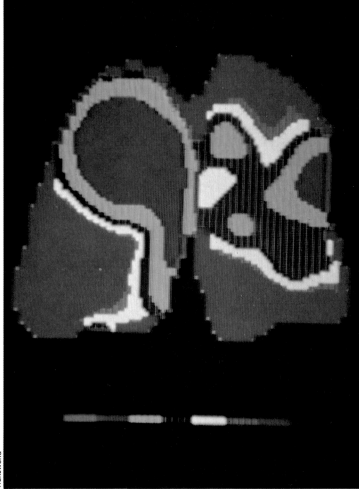

Transworld

Left and below left: A new method of measuring lung efficiency: the pictures are obtained by the inhalation of radioactive gas which emits gamma rays. These are picked up by a special camera. The more gas the lung has absorbed the more efficient it is. Dark red represents the highest level of efficiency and light blue the lowest. The pictures can also record changes in the lungs. Above is a healthy lung, below is a diseased lung.

Right: In Britain alone, some 8,000 babies each year (2,500 of whom die) suffer breathing difficulty within minutes of birth. Known as Respiratory Distress Syndrome it is the result of a lack of surfactant, a fatty substance lining the alveoli (the air pockets where gases diffuse into and out of the blood) which helps diffusion. A 'space helmet' pressure chamber prevents the alveoli from collapsing by raising atmospheric pressure enough to keep the baby's lungs inflated for the first 48 hours until it can produce its own surfactant.

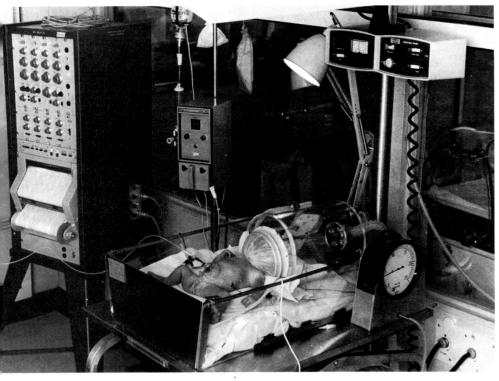

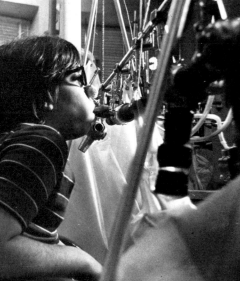

rocks, stone cutting and dressing, foundry work and boiler scaling. Although coal miners are the largest group to develop industrial dust disease or *pneumoconiosis*, it is less clear how coal dust causes fibrosis. About 900 people die each year in England and Wales from pneumoconiosis but only after suffering increasing breathlessness for many years. The amount of coal dust in their lungs may be up to 200 grams with less silica dust—10-30 grams. Only one milligram of asbestos, however, is enough to kill.

Fungal spores are the cause of another type of allergy to which farmers are particularly sensitive. The condition known as 'farmer's lung' is characteristically an occupational fibrosis caused by the fungal spores released when mouldy hay is disturbed. The disease becomes worse with every exposure to the spores, often in the spring when stored hay is forked out to feed stock.

Some bacteria are always present in the upper respiratory tract but the lower respiratory tract and lungs are normally sterile. However, ventilation of the lungs can be prevented by bacteria and viruses which infect the alveoli, the tiny pockets at the ends of the air passages in the lungs from which the oxygen diffuses into the blood. When the air spaces fill with fluid and cells which leak from the blood vessels, this results in pneumonia. Blood passing through the area cannot be oxygenated and if the lack of oxygenation persists the patient develops *cyanosis*—he becomes a dusky blue colour—which is a serious sign. When ventilation is obstructed by blockages of the large airways by inhaled food or by strangulation, cyanosis is again the result.

Ventilation can also be impeded by fluid reaching the alveolar spaces, from outside. This is what happens when someone is immersed in water; in effect, he drowns.

Poisons and pollutants

Gases other than air can penetrate the alveoli. The atmospheric pollutants sulphur dioxide and the oxides of nitrogen from car fumes produce substances which are both poisonous and corrosive—sulphurous acid, produced by dissolving sulphur dioxide in water vapour, dissolves buildings as well as human lungs. Carbon monoxide, however, is thought to be one of the most dangerous pollutants. It mixes with the haemoglobin at 300 times the rate of oxygen; displacement of half the oxygen in the blood by carbon monoxide is lethal.

People with any one of the chronic lung diseases have been found to be more susceptible to infection in general. Particularly vulnerable are those infected with tuberculosis—the tubercle bacilli produce local fibrotic areas in the lung, gradually destroying it.

Any constraint on breathing produces the rather ill-defined sensation we call breathlessness, also known as *dyspnoea*. Since it has been found that interference with the flow of air through the air passages generally affects expiration rather than inspiration, ventilatory tests tend to concentrate on the former. The simplest test is to hold a lighted match six inches from the open mouth. Anyone with normal ventilatory function can blow it out; but it is also useful for a doctor to know the volume of air a patient can blow out in one second since this indicates the rate at which air can be exchanged.

Left: Children suffering from asthma can now be greatly helped by a machine which tests sensitivity. This young patient is inhaling air from separate containers containing various antigens so that his response to each can be monitored.

Below and below left: Although human lungs are capable of adapting to extraordinary conditions, the process is very gradual. The increased lung capacity of Japanese pearl divers and many mountain dwellers cannot be attained in short periods, so that divers (below left) and mountaineers (below) require additional oxygen.

BIPS

Transworld

Dr. H. E. Dobbs/Bruce Coleman

Chris Bonnington/Bruce Coleman

Respiratory conditions

People who suffer from asthma and chronic bronchitis have difficulty in expiration because their airways are partly obstructed. Their peak expiratory flows (measured on a peak flow meter in litres per minute) may be very low. But in asthmatics the flow can be improved if they inhale *bronchodilator* drugs. Bronchitis sufferers, however, do not respond to them.

Breathlessness can sometimes be caused by high blood pressure in the pulmonary circulation, a common complication amongst people suffering from chronic bronchitis. Excessive carbon dioxide in the blood adversely affect the cells of the inspiratory centre in the brain forcing them to reduce the respiration rate. This results in compression, and subsequently

Right: An X-ray of the lungs of a miner with pneumoconiosis, the disease caused by the inhalation of coal dust, shows the lungs (relatively transparent in a healthy person) as two dark patches.

Below: This slide prepared in the 1880s from the tissue of a saw-grinder's lung embedded with stone particles, helped in the demand for legislation to control working conditions.

Bottom: A dandelion pollen grain magnified 12,000 times. Inhalation of these micro-organisms, which penetrate the alveoli, causes antibodies to form in the blood of hay-fever sufferers and results in their unpleasant symptoms.

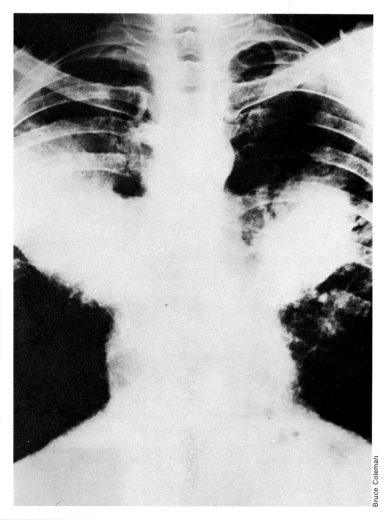

Bruce Coleman

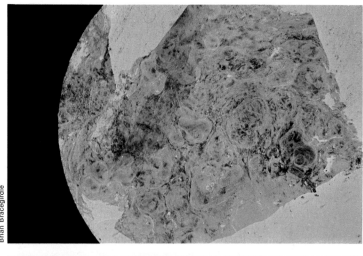

Brian Bracegirdle

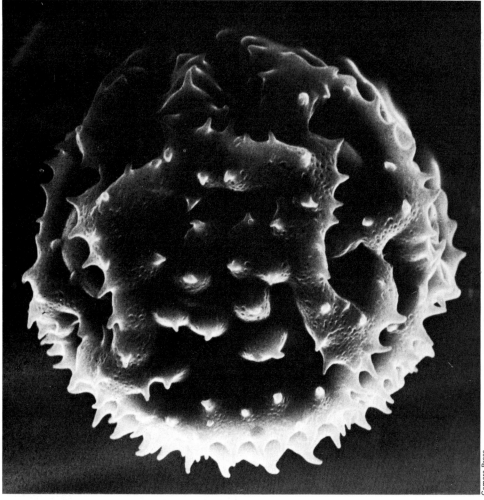

Camera Press

damage, to the capillaries around the alveoli. Increased pressure in the pulmonary artery forces the heart to overwork in the effort to force the blood through the capillaries unaffected by the bronchitis.

Detection and diagnosis

Although a certain amount can be learned from listening to the sounds of breathing, a respiratory malfunction generally requires a more detailed examination. Some conditions can be diagnosed through the use of a *bronchoscope*, a lighted tube which is passed down the trachea into the bronchus. Minor surgery may even be carried out with the help of this instrument—the removal of a fragment of tissue for analysis, for example.

Although they have definite limitations X-rays are a more reliable method of examination. Some conditions such as fibrosis, tuberculosis, pneumonia and tumours are fairly easily recognized. X-rays normally pass through the air in the lungs freely, recording them as transparent except for their fine branch-like blood vessels. But because of these respiratory conditions, the air is displaced by fluid or tissue, through which the X-rays have difficulty in passing, a shadow therefore appears on the picture. Some lung diseases, however, cannot be so easily diagnosed from X-ray plates. The shadows they throw up may often diffuse with the shadows cast by X-rays passing through massive organs like the heart, resulting in an indeterminate shape which cannot be interpreted accurately and the patient may have to undergo surgery for a more detailed examination.

Speech

Speech is so fundamental to human existence that it is difficult for us to believe that our pre-historic ancestors did not have this facility. Indeed, much time and energy has been expended on the question of the origins of language. Some investigators believe that language developed from the grunts and groans of physical exertion, popularly known as the Yo-He-Ho theory; others think that the first words were onomatopoeic, that is, they resulted from the sound of the object they symbolized. For example, it is easy to see why the cuckoo is so called or why bells are said to 'clang'. However, it does seem likely that the skill evolved from primitive man's need to share information with his fellows as a means of protecting himself from predators, and in the process of evolution man's physiology gradually adapted to expand this skill.

The human speech apparatus is capable of producing an infinite number of sounds but each language uses only a small selection of these and has rules governing their occurrence.

The full potential of the vocal tract can be demonstrated by the range of sounds produced by a baby before he learns to speak—he effortlessly practices English sounds, African clicks, German gutterals and occasionally employs a fist or a rattle to help him produce an unknown sound. Gradually his repertoire reflects more and more the sounds of the langu1age he hears around him and later still he will begin the process of attempting to speak by reducing that repertoire to only one or two sounds.

The act of speaking involves hundreds of muscles moving in split-second co-ordination. An idea is formulated into language and the region of the cerebral cortex known as Broca's area, which contains the brain's motor speech centres, fires off signals to all the muscles involved.

The respiratory apparatus first of all provides the 'hot air', the raw material for speech. The primary function of this mechanism is the inspiration (breathing in) of air containing oxygen, which is absorbed by the blood when it reaches the lungs. Carbon dioxide is the blood's waste matter and this is excreted into the air which is then expired (breathed out). Air is taken in through the nose, it passes through the nasal pharynx and the larynx, down the trachea (the windpipe) through the bronchial tubes to the lungs. The exchange of gases then takes place before the air begins its return journey.

We are totally unaware of normal quiet breathing, but during exercise or physical work we automatically breathe more deeply as the body's demand for oxygen increases and in order to rid the body of the resulting increase in carbon dioxide. If we interfere with our body's demands for oxygen we will experience discomfort in various forms, such as fainting. It is thus all the more remarkable that during speech our breathing can be substantially modified for a substantial length of time without such ill effects. A speaker's words will become slurred from general fatigue, his audience may fall asleep, but neither will experience respiratory problems. It has been suggested that this is one of the ways our physiology is specifically adapted for speech.

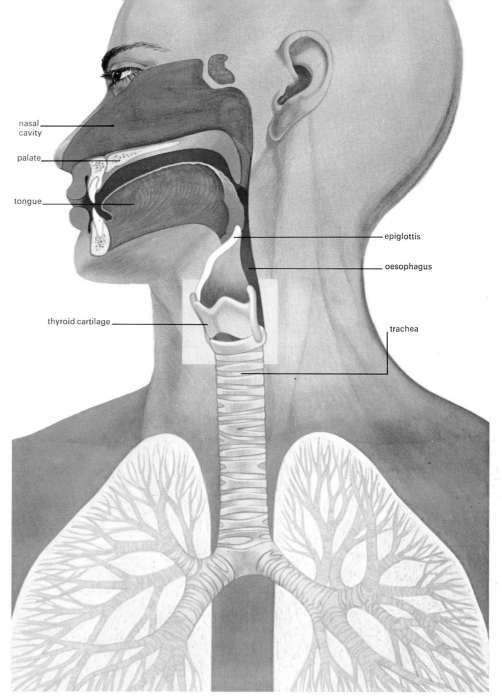

nasal cavity

palate

tongue

thyroid cartilage

epiglottis

oesophagus

trachea

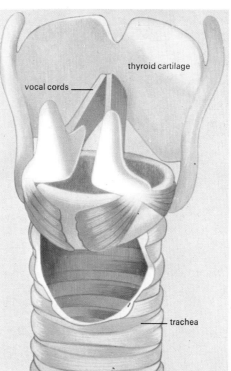

thyroid cartilage

vocal cords

trachea

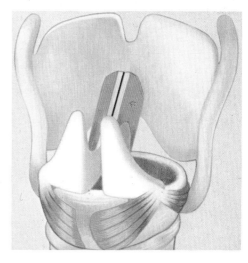

Left: The vocal cords, are formed from bands of elastic cartilage attached to the skeletal muscles. When the muscles are at rest the cords are open.

Below: Contraction closes the vocal cords, altering the pitch of the voice—the tenser the cords the higher the pitch.

Above: Speech requires split second co-ordination involving not only the vocal cords, nose, lungs and air passages but all the muscles which control those organs. The sounds of speech are produced when the vocal cords, housed in the larynx, or voice box, are set in vibration by the passage of air.

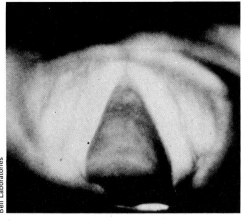

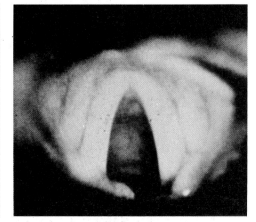

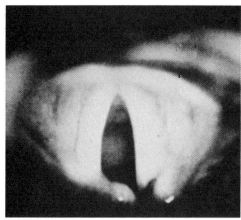

Above: A series of high speed photographs showing the changes in position of the vocal cords—from normal respiration, when they are at rest, to the closed positions required for speech.

Right: The vocal cords create a triangular opening; to the left is the epiglottis which prevents food entering the air passage. The cameras used to take pictures like these have elongated lenses.

During speech air is inhaled briskly through the nose and then exhaled smoothly. It is the amount of pressure brought to bear on the exhaled air by the diaphragm and intercostal muscles that determines the loudness of the actual utterance. On its return journey through the larynx the air passes between two folds of tissue known as the vocal cords. These are rather like tiny curtains which can be 'drawn' by the action of the small cartilages to which they are attached. Their primary function is to assist the body in such tasks as the lifting of heavy weights by sealing a rigid column of air in the windpipe. At rest the vocal cords are open; during speech they are brought together and caused to vibrate by the exhaled air passing through them. This determines the pitch of an individual's voice: the tenser the cords the higher the pitch.

Speech is quite a complex act and not all speech sounds are accompanied by voice, that is, shaped by the larynx. Many sounds are formed by the lips and tongue without vibration of the vocal cords. All vowels, however, are vocalized and they provide the volume and carrying power of speech. Consonants are important in signalling differences in meaning and the presence or absence of voice during certain consonants may be the distinguishing feature between two otherwise similar sounds. The word *bib*, for example, is voiced throughout. While in the word *pip*, since *p*s are not voiced the vocal cords are therefore apart, they are closed for the *i* and opened again for the final *p*.

Whispering brings the cords close enough together to provide a stricture through which escaping air causes friction, but not close enough to produce voice. This is combined with low pressure expiration High pressure expiration combined with tense vocal cords occurs in screaming or, with finer control, in singing.

The exhaled voiced (controlled by the larynx) air continues its upwards journey to the surface via the nose and mouth. It is an individual's unique combination of shape and size of these anatomical structures that determines the quality of his voice and ensures that it will be instantly recognizable to those who know him. The nose, sinuses, pharynx and oral cavity act as resonating chambers,

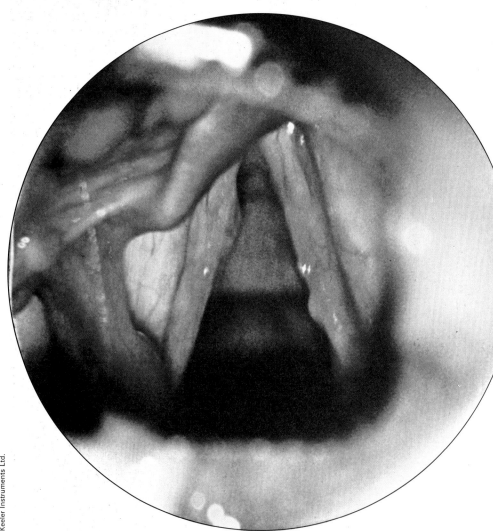

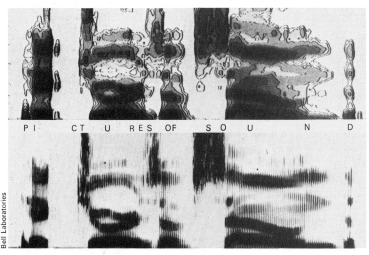

PI CT U RES OF SO U N D

Left: The words 'pictures of sound' are analysed on a speech spectogram. In the top picture the frequency (or pitch) is recorded on the vertical scale; the intensity or loudness is recorded by the depth of the shading —the louder the sound, the darker the shading. The lower picture uses contours to represent similar intensities of sound. Note the high frequency of the S in the word 'sound'.

Right: A computer voice identification system checks a voice against a sample voice print stored in its memory. Dotted lines (not visible here) representing the sample, are compared with the solid line produced by the speaker pronouncing the same phrase.

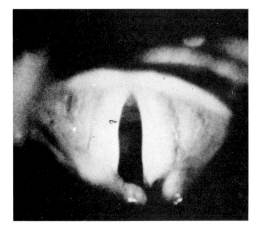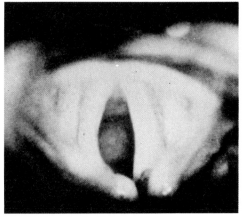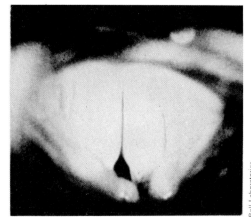

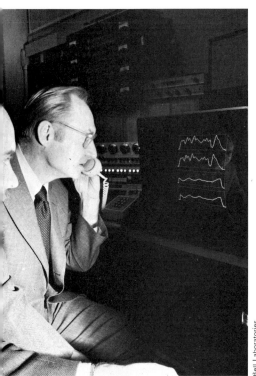

Left: The devastating effect of deafness, which limits a child's ability to communicate through speech, can be indicated by an audiogram-analysis of his hearing pattern. This indicates the degree of deafness with which he is afflicted so that auditory training can be designed to suit his personal needs. Special apparatus amplifies the teacher's voice to help a partly-deaf child hear normally.

lowered to allow passage of air to the lungs. During speech, the soft palate is raised for the production of vowels and oral consonants, and lowered for the articulation of nasal sounds.

The movements of the tongue against the palate and the shaping of the lips bring about the transformation of the voice into the sounds of language. Here again many muscles move with such speed and precision that if we stopped to think about how we were saying a sentence, we would grind to a halt.

Speech is, in fact, the agitation of a pocket of air in such a way as to set up vibrations that will be picked up by another person's hearing apparatus, transmitted to the hearing centres in the brain where they are interpreted as speech. Our own voices are also heard by means of vibrations transmitted via the bones of the skull. This is why our voices recorded on tape sound so strange to us: we are used to hearing ourselves via both bone and air vibrations but the tape recorder receives and reproduces only sounds conducted through the air.

The hearing mechanism plays a vital role in the maintenance of normal speech. It acts as a source of instant feedback by which the brain can monitor the sounds we produce. Its importance can be demonstrated by interfering with this mechanism and observing the effects. For example, if one speaks into a tape recorder which is fitted with a delaying mechanism, one can hear one's own voice through ear phones a fraction of a second later. This delay totally disrupts speech and makes it impossible to continue speaking fluently. This sometimes happens in deafness, which may result in slurring and voice distortion—and cannot be corrected unless special treatment is given involving alternative forms of sensory feedback.

The images provided by visual feedback can be used to help deaf people learn to speak. For example, talking into a microphone connected to an oscilloscope supplies visual feedback in the form of patterns of pitch and amplitude. The characteristic pattern which each sound has is shown on the oscilloscope screen. The deaf person attempts to make the appropriate sounds by reproducing these patterns and gradually regains his speech facility when they are committed to memory.

modifying the vocal tone produced by the vocal cords in the same way that a violin case modifies the notes produced by its strings. Temporary changes in these structures such as enlarged adenoids, a cold in the nose or blocked sinuses will affect the voice.

The primary function of the nose, which is lined with little hairs, is to warm and clean the inhaled air before it travels down to the lungs. It also, of course, houses the receptors of our sense of smell. The resonating function of the nasal cavities can be easily demonstrated. If you hold your nose and say 'I have brought two apples for the teacher today' you will hear that your voice is altered in quality but the sentence can still be understood. However, if you then attempt to say 'Dawn is singing in the summer concert' you may have difficulty making yourself understood. This is because *m*, *n* and *ng* are nasal sounds and when they are pronounced the voiced air is diverted up through the nose by the action of the soft palate—the mobile back section of the roof of the mouth, from which the uvula dangles—whose primary function is to stop food being regurgitated through the nose during swallowing; it is raised to seal off the nose at such times. At rest it is

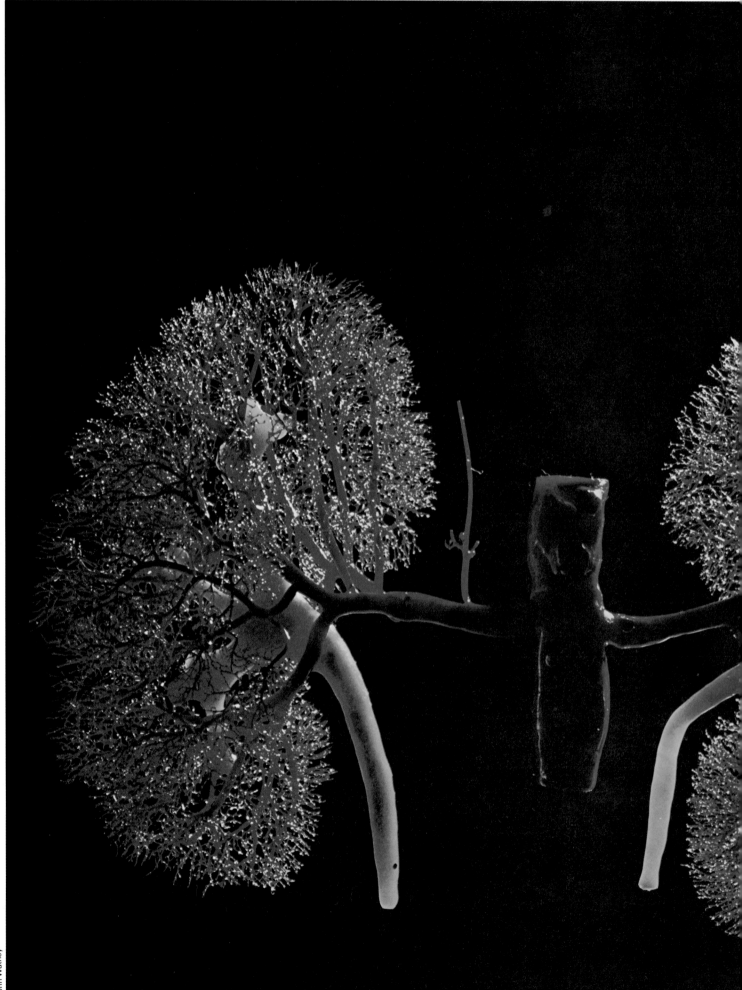

Chapter 5

Digestion and Filtration

The kidney is a complex system of tubes, capillaries, arteries and veins, forming approximately a million identical *nephrons*. These are miniature chemical filtration plants, balancing the composition of the blood and producing urine.

Digestion in the Mouth

All living things require food in order to survive. Oxygen inhaled from the atmosphere is not enough by itself to provide the raw materials for maintenance and repair and for the supply of energy. Most of the food for human consumption is derived from plants and animals, since they have already built up the complex molecules of carbohydrates, proteins and lipids (fats).

Food in this form, however, is difficult for living creatures to absorb and must be turned into a soluble form in order to reach the cells which require it. In simple animals like the worm this is accomplished when the food is taken in at one end of the body and passed along a tube, through the walls of which *enzymes* (chemicals which speed up reactions in the organism) flow, mixing with the food. It is then broken down and absorbed through the walls of the tube or tract and the residue of rejected materials passes out the other end. The larger the animal, however, and the larger the portions of food it is capable of taking in, or ingesting, the more complex the mechanism required to make the breakdown process possible.

The development of digestion

In man the simple tube, or *alimentary canal*, has lengthened in the course of evolution to provide the maximum area along which the food can be exposed to the enzymes. In this way, the greatest amount of necessary materials can be derived with the minimum amount of wastage.

Food spends possibly the shortest time of the whole process in the opening of the alimentary canal, the *mouth*. Nevertheless, it is one of the most important parts of the digestive process since it is here that the food undergoes its first stage of conversion into a substance which can eventually be more readily absorbed by the cells of the body.

Even in simple animals like the worm a band of muscle is necessary at the entrance to the digestive tube which can contract and stop the food from falling out. In man, the circular band of muscle known as the *orbicularis oris* (little circle around the mouth) serves this function. Strictly speaking, the mouth is the entrance to the alimentary canal which is visible as the orbicularis oris relaxes, and the lower jaw drops, but the outer layer of tissue covering that circle of muscle, the lips, is generally included in that term.

The lips have several functions, but they are primarily concerned with manipulating the food into the mouth in the most economical way possible. The thin outer membrane covers an abundant supply of blood vessels, giving the lips their red colour. They are also well supplied with nerve endings, making them highly sensitive to the size, texture and temperature of the food they are handling.

The movement of the food around the mouth so that it can be chewed requires skilfully co-ordinated movements of all the parts involved in the process—the tongue, jaws and the muscles of the cheeks. As soon as an adequate portion of food has been taken into the mouth, the muscles of the lips and cheeks stiffen, to assist the tongue in moving the food around the mouth and to prevent it escaping from the chewing action of the teeth. The movements of the jaw during the chewing of the food are reflex actions, but they can be voluntarily controlled by conscious direction from centres in the brain. The movements of the muscles are extremely important since they are responsible for aligning the top and bottom teeth to pulverize the food without damaging the tongue or the other tissues of the mouth, or indeed, the teeth themselves.

Humans are provided with two sets of teeth during their lives. The first set—the *deciduous* or milk teeth—are temporary and come through the gums during the first two years of life. From the sixth year onwards, they are gradually replaced by permanent teeth, about 32 of them by the time adulthood is reached. The permanent teeth have slightly different shapes and sizes, depending on their function in the eating process. The eight incisors at the front of the mouth (four on the top set, four on the bottom) are

Rank Xerox

Above: A dramatic view of the bones and tissue of the head and neck. The xeroradiography technique uses very low doses of X-rays and a photocopying process to produce the image, giving much greater definition than the conventional X-ray photo. The patient has an artificial plate in his skull.

Below: A warrior of the Txukahamae in the Amazon appears to have no difficulty eating with a large lip-plate. Accentuating the lips is thought by many peoples to enhance beauty. The lips, however, have a highly practical function, being very sensitive to the texture and temperature of food.

Transworld

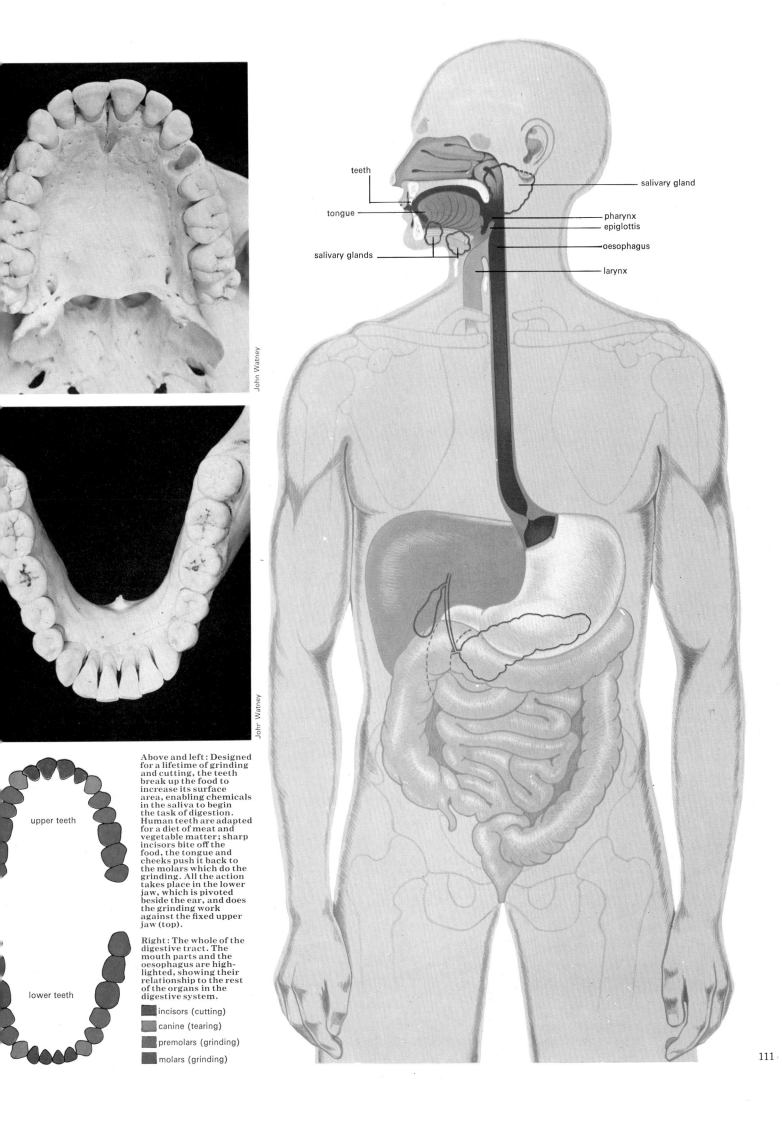

teeth

tongue

salivary glands

salivary gland

pharynx

epiglottis

oesophagus

larynx

upper teeth

lower teeth

Above and left: Designed for a lifetime of grinding and cutting, the teeth break up the food to increase its surface area, enabling chemicals in the saliva to begin the task of digestion. Human teeth are adapted for a diet of meat and vegetable matter; sharp incisors bite off the food, the tongue and cheeks push it back to the molars which do the grinding. All the action takes place in the lower jaw, which is pivoted beside the ear, and does the grinding work against the fixed upper jaw (top).

Right: The whole of the digestive tract. The mouth parts and the oesophagus are high-lighted, showing their relationship to the rest of the organs in the digestive system.

- incisors (cutting)
- canine (tearing)
- premolars (grinding)
- molars (grinding)

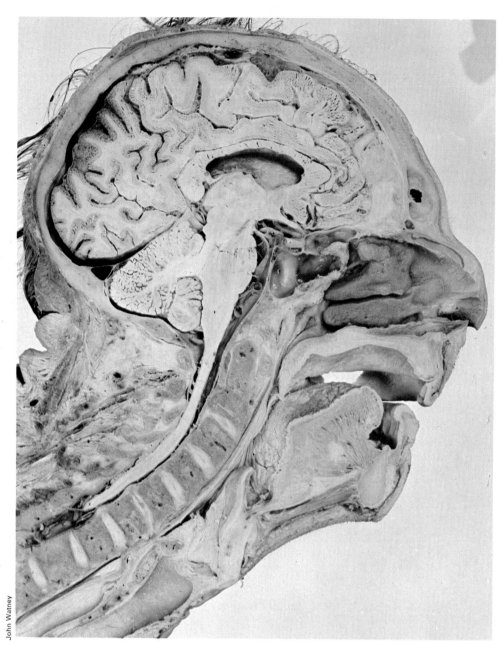

John Watney

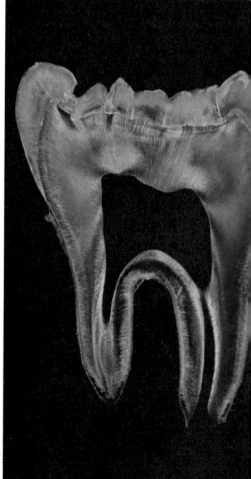

Brian Bracegirdle

soft palate

pharynx

epiglottis

larynx

hard

bolus

tongue

chisel-shaped with sharp, bevelled edges for cutting the food; the four canines, one on each side next to the incisors, tear the food (meat off a bone, for example) while the eight premolars (small 'double' teeth) and the 12 molars at the back of the mouth near the throat grind the food up.

Grinding the food up is essential in the digestive process to increase the surface area of the food so that chemicals (enzymes) in the saliva can begin the task of breaking down the food into smaller molecules. Three pairs of salivary glands secrete *saliva* into the mouth. Saliva is a slightly sticky substance made up of about 98 per cent water and containing enzymes one of which is *amylase*. This works on the carbohydrates (starch) in the food converting them into simple sugars.

A small amount of saliva is secreted into the mouth, even when eating is not taking place, to keep the tongue, teeth and cheeks from rubbing against each other during speech and causing irritation. Another of the enzymes in the saliva, *lysozyme*, which has an anti-bacterial action, is useful in keeping the mouth free from infection.

The mouth is particularly susceptible to infection during fever when salivary secretion is suppressed to conserve water.

The lips, teeth and mouth become coated with dead cells, food particles and dried mucus (the substance which gives saliva its stickiness) and if it is not cleaned the mouth becomes infected. Secretion is also reduced during exercise, emotional stress and dehydration; one result is the sensation of thirst.

The flow of saliva is instantly increased at the sight, smell or even thought of food. The glands are stimulated by the reflex action of parasympathetic nerves. They release the saliva through between 10 and 20 small ducts. In the case of the walnut-sized *submandibular* gland under the back teeth, these ducts open out at either side of the tongue. The *sublingual* gland, the smallest of the three, opens out in the floor of the mouth behind the chin. The saliva from the *parotid* gland at the root of the cheekbone in front of the ear emerges from the duct which opens into the cheek.

The salivary glands are supplied with both sympathetic and parasympathetic nerves, although the exact distribution and function of these nerves is not yet fully understood. Parasympathetic stimulation through the *chorda tympani nerve*, however, is known considerably to increase the blood flow through the gland

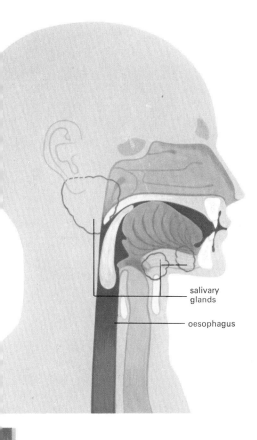

salivary glands

oesophagus

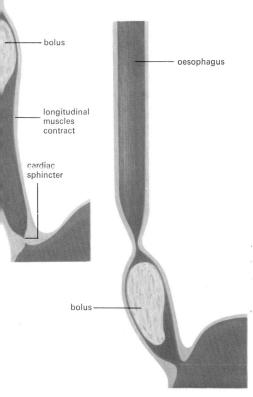

oesophagus

oesophagus

circular muscles contracted

bolus

longitudinal muscles contract

cardiac sphincter

bolus

and to produce a profuse secretion of saliva, consisting mainly of water and salts.

Stimulation of the sympathetic nerve, on the other hand, reduces blood flow and the volume of secretion is less and low in protein, mucus and enzymes. It is these nerves which are stimulated when we are frightened and contribute to the sensation of a dry mouth; even in less frightening situations, acute nervousness can produce the same effect, interfering with the ability to speak; but little is known about the psychological factors involved in the composition and flow of saliva.

As much as 1,500 mls (2.5 pints) of saliva are secreted each day and one of its functions is to maintain the level of acidity in the mouth so that enzymes can be effective. If food becomes lodged in the teeth after salivary flow has stopped, bacterial action can increase the acidity level. At this point the calcium in the teeth begins to dissolve and is lost.

The organic constituents

The main organic constituents of saliva are the glycoprotein, *mucin*, which gives saliva its viscous and lubricating properties, and the enzymes, *ptyalin*, which breaks down starch, and *lysozyme*, which destroys bacteria. Some dissolved gases, urea, uric acid, albumin and globulin are also present in small amounts. The water in saliva dissolves some of the food's components so that the digestive reactions can take place. Bicarbonates and phosphates keep the acidity level of the mouth constant. The blood groups of about 80 per cent of the population can also be determined from their saliva, since it usually contains some of the substance

essential to blood clotting, known as the *ABO* soluble polysaccharides or blood agglutinogens (meaning to stick together).

The swallowing process

When the food has been chewed, moistened and to some extent broken down by enzymes, the tongue shapes it into a ball or *bolus* ready to be swallowed. The act of swallowing only takes a few seconds and is, in fact, a highly complex action requiring accurate co-ordination. The tongue firstly pushes the bolus to the back of the mouth and into the pharynx. At this point there is the danger of food entering the trachea instead of the oesophagus as they both open into the pharynx. Food entering the trachea by mistake immediately initiates the cough reflex, an important protective device which expels the food from the trachea back into the mouth to prevent choking.

During swallowing respiration is inhibited. The larynx rises to meet the epiglottis (a piece of cartilage behind the tongue) which seals off the entrance to the trachea. The rear entrance to the nose is closed by the soft palate, and the tongue, assisted by other throat muscles, acts as a plunger, pushing the bolus backwards with considerable force into the oesophagus connecting the mouth with the stomach.

The act of swallowing involves many muscles, their controlling motor nerves and a specialized centre in the medulla at the base of the brain. It is nevertheless a voluntary one. But once the bolus has entered the oesophagus a different set of mechanisms, involuntarily controlled, come into play to ensure its safe passage into the stomach.

Above: A wave of muscular contraction squeezes the bolus of food along the oesophagus into the stomach. Glands in the walls secrete mucus to lubricate its passage.

Left: This striking photograph is a section through a molar tooth. The black region in the centre is the pulp

surrounded by hard enamel. The roots are buried deep in the jawbone and carry blood to nourish the pulp.

Right: Fortunately for astronauts the body does not rely on gravity to push food through the digestive tract. These astronauts are practising drinking without gravity.

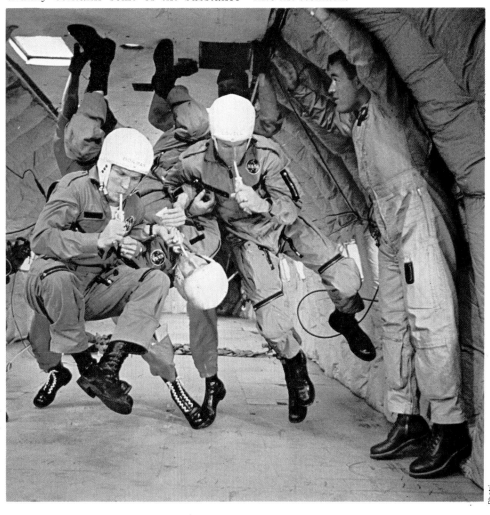

Cruickshank's vivid illustration (1835) of the effects of bad eating habits. These can cause an imbalance of acids in the stomach, leading to *dyspepsia* and *ulcers*. Proper digestion of proteins in the stomach is achieved mainly by the enzyme *pepsin*.

Digestion in the Stomach

Digestion includes all the activities of the digestive tract, involving the preparation of foods to be absorbed by the body and the rejection of the residues. Some constituents of food such as glucose, water and soluble salts require no digestion, but the bulk of the components need to be considerably changed to enable them to pass through the lining of the intestine and into the blood or lymph transportation systems.

Foods, as we know them, are a mixture of nutrients, and to maintain health the human diet must contain certain proportions of proteins, carbohydrates, fats, salts, vitamins and water. All of these can be obtained from either plant or animal sources.

Different species of animals have widely different methods of obtaining their foodstuffs; for instance, horses, cattle and sheep eat only vegetable products and are known as *herbivores*. Some species like pigs and man will eat both animal and vegetable foods and are known as *omnivores*. Obviously, in order to deal with the various forms of diet, different species have specialized digestive systems and it is interesting that both pigs and man have a similar and relatively unspecialized digestive tract.

The process of digestion begins at the lips and ends at the rectum. Once the preliminary breaking up, moistening and chemical breakdown of the food has taken place in the mouth, the next stage is the transfer of the food from the mouth to the stomach. This process is initiated by the

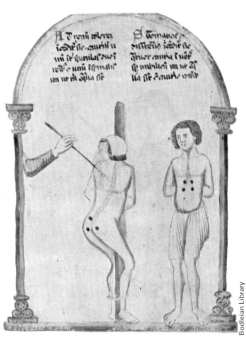

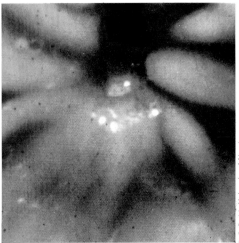

Left: Searing with a hot iron, or cauterizing, was used to treat both internal and external complaints. Taught by the Arabs, it became popular in the West when the knife was forbidden. Here the stomach is cauterized.

Below: The dark area is a gastric ulcer, seen with an endoscope, a tube passed into the stomach.

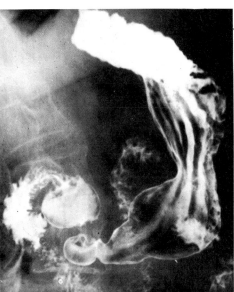

Below: The interior of the stomach lies in folds called rugae, which allow it to expand to hold large quantities of food. As the stomach distends the rugae smooth out.

Right: A wave of peristalsis, seen in the centre of this X-ray of the stomach, squeezes food down to the pyloric sphincter, into the intestine.

reflex action of swallowing, which pushes the bolus of food down the pharynx and into the oesophagus.

The oesophagus is a muscular tube with special rings of muscle known as *sphincters* at either end which are capable of opening and closing. The *oesophageal sphincter* opens as food is passed from the pharynx; it then closes and a wave of muscular contraction pushes the food down the oesophagus.

This wave of muscular contraction is known as *peristalsis* and is the basis of the movement of food through the whole of the digestive tract. The mechanism of peristalsis works independently of gravity; this enables us to eat and drink standing on our heads and allows astronauts to function for long periods in space without gravity.

Contraction of the circular muscles lying just above and around the top of the bolus, coupled with contraction of longitudinal fibres lying around the bottom of the bolus, forces the food down the oesophagus. These contractions are repeated in a wave moving towards the stomach, and movement of the bolus is made easier by secretion of mucus from glands in the wall of the oesophagus.

The food has now arrived at the lower end of the oesophagus where a valve, the *cardiac sphincter*, controls entry to the stomach. A sphincter is an opening with a circular set of muscles around it; when these contract the opening closes and when released the passageway opens. The fact that the stomach contents are at a higher pressure than those of the oesophagus presents a potential problem, in that the acid contents of the stomach might reflux up into the oesophagus when the passageway is open. However, there is one small portion of the smooth muscle of the oesophagus which contracts just as food is about to enter the stomach, raising the pressure sufficiently to prevent this reflux of the stomach contents, and the cardiac sphincter opens just long enough to permit the passage of the bolus into the stomach.

Belching, or *eructation*, is socially unacceptable in many cultures but in fact it plays a useful role in the digestive process. Stomach gas, derived from air swallowed with the food or drink, builds

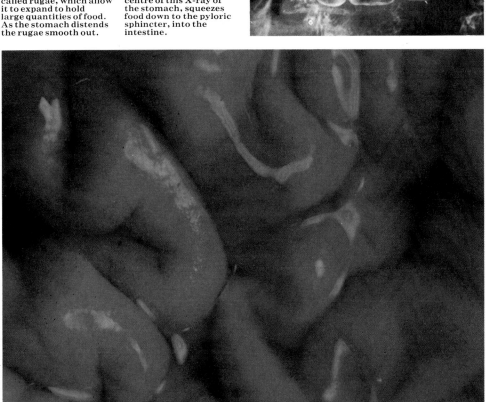

up in the upper part of the stomach until the cardiac sphincter allows it to escape into the oesophagus; from there it is expelled through the mouth by an active muscular contraction.

The process of vomiting is a complex nervous process involving an area in the base of the brain called the *vomiting centre*. Vomiting—usually only found in carnivores (meat-eaters)—has a wide range of causes. It takes place after the hind part of the stomach has closed off and the oesophageal end has relaxed. The main force for vomiting comes from violent abdominal contractions forcing the stomach against the diaphragm which then forces food up the oesophagus and into the mouth.

The stomach and its secretions
The most obvious and important function of the stomach is to act as a store for ingested food. It also provides a site where digestive processes can occur, and where chemicals which cause the breakdown of the foodstuffs are secreted. Local 'messenger' chemicals (hormones) for other parts of the gut are also secreted in the stomach. Despite these many functions the stomach is not absolutely essential to life and there are many reported instances of total removal of the stomach (although the operation does produce an increased burden for the rest of the digestive system).

The stomach consists of a J-shaped bag which can be divided into three functional parts: the *cardiac area*, the *fundic area* and the *pyloric area*. These three areas are quite distinct from one another; they not only have a distinctive microscopic structure but also produce different secretions. The stomach as a whole has a muscular coat enabling it to produce a churning action which breaks up the food particles and mixes them with the secretions which cause chemical breakdown of the food. This muscular contraction is under the control of the nervous system, particularly the *vagus nerve*, which also controls the production and secretion of the digestive chemicals. The net result of this activity is that the food is mixed up into a milky liquid known as *chyme*.

The secretions produced by the stomach can be divided into different components each having specific functions. Perhaps the best known component is *hydrochloric acid*. The stomach is unique in the body in that it produces large amounts of strong acid from cells known as *parietal cells* present in the fundus region of the stomach. Hydrochloric acid is very important in digestion as it activates enzymes (biological catalysts) which are released from other cells. It also helps in the digestion of protein, sterilization of the ingested food and destruction of bacteria.

In man, however, hydrochloric acid is well known for the problems it can cause in relation to *dyspepsia* and *ulcers*. These problems usually arise when acid is produced in the wrong quantity at the wrong time as a result of bad eating habits. We usually resort to treating this inbalance by taking alkali substances (such as bismuth, sodium bicarbonate or other alkaline salts) which neutralize the acid, or by taking drugs (such as atropine) to suppress impulses travelling along the vagus nerve which stimulate the stomach secretions. Too much acid can erode parts of the stomach wall, causing ulcers; in

some cases surgery may be necessary to remove the damaged portion to prevent the damage spreading to a blood vessel, resulting in a possibly fatal haemorrhage.

The principal chemical activity of the stomach is to begin the digestion of proteins. In adults this is mainly achieved by the enzyme *pepsin*, which is produced by *chief cells* in the fundic region.

Pepsin starts the breakdown of the long chain-molecules of proteins into *proteoses* and *peptones*, which are smaller fragments of the original proteins. However, the food does not remain in the stomach long enough for this breakdown to be completed.

The function of the enzyme pepsin is to digest proteins, which poses the question of why the stomach does not digest itself, since all living cells are composed, in part, of proteins. Pepsin, when first secreted, is in an inactive form called *pepsinogen*, to prevent it from digesting the cells which produce it. Hydrochloric acid is necessary to convert pepsinogen into active pepsin, and this does not occur until pepsinogen is free within the stomach. The stomach cells are protected by a coating of mucus secreted by *mucous cells* which forms a barrier between the gastric juice and the cells. Failure of the protective mucus

barrier allows the pepsin and hydrochloric acid to eat a hole (a gastric ulcer) in the stomach wall.

One other component of gastric secretion is the enzyme *renin* which may be familiar as a milk-curdling agent. Its function is to break up the molecular chains of the protein *casein* which is found in milk. The product of this partial digestion reacts with calcium to form *curds*, the remainder being known as *whey*. Renin is important in the infant digestive processes, but is probably not used in adults since it works better in the much more alkaline environment of the infant stomach. Hydrochloric acid takes over the job of milk-curdling in adults.

The third enzyme of the stomach, which again operates best in the less acidic infant stomach, is *gastric lipase*. This acts on the butterfat molecules of milk, splitting them into smaller parts. Adults rely on an enzyme found in the small intestine to perform this function.

Gastric secretion is under nervous and hormonal control. Initially secretions are produced by nervous stimulation as a result of the thought, sight, taste and smell of food. The stomach is thus prepared to receive the food in advance, but problems may well occur if the promised

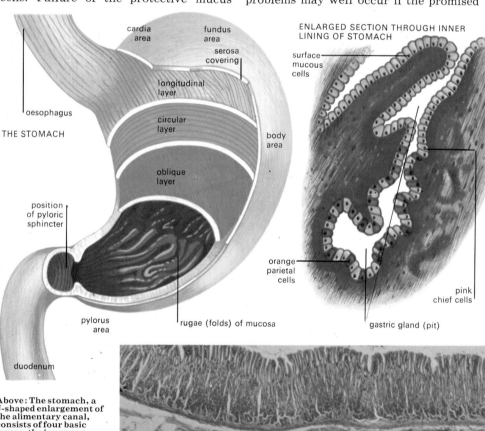

THE STOMACH

cardia area
fundus area
serosa covering
longitudinal layer
circular layer
oblique layer
oesophagus
body area
position of pyloric sphincter
pylorus area
duodenum
rugae (folds) of mucosa

ENLARGED SECTION THROUGH INNER LINING OF STOMACH
surface mucous cells
orange parietal cells
pink chief cells
gastric gland (pit)

Above: The stomach, a J-shaped enlargement of the alimentary canal, consists of four basic layers, the inner one being folded to enable it to expand. Layers of muscle are arranged to allow it to contract to churn, break down and mix together food and gastric juices. Microscopic examination of the inner layer, the mucosa, (above right and far right) reveals columns of cells containing pits, known as gastric glands, lined with three types of cells: chief cells secrete digestive enzymes into the stomach; parietal cells secrete hydrochloric acid to activate one of the enzymes; the mucous cells secrete mucus to protect the stomach from self-digestion.

Picturepoint

food does not materialize, as the acid present in the stomach will be undiluted by food. Further secretion is stimulated by the presence of food in the stomach. This secretion is initiated by the local production of a hormone called *gastrin*—which is secreted by the pyloric region of the stomach when protein foods are present—and by the activity of nerves which are stimulated by the presence of any type of foods.

When the food is thoroughly mixed and in the form of chyme, vigorous peristaltic waves beginning about the middle of the stomach push the partly digested food towards the *pyloric sphincter*, another valve formed by a muscular ring, preventing food passing into the duodenum (the first part of the small intestine). When the pressure in the stomach is greater than that in the duodenum, chyme is forced through the pyloric sphincter. The pressure in the stomach is increased mainly by peristaltic waves (about two to five millilitres of chyme pass into the duodenum with each wave of peristalsis). It takes from two to six hours for the stomach to empty all its contents; foods rich in carbohydrates leave in a few hours, followed by protein foods; fatty foods are the last to leave.

The stomach itself does very little in the way of absorption of foods into the blood. Only some water, salts, certain drugs and alcohol pass through the stomach wall—which explains why we notice the effects of intoxication so soon after drinking. The major breakdown and absorption processes take place in the small intestine, the next stage in the digestive system.

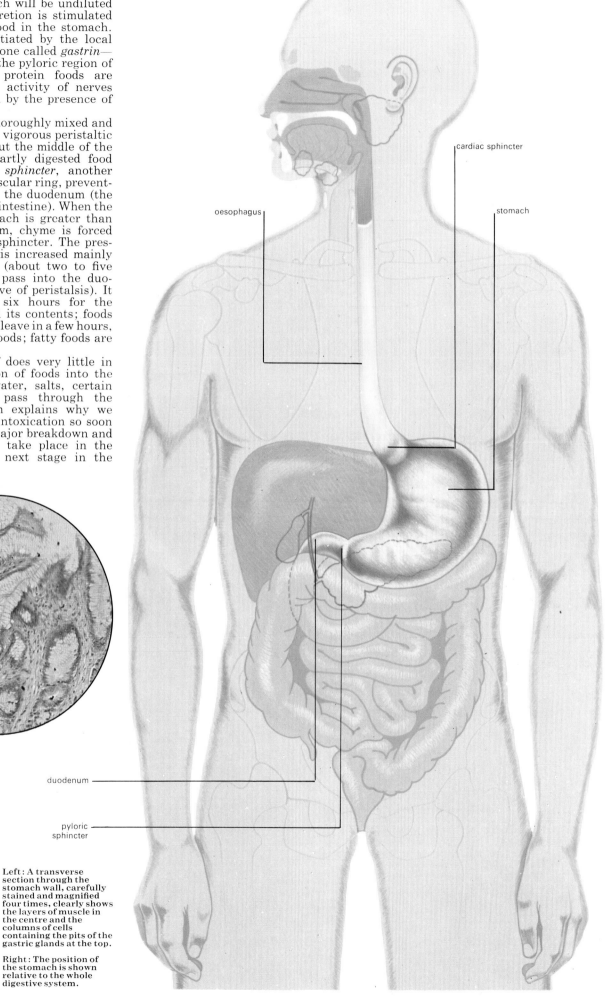

Brian Bracegirdle

cardiac sphincter

oesophagus

stomach

duodenum

pyloric sphincter

Left: A transverse section through the stomach wall, carefully stained and magnified four times, clearly shows the layers of muscle in the centre and the columns of cells containing the pits of the gastric glands at the top.

Right: The position of the stomach is shown relative to the whole digestive system.

Pancreas, Liver and Gall Bladder

Reduced to a thin liquid called *chyme*, thoroughly mixed with digestive juices and partly digested, food is squirted out of the stomach and into the first part of the small intestine—the *duodenum*—to continue its journey through the digestive system. The acid and fat content of the chyme stimulates cells lining the wall of the duodenum to produce a number of hormones, some of which travel to their target organs the *pancreas*, *liver* and *gall bladder*, bringing into play the full functioning of these accessory organs in the digestive process.

Storage by the gall bladder

One of these hormones, *cholecystokinin*, released into the blood when acid and fat together come into contact with the hormone secreting cells of the *duodenum*, acts on the gall bladder—a pear-shaped bag attached to the underside of the liver. This stimulus causes the gall bladder to contract, squeezing its contents of a yellow/green liquid (*bile*) into a tube (*the common bile duct*) which opens into the duodenum a few centimetres below the stomach. This sudden rush of bile flows past a valve called the *sphincter of Oddi*, located in the common bile duct. Normally closed, under stimulation from the hormone cholecystokinin this valve opens to allow the bile into the duodenum.

Once in the duodenum, with the characteristic split-second timing of the body, bile meets the chyme, swamping it with bile salts which split the fats into tiny droplets (a process known as *emulsification*)—the first stage in their breakdown process.

The gall bladder does not manufacture bile, but receives it from the liver and stores it ready for release when food enters the duodenum. Each day the liver secretes about 800 to 1000 cc (about 2 pints) of watery bile, consisting of water, *bile salts*, *bile acids*, *cholesterol* and two pigments. One of these pigments *bilirubin*, is eventually broken down in the intestine and gives faeces its characteristic brown colour.

Bile trickles down the common bile duct from the liver to the sphincter of Oddi; if this valve is closed, the small intestine is empty and bile is not required, so it accumulates in the duct and is forced into the gall bladder to be stored. The gall bladder is far too small to hold the 1000 cc of bile produced daily by the liver, so to overcome this problem it has the ability to concentrate the bile up to 20 times. This attribute is brought about by the inner walls of the gall bladder which consist of a *mucus membrane* able to absorb water from the bile. This produces a strong sticky fluid which is accommodated in a similar fashion to the stomach—by expansion of the folded walls (*rugae*) of the inner lining of the gall bladder. The wall also has a middle muscular coat which is able to contract, squirting the concentrated bile towards the duodenum.

Under normal conditions concentration of the bile takes place to produce a deposit-free liquid, the bile salts keeping the cholesterol dissolved. However, if for

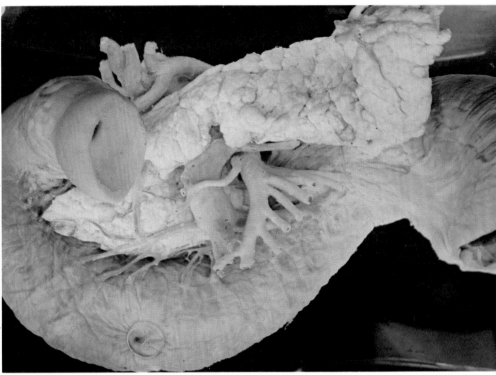

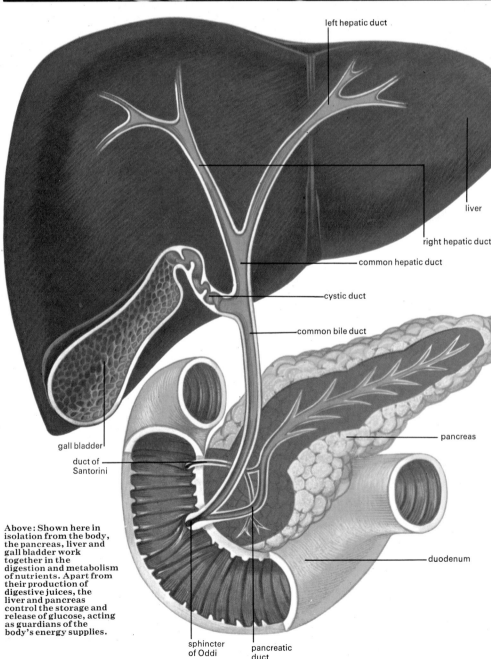

left hepatic duct

liver

right hepatic duct

common hepatic duct

cystic duct

common bile duct

pancreas

gall bladder

duct of Santorini

duodenum

sphincter of Oddi

pancreatic duct

Above: Shown here in isolation from the body, the pancreas, liver and gall bladder work together in the digestion and metabolism of nutrients. Apart from their production of digestive juices, the liver and pancreas control the storage and release of glucose, acting as guardians of the body's energy supplies.

John Watney

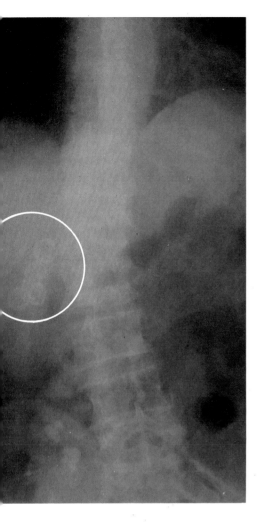

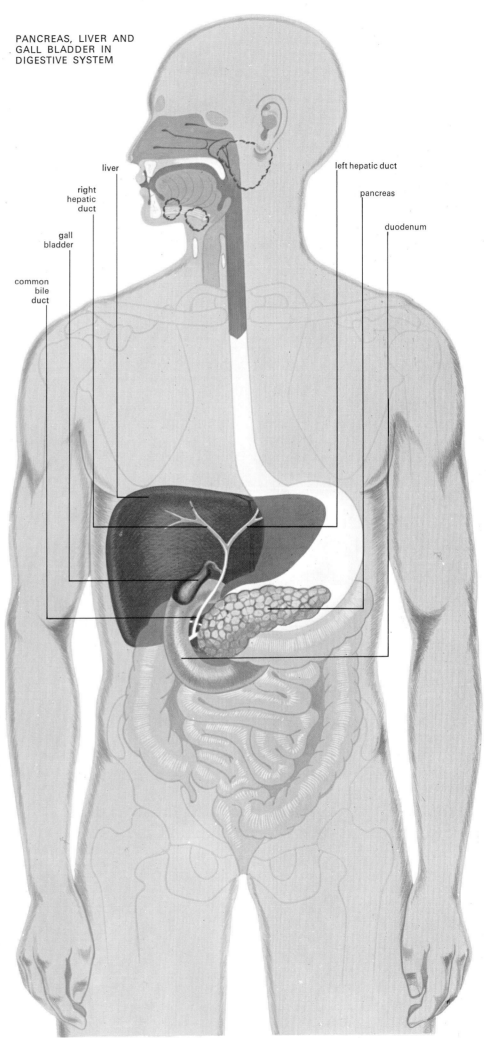

liver

right
hepatic
duct

gall
bladder

common
bile
duct

left hepatic duct

pancreas

duodenum

Above left: Secreting
the most powerful
digestive enzymes in the
body, the pancreas
avoids digesting itself
by relying on the
duodenum to activate
its enzymes.

Above and below:
Gallstones can form
when the bile is being
concentrated in the gall
bladder. Consisting of

cholesterol, calcium and
bile pigments, they can
grow to the size of a
goose egg, preventing
the flow of bile to the
duodenum, resulting in
jaundice. The X ray
above shows five fairly
large stones in the gall
bladder, which may be
dislodged as bile is
squeezed out. A section
through a gallstone is
shown below.

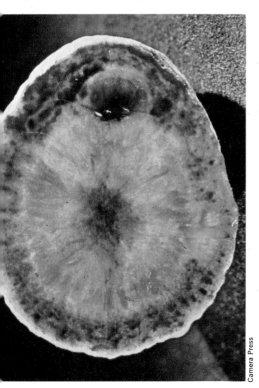

Camera Press

119

some reason the proportions are changed, the result can be that crystals of cholesterol are deposited inside the gall bladder. These crystals combine with the bile salts and bile pigments to produce *gallstones*—beautiful yellow-green tinted stones ranging in size from tiny crystals to a large stone weighing as much as five hundred grams (one pound). Three times as common in women than men, gallstones can pass out of the intestine without causing any problems, but they occasionally become lodged in the duct leading to the duodenum, particularly during times of festivity when the duodenum is flooded with fats. Obstruction of the duct stops the flow of bile—a painful and potentially dangerous condition if left untreated.

The many roles of the liver

The liver itself is an amazing chemical factory within the body, underrated and grossly abused by many people, it has such margins of safety that three quarters of it can be destroyed before life is threatened and, even when badly damaged, its cells have enormous powers of regeneration. Not only is it the body's most important biochemical organ, it is also the largest. Weighing about 1.4 kgs (4 lbs) in the average adult, it lies just below the diaphragm in the right quarter of the abdomen. The two lobes of the liver are supplied with oxygen-rich blood from the *hepatic artery*, and deoxygenated blood, rich in newly digested nutrients, from the *hepatic portal vein*. These two large blood vessels divide and subdivide into a network of thousands of tiny capillaries weaving their way between the millions of specialised cells of the liver. These cells are themselves arranged in functional groups called *lobules*.

All the products of digestion and oxygen are therefore brought to each liver cell, providing them with the raw materials and fuel to fulfil their biochemical role.

The formation of bile is only one of the many functions of the liver cells. It is made inside the cells and secreted into small channels (*bile ducts*) running between the columns of cells. It eventually empties into the duct leading to the gall bladder for storage, or directly into the duodenum. Some of the components of bile are identical in concentration to that of the blood plasma which indicates that the liver cells simply filter the blood plasma, allowing molecules and ions of a certain size to pass through, and holding back the larger proteins. Other constituents are actively secreted by the liver cells; they include the *bile salts* which are responsible for breaking globules of fats into tiny droplets, and the pigment *bilirubin* which is removed from the body in the bile.

The normal life of red blood cells is about 100 days and, when they are worn out, certain cells of the liver break them down releasing bilirubin (a golden yellow colour) to be excreted. If for some reason the liver is unable to remove bilirubin from the blood, or there is an obstruction of the bile ducts, preventing excretion of the bilirubin in the bile, large amounts of this golden-yellow pigment will accumulate in the bloodstream. This in turn will collect in other tissues of the body, including the skin and eyes, giving them the yellow colour characteristic of the condition known as *jaundice*.

The bile salts are not lost after fulfilling their role in the digestive process, but are reabsorbed from the intestine where they pass into the *hepatic portal vein* and are carried back to the liver to be re-secreted into the bile. This type of action illustrates the efficiency of the digestive system which is so finely balanced that it recycles even the very small amount (3 to 4 gms) of bile salts present in the adult.

Besides being responsible for the destruction of worn out red blood cells, the liver has the task of supplying certain proteins to the blood plasma, and *heparin*, a chemical which prevents blood clotting inside the vessels. The liver also produces *fibrinogen*, one of the plasma proteins, which plays an essential part in the formation of blood clots.

All the absorbed nutrients from digestion pass through the biochemical factory of the liver. Carbohydrates arrive here as simple sugars where they are immediately converted to glucose—the body's most direct source of energy. If the cells require immediate energy, the liver releases some of the glucose back into the bloodstream to be carried to the cells. The remaining glucose presents a small problem in that the liver cannot store it. To overcome this the liver changes it into a larger carbohydrate molecule—*glycogen*—which can be stored in the liver and in some of the skeletal muscle cells. When all the glycogen storage areas are filled up the liver transforms the remaining glucose into fat which can be stored below the skin and in other areas of the body. Later, when more energy is required, the glycogen and fat can be converted back to glucose. Even proteins can be converted into glucose by the liver should all the other energy sources be used up, but this

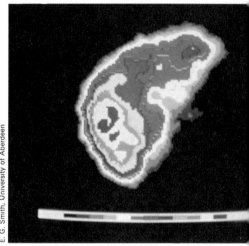

Above and below left: Measuring the amount of a radioactive substance taken up by the liver gives the remarkable picture shown above. Radioactive isotopes injected in very small quantities into the blood accumulate in organs like the liver where the blood flow is slow. By measuring the gamma radiation emitted (shown below left) a colour scan is produced, the colours representing the amount of the isotope absorbed by a normal liver. Obstruction to the blood supply is shown as a light colour, dark areas show fast blood flow.

Below: Over indulgence in fatty foods can cause fat droplets like these to accumulate in the liver.

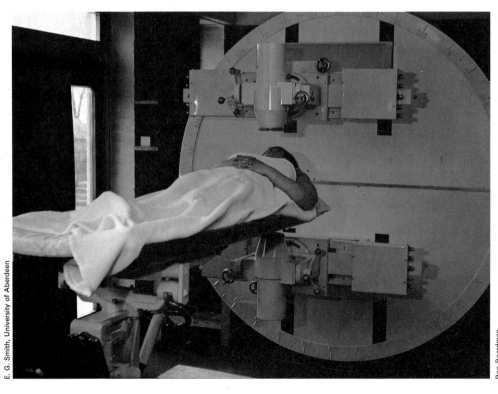

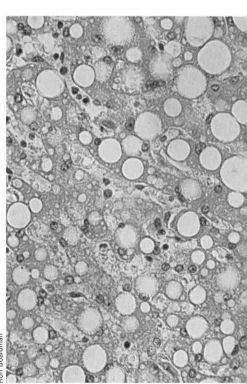

is unusual on a large scale; it produces poisonous waste products which the liver rapidly converts into *urea*. Moderate amounts of urea are harmless and are excreted by the kidneys into the urine, and in the sweat.

All these conversions of carbohydrates, proteins and fats illustrate the inter-changeability of biological chemicals; they do, however, require certain enzymes to make them take place, and the liver has the proper enzymes to carry out these processes.

Glycogen, then, occupies most of the storage space of the liver, but other materials are also stored; notably the *vitamins A, D, B¹² and iron*. One interesting example of the liver's storage of vitamin A can be seen in the liver of the polar bear, whose rich diet of fish gives it a very large store of the vitamin. When the liver has been eaten by humans it has led to severe poisoning and even death.

The liver also secretes certain poisons which cannot be broken down by the body. *DDT*, for example, is found in high levels in the livers of animals and humans who eat sprayed fruits and vegetables. Other poisons like *strychnine, nicotine*, some *barbiturates* and, of course, *alcohol* are destroyed by the liver. Although the liver's capacity for dealing with substances like alcohol is very great, prolonged and excessive intake will damage the cells making regeneration necessary to replace them. If this repair is to be extensive, or is continued over long periods of time, fibrous connective tissue replaces the normal liver cells, causing scarring. This condition is known as *cirrhosis* and, if left untreated, will prevent the liver carrying out its normal functions resulting in jaundice and eventually coma.

The pancreas

Situated behind and just below the stomach is the most important producer of digestive juices in the whole alimentary canal—the *pancreas*. This organ resembles a flask lying on its side, and secretes a variety of the most powerful digestive enzymes in the body. These are essential for the breakdown of carbohydrates, proteins and fats.

Each day the pancreas produces 1200 to 1500 cc (about 2.5 pints) of a clear, colourless liquid called *pancreatic juice* which pours down the *pancreatic duct*, to join with the common bile duct from the liver and gall bladder, and into the duodenum. The pancreas is well prepared for the surge of chyme into the duodenum, for as soon as food enters the mouth, the taste buds send impulses to the brain which responds by stimulating the pancreas (via the *vagus nerve*) to secrete its juice.

This, however, is only a preliminary preparation. The main secretions begin when the acidic chyme comes into contact with the hormone-producing cells of the duodenum. These cells secrete two hormones into the blood which act on the pancreas: *secretin*, which stimulates the pancreas to make pancreatic juice rich in sodium bicarbonate, and *pancreozymin*, which stimulates the production of enzyme-rich pancreatic juice. Sodium bicarbonate neutralises the acid of the chyme, thereby creating the proper environment for the rest of the enzymes in the smaller intestine to work.

Pancreatic juice has five main enzymes. Three of these complete the digestion of proteins begun in the stomach; the others are *amylase*, which digests carbohydrates, and *lipase*, the only fat digesting enzyme in the body, which works on the tiny fat droplets prepared by the bile.

The main protein digesting enzyme, *trypsin*, is potentially a very dangerous chemical. To prevent it digesting the proteins in the cells of the pancreas it is secreted in an inactive form, to be activated when it comes into contact with one of the intestinal enzymes in the duodenum. If the pancreatic duct becomes blocked, the pressure of the juices which are unable to escape can rupture the trypsin producing cells, releasing active trypsin which proceeds to digest the pancreatic tissue and the blood vessels.

Apart from its digestive function, the pancreas produces the essential hormones *insulin* and *glucagon* from groups of cells (the *islets of Langerhans*) scattered throughout the organ. Glucagon accelerates the conversion of glycogen to glucose in the liver in response to the blood sugar level—as the blood sugar level falls, glucagon is secreted to raise it. Insulin, on the other hand, opposes glucagon, decreasing the blood sugar level by accelerating the transport of glucose into the cells and increasing the rate of conversion of glucose to glycogen in the liver. Working together these two hormones exercise control over the body's energy supplies.

Although we are hardly aware of them, these so-called accessory organs perform a phenomenal multiplicity of biochemical functions unequalled by any other organs in the body.

London School of Hygene and Tropical Medicine

Above and right: Often mistaken for malnutrition, an enlarged abdomen can be caused (as in this case) by cysts in the liver making it swell to gross proportions. This Turkana child from Kenya had the hydatid cysts (shown right) removed from her liver. Hydatid cysts are formed by the larval stage of a tapeworm whose mature form exists in dogs. Man in this case plays the role of intermediate host for the tapeworm, and is infected by the embryo worm if the dog contaminates his food or licks his hands. The mature worm is very small in dogs, but the encysted form in man can become the size of a football before becoming dangerous.

London School of Hygene and Tropical Medicine

121

The Small Intestine

About 90 per cent of the absorption of the food constituents into the bloodstream takes place in the segment of the gastro-intestinal tract known as the small intestine, which connects the stomach to the large intestine. By the time it reaches the small intestine, food from the mouth, lubricated and chewed into a ball to enable it to pass down the oesophagus into the stomach, has been reduced by the action of digestive juices to *chyme* and is almost entirely fluid. Digestion, however, is far from complete.

In the mouth carbohydrates are not fully broken down, and further digestion takes place in the stomach before the nutrients pass on. Similarly, although proteins are broken down into short chains of *amino acids* (the molecules which are chemically linked to form proteins, the essential stuff of all living tissue) in the stomach, further breaking down takes place in the small intestine until the molecules can be properly absorbed.

The pyloric sphincter, the muscular valve between the stomach and the small intestine, prevents the passage of partially digested food, or chyme, until it is sufficiently broken down and mixed by the stomach. When the food finally passes into the *duodenum*, the first of the three convoluted, winding tubes which make up the small intestine, it is again thoroughly mixed by the contraction of the muscular walls.

The longitudinal and circular muscles of the intestinal walls are capable of performing three different types of movement for different purposes. Contraction of the circular muscles firstly divides the tube into segments. Further contraction of the muscles between these segments occurs making smaller segments, then the first set of muscles relax. The resulting sloshing action, known as *rhythmic segmentation*, takes place between 12 and 16 times a minute. Together with the alternating contraction and relaxation of the longitudinal muscles, known as *pendular movements*, this action thoroughly mixes the chyme with the digestive juices. It is then propelled down the small intestine by *peristalsis*, a wave of contraction that flows from the duodenum to the *ileum*, the third part of the intestine.

Peristaltic action is made possible by the nervous organization of the intestinal walls. The walls contain tiny collections of nerve cells (ganglia) connected to one another, and to muscle cells, by nerve fibres, to form groups or *plexi*, which can operate by means of voluntary control to synchronize the contraction of groups of muscle fibres. Normal muscular activity of the intestine is not usually felt, although violent and painful spasms may occur if food contaminated with the toxin-producing bacteria which causes food poisoning is eaten. (Vomiting and diarrhoea, the two main symptoms of food poisoning, are both reactions to irritations of the stomach and bowel caused by toxic material. They are often early warning symptoms of certain diseases such as typhus and cholera.)

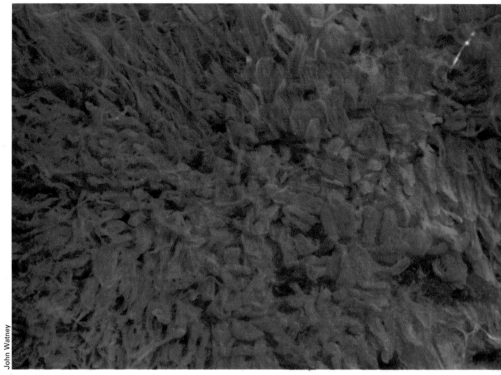

John Watney

The digestive juices

When the chyme enters the duodenum it is highly acidic. It contains a large proportion of hydrochloric acid from the stomach and enzymes which are necessary to break down the large molecules to a size more easily absorbed. The secretions released into the small intestine, however, contain bicarbonate, an alkaline substance, and they therefore neutralize the acid. These secretions come from special cells in the wall of the intestine and from the pancreas and gall bladder by way of the pancreatic duct.

The gall bladder secretions contain bile salts, originally produced in the liver, which act rather like detergents to emulsify the fatty acids and glycerides thus making very small particles which are readily absorbed by the walls of the small intestine.

The small intestine controls its digestive processes by hormones secreted into the bloodstream. The presence of food and hydrochloric acid in the duodenum and the first part of the *jejunum*, the second section of the intestine, stimulates the intestine to produce the hormones *secretin* and *pancreozymin* which stimulate the secretion of bicarbonate and enzymes from the pancreas. *Cholecystokinin* is another intestinal hormone which stimulates the contraction of the gall bladder and the release of bile into the pancreatic duct.

The absorption process

The structure of the small intestine is specialized so that the absorption of nutrients can proceed most efficiently. The wall of the intestine is quite thin but folded rather like the corrugated hose of a vacuum cleaner, providing a large inner surface area. The inner surface has special finger-like structures, called *villi*, which project into the intestinal contents.

The individual cells which line the villi have tiny villi of their own, increasing still further the surface area available for absorption. In an average adult this total area is over 20 square metres (200 sq ft).

In the small intestine, the tiny mole-

Above and above right: The surface of the mucosa or innermost layer of the small intestine (above magnified x 2, and above right x 400) is covered with minute, hair-like projections called villi. These greatly increase the surface area coming in contact with the food and contain specialized cells for absorbing it.

Right: The walls of the small intestine, formed from a mucous membrane and two layers of muscle cells. The muscle cells contract and expand, a movement ensuring that the food has maximum contact with the mucosal layer. The submucosal layer contains lymphoid tissues which destroy bacteria.

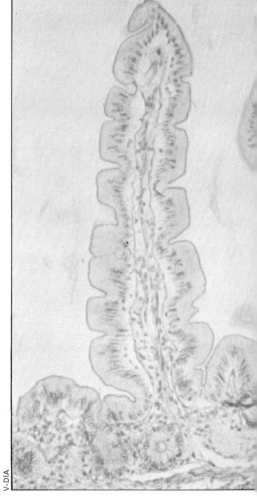

V-DIA

Right: The small intestine—shown here in relation to the other digestive organs—fills the major portion of the abdominal cavity, its six-metre long tube tightly coiled into this small space. It is divided into three sequential sections: the *duodenum* starts at the pyloric sphincter, a valve which prevents the premature passage of food from the stomach, the slightly narrower *jejunum* and the *ileum*, ending at another valve, the *ileocaecal*, which joins it to the large intestine. The small intestine is largely concerned with the absorption of food into the bloodstream, for which its secretions and muscular structure are specially adapted.

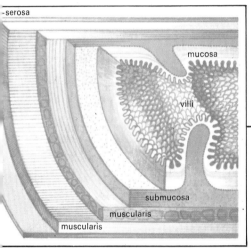

serosa

mucosa

villi

submucosa

muscularis

muscularis

Left and below: An electronmicrograph picture and a longitudinal section through a villus showing the network of blood capillaries through which protein products and carbohydrates are passed. They are then transported through the venules (into which the capillaries collect), the veins and the portal vein to the liver.

capillary network

villus

goblet cell

lacteal

lymph vessel

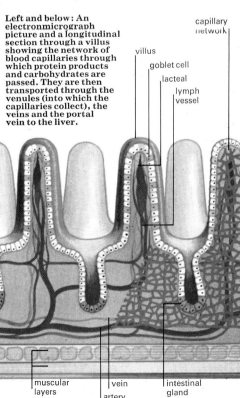

muscular layers

vein

artery

intestinal gland

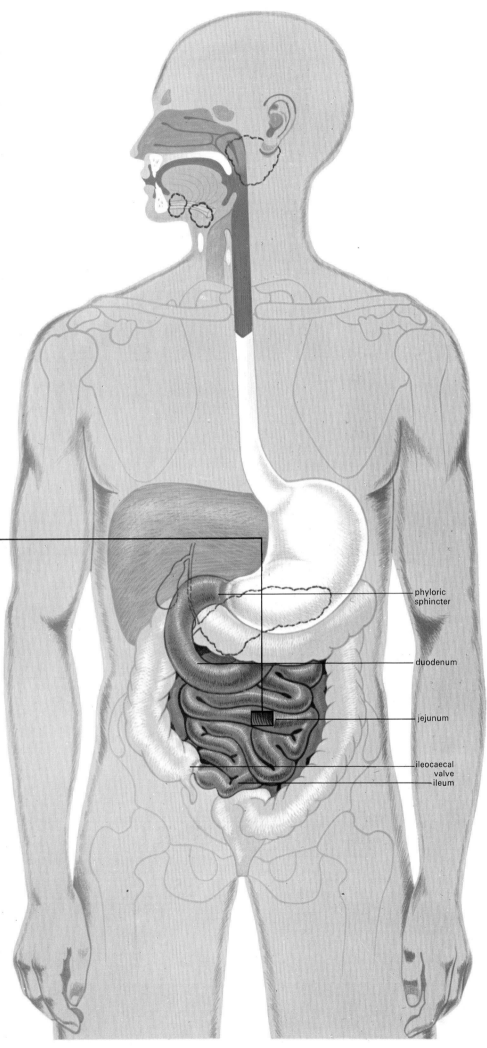

phyloric sphincter

duodenum

jejunum

ileocaecal valve

ileum

cules produced by breaking down carbohydrate and protein foods pass into the cells lining the villi and then travel into tiny blood capillaries which run into the small blood vessel draining each villus. These small vessels run into larger ones and then eventually into the *hepatic portal* (carrying) *vein* which leads to the liver, where the next steps of the breakdown processes continue before, finally, the nutrients are delivered to other cells in the body.

The products of fatty foods, on the other hand, do not enter the blood stream directly. They are absorbed from the gut through special ducts in the villi called *lacteals*. These connect with the lymphatics which eventually drain into the thoracic duct. This empties into the vena cava in the neck region, allowing the fats

into the blood stream so that they too can travel to the liver for further breakdown.

The small intestine, particularly the ileum, contains nodules of lymphoid tissue (known as 'Peyer's patches' after their discoverer). These nodules contain white scavenger cells or lymphocytes which may have a protective function by destroying bacteria. In some diseases, however, the patches themselves are attacked and in typhoid fever, for example, they may become intensely inflamed, damaging the intestinal wall as a result.

Parasites, such as tapeworms, are also found in the small intestine. Although common in tropical countries, tapeworms are now rare in most of Europe, but domestic animals like dogs and cats may still be infected. But not all the

inhabitants of our gut are dangerous parasites. Millions of mutually helpful, or *symbiotic*, bacteria live in our intestines and cause us no harm; they may indeed protect us from attack by harmful micro-organisms.

Absorption of the broken-down food constituents mainly takes place through the villi, the tiny-hair-like projections covering the inner surface of the small intestine. Depending on the size and complexity of their molecular structure, they may pass immediately into the bloodstream by simple diffusion, osmosis or by active transport systems through the cell membrane. The inner wall of the intestine is covered with a mucosal layer which will only allow lipid (fat) soluble substances to dissolve in it and diffuse into the blood vessels and lacteals. Specialized transport processes are present in the membranes of the mucosal cells which deal with larger soluble substances and ions.

Passive diffusion only enables the same concentration of substances to exist on either side of this semi-permeable membrane, since the diffusion can occur equally readily in either direction. But the active transport processes are like pumps, they only operate in one direction, and can concentrate the transported substance, amino acids for example, on the inside of the intestinal mucosa.

The proteins in the diet are absorbed mainly in the form of individual *amino acids* by these active transport systems. Some proteins can be absorbed in their natural, undigested form and many food allergies seem to develop because these proteins pass from the gut into the bloodstream, increasing sensitivity to future doses of food containing that particular protein. The nature of these proteins is not known, but many people appear to suffer violent reactions whenever they eat shellfish or other sea foods which may contain some specific absorbable protein.

Carbohydrates are absorbed in the form of *monosaccharides* (mainly fructose and glucose) by a separate, active transport process. Fats and lipids will passively pass through the intestinal mucosa as long as they are in sufficiently small droplets. As a result of the emulsifying action of the bile salts they are usually in the form of small droplets about 0.5u (0.00002 in) in diameter. The mucosal cells send out a small tentacle of cytoplasm which surrounds the droplet and takes it into the interior of the cell. This is very similar to the way in which an amoeba ingests food particles. About 94 per cent of the dietary fat is absorbed in this way as *triglycerides*.

Some aspects of the absorption of trace elements are still not fully understood, although they are vitally important to the body. For example, the importance of minute quantities of fluoride (found in the mineral structure of bone) for the health of the teeth is now recognized.

Once absorbed by the body, the broken down substances provide the raw materials for the building of longer and more complicated molecules better suited to human needs. They can be combined with oxygen to form water, carbon dioxide and nitrogen-containing wastes, so releasing vital energy for activity and regeneration. What remains of the food after assimilation then passes into the large intestine, where the final stage of the digestive process takes place.

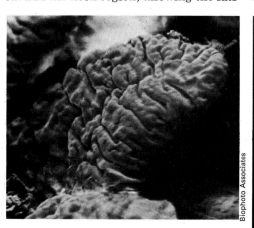

Biophoto Associates

Above: A section of tissue taken from a mouse's small intestine shows a single villus magnified 1,000 times. The outer surface is greatly folded to provide the maximum area for absorption.

Below: 'The cholic', a common digestive complaint, by a 19th-century cartoonist.

Right: This X-ray photograph shows the convolutions of the small intestine. Patients with suspected digestive disorders are given barium sulphate in a meal or an enema so that the intestines— which would usually be transparent on an X-ray plate—become opaque and can be seen in detail.

The Cholic

Mary Evans

The small intestine photographed by light microscopy. The small intestine has a large surface area (over 20 square metres in the average adult) to enable nutrients to be easily absorbed.

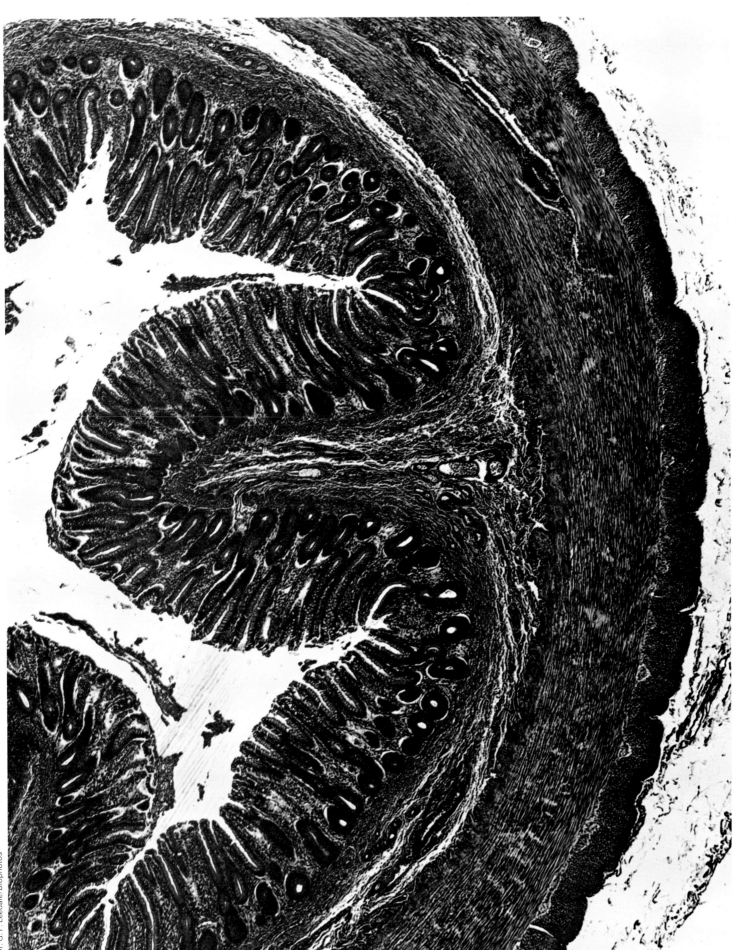

The Large Intestine

By the time the contents of the gut reach the end of the small intestine—about five or six hours after leaving the stomach—the digestive processes are almost complete. The partly digested food passes from the ileum into the first section of the large intestine, to begin the final stages of digestion.

The structure of the large intestine
The large intestine is divided into four main sections: the *caecum, colon, rectum* (these are also known as the large bowel) and *anal canal*. Altogether it is about 1.5 metres (5 ft) long and 6.5 cms (2.5 ins) in diameter—three times the diameter of the small intestine. The caecum is a blind pouch hanging below the ileo-caecal valve, the sphincter separating the small and large intestines. The open end of the caecum joins the colon, a long tube which forms the greater part of the large intestine. The mucous membrane lining the colon—unlike the small intestine—is smooth and devoid of villi. A muscular coat surrounds the mucous layer, consisting of circular internal muscles and longitudinal external muscles, similar to the small intestine. These muscular walls contract to gather the colon into a large number of bulbous pouches called *haustra*, giving it a puckered appearance and creating an enormous capacity for expansion.

The colon terminates in the rectum, a passage about 12 centimetres (5 ins) long; the last three or four centimetres of the large bowel are the anal canal. The exterior opening, referred to as the anus, is held closed most of the time by a muscular valve—the anal sphincter.

The mucous membrane inside the anal canal is arranged in length-wise folds that contain a network of arteries and veins. Unlike the rest of the gastro-intestinal tract, the final part of the rectum and the anal valve are continuations of the skin and are very well endowed with sensory nerves—this is what makes inflammation and enlargement of the anal veins (known as piles or haemorrhoids) so painful.

A peculiar feature of the large intestine is a narrow, worm-like sac called the appendix, about eight cms (3 ins) long, connected to the caecum. This is a remnant from the time when man's ancestors were herbivores, living solely on plant foods. In herbivorous animals it plays a part in digesting the large quantities of cellulose found in plant material—the equivalent organ in a horse is about 1.25 metres (approx. 4 ft) long. But in man it no longer serves a useful function and has a tendency to become inflamed when irritating particles become lodged in it—sometimes resulting in the chronic or acute inflammation called appendicitis.

The activity of the large intestine
Chyme is squirted into the caecum through the ileo-caecal valve, which opens to allow only about two cc maximum through at a time. At this stage the fluid consists of undigested or undigestible food residues, water and secretions from the intestines. Water is extracted particularly

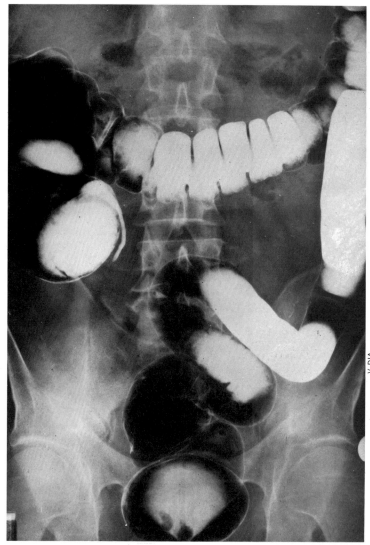
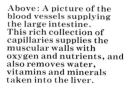

Above: A picture of the blood vessels supplying the large intestine. This rich collection of capillaries supplies the muscular walls with oxygen and nutrients, and also removes water, vitamins and minerals taken into the liver.

Left: An X-ray of the large intestine. The bulbous pouches called *haustra* are visible in the colon (top, left to right). The worm-like appendix can be seen (centre left) coming out of the caecum.

in the caecum and first part of the colon, so that the chyme becomes solid or semi-solid; in this state it is called *faeces*. Numerous cells secrete mucus from glands which line the walls of the large intestine, to lubricate the passage of the faeces and protect the walls from attack by any remaining digestive enzymes.

There is a constant to and fro movement of the chyme within the colon due to muscular activity known as *haustral churning*. The haustra are relaxed and stretched while they fill up with chyme, then at a certain point the wall contracts, squeezing the food residues into the next haustrum. Peristalsis also occurs, but at a much slower rate than elsewhere, culminating in a strong movement known as *mass peristalsis*, which pushes the colon's contents towards the rectum. This movement is brought about by the presence of food in the stomach; it empties the caecum ready for the newly digested chyme from the small intestine. Mass peristalsis, normally taking place three or four times a day, during or soon after a meal, is the cause of some of the 'rumblings' in the abdomen after eating.

The role of bacteria
The bacteria found in the large intestine play an essential role in nutrition and digestion. One of their most important functions is to synthesize several vitamins, particularly some B vitamins and vitamin K—which is vital in helping the liver to manufacture substances used in the blood-clotting process. The bacteria

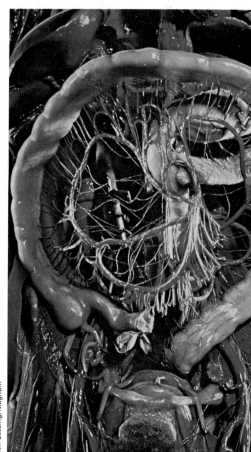

V-DIA

Erich Lessing/Magnum

126

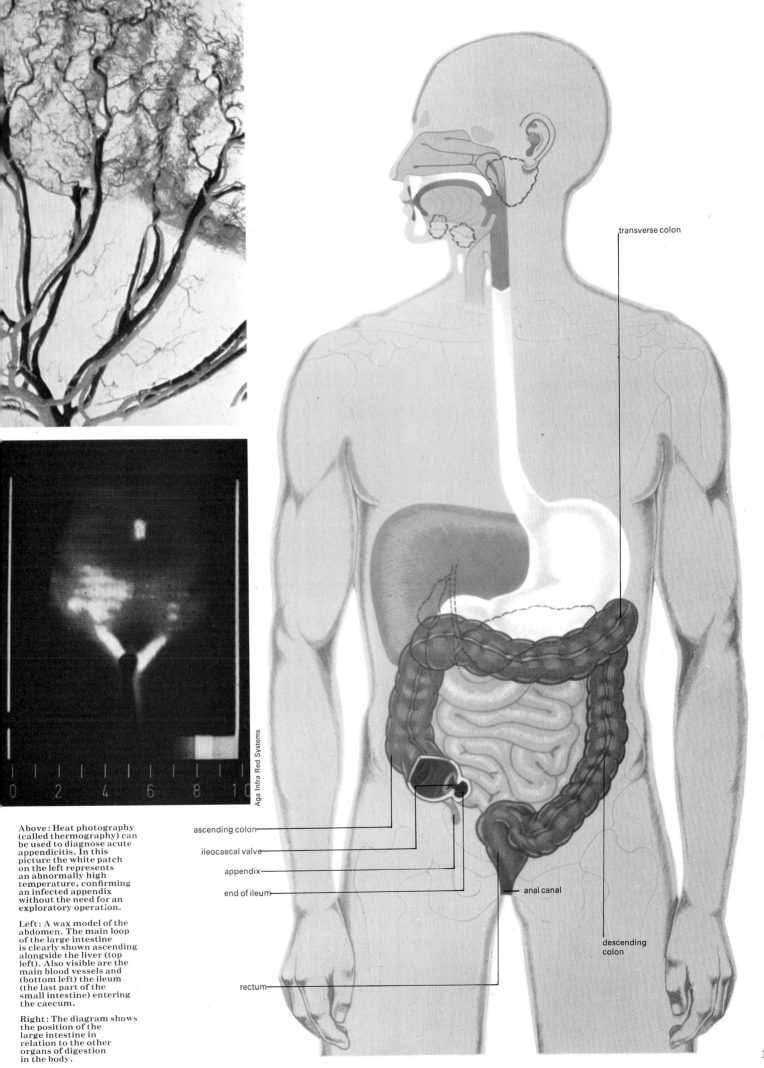

Above: Heat photography (called thermography) can be used to diagnose acute appendicitis. In this picture the white patch on the left represents an abnormally high temperature, confirming an infected appendix without the need for an exploratory operation.

Left: A wax model of the abdomen. The main loop of the large intestine is clearly shown ascending alongside the liver (top left). Also visible are the main blood vessels and (bottom left) the ileum (the last part of the small intestine) entering the caecum.

Right: The diagram shows the position of the large intestine in relation to the other organs of digestion in the body.

Aga Infra Red Systems

transverse colon

ascending colon

ileocaecal valve

appendix

end of ileum

anal canal

descending colon

rectum

Right: A cross-section of the alimentary canal which runs the whole length of the digestive tract. Its function varies at different stages, but it has the same basic structure throughout. One obvious difference between the small and large intestines is that the latter has no villi lining its inner walls.

mesentery

smooth mucosa as found in the large intestine

mucosa

submucosa

muscularis

lymph node

glands in submucosa

villus

circular muscle

longitudinal muscle

serosa

muscle with villi as found in the small intestine

gland outside canal

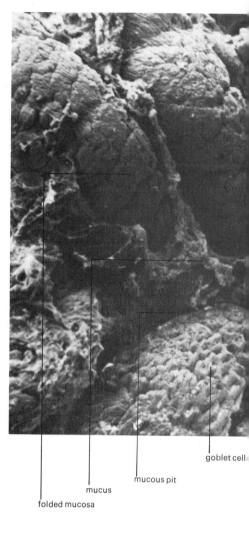

goblet cell

mucous pit

mucus

folded mucosa

muscular layer

connective tissue

capillary

red blood cells

break down any remaining proteins into amino acids and then into simpler substances, such as indole, skatole, hydrogen sulphide and fatty acids. Much of the indole and skatole is transported to the liver, where it is converted into less poisonous compounds and passed out of the body in the urine, but some remains in the faeces and is the chief cause of their distinctive smell.

Remaining carbohydrates are fermented by bacteria, releasing hydrogen, carbon dioxide and methane gas. A variable amount of gas is found in the colon, which may be released explosively when the pressure inside the colon and rectum forces the anal sphincter open. The bacteria also decompose bilirubin (the pigment produced by the breakdown of red blood cells) which is excreted in the bile, and the presence of this in the faeces gives them a brown colour.

By the time the faeces reach the rectum they are approximately 70 per cent water. Bacteria represent 30 per cent of the dry weight and the rest is made up of food residues (mainly cellulose from plant sources which cannot be digested or absorbed by man), a certain quantity of the breakdown products mentioned above, intestinal secretions and dead cells from the lining of the intestine. An average adult on a normal diet will excrete 75 to 170 grams (up to 2.5 oz) of faeces daily.

Expelling the waste

It usually takes from 12 to 24 hours for the chyme to travel from the caecum, turn into faeces and reach the point where it accumulates at the end of colon, but this can be longer, depending on the amount of roughage in the diet. The colon works best when it is moderately full, so the indigestible material found in roughage is useful in increasing the bulk of the contents of the colon. The movement of faeces into the rectum prior to being expelled is not stimulated until the colon is relatively full. The longer this takes, the more water will be absorbed. making

Biophoto Associates

SUMMARY OF THE FUNCTIONS OF THE DIGESTIVE SYSTEM

Biophoto Associates

Above: The inner surfaces of the colon (the second region of the large intestine) magnified x 60 by an electron microscope. The folded inner layer is covered in mucus secreted by the goblet cells. This provides lubrication for movement of the intestinal contents.

Below left: The muscular layer of the colon magnified x 600. Layers of muscle responsible for peristalsis have been cut through, and a capillary is visible (with red blood cells inside). The connective tissue is at the top of the picture.

Below: A section through the mucosa (inner layer) of the colon showing the mucous pits magnified x 10. The goblet cells are stained purple.

STRUCTURE	DESCRIPTION	ACTIVITY	TIME TAKEN
Mouth	Contains the cheeks, lips, tongue, taste buds, opening of the salivary glands and the teeth	The cheeks and lips keep the food between the teeth which grind and break down the food to increase the area exposed to chemicals in the saliva. The tongue manoeuvres the food and rolls it into a bolus to be swallowed. Nerve impulses from the taste buds to the brain stimulate salivation, moistening and softening the food and cleansing the mouth. From 1/2 to 2 litres (about 3 pints) produced daily	Minutes
Pharynx	Muscular passage between the back of the mouth and the oesophagus	The tongue forces the bolus of food into the pharynx which continues the swallowing process by reflex action. The air passageways are closed and the opening to the oesophagus is widened.	Seconds
Oesophagus	A muscular tube connecting the pharynx and the stomach. About 25cms (10 inches) long	Forces the bolus into the stomach by peristaltic waves of muscular contraction. Secretion of mucus aids the process	5-10 seconds for solids, 1 second for liquids
Cardiac sphincter	A muscular band closing the entrance to the stomach	The sphincter opens to receive food pushed along by peristaltic waves in the oesophagus. Normally it is shut to prevent reflux of contents	Seconds
Stomach	A J-shaped muscular sac, folded into rugae to increase the surface area. Has a capacity of about 1 litre; gastric and mucous glands secrete about 2 litres (3.6 pints) of gastric juice each day	The rugae allow the stomach to distend. The muscular walls churn and macerate the food, mixing it with gastric juices and reducing it to chyme. Peristaltic waves force the chyme through the stomach to the pyloric sphincter. The storage of food in the stomach prevents the need for many small meals	2-6 hours
Pancreas	A soft, oblong shaped organ lying behind and below the stomach. It is made up of islets of Langerhans which secrete glucagon and insulin, and other masses of cells which secrete about 800 cc pancreatic juice daily. Connected to the duodenum by the pancreatic duct and the duct of Santorini	Pancreatic juice consists of three protein digesting enzymes, one carbohydrate and one fat digesting enzyme. Hormones from the duodenum stimulate the activity of the gland. Glucagon and insulin control the fate of digested and absorbed carbohydrates	
Liver	The largest organ in the body, located below the diaphragm on the right of the abdomen, and divided into two lobes. Connected to the duodenum by the common bile duct	A complex organ which has a variety of vital functions. As far as digestion is concerned, it manufactures and secretes watery green bile, used in the small intestine to emulsify fats	
Gall bladder	A small sac attached to the underside of the liver, folded into rugae to enable it to expand. Connected to the duodenum by the common bile duct	Stores bile which it concentrates until stimulated to contract by the presence of acid and fat in the duodenum, when it ejects bile into the duodenum	
Small Intestine	A tube about 3 metres (10 feet) long beginning at the pyloric valve of the stomach and coiling through the central and lower abdomen to merge with the large intestine. Divided into three segments: the duodenum, jejunum, and ileum. Intestinal and mucous glands secrete about two to three litres of intestinal juice daily. The inner wall has villi, increasing the surface area	Most digestion and absorption of food occurs here. Hormones secreted here stimulate the pancreas, liver and gall bladder to pour their digestive juices into the duodenum. The muscular walls mix the chyme with digestive juices and bring all the food particles into contact with the villi for absorption. Peristalsis moves the chyme forward.	5-6 hours
Appendix and Caecum	Closed sacs at the junction of the small and large intestine	Have no function in man. In herbivores they contain bacteria which digest cellulose	
Large Intestine	A tube about 1.5 metres (5 feet) long extending from the ileum to the anus. Divided into four regions: the caecum, colon, rectum and anal canal. The ileocaecal valve ensures one-way movement of materials. Mucous glands secrete mucus into the large intestine	Bacteria digest any remaining foods. Water is absorbed, creating solid or semi-solid faeces which are excreted from the anus by muscular action. Mucus lubricates the faeces and protects the tissue from the small intestine's digestive juices	12-24 hours

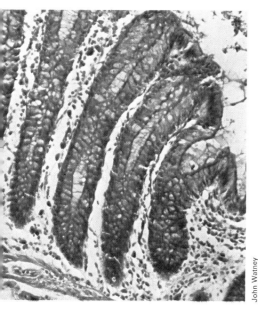

John Watney

the faeces compacted and hard, so it is increasingly difficult to expel them.

The process of expelling waste through the anal sphincter is known as *defaecation*. Pressure of faeces in the rectum is the main stimulus, causing a peristaltic movement of the muscular wall of the rectum. This is under a certain degree of voluntary control which has to be learnt in early childhood and is largely absent in babies.

To expel the faeces, a conscious effort is made to force the diaphragm down thus increasing pressure in the abdominal cavity and propelling the faeces into the rectum. Once this process has begun, the rectum stretches to receive the entire contents of the lower part of the colon. The stretching triggers off the reflex contraction of the rectal muscles, the anal sphincter relaxes, and the faeces are pushed out of the body.

Neglecting the urge to defaecate, as well as eating foods that have insufficient roughage, will lead to constipation—the

contents of the colon become hard and can only be passed out with some difficulty. Laxatives, taken as a cure for constipation, either act to increase the amount of water retained by the contents of the colon, so that the muscles find the waste softer and easier to propel, or some, like liquid paraffin, act as a lubricant for the passage of the faeces. Other drugs directly stimulate the gut walls to contract and expel the faeces. Doctors disapprove of the frequent use of laxatives, as it is easy to grow so dependent on such drugs that the bowel function becomes permanently abnormal.

Diarrhoea—the frequent expulsion of liquid faeces—can be produced by a number of factors, such as nervous stress, excessive use of laxatives or infection. Infection may prevent the large intestine from doing its job of reabsorbing water from the gut contents, so the faeces remain in a semi-liquid state, making the conscious control of defaecation much more difficult.

The Kidneys

The solid appearance of our bodies belies the fluidity of our internal environment. Inside we are awash with fluids: something like 60 per cent of our body weight is water, over half of which is contained inside the cells. The rest is mixed with salts (rather like diluted seawater) and bathes all the cells of the body.

The importance of the surrounding fluid can be demonstrated by the fact that the cells of a drop of blood placed in tap water will swell and burst. Placed in a five per cent solution, on the other hand, they will shrink and wrinkle up. In the first case water is rushing into the cells by osmosis, and in the second it is rushing out of the cells. In the body such gross changes in cell volume would be fatal to the functioning of cells. So it is vital that the bathing fluids are maintained at exactly the right concentrations.

The internal sea

Nearly every cell of the body is surrounded by a network of tiny capillaries, from which blood plasma diffuses into the internal sea. This salty fluid carries nutrients to the cells and removes their waste products, diffusing back through the capillary walls to mix with the other blood constituents. One particularly dangerous waste product is ammonia, produced when proteins are broken down to provide energy. This is a highly poisonous gas which dissolves readily in water. One thousandth of a milligram of

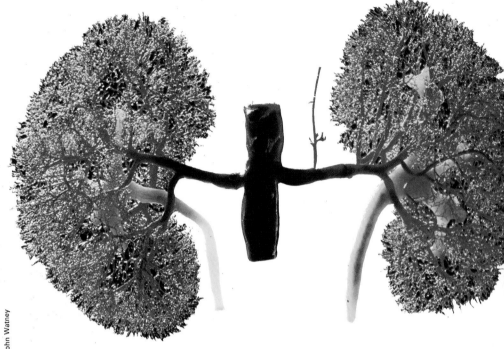

John Watney

Above: Human kidneys treated with resin to show the blood vessels. Each of the kidneys contains about one million nephrons—twisted hollow tubules through which the blood is filtered.

Right: Diagram showing the position of the kidneys, ureter and bladder.

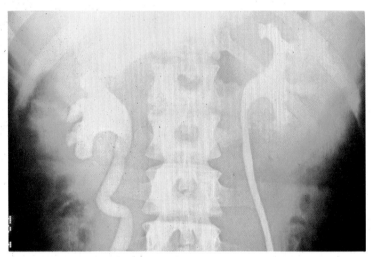

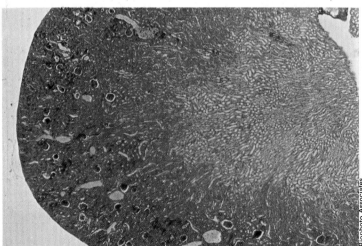

Biophoto Associates

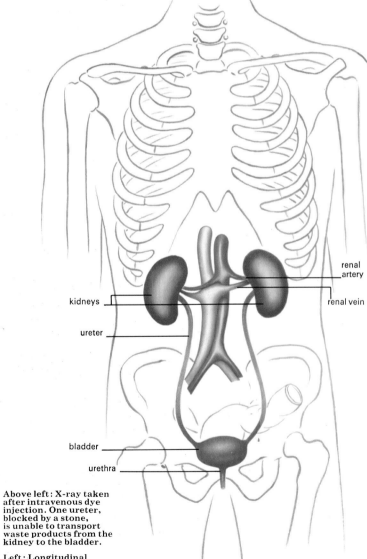

renal artery

renal vein

kidneys

ureter

bladder

urethra

Above left: X-ray taken after intravenous dye injection. One ureter, blocked by a stone, is unable to transport waste products from the kidney to the bladder.

Left: Longitudinal kidney section. The inner medulla is densely packed with nephrons, supplied with blood by the glomeruli (the dark spots).

ammonia per litre of blood is sufficient to kill a man, so the body must eliminate this as fast as possible. It is sent to the liver to be converted into a substance called urea which is still poisonous, but can be tolerated by the body in quantities one hundred thousand times greater than ammonia.

It is vital that the urea be eliminated and the salt concentration of body fluids balanced. It is also essential for the body to regulate the acidity of the bathing solution and control the volume of circulating water which will dilute the body fluids. All of these important functions are performed by the kidneys, which exert a fine degree of control over the substances comprising our internal sea. They chemically process and filter our body fluids and produce urine containing unwanted substances, which is then eliminated from the bladder.

Kidney structure

The two kidneys are attached to the abdominal wall and their surrounding structures by a layer of fibrous connective tissue. This holds them in place, one on either side of the backbone, above the small of the back just behind the stomach and liver. They are bean-shaped and engorged with blood brought to them by the large renal artery.

Microscopic examination of the kidney reveals a complex system of tubes, capillaries, arteries and veins, carefully packed together to form approximately one million identical units known as *nephrons*. The nephrons are miniaturized chemical filtration plants: they balance the composition of the blood and form urine which collects in the renal pelvis, a large cavity in the centre of the kidney. From here the urine drains out through the ureter to the bladder.

The filtration units

The nephron is a twisted, hollow tube surrounded by a network of blood vessels. Each of these tubules is about 31 mm (1.25 inches) long, compacted into the smallest possible space. If placed end to end, the two million tubules of the two kidneys would form a pipe about fifty miles long.

At its closed end, the nephron has a cup called the *Bowman's capsule* which encloses a dense ball of blood capillaries. The tubule leading away from here immediately convolutes itself into a complex, twisted shape. Together with the Bowman's capsule they constitute the outer reddish-brown layer of the kidney—the *cortex*. The tubule straightens out and descends into the medulla, or interior of the kidney. Here it bends back on itself forming a hairpin bend (the *loop of Henle*) and ascends to the cortex again, makes another series of twists and joins up with a straight urine-collecting duct. This goes down through the medulla collecting urine from several nephrons, and discharges it into the pelvis of the kidney.

Below left: A cross section through the kidney showing the cortex, medulla and position of the nephrons.

Below: Diagram showing the arrangement of the kidney filtration units and the vessels which supply them. The renal artery divides into arterioles which subdivide into a spherical cluster of capillaries (known as the glomerulus) at the end of each nephron. Large molecules (protein and blood cells) are filtered out by the pressure of blood in the departing arteriole. Salts in solution are passed along the tubule for reabsorption by the cells lining the walls. Unwanted products (urine) are passed to the bladder.

The nephron is the centre of chemical balance and filtration in the body. To understand how it works it is necessary to follow the path of the blood which transports materials to the kidney.

One quarter of the total blood output from the heart comes to the kidneys along the renal arteries—approximately 1,200 cc (about 2 pints) every minute. The incoming artery divides up repeatedly inside the kidney, eventually forming arterioles, each one of which leads to a Bowman's capsule.

The arteriole splits into tiny, thin-walled capillaries which form a ball known as the glomerulus (little ball). These capillaries reunite to form the arteriole which leaves the capsule. The departing arteriole is narrower than the incoming one, which has the effect of increasing the resistance to the blood flow. This, in turn, increases the pressure in the glomerulus to something like three times the normal pressure, so that the blood is pressing very hard against the thin walls of the capillaries.

The capillary walls are riddled with minute pores which are so small that they act, in effect, like a miniaturized filter, allowing the water, glucose, salts, amino acids, vitamins and urea from the blood to pass through into the tubule, but preventing the passage of blood cells and proteins. The amounts of substances passed through are quite amazing: 125 ccs ($\frac{1}{4}$ pint) of fluid is filtered every minute, 180 litres a day, about four times the amount contained in an average size car petrol tank. This fluid contains something like one kilo ($2\frac{1}{4}$ lbs) of sodium chloride (common salt), .45 kilo (one lb) of sodium bicarbonate, .15 kilo ($\frac{1}{3}$ lb) of glucose.

Obviously the body cannot afford to lose such large amounts of these substances, so it reabsorbs about 99% of the fluid back into the bloodstream. In fact, the kidneys filter and reabsorb our entire internal sea nearly fifteen times every day, which amounts to a remarkably thorough cleansing operation.

The reabsorption process

Once it has passed out of the blood vessels of the glomerulus the fluid enters the tubule of the nephron. This is surrounded by a network of capillaries whose function is to reabsorb the valuable and useful blood components, leaving excess and waste products inside ready to be discharged as urine (about one per cent of the total filtered fluid).

During its passage through the first twisted part of the tubule (the *proximal convoluted tubule*) about 85 per cent of the water, sodium chloride and bicarbonate, together with virtually all the glucose, vitamins and amino acids, are reabsorbed. This is accomplished by the millions of cells lining this part of the tubule which have millions of microscopic villi—minute protrusions similar to those found in the lining of the small intestine—vastly increasing their surface area, so that they can absorb quickly and easily.

Most of the water passes through the tubule walls by osmosis, the process by which water is passed through a semipermeable membrane to equalize two different concentrations; other materials such as glucose. amino acids and vitamins have to be actively transported back into the blood by special carrier molecules. These pick up a particular molecule and carry it across the tubule cells and into

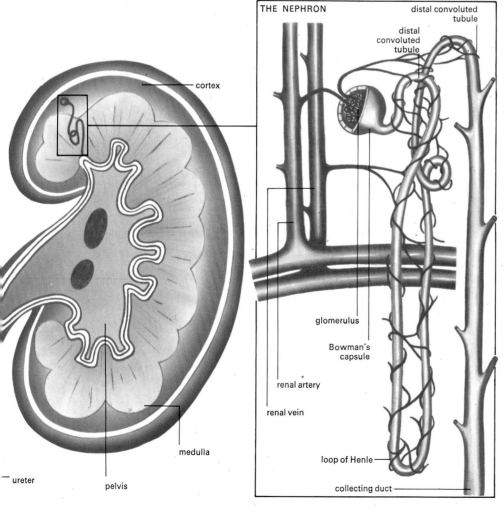

THE NEPHRON

distal convoluted tubule

distal convoluted tubule

cortex

medulla

ureter

pelvis

glomerulus

Bowman's capsule

renal artery

renal vein

loop of Henle

collecting duct

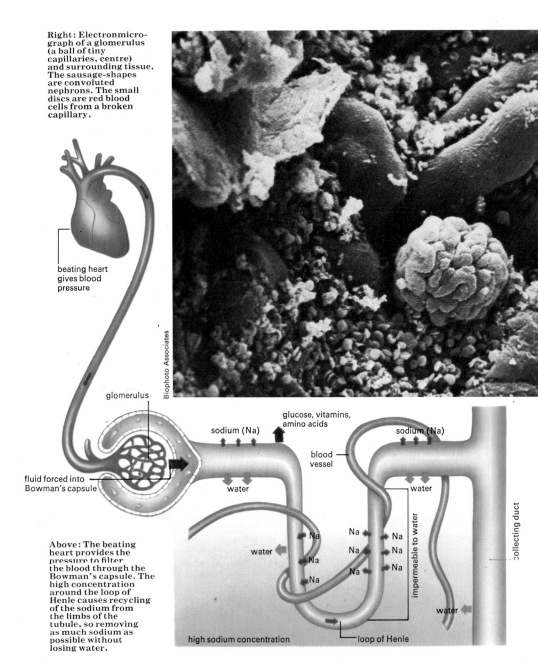

Right: Electronmicrograph of a glomerulus (a ball of tiny capillaries, centre) and surrounding tissue. The sausage-shapes are convoluted nephrons. The small discs are red blood cells from a broken capillary.

beating heart gives blood pressure

glomerulus

fluid forced into Bowman's capsule

sodium (Na)

glucose, vitamins, amino acids

sodium (Na)

blood vessel

water

water

Na Na Na
Na Na Na
Na Na
Na

water

impermeable to water

collecting duct

water

water

high sodium concentration

loop of Henle

Above: The beating heart provides the pressure to filter the blood through the Bowman's capsule. The high concentration around the loop of Henle causes recycling of the sodium from the limbs of the tubule, so removing as much sodium as possible without losing water.

ACTIVE TRANSPORT FROM TUBULES

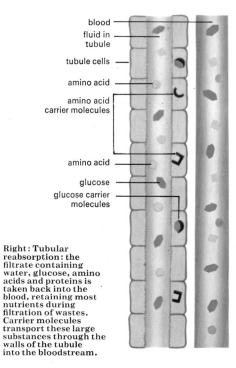

blood

fluid in tubule

tubule cells

amino acid

amino acid carrier molecules

amino acid

glucose

glucose carrier molecules

Right: Tubular reabsorption: the filtrate containing water, glucose, amino acids and proteins is taken back into the blood, retaining most nutrients during filtration of wastes. Carrier molecules transport these large substances through the walls of the tubule into the bloodstream.

the blood. Active transport needs energy, so the cells of the tubule have large numbers of mitochondria, the 'powerhouse' organelles in the cell, to produce the necessary ATP (adenosine triphosphate), 'high grade' energy fuel.

Water conservation

The remainder of the fluid passes down to the loop of Henle, and begins its ascent up the other limb towards the cortex. The ascending limb of the tubule does not allow water to pass through, but it actively absorbs sodium which it pumps out into the surrounding tissue. Since the descending and ascending limbs are very close together some of the sodium diffuses back into the descending limb to mix with the fluid coming from the capsule, hence recycling itself. The result of this is a very high concentration of sodium around the loop of Henle, and the more sodium there is, the more sodium will be pumped out of the ascending limb of the tubule. This is a method of removing as much sodium as possible in a very short tubule; the chloride follows the movement of sodium, enabling the body to retain its valuable salt.

132   The fluid travels up to the cortex in the

ascending limb into the twisted, *distal convoluted tubule* where water is once again absorbed. From here it enters the collecting duct which carries it down to the pelvis of the kidney. It again comes across a high concentration of sodium as it goes down through the inner area, the medulla, and past the region around the loop of Henle. This time, however, the walls of the tubule will allow water to pass through them by osmosis into the tissue and the blood. This rather complicated procedure is an ingenious method of concentrating the fluid to conserve water and keep as much salt as possible back from the urine.

Waste removal

The unwanted urea and excess materials pass straight through the tubule and into the collecting duct where they are then known as urine. A certain amount of water is essential to keep all these substances dissolved, which is one reason why we cannot survive for long periods without water. The body concentrates the urine to the maximum possible amount, but it must dispose of the poisonous urea, so urine must be expelled.

Besides removing substances from the blood, the kidney can also contribute small, but significant amounts of materials. Into the first twisted part of the tubule from the surrounding capillaries it secretes substances such as hydrogen ions which keep the acidity of the blood at a constant level (adding hydrogen ions will increase the acidity, and taking them away will decrease the acidity). The kidneys' efficient filtration system, however, also means that certain drugs, such as penicillin and one of the anti-malarial drugs, are immediately secreted into the urine. In order for them to be effective in the fight against invading bacteria, they must, therefore, be taken regularly.

The kidney is a very discriminating processing plant, carefully regulating our internal sea. Survival of the whole body relies on the delicate balancing processes of these two organs, each no bigger than the size of a clenched fist.

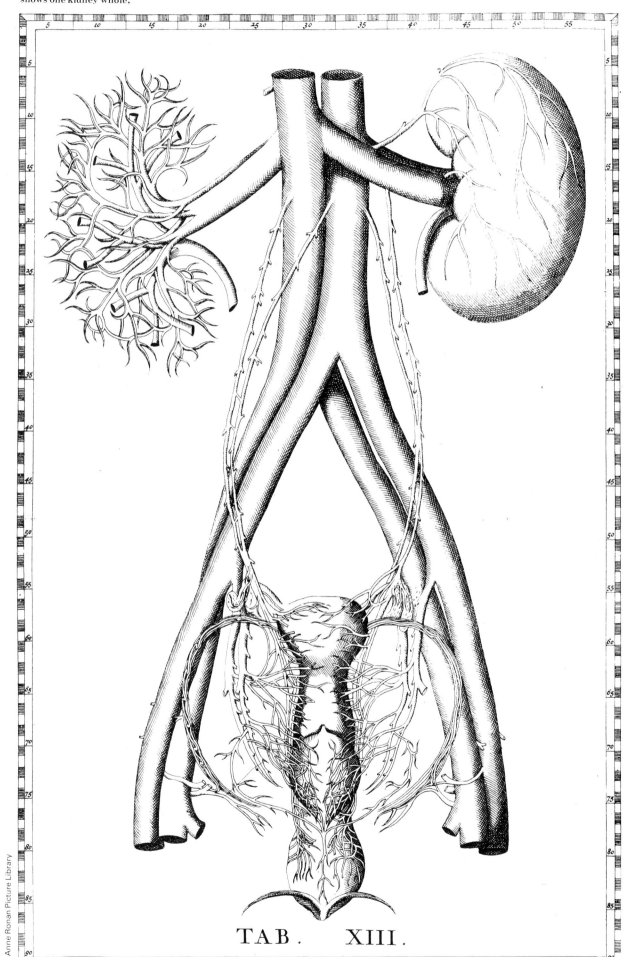

TAB. XIII.

Kidney Action

The kidney regulates the composition of our body fluids, excreting unwanted chemicals in the solution called urine. To make this solution we must drink water, and our intake is regulated by a special drinking centre in an area of the hypothalamus of the brain.

When our body fluids have decreased by about one per cent of the body weight the hypothalamus induces the sensation of thirst which stimulates us to drink. This is achieved by a reduction in the production of saliva, leaving the mouth feeling dry and parched. When the water loss reaches over 10 per cent of the body weight, the cells can no longer function efficiently and death is likely to follow. This can occur in a matter of a few days, whereas we can withstand hunger for weeks, using our fat and protein reserves.

The drinking centre also affects the kidneys by causing them to conserve water. The urine produced in this way is more concentrated and much less in volume. Shipwrecked sailors, for example, cannot quench their thirst by drinking seawater because the salt concentration is three times that of the blood. The kidney has to excrete the excess salts, and this requires much more water than the amount of seawater drunk. The body, therefore, becomes even more dehydrated than before, accelerating the onset of death.

Water concentration control

The kidney's degree of control over the water content of the body is remarkable. If we drink a litre of water quickly, the urine production will increase by almost exactly one litre. The kidneys appear to know exactly how much water is present, and maintain this level by increasing or decreasing the amount of urine formed. How does the body accomplish this regulation?

If we become slightly dehydrated by sweating or not drinking enough, the concentration of water in the blood will fall. As the blood circulates through the brain the *osmoreceptors*—special receptors in the hypothalamus at the front of the brain—become active: they send out nerve impulses which travel down to the posterior lobe of the pituitary gland. Here they stimulate the gland to release the *ADH* (antidiuretic hormone) which pours into the blood capillaries and so into the blood circulation. It travels to the kidney by the renal artery where it reaches its site of action—the distal convoluted tubules and the collecting ducts. ADH causes the cells lining these tubules to become permeable to water, thereby increasing the passage of water out of the urine and back into the blood. As a result of this, the urine volume is decreased and the body water conserved.

If, on the other hand, an excessive amount of water has just been drunk, the concentration of the water in the blood will rise; the osmoreceptors in the hypothalamus will no longer be stimulated, and ADH will not be secreted into the blood. The kidney tubule cells become less permeable to water; the urine volume then increases and becomes much more dilute, and the excess water is excreted.

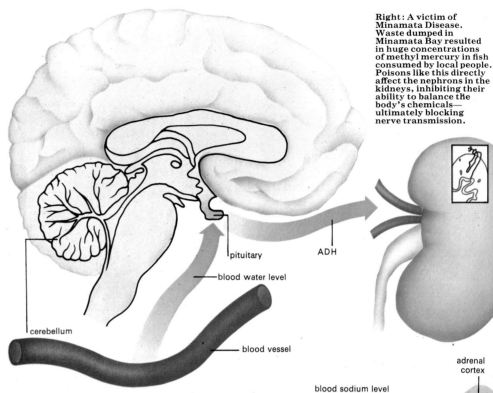

cerebellum

pituitary

blood water level

ADH

blood vessel

adrenal cortex

blood sodium level

aldosterone

Above: The regulation of body fluids is controlled by a mechanism in the brain which directs the kidneys to make adjustments in urine production in relation to fluid intake, thus releasing or conserving water. When the body fluid is low, the osmoreceptors (specialized sensory receptors) in the hypothalamus send nerve impulses to the posterior pituitary lobe, stimulating it to release ADH (antidiuretic hormone). This hormone is carried in the blood to the kidneys. There it stimulates the cells in the urine-collecting ducts to reabsorb more water.

Below: Longitudinal kidney section x 35,000.

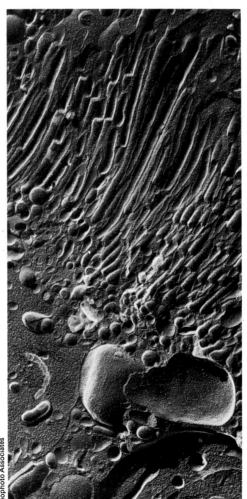

Biophoto Associates

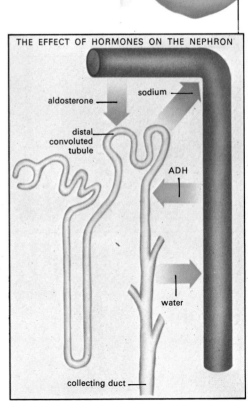

THE EFFECT OF HORMONES ON THE NEPHRON

aldosterone

sodium

distal convoluted tubule

ADH

water

collecting duct

Right: A kidney stone can result from over-concentrated urine. The dissolved chemicals crystallize and develop into stones. These may obstruct the flow of urine, stretching the walls of the ureters.

Left and below left: The osmoreceptors in the hypothalamus respond to low blood-water concentration and stimulate the posterior pituitary to release ADH which in turn stimulates the renal cells to reabsorb more water. Similarly low blood-sodium results in reabsorption (below) through the agency of aldosterone hormone.

Below: An X-ray of a staghorn calculus kidney stone, so-called because it fills up the horn-shaped pelvis of the kidney. Small stones pass out naturally, some larger ones can be dissolved chemically, but a stone of this size would be removed surgically.

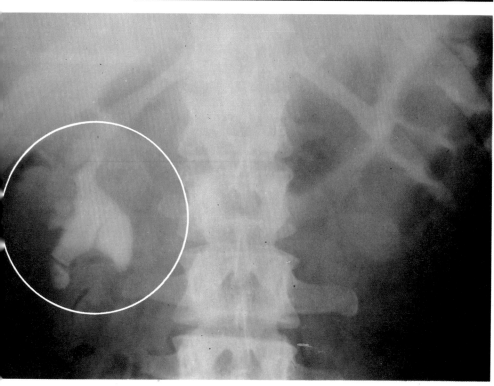

A deficiency of ADH causes a rare disease known as diabetes insipidus, where copious amounts oı urine are produced—up to six gallons a day—compared to the normal 2-3 pints. Lack of ADH means that the kidneys do not reabsorb enough water from the urine, hence the excessive urine production.

The more common condition, sugar diabetes, also causes a reduction in the amount of water reabsorbed. People suffering from this disease excrete large quantities of water and glucose and this leads to dehydration of the body. It can be very easily controlled, however, by regular injections of the hormone insulin, lowering the blood-glucose level.

Sodium control

Intimately connected with the water content of the body is the sodium level; if the level of sodium is too high the kidneys excrete the excess in the urine; but this causes water to be retained in the urine as well. This is again due to the osmotic effect where water moves from a low to a high concentration, and we are again reminded of the shipwrecked sailor who cannot drink salty water without having to excrete large quantities of water along with the salt.

Sweating, on the other hand, lowers the level of sodium in the body: sodium is excreted in the sweat. To try to maintain the level of sodium in the body the kidneys reabsorb it back into the blood. Water, by the process of osmosis, follows the sodium, hence the amount of water excreted in the urine is decreased.

This osmotic reabsorption of water accounts for 80 per cent of the total water transport into the blood, and this cannot be controlled by the kidneys. It is only the remaining 20 per cent which can be controlled by the ADH levels. If total water movement could be controlled we would be much less dependent on our daily water intake.

The actual movement of sodium through the tubule cells is accomplished by special carrier molecules which actively transport the sodium into the blood. Therefore, it is the control of this transport process which regulates the sodium content of the body. When the blood-sodium level is low, the cortex of the adrenal gland (which is on top of the kidney) is stimulated to release the hormone aldosterone. Once in the blood, aldosterone acts on the cells lining the distal convoluted tubule causing them to pump large quantities of sodium, and hence water, back into the blood. As soon as the sodium level in the blood returns to normal the secretion of aldosterone is reduced, and the sodium reabsorbtion decreases. A high blood-sodium concentration will completely stop the secretion of aldosterone, and the kidneys will excrete large quantities of sodium in the urine.

This regulatory mechanism is so precise that the levels of sodium in the body are maintained to within two per cent of normal. If, however, something goes wrong with this system, and the kidneys fail to excrete enough sodium, it will accumulate, together with water, in the tissues of the body causing swellings—a condition known as oedema.

The effects of diuretics

Most people have probably noticed that drinking tea, coffee and alcohol increases the volume of urine produced. These

Eugene Smith/Magnum

Dr. P. Slatter/ZEFA

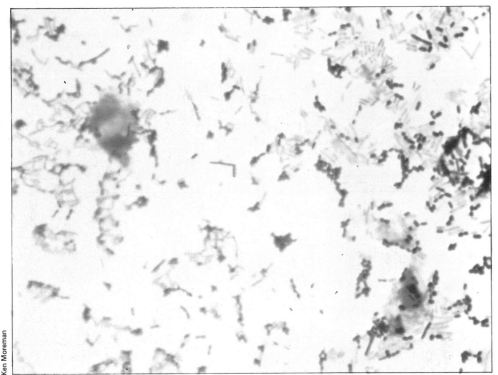

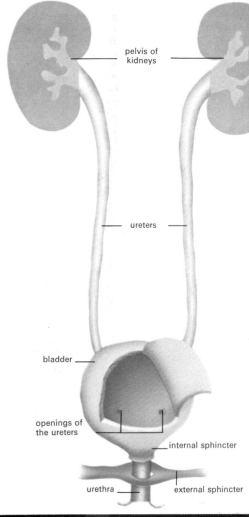

pelvis of
kidneys

ureters

bladder

openings of
the ureters

internal sphincter

urethra

external sphincter

substances are common examples of *diuretics*, and the abnormal increase in urine flow is called *diuresis*. Caffeine (found in coffee and tea) and alcohol inhibit the excretion of ADH by the pituitary which decreases the amount of water reabsorbed by the kidneys.

Drinking whisky in the desert causes rapid dehydration due to its diuretic effect and can be fatal. Something like 100 cc of water need to be excreted for every 10 gms of alcohol drunk. Beer is a much better thirst quencher: it contains only about 4 per cent alcohol, its diuretic effect being due more to the amount of water drunk than its alcohol content.

The characteristics of urine

Once formed, urine travels down the two ureters into the bladder. Here it is stored until discharged through the urethra. Like the stomach, the bladder is folded into rugae which allow it to stretch to its average capacity of holding 700 to 800 cc of urine, prevented from leaving by internal and external sphincter muscles which squeeze shut the urethra.

When the bladder has more than about 400 cc of urine in it, the stretch receptors lining its walls send a message to the central nervous system which responds by causing the internal sphincter to relax—if the external sphincter is relaxed urine will pour down the urethra. But this sphincter is under conscious control, and it is possible to prevent urination until the bladder becomes fuller. Children do not develop conscious control over this reflex until they are about two years old, and hence urinate whenever the bladder is full enough to initiate the reflex.

Examination of the urine can give vital clues about the internal condition of the body, and has thus become a routine diagnostic procedure. If certain of the body's chemical processes are not working correctly, traces of unusual chemicals may appear in the urine, or normal urine constituents may be present in abnormal amounts. If, for example, dead cells from the bladder walls and urethra (these are constantly being shed and passed out in

Above and below: Urine analysis is now a routine process in diagnosis. Samples are spun on a centrifuge to separate the water and the sediment may be dried out or left wet for microscopic inspection. The dry preparation (above) stained with a dye, may turn red or blue depending on the bacteria present. The large red spots are pus cells, indicating infection in the urinary system. Uric acid crystals present in the wet preparation (below) can be more easily seen through polarized light—light in which all the waves are vibrating in the same direction. Excess uric acid in the blood causes gout; it accumulates in joints, causing inflammation.

136

Left: The kidneys, ureters and bladder.

Below: The artificial kidney machine maintains the chemical balance of body fluids by dialysis, the process by which chemical substances are separated by the use of semi-permeable membranes. Blood is pumped through a series of spiral grooves between two thin membranes. Dialyzing fluid—similar in composition to purified blood plasma—flows in the opposite direction through channels on the outside of the membrane, which allows urea and wastes to pass into the outer channel but not larger molecules such as proteins and blood cells.

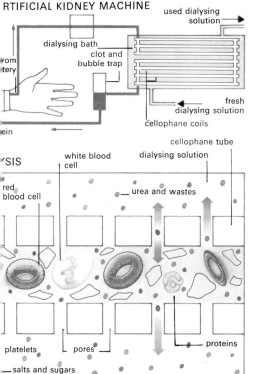

RTIFICIAL KIDNEY MACHINE

used dialysing solution

dialysing bath

clot and bubble trap

om tery

ein

fresh dialysing solution

cellophane coils

SIS

cellophane tube

dialysing solution

white blood cell

red blood cell

urea and wastes

platelets

pores

proteins

salts and sugars

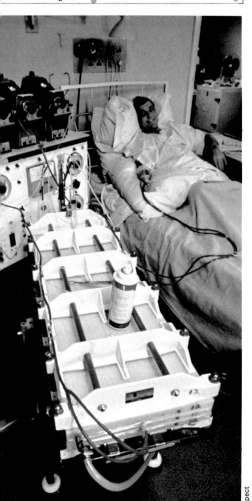
Aspect

Below left: A hospital patient linked to a kidney machine may be able to use the machine at home depending on his ability to monitor the control units. These show the dialyzate temperature and conductivity which must be maintained at precise levels. Kidney failure resulted in certain death before the advent of this machine.

Above: A scene from Lewis Carroll's famous book *Alice's Adventures in Wonderland* (1865). The character of the Mad Hatter (right) is a parody of the many hatters of that period who suffered from mental derangement and nervous disorders as a result of poisoning from the fumes of mercury used in the making of beaver hats.

the urine) are present in unusually large quantities, or different types of cells are present, the person may be suffering from a kidney infection.

Occasionally the dissolved salts in the urine may solidify to form kidney stones—small gritty particles or large stones. Very small stones usually cause no problems, and simply pass out in the urine; large ones, however, require surgical removal. This is one of the oldest operations in the history of medicine: travelling 'stone-removers' in medieval times used to perform these operations in public to attract new patients. However, the patients often died from post-operative infections, due to lack of sterilization.

The kidney machine

Total or partial kidney failure results in the accumulation of poisonous wastes in the body, a disease known as uremia (urea in the blood). It is a progressive toxic condition which kills thousands of people each year. Recent technology has developed an artificial kidney machine, however, which mimics the action of the real kidneys, filtering the blood, and regulating the body fluid concentration. It has been developed from a technique known as *dialysis*, the basic principle of which is osmosis—the migration of certain molecules through a semi-permeable membrane.

The kidney machine pumps the blood from the patient's artery through a long cellophane tube immersed in a warm bath containing chemicals which match the normal blood plasma. The remarkable property of cellophane is that it is per-forated with pores corresponding to the size of the pores in the capillaries clustered inside the glomerulii, the small spheres at one end of the nephrons, the millions of convoluted tubes which make up the kidney's filtering system. It is therefore able to act as a filter in exactly the same way as the glomerulus filters the blood, allowing small molecules to pass through out of the cellophane tube and into surrounding solution.

By carefully controlling the concentrations of the chemicals in the bath it is possible to remove all the unwanted chemical and waste products from the blood. They will pass out of the cellophane tube from the blood and into the bathing solution as long as the concentrations of these substances are lower in the bath. When the concentrations are equal, no movement will occur, and the blood will be free of its wastes.

This process takes from six to ten hours, and might have to be repeated twice or three times a week in serious cases.

Some patients are fortunate enough to be able to have a kidney machine at home after they have received a course of instructions. An arterio-venous shunt, prepared from two catheter tubes, is inserted—one into an artery and the other a vein—in a wrist or ankle. The concentrated dialyzing solution is introduced to the reservoir and checked for its conductivity (ability to conduct electricity). When the solution is within the limits set for that particular patient, he removes the short tube connecting the two catheters and connects them to the machine input and output. Patients must learn, however, to monitor the control units which show the temperature of the dialyzing fluid and conductivity with great accuracy, since these must be held at precise levels during treatment. A variation of as little as a few degrees in temperature could prove fatal.

Unfortunately treatment is very expensive, and the machines scarce. There are, in fact, many more people suffering from kidney failure than there are machines to treat them, but hopefully the apparatus will eventually be simplified and brought within reach of all who need it.

Lymph vessels carry
nutrients to the spaces
between tissue cells.
Lymphocytes, white cells
found in large numbers
in the lymphatic
system, help
manufacture antibodies
and destroy invading
organisms.

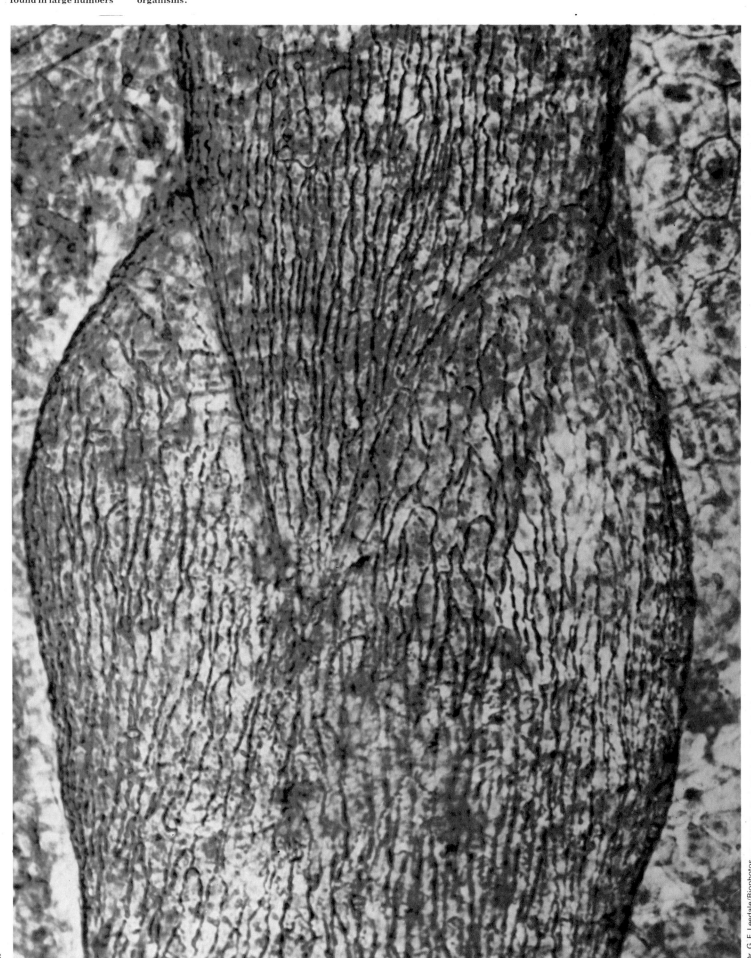

Body Fluids

The distant ancestors of all land animals were water creatures: their fluid environment transported food and raw materials to them, and carried away the waste products of their energy functions and body activities. The surrounding fluid helped protect them against buffeting, maintained tolerably constant living quarters, and yet permitted a fair degree of mobility without endangering the basic body functions.

Evolution into land creatures has turned the human environment outside in. Within the human frame, a series of fluid compartments serve the same functions, on an internal basis, that were possible in the old sea water and freshwater environments.

The internal fluids supply food and oxygen to nourish body cells and tissues, and remove carbon dioxide and waste products. But they may also have specialized functions: containing salts, for electrolytic influence on nerve and muscle cells, chemicals such as digestive enzymes for food breakdown, or hormones which act on distant target organs. Fluid may still also have a protective function: the brain, for example, is surrounded by cerebro-spinal fluid.

Fluid also protects the human organism by transporting the antibody agents that repel foreign materials—bacterial, viral and inanimate substances. Just as water once provided a tolerably constant external environment, it now has an important role in maintaining the internal body temperature within the fairly narrow range in which body metabolism works most efficiently.

Fluids forms part of the bulk of the human body, not only in terms of specialized fluid holders—like the heart, blood vessels, bowels and bladder—but actually within each individual human cell. Water in fact constitutes 80 per cent of an individual cell's total weight.

The proportion of body weight accredited to water differs between the sexes and according to age. While 65 per cent of infant weight is water, this drops to 60 per cent in the mature man and about 50 per cent in the adult woman. The more fat the individual has stored, the lower the proportion of body weight due to actual water. In an adult man who weighs 70 kilograms, a remarkable 42 litres is being carried about daily.

Human body fluids are considered in terms of the space or compartment they usually occupy. The largest of the compartments is the *intracellular* space where the fluid is built into the individual cell substance. In the 70-kilogram man this accounts for 60 per cent of the 42 litres—representing about 25 litres. The remaining 17 litres lies in the *extracellular* space. This is itself subdivided into the fluid which bathes the tissue cells—*interstitial fluid*—and blood plasma, the fluid in the *intravascular space.* The total figures are rounded off by including the relatively small volumes that make up the cerebrospinal fluid, and those occupying the lymphatic vessels and ducts, the lining sacs known as the pericardium, which surrounds the heart, the peritoneum in the abdominal cavity and the pleura, the membrane surrounding the lungs. The

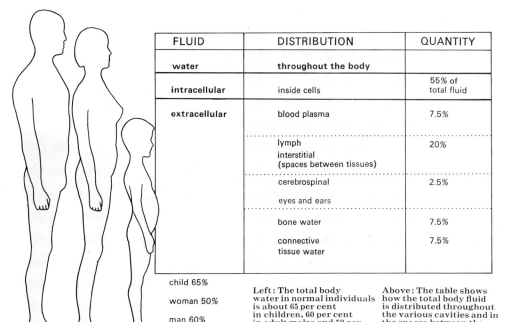

FLUID	DISTRIBUTION	QUANTITY
water	**throughout the body**	
intracellular	inside cells	55% of total fluid
extracellular	blood plasma	7.5%
	lymph interstitial (spaces between tissues)	20%
	cerebrospinal	2.5%
	eyes and ears	
	bone water	7.5%
	connective tissue water	7.5%

child 65%

woman 50%

man 60% of body weight

Left: The total body water in normal individuals is about 65 per cent in children, 60 per cent in adult males and 50 per cent in adult females.

Above: The table shows how the total body fluid is distributed throughout the various cavities and in the spaces between the cavities.

Right: A Holbein woodcut of a physician examining a urine sample. As early as 1537 it was recognized that since urine is the solution in water of the various waste products of body processes, the colour and density of the urine would reflect the health of the patient.

Below: An engraving of the cholera pandemic which swept India and Europe late in the 19th century. Within 24 hours a cholera victim may lose as much as 25% of his body weight as a result of diarrhoea. This heavy water loss can itself be fatal, but potassium salts are also lost and this can disturb the conduction of nerve impulses as well as interfere with the way the body balances its fluid distribution.

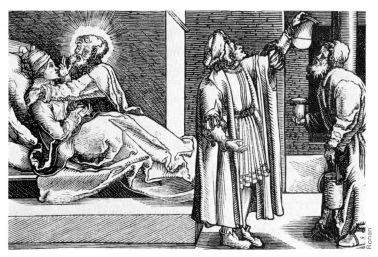

Ronan

Mansell

blood plasma volume is about 3.0 litres.

In the fluids within the various compartments, a wide range of substances are dissolved and transported. Proteins, for example, are carried to the cells all over the body; salts are vital not only in the transmission of nerve impulses, but to provide a means of maintaining the balance of fluids as well as the relative concentration of the major substances in the compartments themselves.

The fluid balance

In maintaining the fluid balance inside and outside individual cells, the presence of sodium and potassium salts is crucial. The main salt in the extracellular fluid is sodium, while in the intracellular fluid it is potassium.

Although the cell membrane is freely permeable to water it does not allow either of these salts to pass through it. In practice, if the concentration of sodium decreases outside the cell (as a result, for example, of excessive sweating) this will lower the osmotic pressure of the extracellular fluid and allow water to move into the cell itself.

An increase in intracellular water concentration results in overhydration, which can disrupt the function of the cell. Lowering the volume of water in the interstitial fluid results in a drop in pressure which means that water will move out of the blood plasma to maintain equilibrium. This can also have serious consequences; it may, for example, lead to shock.

Fluid exchange

In the blood plasma of the intravascular space, the concentration of proteins also exerts an osmotic pressure which can reclaim water and salts from the tissue fluids, and ensure a continuous exchange of fluids to and from the capillaries. If, for example, the proteins drop below normal levels, the intravascular osmotic pressure falls and fluid will leak into the tissue fluid space, increasing the volume of interstitial fluid. In a healthy individual, however, the level of protein is maintained by both protein intake in food and by its manufacture in the liver.

The body salts are derived from the daily food intake. Their levels in the intracellular and extracellular fluids, like the body's water level itself, are regulated by the kidneys through the mechanisms of excretion and reabsorption in the specialized filters called the *tubules*.

This reabsorption process is under hormonal control: for example, ADH (antidiuretic hormone) is secreted by the posterior pituitary gland when body fluid level is low. ADM acts directly on the urine collecting ducts to reabsorb more water. Similarly, when blood volume falls, aldosterone is secreted by the adrenal cortex to encourage sodium and therefore water retention.

Daily fluid levels

In the healthy human being, a constant balance has to be maintained in the fluid levels. This involves matching up daily fluid intake with daily fluid losses. Fluid intake is derived from water, tea, coffee, milk and other beverages, as well as the water present in solid foods and fruit. In addition, water is produced as the 'end product' of cell activity. Fluid losses occur through the bowels as part of excreted faecal material. There is also

water loss through the skin in insensible perspiration in which water diffuses through the epidermis over the whole body surface. These two losses respectively account for about 150 millilitres and 600 millilitres each day.

Water is also evaporated from the lungs in the air that is breathed out, and this accounts for about half a litre daily. Urine excretion from the kidneys adds 1.5 to 2 litres to the daily loss. Thus for a healthy individual average daily fluid intake has to be at least around 3 litres to match the total regular losses.

There is a large daily turnover of fluids in some parts of the body, particularly in the stomach and bowels, mouth and pancreas. Stomach and intestinal juices, saliva fluid and pancreatic fluid may each attain an output of under two litres daily. Liver bile production is well over half a litre. However, most of this fluid is reabsorbed on its way through the alimentary pathways, leaving a small amount of faecal fluid as actual loss.

Left: Diagram showing blood circulation and the lymphatic system, the two main life-support systems of the body. Blood and lymph are constantly circulating extra-cellular fluids, delivering vital nutrients and chemicals to the spaces between the tissue cells, where they can be absorbed into the cell by osmosis or diffusion.

Bottom: Section showing the movement of fluid between the cellular and interstitial spaces, and the blood and lymphatic vessels.

lymph

arterial blood

heart

venous blood

lymph node

MOVEMENT OF FLU

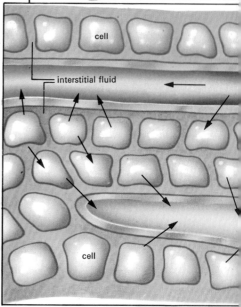

cell

interstitial fluid

cell

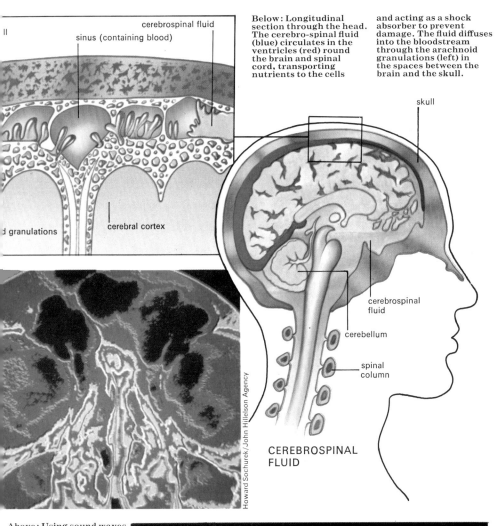

cerebrospinal fluid

sinus (containing blood)

d granulations

cerebral cortex

Below: Longitudinal section through the head. The cerebro-spinal fluid (blue) circulates in the ventricles (red) round the brain and spinal cord, transporting nutrients to the cells

and acting as a shock absorber to prevent damage. The fluid diffuses into the bloodstream through the arachnoid granulations (left) in the spaces between the brain and the skull.

skull

cerebrospinal fluid

cerebellum

spinal column

CEREBROSPINAL FLUID

Howard Sochurek/John Hillelson Agency

Above: Using sound waves instead of X-rays, this picture shows infected areas ((black outlined with red) of the sinus cavities behind the forehead. As a result of this condition—known as sinusitis—the cavities fill with fluid which may carry the infection elsewhere.

Right: An X-ray technique reveals some of the spaces—note the two dark 'holes' on top of the skull—between the brain and the skull. Cerebro-spinal fluid fills these spaces, nourishing the brain.

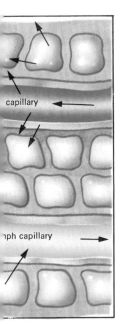

capillary

ph capillary

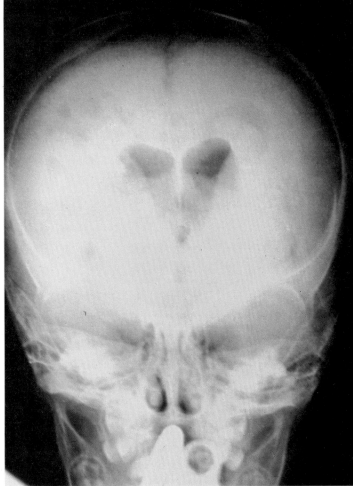

Derek Ellis

Fluid intake may only safely exceed fluid loss in two situations: in the growing infant and child who requires additional fluid as part of the expanding cells and tissue development; and in pregnancy when cellular growth is taking place in the foetus. There is also evidence that the fluid intake requirements may rise in the convalescent phase after illness.

Fluid disturbance

The fluid balance in the compartments of the body can be upset by various conditions. Severe dehydration due to shortage of water can occur in tropical and semi-tropical climates but not usually as pure water deficiency in temperate climates. Old people living alone and people unconscious for prolonged periods frequently suffer from lack of body water. The intracellular space and extracellular space fluid volumes both shrink; usual symptoms are thirst and a dry mouth and sometimes the mind becomes muddled and confused. Only water should be given to correct this condition, either by mouth or (mixed with glucose) by drip infusion.

Sodium and potassium loss

In severe vomiting or diarrhoea, excessive amounts of water and sodium and potassium salts are quickly lost. The extracellular fluid volume shrinks resulting in weakness and cramps in the limbs; the individual looks tired, the face having a 'sunken' appearance, and he has low blood pressure.

A similar condition can occur in places like the tropics, where excess sweating causes water and sodium loss but only pure water is drunk, so that salt is not replaced. Hospital care is often necessary if the condition is severe so that the water and sodium loss can be corrected by intravenous infusion of saline. Potassium loss produces marked muscle weakness, and is corrected by taking both potassium salt tablets and drinking plenty of fresh orange juice and tomato juice.

Excessive retention and loss

Specific illnesses can cause fluid imbalance in the human body. Stagnation of the venous circulation in chronic heart disease causes a marked loss of fluid into the interstitial tissues. This is known as *oedema* when the excess fluid in the tissue is recognized by swelling of the feet and ankles. Oedema can spread to involve the limbs, abdomen and even the chest. The fluid imbalance is corrected by giving drugs called *diuretics* which force the kidneys to push out salt, mainly sodium. The sodium draws out water with it, the urine output greatly increases, the excess interstitial fluid returns to the intravascular space, and balance is restored.

In *hyperthyroidism*, overactivity of the thyroid gland, the basal metabolic rate of cellular processes is considerably increased. Sweating becomes profuse and there may also be diarrhoea, which, of course, is likely to cause fluid loss. However, any tendency to imbalance is usually corrected by the increase in 'end product' water derived from excessively active cellular metabolism.

Starvation reduces the plasma proteins in the intravascular space, causing the shift of fluid into the interstitial space. Oedema may again appear, and this type of fluid imbalance is corrected by giving high protein compounds and plenty of meat, fish and eggs.

The Body's Internal Balance

The body's myriad chemical processes go on largely without our awareness. We know, for example, that every cell in the body is constantly metabolizing, breaking down foodstuffs to produce energy—some of which is released as heat—or building up new tissue, but these processes cannot be seen, felt or consciously controlled.

Although we know that eating and drinking are necessary to live, it is completely beyond our power to calculate exactly how much food or water we need at any one time. However, our bodies tell us by creating the sensations of hunger and thirst which are satisfied by certain quantities of food or liquid.

Similarly, the production of energy by the body's cells needs oxygen, which the lungs take in at every breath. The amount of oxygen needed varies constantly but the body automatically ensures that we inhale the right amount.

It is clear that we must have a most efficient control centre which governs these and many more activities.

This process of keeping conditions constant in the face of constant change is called *homoeostasis*. The internal monitor and co-ordinator is the *hypothalamus*, in the middle portion of the brain. It exerts its control by two main pathways: the autonomic nervous system and the endocrine system. The effect of the autonomic nervous system is immediate but rapidly dies away; endocrine response takes longer but once in action its effect is longer lasting. The autonomic nervous system, consisting of the sympathetic and parasympathetic nervous systems, is responsible for all the continual adjustments needed for effective functioning of our internal organs, including the heart, blood vessels and digestive tract. The sympathetic nervous system speeds things up: it causes an increase in the rate of the heartbeat and the force with which the heart pumps the blood round the body; it also increases blood pressure and the level of the sugar in the blood—in other words, the sympathetic nervous system prepares the body for action.

Under stress, the sympathetic nervous system will direct more blood to the voluntary muscles controlling movements like running. It does this by constricting blood capillaries and veins, cutting down the blood flow to the skin and abdomen.

The parasympathetic nervous system acts in the opposite way: it lowers heart rate and blood pressure. The two systems are complementary, however, and the adjustments minute. They are too finely balanced to be merely a matter of one system modifying an over-reaction by the other.

The hypothalamus is able to co-ordinate the actions of the autonomic nervous system by the messages it receives from various parts of the body. It is like a control room or telephone exchange: messages come in, the hypothalamus 'decides' what action to take on the basis of the information and the autonomic nervous system carries out its instructions which may, for example, instruct the heart to slow down. This decreases the volume of blood pumped per minute and so lowers the blood pressure.

Certain processes, such as enzyme reactions, however, have their own in-built control so that just enough of the products are made when needed. But this control depends on the maintenance of an optimum environment to enable the enzymes to work—enzymes are highly sensitive to changes in the pH (acidity or alkalinity) of their surroundings, the concentration of salts and the temperature. And yet, every reaction itself alters these conditions.

It has been calculated, for example, that over a period of 24 hours, 95 per cent of the total 3,000 kilocalories released by energy production is given off as heat. But, in a healthy person, the body temperature does not vary much around 37°C (98.6°F).

Likewise, many enzyme reactions have water as one of their products; this will tend to dilute the solution of salts which bathes the area the enzyme works in. Reactions producing hydrogen ions and increasing the acidity of the enzyme's environment are also going on all the time. The body must, therefore, have a monitoring system which not only ensures that each and every process is functioning properly but which also maintains the status quo: supplying food, water and oxygen as and when needed and keeping the composition of the blood and other body fluids constant.

Fluid control

Water is the basic ingredient of the body. Its turnover is rapid and occurs over a large area. Water loss could be cut down by the constricting action of the autonomic nervous system on blood vessel walls, but the effects of the endocrine system, through its chemical secretions called hormones, are far more powerful and long-lasting.

The hypothalamus is also in control of the intake, movement and elimination of water. It can detect the concentration level of the blood when it flows over its receptors. If the amount of water in the blood falls, the hypothalamus sends a message to the pituitary, the main gland in the underside of the brain. The pituitary then releases a hormone called vasopressin or ADH (antidiuretic hormone). ADH makes the kidney tubules, which are responsible for reabsorbing the water the body produces, more permeable to water. So, when ADH is released, more water is reabsorbed and, because less water is excreted, the urine becomes more concentrated. At the same time, the hypothalamus makes us feel thirsty, so that we drink more and maintain the correct water balance.

After drinking alcohol, the fine control of the hypothalamus is thrown off balance. The output of ADH is cut down increasing the flow of dilute urine. But we do not feel thirsty—even though we need to make up the water lost—until after the effects of the alcohol have worn off.

Temperature control

The role of the hypothalamus in controlling body temperature is intriguing and, as yet, not completely understood. There are differing opinions among researchers as to how the hypothalamus 'knows' which temperature is correct. Some believe that the temperature is preset by a particular concentration of sodium and

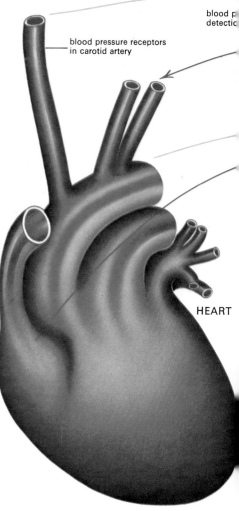

blood pressure receptors in carotid artery

blood p
detectio

HEART

Diagrams to illustrate how homoeostasis, a stable state, is maintained in the body. A constant environment is essential to ensure the correct conditions for chemical and physical processes and this is controlled by the hypothalamus in the middle of the brain above the roof of the mouth. The hypothalamus monitors and initiates control over body temperature and fluid balance, blood pressure, acidity and ionic composition. It does this through the complementary stimulating and inhibiting action of the sympathetic and parasympathetic divisions of the autonomic nervous system.

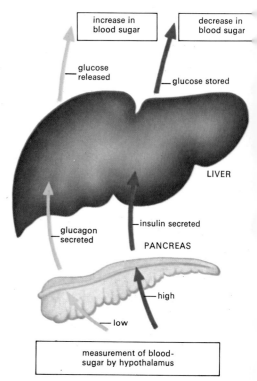

| increase in blood sugar | | decrease in blood sugar |

glucose released

glucose stored

LIVER

glucagon secreted

insulin secreted

PANCREAS

high

low

measurement of blood-sugar by hypothalamus

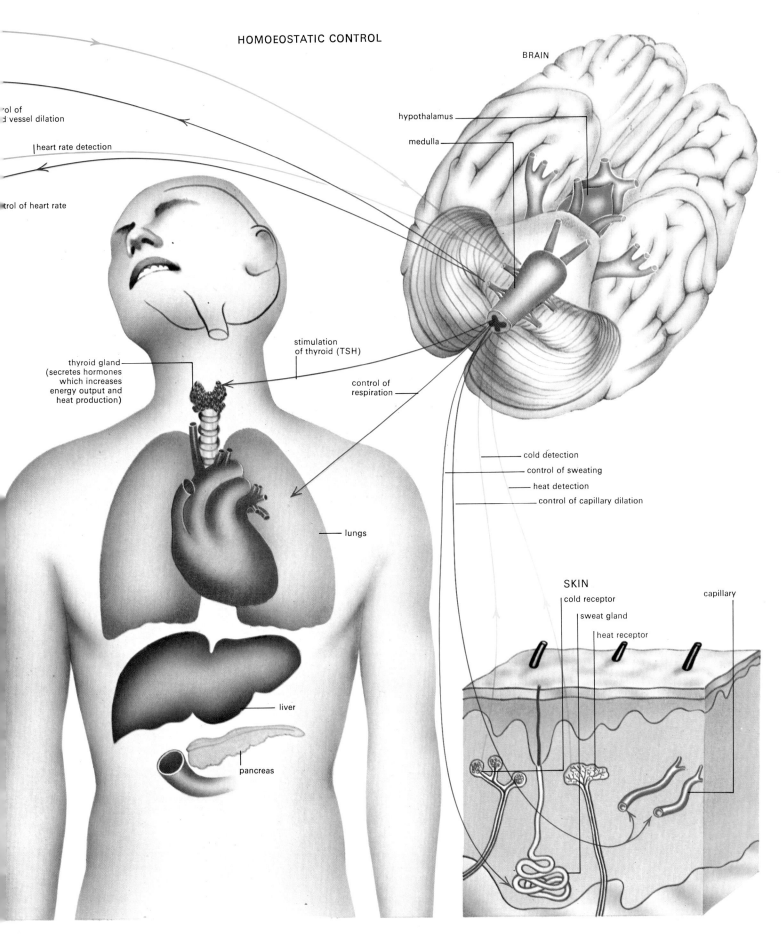

BRAIN

hypothalamus

medulla

rol of
d vessel dilation

heart rate detection

trol of heart rate

thyroid gland
(secretes hormones
which increases
energy output and
heat production)

stimulation
of thyroid (TSH)

control of
respiration

lungs

liver

pancreas

cold detection

control of sweating

heat detection

control of capillary dilation

SKIN

cold receptor

sweat gland

heat receptor

capillary

Above: Blood pressure is controlled by nervous feedback. When blood pressure is too high, for example, pressure receptors in the aorta—the main heart artery which carries oxygenated blood to the rest of the body—and the carotid artery (top left) supplying the brain, send 'messages' via the spinal nerves to the hypothalamus in the mid-brain. It then instructs the heart to slow down, decreasing blood volume rate, thereby lowering blood pressure. The hypothalamus also ensures that the body temperature is maintained at the normal level of 37°C (98.6°F) even when the external temperature rises. It relays signals via the autonomic nervous system to dilate the blood vessels, allowing more heat to be carried to the skin (see diagram right) to be cooled. The sweat glands are also activated so that water can be lost through sweating. When the water level falls, it can be corrected by the secretion of ADH. Heat loss also has to be cut down during cold weather. The hypothalamus sends instructions not only to reduce skin blood flow, but to step up heat level. The pituitary is directed to release TSH (thyroid stimulating hormone) which increases thyroxin, which speeds up the metabolic rate by breaking down glycogen stored in the liver (left) and muscles at a much faster rate and thereby providing more fuel for heat and energy. The sugar level is adjusted by the secretion of insulin and glucagon from the pancreas. Glucagon increases blood sugar level; insulin decreases it.

143

calcium ions because this concentration has been found to be altered when fever is induced in experimental animals. It is even more interesting that antipyretics—drugs like aspirin which reduce fever—bring the altered concentration back to normal.

Whatever the basis for a set temperature of 37°C in humans, the hypothalamus normally ensures that it does not vary much. Even in fever, the hypothalamus still seems to regulate temperature quite finely round a fixed point—but it is as though this point is set higher.

When the external temperature rises, the hypothalamus sends messages via the autonomic nervous system to the sweat glands. Through sweating, water is lost and this loss is made good by the water-monitoring system. At the same time, signals are relayed—again by the autonomic nervous system—to the pre-capillary valves of the skin. These valves open up allowing more blood to be carried to the body surface to lose heat.

When the external temperature drops, the hypothalamus directs the autonomic nervous system to raise the body hair. In humans this is ineffective as a means of conserving heat and merely results in 'goose pimples'; but in animals, the erect hair traps an insulating layer of air next to the skin. In cold weather, the autonomic nervous system also restricts the blood flow to the skin capillaries and so succeeds in reducing the amount of heat lost. A drop in the blood supply to the skin also means there is more blood available to carry oxygen and fuel to the inner parts of the body. This extra fuel is needed because the metabolism speeds up in cold weather to produce more energy.

Increased metabolic rate is under hormonal control. As well as instructing the autonomic nervous system to cut down on heat loss immediately, the hypothalamus also sends out signals to the pituitary to step up heat production. The pituitary produces TSH (thyroid stimulating hormone) which increases the production of thyroid hormone from the thyroid gland in the neck. This, in turn,

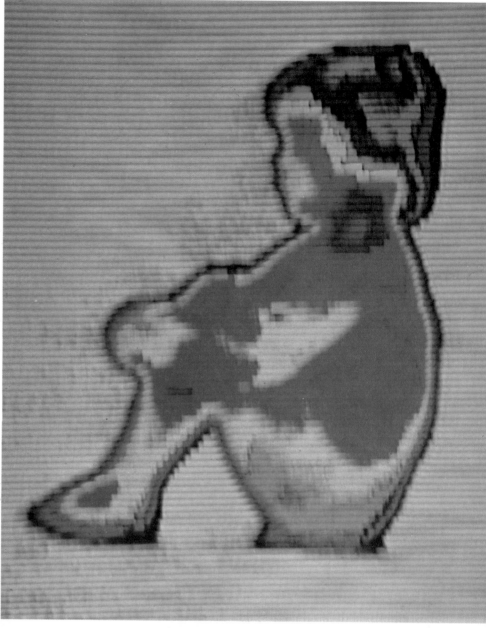

Howard Sochurek/John Hillelson Agency

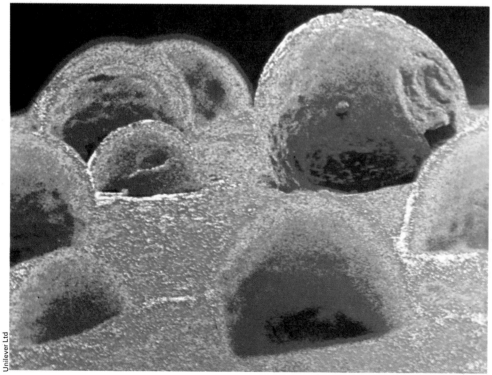

Unilever Ltd

144

Above: Thermograph of a child sitting on a cold floor. The surface temperature has dropped and if exposure to cold is prolonged, the child will start shivering as a result of signals sent by the skin receptors to the hypothalamus which will activate the muscles to generate heat. The blood vessels also receive signals to constrict, reducing blood flow through the skin, preventing heat loss through radiation.

Left: Scanning electron-microscope picture (magnified x 900) of sweat droplets on the surface of the thumb. When the humidity of the air is high, the body sweats to regulate the temperature, in the usual way, but the sweat cannot evaporate into the air which is already saturated with moisture and so it merely accumulates on the skin.

Right: Section of the anterior lobe of the pituitary. The blue cells produce a hormone which regulates blood sugar. The red areas secrete TSH and ACTH to regulate the thyroid and adrenals, so altering metabolic rate as the temperature changes.

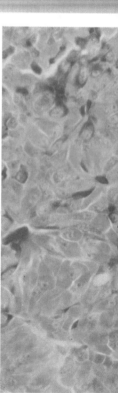

Biophoto Associates

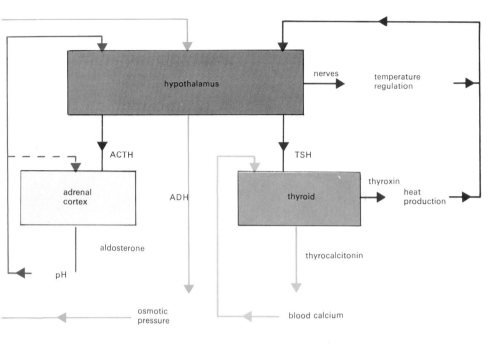

Above: Diagram of the principal mechanisms of homoeostasis governed by the hypothalamus. Although every part of the human body from the cell onwards is capable of individually maintaining constant conditions despite external changes, overall control is nevertheless essential to ensure that the body works as an integrated whole.

Right: African Bushmen are able to cope with the extreme temperature changes of the Kalahari Desert. The hypothalamus keeps blood vessels constricted to prevent heat loss during the icy winter nights and dilated during the scorching days to keep blood flow near the skin's surface from which heat can radiate.

increases the metabolic rate.

The way thyroid hormone works is not clear. It appears to produce an increase in protein synthesis and so probably makes more enzymes for use in the energy-releasing steps of metabolism—principally those in the mitochondria, the 'power-houses' of the cell.

Another hormone, called adrenalin, is also released in response to cold, as a direct action of the autonomic nervous system on the adrenal glands, lying just above the kidneys. Adrenalin increases the breakdown of glycogen (stored in the liver and muscles) to glucose, so giving more fuel for energy and heat production. Adrenalin also frees fatty acids—an even better fuel than glucose—from fat stores.

The body obviously has a tremendous capacity for producing and preserving its heat. In cold weather, however, body temperature may still fall. Death follows if it gets as low as about 26°. This often fatal drop in body temperature is called *hypothermia* and usually affects only the very old and the very young. Old people may fail to make the correct adjustment because they do not eat enough, or because they do not feel cold and therefore do not take proper measures to keep themselves warm with extra clothing and food.

Calcium balance and hormonal control

Almost all the calcium in the body, more than 99 per cent, is in the bones and teeth. The remaining one per cent, in the blood and other body fluids, is vitally important in blood coagulation, for the action of the heart and muscles and in controlling the permeability of membranes—not least those of the nervous system.

Bones may appear to be fairly static metabolically, but, in fact, they are constantly being renewed, even if very slowly. The concentration of calcium in the body fluids can do its job properly only if kept within very narrow limits. Some control is needed, therefore, to make sure that, despite wide variations in calcium intake (with food) and its removal and laying down in bones, blood levels do not fluctuate wildly.

This control is largely exerted by the parathyroid hormone, secreted by the parathyroid gland which lies near the thyroid in the neck. Parathyroid hormone increases the output of calcium from the bones into the blood, and it affects the kidney so that more calcium is reabsorbed. Thyrocalcitonin, another hormone, on the other hand, secreted by the thyroid gland, works in the opposite direction to parathyroid hormone by making bones take up calcium and by increasing calcium excretion by the kidneys.

Not only does the kidney help maintain the right levels of body water and of calcium, but it has a similar role in maintaining levels of other ions and in keeping the correct acid-base balance of the blood. Acids produced by metabolism are filtered out by the kidney, the hydrogen ions removed and the rest of the molecule reabsorbed through the kidney tubule. The hydrogen ions are eventually excreted in the form of soluble ammonium salts.

Each individual cell in the body is perfectly capable of self-regulation, but the human organism nevertheless requires specialized control mechanisms to allow it to work as the integrated whole that it actually is.

Brian Brake/John Hillelson

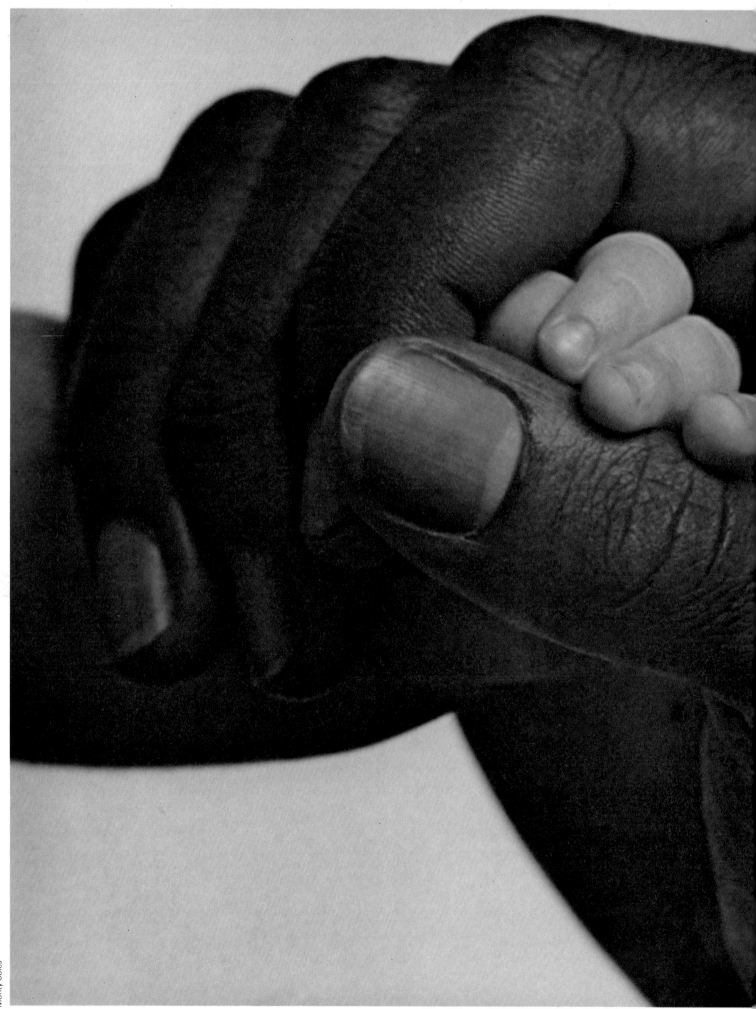

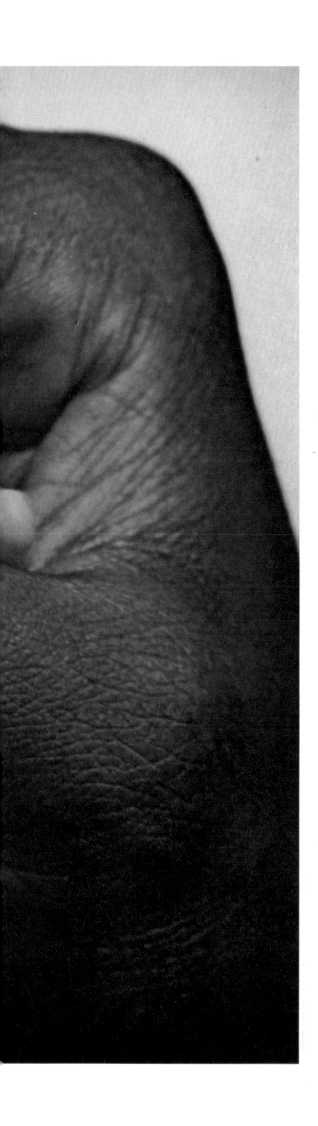

Chapter 6
The External Coverings

The skin's pigmentation is determined by *melanin*. In fair skinned races *melanin* appears in the first two skin layers, and is found in all skin layers of peoples originating in tropical climates.

Skin

The skin is rightly described as the largest functional organ of the human body, since it covers an area of 1.5 to 2 square metres in an average adult person. Throughout life, the skin has a wide variety of tasks to perform in protecting the internal environment of the human body from the ravaging effects of the outer environment and in maintaining communication between the two.

The evolution of skin

During the course of evolution, this outer covering developed to protect the organs engaged in the basic tasks of survival—ingesting food, respiration and excretion of waste products. Since these inter-actions were no longer taking place on the surface because of increasing complexity—the elongation and convolution of the digestive tract, for example—less and less of the outer area was in direct contact with these processes and the outer layers of the body, like other organs, became specialized. Although responsible for a number of other activities, the skin is primarily involved in protection and communication and the two principal layers, the *epidermis* and *dermis*, are specifically adapted to carry out these tasks.

The skin layers

The *epidermis* is the outer layer of skin and is itself made up of some five layers of cells. The innermost layer of the epidermis, the *stratum basale*, or basal layer, of cells, formed in a column-like structure, is continually dividing and pushing toward the surface, during which time the nuclei degenerate and the cells die. This forms the outermost *stratum corneum*. This layer, 25 to 30 dead cells deep, contains an insoluble, indigestible protein called *keratin*, which is the main component of hair and nails. Keratin production varies throughout the body: it is much thicker, for example, on the palms and soles of the feet where pressure and friction is greater. This is what forms the *stratum lucidum*, a fifth layer, which is seen only in these thickened areas. The cells of this layer contain *eleidin*, a clear or 'lucid' substance formed from *keratohyaline* from which keratin is produced.

The keratin lies in a loose, basket-weave pattern allowing great mobility (particularly on the bodies of animals, where it forms scales) but nevertheless preventing the entry of bacteria, the absorption of water from outside or the loss of body water through evaporation.

Just above the innermost layer of the epidermis, the *stratum spinosum* (prickly layer) is formed from 8 to 10 rows of polygonal (many-sided) cells which have a prickly appearance. Like the stratum basale, this layer contains the pigment, *melanin*, which forms granules. These are gradually broken down as they are carried towards the surface with the basal cells and are finally shed with the keratin. Melanin protects the skin from excessive exposure to ultra-violet radiation: the light energy is absorbed by the melanin, the pigment becomes oxidized and therefore darker. This is what produces a 'sun-tan' when skin is exposed to the sun only for short periods. If the epidermal cells are damaged by excessive exposure, the melanocytes are stimulated to produce more melanin and thus a darker tan.

Melanin appears in the first two layers in the fair skin of northern peoples and in all the epidermal layers of the dark skin of peoples originating from tropical climates. Some oriental peoples, such as the Chinese, have an additional pigment called *carotene* in the corneum and the dermis giving the skin its characteristic yellow colour.

The third layer of the epidermis is formed from two or three layers of cells which are the source of keratin production. These cells contain granules of keratohyaline which give this layer its name, *stratum granulosum*. The epidermis is always busy rebuilding its cast off layers—this is an important factor in healing after disease or injury or in regrowing if transplanted to a new site in a skin graft. The epidermis is purely cellular. Nourishment of the five layers is provided by tissue fluids diffusing up from the spaces among the cells of the dermis, the area below.

The dermis is more active than the epidermis since it contains the skin's means of nourishment, communication and temperature control. The dermis has two layers, the upper one of which is rich in blood vessels that weave in and out of the tough *collagen* and *elastin* connective tissue. Collagen is formed from bundles of fibrous protein, in some of which the protein elastin, which gives the skin its elasticity, is present. The spaces between the bundles are thought to be filled with a watery substance. This upper layer is known as the *papillary layer* because its surface area is greatly increased by *papillae*, small, finger-like projections similar to the villi in the small intestine. Since the layers of the epidermis are built on top of these projections, the outer layer is structured in a series of hollows surrounded by ridges, known as the *epidermal* ridges, which change the outer appearance of the skin. These are what provide the easily recognizable differences between individuals in the patterns called fingerprints.

Above: The skin has to withstand a lifetime of wear and tear not least of which is the process of ageing. Although the epidermal, the outer, layers are constantly being shed and replaced from the inner dermis, the dermis itself gradually deteriorates. By the early 50s, the absence of the hormone oestrogen reduces the skin's bloom; elastin, the protein which gives the skin its elasticity, wastes away by the age of 60, and by the age of 70, the activity of the sweat glands is considerably reduced, probably due to the narrowing of the blood vessels. But despite these changes the skin retains its marks of individuality.

Dennis Stock/Magnum

John Watney

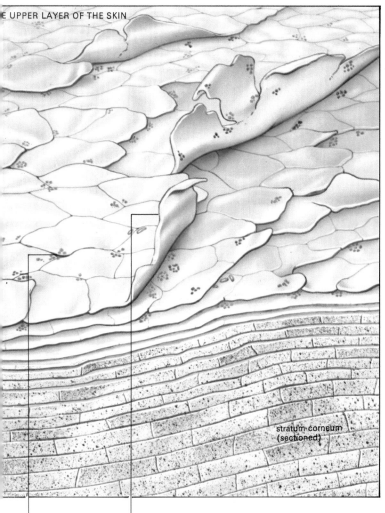

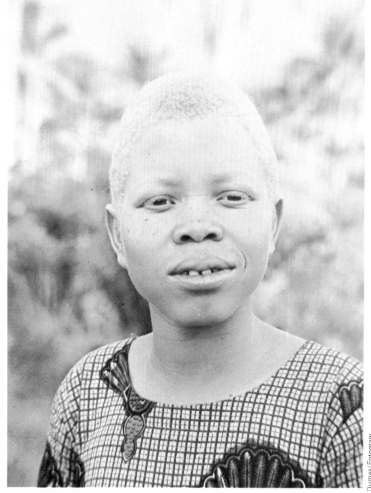

bacteria
living on
the surface

flat dead cells
containing keratin,
continually
peel off

stratum corneum
(sectioned)

Below left: Fingerprints, the most distinctive characteristics of the skin, are formed by layers of cells built on tiny projections called papillae. The outermost layer is structured in a series of hollows and ridges, which are profusely covered with sweat, leaving impressions on all objects they touch.

Above right: Albinos are extremely sensitive

Above: Diagram to illustrate a section of the epidermis, the outer layer of the skin. The constant shedding of dead cells allows bacteria to penetrate under the surface where they feed off the oily sebum secreted by the sebaceous glands.

to ultra-violet rays as they are born with a deficiency of the melanin pigment which normally provides a protective coat in the epidermal layers of the skin.

Below: Skin section stained to show blood vessel supply (pink) and the elastic fibres (red) in the two layers of the dermis.

Communication and protection

Capillary blood vessels loop in and out of the papillae. Together with the arterial supply and venous drainage network, they provide a certain amount of control over heat loss and retention by altering the flow of blood to the skin. They also facilitate the healing process by ensuring a prompt supply of nourishment since the blood transports a variety of nutrients: fatty acids, glucose, amino-acids and various types of salts. There are some nerve endings present in this layer which are receptive to touch (Meissner's corpuscles), pressure (Pacinian corpuscles) pain and temperature. They communicate the presence of potential danger in hot, cold, heavy or sharp objects, by transmitting signals to the brain via the spinal nerves. The muscles are then directed, via the transmission of impulses from the brain, to remove the endangered body area—a hand from extremely hot water, for example—instantly.

Below the papillary layer of the dermis lies the *reticular region*. This also contains collagenous and elastic fibres and blood vessels, but the spaces in between the bundles are occupied by the accessory organs: sweat glands, hair follicles and sebaceous glands. The reticular region is joined to the skeleton and muscles by the *subcutaneous layer*, throughout which fat cells, collected together to form *adipose tissue*, provide a cushioning layer. The adipose tissue not only acts as an emergency fuel store, but insulates the body from the cold by preventing heat loss.

Further protection is provided by the *sebum*, an oily substance secreted by the *sebaceous glands*. The sebum constantly flows along the ducts which connect it 149

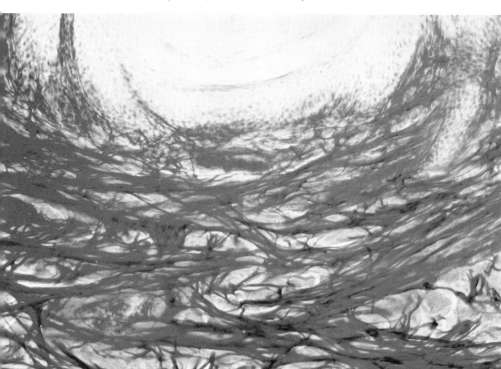

Dumas/Fotogram

John Watney

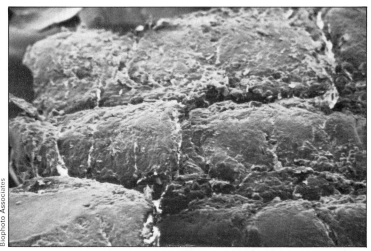

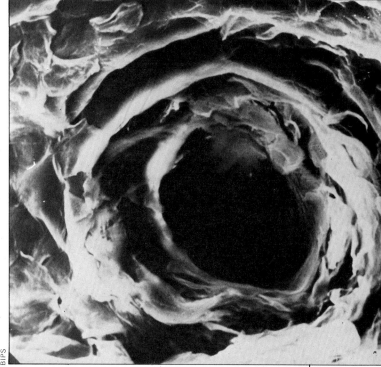

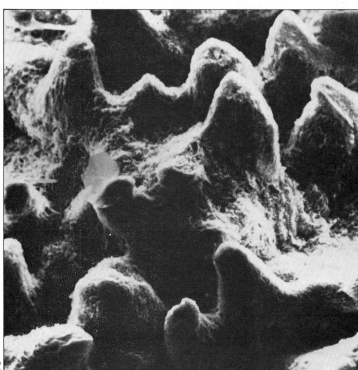

Above: A sweat pore magnified x 150. Sweat glands develop in the embryo as tubular downgrowths of the epidermis, ending in a spiral in the dermis from which the sweat is actually produced. Millions of these ducts open out as pores on the surface of the skin—they are more numerous in some areas: the palms, for example, have 350 per sq cm, while the backs of the hands have 200. Sweat glands can pour out as much as 1,500 millilitres of sweat in an hour which can enable the body to lose nearly 1,000 calories of body heat.

A SECTION THROUGH THE SKIN

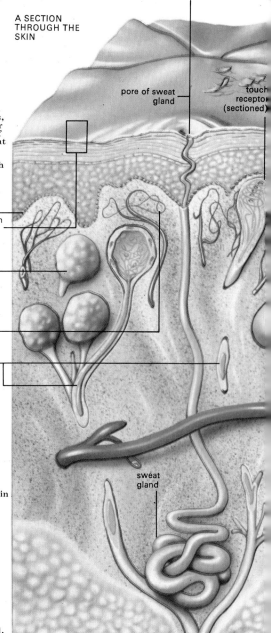

pore of sweat gland

touch receptor (sectioned)

see enlarged section (on previous page)

cold receptor (external view)

nerve fibres

sweat gland

Top left: Electron-micrograph of the outer layer of the skin magnified x 90. It shows the epidermal ridges, or fingerprints, formed by the papillary projections in the upper region of the dermis.

Above left: Electron micrograph of papillae, tiny projections in the outermost layer of the dermis which gives the outer layer its uneven, ridged surface.

Left: An electron-micrograph of the dermis, the inner layer of the skin, magnified x 2,200. It shows the disc-like red blood cells, the spiky platelets which form to seal damaged areas, and the collagen, connective fibres, in the background.

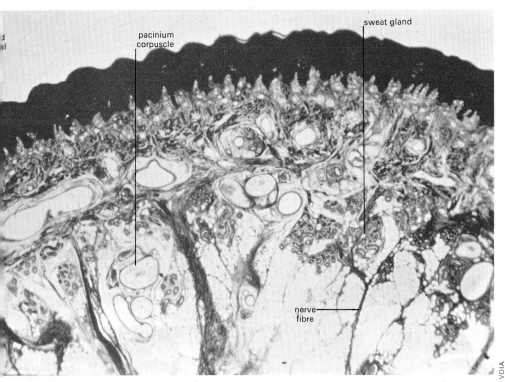

pacinium
corpuscle

sweat gland

nerve
fibre

VDIA

Above: Section of the skin stained red to show the epidermal and dermal layers clearly. The serrated effect of the outer, cornified layer can be distinctly seen to be made by the papillae.

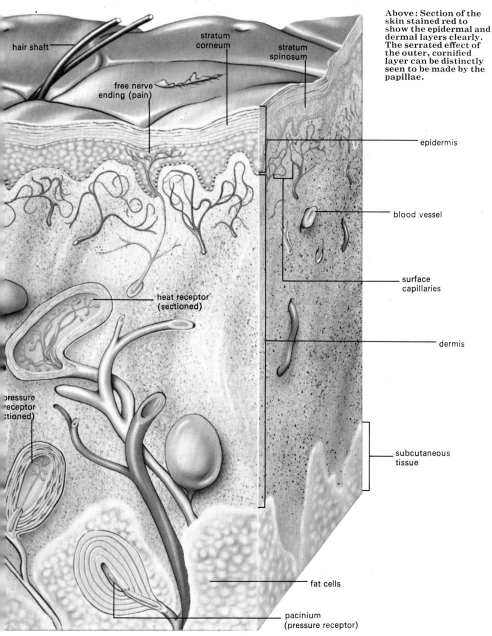

hair shaft

stratum
corneum

stratum
spinosum

free nerve
ending (pain)

epidermis

blood vessel

surface
capillaries

heat receptor
(sectioned)

dermis

pressure
receptor
sectioned)

subcutaneous
tissue

fat cells

pacinium
(pressure receptor)

with the dip in the epidermis known as the *follicle* (little bag) in which each hair is rooted. Sebum is described as a *holocrine* type of secretion as the cells of the gland itself are broken down and form part of the secretion. After lubricating the hair in the follicle, the sebum flows over the skin surface, mixing with the outer keratin layers and so helping to protect against physical damage. The sebum also provides the first line of defence against invasion by bacteria as it is slightly antiseptic.

The secretion of sebum is particularly important in tropical climates where the surface layer is constantly being dried out and rubbed off. Without this slightly greasy protective lubricant, the skin would not be able to withstand daily wear and tear and the natural moisture of the skin would be lost, constantly endangering the body through dehydration.

Temperature regulation

The reticular region of the skin also contains the sweat glands which are vital to the regulation of body temperature. Unlike the sebaceous glands, the sweat glands are true or *eccrine* glands since the secreting cells do not form part of the secretion. The clear watery fluid known as sweat is produced by the cells lining the lower portion of a coiled tube embedded in the dermis. It flows along a straight duct which becomes spiralled (to control the amount of secretion) as it penetrates the epidermis before opening into a pore on the surface of the skin. Sweating enables the body to lose excess heat as the moisture evaporates into the atmosphere. Sweat glands are distributed throughout the body, particularly on the soles of the feet and palms, in the armpits and on the forehead. Another set of glands, the *apocrine glands*, similar to the sweat glands, are also present in the dermal layer. They are only found, however, in special sites related to the sexual areas—on the pubis, around the genitalia, in the axillae (armpits) and around the nipples. Like the sebaceous glands, the apocrine gland pours its secretion into the hair follicle rather than directly onto the surface of the skin.

The feedback system

Control of body temperature is very finely balanced in all warm-blooded mammals. This remarkable ability to maintain the internal environment of the human body at a constant 37°C (98.6°F) relies on a complex and delicate feedback system involving skin receptors, nerves, control centres in the brain and sweat glands.

A rise in external temperature is sensed by the specialized nerve endings in the skin, which relay the message to the hypothalamus, the temperature-regulating area of the brain. The brain sends nerve impulses to the sweat glands stimulating them to release sweat until the skin receptors detect that the skin temperature has returned to normal. They inform the brain accordingly and it ceases its messages to the sweat glands.

These adjustments to changes in the outer environment could not be made without the specialized organ we know of as skin. Without its protection we could not survive dehydration, abrasion or bacterial invasion encountered in daily activities in temperate climates, let alone survive the extreme conditions of desert or arctic regions.

151

Hair and Nails

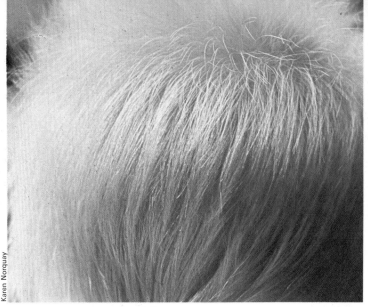

Both our hair and our nails are essentially waste products. They are made by specialized cells but, because of our evolutionary development, they are no longer needed to carry out specialized tasks. Our nails were once used as claws and were particularly useful in grubbing for food. The function of the luxurious covering of hair possessed by our ancestors was to trap tiny pockets of warm air around the body, thereby conserving heat.

Although we have now discarded this thick coat of hair, it still grows strongly in one or two places, notably on the head, under the armpits and around the genital areas. Most of the human body is, in fact, still covered with hair, although it is mainly very fine. The only parts which are now entirely hairless are the lips, the nipples, the palms of the hands, the fingers from the second joint to the tip, the penis, and the soles of the feet.

Despite its decrease, the hair does still perform some useful functions. For instance, it protects the head from the harmful effects of the sun's rays. Certain brain proteins are particularly susceptible to heat and excessive exposure to the sun will affect the brain and cause sunstroke. The even, wool-like growth of hair covering the heads of African people is especially effective in this respect. In addition, the hair of the brows and lashes protects the eyes, and hair in the nostrils and the external ear filters out large dust particles to stop them entering the body.

One protective, but now ineffectual, device is still retained from the days when thick hair covered the human body. It can be compared with a parallel reaction in animals. In response to cold, the fur of animals puffs out, creating a thicker, more insulating layer; this also occurs in response to fright, as can be seen when a cat's fur stands on end. (The intention is presumably to make the animal, in a confrontation, look larger and more terrifying.)

In humans, under the stresses of cold or fright, the arrectores pilorum muscles lying near the surface of the skin, can tighten the skin and pull the hairs into a vertical position. This results in gooseflesh because of elevations of the skin around each hair.

The first growth of hair occurs while a baby is still in the womb and is a down-like covering of very fine hair called *lanugo*. By the time the baby is born, this has usually disappeared, although it may sometimes be seen in premature babies. Lanugo is replaced by stronger, though still soft, hair called *vellus* which normally has no colouring pigment and seldom grows much longer than 2.5 centimetres (1 inch). This then gradually begins to thicken and coarsen into the type of hair which will last through adult life, and it is at this stage that the hair takes on its true colour.

All hair growth does not, however, begin before and at birth, and later growth is largely associated with sexual development. At puberty, major changes in the sex hormones in both males and females stimulate the growth of hair under the armpits (*axillary hair*) and around the genital areas (*pubic hair*). In the later teens, males also begin to grow hair along

Karen Norquay

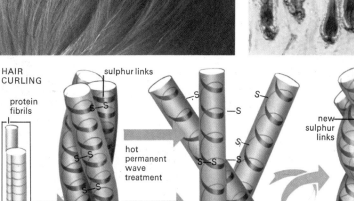

Above: The fine hair of an infant. Hair is essentially a waste product which in later life may serve the purpose of sexual attraction as much as any practical function like conserving heat.

Right: Hair is made up of twisting protein chains coiled round each other and linked together. *Denaturation*, by permanent waving, destroys the structure of the protein chains in hair. (A) shows normal coiled protein fibrils; (B) fibrils separated; (C) fibrils recoiled.

HAIR CURLING

sulphur links

protein fibrils

hot permanent wave treatment

cold-wave treatment

hair curled around roller

new sulphur links

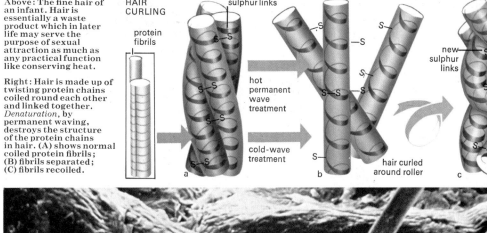

Patrick Thurston/Daily Telegraph Colour Library

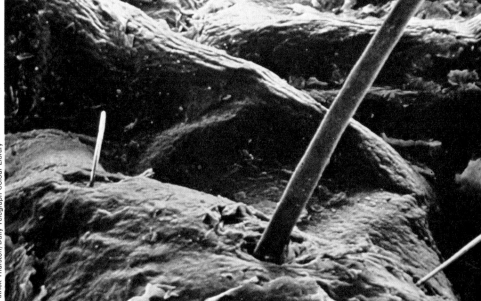

Above: A magnification of a hair in a man's beard. Beard growth is a sexual characteristic, and scientific tests suggest that sexual activity, anxiety and mental fatigue may accelerate such growth.

Right: Each hair is covered with overlapping scales of keratin. Our reptilian ancestors adapted the keratin in the epidermis to form a protective coating of scales, and the scale has continued in specialized form on birds' legs and in the human nail. The hair of mammals and the feathers of birds also developed the scale, making it looser and so more able to trap warm air round the body and insulate it.

Biophoto Associates

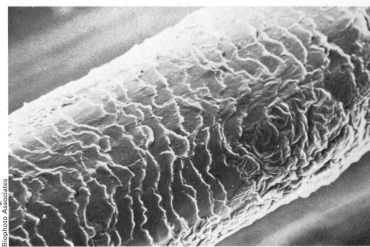

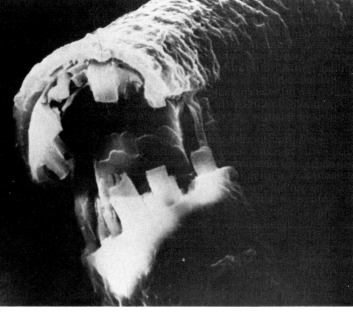

Left: A cross-section of the skin, showing hairs growing out of the follicles embedded in the dermis. See diagram below.

Right: The picture shows a broken hair, which can result both from over-washing and from over-brushing. Too frequent washing removes the film of sebum, the oily secretion from the sebaceous gland, which lubricates each hair and keeps it from drying out and becoming brittle. While occasional brushing is beneficial to stop the hair becoming matted, too vigorous brushing can knock the keratin scales off the hair, which will then split or break more easily, leaving the hair vulnerable to invasion by bacteria.

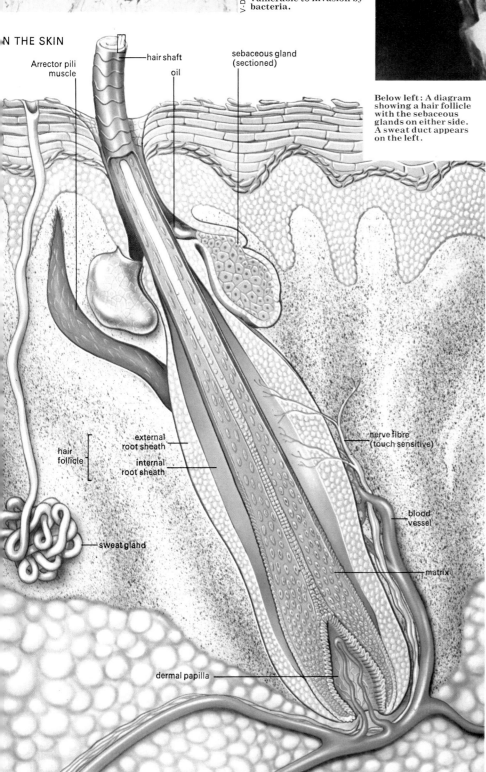

N THE SKIN

Arrector pili muscle

hair shaft

oil

sebaceous gland (sectioned)

external root sheath

internal root sheath

hair follicle

sweat gland

nerve fibre (touch sensitive)

blood vessel

matrix

dermal papilla

Below left: A diagram showing a hair follicle with the sebaceous glands on either side. A sweat duct appears on the left.

the cheeks, under the chin and on the upper lip, and also to develop longer hairs on the chest and shoulders. Since these features do not serve any vital purpose (although hair around the mouth may provide some protection for it), they are generally classified as secondary sexual characteristics, which distinguish the male from the female.

Hair growth

Each of us possesses between 100,000 to 200,000 hairs on our heads, which grow at the rate of about 1.25 centimetres ($\frac{1}{2}$ inch) a month. All hair grows out of the *hair follicles*, specialized pockets in the skin. These are actually cells from the upper skin layer—the epidermis—which have penetrated back into the lower layer, the dermis. The number and distribution of the follicles, and therefore the thickness of the hair, is a matter of heredity, being determined by our genes. All the follicles are established when in the womb, between the second and fifth months of pregnancy. Hair colour is genetically determined too, although a child does not necessarily inherit the hair colour of its parents: it could be a throwback from several generations.

One further aspect of hair is also determined by heredity: whether it will be curly, wavy or straight. This depends on the cross-sectional shape of the hair which is in turn dependent on the cross section of the follicle. Round hairs grow straight while oval or flattened follicles produce curly or wavy hair. There are broad differences in follicle shape between ethnic groups. Races such as the Chinese, the Mongolians and the North American Indians tend to have coarse, straight hair almost circular in cross section, and almost always black in colour. Most of the negroid races have short, crisp wool-like hair with an elliptical or kidney-shaped cross section, again invariably black. European hair tends to be silkier and to be wavy or curly, due to its oval cross-section, and although fair colours predominate there is a wide variety from light blonde through flaming red to deepest black.

The structure of hair

Hair is composed of a number of parts. The lower end of each follicle is enlarged

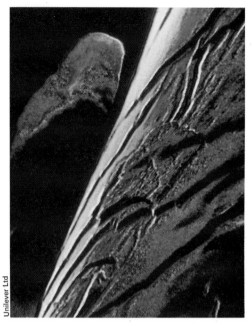

to form a bulbous shape which holds the *papilla*, a section of loose connective tissue. The papilla is richly supplied with dendrites, branch-like nerve endings, and with blood vessels which nourish the growing hair. The hair itself is actually formed by the division of cells in the *matrix*, a region of cells around the papilla. The basic material of which hair is comprised is a tough protein called *keratin*, produced in the fluid layer of the epidermis from a granular substance called keratohyaline. The centre of most hairs is hollow although some have a central pith of softer cells. The outer surface is covered with overlapping scales of keratin.

From the matrix, the hair moves as a shaft towards the skin's surface. Curiously, when it begins to grow it moves downwards in the follicle but after a few days the confined space forces it upwards. By the time the hair reaches the surface of the skin the cells comprising it are dead.

Hair does not grow continuously out of

each follicle: there is a distinct pattern of activity. First, there is the active phase with the hair steadily pushing itself out of the follicle, which usually lasts for between two and four years. Then there is a period of withering, lasting a few weeks, after which the hair falls out. The follicle may then be dormant for three or four months before hair growth begins again. As each hair has its own life cycle, independent of its neighbours, hair is actually being shed all the time, at an average daily rate of between 40 and 100 hairs. Similarly, some hairs are always being replaced, so, in general, the thickness of the hair remains fairly constant.

The rate at which hair grows varies from person to person, as it does from one part of the body to another. The average rate for hair on the head is about 15 centimetres (six inches) a year, and since the active period is usually only up to four years it is difficult for the average person to grow tresses more than a few feet long.

Both skin and hair are kept supple by a substance known as *sebum*, a mixture of fats, cholesterol, proteins, and inorganic salts. Sebum is secreted by the sebaceous (grease) glands, which lie at the side of each follicle, and are connected to the latter by short ducts. The glands vary in size and shape in different parts of the body, and are absent in the palms of the hands and the soles of the feet.

Hair loss

Just as increased growth of hair in adolescence is more a male concern, so loss of hair is also predominantly a male problem. Women rarely go bald. Some thinning of the hair may occur after the menopause, however, and excessive hair loss may also be experienced after giving birth. During pregnancy, changes in hormone levels cause the hair to grow luxuriantly, but after the birth the follicles become dormant and hair loss reaches as much as tens of thousands of hairs per week. Within six months, however, the follicles regain their rhythm.

Baldness in men is dependent both on a hereditary predisposition in each man, and on an overproduction of *androgens*, the group of male sex hormones.

Alopecia areata is a form of nervous illness characterized by sudden loss of hair in patches. In *alopecia universalis* all body hair is lost and in *alopecia totalis* all hair on the head including eyelashes and eyebrows.

The nails

Like the hair, the nails are made of keratin and are simply adaptations of the skin's outer layer. They consist of four parts. The first is the outermost layer of the epidermis which protrudes a short way above the nail and is known as the scarf nail or the cuticle. The nails themselves are formed by a specially thickened and so more protective layer of keratin, which exists only in those parts of the body where pressure and friction is greatest, such as the soles of the feet.

Below the nails lies a white granular layer made up of a different cell. It ends abruptly just above the point where the nail emerges, and can be seen in the white, semi-circular section at the base of each nail, known as the lunule or half-moon. Finally a layer composed, unlike the others, of living cells forms the nail bed or quick of the nail. It takes about six months for the nail to grow out from its base to the fingertip.

Above: A hair magnified and colour-coded according to brightness—light areas are shown as orange and dark areas as dark green and black—so that contours and dimensions can be more readily seen. The cuticle cells are shown as black criss-crossed lines and a particle of skin is attached to the left of the hair.

Below: A human hair with nits—the eggs of a louse. Several species of these insects are parasitic to man but they only flourish in unclean and overcrowded conditions. They transmit epidemic diseases such as typhus and the occupants of overcrowded public institutions are most susceptible.

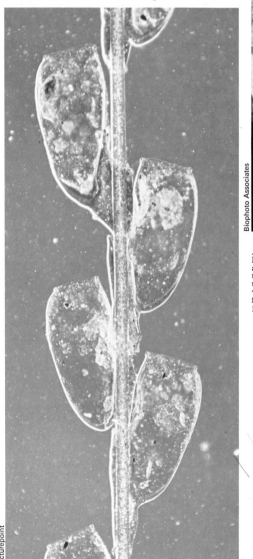

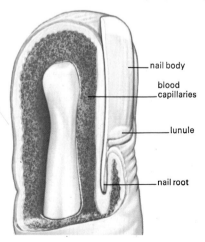

Above: Section of a human nail, viewed with a polarized light technique, in which all the light waves are vibrating at the same frequency so giving a prism effect under the electron-microscope. It shows the only layer of living cells which forms the quick or nail-bed.

Below: Diagram showing the layers which make up the nail.

SECTIONED FINGER TO SHOW THE NAIL

nail body

blood capillaries

lunule

nail root

Hair colour and texture are determined by heredity. Whether the hair is curly or straight, blond or dark, is a matter of genes. These are not necessarily derived from the parents but may be a throwback from previous generations.

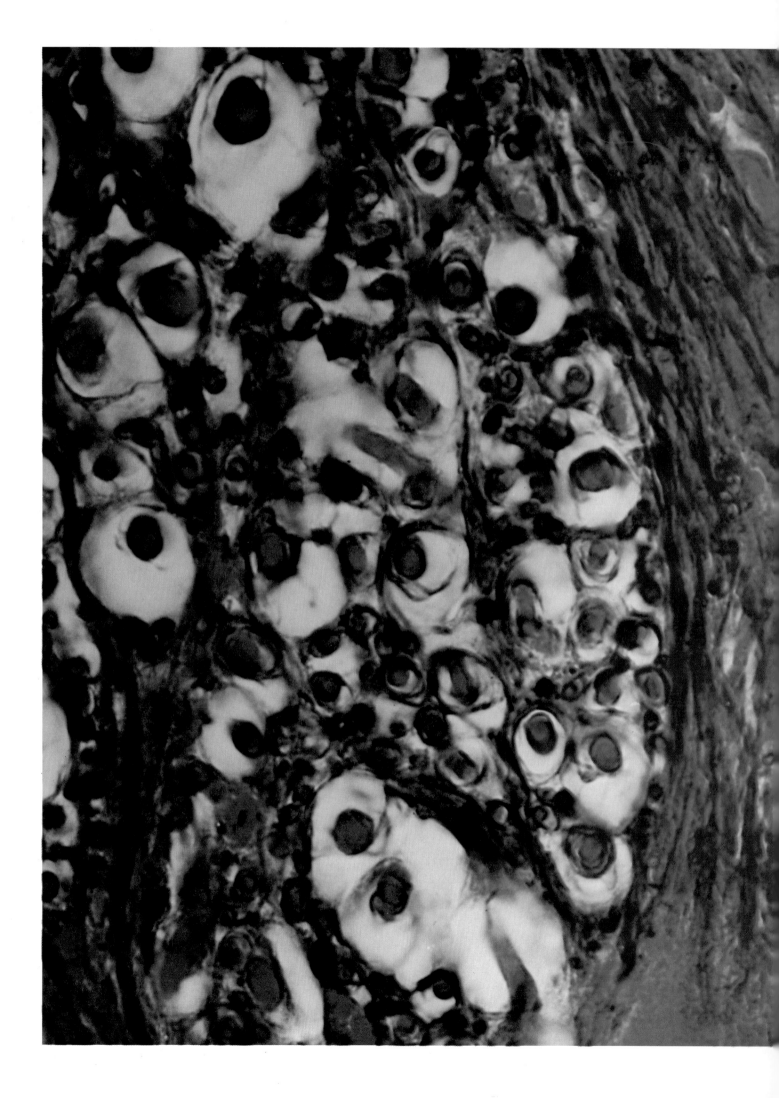

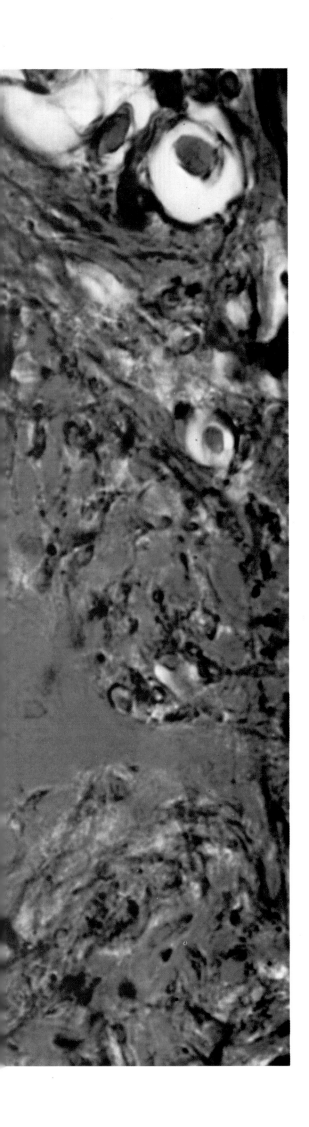

Chapter 7
How the Body Works

A motor *neurone,* or nerve cell, in the
spinal cord, magnified 350 times.
Motor nerve fibres conduct impulses
from the central nervous system to
the muscles in the head, neck, trunk
and limbs.

Body Chemistry

To understand what really makes the body tick it is necessary to look beyond the functioning of the organs and investigate what is happening inside the billions of individual body cells. Each of these is, in effect, a miniature factory where hundreds of life-sustaining chemical reactions are carried out simultaneously. Many of these biochemical reactions, such as the synthesis of proteins, are highly complex, requiring a high input of energy to bring them about. Others, such as the oxidation of glucose, release large amounts of energy.

Before looking more closely at these reactions, however, it may be helpful to know something about the body's chemical composition; by weight, it is about 70 per cent water and 30 per cent solids. These solids are mainly the well known organic compounds of living matter—proteins, lipids (fats), and carbohydrates together with their derivatives—and a relatively small proportion of inorganic compounds, for example sodium chloride (common salt) and calcium phosphate, the structural material of bones. Iron, magnesium, copper, cobalt, manganese and iodine occur only in trace amounts, but are nevertheless vital.

The energy factor

Like any machine the body needs energy to keep it working. This energy is required not only for muscular action but also for other essential body processes such as the maintenance of body temperature and the synthesis of complex molecules, such as proteins and fats. The total energy requirement of the body is made up of the individual needs of the billions of body cells, and this energy is derived from the food we eat. Just as a lump of coal is burnt to obtain energy in the form of heat, so too is the body's fuel, food, burnt or, in chemical terms, oxidized to obtain energy. Supplies of oxygen reach the cells via the circulating blood. The food, however, reaches the cells only after it has been broken down into relatively simple molecules by the digestive process—the proteins are broken down into amino acids, the carbohydrates into sugars, and the fats into glycerol and fatty acids. Only small molecules can pass through the intestinal walls (passing directly in the case of sugars and amino acids, and indirectly in the case of fats) into the bloodstream to be circulated throughout the body. Thus the cells are assured of a satisfactory supply of nutrients.

Biochemical reactions which break down complex molecules into simpler ones tend to be 'energy-producing' or *catabolic*, while the synthesis of complex molecules, for example, proteins, are 'energy-using' or *anabolic* reactions. Both types of reaction come under the umbrella of *metabolism*, which refers to the sum total of all chemical reactions in the body. It is therefore important that the cell strikes a balance between input and output of energy. Any excess energy produced is not frittered away but stored in a sort of energy bank in the form of the energy rich chemical compounds. *Adenosine triphosphate*, known universally as ATP, is the best known of these. This can be converted to *adenosine diphosphate* (ADP)

releasing the stored energy when required.

ATP tends to be made during the breakdown of glucose, amino acids and fatty acids. It is then put into service to yield the energy needed for muscular contraction, protein synthesis, and the transport of wanted substances through the cell membrane into the cell and unwanted substances out of it. Cell reactions overall, however, use more ATP than they create—for this reason we need to eat enough to replenish supplies.

Most of the cell's reactions are carried out in steps which are sometimes referred to as *metabolic pathways*. For example, glucose is oxidized to carbon dioxide and water in about 20 steps. This is necessary because so much energy is released, about 673,000 calories, that to oxidize glucose in one massive step would overheat and probably destroy the cell. (Living tissue is very sensitive to heat largely because the proteins in it become *denatured*—irreversibly changed by too much heat, as can be demonstrated by boiling an egg when the albumen, normally liquid, hardens into egg white).

Many of the complex cell reactions, such as the synthesis of large molecules of fats or proteins, remain unique to the living cell. Even with all his expertise and equipment, the chemist in his laboratory has failed to synthesize most of these compounds. And it is even more remarkable that the body's cells can do the job when we consider the rather bland conditions in which they must operate. For example, the cell must not be subjected to strong heat and is maintained at a neutral pH, that is neither acid nor alkaline. A chemist working in the laboratory would have the advantage of being able to use intense heat, and strong acids or alkalis to bring about a reaction. However, by using its high-energy tool, ATP, the cell brings about syntheses, effortlessly.

Enzymes for activation

Often chemical reactions need an activating agent or *catalyst* to make them proceed efficiently. In margarine production, for

Above: Vitamin A crystals. In the body vitamins act as co-enzymes, helping to bind an enzyme to the substance on which it acts, or removing one of the products of the reaction. The body does not manufacture vitamins.

Below: Lazzaro Spallanzani was one of the pioneers of research into the effects of digestion. In 1783 he experimented with a crow, feeding it meat then forcing it to vomit to study the action of digestive juices. He was one of the first to discover the importance of chemicals in the body and their role in breaking down food so that it could be absorbed.

Lazzaro Spallanzani

159

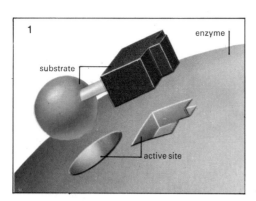

1

substrate

enzyme

active site

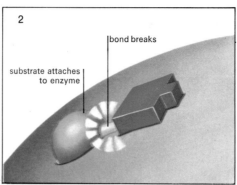

2

bond breaks

substrate attaches to enzyme

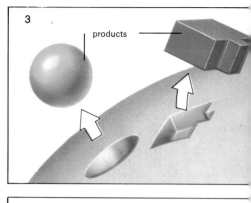

3

products

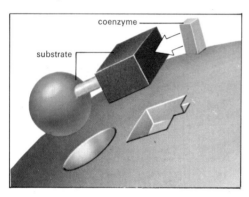

coenzyme

substrate

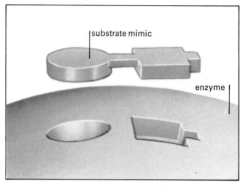

substrate mimic

enzyme

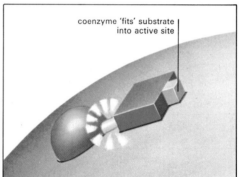

coenzyme 'fits' substrate into active site

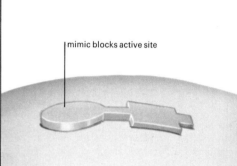

mimic blocks active site

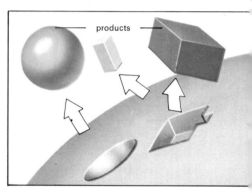

products

Above: This series of illustrations shows enzymes in action. (1) The enzyme and the substrate (the substance on which it acts) are shaped to allow them to fit together. They form a chemical complex (2) when the enzyme steers the substrate's electrons into new orbits, thereby making or breaking bonds between the molecules to produce new substances necessary to the body. These are then released (3) and the enzyme is again free to participate in new reactions in the digestion of food compounds.

Right: These two illustrations show enzyme inhibition which results from certain molecules having a similar shape to the substrate but dissimilar chemical components. They attach themselves to the enzyme, thus preventing any substrate attaching to it.

Below: Vitamins act as co-enzymes, in effect adapting the shape of a substrate to fit the enzyme. After the reaction the co-enzyme is released and is free to attach itself to another substrate.

example, a nickel catalyst is used to get more hydrogen atoms added to the oil molecules so that they become solid. Normally the reactants come together to form a temporary compound with the catalyst, which having done its job drops off to be used over and over again. Thus a catalyst promotes a reaction without itself being changed in the process—rather like oil on a rusty bearing.

This mechanism is widely used for biochemical reactions, and in the body the catalysts are called *enzymes*. For a long time enzyme action has been put to good use in winemaking where the natural sugar in the grape juice is converted to alcohol and carbon dioxide by enzymes present in the yeast on the grape skin. In fact, when the study of enzymes was begun seriously in the early twentieth century it was so related to yeast that the name itself was chosen from the Greek words meaning 'in yeast'.

The human body contains literally hundreds of different enzymes. Many are contained within the cells, but others, such as those used for the digestive process, act outside cells in the gut itself. Enzymes are involved in almost every chemical reaction taking place in the body. They are normally highly specific, promoting just one particular reaction. For example, the enzyme which breaks down sucrose into glucose and fructose, is called *sucrase*. (This ending *-ase* is often used for naming enzymes.)

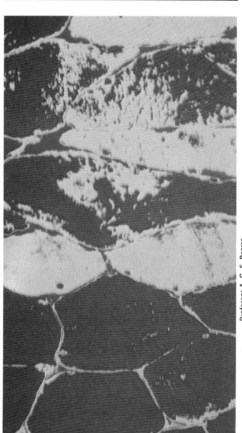

Professor A. G. E. Pearse

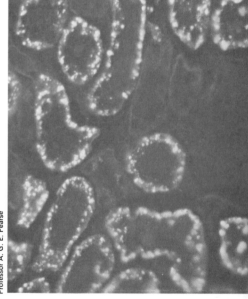

Professor A. G. E. Pearse

Above: This picture shows lysosomes (yellow) in the kidney. Lysosomes are bags of enzymes inside the cell which are capable of breaking down and destroying certain cell constituents.

Left: Distribution of the enzyme phosphorylase in muscle cells. Shown as yellow-green in colour, it acts as a catalyst in the

conversion of glycogen into glucose, one of the body's major sources of energy. Blood vessels are shown in red and other muscle as blue.

Right: A molecular model of the enzyme lysozyme. This is present in both saliva and tears and kills bacteria by breaking down their cell walls.

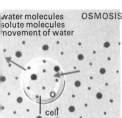

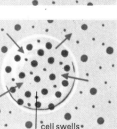

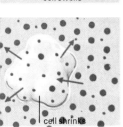

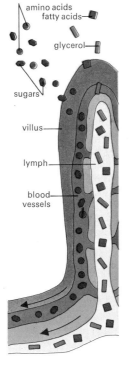

water molecules
solute molecules
movement of water

OSMOSIS

cell

cell swells

cell shrinks

amino acids
fatty acids

glycerol

sugars

villus

lymph

blood
vessels

Above: The process by which water moves into and out of a cell through the semi-permeable membrane is known as osmosis. The top picture shows a state of equilibrium in which the concentration of water molecules inside and outside the cell is equal. (The solute molecules are those dissolved in water). The second picture shows a higher concentration of water molecules outside the cell, thus water moves into the cell, causing it to swell and diluting the internal solution. The third picture shows the reverse: there is a greater concentration of water molecules inside the cell. As a result water moves out, causing the cell to shrink.

Above: Mustard gas, used in the First World War with terrible consequences, chemically alters certain cells in the body. A derivitive of the same gas is used to alter the genetic code in the treatment of some cases of diseases like leukemia.

Right: This illustration shows the diffusion of molecules from a higher concentration to a lower concentration. It plays an important role in the entry and distribution of molecules within the living cell.

Left: The action of enzymes during digestion produces small molecules which diffuse through the cells lining the villi surface. They then travel into blood or lymph vessels.

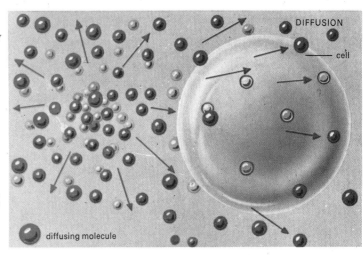

DIFFUSION

cell

diffusing molecule

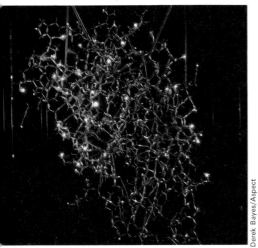

The activity or work rate of an enzyme depends both on the temperature, the pH (that is, the degree of acidity or alkalinity) and the amount of *substrate*—the substance upon which the enzyme acts. However, a small amount of enzyme goes a long way because it can be used again and again, often amazingly quickly. In a few seconds a single enzyme molecule may bring about the required changes on hundreds of molecules of the substrate.

Enzymes are themselves proteins and are therefore composed of amino acids strung together. Normally there is one part of the amino acid chain, known as the *active centre*, which interlocks readily with the substrate molecule. As soon as the substrate has formed its reaction products it no longer fits and so breaks away from the enzyme. Many enzymes are not solely protein, they include other substances which tailor the enzyme to fit the substrate, and without which the enzyme would be useless. Such substances are known as *coenzymes*, *activators* or *prosthetic groups*, and may be loosely or firmly attached to the enzyme. Frequently they contain metal *ions* (metal atoms which have been stripped of electrons and carry a positive charge as a result) such as manganese or magnesium. Often *vitamins* act as coenzymes; for example, biotin, one of the B vitamins, is used in reactions for transferring carbon dioxide. In fact, most of the B complex vitamins function as coenzymes.

Enzyme action can be blocked, either temporarily or permanently. Mercury, lead and arsenic, for example, poison us by affecting the activity of the enzyme. They bind to it at a site remote from the active centre, altering the conformation of the enzyme and making it unable to form an active complex with the substrate. Other chemicals poison us because they are structurally so similar to the enzyme's normal substrate that they can fool the enzyme, combine with it and so prevent the real substrate from reaching it. Normal metabolism is thus prevented.

Enzymes are classified according to the type of reaction involved. *Oxidases*, for example, bring about oxidation by adding oxygen, while *dehydrogenases* remove hydrogen from molecules to oxidize them. *Hydrolases* speed up the process of hydrolysis—the splitting of molecules by the addition of water molecules. Most of the digestive enzymes are in this particular category.

Monitoring systems

Although most biochemical reactions occur within cells, they cannot be isolated from the workings of the body as a whole. Cellular activity tends to alter the temperature, the composition and even the pH of a cell. As already mentioned these are factors that need to remain fairly constant, so there are systems which monitor conditions and make adjustments where necessary. The job of the lungs is to supply the necessary amounts of oxygen, remove carbon dioxide, a waste product of metabolism, and help to regulate the pH. The kidneys also help to control the pH and monitor the chemical composition of the blood. A steady supply of nutrients and water is supplied by the gut and the kidneys. Overall the entire network is monitored by the nervous system and the endocrine glands, which release hormones to keep certain events under control.

The Body's Fuels

The main function of the *carbohydrate* and *fat* we eat is to fuel all the body processes which require energy.

Much of our dietary carbohydrate is converted to fat, which is a far more efficient fuel, yielding over twice as much energy for the same weight. But carbohydrate is still needed because its main product, *glucose*, is the only form of energy that the brain can use.

Some of the energy released from the metabolism of carbohydrates and fats will be given off directly as heat and this is necessary to maintain the body's temperature. However, a considerable amount of energy is harnessed in the form of the chemical *ATP* (adenosine triphosphate) which is stored in the cells. It can then be used to drive processes needing an energy input—such as the synthesis of the body's structural components, or muscular contraction. The carbohydrates and fats that are not needed immediately as fuel may be stored until they are incorporated more or less permanently into the tissues.

Carbohydrates, as well as being broken down to provide energy, are also important constituents of connective tissue, such as cartilage and bone. Lipids, together with proteins, form the membranes of cells and the organelles, structures inside the cell.

Apart from helping to form the basic structure of the body, fats and carbohydrates also protect it: carbohydrates lubricate joints, and fats act as thermal and electrical insulators.

The white matter of the brain and spinal cord is made of a substance called *myelin* which contains a high proportion of fat. This insulates the nerves and prevents the short-circuiting of nervous impulses. When the myelin sheath is lost, nerves

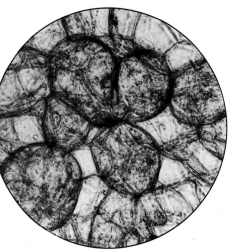

Biophoto Associates/Gordon Leedale

Biophoto Associates/Gordon Leedale

Left: A section of potato tissue magnified x 250. It shows the accumulation of the carbohydrate starch in some of the cells.

Below left: When the potato is boiled, the starch grains swell. In the body the starch is broken down into glucose to provide energy for many of the body's processes, such as muscular contraction.

Right: Part of the colon, or large intestine, which has been stained with a fluorescent dye. The dye has attached itself to the carbohydrates present in the mucus lining the colon, which is secreted to lubricate and protect the colon.

Below: A model of a cholesterol molecule. The hydrogen atoms are represented as white and the oxygen as red. Cholesterol is a lipid (fat), an essential component of most animal tissues.

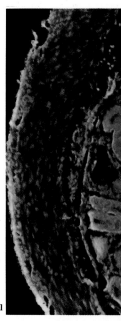

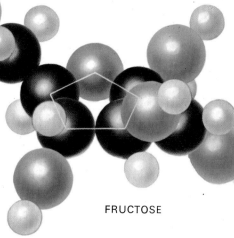

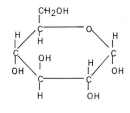

GLUCOSE

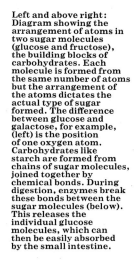

FRUCTOSE

Left and above right: Diagram showing the arrangement of atoms in two sugar molecules (glucose and fructose), the building blocks of carbohydrates. Each molecule is formed from the same number of atoms but the arrangement of the atoms dictates the actual type of sugar formed. The difference between glucose and galactose, for example, (left) is the position of one oxygen atom. Carbohydrates like starch are formed from chains of sugar molecules, joined together by chemical bonds. During digestion, enzymes break these bonds between the sugar molecules (below). This releases the individual glucose molecules, which can then be easily absorbed by the small intestine.

hydrogen

oxygen

carbon

changing these groups makes galactose

glucose molecules

STARCH

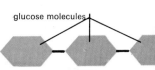

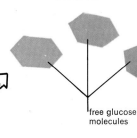

free glucose molecules

enzyme breaks bonds

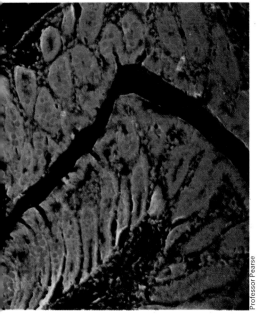

RUCTOSE

Below and below right:
Cross-section of a
normal coronary artery.
It conveys blood to
the heart muscles, the
red area below. The
yellow area shows normal
fat deposits. Cholesterol
deposits, (yellow area,
below right) present in
some diseases such as
arteriosclerosis, block
the arteries and prevent
the flow of blood.

can no longer conduct impulses resulting
in crippling conditions such as multiple
sclerosis.

The layer of fat under the skin acts as a
thermal insulator, cutting down the heat
loss from the body. Carbohydrate and
protein linked together will form *glycoprotein*, a protective coat of mucus in the
intestinal wall, whereas the pure protein
would be digested by the enzymes of
the intestine. But the glycoprotein—
which lines the intestinal wall with
mucus—cannot be digested and thus
stops the gut enzymes from destroying the
gut itself. Carbohydrates are also an
integral part of the genetic material, DNA
and RNA, in all living creatures.

Structure of carbohydrates
The carbohydrates are all made up of
chains of small molecules—the sugars.
The most important of these from a metabolic point of view is glucose.

Glucose is the end product of starch
breakdown. It is also released when
sucrose (cane sugar) is digested. Glucose
and fructose (another sugar) are known as
monosaccharides (mono: single; saccha-
: sugar) and are the smallest structural
units of carbohydrates. Sucrose, because
it is made up of glucose and fructose, is a
disaccharide (two sugars) and starch is a
polysaccharide (many sugars), each molecule containing at least 300 molecules of
glucose. *Cellulose*, the chief constituent
of plant walls, is also a polysaccharide.
Another important monosaccharide is
galactose, which is a constituent of the
milk disaccharide, *lactose*.

Digestion of carbohydrates
Humans cannot digest cellulose and,
although herbivores like cattle can, they
depend on the enzymes of bacteria in
their gut to do the job.

The final product of all carbohydrate
digestion is a monosaccharide. Digestion
of starch begins in the mouth by an
enzyme called salivary *amylase* or *ptyalin*.
This starts to break down starch into the
disaccharide, *maltose*, but because the
food stays in the mouth for a short time

only, most of the digestion still has to
occur when the starch reaches the
stomach.

No starch is digested in the stomach
itself, but once it reaches the duodenum—
the first part of the small intestine—it
comes into contact with the pancreatic
enzyme amylase which degrades the
starch completely into *maltose*. In the
next metabolic stage, glands in the small
intestinal wall produce enzymes known
as *maltases* which break the maltose into
glucose. Other specific enzymes attack
sucrose and lactose.

Absorption, storage and utilization
Carbohydrates cannot be absorbed across
the intestinal wall until they are broken
down into monosaccharides. But absorption does not appear to take place by
simple diffusion because they are absorbed rapidly and at a fixed rate no matter
what their concentration inside the
intestine. This indicates that they must
be absorbed by facilitated diffusion or
active transport.

Once in the bloodstream, the sugars are
carried round the body to the tissues.
Where energy is needed immediately,
glucose is broken down completely to
carbon dioxide and water. Glucose provides the energy needed to combine ADP
and phosphate into ATP, yielding 38
molecules of ATP for every molecule of
glucose. 'Spare' glucose may be converted to *glycogen*, a polysaccharide, in
the liver and muscles where it can be
quickly mobilized and broken down as
required.

Glycogen is relatively insoluble in
water. This makes it ideal for storage as it
remains in one place and does not exert
such a high osmotic pressure as it would
if stored as the equivalent amount of
glucose. An increase in osmotic pressure
means that water would enter the cells
and eventually burst them.

The complete breakdown of glucose
needs oxygen although a considerable
amount of energy can be generated without it. This is known as *anaerobic* respiration (without oxygen). It occurs in

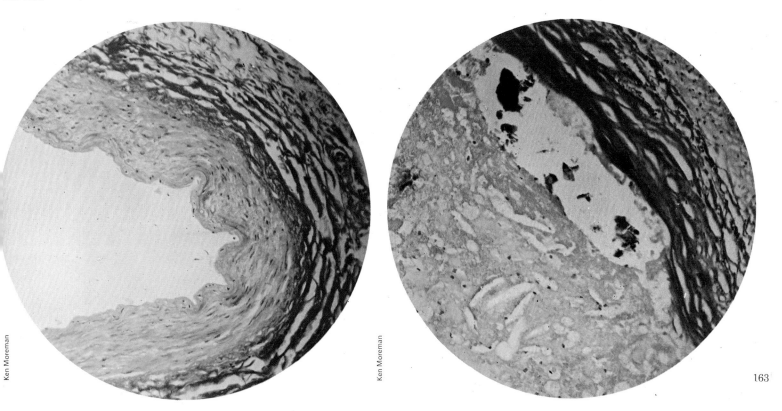

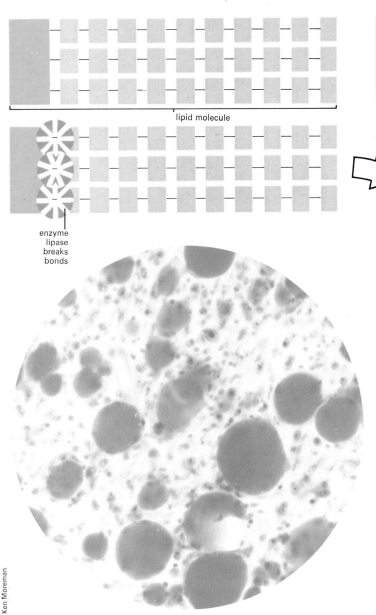

lipid molecule

$$H-C-O-C=O \quad C_9H_{19}$$
$$H-C-O-C=O \quad C_9H_{19}$$
$$H-C-O \quad C=O \quad C_9H_{19}$$

enzyme lipase breaks bonds

glycerol

fatty acid

fatty acid

fatty acid

Ken Moreman

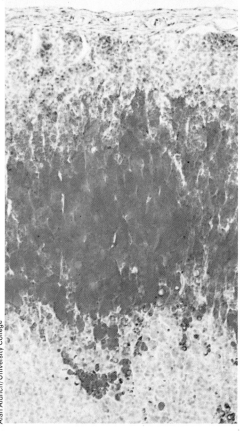

Alan Aldrich/University College

Above: Diagram showing structure of lipids which are composed of fatty acids. These are formed from carbon, hydrogen and oxygen atoms attached to a glycerol molecule which is also composed of carbon, hydrogen and oxygen atoms but with a different arrangement. During digestion, enzymes break the bonds between the glycerol and the fatty acids, producing free fatty acid and glycerol then small enough to be absorbed through the intestinal wall into the bloodstream.

Left and below: Cross section of tissue showing fat cells stained in red. Deposits of fat are a kind of mobile store constantly moved around to meet the energy requirements.

micro-organisms such as yeasts and it does not extract the full amount of energy from the glucose molecule since oxygen is needed to complete the breakdown.

In muscle, for example, oxygen may not get to the tissues quickly enough for complete oxidation of the glucose to occur. When this happens, glucose is metabolized to a substance known as *lactate* which builds up and causes cramp. However, once muscle work slows down or stops, oxygen transport can once more keep pace and the lactate is removed.

Structure of fats
Fats or lipids can be divided into several different groups. All fats contain fatty acids linked to alcohols. The simplest fats, *triglycerides*, have a 'backbone' of glycerol joined to three fatty acids. More complex lipids may have other alcohols and additional groups containing nitrogen and phosphorus.

Phospholipids are the most important lipids in cell membranes. They are long molecules each having a short 'head' end which is attracted to water and a long hydrocarbon 'tail' which is water repellant. So the molecules naturally arrange themselves in the cell membranes with the heads pointing outwards in contact with the surrounding body fluid while the tails point inwards. Cell membranes are thought to be made up of layers of phospholipids. Despite their

importance in the body's structure, however, phospholipids form only a small part of the diet—the body normally makes them for itself.

Another small part of the fat we eat, which is nonetheless essential, is the *polyunsaturated fatty acids*. The body cannot make these and they are found only in certain plant seeds such as peanuts. The essential fatty acids are used, among other things, to synthesize *prostaglandins*, which are involved in the control of contraction of smooth muscle, including the walls of blood vessels.

Digestion of fats
The bulk of our dietary fat is triglyceride. Very little of it is digested in the stomach, in adults at least. In infants, the more alkaline environment of the stomach and the highly emulsified state of milk lipid may be more favourable to the digestion of fat by the stomach enzyme, *gastric lipase*.

The major site of lipid digestion is the small intestine. In the duodenum, bile from the gall bladder breaks the lipids up into minute globules, a process known as emulsification. This increases the surface area exposed to the enzymes and also makes sure that lipids do not coat other food and hamper *its* digestion.

Pancreatic lipase hydrolyses (breaks down) the triglycerides to fatty acids, glycerol, monoglycerides and diglycerides. Because the second and third fatty acids are removed from triglycerides with difficulty, three-quarters of the total fat we eat ends up as monoglycerides and only one quarter is completely broken down into its constituents.

Absorption
Within the intestinal wall the monoglycerides are further hydrolysed to glycerol and fatty acids. The glycerol then recombines with the free fatty acids present in the wall to form triglycerides again. These are carried round the body in the lymphatic vessels as minute particles known as *chylomicrons*, which eventually enter the blood. Chylomicrons contain a small proportion of protein which is essential if the fat is to be delivered to other sites in the body where it is stored or broken down as the energy requirements of the body demand.

Carbohydrates and fat
fuel all the body
processes which require
energy. Fat is the more
efficient fuel, but

carbohydrate's main
product, glucose is
essential for the supply
of energy to the brain.

Paul Kemp

The Chemistry of Proteins

Every single part of the human body requires *protein*. It is one of the most essential elements since it forms the basic structure of all cells and is therefore found in the blood as well as the brain, in the enamel of the teeth as well as in the muscle tissue. All other animals and plants are predominantly built of protein —even down to the smallest viruses which inflict man with disease.

Although all life forms are composed of protein, human protein is different from the proteins found in both animals and plants. When we absorb the source of protein required for our own needs from the animal and plant foodstuffs we eat, it therefore, has to be broken down and rebuilt into a form which is useful to us as human beings.

The first part of this process takes place during digestion, when the protein is broken down into its constituent elements, *amino acids*, which are known as the basic building blocks of protein. These amino acids are *molecules* made up from smaller units called *atoms*, of carbon, oxygen, hydrogen and nitrogen.

There are 20 basic types of amino acids which combine in formations in much the same way as letters of the alphabet combine to form words. The resulting formations not only produce different species of plant and animal life, but individuals who differ from each other.

The myriad roles of proteins

Within the human body, protein provides the structural material of the tissues, but the function and type of protein present depends on the tissue itself. By far the largest group of proteins are *enzymes*, responsible for controlling and regulating all the essential life-sustaining reactions in the body. These large, globular molecules are employed as *catalysts*—agents which speed up chemical reactions in the cells of the body without changing themselves. One way in which they do this is by providing a site or meeting place to which the *substrate* (the substance which is to be acted upon chemically) is attached. The substrate is chemically acted upon so that it is forced to release its product—a molecule of amino acid which is 'chopped off' and released into the cell where it is taken up as a constituent to be rebuilt into a new protein.

The particular formation of amino acids which make up an enzyme may vary slightly between species, but the biological activity will be the same. For example, diabetics are treated with a purified preparation of insulin, a protein derived from pig or ox pancreas which works equally well in man.

Not all proteins involved in chemical regulation are enzymes, however. Protein hormones form another important group. These are the 'chemical messengers' of the body which carry substances to target cells, stimulating them into releasing other substances, such as insulin from the pancreas, into the bloodstream to regulate activity in another part of the body. In the case of insulin this promotes the

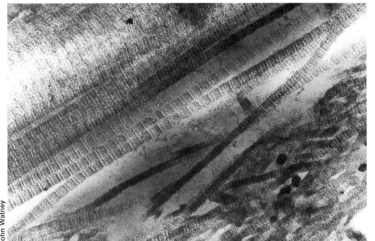

John Watney

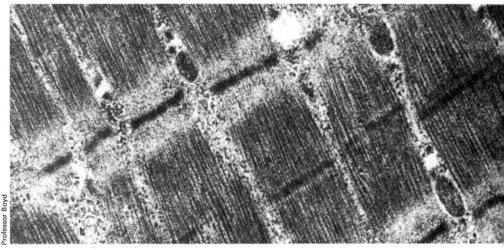

Professor Boyd

Left: An electron-micrograph of collagen fibrils.

Right: Collagen fibrils form a major part of skin, tendon, cartilage and bone tissue. To build the fibril, chains of amino acids are coiled into a helix; three chains are then intertwined to form molecules which line up and overlap each other. These illustrations show the structure of collagen fibrils (1 & 2) and how a lack of order in their arrangement can produce arthritic joints.

Below: A picture of muscle tissue magnified x 40,000. The striped bands are the cylindrical protein fibrils which interlock and cause contraction by sliding over each other.

Right and below: Diagram to illustrate the formation of proteins. The building blocks of proteins consists of a basic 'alphabet' of 20 amino acids. These are nitrogenous compounds with an amino-(NH_2) group, a carboxyl group and a variant known as an 'R' group of atoms. The combinations of these amino acids form thousands of different proteins in much the same way as the letters of the alphabet form thousands of different words. These variations not only produce species which are different from each other, but humans, animals and plants which are individual. (1) The amino acids are linked together by a peptide bond. This is formed by a chemical reaction known as condensation reaction, in which a water molecule between the two amino acids is lost. (2) The linking up of 100 or more amino acids by this means results in the formation of a polypeptide chain (3) which is called a protein. (4) These chains coil, forming a helix (spring-like) shape which often re-coils, giving the protein its final individual shape.

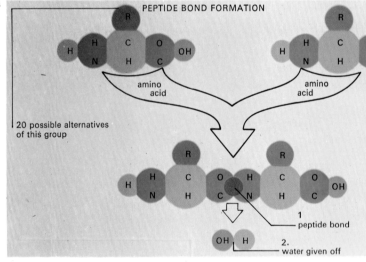

PEPTIDE BOND FORMATION

amino acid

amino acid

20 possible alternatives of this group

1
— peptide bond

2.
— water given off

KEY TO ATOMIC STRUCTURES

R = variable group of atoms
H = hydrogen
N = nitrogen
C = carbon
O = oxygen

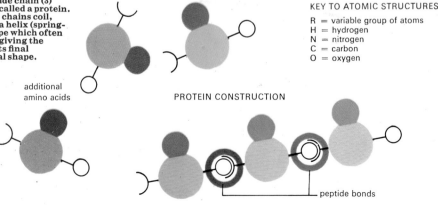

additional amino acids

PROTEIN CONSTRUCTION

peptide bonds

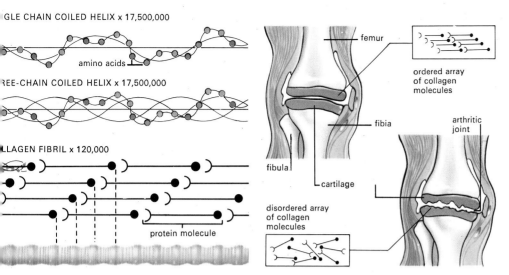

SINGLE CHAIN COILED HELIX x 17,500,000

amino acids

THREE-CHAIN COILED HELIX x 17,500,000

COLLAGEN FIBRIL x 120,000

protein molecule

femur

ordered array
of collagen
molecules

fibia

arthritic
joint

fibula

cartilage

disordered array
of collagen
molecules

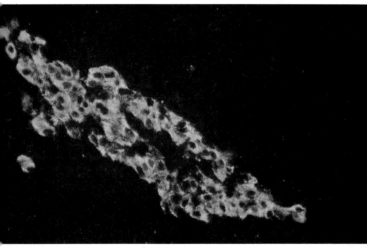

Left: Insulin, one of
the most vital hormones
in the human body. Its
chemical structure,
discovered by F. Sanger,
is a chain of 51 amino
acids and is described as
a lightweight protein.
(Proteins can be
composed of thousands
of amino acids making
them among the largest
molecules in the body.)
Secreted by the pancreas,
insulin is thought to
be responsible for
facilitating the passage
of glucose from the
bloodstream through
the outer membranes of
the cells. An excess of
insulin dangerously
decreases the amount of
glucose in the
bloodstream, leading to
hypoglycaemia; excess
glucose accumulation in
the blood results from a
deficiency of insulin
and causes diabetes.

uptake of glucose from the bloodstream.
But not all hormones are proteins. Some
are cholesterol, formed from a fat-like
substance.

Proteins have a variety of functions
other than chemical ones, which are vital
to the body processes. One of the most
important of these is in the formation of
collagen—the fibrous connective tissue
which binds bones, ligaments, cartilage,
muscles and skin together. Mucoproteins
are the body's lubricants—they aid
swallowing and the movement of joints.
Some proteins are involved in the transport of various substances around the
body: they have the capacity to bind
molecules and carry them in the bloodstream or across the membranes into cells.
One of the most important of these is
haemoglobin, the red pigment in the blood
which carries oxygen from the lungs to
the tissues.

Protection of the body against disease-
carrying viruses is also the responsibility
of the proteins. Each species has its own
type of *immunoglobulins*, or antibody
molecules, which appear in the blood and
tissues in response to foreign bodies, such
as grass pollen, entering the body through
the respiratory passages or in response to
dietary allergies arising from particular
types of foods.

Emergency supplies

In addition to these active roles, proteins
are also the body's emergency source of
energy. If the necessary minimum of 2,000
kilocalories of energy required daily to
maintain the body functions cannot be
obtained from food, due to starvation,
severe dieting or some types of illness,

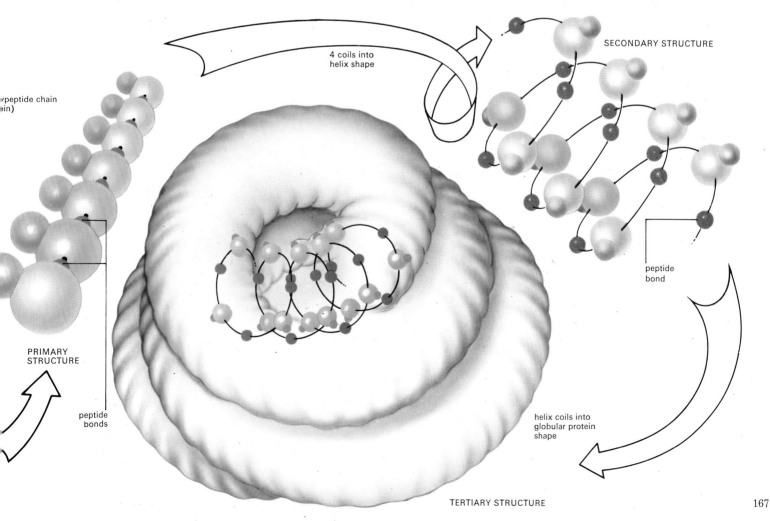

4 coils into
helix shape

SECONDARY STRUCTURE

peptide chain
(in)

peptide
bond

PRIMARY
STRUCTURE

peptide
bonds

helix coils into
globular protein
shape

TERTIARY STRUCTURE

the glycogen stores in the liver are used up within a few days, the fat stores in the adipose tissue under the skin are consumed and the breakdown of the proteins of the tissues begins.

This process is regulated by the hormones which ensure that the muscles, liver and spleen lose more than the vital organs such as the brain and the heart—the maintenance of the blood glucose level is vital if the brain is to stay in operation. In complete starvation, death usually follows some six weeks after the fat stores have been completely used up. But the exact extent of endurance depends on the individual's fat distribution. Since women have a greater proportion of body fat than men, they are obviously better able to cope with starvation.

Besides being the structural fabric of the cells, protein contributes to the shape and development of the body as a whole. In children, the rate of *protein synthesis*—a process known as *anabolism*—is high, since they are growing and forming new tissues. When adulthood is reached, however, the function of protein synthesis is mainly concerned with the repair and replacement of existing tissues.

One particular group of proteins, known as *anabolic steroids*, are involved in the development of the muscles and other tissues and the changes in secondary sexual characteristics (growth of facial and body hair and so on) which take place at puberty. Anabolic steroids are used to restore the wasting tissues of people suffering from debilitating diseases. They have also been used by some athletes to increase their strength and weight. However, they do have serious consequences when used in this way: since they are primarily concerned with the stimulation of the *androgens*, the male sex hormones, they frequently result in the development of secondary male sexual characteristics in women athletes.

The structure of protein

Protein molecules vary in size and some of the larger proteins found in the body may contain hundreds or even thousands of amino acids, depending on how many are linked together in the structure known as the *polypeptide chain*. The molecular weight of a protein is calculated from the combined weight of its atoms. It may be as much as 45 times the weight of a molecule of fat or 120 times a molecule of sugar.

A polypeptide chain is usually formed from at least 100 amino acids joined together by *peptide bonds*. The bond is formed between two amino acids when the amino (NH_2) group of one joins the acid ($CO\,OH$) group of the next with the loss of a water molecule between them—an OH from the acid (carboxyl) group and an H from the amino group.

This polypeptide chain makes up the *primary structure* of the protein, but few proteins are simple straight chains. They are generally coiled into a *helix*, a spring-like shape, the most common type of which, the alpha helix, has a turn of the helix every 3.6 amino acids. These turns are held or stabilized by hydrogen bonds formed between the C and O group of one amino acid and the NH group of another. This *secondary structure* may undergo further contortions into a *tertiary structure* which can be globular, elongated or twisted into a variety of different shapes. The structure and properties of a

George Rodger/John Hillelson

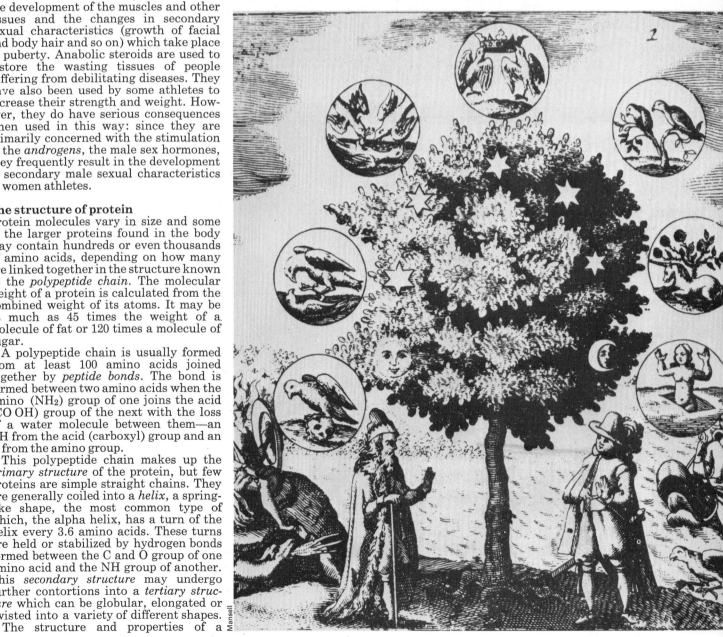

Mansell

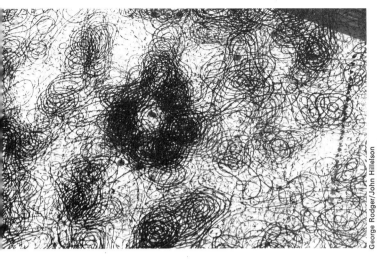

George Rodger/John Hillelson

George Rodger/John Hillelson

Left and above: Three-dimensional mapping of myoglobin molecules which temporarily store oxygen in the muscle cells. Electron densities of the molecule are measured from the clusters of atoms around them—see close-up (above)—and the map is built up on sheets of transparent plastic, from which the model was made.

Above right: A model of a myoglobin molecule, the oxygen-carrying pigment in the muscle which has a similar function to the haemoglobin in the blood. It belongs to the group of conjugated proteins—chains of amino acids coiled into a helix (white) plus an iron molecule to which stored oxygen is attached.

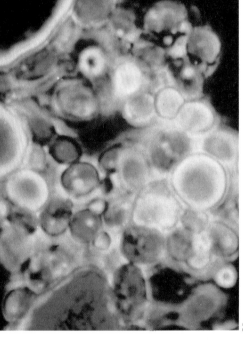

BP

protein may be altered by changing its environment. Heat, excessive acidity, chemical agents or radiation can alter the secondary and tertiary structures. This alteration process, known as *denaturation*, may be reversible or .irreversible. The secondary structure of albumen (white of egg), for example, is irreversibly altered when it is boiled. Coagulation results when the spiral arrangement is altered, although the acid sequence in the protein is unchanged. The helix is unable to reform and the molecule loses its original properties. The necessity of maintaining a stable environment for some proteins—for example, the refrigeration of blood plasma for transfusion purposes—is therefore paramount, since the weak hydrogen bonds which hold the fragile tertiary structures are vulnerable to the slightest changes in temperature.

Conjugated proteins

Although most proteins are made up entirely of amino acids, there are some which contain other components. These are known as *conjugated proteins* and the additional elements as *prosthetic groups*. Haemoglobin, the red, oxygen-carrying pigment in the blood, is a typical conjugated protein. Its basic structure consists of four polypeptide chains (two alpha chains of 141 amino acids and two beta chains of 146 amino acids), each of which carries a molecule of the iron compound, *haem*, which can take up and release one molecule of oxygen. The haem forms a ring structure to which the *globin*, the globular protein part of the molecule is conjugated (bound).

Chlorophyll, the green pigment in plants responsible for production of the basic elements of food—carbon and hydrogen—and oxygen, needed to support all forms of life, is an important conjugated protein akin to haem in its structure, except that its prosthetic group is magnesium. Like the proteins proper of the body, conjugated proteins are involved in different types of functions. Some like the *cytochromes*, the group of compounds found in all the tissues, are concerned with energy production through the transfer of blood to the cells; the *glycoproteins*, (carbohydrate plus proteins) found on the surface of the *erythrocytes* (red blood cells) are responsible for blood types, while the *lipoproteins* (lipid plus protein) form part of the structure of the cell membranes.

Molecule degradation

Protein in its pure form is never broken down to supply energy unless the body is totally devoid of fat resources. It does, however, undergo a chemical breakdown in which it 'co-operates' with a number of other substances in the release of energy.

Carbohydrates, fatty acids and amino acids can all be degraded, chemically changed, to a common denominator of simpler molecules known as the *acetyl group*. This enables them to take part in a series of chemical reactions called the Krebs cycle. They are then broken down further with the use of oxygen, so that the energy tied up in the molecular bonds is released, producing ATP (adenosine triphosphate), the high grade fuel required by the cells to carry out their vital rebuilding processes.

Above: Micro-organisms growing on petroleum, a cheap and efficient method of producing protein—a possible solution to the world food problem.

Left: The foundations of biochemistry were laid by the alchemists. The Tree of Knowledge, shown here, symbolized the knowledge they gained in their search for the 'elixir of Life'.

Right: Crystals of ceparin, a broad spectrum antibiotic with the property of being able to attack different types of bacteria. It is effective in the fight against disease simply because it does not bind readily with the proteins of the body and is therefore free to move around, controlling invasion by foreign substances.

Glaxo

169

The Cell

All living things are made up of cells. These minute organisms, the smallest units of the body, are responsible for carrying out all the processes fundamental to life.

All cells have the same basic structures but, although it is possible to describe a 'typical' animal cell, it must be remembered that within an organism as large and complex as man there are many different cell types—each one specialized to carry out a particular task—despite having the same basic organizational structure.

The cell is a chemical machine able to take in and channel energy, thereby maintaining its internal organization as well as doing useful work. As soon as the energy supply stops, however, the cell reverts to a greater state of disorganization—in effect it dies.

Human beings and animals are utterly dependant on plants to provide the basic raw materials for the foodstuffs from which they derive energy. Plant cells utilize the sun's energy directly, trapping it and building up large molecules of carbohydrates, proteins and fats from carbon dioxide, nitrogen and water; animals ingest these substances, breaking them down again to release their energy. These molecules are really only the 'crude fuels' of life; the cell uses this released energy to make its own 'high grade' fuel, a substance known as *ATP* (*adenosine triphosphate*) which, in turn, runs the machinery of the cell.

The cell machine, therefore, does a great deal of chemical work, constantly replacing and repairing all the enzymes which are essential to release this energy and manufacture ATP. And this is not all: cells also duplicate and extend themselves, a process which requires large scale synthesis of proteins.

The cell has to have a great deal of control over its internal environment to carry out all this chemical work, which means that it must be able to retain certain molecules and remove others. This would be impossible were the cell not enclosed in a semi-permeable sac (the *plasma membrane*) which allows molecules of a certain size to pass through by the simple processes of diffusion and osmosis. Glucose, for example, travels easily through the plasma membrane, and is, in fact, the main source of energy for the cell. To prevent it travelling back out again, certain cells join the glucose molecules together to make a large carbohydrate molecule (glycogen) which cannot escape through the plasma membrane, hence the glucose is stored to meet future energy needs.

In general, molecules that are small, have no electrical charge and will dissolve in lipids (fats), penetrate the membrane easily. Electrically charged molecules which are needed by the cell are 'pumped' in and out of the cell by a process known as *active transport*. This is thought to take place by the use of special carrier molecules, which shunt backwards and forwards across the plasma membrane, picking up and dropping off required substances which cannot travel in by osmosis or diffusion.

Movement of the carrier molecule, and

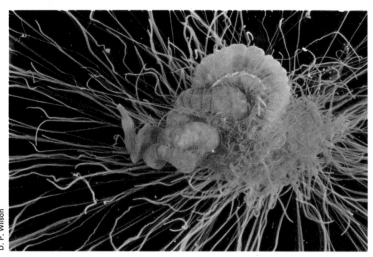

D. P. Wilson

Left: When disturbed in the dark, *Terebellid polychaete*, a species of luminescent worm, gives off a brilliant light. This is the result of the conversion of ATP (adenosine triphosphate, the chemical form in which energy is stored in its cells) back into energy.

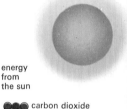

energy from the sun

carbon dioxide

water

nitrogen

Right and below: Diagram showing energy flow. Plant cells produce carbon dioxide, nitrogen and hydrogen from the sun's rays. These are built up into molecules of carbohydrates, proteins and fats which are digested by animals and humans. In the cell the molecules are broken down to release energy, which is stored as ATP.

ENERGY FLOW THROUGH BIOLOGICAL SYSTEMS

carbon dioxide

water

ammonia

WASTE

synthesis of 'low grade fuel'

plant cell

proteins
carbohydrates
fats

'high grade fuel' ATP

respiration

animal cell

Below: A replica of plasma membrane, the outer covering of the cell magnified x 132,000. The tiny raised dots are molecules. The surface is intricately folded to allow greater contact with the substances being absorbed into the cell. In some places, folding creates *microvilli*, (projections), ensuring more efficient absorption.

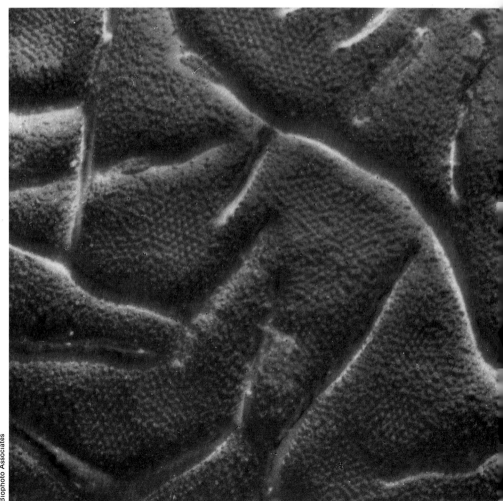

Biophoto Associates

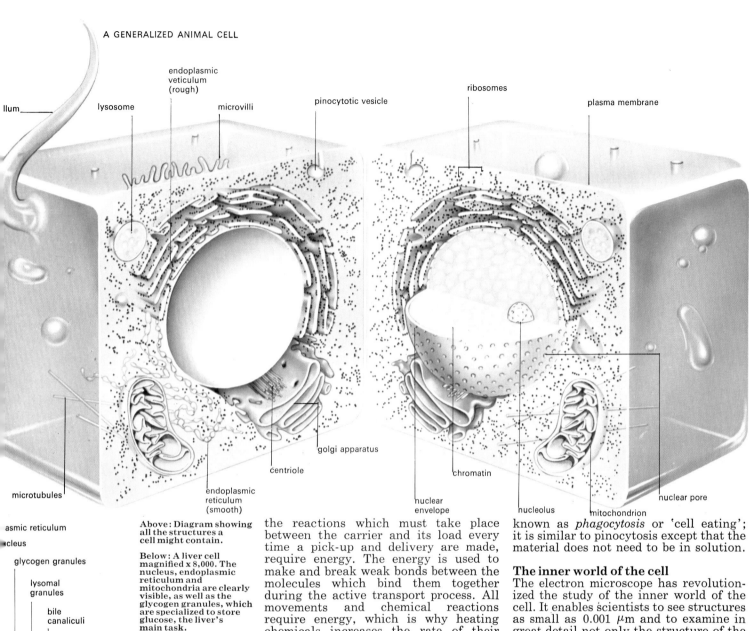

A GENERALIZED ANIMAL CELL

llum

lysosome

endoplasmic
veticulum
(rough)

microvilli

pinocytotic vesicle

ribosomes

plasma membrane

microtubules

centriole

golgi apparatus

endoplasmic
reticulum
(smooth)

chromatin

nuclear
envelope

nucleolus

mitochondrion

nuclear pore

asmic reticulum

cleus

glycogen granules

lysomal
granules

bile
canaliculi

**Above: Diagram showing
all the structures a
cell might contain.**

**Below: A liver cell
magnified x 8,000. The
nucleus, endoplasmic
reticulum and
mitochondria are clearly
visible, as well as the
glycogen granules, which
are specialized to store
glucose, the liver's
main task.**

Ken Moreman

the reactions which must take place
between the carrier and its load every
time a pick-up and delivery are made,
require energy. The energy is used to
make and break weak bonds between the
molecules which bind them together
during the active transport process. All
movements and chemical reactions
require energy, which is why heating
chemicals increases the rate of their
reaction (heat being one form of energy).

The cell must use energy to release
energy. The breakdown of glucose, for
example, requires expenditure of energy,
although in this case the cell gains in the
process because more energy is released
than is used. A great deal of the energy
channelled into the cell is used to maintain its own environment, thus, the
maintenance of order requires energy for
without it organization reverts to total
disorganization, or chaos.

Cell drinking and eating

The cell has two other ways of taking in
materials which cannot enter by osmosis,
diffusion or active transport. One of these
is *pinocytosis* (from the Greek, meaning
'cell drinking'). By sending out finger-like
projections the cell is able to pinch off and
enclose tiny droplets of its surrounding
fluid. In time, this mixes with the
materials inside the cell and the cell is
able to select from the salts, amino acids
and proteins dissolved in the fluid the
substances it requires.

Solid particles like bacteria, cell debris,
foreign material or even damaged cells
can be engulfed by some cells—white
blood cells do this, for example—and
degraded (broken down) into harmless
forms by the action of enzymes. This is

known as *phagocytosis* or 'cell eating';
it is similar to pinocytosis except that the
material does not need to be in solution.

The inner world of the cell

The electron microscope has revolution-
ized the study of the inner world of the
cell. It enables scientists to see structures
as small as 0.001 μm and to examine in
great detail not only the structure of the
cell but the activities that take place in
its interior.

The plasma membrane encloses the cell
in a semi-permeable skin, controlling the
entry and exit of molecules. Something
like 75 Anstrom units thick (approx. one
millionth of a millimetre). It is made of a
double layer of protein with a layer of
lipid molecules between.

A closer examination of the cell's surface reveals that the plasma membrane is
not tightly stretched over the cell. It
sometimes projects outwards to form
microvilli, or folds inwards into channels
which form a complex network of spaces
interlacing the interior of the cell. This
inward folding is known as the *endoplasmic reticulum*.

The complex network of the endoplasmic reticulum is sometimes smooth, and
at other times it is rough, being studded
on its interior side with numerous tiny,
closely spaced granules. These granules
are the *ribosomes*, which synthesize
protein for growth and maintenance of
the cell. They are found in greater numbers in cells which are actively synthesizing proteins. They are not always attached
to the endoplasmic reticulum, however,
but are sometimes found free or in clusters
known as *polyribosomes* inside the cell.

Near the nucleus of the cell (the 171

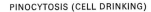

PINOCYTOSIS (CELL DRINKING)

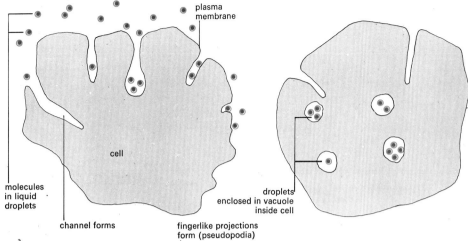

plasma membrane

cell

molecules in liquid droplets

channel forms

droplets enclosed in vacuole inside cell

PHAGOCYTOSIS (CELL EATING)

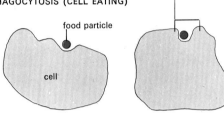

food particle

cell

fingerlike projections form (pseudopodia)

food particle enclosed in vacuole

Above and left: Two ways in which the cell obtains food. In pinocytosis (cell drinking) the cell surrounds molecules of substances enclosed in droplets of water (above). In phagocytosis (cell eating) larger food particles are taken in. The cell projects finger-like pseudopodia (left) which surround and engulf the particle.

Ken Moreman

kernel which directs the cell's activities) the endoplasmic reticulum opens into a system of tightly packed *vesicles* (spaces) named in 1898 the *Golgi apparatus* after their Italian discoverer Camillo Golgi. After much controversy, the existence of the Golgi apparatus was finally demonstrated clearly with the electron microscope. Its role is still not totally understood, although it is known to be concerned with the packaging of materials secreted by the cell.

The endoplasmic reticulum joins in places with the outer of two other membranes which surround the nucleus. This double membrane structure—the *nuclear envelope*—has pores along its surface which are not simple holes, but are often plugged with proteins, enabling it to be very selective about the type of materials allowed to pass into and out of the nucleus. The endoplasmic reticulum, therefore, gives the nucleus a direct link with the interior of the cell.

So far, only the outside of the cell has been examined, but through the plasma membrane is the *cytoplasm*. Around the nucleus, the cytoplasm is constantly changing, capable of being liquid at times and jelly-like at others. It consists mostly of water (70%-90%), some lipids (fats), carbohydrates, minerals and salts, being generally more solid near the outer membrane, and liquid in the interior. Much of this, however depends on the type or state of the individual cell.

Suspended in the cytoplasm are a number of small structures known as *organelles* (little organs), which are the functional units of the cell. Perhaps the most noticeable of these are the *mitochondria* of which there may be any number from one to a thousand in a cell. They change their shapes and sizes and aggregate where energy is required. They have an inner membrane folded in pleats to greatly increase their surface area, and a tightly stretched outer membrane. It is here, along the folded inner membrane of the mitochondria, that the 'crude fuels' of the cell are oxidized to release the energy needed to build ATP, the 'high

172

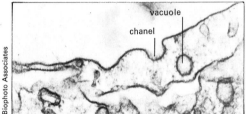

vacuole

chanel

Biophoto Associates

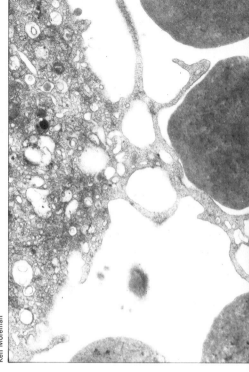

Ken Moreman

Left: Pinocytosis in action in a living cell magnified x 40,000. It shows how the cell produces a fine channel from the finger-like projection emerging at the surface of the plasma membrane. Certain soluble substances such as salts, amino acids and some proteins are enclosed in droplets of water, and are taken

through the plasma membrane and mixed with the cytoplasmic contents.

Above: Phagocytosis in a living cell magnified x 25,000, a similar process to cell drinking except that it is adapted to absorb solid particles. Here a red blood cell (right) is about to be engulfed by the membrane

nucleus

endoplasmic reticulum

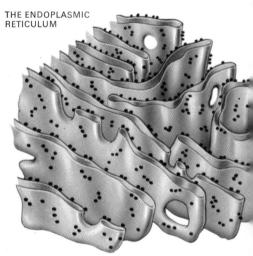

Ken Moreman

THE ENDOPLASMIC RETICULUM

Left: Section of a pancreatic cell x 10,000. It shows the intricate network of endoplasmic reticulum, interlaced throughout the cell.

Below: Section through the plasma membrane, the outer covering of a cell. It is made up of a layer of lipid sandwiched between two layers of protein.

Above right: Diagram of the molecular structure of the plasma (outer) membrane of a cell. Water soluble ends of the fatty molecules in the middle layer face outwards and contact the protein layer.

Above: Diagram of the endoplasmic reticulum, the folded membrane inside the cell.

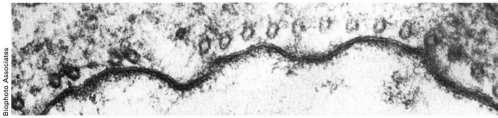

Biophoto Associates

THE CENTRIOLE

microtubule

CILIA AND FLAGELLA

doublet microtubules

cilium or flagellum

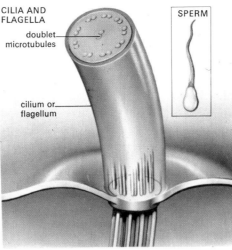

SPERM

Left: The centriole or 'central body', an organelle (structure) specially adapted for cell division. Formed from a circlet of nine microtubules, each subdivided into three smaller tubules, centrioles push their way up to the cell's surface (below right) where they emerge as whip-like projections or hair-like cilia. The flagella (above) may be adapted to propel some types of cells to other parts of the body. They form the tails on sperm cells, for example, guiding them towards the ovum (egg) for fertilization. The cilia line the surface of the cells of the trachea (above right), undulating constantly to sweep mucus and dust particles towards the mouth.

dirt particle

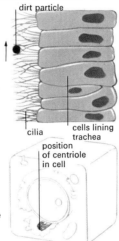

cilia

cells lining trachea

position of centriole in cell

PLASMA MEMBRANE STRUCTURE

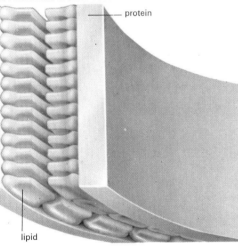

protein

lipid

ACTIVE TRANSPORT ACROSS THE PLASMA MEMBRANE

plasma membrane

transported molecules

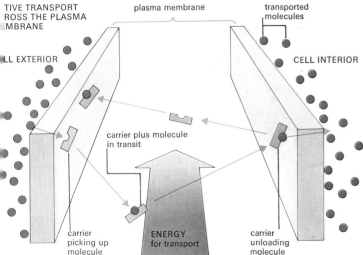

CELL EXTERIOR

CELL INTERIOR

carrier plus molecule in transit

carrier picking up molecule

ENERGY for transport

carrier unloading molecule

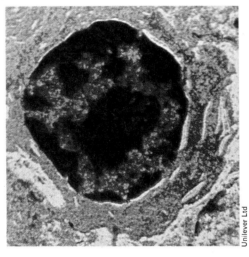

Above: An artificially coloured electronmicrograph of a cell. The nucleus (blue), actively involved in splitting, has chromosomes (collections of genes) spread out over it. The cytoplasm is shown as green and yellow.

Left: Diagram to illustrate active transport, the method by which substances required for synthesis (rebuilding) are absorbed into the cell. Carrier molecules (proteins), specially adapted to carry specific substances, attach themselves to molecules outside the cell, carry them through the lipid layer, deposit them inside the cell and return to the outer membrane to repeat the process.

grade fuels' in the process known as *respiration*. Within the cytoplasm there are also spherical sacs of enzymes called the *lysosomes*, which are responsible for the digestion of dead and redundant cells.

The two *centrioles* are small central bodies near to the nucleus and very important in the division of animal cells. They are made of a circle of nine *microtubules*, each divided into three smaller tubules, the whole structure forming a short, hollow cylinder.

Besides taking part in cell division, the centrioles can reproduce themselves, their copies travelling up to the cell surface and giving rise to the short hairlike *cilia*, or long whiplike *flagellae*. These appendages are found on many cells: on cells lining the trachea, for example, undulating cilia move mucus across the cell surface and the lashing tails (flagellae) of sperm cells propel the sperm towards the egg.

The control centre

A marvel of chemical organization has been achieved by the nucleus of the cell. It is the largest and most conspicuous of the cell constituents, and is responsible not only for the organization of the cell itself, but for the make up and appearance of each individual person. Since we are composed of cells, it follows that the way each cell grows, how it arranges itself with surrounding cells, how long it survives, in what ways it specializes, in fact, the whole behaviour of the cell, will determine the overall appearance of each individual. This is no simple achievement. It depends on the information held in the genetic material of the cell, which controls the manufacture of cell components, which, in turn, control the behaviour of the cell.

The nucleus is surrounded by its own porous double-layered envelope which connects it with the rest of the cell via the channels of the endoplasmic reticulum. Minute pores in the nuclear envelope are thought to allow substances to enter and leave the nucleus. In particular, parts of the ribosomes which are manufactured inside the nucleus, pass out of the pores and into the cytoplasm where they are assembled into functioning ribosomes. They are manufactured in a small, dense, spherical body inside the nucleus, known as the *nucleolus* (of which there may be one or more) which is absolutely essential for the growth of the cell. If there is no nucleolus, ribosomes are no longer manufactured, and protein synthesis stops. Without protein the cell cannot grow or maintain itself.

One of the substances in the nucleus which is readily visible by artificial staining, is DNA (*deoxyribonucleic acid*), the genetic material of the cell. This chemical structure is organized into *chromosomes* which are short, thick, rod-shaped bodies during and immediately before the cell begins to divide. In the non-dividing cell they are spread out into a threadlike mass throughout the nucleus, and in this state they are in their most active form—directing the cell's activities. Certain cells, such as mature red blood cells and cells in the centre of the eye, have no nucleus, being so highly specialized that they are capable of only a very limited amount of chemical activity. Lacking a control centre, they are not capable of self-reproduction, so they must be regularly replaced by new cells.

Inside the Cell

Energy production is essential to the life processes: it enables the body to carry out the chemical and mechanical work necessary to sustain order inside the cell.

The source of this energy is in the production of the 'high grade' fuel ATP (adenosine triphosphate). ATP is a molecule consisting of three phosphate groups attached in a chain to one adenosine group. The interesting and useful attribute of this molecule is that the third phosphate group can be removed easily and efficiently by the cell, releasing something like six times the amount of energy usually produced when chemical bonds are broken and giving out the energy needed for the thousands of chemical reactions carried out in the body. This leaves the lower energy ADP (adenosine diphosphate) which can be 're-charged' by addition of another phosphate group and the input of energy forming ATP.

But in order to understand how this energy is released, the mechanisms involved in the process, including the site itself, must be examined. Since 90 per cent of the cell's energy is derived from the reactions which take place in the *mitochondria* these organelles are obviously crucial to cellular metabolism.

The powerhouse of the cell

Mitochondria are found only in the cytoplasm of the cell. They are usually rod-like structures, although their shape and size varies depending on the chemical state of the cell. A cell may contain one or a thousand or more, again depending on the type and state of the cell—muscle cells for example, are packed with mitochondria to cope with their high energy requirements. Seen with the light microscope they are very active little structures, moving around the cytoplasm congregating where energy is required, changing shape and fragmenting to form new mitochondria.

When the mitochondria are examined with the electron microscope, they are found to have the same basic structure. A smooth outer membrane covers the outside, separated by a small space from a highly folded inner membrane. These folds are known as *cristae* and often extend right across the width of the mitochondrion to vastly increase its inner surface area. Here again variation arises in different cells: high-energy producing cells will have a great deal of cristae tightly packed into the organnelle. Observations of these details are, in fact, what gave early researchers the idea that mitochondria are intimately connected with the release of energy.

The inner surface of cristae are studded with minute stalks with round 'head-pieces' on top extending out into the inner space of the mitochondrion (the *matrix*). The functioning of the headpieces is not really understood: some researchers think they are concerned with the addition of the third phosphate group to ADP.

The matrix between the inner membrane has a fine granular appearance which changes its consistency depending on the state of the mitochondrion at the time (it is similar to the cytoplasm which is sometimes gel-like and sometimes liquid).

matrix · cristae · inner mem · outer memb · RESPIRATO ASSEMBLY · headpieces

Above: Diagram to show structure and position of the mitochondria in the cell (far left). The mitochondrion 'cut open' (centre) reveals the cristae, the highly folded inner membrane. This increases the surface area and exposure to enzymes which are involved in the production of ATP (high energy fuel). The magnified view of the inner membrane shows the 'head pieces', thought to be the conversion sites of ADP to ATP, the process by which energy is stored. Some researchers think that the headpieces add the third phosphate group to ADP. Others, however, have suggested that they do not really exist in the intact mitochondrion but are created during the preparation of the structure for study.

Left: Surface view of kidney tissue magnified x 25,000 showing mitochondria (sausage-shaped outlines to right of centre) above the nucleus.

Below: Section through a series of cells showing variety of mitochondrial shapes with their tightly packed cristae.

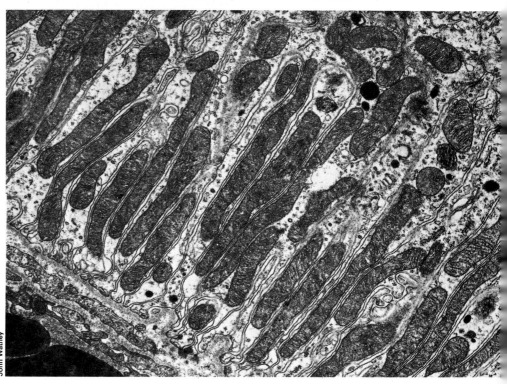

Biophoto Associates

John Watney

174

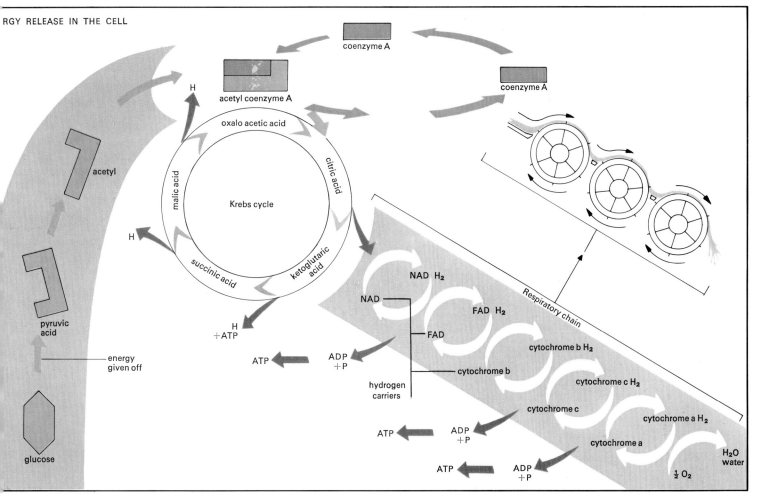

coenzyme A

acetyl coenzyme A

coenzyme A

oxalo acetic acid

malic acid

citric acid

Krebs cycle

acetyl

H

succinic acid

ketoglutaric acid

pyruvic acid

energy given off

H
+ATP

H
+ATP

ATP

ADP
+P

NAD H₂

NAD

FAD H₂

FAD

Respiratory chain

hydrogen carriers

cytochrome b H₂

cytochrome b

cytochrome c H₂

glucose

ATP

ADP
+P

cytochrome c

cytochrome a H₂

ATP

ADP
+P

cytochrome a

H₂O
water

½ O₂

Above: Energy release process. The glucose molecule is broken down to an acetyl group by the release of high energy hydrogen. The acetyl group is taken into the mitochondrion by co-enzyme A. It enters the Krebs cycle for further breakdown with the aid of oxygen, releasing carbon dioxide. All the high energy hydrogens released enter the respiratory chain, likened to a waterfall driving the cell's water wheels, to produce ATP.

Below: Diagram showing how energy is stored in the cell. The high energy bond joins the final phosphate to ADP (adenosine diphosphate). Energy is released when this bond is broken.

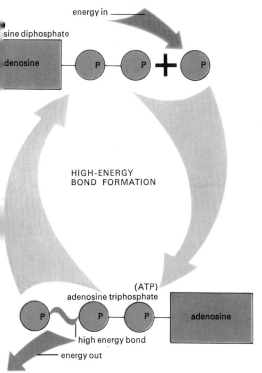

energy in

sine diphosphate

denosine

P

P

P

HIGH-ENERGY BOND FORMATION

(ATP)
adenosine triphosphate

P

P

P

adenosine

high energy bond

energy out

Within this space are found all the enzymes necessary to build up ATP.

Recent studies have revealed that the matrix also contains a full complement of the apparatus needed for protein synthesis, including DNA.

It was originally thought that DNA was only present in the nucleus of the cell; since DNA is essential for the synthesis of proteins, and since proteins are essential to form cell constituents, this made the cell the smallest unit of the body able to reproduce itself. The fact that mitochondria possess the apparatus for protein synthesis raises the interesting possibility that they are independent organisms existing inside the cell.

In the early stages of evolution, mitochondria may have been simple, bacteria-like organisms, which at some point adopted an existence actually inside other cells. This resulted in symbiotic co-existence between the cell and the mitochondria—the mitochondria benefiting from the protected, nourishing environment and the cell having its energy production greatly increased. The cell appears to be unable to make new mitochondria. They independently reproduce themselves by a process known as *budding*: splitting into two or more.

The release of energy
The production of ATP from ADP requires energy to form the bond between the third and second phosphate groups. But where does this energy come from? To answer this question we must go back to the cytoplasm and the glucose molecule.

Enzymes in the cytoplasm act on each glucose molecule, breaking some of its chemical bonds to release their energy.

This is quite a complicated procedure which eventually converts each glucose molecule into two molecules of a substance called *pyruvic acid*. These series of reactions are together known as *glycolysis*, and the energy released is used mainly to make two molecules of ATP. The rest of the energy is in the form of heat and helps to maintain the body temperature.

Glycolysis does not require oxygen to take place; for this reason it is called *anaerobic respiration* (the release of energy without oxygen)—it is the process carried out by yeasts, for example, when they ferment sugar. If no oxygen is present the breakdown of glucose stops here. When oxygen is available, however, the cell continues the energy release process by breaking down the pyruvic acid molecules, but this time inside the mitochondria. This is called *aerobic respiration* (the release of energy with oxygen) and is where the cell really begins to extract the full amount of energy.

Pyruvic acid molecules formed by the breakdown of glucose in the cytoplasm must be carried to the mitochondrion to have their energy extracted. First of all, however, they must be prepared for transport and entry into the mitochondrion. They are, therefore, converted from the three-carbon pyruvic acid molecule into a smaller two-carbon one called an *acetyl group*, releasing carbon dioxide in the process. This carbon dioxide is excreted from the cells into the bloodstream and thence to the lungs.

The acetyl group attaches itself to a coenzyme (these help enzymes to carry out reactions) which carries it to a spot on a mitochondrion, detaches itself and goes back through the cytoplasm to pick

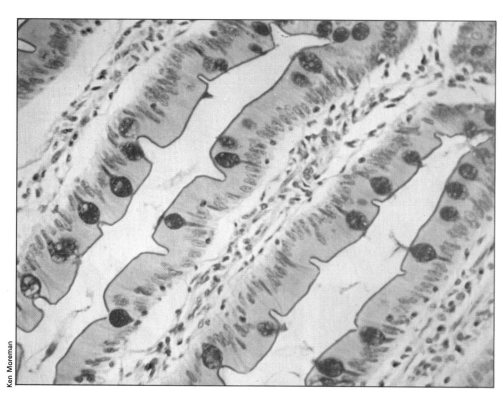

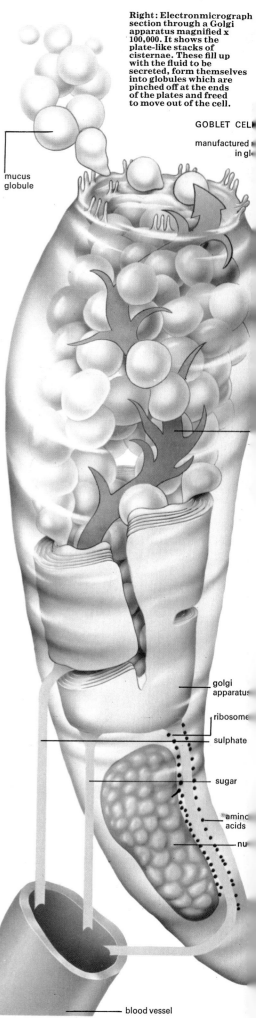

GOBLET CEL▮

manufactured ▮
in gl▮

mucus
globule

up another acetyl group—a sort of cyto-plasmic shuttle service.

The outer membrane of the mitochon-drion readily allows acetyl groups through to the matrix where they enter a unique cycle of chemical reactions called the *Krebs cycle* (or the *citric acid cycle*).

This is really a means of gradually removing the carbon atoms from the incoming acetyl group until there is nothing left of the original molecule. Every time a carbon atom is removed energy is released, making more and more molecules of ATP. The original substance which combines with the acetyl group at the beginning of the Krebs cycle remains intact at the end, ready to combine with another acetyl, so completing the cycle.

Each turn of the Krebs cycle actually releases excited hydrogen atoms and one molecule of ATP, hence the energy of the original glucose molecule is now in the form of ATP and excited hydrogen atoms. The latter are not much use to the cell as far as fuel is concerned, so the mitochon-drion is also charged with the task of lowering the excited hydrogen atoms to a less energetic state and trapping the energy in ATP molecules.

Recent research has revealed a chain of enzymes and coenzymes attached to the inner surface of the mitochondrion. Hydrogen atoms from the Krebs cycle enter this chain and are passed along from compound to compound. At each stage their energy level is reduced until the hydrogen finally combines with oxygen to form water which the cell excretes.

At three points along this chain the energy is used to convert one molecule of ADP into ATP. This sequence of events is known as the *respiratory*, or *electron transport chain*, and can be likened to a waterfall; the excited hydrogen atoms can be represented by the water which drives a series of water-wheels (converting ADP to ATP) as it falls down the cliff face, losing energy in the process.

The Krebs cycle represents the energy hub of the cell. Each turn results in the complete breakdown of one acetyl group derived from glucose, releasing energy

Above: Goblet cells (red) lining the villi of the small intestine. They secrete mucus which protects the intestinal lining from erosion by digestive enzymes.

Below: A single goblet cell x 6,500. The mucus is being secreted into the interior space of the gut, known as the lumen.

Right: Mucus is manufactured from proteins, sugars and sulphates which are packaged inside the cup-like Golgi apparatus. The proteins are formed by the ribosomes, small spherical bodies inside the cell, from amino acids from the blood. These are then combined with sugars and sulphate to form the mucus.

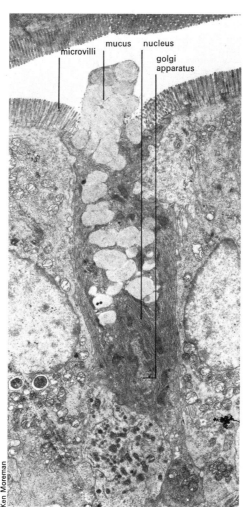

microvilli   mucus   nucleus

golgi
apparatus

golgi
apparatus

ribosome

sulphate

sugar

amino
acids

nu▮

blood vessel

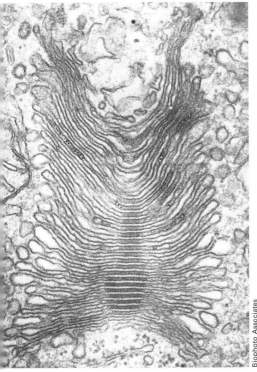

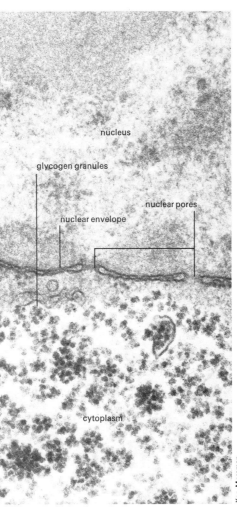

nucleus

glycogen granules

nuclear pores

nuclear envelope

cytoplasm

Biophoto Associates

Ken Moreman

Below: Micrograph of the nucleus of a cell viewed from the outside magnified x 30,000. The surface of the outer covering, the nuclear envelope, is pitted with pores through which large molecules can travel in and out. The passage of these molecules is controlled by cylinders of protein which plug up the pores.

Right: Section through the nuclear envelope magnified x 135,000. The two-layered structure of the envelope with the pores (the points at which the line is broken) dividing the nucleus (top) from the cytoplasm is clearly visible. The glycogen granules (derived from glucose) in the cytoplasm indicate that it is a liver cell.

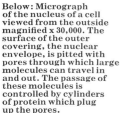

which drives the turbines of the respiratory chain to produce the 'high grade fuel'.

The Golgi apparatus

The cell is a kind of manufacturing complex, using the energy released by the mitochondria to form chemical products, some of which are passed out of the cell—for example, the intestinal goblet cells secrete mucus. This necessitates a transporting system inside the cytoplasm to collect and distribute the manufactured products of the cell's activities. This is done by the *Golgi apparatus*, an organelle discovered by Camillo Golgi in 1898, although it could not be confirmed until the advent of the electron microscope some 40 years later.

The Golgi apparatus is much more developed in secretory cells—those which secrete mucus and hormones, for example. Generally found near the nucleus of the cell, the Golgi apparatus consists of stacks of plate-like structures called *cisternae*. These are parallel membranes which form flattened sacs, thin at the centre, swollen at the edges. The whole structure is bent to make a concave series of discs. They are filled with fluid which travels to the swollen edges making *vacuoles* which pinch off from the cisternae when they reach a critical size. From here they migrate through the cytoplasm and out of the plasma membrane of the cell where they rupture, releasing their contents.

The cisternae derive their proteins from the rough endoplasmic reticulum, which synthesizes them from the incoming amino acids. Inside the sacs of the cisternae the protein is joined onto carbohydrate molecules. These are synthesized inside the Golgi apparatus, making carbohydrate-protein complexes called *glycoproteins*. The assembled glycoproteins accumulate in the vacuoles at the edges of the cisternae ready to be exported.

This activity is very noticeable in the goblet cells lining the duodenum, which produce mucus to lubricate the passage of food and protect the lining of the intestine. The mucus is, in fact, a glycoprotein, and is packaged and transported throughout the cell by the well-developed and highly active Golgi apparatus of the goblet cells.

The lysosomes (sacs of enzymes) are thought to be formed by the Golgi apparatus. The enzymes are made by the rough endoplasmic reticulum and passed to the Golgi apparatus where they are packaged up inside a membrane, and pinched off into the cytoplasm.

The nuclear envelope

The nucleus, the control centre of the cell, is isolated from all this chemical activity by its own special membrane—the nuclear envelope. This double-layered structure controls the entry and exit of materials in and out of the nucleus. It is dotted with holes called *nuclear pores* which control the passage of large molecules by becoming plugged with cylinders of protein, thereby actively regulating the flow. Small particles like sodium and potassium ions do not depend on the pores for entry, but can pass through the envelope walls unhindered.

Far from being a homogeneous bag of chemicals, the cell is a compartmentalized organ. The membranes act as guardians of the different structures, isolating them and enabling each part to carry out its task with minimum interference.

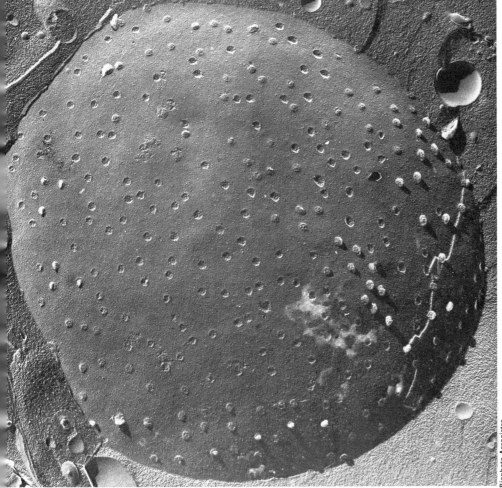

Biophoto Associates

177

Blueprint of the Cell

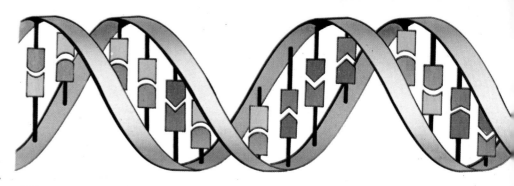

The nucleus of each human cell, although only a minute fraction of a millimetre wide, contains a staggering amount of 'information'—all the information needed, in fact, to make a complete human being. This information is all 'written' along the strands of that remarkable molecule, DNA (deoxyribonucleic acid).

The DNA molecule lies in the nucleus of the cell, where it is protected from damage. Here, tightly coiled strands of the DNA are bound together with a protein to form threads called *chromosomes* (which will absorb a particular dye, making them visible under the light microscope). The number of chromosomes in a cell varies from species to species—in every human body cell (except the reproductive cells), for example, there are 46, while rats have 42 and pea plants have as few as 14.

The model of DNA—first constructed by Watson and Crick in 1953—looks something like a ladder; the uprights being made of an alternating sequence of sugar and phosphate molecules, and the rungs are pairs of molecules containing nitrogen (known as nitrogenous bases). The whole ladder, called the *double helix*, is twisted so that it resembles a spiral staircase. Each rung is composed of two bases joined end to end and extending out from each side of the ladder. There are four varieties of base: *adenine, guanine, thymine* and *cytosine* (*A, G, T,* and *C*), which pair off to form the rungs. The pairing off, however, is not random: adenine can only pair with thymine, and guanine with cytosine. The 4,000 million rungs making up the DNA strands in one cell follow each other in any order. They extend the whole length of the double helix DNA molecule (AT, GC, AT, TA, CG, TA, CG, CG, etc) giving an incredible number of possible combinations.

The secret of the DNA molecule lies in the order of the bases which make up the rungs. They form a code which contains all the information necessary to build a new cell; since the human body is composed of cells, the information must be sufficient to code for an entire human being. If the bases were letters of an alphabet (A, G, T and C) and these were used to construct words consisting of three letters each, it would be possible to compose a total of 64 words from the four letters. These 'words' can be arranged in any order along the length of the DNA molecule to make up 'sentences' each of which provides the instructions for the cell to synthesize one protein. These proteins are, in fact, enzymes—which cause all the reactions of the body to be carried out.

The genetic code
Proteins are made up of chains of amino acids arranged in a particular order, and each 'word' of a coding-sentence will specify one of the 20 amino-acids. (The sentence-coding for each protein is called a *gene*, and the whole of the code is called the genetic code). But as there are 64 possible 'words' in the arrangement of bases, there must be some words which

code for the same amino acid: the amino acid alanine, for example, is coded for by the words CGA, CGG, CGT, and CGC. Some words, however, signify a full stop which ends the 'sentence' thus completing the protein synthesis, and others the capital letter which begins it.

The genetic code has been found to be universal; the three letter words code for the same amino acids in all organisms. But the difference between a man and a fly is in the information stored in the DNA molecule since the different combinations of codes produce different species. The particular message for each living organism is like a master template from which the characteristics of the organism can be fashioned again and again.

Transcription of the genetic code
Since the DNA strand containing the genetic code must remain in the nucleus of the cell for protection it therefore delegates its duties by producing a replica of itself. The replica, known as *mRNA*

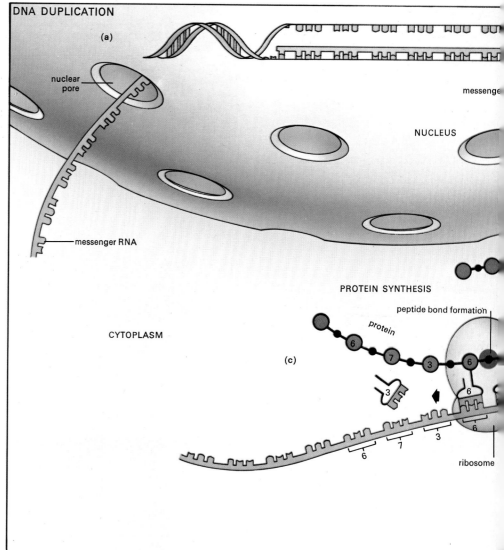

DNA DUPLICATION

(a)

nuclear pore

messenger RNA

NUCLEUS

messenge

CYTOPLASM

PROTEIN SYNTHESIS

peptide bond formation

protein

(c)

ribosome

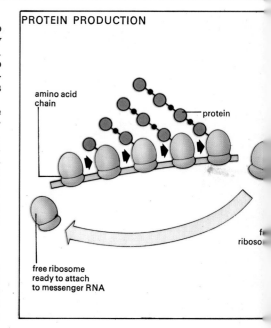

PROTEIN PRODUCTION

amino acid chain

protein

free ribosome ready to attach to messenger RNA

Left: A DNA molecule resembles a spiral staircase, the uprights formed from two strands of sugar phosphate coiled into a helix. Each 'rung' is formed from one of four nucleotides—nitrogenous bases— paired off with a structurally similar partner: adenine with guanine and thymine with cytosine.

Right: Section of a cell x 50,00 in the process of synthesizing proteins. The black dots are the ribosomes by which the genetic message in the mRNA strand is read and the appropriate proteins are manufactured from chains of amino acids.

mitochondrion
polyribosome
endoplasmic reticulum

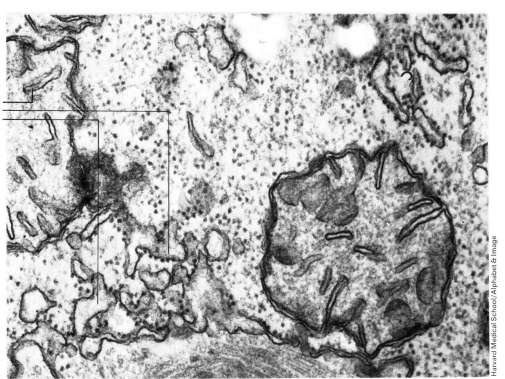

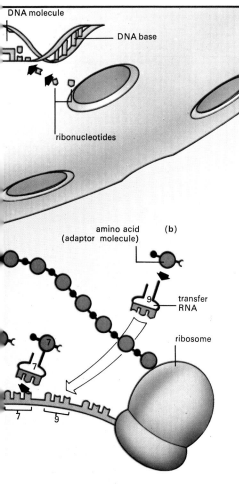

DNA molecule

DNA base

ribonucleotides

amino acid   (b)
(adaptor molecule)

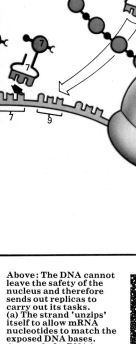

transfer RNA

ribosome

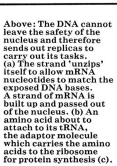

Above: The DNA cannot leave the safety of the nucleus and therefore sends out replicas to carry out its tasks. (a) The strand 'unzips' itself to allow mRNA nucleotides to match the exposed DNA bases. A strand of mRNA is built up and passed out of the nucleus. (b) An amino acid about to attach to its tRNA, the adaptor molecule which carries the amino acids to the ribosome for protein synthesis (c).

Left: As the ribosome moves along, the amino acid chain grows to form the protein. The protein and the ribosome detach from the mRNA and the free ribosome is ready to resume the process.

Right: Portion of a DNA strand isolated from a virus magnified x 80,000. The tightly coiled strands would stretch 1.7 metres if uncoiled. Each DNA is composed of 23 pairs of chromosomes, made up of hundreds of genes (molecular units).

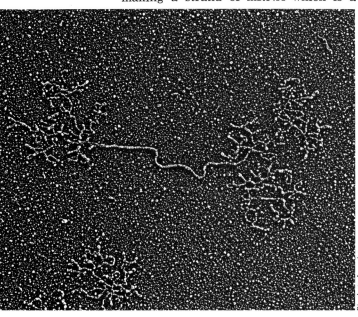

(messenger ribonucleic acid), can travel out of the nucleus, through the nuclear pores to join up with the *ribosomes*—the apparatus for protein synthesis—to direct their activities.

Messenger RNA is similar to DNA in its structure except that it is only single stranded—like a ladder split in half by cutting through the rungs. It contains an exact copy of the code words of the DNA molecule.

DNA duplication
The double helix DNA molecule first 'unzips' itself, exposing the sequence of bases attached to one side of the ladder. Floating freely in the nucleus are *nucleotides*, building blocks of the mRNA molecule, which consist of a length of the sugar-phosphate 'upright' plus one base as the rung. The nucleotides line up along the 'unzipped' DNA molecule and match the exposed DNA bases with the complementary mRNA bases. Once aligned they are bonded together with an enzyme, making a strand of mRNA which is a complementary copy of the base sequence along the DNA strand. The 64 different three letter words of the code now transcribed onto the mRNA strand are called *codons*, and each codon codes for one particular amino acid. When the copying process is complete, the DNA 'zips' itself back up again.

The messenger RNA strand moves out of the nucleus and into the cytoplasm where it attaches to a ribosome, the organelle which synthesizes protein. It 'reads' the message of the mRNA strand, joining the amino acids together to make the exact proteins specified by the genetic code.

Protein manufacture
The amino acids are gathered and taken to the ribosomes by special adaptor molecules known as transfer RNA. One end of the tRNA molecule has a special site to which a particular amino acid can attach itself; the other end has three bases which are complementary to a particular mRNA codon. The tRNA picks up its amino acid, goes along to the ribosome, and when its complementary mRNA codon comes along, it locks onto it. At the same time another tRNA with its own amino acid will be doing exactly the same thing, but locking onto the next codon on the mRNA strand. In this way the amino acids are brought together in the correct sequence. With the aid of two enzymes and some energy a peptide bond is formed between the two amino acids, and the protein chain begins to form.

The role of the ribosome in this process is to hold the two tRNAs together onto the mRNA strand. The ribosome moves along the strand reading codon after codon; with each reading an amino acid is brought into position and joined to the one before it, and the protein chain grows. The tRNA detaches from its amino acid, is released from the ribosomes as the next one comes into position, and is free to pick up another amino acid.

When the protein is complete, the last one or two codons will signal a full stop. The ribosome then releases the last tRNA and detaches itself from the mRNA strand. Sometimes the mRNA strand is thousands of codons long, and has several ribosomes reading it at the same time, each one producing a protein chain. This chain of ribosomes is called a *polyribosome*.

The dividing cell

Cells, like people, are not immortal. Some 500 million body cells die each day of our lives, and an approximately equal number take their place. They have varying life spans: nerve cells live for 50 years or more, whilst an intestinal cell might only survive for 36 hours. Replacement is accomplished by the division of one cell into two—the process known as *mitosis*.

Cell division is part of the normal life cycle of a cell. A cell which is not dividing is said to be in *interphase*. During this period it is actively synthesizing RNA, proteins and the chemicals it will need when the division process begins. One of the most important events of interphase is the complete duplication of the nuclear DNA. This is accomplished in a similar way to mRNA synthesis: the DNA strand 'unzips', and new bases pair up to form an exact replica. The chromosomes are not visible at this stage, the DNA being distributed around the nucleus in its most synthetically active form known as *chromatin*.

When the cell has completed its DNA replication and prepared itself for division, the chromatin forms itself into the dense chromosome threads. The centrioles —the tube-like central bodies—divide and move to the opposite poles of the cell where they spread a network of protein *spindle fibres* across to each other. This

Below: A section of a cell showing a lysosome magnified x 50,000. Known as 'suicide bags', they release enzymes which digest dead cells.

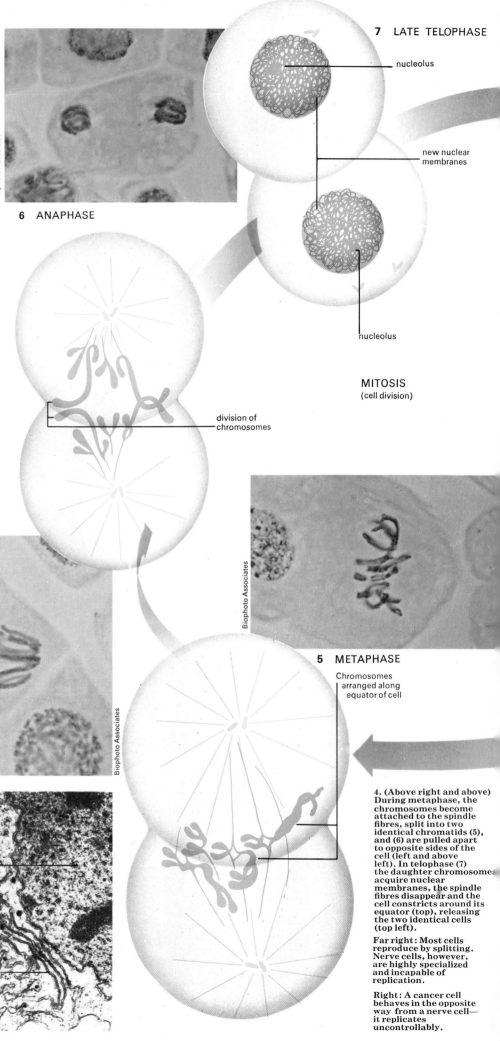

7 LATE TELOPHASE

nucleolus

new nuclear membranes

nucleolus

6 ANAPHASE

MITOSIS
(cell division)

division of chromosomes

5 METAPHASE

Chromosomes arranged along equator of cell

4. (Above right and above) During metaphase, the chromosomes become attached to the spindle fibres, split into two identical chromatids (5), and (6) are pulled apart to opposite sides of the cell (left and above left). In telophase (7) the daughter chromosomes acquire nuclear membranes, the spindle fibres disappear and the cell constricts around its equator (top), releasing the two identical cells (top left).

Far right: Most cells reproduce by splitting. Nerve cells, however, are highly specialized and incapable of replication.

Right: A cancer cell behaves in the opposite way from a nerve cell— it replicates uncontrollably.

nucleus

cytoplasm

nucleus

lysosome

endoplasmic reticulum

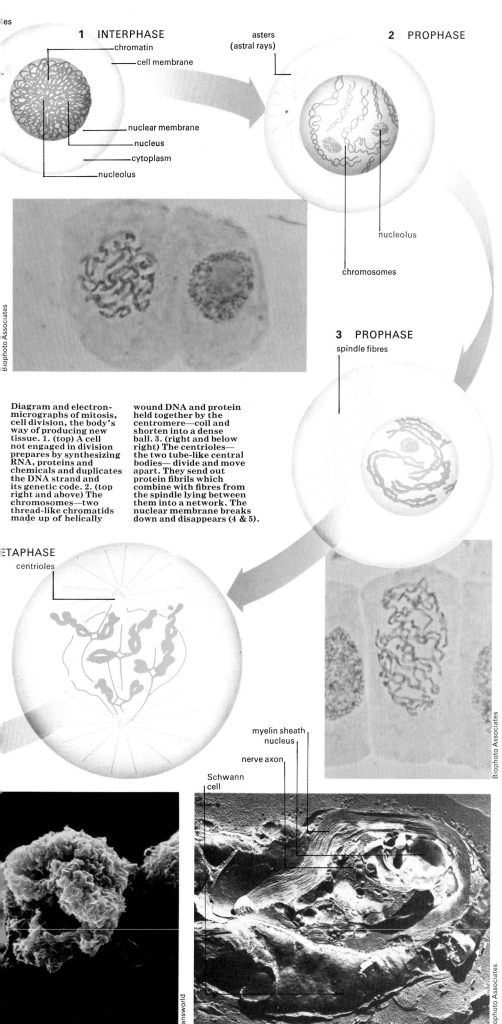

1 INTERPHASE
— chromatin
— cell membrane
— nuclear membrane
— nucleus
— cytoplasm
— nucleolus

asters (astral rays)

2 PROPHASE
nucleolus
chromosomes

3 PROPHASE
spindle fibres

ETAPHASE
centrioles

myelin sheath
nucleus
nerve axon
Schwann cell

Diagram and electron-micrographs of mitosis, cell division, the body's way of producing new tissue. 1. (top) A cell not engaged in division prepares by synthesizing RNA, proteins and chemicals and duplicates the DNA strand and its genetic code. 2. (top right and above) The chromosomes—two thread-like chromatids made up of helically wound DNA and protein held together by the centromere—coil and shorten into a dense ball. 3. (right and below right) The centrioles—the two tube-like central bodies— divide and move apart. They send out protein fibrils which combine with fibres from the spindle lying between them into a network. The nuclear membrane breaks down and disappears (4 & 5).

stage is known as *prophase*. Close examination of the chromosomes shows that each one is, in fact, a pair of identical structures called *chromatids* attached to each other by the *centromere*, a small spherical body. The nuclear membrane disappears during prophase, and the chromatid pairs line up around the centre of the cell, beginning *metaphase*, the next stage of division.

The centromere of each chromatid pair attaches to one of the spindle fibres and splits itself into its two identical chromatids; these are then pulled to opposite sides of the cell by the contracting fibres. The movement of these daughter chromosomes (the separate chromatids) to the opposite poles of the cell is known as the *anaphase* and the final stage of mitosis is called *telophase*. This stage is essentially the reverse of prophase (the first stage): each set of daughter chromosomes is surrounded by a nuclear membrane; the spindle fibres disappear and the cell constricts in a tight band around its equator finally releasing the two independent daughter cells each with exactly the same DNA structure.

Specialized cells

The appearance and functioning of the human body is a direct result of the subtle action of the thousands of enzymes produced by the genes in the nucleus of each living cell.

It is obvious that all our cells are not alike: some produce hair, for example, and others hormones. All cells, however, have the same amount and type of DNA, so there must be a method of controlling the expression of the coded message in the DNA strand.

The cell does this by 'switching' genes 'on and off'. Every cell has the gene for making haemoglobin, for example, but only young red blood cells actually produce this protein. The gene is therefore 'switched off' in all the other body cells. Cells thus become specialized in this way for a particular task. Control is exerted to the point in some cells where they actually lose their ability to divide —mature red blood cells for example; in others cell growth and division takes place exactly when and where required. In skin cells, division is constant: the outer covering is continually being shed and replaced from the layer below. The speed at which this takes place is vital in healing wounds and abrasions through which infection can attack the body. Nerve cells are probably the most highly specialized cells and among the most vital, since their destruction can mean paralysis and sometimes death.

The death of a cell

Cells become old and damaged and eventually die. But unlike the body as a whole, they contain their own self-destruct mechanism in the form of 'suicide packets' called *lysosomes*. These packets contain powerful digestive enzymes which are normally isolated from the cell contents by an impermeable membrane. Their role in normal life is to digest certain food particles and keep the body free from bacteria and debris. When a cell is injured, however, its own lysosome releases its content of digestive enzymes which proceed to digest the cell from within. The cell constituents can then be re-used or excreted—recyling the components of life.

181

Part II

Development and and Behaviour

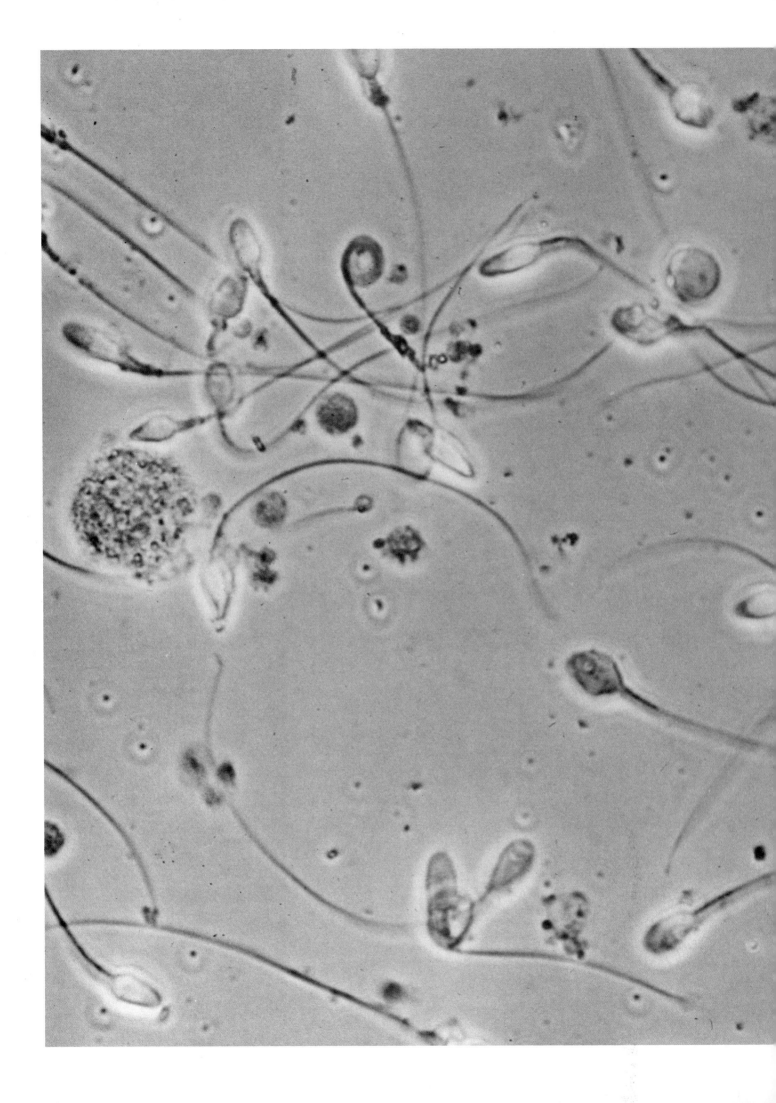

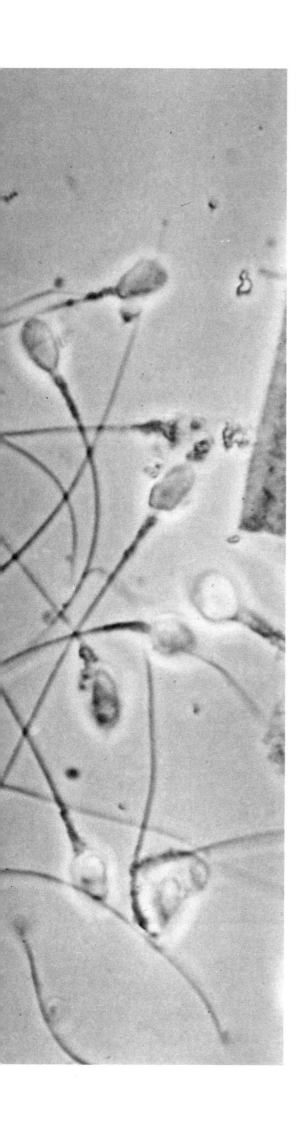

Chapter 1
Human Life

Sperms, magnified 400 times. The head
of a single sperm is only about 5
thousandths of a millimetre across.
The tail is formed from cylindrical
fibres and propels the sperms with a
whip-like motion.

The Beginning of Life

It has taken hundreds of years to realize that the smallest living part of all living things is *the cell*. It has an inherent similarity in all plants and animals, including man. The basic process of a cell is utterly dependent upon chemical units which build up and function to a basic pattern or coded message. This patterned and coded cellular unit has been likened to a factory, and the workings within this factory have been slowly brought to light by many dedicated and imaginative researchers.

Discovery of the cell

Surprisingly enough, one of the first molecular studies was done as early as 1665 by the biologist Robert Hooke, using a simple magnifying glass. The object of his study was a piece of cork. Hooke found that his piece of cork was 'perforated like a honeycomb' and that this honeycomb structure was composed of tiny box-like *cells*. His use of the term 'cell' was retained by those who followed him, and although to Hooke it simply meant a tiny room or space, it eventually became the term for a living organism in which highly complex chemical processes take place.

The basic *cell theory* first came into being with the independent researches of Theodor Schwann and Matthias Schleiden in 1838. During these researches into plant cells, both men were so struck by the similarity of their observations that they simultaneously proposed that cells were the fundamental particles of life from which all living organisms were composed. However, it was not until 1859 when Rudolf Virchow, the Prussian pathologist, stated that 'cells were the unique elements of life from which all other cells arose', that the subject of molecular biology was properly born.

With the invention and perfection of the microscope, the divergent variety of plants, animals and micro-organisms became understandable for the first time. The cell was recognized as a basic sub-unit of all living organisms. Its similarity of pattern from one organism to another was interpreted as meaning that all organisms, whatever their size, shape, colour or complexity of function, probably belonged to one fundamental cellular unit.

Over the last hundred years, the image of the cell—that of a blob of jelly surrounding a nucleus or centre—has been replaced by the idea of a structure enveloping many highly developed and specialized sub-cellular organs called *organelles* (a specialized part of a cell serving as an organ). These organelles, it was noticed, carried out the various life-building processes because of information in the form of a code fed to them from the cell nucleus. The examination of cell structures from many parts of a living organism, although showing certain differences, did reveal that the basic function of a cell and its organelles were fundamentally the same. The often translucent and transparent cellular bodies were found to be susceptible to staining with dyes and allowed researchers to

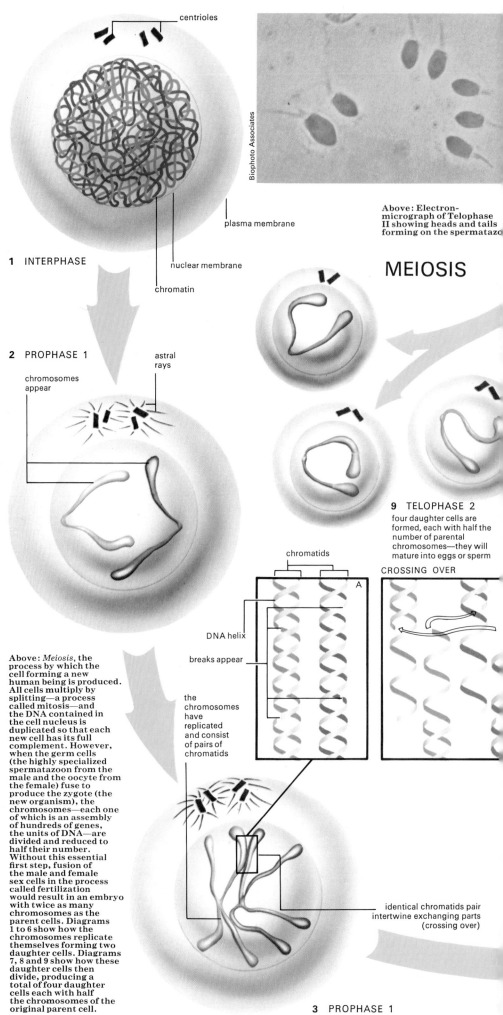

1 INTERPHASE

centrioles

plasma membrane

nuclear membrane

chromatin

2 PROPHASE 1

chromosomes appear

astral rays

Biophoto Associates

Above: Electron-micrograph of Telophase II showing heads and tails forming on the spermatazoa

MEIOSIS

9 TELOPHASE 2
four daughter cells are formed, each with half the number of parental chromosomes—they will mature into eggs or sperm

chromatids

DNA helix

breaks appear

the chromosomes have replicated and consist of pairs of chromatids

CROSSING OVER

identical chromatids pair intertwine exchanging parts (crossing over)

Above: *Meiosis*, the process by which the cell forming a new human being is produced. All cells multiply by splitting—a process called mitosis—and the DNA contained in the cell nucleus is duplicated so that each new cell has its full complement. However, when the germ cells (the highly specialized spermatazoon from the male and the oocyte from the female) fuse to produce the zygote (the new organism), the chromosomes—each one of which is an assembly of hundreds of genes, the units of DNA—are divided and reduced to half their number. Without this essential first step, fusion of the male and female sex cells in the process called fertilization would result in an embryo with twice as many chromosomes as the parent cells. Diagrams 1 to 6 show how the chromosomes replicate themselves forming two daughter cells. Diagrams 7, 8 and 9 show how these daughter cells then divide, producing a total of four daughter cells each with half the chromosomes of the original parent cell.

3 PROPHASE 1

186

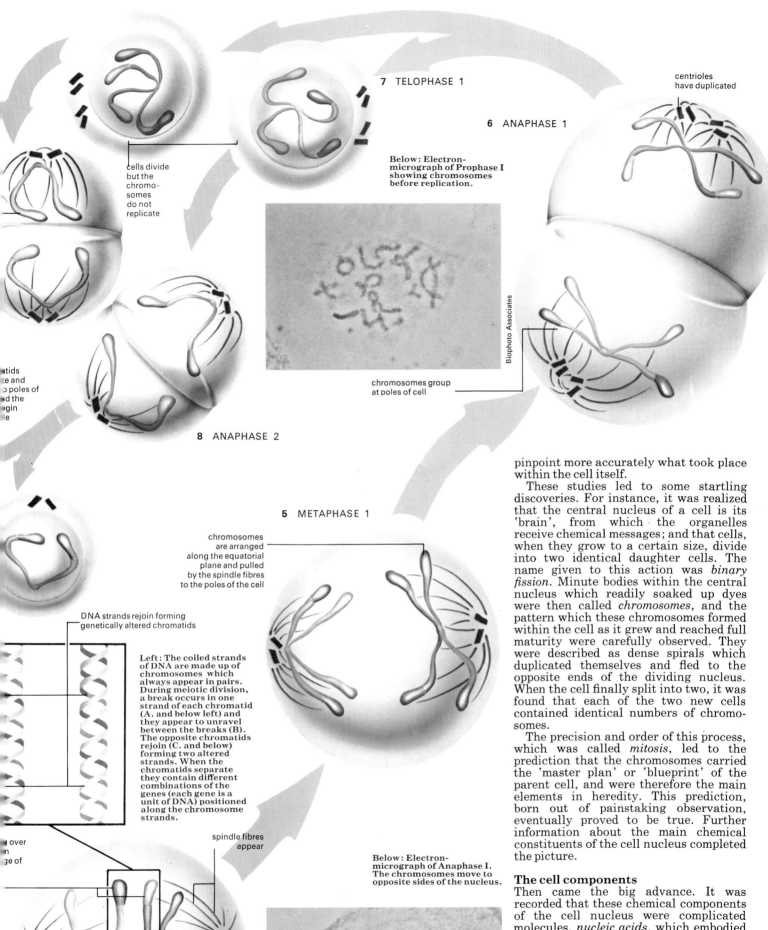

7 TELOPHASE 1

centrioles
have duplicated

6 ANAPHASE 1

cells divide
but the
chromo-
somes
do not
replicate

Below: Electron-
micrograph of Prophase I
showing chromosomes
before replication.

Biophoto Associates

chromosomes group
at poles of cell

...tids
...e and
...o poles of
...d the
...gin
...e

8 ANAPHASE 2

5 METAPHASE 1

chromosomes
are arranged
along the equatorial
plane and pulled
by the spindle fibres
to the poles of the cell

DNA strands rejoin forming
genetically altered chromatids

Left: The coiled strands
of DNA are made up of
chromosomes which
always appear in pairs.
During meiotic division,
a break occurs in one
strand of each chromatid
(A. and below left) and
they appear to unravel
between the breaks (B).
The opposite chromatids
rejoin (C. and below)
forming two altered
strands. When the
chromatids separate
they contain different
combinations of the
genes (each gene is a
unit of DNA) positioned
along the chromosome
strands.

...over
...n
...ge of

spindle fibres
appear

Below: Electron-
micrograph of Anaphase I.
The chromosomes move to
opposite sides of the nucleus.

...romosomes
...me attached
...pindle fibres

4 PROPHASE 1

Biophoto Associates

pinpoint more accurately what took place
within the cell itself.

These studies led to some startling
discoveries. For instance, it was realized
that the central nucleus of a cell is its
'brain', from which the organelles
receive chemical messages; and that cells,
when they grow to a certain size, divide
into two identical daughter cells. The
name given to this action was *binary
fission*. Minute bodies within the central
nucleus which readily soaked up dyes
were then called *chromosomes*, and the
pattern which these chromosomes formed
within the cell as it grew and reached full
maturity were carefully observed. They
were described as dense spirals which
duplicated themselves and fled to the
opposite ends of the dividing nucleus.
When the cell finally split into two, it was
found that each of the two new cells
contained identical numbers of chromosomes.

The precision and order of this process,
which was called *mitosis*, led to the
prediction that the chromosomes carried
the 'master plan' or 'blueprint' of the
parent cell, and were therefore the main
elements in heredity. This prediction,
born out of painstaking observation,
eventually proved to be true. Further
information about the main chemical
constituents of the cell nucleus completed
the picture.

The cell components

Then came the big advance. It was
recorded that these chemical components
of the cell nucleus were complicated
molecules, *nucleic acids*, which embodied
the essence of life in their ability to copy
or replicate themselves. Further study
showed that only one variety of nucleic
acid—known as deoxyribonucleic acid, or
DNA for short—carried the entire
heredity blueprint for the manufacture
and assembly of another complete cell.
This particular nucleic acid or macro-
molecule contained the exact specifica-
tions for that replication in the form of a
chemical code.

One curiosity found in this building   187

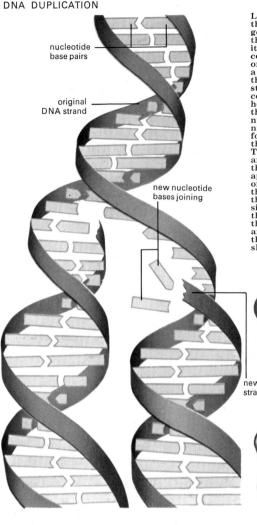

nucleotide
base pairs

original
DNA strand

new nucleotide
bases joining

new DNA
strand forming

Left: DNA, which holds the hereditary code, or genetic blueprint, has the ability to duplicate itself. Every new cell formed by mitosis, or splitting, contains a replica of the DNA in the fertilized ovum. The strands of DNA, normally coiled into a double helix, are uncoiled and the bonds between the nucleotides—the nitrogenous bases forming the 'rungs' of the ladder—are broken. Two new strands of DNA are then paired off with the old strands, the appropriate nucleotides of the new strand lining themselves up opposite their structurally similar partners. When this process is completed, the two DNA molecules are then rewound into their original helical shape.

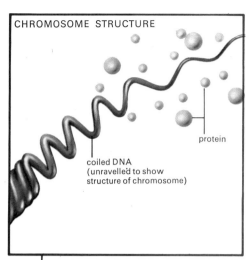

CHROMOSOME STRUCTURE

protein

coiled DNA
(unravelled to show
structure of chromosome)

Left and below: Diagrams to illustrate one theory of how a chromosome is constructed. The chromosome is made up of tightly wound strands of DNA packed in protein. To enable duplication of the DNA to take place, the strands are uncoiled (see far left) to reveal the nucleotide sequence. Depending on this sequence, which is formed by the order in which the nitrogenous bases are arranged, the DNA will contain the blueprint for the manufacture of a specific type of protein. Since it is the most essential ingredient in all living matter, the arrangement of the chain of amino acids which make up a protein molecule determines the protein's exact function in the body.

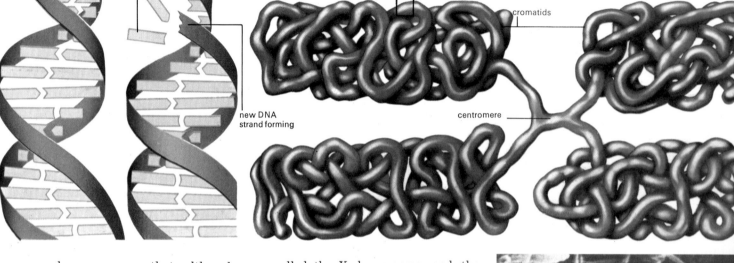

cromatids

centromere

process, however, was that although every cell carried the complete potential, or the total manufacturing message, of DNA to make a man, animal or plant, the sperm and ovum (egg cells of the male and female) did not; that is, they each contained only half of the blueprint, and in essence were only half cells carrying half the number of genes to produce a living form. The total instruction for the creation of a living organism could therefore only come about through *fertilization*—the joining of the sperm and ovum cells—so allowing the total message or blueprint for the production of life to take place. In the moment of fertilization, the two half cells become one complete cell, and in doing so are then capable of dividing over and over again to build slowly the particular form in question.

Chromosomes: the matching pairs

During this process of observation and discovery it was also realized that the inherited differences between one person and another are due to the very small differences in sections of the chromosomes each person possesses and that the basic difference of whether a child will be male or female is the difference of one whole chromosome. Microscopists were soon able to group the chromosomes of the male and female into matching pairs to show how this comes about: the 46 chromosomes in a woman produce 23 matching chemical pairs, whereas the 46 chromosomes in a man produce only 22 matching pairs—this leaves two chromosomes which do not resemble each other in any way. One of these chromosomes, being much larger than the other,

was called the X-chromosome, and the smaller of the two called the Y-chromosome. It was noted that the X-chromosome in the male was equal to the X-chromosome in the female. The X and Y chromosomes were then called the *sex determining chromosomes*, while the many others in each separate chain were given the title of *autosomes*.

The sex of a child is therefore governed and determined by whether the father contributes an X or a Y-chromosome from his non-matching pair, whereas the mother has no choice in the matter but to contribute one of her two matching X-chromosomes. The X-chromosome from the mother and the X-chromosome from the father together produce a female child; the X-chromosome of the mother plus the Y-chromosome of the father dictates that the child will be male. So the mother can only complete the DNA information code in accordance with what she is offered from the male. But her contribution, within the terms of a female child in particular, will be seen to be slightly unusual because although the Y-chromosome seems to dominate the X-chromosome—so producing, on average, more male children than female—the death rate in boys and men is higher than that in women.

Inheritance information

Within the terms of heredity, all the information for human inheritance is embodied in the nucleic acid DNA. This is made up of two chains of chemicals called *nucleotides* which are wound round one another like two intertwining springs. These chains contain compounds known

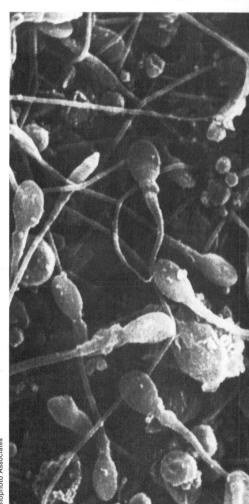

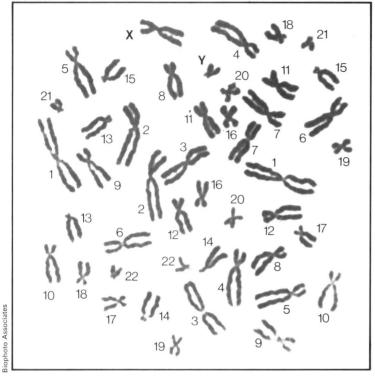

DNA DAMAGE AND REPAIR

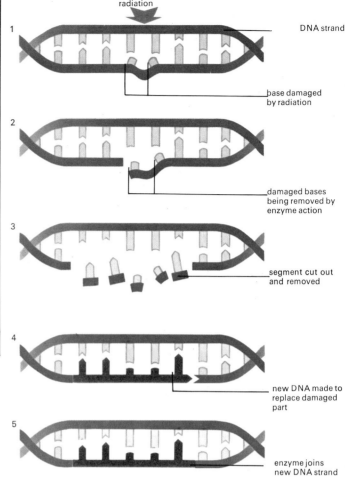

radiation

1 — DNA strand

base damaged
by radiation

2 — damaged bases
being removed by
enzyme action

3 — segment cut out
and removed

4 — new DNA made to
replace damaged
part

5 — enzyme joins
new DNA strand
to old one

Above: The 46 chromosomes of a human cell. Cells have 22 matching pairs plus two Xs in a woman and an X and a Y in a man. The sex of the fertilized ovum will depend on whether the man contributes his X which is female or his Y which is male.

Below left and below: Electronmicrographs of sperm, the male sex cells. The enlarged sperm in the centre (below) is a mutation arising from a fault in the way DNA has replicated itself.

Right: DNA is extremely stable, but may be damaged and replicated inaccurately. It can, however, sometimes repair itself depending on the extent of the damage. 1. A section of nucleotide bases damaged by radiation. 2 and 3. An enzyme travels to the spot, cuts out and entirely removes the damaged section. 4. New DNA is synthesized and inserted in the gap. 5. The new section is joined to the old by another enzyme called a ligase.

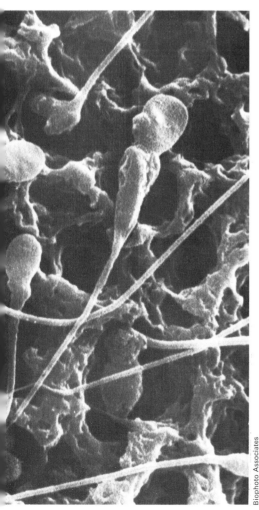

as *bases* of which there are four types. These four different bases constitute the 'letters' of the 'genetic alphabet'. It is the arrangement of these bases which determines the genetic information passed on when a fertilized cell splits into two identical daughter cells. These cells in turn split to form the plant, animal or human 'image' written in the basic DNA code of instruction. The basic building block produced through the passing on of this coded information is a protein. The structure of the protein is governed by the arrangement of amino acids coded by the sequence of bases on the nucleotide chain.

In man, about 20 different amino-acids are found in the proteins which make up his body. However, if only one amino-acid is altered in the sequence leading to the production of protein, this may profoundly change the structure of those proteins being manufactured. It may subsequently change the structure of the body in either a plant, animal or man in some way.

The mutation factor

This disturbance in the nucleotide chain of the bases which are the code for the amino-acid chain is called *mutation*. For example, haemoglobin is the protein in the blood which carries oxygen to the body's tissues. If one of the bases in the DNA strands governing the production of the amino-acids in haemoglobin is damaged or removed, then this minute change is sufficient to alter completely the properties of the haemoglobin protein. Such an alteration could lead to oxygen starvation and death in an otherwise perfect organism.

Experiments have shown that only one germ (sex) cell in 100,000, or perhaps only one in a million according to some estimates, carry such a mutation. The basic reason for this is that the DNA molecule is extremely steady as a chemical unit, and the chances of such mutations taking place are slight. The only problem, of course, is that if a mutation does take place, then the very stability of the DNA molecule leads to the passing on of the genetic defect through generation upon generation. The protruding lip of the Hapsburg royal family is a good example of this.

The mutation factor can be more clearly understood if one can appreciate what happens in everyday language when a common letter such as *a* is removed from a simple sentence. Take the sentence, *and the cat sat still.* The meaning is clear, but if one removes the letter *a* (which genetically would have an effect on the whole structure of the amino-sentence), the result could very well be: *ndt hec tst sti ll.* This nonsense sentence represents the kind of message which would result from damage to one type of base.

Luckily enough, few breakdowns in the genetic code produce anything more than slight 'oddities'. But sometimes overt disturbance of the physical body and/or the neurological processes can be extensive. The paralysis of Minamata Disease—acute mercury poisoning—and recurring scar tissue as a result of nuclear fall-out, are only two reminders that man's future ability to survive through evolutionary adaptation can be weakened as well as strengthened by the passing on of hereditary characteristics.

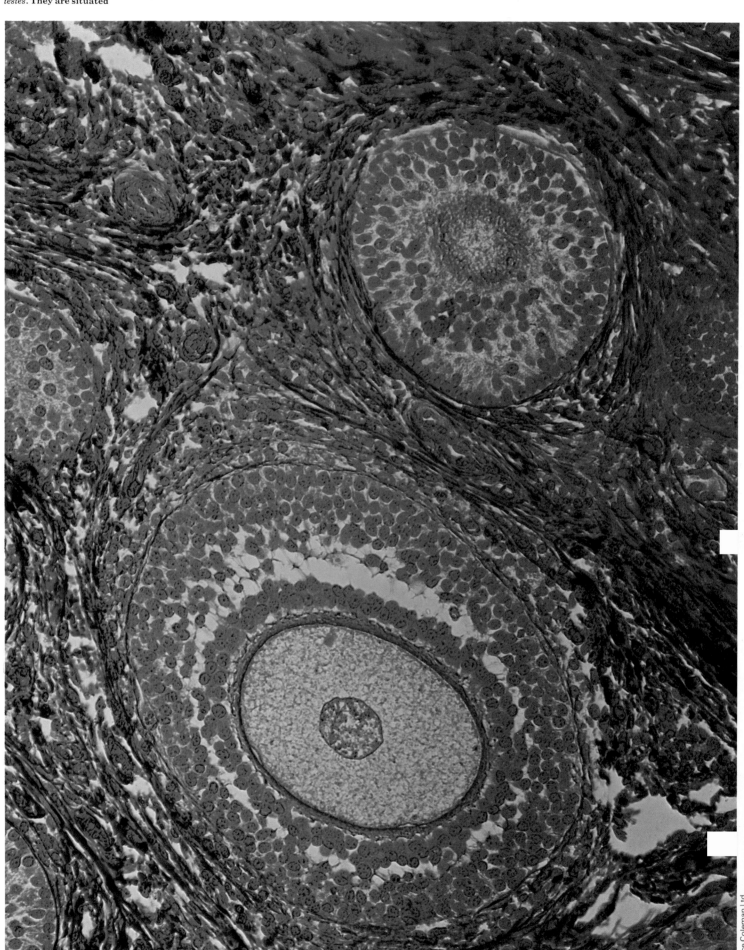

Conception

The birth of a new individual has always been regarded as a highly significant event, but not until the beginning of the nineteenth century was an accurate understanding of the reproductive process achieved.

All mammals, including man, produce offspring by a process of sexual reproduction involving the union of male and female. During the seventeenth century the celebrated Dutch microscopist, Anton von Leewenhoek, invented a microscope which enabled him to see that *semen*—the male fluid emitted during intercourse—contains tiny tadpole-shaped cells, the male sex cells or *sperm*. But not until 1827 did Karl Ernst von Baer—the pioneer of embryology—observe the corresponding female sex cell, the *ovum* or egg. Until this discovery, the role of sperm and ovum were hotly disputed. Some believed that the sperm contained the *homunculus*, a miniature, but perfectly formed, human which was merely nourished by the ovum. Rivals contended that the role of the sperm was to activate a preformed human in the ovum. We now know that homunculi do not exist: complex organisms are built by the division of simple cells, each containing genes which control the development of the whole. This explains how both sperm and ovum are equally important in reproduction and also why children share the characteristics of both parents.

The development of the sex cells

The first stage of reproduction, *conception*, involves the development of sperm and ova in the *gonads*—the primary reproductive organs—of the male and female and the joining together of these cells in the body of the female.

Both sexes possess two symmetrical gonads. The *testes*, the male gonads, are two oval bodies about five cm (two in.) long, suspended in a sac outside the body to maintain the lower temperature necessary for efficient sperm production. Each testis is divided into about 250 small lobes filled with tubes called *seminiferous tubules*. Within these tubes, cells known as *spermatagonia* are constantly developing and during the process of *spermatogenesis*, which lasts several weeks, they become mature sperm.

Spermatagonia, like normal body cells, contain 23 pairs of *chromosomes*. They carry the characteristic determining genes. The formation of both sperm and ovum must involve a reduction of this number by a half, to 23 single chromosomes, so that the new cell produced by their subsequent union will have a normal complement of 46 chromosomes. This is achieved by a specialized process of division known as *meiosis*. The spermatagonium which has matured to the point where this process may start is called the *primary spermatocyte:* chromosome pairs separate, one member of each pair moving into each of the two new cells formed by the division. These new cells, the *secondary spermatocytes*, now contain only 23 chromosomes and each of them undergoes a second meiotic division. The strands of each chromosome divide, half going to each spermatid, in which they then develop into complete chromosomes.

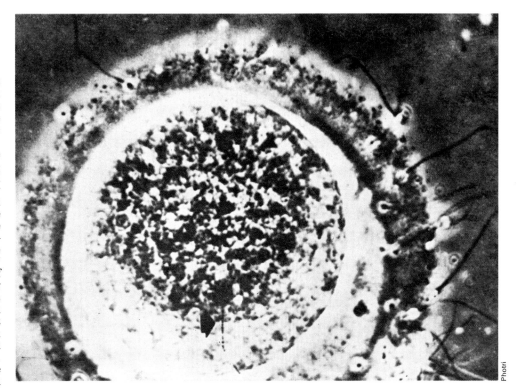

Photri

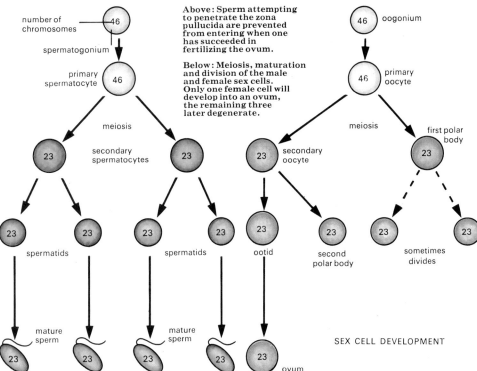

Above: Sperm attempting to penetrate the zona pullucida are prevented from entering when one has succeeded in fertilizing the ovum.

Below: Meiosis, maturation and division of the male and female sex cells. Only one female cell will develop into an ovum, the remaining three later degenerate.

SEX CELL DEVELOPMENT

Up to this point, the spermatids are round and must undergo many physical changes to become fully fledged sperm with head, mid-piece and tail, specially adapted to transmit their genetic material to the ovum. They are aided in these changes by *Sertoli*, or nurse, cells, large pyramidal-shaped cells which project from the edge to the centre of the seminiferous tubule. Each spermatid embeds itself in a Sertoli cell. This helps it to reduce the cytoplasmic material which normally surrounds the chromosomes, and this densely packed genetic material will form the head of the sperm. The head is elliptical in shape, slightly flattened and acquires a covering cap known as the *acrosome*.

A tail is formed from cylindrical fibres which eventually propel the sperm by contracting in length—first on one side of the tail then the other—and producing whip-like movements. These make it move in a forward direction. The spermatidal mitochondria, containing enzymes which break down food to provide energy for the mature sperm, migrate to a position where they will form a mid-piece between head and tail. The sperm detaches itself from the Sertoli cell and moves to the *epididymis*, a convoluted tube lying along the back of the testis, where final maturation occurs and the entire sperm is then covered by a cell membrane. They can wait here for up to three or four weeks before they are used but after this period they will be reabsorbed.

The mature sperm is invisibly small: van Leewenhoek was certainly not far wrong when he asserted: 'I judge a million of them would not equal the size of a grain of sand'. Powerful electron microscopes 191

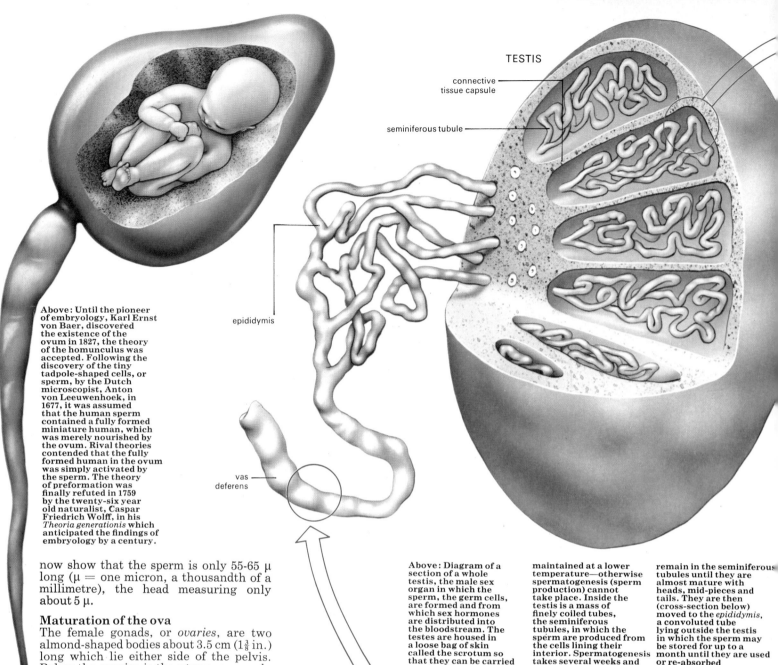

TESTIS

connective tissue capsule

seminiferous tubule

epididymis

vas deferens

Above: Until the pioneer of embryology, Karl Ernst von Baer, discovered the existence of the ovum in 1827, the theory of the homunculus was accepted. Following the discovery of the tiny tadpole-shaped cells, or sperm, by the Dutch microscopist, Anton von Leeuwenhoek, in 1677, it was assumed that the human sperm contained a fully formed miniature human, which was merely nourished by the ovum. Rival theories contended that the fully formed human in the ovum was simply activated by the sperm. The theory of preformation was finally refuted in 1759 by the twenty-six year old naturalist, Caspar Friedrich Wolff, in his *Theoria generationis* which anticipated the findings of embryology by a century.

now show that the sperm is only 55-65 μ long (μ = one micron, a thousandth of a millimetre), the head measuring only about 5 μ.

Maturation of the ova

The female gonads, or *ovaries*, are two almond-shaped bodies about 3.5 cm (1⅜ in.) long which lie either side of the pelvis. Below the ovaries is the *uterus*, or womb, in which the embryo develops. This organ is about eight cm (roughly three in) long and connects at the top with the Fallopian tubes. These are narrow ducts, about 10 cm (four in) long. Their wider open ends are near the ovaries. At the lower end of the uterus is its *cervix*, the neck, which contains a narrow opening and projects into the *vagina*—the wider channel which connects the reproductive system with the outside of the body.

The *oogonia*, the female equivalent of spermatagonia, are not produced continuously. A baby girl possesses about a half a million potential ova which do not multiply. Many of these never develop further but degenerate, a process known as *atresia*. In a woman between the age of 35 and 40 only about 8,000 oogonia remain. Some will have been used during *oogenesis*, the female equivalent of spermatogenesis.

In the first stage of ovum maturation, the primary *oocytes* develop from *oogonia* which are surrounded by a protective sac of cells known as the *follicle*. Like the male primary spermatocytes they contain 23 pairs of chromosomes and will divide by meiosis. A band of dark material forms between the cell membrane of the oocyte and the surrounding cells, thickening to become an almost transparent membrane

Above: Diagram of a section of a whole testis, the male sex organ in which the sperm, the germ cells, are formed and from which sex hormones are distributed into the bloodstream. The testes are housed in a loose bag of skin called the scrotum so that they can be carried outside the body to be maintained at a lower temperature—otherwise spermatogenesis (sperm production) cannot take place. Inside the testis is a mass of finely coiled tubes, the seminiferous tubules, in which the sperm are produced from the cells lining their interior. Spermatogenesis takes several weeks and the spermatogonia remain in the seminiferous tubules until they are almost mature with heads, mid-pieces and tails. They are then (cross-section below) moved to the *epididymis*, a convoluted tube lying outside the testis in which the sperm may be stored for up to a month until they are used or re-absorbed by the body.

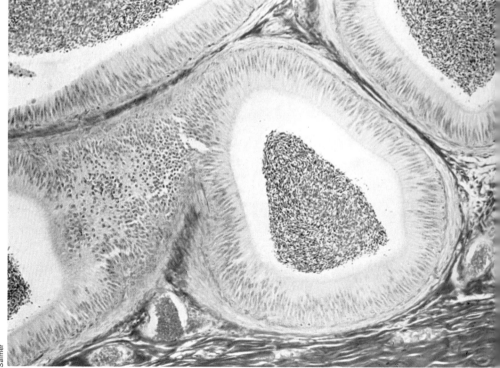

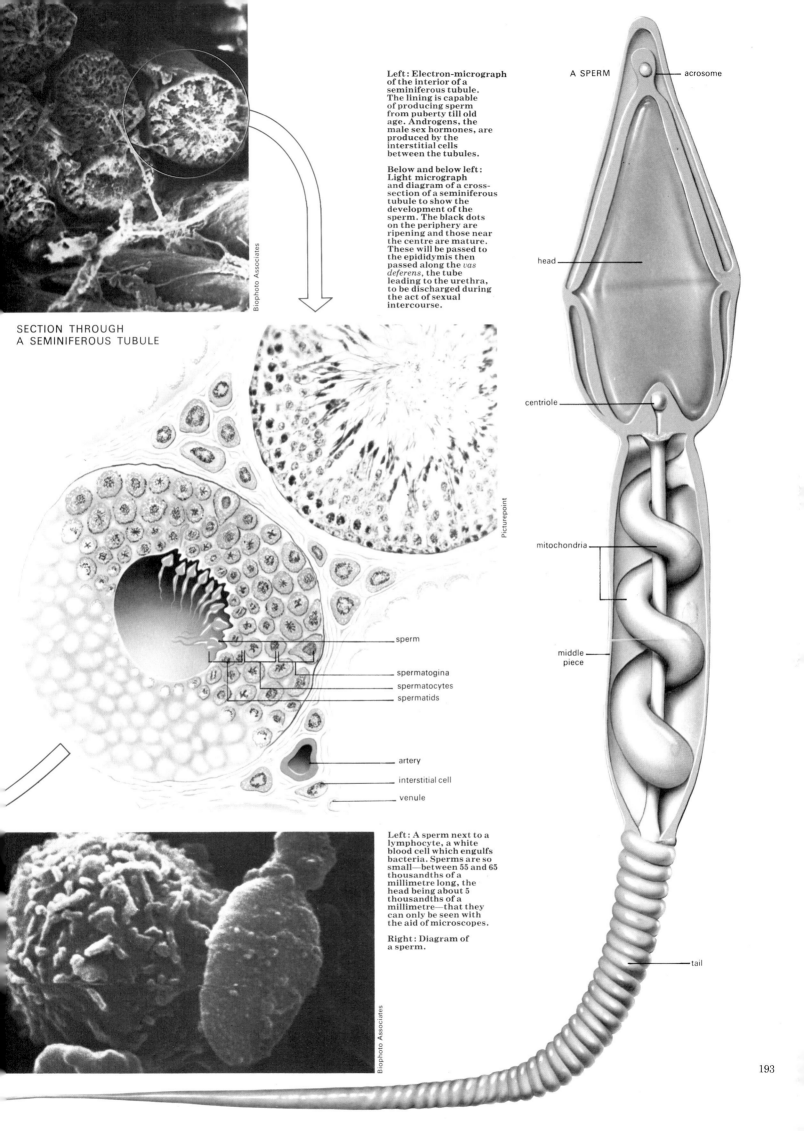

Left: Electron-micrograph of the interior of a seminiferous tubule. The lining is capable of producing sperm from puberty till old age. Androgens, the male sex hormones, are produced by the interstitial cells between the tubules.

Below and below left: Light micrograph and diagram of a cross-section of a seminiferous tubule to show the development of the sperm. The black dots on the periphery are ripening and those near the centre are mature. These will be passed to the epididymis then passed along the *vas deferens*, the tube leading to the urethra, to be discharged during the act of sexual intercourse.

A SPERM

acrosome

head

centriole

mitochondria

middle piece

tail

SECTION THROUGH A SEMINIFEROUS TUBULE

sperm

spermatogina

spermatocytes

spermatids

artery

interstitial cell

venule

Left: A sperm next to a lymphocyte, a white blood cell which engulfs bacteria. Sperms are so small—between 55 and 65 thousandths of a millimetre long, the head being about 5 thousandths of a millimetre—that they can only be seen with the aid of microscopes.

Right: Diagram of a sperm.

193

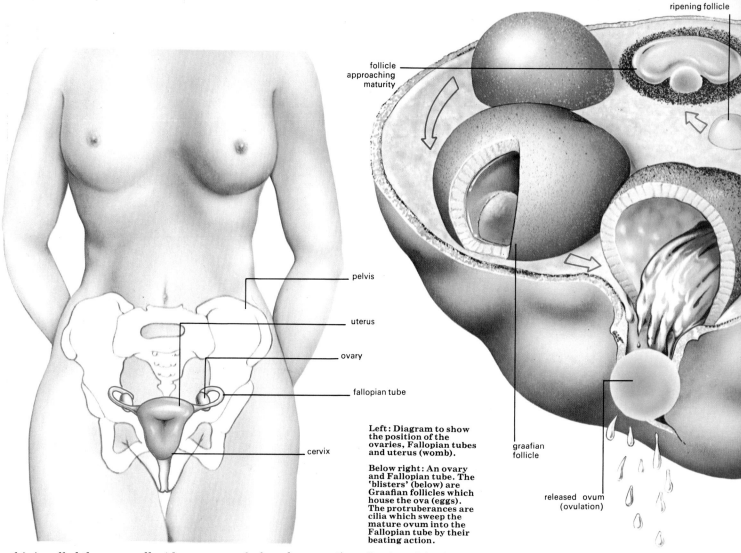

pelvis

uterus

ovary

fallopian tube

cervix

ripening follicle

follicle approaching maturity

graafian follicle

released ovum (ovulation)

Left: Diagram to show the position of the ovaries, Fallopian tubes and uterus (womb).

Below right: An ovary and Fallopian tube. The 'blisters' (below) are Graafian follicles which house the ova (eggs). The protruberances are cilia which sweep the mature ovum into the Fallopian tube by their beating action.

—this is called the *zona pellucida*.

The surrounding cells increase rapidly in number to form the *Graafian follicle*, a cavity filled with fluid forming between the follicle and the developing egg it contains. Some follicular cells remain around the zona pellucida. They are attached by a gelatinous substance and are known collectively as the *corona radiata*.

Once a month, ovulation occurs, when a single follicle is ruptured to release a developing egg cell. About two days before this the primary oocyte undergoes its first meiotic division to reduce its chromosome number by half. The outcome of this meiosis is different from division in the corresponding male cell in that two separate secondary oocytes are not formed. One of the two bodies formed during the division is larger than the other and remains in the egg as the secondary oocyte containing 23 chromosomes. The smaller one is known as the first polar body and moves out into the zona pellucida where it normally degenerates.

The maturing egg is now much larger than the sperm or a normal body cell. It is spherical, with a diameter of about 110-160 μ including the zona pellucida which is 10-20 μ thick. The egg does not begin its second meiotic division until ovulation, when it journeys down the Fallopian tube to the uterus.

The egg cannot move by itself but is collected by the *fimbria*, finger-like projections from the open end of the Fallopian tube. A current formed by the beating of tiny hair-like structures on the fimbria, together with contractions of the tube itself, carries the egg downwards. The egg can survive for about 24 hours

before degenerating. During this time it must be reached by the sperm if fertilization is to take place.

The union of the sex cells

During intercourse the sperm travel from the epididymis through the *vas deferens*, and finally the urethra, a tube in the male organ which transmits them to the vagina. They are suspended in fluid known as *seminal plasma* and deposited around the cervix of the uterus. On average about 250 million sperm will be emitted and will normally survive for little more than 24 hours, when they must reach the egg.

Ovulation

In all mammals except humans the female is only receptive to the male for a short period before ovulation, so that the sperm arrive in the female tract at exactly the right time to fertilize the egg. But the human female is potentially receptive at all times of her monthly cycle. Consequently the likelihood that both sperm and egg will be in the right state for fertilization is very much reduced. For fertilization to occur while both egg and sperm are in optimum condition intercourse must occur just a few hours before ovulation: when the egg begins to age, or if the sperm have been present for a considerable time before ovulation, the possibility of truly healthy children decreases.

One cause of male infertility is known to be a low sperm count—too few sperm per millilitre of semen. Although this may be accompanied by slow-moving sperm, or an abnormally high number of poorly-formed sperm which are incapable of fertilization, quantity is still important. Comparison of the dimensions of the

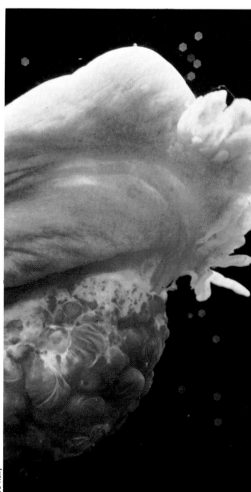

Dave Kelly

194

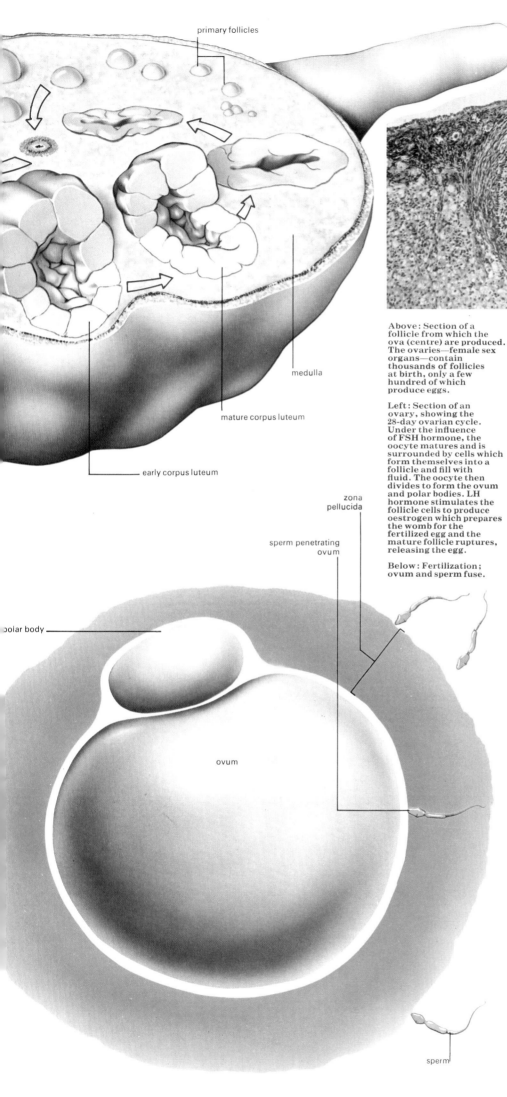

primary follicles

medulla

mature corpus luteum

early corpus luteum

zona
pellucida

sperm penetrating
ovum

polar body

ovum

sperm

Salmer

Above: Section of a
follicle from which the
ova (centre) are produced.
The ovaries—female sex
organs—contain
thousands of follicles
at birth, only a few
hundred of which
produce eggs.

Left: Section of an
ovary, showing the
28-day ovarian cycle.
Under the influence
of FSH hormone, the
oocyte matures and is
surrounded by cells which
form themselves into a
follicle and fill with
fluid. The oocyte then
divides to form the ovum
and polar bodies. LH
hormone stimulates the
follicle cells to produce
oestrogen which prepares
the womb for the
fertilized egg and the
mature follicle ruptures,
releasing the egg.

Below: Fertilization;
ovum and sperm fuse.

female organs and the sperm shows that a
formidable journey awaits them; propelled
partly by movements of their tail and by
contractions of the female organs the
sperm pass through the cervix and uterus
and only a few thousand ever reach the
Fallopian tubes. Hence there must be an
allowance for this great loss.

Capacitation

It was discovered during the 1950s that
the sperm must spend a certain time in the
female system to become capable of
fertilizing the egg. The process they
undergo there is known as *capacitation*.

In humans it takes about seven hours,
and involves activation of the acrosome
reaction by substances in the female
organs. The *acrosome*, or tip, of the sperm
contains *hyaluronidase*, an enzyme
capable of dissolving the gel of the corona
radiata which is held together by hyal-
uronic acid. This allows the sperm to
move through the corona and to penetrate
the zona pellucida. The acrosome reaction
must occur in many sperm around the egg,
since the enzyme produced by a single
sperm is insufficient to break down the
barrier, but only one sperm will actually
penetrate the egg.

The fertilized egg

Once penetrated by a sperm the egg
becomes resistant to any other. Its surface
layer moves out to engulf the sperm, the
cell membranes surrounding sperm and
egg fuse so that they constitute a single
cell. The sperm has now fertilized the egg.

The entry of the sperm activates the
egg which only now completes its second
meiotic division. This is similar to the
second division in the male, but, again in
the female, two new cells do not form.
The strands of chromosome which will
eventually unite with those of the sperm
remain in the egg to complete themselves.

The chromosomes of both the sperm and
egg then form two separate units known
as the male and female *pronucleus*. These
enlarge and move towards each other,
meeting in the centre of the egg. The
membranes surrounding them finally fuse
so that their respective groups of chromosomes come together. The maternal and
paternal contributions of hereditary
material are at last united into a single
cell called the *zygote*. This cell with its
full complement of 46 chromosomes (half
of each pair from each parent) now contains all of the information necessary to
guide the development of a new individual
who will share the characteristics of both
parents.

Pregnancy is divided into three periods known as *trimesters*. The first is from the beginning of the last menstrual period to the 14th week, the second from the 15th to the 28th week, and the third from the 29th to the 40th week, around which time the baby is delivered.

The Developing Being

The *zygote*, which is formed by the union of the male and female sex cells, the ovum and sperm, is one of the biggest cells in the body. There is about twice as much cytoplasm as nucleus, which is much higher proportionally than in a normal cell.

Almost immediately after it is formed, the zygote begins to divide by *mitosis*, or splitting, and in less than 30 hours has become two cells, called *blastomeres*. Repeated mitotic divisions, known as cleavage, rapidly increase the number of blastomeres. This occurs without increasing the total size of the zygote—it remains within its zona pellucida, the thick jelly-like layer beneath the outer layer of cells—and results in further reduction and equal distribution of the nucleus throughout the group of cells.

While undergoing cleavage the zygote is passed along the Fallopian tube partly by currents created by the beating of the *cilia* the hair-like structures lining the tube, and partly by muscular contractions of the tube itself. By the time it reaches the uterine cavity, or womb, some three to five days after ovulation, it consists of 20 to 50 blastomeres enclosed within the zona pellucida, and is known as a *morula* or mulberry. The zygote's nutritional requirements for this journey along the Fallopian tube are slight. Its needs are chiefly met by secretions from the tube permeating through the zona pellucida, although some nutrition is provided by the yolk granules of the egg.

At about four to six days the morula takes in uterine fluid and develops into what is known as the hollow *blastocyst*. It consists of a *trophoblast*, a circle of peripheral cells and an inner cell mass, a cluster of centrally placed cells at one pole. The change from morula to blastocyst doubles the size of the conceptus—the embryo—and causes the zona pellucida to become thin and eventually disappear.

The trophoblast is now exposed and attaches itself to the *endometrium*, or lining, of the uterus, usually implanting itself high up and toward the back of the uterus. It is not yet known what factors are involved in choosing any one particular place in the uterus rather than another. But the relationship between the blastocyst and the endometrium is influenced by the hormone secreted to prepare the lining for implantation.

The blastocyst becomes completely buried in the endometrium in about 10 days. Its point of entry is marked by a slight swelling and, for a time, a small plug of fibrin—fibrous protein which forms the scars during blood clotting. This later disappears and the endometrium heals over completely.

At this stage nutrition is supplied to the embryo by diffusion through the outer trophoblast layer. During the process of invasion of the endometrium by the blastocyst, the trophoblast puts out finger-like projections or villi, which can absorb dissolved substances such as nutrients from maternal blood as soon as they make contact with it. At first, villi

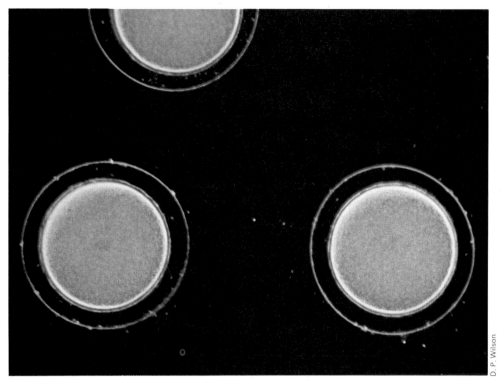

D. P. Wilson

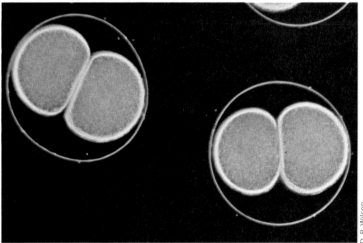

D. P. Wilson

Above, left and below: Three stages of the fertilization process in the sea urchin. The thin lines surrounding the ova (above) are the membranes, reinforced to prevent the surrounding sperm from entering. This indicates that the eggs have already been fertilized. Some two hours later the ova have begun mitotic division (left) into two blastomeres, which continue to split into eight, 16 and 32 (below). This process, known as *cleavage*, continues until there are 128 cells within the ovum. By this stage, some three hours after fertilization, the membrane splits and the blastocyst—a ball of cells with a hollow interior filled with fluid —emerges.

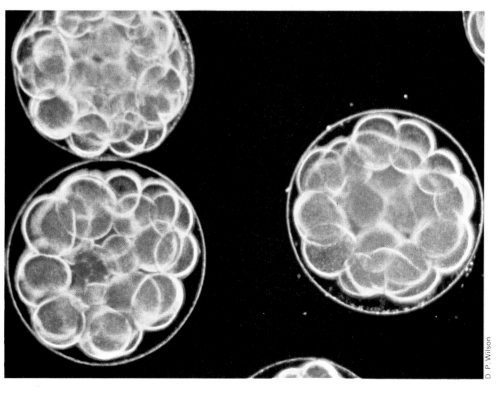

D. P. Wilson

197

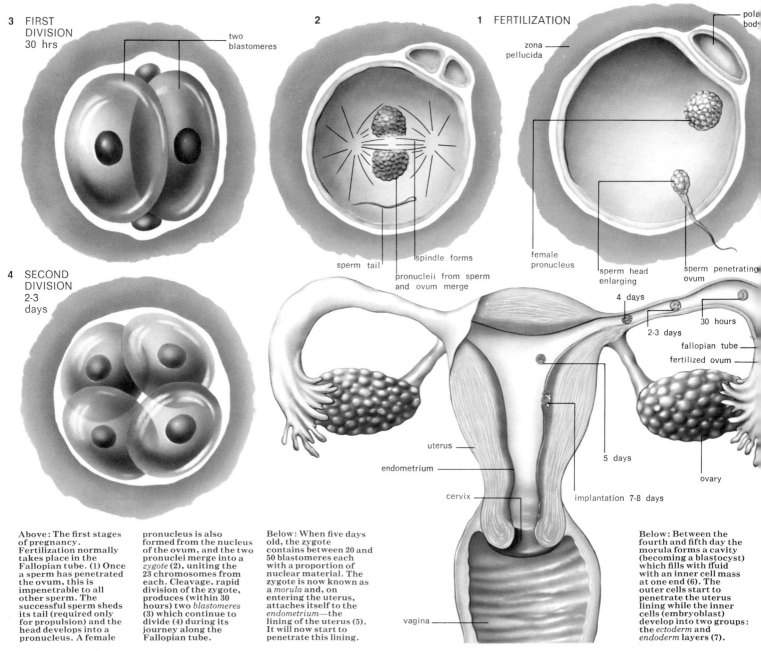

3 FIRST DIVISION 30 hrs

two blastomeres

2

sperm tail

spindle forms

pronucleii from sperm and ovum merge

1 FERTILIZATION

polar bod[y]

zona pellucida

female pronucleus

sperm head enlarging

sperm penetrating ovum

4 SECOND DIVISION 2-3 days

4 days

30 hours

2-3 days

fallopian tube

fertilized ovum

5 days

ovary

uterus

endometrium

implantation 7-8 days

cervix

vagina

Above: The first stages of pregnancy. Fertilization normally takes place in the Fallopian tube. (1) Once a sperm has penetrated the ovum, this is impenetrable to all other sperm. The successful sperm sheds its tail (required only for propulsion) and the head develops into a pronucleus. A female pronucleus is also formed from the nucleus of the ovum, and the two pronuclei merge into a zygote (2), uniting the 23 chromosomes from each. Cleavage, rapid division of the zygote, produces (within 30 hours) two blastomeres (3) which continue to divide (4) during its journey along the Fallopian tube.

Below: When five days old, the zygote contains between 20 and 50 blastomeres each with a proportion of nuclear material. The zygote is now known as a morula and, on entering the uterus, attaches itself to the endometrium—the lining of the uterus (5). It will now start to penetrate this lining.

Below: Between the fourth and fifth day the morula forms a cavity (becoming a blastocyst) which fills with fluid with an inner cell mass at one end (6). The outer cells start to penetrate the uterus lining while the inner cells (embryoblast) develop into two groups: the ectoderm and endoderm layers (7).

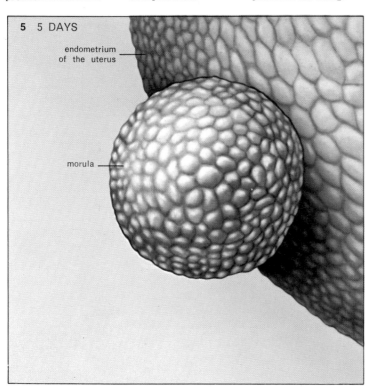

5 5 DAYS

endometrium of the uterus

morula

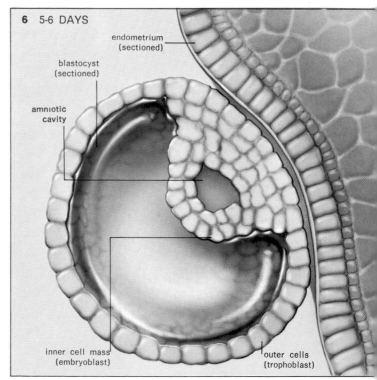

6 5-6 DAYS

endometrium (sectioned)

blastocyst (sectioned)

amniotic cavity

inner cell mass (embryoblast)

outer cells (trophoblast)

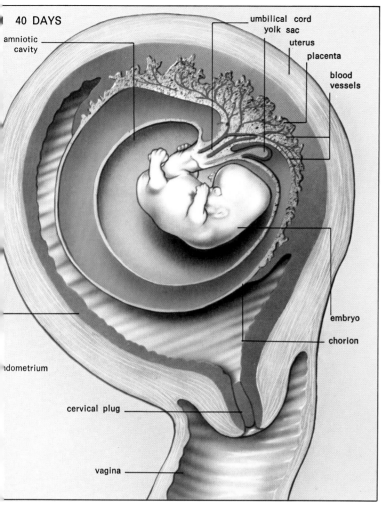

40 DAYS

amniotic cavity

umbilical cord
yolk sac
uterus
placenta
blood vessels

endometrium

embryo

chorion

cervical plug

vagina

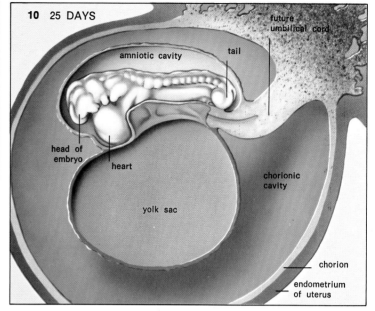

10 25 DAYS

amniotic cavity

future umbilical cord

tail

head of embryo

heart

chorionic cavity

yolk sac

chorion

endometrium of uterus

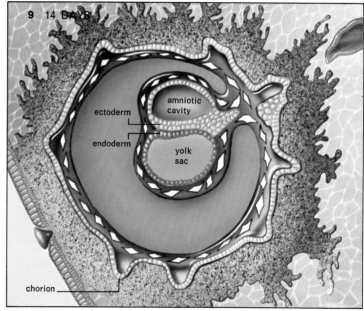

9 14 DAYS

ectoderm

endoderm

amniotic cavity

yolk sac

chorion

Below and below right: By the seventh day a cavity appears between the ectoderm and the trophoblast—the *amniotic cavity* (7). Endoderm cells form a layer around the other cavity creating the *secondary yolk sac*. The trophoblast splits into two layers with a cavity in between called the *chorionic cavity*. (8).

Right: By the 13th day the embryoblast's only connection to the trophoblast is the *connecting stalk* (future umbilical cord). The two layers between the amniotic and secondary yolk sac flatten out into the *bilaminar germ disc* (9) from which the embryo will develop. The ectoderm layer develops into the skin and nervous system. The endoderm becomes the digestive organs and lungs. Between these two layers the *mesoderm* forms from which bones, blood and muscles form. The *umbilical cord* and *placenta* develop (10). The ectoderm folds in on itself, squeezing off most of the yolk sac, and becomes surrounded by the amniotic sac (11).

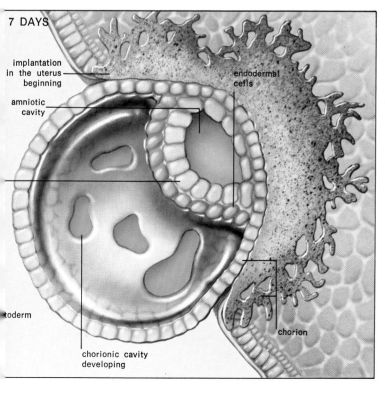

7 DAYS

implantation in the uterus beginning

amniotic cavity

endodermal cells

ectoderm

chorionic cavity developing

chorion

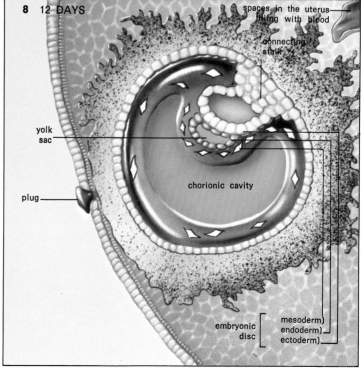

8 12 DAYS

spaces in the uterus filling with blood

connecting stalk

yolk sac

plug

chorionic cavity

embryonic disc

mesoderm)
endoderm)
ectoderm)

sprout into the endometrium all around the blastocyst but quite quickly most of them die so that only those lying deep in the lining of the uterus continue to grow. The rest of the trophoblast forms itself into a tough, protecting membrane around the embryo, the *chorion*.

Development of the placenta

About two weeks after implantation, blood vessels are formed within the villi. These link up with the embryonic circulatory system which develops at the same time. The villi come together to form the *placenta* (literally 'flat cake'), an extraordinary and elaborate organ with many highly sophisticated functions, mainly anchoring the conceptus firmly to the uterine wall, but also able to detach itself at birth without injury to mother or baby. It allows food and respiratory gases to reach the embryo and transport embryonic waste back to the mother. In this way it acts as lungs, liver and kidneys for the embryo.

The placenta can store certain substances such as glycogen—a carbohydrate formed from large glucose molecules. In conjunction with the embryo, it manufactures various hormones which prevent the uterus from expelling its contents too soon and which prepare the mother's breasts for milk production. The placenta also serves as a barrier between embryo and mother, keeping out a variety of toxins, hormones and metabolites (chemical substances involved in metabolism) present in the maternal circulation which could harm the embryo. The blood of the foetus and the mother do not come into direct contact. The maternal blood forms pools in the spaces around the placenta villi.

The formation of the embryo

Soon after implantation has begun—about one week after ovulation—the cells comprising the inner cell mass of the blastocyst begin to differentiate, that is, to become specialized to carry out different tasks. This process eventually results in the formation of the embryo.

A cavity forms between the cells of the inner cell mass close to the trophoblast lying immediately next to it. It is within this cavity, lined with the *amnion* (membrane) and filled with fluid, that the embryo actually develops. The tissues of the inner cell mass now form a disc with the *amniotic cavity* on one side and the blastocyst cavity on the other. At the same time a layer of cells lines the base of the disc and the whole inner surface of the trophoblastic shell. This lining then separates from the trophoblast to form the 'yolk-sac' cavity. In common with other mammalian eggs—and unlike a bird's egg—this sac does not contain yolk. Unlike the amnion, it does not persist and grow with the embryo, but disappears by mid-pregnancy.

By the twelfth day after fertilization the embryo has developed into a flattened two-layered disc bounded by two fluid-filled spaces. It is joined to the inner surface of the trophoblast by a connecting stalk which later contains the umbilical cord. Facing the amniotic cavity is the embryonic ectoderm (outer layer), while the embryonic endoderm (inner layer) faces the yolk-sac cavity. About three days later, the embryonic mesoderm, a third or middle layer, appears.

Although the division of the early em-

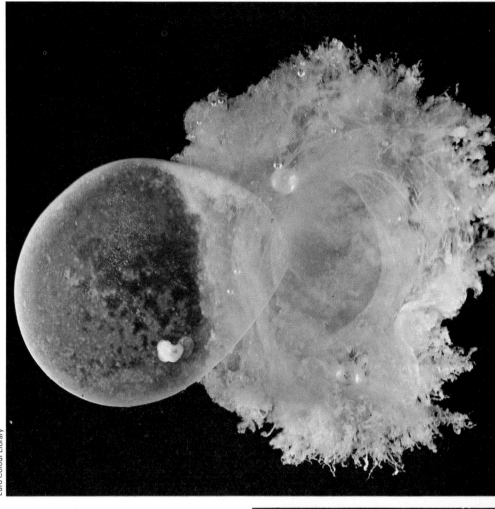

Euro Colour Library

Above: A two-week-old embryo surrounded by the amnion, or amniotic sac, a liquid-filled balloon which protects the growing child and which expands with it.

Right and below: The embryo between its fourth and fifth weeks. Still only the size of a pea, it is already beginning to show quite dramatic changes. During this time the arches which will become the upper and lower jaws become visible. The regions where the eyes and ears will eventually develop are also differentiating and becoming distinct. Somites indicate where muscles will develop.

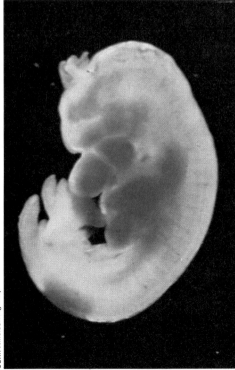

John Hillelson Agency

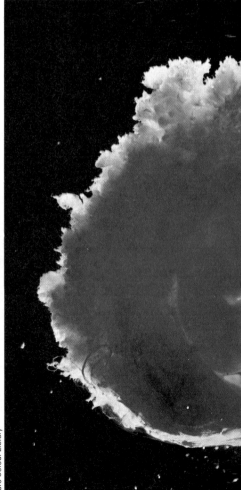

Euro Colour Library

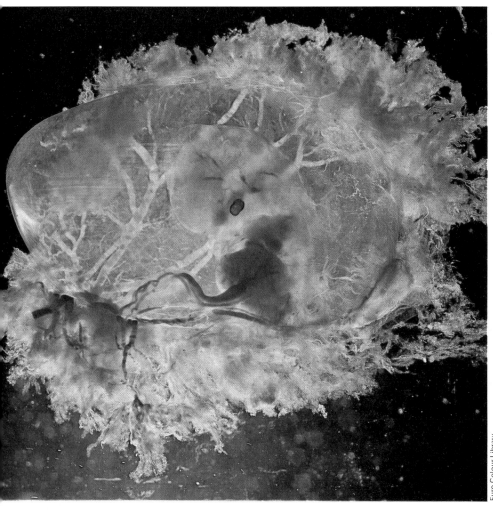

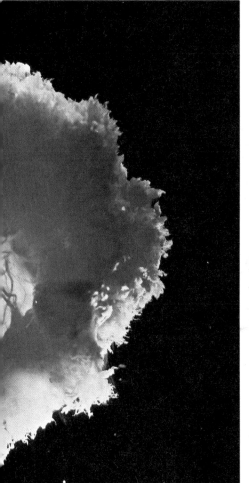

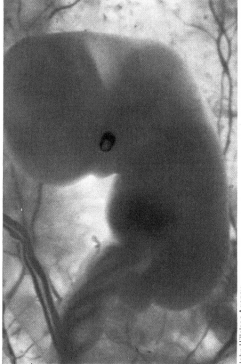

Above: By the sixth week most of the basic systems have appeared in a primitive form and its heart has begun beating. Tiny limb buds—first hands then feet—also emerge.

Below: At seven weeks the embryo is beginning to look more human. The swelling of the nose and the shape of the jaw are well established, the brain continues to develop and the eyes are forming. Although it is still only about 3 cm long, the limb buds are well defined. Paddle-shaped at first, they later become web-like, finally flattening out and separating so that the thumb- and finger-prints can be seen.

Euro Colour Library

John Hillelson Agency

bryo into these three primary germ (cell) layers is mainly for descriptive convenience, it does seem that the endoderm produces the lining of many different organs, including the lungs and the alimentary canal; the mesoderm is responsible for the formation of muscles, connective tissues and blood; while from the ectoderm develop the skin, the lens of the eye and the nervous system.

At about the time the embryonic mesoderm is formed—roughly two weeks after fertilization—the ectodermal cells heap together into what is called the primitive streak. Along this line develops the neural groove. Its edges then fold over, forming the neural tube. Ultimately this gives rise to the brain, spinal cord and entire nervous system.

Some 20 days after fertilization, and two weeks after implantation, a circulatory system begins to develop in the mesoderm of the embryo. At first the embryonic heart is no more than a straight tube. The chambers and valves do not develop until much later. But even an organ as rudimentary as this is capable of function and heart beats may be recorded from a six-week old embryo.

The emerging human

At the end of the third week, the cells of the mesoderm, already heaped up on either side of the neural groove, begin to group themselves into a series of paired mesodermal *somites* (little bodies) which are a prominent feature during the fourth and fifth weeks after fertilization. Most of the skeleton and muscles eventually develops from these somites.

Arm buds appear at the beginning of the second month, and leg buds a little later. At first the hands and feet are paddle-shaped. Later they take on a webbed appearance and, finally, the fingers and the toes separate from each other. By the seventh week, the ends of the digits are flattened and thumb and fingerprints can be seen. During the third month these flat-ended pads grow smaller and disappear, so that the hands, then the feet, become truly human.

The second month also sees the development of several structures of the head and face. The neck becomes more visible making the head distinct from the body. The ears develop from two folds of tissue very low down along the sides of the head. The eyes, located on either side of the head (as are the nostrils at this stage), are visible by the sixth week but are lidless at first. The mouth at six weeks is merely a broad gash.

At this time the embryo appears grotesque, a monstrous caricature of a human. But within about two more weeks, by the end of the second month, the humanity of the embryo is beyond question. The eyes are in place and sealed by the eyelids; the nostrils have moved closer together and the nose is almost completed; the ears have developed tiny lobes, and the mouth has acquired lips.

By the eighth week of development, therefore, the ground plan of physical individuality has been established. All the human features are present, although not in proportion. The head, for example, takes up half the total length of the embryo, which from this stage onwards becomes known as the *foetus*. Incredible though it seems, it is still barely 2.5 cm (1 in) long and weighs about one gramme. Its major task now is to grow.

The Foetus

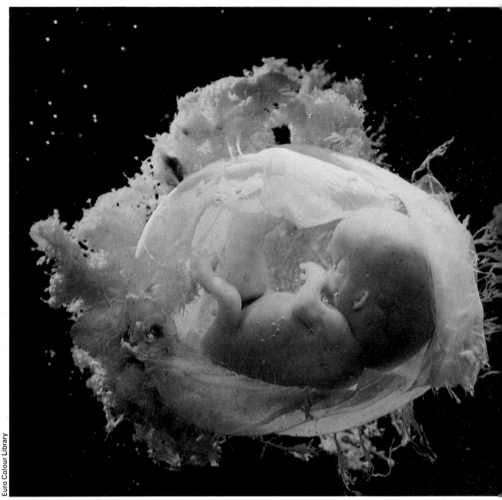

By the end of the embryonic stage, about eight weeks after fertilization, the embryo takes on a recognizably human form although it is still barely an inch (2.5 cm) long. The main external features (limbs, eyes, ears, mouth, nose and sexual organs) can be clearly seen and internal organs such as the heart, lungs, liver, kidneys, digestive tract and brain have formed but are not yet fully developed. The embryo is now called a foetus and for the remainder of its time in the womb the changes it will experience concern size and sophistication.

The cardiovascular system

A primitive cardiovascular system (CVS) has already been established by the end of the embryonic period, but during the next stage of development it becomes much more elaborate. The foetal CVS has adapted to cope with the fact that the placenta functions as the organ of respiration rather than the lungs. It must also, however, be capable of carrying out the changeover at birth from placenta to lungs with minimal delay and no loss of efficiency. The key factors in this special circulation system are three 'short circuits' whereby blood can bypass specific organs.

The placenta and the foetus are joined through the umbilical cord by three great blood vessels—two arteries carrying blood from the foetus and one vein carrying blood from the placenta. Blood

Euro Colour Library

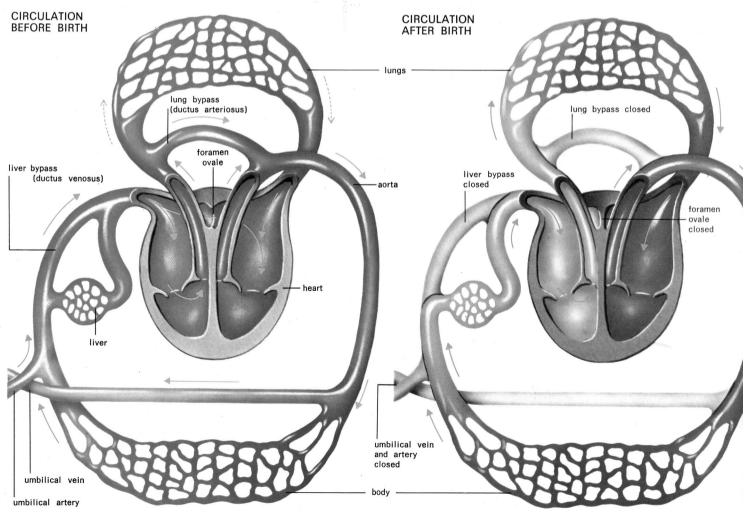

CIRCULATION
BEFORE BIRTH

CIRCULATION
AFTER BIRTH

lungs

lung bypass
(ductus arteriosus)

foramen
ovale

liver bypass
(ductus venosus)

aorta

heart

liver

umbilical vein

umbilical artery

lung bypass closed

liver bypass
closed

foramen
ovale
closed

umbilical vein
and artery
closed

body

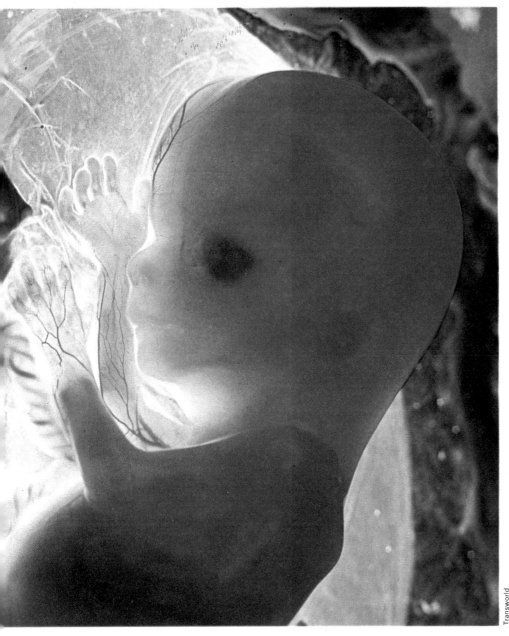

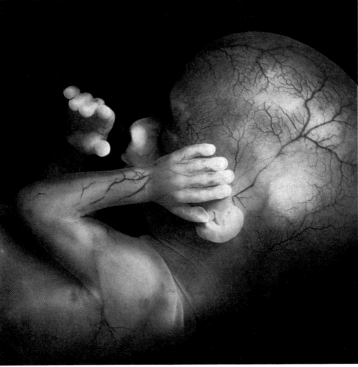

returning from the placenta through the umbilical vein flows towards the liver. Some of it passes through the liver and into the inferior *vena cava* (large vein) while much of it bypasses the liver through the first short circuit, the *ductus venosus*. The blood now moves toward the heart. Entering the right side of the heart, most of the blood is sent through the second short circuit, the *foramen ovale*, which is a flap valve in the tissues dividing the right and left sides of the heart.

Having entered the left side of the heart, this highly oxygenated blood is pumped into the systemic circulation, whose first branches go to the head and upper limbs. The blood which does not pass through the foramen ovale remains in the right side of the heart and mingles with blood returning from the head and upper limbs. Now partially deoxygenated, this mixture of blood leaves the heart and travels towards the lungs. But, instead of entering the lungs, nearly all of it enters the third short circuit, the *ductus arteriosus*, and thereby enters the lower half of the body, returning to the placenta through the two umbilical arteries. Thus, foetal liver and lungs receive very little blood while the placenta performs their future functions.

The Head

The three short circuits in the foetal circulation mean that arterial and venous blood are not completely separated. The most fully oxygenated blood passes to the upper body first, ensuring adequate nutrition for the brain. The consequences of this preferential supply of blood to the upper half of the body are easily seen in its much more advanced development at birth. The arms are longer than the legs, and the circumference of the head is a little greater than that of the chest. This latter feature is a result of the size of the cranium (the bony casing around the brain), the facial features being in fact quite small, especially the jaws which are particularly underdeveloped at birth. The skull bones are soft, with gaps between them called *fontanelles*. This allows for considerable moulding of the head to occur during birth without getting crushed by the birth canal.

Formation of the brain begins early, even before the neural tube is fully sealed which is during the fourth week. By the time closure is complete, the three main subdivisions of the brain are recognizable. The forebrain shows the greatest degree of subsequent differentiation, forming as it does the complex folds of the cerebral cortex. The midbrain and hindbrain undergo much less differentiation, and the cerebellum, which is concerned with the unconscious control of willed movements, does not begin to develop until late in foetal life.

The head and face, so large and apparently misshapen during the first few weeks, soon become obviously human. The eyes, which begin to form by the third week and are clearly visible by the sixth week, start as cup-shaped growths emerging from the forebrain. This growth closes in on itself to form the optic stalk (within which the optic nerve fibres will develop) and the optic cup. The overlying ectoderm layer (the layer of cells in the embryo from which the skin and nervous system develop) follows the contours of these forebrain outgrowths. It bulges

Top left: The foetus at nine weeks enclosed in its amniotic sac. At this age the foetus is about 3¼ cm long and weighs approximately one gram. Yet even at this age and size it has all the external human features and the rudiments of all the internal organs.

Above: When the foetus is 11 weeks old it is 6¼ cm in length. Notice that the eyelids are fused together—they will remain so until the sixth month. The mother can at last feel her uterus enlarging. Individual facial expressions appear and the sex of the foetus can be identified.

Left: The foetal circulation includes three short circuits which bypass the liver, heart and lungs. The lungs are not functional until birth and receive only 10% of the blood. Oxygen comes from the placenta which also acts as a liver. At birth, during the transition from water to air, these bypasses close.

Right: Foetus at 14 weeks (length 13 cm). During the fourth month the blood system develops and simple reflexes start.

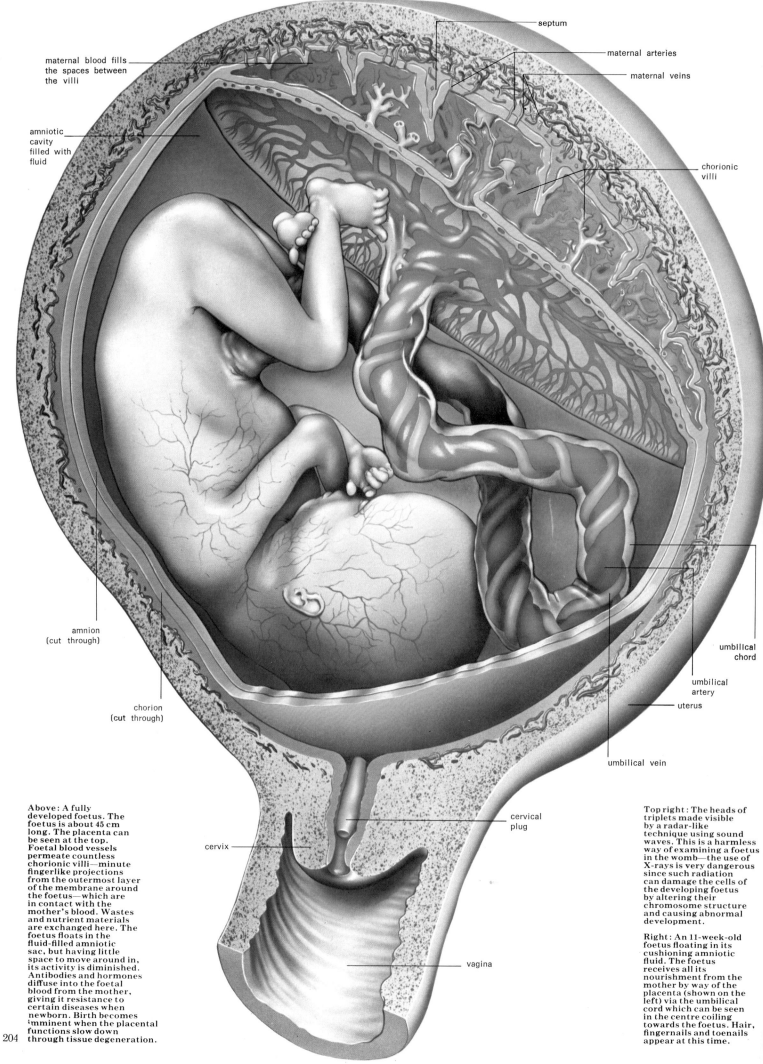

septum

maternal blood fills
the spaces between
the villi

maternal arteries

maternal veins

amniotic
cavity
filled with
fluid

chorionic
villi

amnion
(cut through)

umbilical
chord

chorion
(cut through)

umbilical
artery

uterus

umbilical vein

cervical
plug

cervix

vagina

**Above: A fully
developed foetus. The
foetus is about 45 cm
long. The placenta can
be seen at the top.
Foetal blood vessels
permeate countless
chorionic villi—minute
fingerlike projections
from the outermost layer
of the membrane around
the foetus—which are
in contact with the
mother's blood. Wastes
and nutrient materials
are exchanged here. The
foetus floats in the
fluid-filled amniotic
sac, but having little
space to move around in,
its activity is diminished.
Antibodies and hormones
diffuse into the foetal
blood from the mother,
giving it resistance to
certain diseases when
newborn. Birth becomes
imminent when the placental
functions slow down
through tissue degeneration.**

**Top right: The heads of
triplets made visible
by a radar-like
technique using sound
waves. This is a harmless
way of examining a foetus
in the womb—the use of
X-rays is very dangerous
since such radiation
can damage the cells of
the developing foetus
by altering their
chromosome structure
and causing abnormal
development.**

**Right: An 11-week-old
foetus floating in its
cushioning amniotic
fluid. The foetus
receives all its
nourishment from the
mother by way of the
placenta (shown on the
left) via the umbilical
cord which can be seen
in the centre coiling
towards the foetus. Hair,
fingernails and toenails
appear at this time.**

into each optic cup until a pocket of cells is formed which breaks from the surface ectoderm. These pockets will eventually become the lenses.

Between the lens and the surface a cavity appears. The tissue forming the outer wall of this cavity becomes the transparent cornea and the inner wall becomes the *pupillary membrane* hiding the pupil. By the beginning of the foetal stage, the surface ectoderm is forming folds which will become the eyelids, by the ninth week the optic stalk has transformed into the optic nerve and by the 25th week the various layers of the retina (formed on the inside of the optic cup) can be distinguished. The eyelids separate at about six months, but the pupillary membrane does not disappear until the seventh month.

Growth

During embryogenesis, organ development and differentiation is the keynote, but during the foetal period rapid growth is the major factor. The foetus grows at about 1.5 mm (1/20 inch) each day, doubling its length during the third month—9 to 18 cm (3½ to 7 inches)—and reaching almost half its full term length by the end of the fifth month (25 cm,

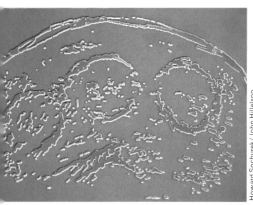

Howard Sochurek/John Hillelson

10 inches). Weight gain as distinct from length increase begins in the seventh month when ordinary white fat is deposited under the skin all over the body. In addition during the last few weeks of life in the womb, a peculiar form of fat called brown fat is deposited across the shoulders and at other sites on the upper body. By the end of pregnancy, the foetus will probably weigh somewhere between 3 and 4 kg (6—9 lbs) and be about 50 cm (20 inches) long.

The late appearance of fat means that up to about seven months the foetus has a decidedly scrawny look. At four months it is pitifully thin, a huge head dominating its appearance and the blood vessels glowing brightly through the fatless, transparent skin. A few weeks later the skin, although very wrinkled, is less translucent because it is covered with a fine downy hair called *lanugo*. This drops out by the end of pregnancy except perhaps across the shoulders. During the seventh month the skin, a little less wrinkled as fat develops, becomes covered in a creamy waxy substance, *vernix caseosa*, which is manufactured by glands under the skin. This is thought to 'waterproof' the skin.

Life in the womb

As the foetus grows, so do the membranes which surround it. The external trophoblast has become the tough chorion, the amniotic sac containing the foetus has expanded inside the chorion and the remnant of the yolk sac usually gets flattened between them. Frequently the chorion and amnion fuse. Secure within the double membrane the foetus floats in amniotic fluid. It can move about freely (at least while still relatively small) and is cushioned from mechanical pressure of the uterine walls or sudden injury should the mother have an accident.

As early as the third month, the foetus begins to swallow some of the amniotic

fluid and excrete drops of urine into it. By late pregnancy it may swallow almost a pint a day. Although most foetal waste enters the placental circulation and is excreted by the mother, a small amount of amniotic fluid is made up of foetal urine. It is uncertain what role, if any, amniotic fluid plays in foetal nutrition.

The rate of growth of the placenta is very different from that of the embryo and foetus. At the end of the third month, it weighs about six times as much as the foetus. Placental growth then diminishes so that by the end of the fourth month it weighs as much as the foetus, and at birth it is only a fifth as heavy.

As well as functioning by itself as the organ of transfer between mother and baby, the placenta should also be considered as part of an endocrine (that is, hormone secreting) structure. The hormones produced by this unit have profound effects on the mother. Her heart rate and output are increased, her kidneys step up production, and her entire metabolism is changed so that digestion is slower and absorption of nutrients more thorough. Progesterone in particular is responsible for softening all tissues and muscles, especially uterus and cervix, which aids implantation, prevents the uterus from expelling its contents too soon by reducing its irritability, and prepares the cervix for the stretching it will undergo during the baby's birth. Foetoplacental hormones are also responsible for preparing the mother's breasts for lactation.

By contrast, maternal hormones cannot normally pass the placenta into the foetus. Any that do are usually neutralized by specific placental enzymes. During late pregnancy, however, the placenta allows a number of antibodies to pass from the mother to the baby so that the newborn child has a degree of immunity to many of the diseases to which its mother has previously built an immunity.

Foetal activity

It has been suggested that the foetus swallows fluid because it needs to practice swallowing. There is increasing evidence to show that the foetus does practice all kinds of complex behaviour patterns such as breathing, swallowing and sucking. Sensory functioning in the uterus may of necessity be limited but it occurs.

There seem to be three distinct states of activity shown by the foetus. During 'deep sleep' it makes few and feeble spontaneous movements and does not react to stimuli. During the 'waking state' its eyes may open and it moves frequently and spontaneously. Foetal movement actually begins as soon as the limbs develop but the mother is rarely aware of the movements until about the fourth month. During waking it responds to stimuli—such as a very loud noise, a sudden flash of light, or a rapid change in the mother's position, and these may evoke a quick and vigorous reaction from the foetus.

The third state is rapid eye movement or REM sleep. During this time, the foetus shows rapid horizontal movements of the (closed) eyes and twitching movements of the limbs, trunk and face and he may practice quite strong rhythmic breathing movements of the chest. We know that in children and adults, REM sleep is associated with dreaming, and it is possible that the foetus also dreams in this state.

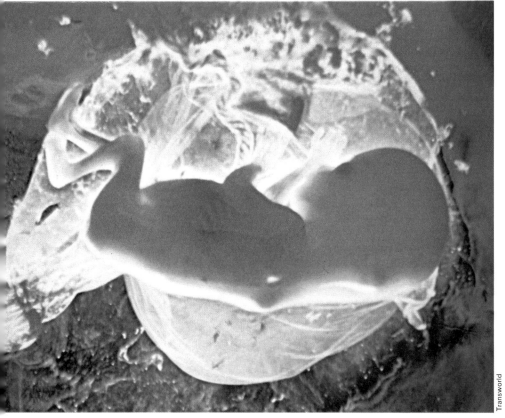

Transworld

Progesterone crystals. This hormone softens up muscles and ligaments – especially the pelvis, uterus and cervix – to make them more elastic for the birth. Levels of progesterone in the blood rise steadily during pregnancy.

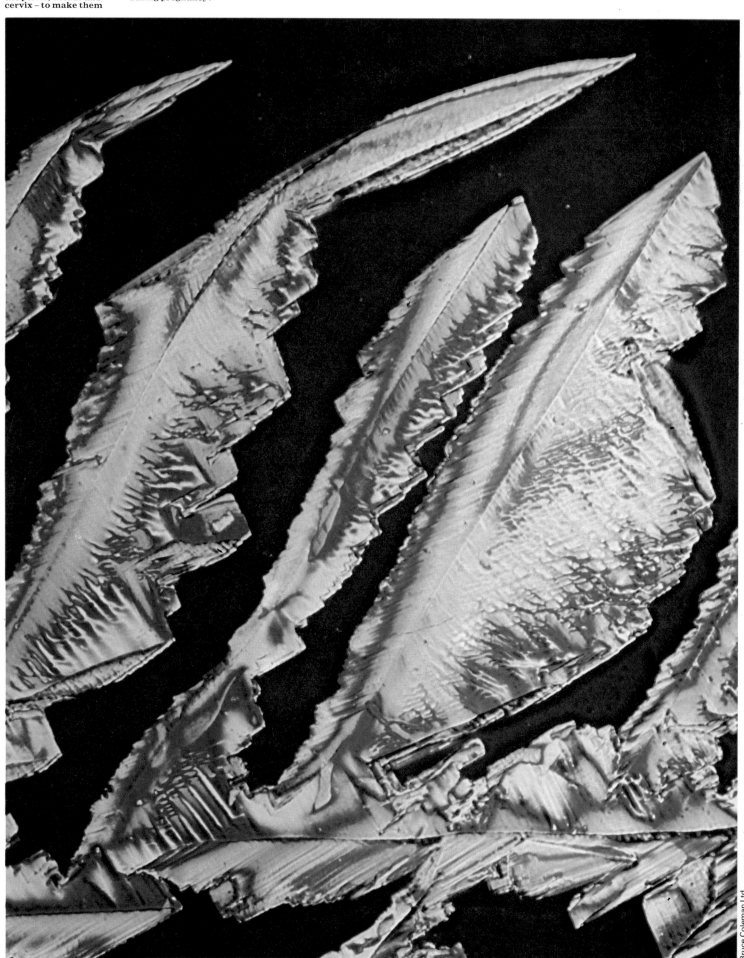

Birth

The mature foetus spends several weeks preparing for the hazardous journey from his mother's womb to the world outside. Most of the preparations are caused by hormones from the adrenal glands.

In a child or adult the adrenal glands, situated just above the kidneys, consist of a *medulla* (core) and a *cortex* (shell). But in a foetus an extra layer of cortex lies between them, making the foetal adrenal relatively huge. After birth the foetal cortex shrinks until at three months the adrenal weighs only half what it did at birth.

Corticosteroids, hormones released by the adrenal cortex, cause large amounts of glycogen to be stored in various parts of the foetus' body, particularly the liver and the heart. The glycogen store in the cardiac muscles is of special importance as it enables the heart to continue beating in the absence of oxygen—thus helping the baby later through the potentially dangerous changeover from placenta to lungs.

During the last two months of pregnancy, the lungs, again due to stimulation by corticosteroids, gradually become ready for the moment that the newborn baby will draw breath. A surface-active compound or *surfactant* is formed within the *alveoli* of the lungs (the minute grape-like air sacs where exchange between air and blood will take place). This surfactant has the distinctive property of exerting a high surface tension when it is stretched, but a low one when its surface is compressed. As a result small alveoli will tend to expand, thus preventing lung collapse following the initial inflation just after birth. Babies born very prematurely, before surfactant has formed, cannot breathe independently for long.

Positions in the womb

The baby's position in the uterus also shows his readiness for birth. Until about six weeks before delivery he may change his position fairly often so that sometimes his head is at the top of the womb, and sometimes at the bottom. As he gets bigger he comes to fill the available space until

British Museum

Above: A medieval caesarean section. The use of such operations has been recorded since Roman times although the survival rate of both mother and child was low because of infection and haemorrhage. The operation, which involves removal of the foetus via an incision of the abdomen and uterus, is widely used today.

Below: Position of the foetus before the onset of labour. This position is known as a *cephalic presentation*—the baby's head will be born first. The baby has already dropped down and its head is in the pelvic cavity—a process known as 'lightening' because it removes the pressure on the mother's lungs caused by the uterus.

POSITION OF THE FOETUS JUST BEFORE BIRTH

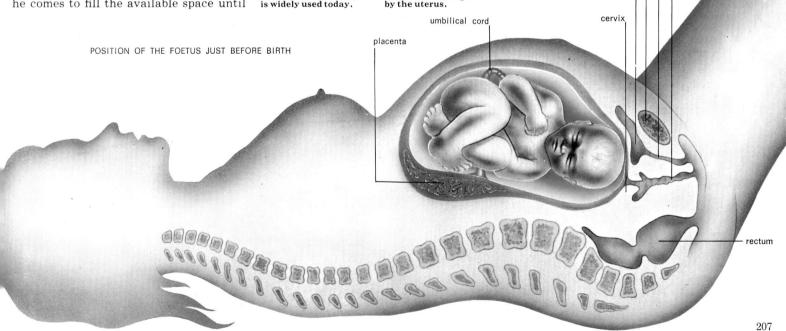

placenta

umbilical cord

vagina

urethra

coxal bone

urinary bladder

cervix

rectum

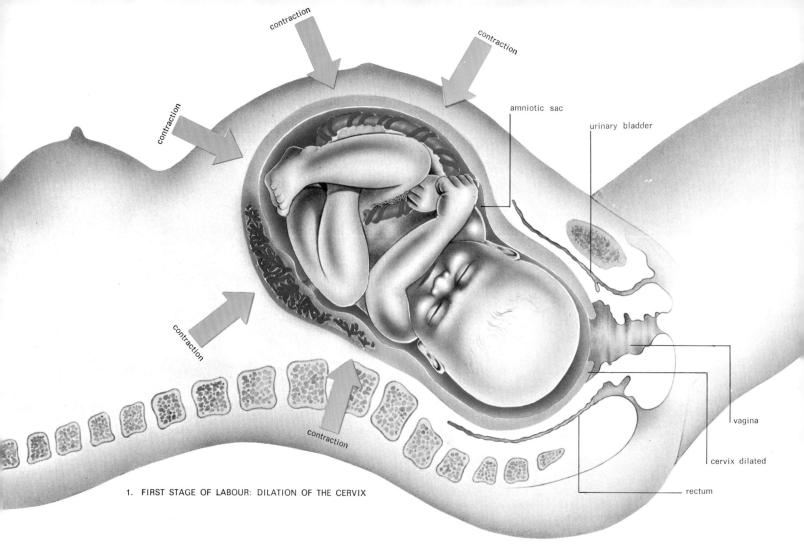

amniotic sac

urinary bladder

vagina

cervix dilated

rectum

1. FIRST STAGE OF LABOUR: DILATION OF THE CERVIX

no more manoeuvring is possible, and he must settle into one position. In the vast majority of cases this is head downwards, called a *cephalic presentation*. Occasionally a baby settles head upwards, so that his bottom is born first. This is called a *breech presentation*. Later on he will 'drop' into the mother's pelvic cavity. The top of the uterus also drops as the baby moves down, and consequently no longer causes pressure on the mother's lungs. Because of the relief of this pressure, the process is known as 'lightening'.

The descent of the foetal head into the pelvic cavity is called the *engagement* of the head. It tends to occur about a month before birth among firstborn children, but not until much nearer delivery, or actually during labour, in second and subsequent deliveries. Its occurrence is a good indication that the mother's pelvic size and shape are adequate for birth.

The onset of labour

Throughout pregnancy the uterus contracts regularly. These practice contractions are mild and rarely detectable by the mother. At some point they begin to increase in strength and duration, and the intervals between them get shorter. It used to be thought that this was caused by a drop in maternal circulatory progesterones. But during recent years evidence has begun to pile up that this change in the nature of uterine contractions, which marks the onset of true labour, is somehow initiated by the foetus itself. A chain of hormonal reactions seems a probable cause, and the foetal hypothalamus is thought to be one of the earliest links in the chain. If the theory is correct, hypothalamic stimula-

Above: The first stage of labour. Contractions increase in intensity and frequency. The amniotic sac (which is incompressible) is forced down against the cervix.

Below: The cervix dilates, the amniotic sac breaks and its contents gush out. At this, the second stage of labour, uterus, cervix and vagina form a continuous *birth canal*.

2. BREAKING OF THE WATERS

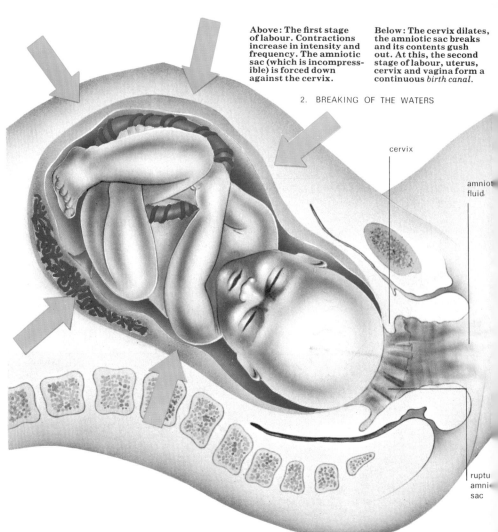

cervix

amniotic fluid

ruptured amniotic sac

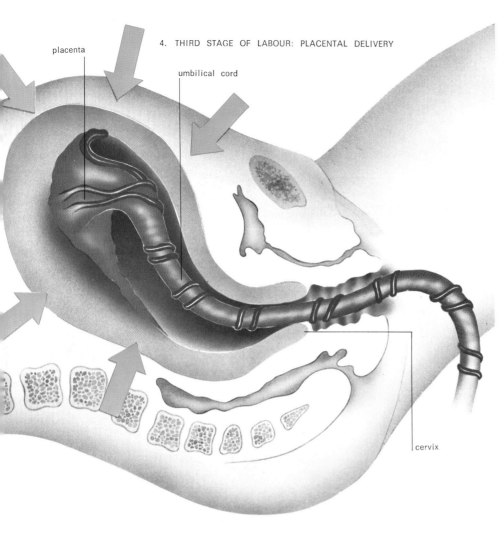

4. THIRD STAGE OF LABOUR: PLACENTAL DELIVERY

placenta

umbilical cord

cervix

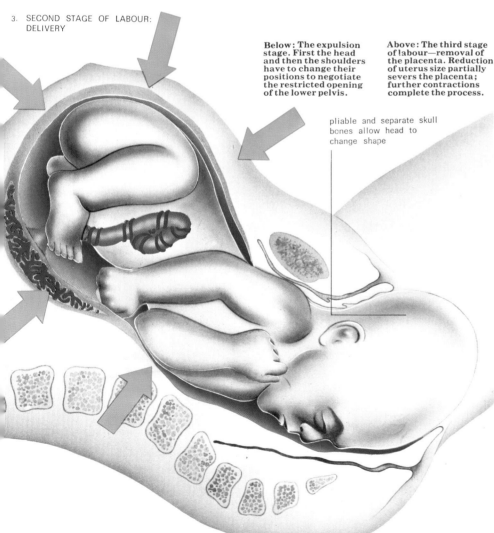

3. SECOND STAGE OF LABOUR: DELIVERY

Below: The expulsion stage. First the head and then the shoulders have to change their positions to negotiate the restricted opening of the lower pelvis.

Above: The third stage of labour—removal of the placenta. Reduction of uterus size partially severs the placenta; further contractions complete the process.

pliable and separate skull bones allow head to change shape

tion causes the pituitary to release ACTH (adrenal corticotrophic hormone) which in its turn stimulates the adrenal cortex to secrete corticosteroids. These steroids cause a change in the hormone balance of the mother and stimulate her tissues to synthesize *prostaglandin*. Minute quantities of prostaglandin cause strong uterine contractions.

The process of childbirth is aptly named labour, for it is a time of extraordinarily hard work. During the first stage most of the efforts of the uterus are directed at opening the neck of the womb, or cervix. The baby flexes his head so that his chin rests on his chest, well tucked in, and the top of his head settles more deeply into his mother's pelvic cavity. As the cervix continues to widen the baby slips down even further so that his head causes pressure on the mother's bladder above and rectum below. When the cervix is fully dilated, the uterus, cervix and vagina form a continuous curved passage —the birth canal—from the baby into the world. At the very end of first stage of labour, although it can occur much earlier, the amniotic sac usually breaks and the amniotic fluid gushes out of the vagina. This is termed the 'breaking of the waters'.

Birth and afterbirth
The second stage of labour begins when the cervix is completely (or almost completely) dilated, and is triggered by the release of another hormone, *oxytocin*, from the maternal pituitary gland. This stage mainly involves the *fundus muscles* which form the top of the uterus. These powerful muscles begin to contract and push downwards on to the baby's bottom, propelling him along the birth canal.

Because of the shape of the muscles across the mother's pelvis, the baby's head is slightly turned so he faces toward her rectum. Evolution has made this, and a complex sequence of other movements, necessary; when man expanded his brain and developed a round skull he made childbirth more difficult. The widest diameter at the entrance to the mother's bony pelvis is the one stretching across it between the hip bones, and the baby adjusts so that the length of his head from the forehead backwards rather than its width, fits into this. In the lower part of the pelvis, the longest diameter stretches backwards from the pubic bone in the front and, having descended this far, the baby must rotate his head to fit the new shape.

Each contraction of the uterus pushes the baby's head nearer the vulval cleft and the outside world until, at last, the top of the back of the head is just visible from the outside at the peak of a contraction. Finally, the head stretches the vaginal entrance and all the tissues around it, and begins to emerge. This is called *crowning*. At this point the baby's shoulders also begin to turn to negotiate their journey through the birth canal. The next contraction pushes the baby down further, his head sweeps over the vulval tissues and emerges into the world: forehead, eyes, nose, mouth and chin appearing successively. Once the head is born the baby turns on to his side, facing his mother's hip. This means that his shoulders and the rest of his body can slip out of the birth canal quite easily, which they usually do with the next contraction. The baby is born.

209

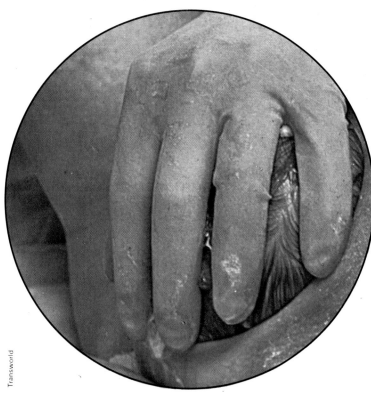

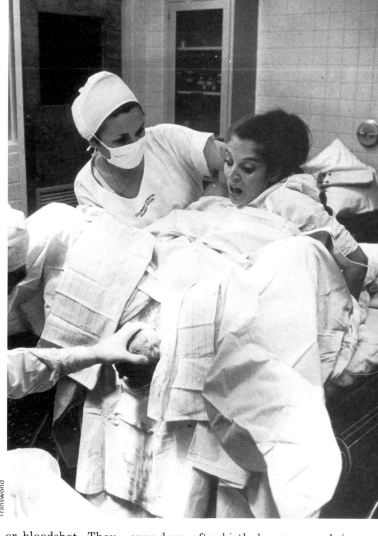

The third stage of labour is the delivery of the *placenta*, also called the afterbirth for obvious reasons. The placenta separates from the uterus during birth, and is usually delivered by uterine contractions within 20 minutes of the baby.

The first few weeks of life

At birth the baby may not be an altogether prepossessing sight. He is greasy and whitish with his covering of *vernix caseosa*, and beneath this he may look grey because his blood circulation has not been fully established. But with the first few breaths his skin turns a healthy pink, although he may still look greasy and wrinkled. The umbilical cord continues to beat for a few minutes after birth to ensure that the baby has time to begin breathing before oxygen supplies from the placenta are completely cut off. The thick muscular walls of the umbilical vessels then contract and pulsation within the cord can no longer be detected. Some obstetricians and midwives prefer not to cut the cord until it has ceased to beat. But usually the cord is tied, which stops the blood flow through it, and cut as soon as the baby is born and has begun to breathe. Because the cord contains no nerves, this cutting does not hurt either mother or baby.

When the baby is properly born, breathing independently and separated from his mother, he is usually wrapped up and given to his exhausted but proud parent for a few minutes. Then he is weighed and examined. Birth weights vary, the usual range being 3 to 4 kg (6 to 9 lb), and boys usually weigh a few ounces more than girls. The medical attendant will wipe off most of the vernix caseosa but not remove it entirely as it protects against skin infections during the first week or so.

The newborn's skull is sometimes lopsided or elongated through pressures from the birth canal on the soft skull bones, but it expands measureably during the first week of life, and gradually returns to a normal shape. The eyes, too, may show the effects of pressure during delivery by

Above: The baby's head, emerging from the vulvo-vaginal orifice, being guided by the obstetrician's hand. The head must be held and turned to match the internal rotation of its shoulders as they negotiate the lower pelvis. Within a few minutes the baby will be born.

Right: Amazement—or exhaustion? A mother's reaction, after hours of extremely hard work, as the baby's head emerges. Labour, the process of childbirth, is usually much easier with the second and later births because the muscles surrounding the uterus are stronger and the birth canal tissues never completely return to their pre-pregnancy size.

being puffy, swollen or bloodshot. They are usually slate blue, and may not attain their individual colour for several weeks.

So that the lungs can function correctly in supplying oxygen, the newborn's cardiovascular system must re-route its blood supplies to receive it. Before birth, the foetus' circulation system contains three shunts or 'short circuits' which by-pass the liver, the heart and the lungs. These are the *ductus venosus*, the *foramen ovale* and the *ductus arteriosus* respectively. When the newborn begins to breathe, the ductus venosus and the ductus arteriosus close down, partly through muscular contraction of their walls.

As the lungs expand the blood vessels inside them open up. The amount of blood returning to the left side of the heart thus suddenly increases, which pushes a membrane against the foramen ovale, thus sealing it shut and irrevocably separating the two sides of the heart. The closing down of the three 'short circuits' is normally rapid and seems to depend on a number of factors. Most of these are not yet fully understood, although the amount of oxygen in the baby's system is important. Blood may still be shunted through the ductus venosus for hours, or

even days, after birth, however, and since this means that it is not passing through the liver, this incomplete closure of the 'shunt' may contribute to the mild and transient jaundice many newborns show. Occasionally, too, blood may pass through the ductus arteriosus for up to two weeks after birth.

The baby's cardiovascular system must also make other adjustments before it can work properly. During the first few weeks it is common for the baby's extremities (hands and feet) to turn blue. Occasionally the side on which the baby is lying becomes a bright red, while his upper half remains pale with a definite line right down his body marking the junction of red and pale areas. This so-called 'harlequin colour change' is thought to be due to gravity causing the blood to pool, before the circulation has fully learnt to adjust to such things.

Unlike most mammals, the human mother does not produce mature milk immediately after delivery. For the first few days she produces *colostrum*, a clear yellowish fluid rich in protein and in antibodies. The baby's needs are met partly through colostrum and partly through the glycogen stored for this purpose in his liver and white subcu-

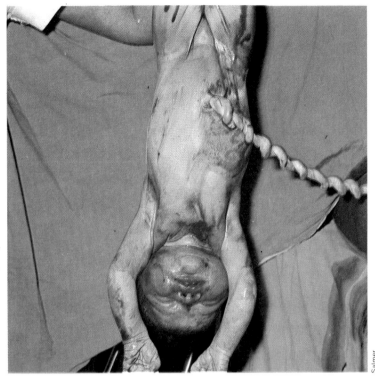

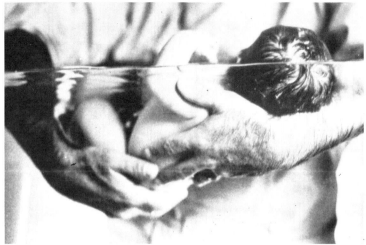

Left: The newly born baby is held upside down to help remove any fluids that may still be in the lungs. If it does not start breathing of its own accord, it may be slapped.

Below: Its umbilical cord cut, the child begins an independent existence. It is then measured and tagged.

Above: Some obstetricians believe that conventional deliveries, with their bright lights, rough blankets and cold scales, overload the baby with extreme sensations which terrify it. Instead, they believe that babies should be eased gradually into life. This baby is being held in a bath of warm water—for comfort, not cleansing.

Below: This baby has been born into a world of soft lights and soft blankets. It is claimed that babies delivered in this way do not show the usual newborn behaviour of clenched, raised fists, screwed up eyes and loud piercing wails. This one certainly looks as if he is enjoying his first few hours outside the womb.

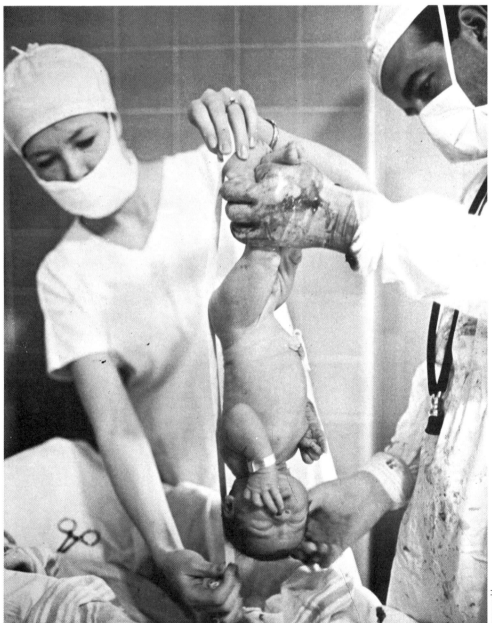

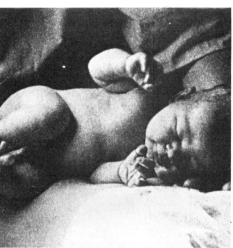

taneous fat. This is why most breast-fed babies lose weight for the first few days after birth. The baby's suckling encourages milk production, which usually begins within five days, and by ten days of age most babies have regained their birth weight.

Changes in environment

Views about prenatal existence and the meaning of birth have changed radically in recent years. Older research tended to consider the foetus as living in a kind of void, oblivious of his surroundings and wholly unprepared for the experiences and activities awaiting him. Now it is known that development is remarkably complete before birth, both in form and function, and that birth represents a transition from one stage of existence to another, rather than a sudden leap from 'nothingness' to 'being'.

Birth remains in all societies a highly significant event in the lives of the parents and the whole network of friends and relatives into which the child is born. It is as well for the survival of the species that successful reproduction evokes such a profound response; but the reverence is no less genuine because it is functional for this remarkable biological event.

211

Heredity

Over 3,000 million people inhabit the earth and, although we all exhibit the same basic features, no two people are exactly alike. The consistency and diversity which can be seen within the human race, and within other forms of life, is a result of the way that information about our form and content is stored within our bodies.

The nucleus of each cell in our body contains a 'blue-print' of ourselves—consisting of a series of instructions, like a string of sentences. Each 'sentence' is called a *gene* and specifies one piece of information. These genes are grouped together in bundles called *chromosomes* and in each cell there is an estimated 100,000 genes which are grouped into precisely 46 chromosomes (except for the specific sex cells which have only 23 chromosomes).

Although we are all different, we do share characteristics in common with our parents and ancestors; the colour of our hair, the shape of the nose, or sometimes unfortunate characteristics such as haemophilia—the bleeding disease. The process of acquiring characteristics from our ancestors and passing them on from one generation to another is known as *heredity* and the study of this is *genetics*.

Chromosomes and sex

To begin to understand genetics we must go back into the microscopic world of the cell and look at those dark-staining threads in the nucleus—the chromosomes. The 46 chromosomes are arranged in pairs (given numbers from one to 23 for convenience), one member of each pair coming from the mother during fertilization, and the other from the father. In males one pair (the sex chromosomes) can be easily distinguished from the rest—they are dissimilar—one is small, hook-shaped and known as the *Y* chromosome, the other is larger, cross-shaped and known as the *X* chromosome. Females, on the other hand, have two *X* sex chromosomes and no *Y* chromosome. The combination *XY* therefore makes a male, and the combination *XX* a female. These *sex chromosomes* are ultimately responsible for the vast range of physical and emotional differences between a man and a woman.

During the production of egg cells or sperm, the cells undergo a special type of division called *meiosis* where exactly half of the original 46 chromosomes are distributed to each egg or sperm. Of these 23 chromosomes one will be a sex chromosome. In a male, therefore, half the sperm will receive 22 plus an *X* chromosome, the other half will have 22 chromosomes plus a *Y* chromosome. During fertilization the 23 chromosomes from the sperm join together with the 23 chromosomes from the egg to form 23 pairs known as *homologous pairs*. The *X* bearing sperm will make an *XX* pair (female), and the *Y* bearing sperm an *XY* pair (male).

Albinism

The two chromosomes in each homologous pair (one from the mother and one from the father) contain genes which

Above: Gregor Johann Mendel, the Augustinian monk who is known as the 'father of genetics.' In 1865 he outlined the principles of inheritance in successive generations of pea plants. At the time his work was ignored as a meaningless obsession. But although he knew nothing about the existence or function of genes or chromosomes, Mendel's laws are still taught because they are fundamental to the science of genetics. The precise structure of the DNA 'code' was not discovered until 1953.

Right: Of the 23 chromosomes paired off during meiosis, one will determine the sex of the child. Males have both X and Y chromosomes and females have two X chromosomes.
Below: Albinism, or the inability to produce melanin (skin pigment) results in a completely white skin. If both genes responsible for skin colour are defective, then albinism will result. But if one of them is normal it will be dominant—melanin will be produced—and skin colouring will be normal.

control the same characteristics. If, for example, a chromosome carries 5,000 genes along its length and the tenth gene is concerned with hair colour, then the tenth gene on the homologous chromosome will also be concerned with hair colour.

These two sets of homologous genes work together to produce the complete internal and external appearance of each individual. To see how they do this we can examine the inheritance of *albinism*—the inability to synthesize the skin pigment *melanin*.

Melanin is a dark yellow pigment formed in special skin cells from the amino acid tyrosine. The conversion of tyrosine to melanin is undertaken by certain enzymes, each of which is coded for by a particular gene. If one of these genes is defective, a defective enzyme will be produced and the synthesis of melanin will not take place. The person will therefore be an *albino* and have completely white skin. There are two genes which code for the enzyme, one on each of the chromosomes making up the homologous pair; and only if both genes are defective albinism will result. The combination of one defective and one normal gene will mean that melanin will be produced—the normal gene masks the effect of the defective gene, and is said to be *dominant* over the *recessive* abnormal gene.

Albinism is an extreme example of the

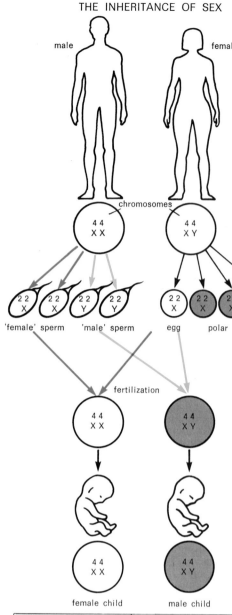

THE INHERITANCE OF SEX

male   female

chromosomes

44 XX   44 XY

22 X   22 X   22 Y   22 Y   22 X   22 X   22 X

'female' sperm   'male' sperm   egg   polar bodie

fertilization

44 XX   44 XY

44 XX   44 XY

female child   male child

A = normal dominant gene for skin colour		
a = recessive defective gene for skin colour		
6 possible combinations of differents parents	normal	normal
genotypes of parents	A A	A A
possible eggs and sperm produced	A A	A
possible children	A A A A A A	
	all normal	

212

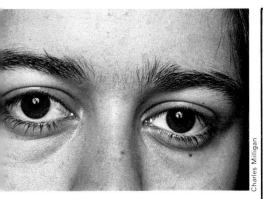

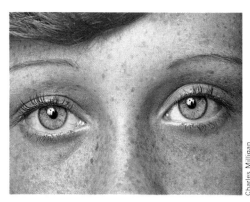

DOMINANT	RECESSIVE
Curly hair	Straight hair
Dark hair	Light hair
Nonred hair	Red hair
Coarse body hair	Normal body hair
Normal skin pigmentation	Albinism
Brown eyes	Blue or grey eyes
Near or farsightedness	Normal vision
Normal hearing	Deafness
Normal colour vision	Colour blindness
Normal blood clotting	Haemophilia
Broad lips	Thin lips
Large eyes	Small eyes
Short stature	Tall stature
Polydactylism	Normal digits
Brachydactylism	Normal digits
Syndactylism	Normal digits
Normal muscle tone	Muscular dystrophy
Hypertension	Normal blood pressure
Diabetes insipidus	Normal excretion
Huntington's chorea	Normal nervous system
Normal mentality	Schizophrenia
Nervous temperament	Calm temperament
Average intellect	Genius or idiocy
Migraine headaches	Normal
Resistance to disease	Susceptibility to disease
Enlarged spleen	Normal spleen
Enlarged colon	Normal colon
A or B blood group	O blood group
Rh blood group	No Rh blood group

Above and below: Example of the mechanism of inheritance: all our characteristics are received through the genetic code. The gene that codes for brown eyes is dominant over that for blue or grey eyes (top right) and the gene responsible for curly hair dominates over that for straight hair (far right).

Below centre: The giant chromosomes of the fruit fly *Drosophila*. Staining reveals light and dark bands along the length of the chromosome. The bands are thought to represent genes arranged along the length of the chromosome, which in turn contains the double-stranded molecule DNA—the blueprint for the new individual.

Left: The current list of hereditary traits as determined by the universal genetic code. It is quite likely that the list will be added to or modified as more research is done in this field—the science of genetics is relatively new. The fatal bleeding disease, haemophilia, for example, which afflicted Queen Victoria's male offspring is now understood to have been due to the passing on of a recessive gene through a line of female carriers, who did not themselves suffer from it. Schizophrenia is also blamed on defective genes and some controversial studies are taking place to determine the role of genetic disturbance among violent criminals.

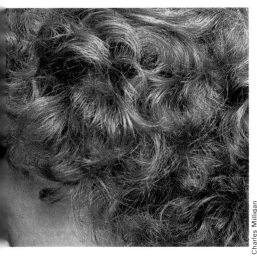

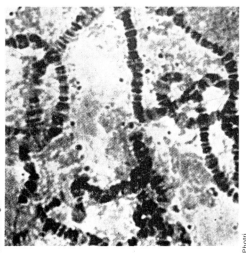

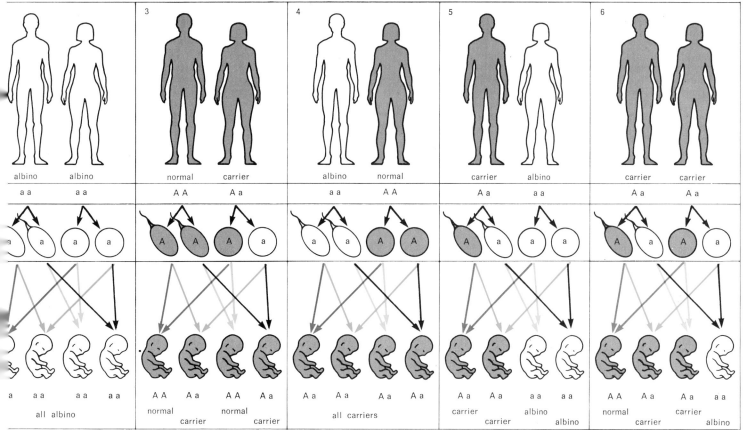

THE INHERITANCE OF ALBINISM

Above: The ill-fated royal house of Hapsburg. The Emperor Maximilian I and his family suffered from massive genetic mutation. The disease known as *acrocephaly* is an endocrine disorder producing distinctive physical and mental abnormalities. The lower jaw protrudes so that its teeth lie in front of the upper ones and the mouth often hangs open. Carlos 'The Bewitched' (below) inherited mental defects, too. Epilepsy, sexual fear and other abnormalities, ascribed at the time to witchcraft, are now seen as a direct result of genetic malformation—due, in turn, to chronic inbreeding which was rife in European royal families until very recent times.

Right: Colour blindness —the inability to distinguish between red and green—is due to a gene found only in the X chromosome. Normal colour vision is actually a dominant characteristic, but a recessive gene can replace the normal colour vision gene. Males, having one X chromosome, need just one recessive gene.

Kunsthistoriches Museum, Vienna

THE SEX-LINKED INHERITANCE OF COLOUR BLINDNESS

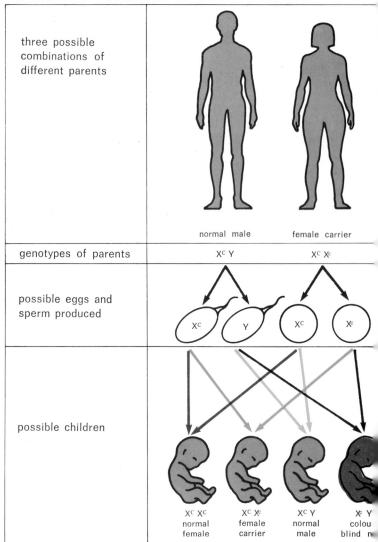

three possible combinations of different parents	normal male	female carrier
genotypes of parents	$X^C Y$	$X^C X^c$
possible eggs and sperm produced	X^C Y	X^C X^c
possible children	$X^C X^C$ normal female — $X^C X^c$ female carrier — $X^C Y$ normal male — $X^c Y$ colour blind m		

X^C female sex chromosome with dominant normal colour vision gene

X^c female sex chromosome with recessive colour-blindness gene

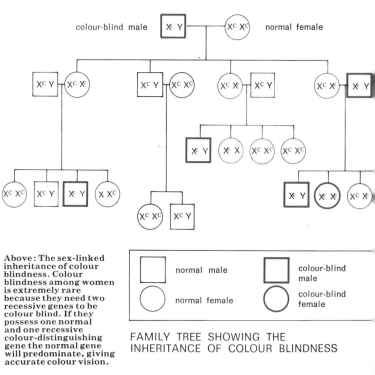

Above: The sex-linked inheritance of colour blindness. Colour blindness among women is extremely rare because they need two recessive genes to be colour blind. If they possess one normal and one recessive colour-distinguishing gene the normal gene will predominate, giving accurate colour vision.

☐ normal male	☐ colour-blind male
◯ normal female	◯ colour-blind female

FAMILY TREE SHOWING THE INHERITANCE OF COLOUR BLINDNESS

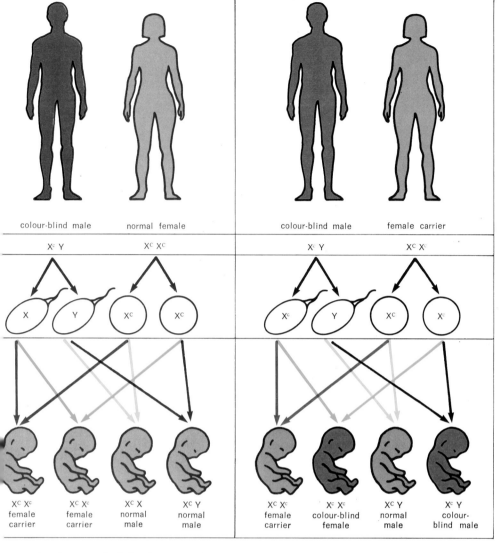

| colour-blind male | normal female |
| X^c Y | X^c X^c |

| colour-blind male | female carrier |
| X^c Y | X^c X^c |

| X | Y | X^c | X^c |

| X^c | Y | X^c | X^c |

| X^c X^c female carrier | X^c X^c female carrier | X^c X normal male | X^c Y normal male |

| X^c X^c female carrier | X^c X^c colour-blind female | X^c Y normal male | X^c Y colour-blind male |

mechanisms of inheritance. All our internal organs are the result of the interactions of the gene combinations received from our parents. The gene for curly hair, for example, is dominant over that for straight hair, whereas the gene for red hair is recessive to that for non-red hair.

There are many more known recessive and dominant genes, and one interesting fact which emerges is that normal characteristics are not always dominant over abnormal ones. Fortunately people who inherit severe disorders often do not live long enough to reproduce and pass the gene onto the next generation. Damaging inherited characteristics are in this way gradually weeded out of the population while advantageous ones (like dark skin in tropical countries) slowly increase.

Sex linked inheritance

The X and Y chromosomes, as we have already said, determine the sex of the child. They also contain certain genes which are not concerned with sexual characteristics. These are known as *sex linked* genes since they are inherited along with the sex chromosomes. Unlike other chromosomes the X and Y chromosomes have no genes in common. The X chromosome in particular contains many genes for which there are no homologous genes on the Y chromosome, one of which is the gene for colour vision.

The ability to discriminate between the colours red and green is completely dependent on a gene located only on the X chromosome. Normal colour vision is a dominant characteristic but there is also a recessive gene which causes colour blindness, and can replace the normal colour vision gene on the X chromosome. As male sex chromosomes have only one X chromosome, if this contains the recessive colour vision gene the male is colour blind. With a female, however, having two X chromosomes, both must have recessive colour vision genes for colour blindness to occur because if one gene is the dominant normal vision type, this will mask the recessive gene.

Recessive sex linked genes like colour blindness are always masked in females who have the dominant gene. Whereas in males they are always expressed when they appear. Men, therefore, are much more likely to be colour blind than women.

Haemophilia is another sex linked recessive characteristic found only on the X chromosome. It is a very rare disease in which the person's blood fails to clot or clots very slowly. The most famous sufferers from haemophilia were the royal family of Queen Victoria in which certain male offspring inherited the disease. The Queen herself was a carrier, and everytime the defective gene was passed on to a male the disease appeared. A female, however, needs a double dose of the gene to inherit haemophilia—the gene itself is very rare, and a double dose almost unknown.

Chromosome abnormalities

Haemophilia and Queen Victoria poses another interesting problem in genetics because none of her ancestors suffered from the disease. Where, then, did the gene come from?

During the early stages in producing a sex cell (by the process of *meiosis*) the chromosomes are carefully copied—this is a complex chemical process. Chromosomes have a 'spiral staircase' structure consisting of a long double-helix DNA molecule with 'rungs' of certain chemicals in between. These rungs are the 'words' which make up the 'sentence instructions' or *genes*. Thus, in copying the genes faithfully (and there maybe 5000 of these in a single chromosome) it is necessary to copy every chemical rung correctly.

It is inevitable, therefore, that out of the millions of times that this process occurs, and the millions of chemicals to be copied each time, that mistakes will occur and even a simple change in the order of the chemicals will change the message coded in that gene. If this change is then passed on during fertilization it will be reproduced over and over again in all the cells of the offspring. It is thought that this chance occurrence (called a *gene mutation*) happened in one of the sex cells of one of Queen Victoria's parents, or in one of her own embryonic cells.

The natural rate of gene mutation is very slow. It can, however, be increased dramatically by the effect of certain chemicals and radiation. X-rays and nuclear fallout are the two main culprits and, for this reason, X-ray photographs are rarely taken of developing foetuses, the ovaries and testes and strict precautions are taken to shield people from nuclear radiation. We cannot, however, shield ourselves from cosmic rays striking the earth, and other sources of natural radiation (like radioactive elements found in the food and soil), all of which contribute to the slow, but highly significant, natural rate of mutation.

It must be stressed that mutations are chance occurrences and, like all chance occurrencies, they can be good or bad. Unfortunately, chance changes in such a complex, delicately balanced system as life are usually for the worse. Yet the advantageous ones are the wheels which propel evolution forward. Genes arise by duplication of genes already in existence, and without the element of change introduced by mutation, evolution would come to a complete standstill. Life would not have progressed from the most primitive, single-celled organisms floating around in the primordial soup. The human race is the result of millions of such advantageous mutations.

Although mutation is the only means available to produce new genes, nature has developed an ingenious method for reshuffling the genes on homologous chromosome pairs. This reshuffling, which greatly increases the number of gene combinations and hence the variety of new individuals is accomplished during meiosis when homologous chromosomes can be seen to curl round each other. They, in fact, exchange genes during this evolutionary dance, which is known as *crossing over*.

There are other types of chromosome abnormalities: crossing over may go wrong, for instance, adding extra pieces onto some chromosomes, or one sex cell

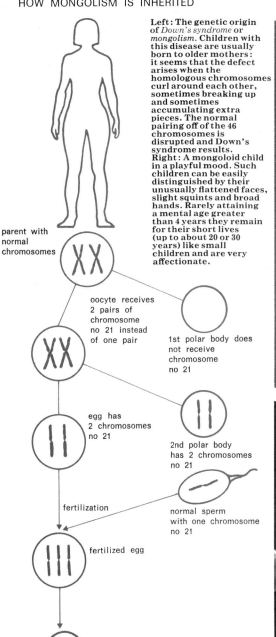

parent with normal chromosomes

oocyte receives 2 pairs of chromosome no 21 instead of one pair

1st polar body does not receive chromosome no 21

egg has 2 chromosomes no 21

2nd polar body has 2 chromosomes no 21

fertilization

normal sperm with one chromosome no 21

fertilized egg

child has 3 pairs of chromsome no 21 instead of two, causing mongolism

Left: The genetic origin of *Down's syndrome* or *mongolism*. Children with this disease are usually born to older mothers: it seems that the defect arises when the homologous chromosomes curl around each other, sometimes breaking up and sometimes accumulating extra pieces. The normal pairing off of the 46 chromosomes is disrupted and Down's syndrome results.
Right: A mongoloid child in a playful mood. Such children can be easily distinguished by their unusually flattened faces, slight squints and broad hands. Rarely attaining a mental age greater than 4 years they remain for their short lives (up to about 20 or 30 years) like small children and are very affectionate.

National Society for Mentally Handicapped Children

Dr. S. M. Lewis

Below: Three 21s in the chromosome pattern always results in mongolism. The loss of 21 is fatal but an extra one, making a total of 24 chromosomes, survives well (even though it results in a genetic mutation). One in six hundred live births is likely to be affected by this or a similar malformation.

Above: Sickle-cell anaemia together with some 1,500 other human disorders, is based on a genetic mutation. In this case a change in a single DNA molecule results in the inability of the red blood cells to transport oxygen, changes their shape and produces many distressing, or even fatal, symptoms including heart disease.

might receive extra chromosomes due to faulty separation of the chromosomes during meiosis. The latter case is fairly common (1 in 600 live births), happening generally in older mothers, and usually involving chromosome 21. One of the egg cells receives an extra chromosome 21, giving it a total of 24 chromosomes, while the other egg cell receives only 22 chromosomes. The loss of chromosome 21 is fatal, but the egg receiving an extra chromosome survives well, producing an embryo with totally 47 chromosomes. The child, however, is severely mentally retarded, has mongolian eyelids, broad hands, a flattened face and other serious defects. This condition is known as *Down's syndrome* or *mongolism*. Mongol children usually never progress above a mental age of a normal 2 to 3 year old. They usually live a happy, if short, life.

Polygenes

The inheritance of characteristics like albinism or haemophilia depend solely on the behaviour of a single pair of genes. The individual will be either albino, for example, or have pigmented skin. When we come to consider characteristics like height or intelligence we find such a wide range that it seems that these characteristics cannot be controlled by such highly specific units as genes. These variable characteristics are, in fact, controlled by a number of genes acting together—called *polygenes*—each one contributing a small part to the total effect.

Many of the characteristics controlled by polygenes (height, weight and skin colour for example) can be strongly modified by the environment. The amount and type of food we eat contributes to our height and weight; exposure to the sun darkens the skin. Even so, it is possible for one abnormal gene to alter completely the effect of polygenes. Genes and the environment can, and do, work together to produce a species—the human race—capable of adapting itself to environments as radically different as the frozen north and the scorching Sahara.

THE CHROMOSOME COMPLEMENT OF A PERSON WITH MONGOLISM

1 2 3 4 5

6 7 8 9 10 11 12 13 14 15

16 17 18 19 20 21 22

Biophoto Associates

Roughly one in every 80 deliveries is a twin birth. Identical, or *monozygotic* twins come from one egg which splits after fertilisation.

Non-identical (*dizygotic*) twins are the result of two eggs being released at the same time, each fertilised by a different sperm.

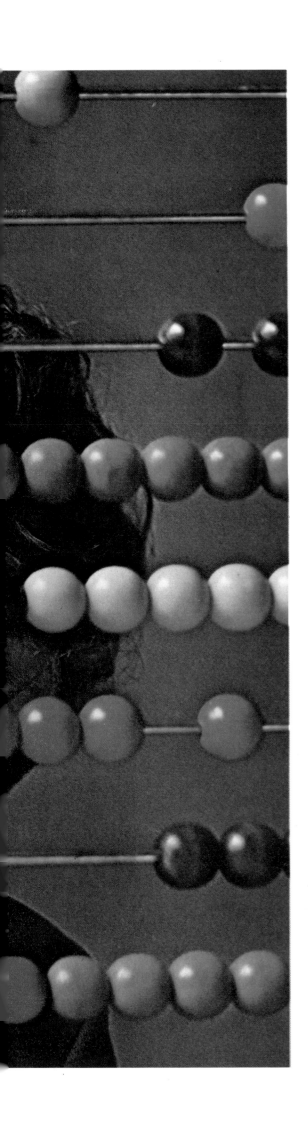

Chapter 2
The Growing Child

Between the ages of five and eleven
the child develops the capacity for
operational thought – the ability to
count, to classify objects, and to order
them into a series, such as size.

Development of the Senses

Information from the senses tells us about the characteristic form, colour, feel, smell and taste of every object around us. This information, along with our experience of time and space, our own bodies and our interactions with other people, is integrated into a complex series of actions and reactions which we call human behaviour.

We know that people are capable of voluntary action but that physical objects are passive and readily subject to our action upon them. However, unlike adult humans, the newborn baby seems passive and helpless. He appears to be incapable of moving, feeding, protecting himself or influencing the world without adult assistance.

For centuries most people believed that the newborn had no basic capacities with which to understand even the simplest aspects of his world. William James, the 19th Century psychologist, claimed that the infant must experience his new environment outside the womb as 'one great blooming, buzzing confusion'.

Developments in psychology since the 1950s, however, involving simple but ingenious techniques of controlled observation and experimentation, show that the newborn is certainly neither passive nor as confused as James believed. At birth he possesses highly organized processes which aid attachment to an adult caretaker. This enables him both to survive and to develop more complex forms of social interaction. His sensory organization also enables him to discover the nature of the world and the consequences of his action upon it.

Brain development

The brain, which is involved in perception, thought and action, is reaching the peak of its growth curve at birth. The head seems abnormally large for the body: the brain constitutes about 12 per cent of the baby's total weight. By the end of the first year the brain will weigh twice as much and by the age of two years will have grown to 80 per cent of its adult size.

At birth many neural (nerve) pathways are partly surrounded by a myelin sheath (the fatty substance making rapid and efficient conduction of neural messages possible) and during the first year, myelination will be completed. More significantly, the growth of the brain involves the formation of many connections between neurons (nerve cells) present at birth. These connections are the basic equipment of learning. The cortex, the highest level of the brain in which complex learning process take place, is only half its adult thickness at birth but becomes thicker as the neural connections develop.

Sensory development

The senses develop more rapidly than motor skills such as sitting, reaching or walking. Vision is of particular importance since it provides most of the information about the world. The eyes are well developed at birth. Both *rods*,

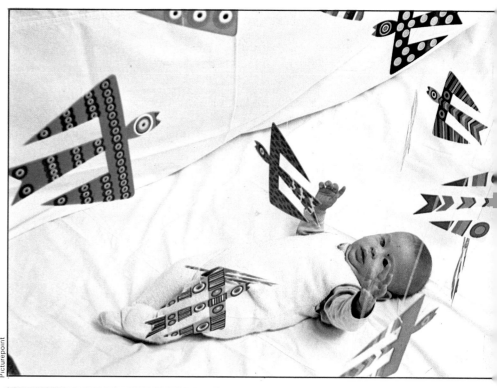

Picturepoint

Left and below: The 'visual cliff', a means of testing depth perception in infants. The baby responds to his mother's calls by crawling towards her until he comes to the 'edge' of the cliff. Although he can feel the glass surface for himself, he refuses to cross what appears to be a sudden drop.

Above: The newborn baby is able to detect colour and brightness changes, follow moving objects and make small exploratory eye movements, but he is unable to perceive detail clearly until about four months old. This five-month old baby is being tested to ensure that his development is normal.

NERVOUS CONNECTIONS AT:
BIRTH
15 MONTHS

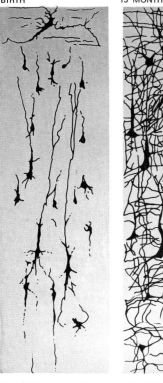

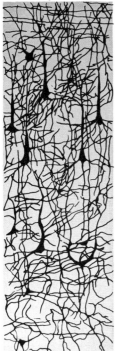

Left: Diagrams showing brain development from birth to 15 months. The cortex, where learning takes place, is made up of inter-connected nerve cells. These connections can form only if the infant is adequately stimulated into exploring and understanding his environment or mental retardation may result.

Camera Press

Above: The glazed look in the baby's eyes denotes 'habituation', the stage at which an object becomes familiar and he stops looking.

Left: This baby, a few hours old, was 'eased into life' with soft lights and voices. The school of thought which proposes gentler methods of delivery claims that the babies do not show the usual newborn behaviour—clenched fists and piercing wails—but are contented and smiling. Babies born conventionally rarely smile until six weeks old.

Below: Results of an experiment to demonstrate that infants prefer patterns to colour or brightness.

Pierre-Marie Goulet/Wildwood House

which detect brightness changes, and *cones*, which detect colours, are functioning. But the *fovea*, the area which makes perception of fine detail possible, is only partially developed at birth. Its growth is completed by about four months.

This highly developed apparatus would be expected to enable the newborn to see quite well, even if he does not understand what he sees. However, a certain lack of response was noted during early vision experiments with many young infants which may be explained by two recent findings. Firstly, the infant's ability to control the lens and muscles of his eyes is limited. His focal length is fixed at about 17—19 cm. for the early months, hence objects must be quite close for him to see them clearly. Secondly, infants tend to be in a drowsy state when flat on their backs, even when awake, whereas they are far more alert when propped up. Even in the first few days of life an infant supported in this way will follow moving objects and may show a highly developed ability to change the direction of his gaze and to make small exploratory eye movements over objects presented to him. This raises the obvious question: does what the infant sees have any meaning for him, or is it received as a coded message which must yet be deciphered?

Depth perception

There is sufficient evidence that the infant has an innate understanding of certain dimensions such as depth. A test known as the *visual cliff* has been devised which consists of a plate-glass table divided into two parts, one of which has a highly textured check fabric fixed directly below it. There is similar fabric several feet below the second half. The infant is placed upon a central board between the two parts and his response noted as his mother calls him from each side of the cliff in turn. One side looks at the same level as the central board, the other appears to be a drop, but the glass ensures that the infant is in no danger of falling. Once a baby can crawl, he will go to his mother only if she is on the 'shallow' side of the cliff. At the 'deep' side he remains firmly on the board, looking apprehensively down at the floor.

To discover whether this response is the result of falling experiences while crawling, much younger infants, not yet able to crawl, can be placed on the cliff and their heart-rate monitored. It has been found that heart-rate changes only when the young infant looks over the 'deep' side of the cliff and experiences anxiety. This type of depth perception is simpler and less accurate than stereoscopic vision, which involves fusion of images from both eyes. The infant's response is probably to the angle presented by the check pattern and by movements of the head from side to side making closer objects appear to move farther than more distant ones. This is confirmed by findings that even infants with vision only in one eye perform competently on the cliff. Also, as the texture of the pattern is reduced more and more, crawling infants will cross the 'deep' side.

If a three week-old baby is propped up and a large object brought increasingly closer to him he shows a very interesting reaction. Besides looking at it he will raise his arms before his face, try to pull back, and may grimace. As with the 'cliff'

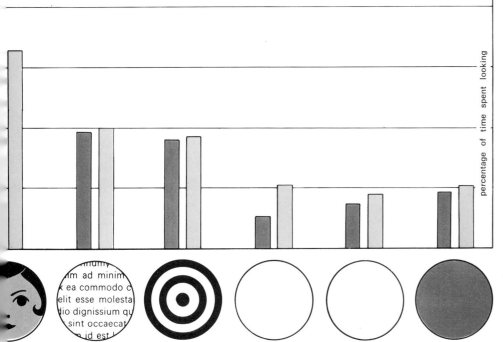

NTS AND PATTERN RECOGNITION

under 3 months

over 3 months

percentage of time spent looking

221

it implies an understanding of depth but is also important for other reasons. Since the response occurs only if the object is on a collision course it implies that the infant understands when the object is coming towards him. In other words, he can differentiate between an external world and objects within it. Perhaps more surprisingly it suggests that he understands that the object will hit him. He seems to know that visual objects have tactile characteristics long before he has been able to link touch and vision through learning.

It is now known, therefore, that very young infants do not just detect unrelated sensations but solid objects in three-dimensional space, despite their two-dimensional retinal image of the world. But how aware is the infant of the detailed form of these objects? A technique known as 'visual preference' has shed some light on this question.

The infant lies in a crib fitted with a roof, into which two different stimulus objects or pictures can be slotted, one to either side of him. By looking through a central peephole the researcher can observe the reflection of the stimuli in the infant's eyes. This shows which one he is looking at and the time spent looking at each is recorded. The stimulus which receives most attention, as measured by the length of time the infant looks at it, is said to be 'preferred'; it is of greatest interest to the infant.

The effects of patterns
Many studies show that infants find pattern the most interesting aspect of objects. An important, though controversial, finding is that the most 'preferred' stimulus is a diagram of a human face. Certain researchers have found that during the earliest months an infant will look just as long at a face in which the features are scrambled as he will at a normal arrangement. This would suggest that it is not the 'facedness' as such which attracts attention. Nevertheless, very soon the human face is of great interest to infants. This reveals that it is not only the adult who is stimulated into responding to a young infant but that both infant and adult possess innate and complementary behaviour patterns to ensure the formation of a bond between them. The infant is not passive but can influence others as much as they influence him.

The meshing of complementary patterns of behaviour is a fascinating example of evolutionary adaptation. The infant who cannot cling or seek food directly will cry. This cry is unnerving to most adults, who respond by picking him up. Usually this makes access to food possible for the infant. The physical contact invariably quietens the infant, who may begin to explore the adult's face which is now within close range. In one study 249 out of 252 newborns ceased to cry when picked up for the first time. Since this occurred before the first feed the behaviour could not have been learned. Needless to say, the adult feels satisfaction when he or she successfully pacifies the infant.

Even very young babies will turn to look at the source of a sound: their hearing is well developed. By about six weeks they smile regularly and most often at the sight of an adult or the sound of a voice. Other sights or sounds are not as effective in producing this smile.

222

John Hillelson

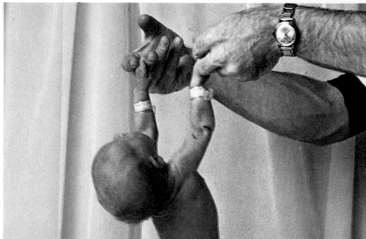

Above: Recent studies have shown the importance of communication between mother and child. Mothers who constantly talk to their babies not only stimulate the development of the baby's sensory apparatus (neural network) but may be inadvertently teaching them how to carry out certain actions and physical movements. Some experiments have shown that babies learn certain movements from the actual rhythm and patterns of speech as well as from watching the speaker's body movements. This process is thought to begin as early as a few hours after birth, long before the neural networks are fully formed.

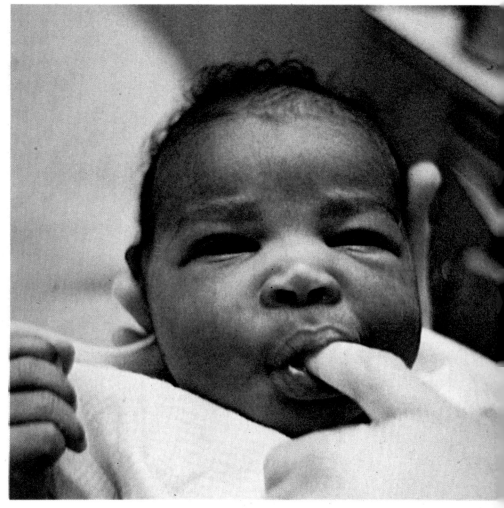

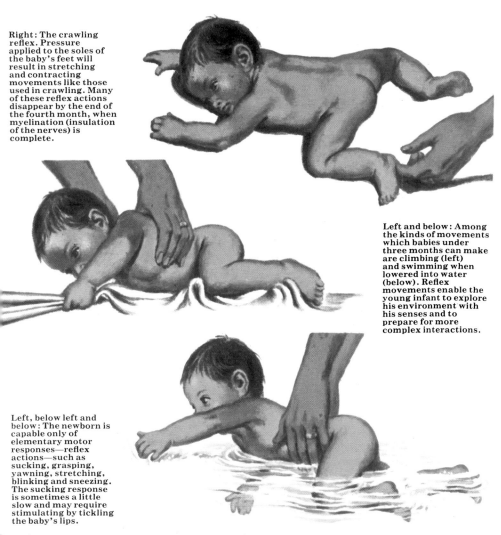

Right: The crawling reflex. Pressure applied to the soles of the baby's feet will result in stretching and contracting movements like those used in crawling. Many of these reflex actions disappear by the end of the fourth month, when myelination (insulation of the nerves) is complete.

Left and below: Among the kinds of movements which babies under three months can make are climbing (left) and swimming when lowered into water (below). Reflex movements enable the young infant to explore his environment with his senses and to prepare for more complex interactions.

Left, below left and below: The newborn is capable only of elementary motor responses—reflex actions—such as sucking, grasping, yawning, stretching, blinking and sneezing. The sucking response is sometimes a little slow and may require stimulating by tickling the baby's lips.

Bill Carter

Smiling at this stage was thought to be caused by wind after a feed, but it has been found that the infant's face and body are relaxed before it occurs, whereas before 'windy smiles' the face may be reddened and facial and bodily muscles contorted.

The smiling response cements the adult-infant bond. Many mothers report that their baby first seems like a real person when he makes eye contact with them and smiles.

The infant's preoccupation with pattern extends beyond the human face. The responses to basic characteristics of the environment, are relatively simple. There appears to be an ability at birth to pick out certain features of objects and space and to give a precise response, such as avoidance, to them.

The complexity and variety of human societies—particularly technological societies—means that the human blueprint must be flexible. The infant cannot 'know' everything about his particular society at birth. His interest in pattern predisposes him to learn the characteristics of the many complex objects he will encounter and need to deal with in everyday life.

Responding to objects

When a newborn infant is presented with an object the intensity of his attention may be very amusing. Body movements cease, the pupils dilate and the eyes take on a glazed appearance. He seems unable to move and is sometimes described as 'stuck' on the object. Eventually he stops looking, but he is not just tired, he has built a 'model' or representation of the object and it is now predictable and uninteresting. This is clear because if given a choice he will now look at a new object, but not at the old one. Hence he must remember the old object, otherwise he would not distinguish between the two.

This form of learning is called *habituation*. It does not occur in infants born without a cortex or in an animal whose cortex has been surgically removed. As the infant's model develops he will become increasingly interested in objects and events which do not fit the predictions he is able to make. This is the basis of exploration and curiosity, processes essential for continued learning. If the newborn is not reared in a stimulating environment he will be unable to learn and his motivation to explore further will not develop.

In a normal stimulating environment an infant is mentally very active. He seeks out novel information and shows great pleasure in being able to understand and predict what goes on about him. Researchers have found that a baby of six weeks will learn to suck on a dummy to bring a picture into focus—he wants to see clearly what is going on. Infants exposed to flashing lights learned very quickly to turn their heads in that direction and began to smile each time they appeared.

The critical period

Learning and the development of the brain during this period proceed at a rapid pace. The first two years are a critical period for brain development. If the right experiences are not provided at this stage development of mental processes may be grossly retarded. This is one of the reasons why infants in institutions may show subnormal performance on mental tests even though they are neurologically normal at birth. They may be left for long periods confined to a cot with little stimulation, physical or social. In recent years research findings have led to a great improvement of conditions for such infants.

For the baby reared in a normal family it is important that tests of vision and hearing are carried out regularly to ensure that the infant is able to make normal sensory contact with the world. Defects such as squint or 'lazy eye' can be detected in the early months and surgically corrected. If left for too long the child can become blind in the eye which was not being used. This would make fine manipulations of objects, for which binocular vision is needed, difficult in later life.

Even if the senses are normal care is still necessary. Each infant is an individual at birth, some are more active than others and in some, certain sense organs are more sensitive than others. It is important that the mother is able to adjust to these variations. If a baby is very inactive he will need encouragement from her to explore his environment; it is unlikely that a very passive baby will show the mental development of which he is capable if left to his own devices.

Fortunately many mothers are able to tune in to the personality of their baby and to provide him with experiences to maintain his curiosity and stimulate learning. Infant research has only recently begun to understand what good mothers have been doing for centuries with no specialized knowledge whatsoever.

The Growing Child

The period of transition from infancy to adulthood, called 'growing up' does not only involve a change in the child's size, but in his basic anatomy and physiology, which alters the structure of both brain and body. As the cells of the brain and body specialize, their overall shape changes enabling them to perform different functions. This process is known as maturation and it is determined by the genetic blueprint laid down at conception.

Maturation and experience interact at all stages of physical and psychological development. Maturation provides a state of 'readiness' in which experience, information acquired by the child in his repeated interactions with the environment through his sensory apparatus, may play their part in fulfilling the potential outlined by heredity. These experiences produce further changes in physical structure and in behaviour. Defects of either maturation or experience prevent a human being from reaching his or her full potential. Height, for example, is genetically determined but without adequate nutrition a child will grow into a shorter adult than he might have been. In the psychological realm, maturation provides the basis for motor and sensory skills, through which understanding of the world becomes possible.

The importance of feeding

Feeding and sleeping are two activities crucial for normal development. Food must provide material for activity, growth and repair of bones and tissues and normal functioning of the endocrine glands—which produce the hormones directing growth.

Protein is the most crucial foodstuff for growth and repair. Certain vitamins and minerals are also needed for formation of healthy bone and tissue. During the First World War and the years up to the Second World War, children were smaller as the quantity and quality of their food was not adequate to enable them to grow to their full height. In underdeveloped countries this is still a problem.

If a mother has a diet rich in necessary nutrients her infant will invariably receive all that he requires from her milk. This will also provide certain antibodies to help build his immunity to disease. Immediately after birth the infant needs food every three to four hours, consuming about 600 ml (one pint) of milk a day. By about 6 weeks his hunger cycle will have lengthened and he may pass a night without needing to be fed.

Many mothers now bottle feed their infants, mixing specially adapted formulas with water. These can be a valuable substitute for breast milk, but there are hazards involved. Unless the formula is weighed precisely the feed may be too concentrated.

Some mothers believe that a stronger mix helps the infant to sleep and grow better, but this is faulty reasoning. An overstrong feed will contain too much sodium and the infant's kidneys must work furiously to eliminate it. This can produce dehydration, a dangerous condi-

tion if maintained for any length of time. A further hazard is that the infant may appear to be growing quickly but in fact he will not be building extra bone and muscle, he will accumulate excess fat. The number of fat cells is determined during the first year of life, consequently a fat baby will probably grow into a fat adult. Obese people have more cardiac and respiratory problems than normal and a shorter life-span. A fat child cannot join fully in games with other children. He may suffer emotionally from isolation and feelings of unattractiveness.

During the second part of the first year the infant is weaned, he progresses from milk to solid food. It is important that a balanced diet is maintained and that sugar is not used too liberally to make food palatable. Pure sugar is unnecessary to the diet and very fattening.

The importance of sleep

Sleep provides a time for growth and restoration of the brain and body. Two-thirds of a newborn's day is spent asleep. Half of this time is in *REM* (rapid eye-movement) sleep, when body, face and eyes are active. The other half is spent in *NREM* (non-REM) or quiet sleep when body, face and eyes are relaxed. During

Syndication International

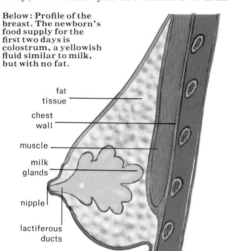

Below: Profile of the breast. The newborn's food supply for the first two days is colostrum, a yellowish fluid similar to milk, but with no fat.

fat tissue
chest wall
muscle
milk glands
nipple
lactiferous ducts

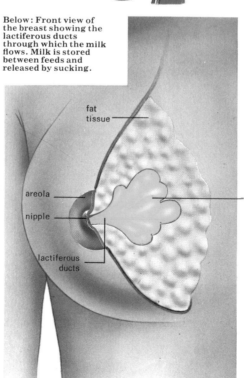

Below: Front view of the breast showing the lactiferous ducts through which the milk flows. Milk is stored between feeds and released by sucking.

fat tissue
areola
nipple
lactiferous ducts
milk glands

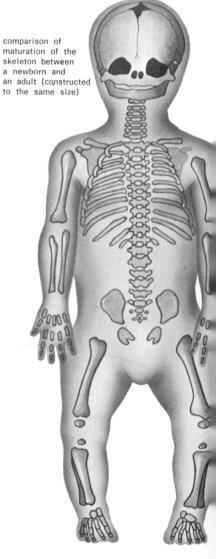

Above: From birth until the age of 10 months, many major developments in a child's life, such as walking, take place. They depend on *maturation*, the process by which the cells of the brain and body become specialized into different types of tissue—for example, bone to form the skeleton (below).

comparison of maturation of the skeleton between a newborn and an adult (constructed to the same size)

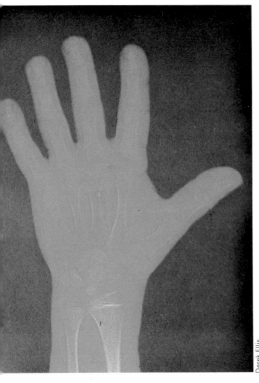

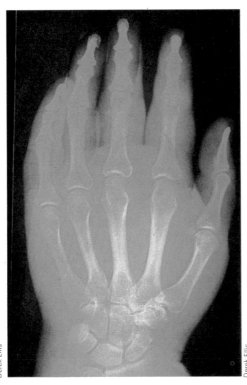

Below left and below: Diagrams to illustrate the beginning and end of maturation in the skeleton. The process takes about 20 years to complete.

Cartilage—the first stage of ossification—is quite soft, and it is several months before the skeleton can fully support the baby's limbs.

Above left and above: X-rays showing the difference between bone development in a child's and an adult's hands. The X-ray process is the only means by which it can be accurately assessed if the child's growth is proceeding at a normal pace. Frequent X-rays are dangerous, however, since they can damage certain organs. Weight and height, therefore, are the usual means of predicting the child's potential adult size.

Below and bottom: X-rays of a child's and of an adult's skull. The main difference is in the chin, which is the last part of the child's skull to mature.

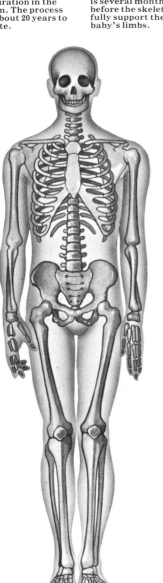

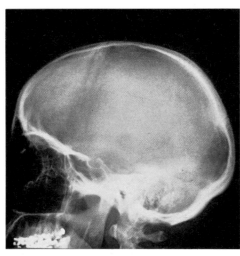

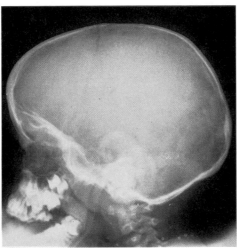

development the total amount of sleep and the proportion of REM sleep decrease. Between three and five years, 11 hours are spent asleep, 20 per cent of this time being REM sleep.

NREM sleep appears necessary for protein synthesis in the body, the process underlying growth and repair. People involved in strenuous exercise increase their amount of NREM sleep. There are differing theories about the function of REM sleep due to its association with dreaming in adults. Several recent theories, however, suggest that the brain needs constant stimulation to develop and function efficiently. REM sleep may be a result of the brain activating itself, particularly in the area of the cortex, during periods of low external stimulation. People who are kept awake but deprived of all sensory input eventually have hallucinations. This may be the brain attempting to stimulate itself, as in REM sleep. Severely mentally retarded people show less REM sleep than normal people, which may be related to the inefficiency of their brains. REM sleep may also be involved in protein synthesis in the brain for its maturation and formation of new neural connections. Even an unborn foetus shows large amounts of REM sleep as do people going through periods of rapid change and learning.

The rapid growth phase

At birth the average full-term infant is about 51cm (20 inches) long and weighs 3-4.5 kg (6-10 lb). During the first year he increases in length by almost 50 per cent, to about 72.4 cm (28½ inches) and the baby becomes three times as heavy. During the second year, a further 11.4 cm (4½ inches) or so will be added to height, (no longer regarded as length since the infant is now able to stand), and the baby will be four times heavier than at birth. This extremely rapid growth now settles to a slower pace. During each successive year height will increase by just over 5 cm (2 inches) and weight by 2.3-3 kg (5-6 lbs). This rate of increase continues until the adolescent growth spurt at puberty.

At birth neither weight nor height can predict adult size since they have already been influenced by conditions inside the womb. A premature baby, or a twin or triplet may be smaller than normal but will grow more rapidly during the early months until he makes up the deficit and returns to his genetically determined growth curve. By the time he is two years old his adult size will be predictable.

During periods of severe malnutrition or illness growth may be restricted. Following such periods the child shows a growth spurt until he regains the size he should have reached by that time with normal development. This process is known as *homeorhesis*.

Physical maturity

Since each individual's size is destined to be unique, measures of height and weight at a particular time are poor indicators of how well growth is proceeding. If a child is shorter than others of his age he may be growing too slowly or he may merely be genetically programmed to become a smaller adult. (He may be gaining weight but this could be due to development of bone and muscle or fat.)

The best index of physical maturity is skeletal age. At birth many bones are formed in cartilage which gradually 225 becomes true bone. X-rays allow the shape of formed bone to be seen and an assessment of the skeleton's maturity to be made.

In young infants, the ankle and knee are generally examined and so is the hand in older children. Since everyone eventually achieves the same skeletal pattern, skeletal maturity provides an absolute guide to the amount of growth completed. This method of prediction has one severe disadvantage, however. Radiation from the X-ray itself is potentially harmful in that it may retard growth of certain parts of the body, particularly the sex glands.

Major developments in the infant

As brain and body mature two major developments of infancy become possible —reaching for objects and walking. These enable a fuller exploration and understanding of the world. Newborns show automatic or reflexive reaching and walking movements. With maturation the cortex of the brain develops inhibitory control of lower motor areas making voluntary control of these behaviours possible.

A two-month-old-infant will swipe at an object with his hand closed but by four months he can open his hand as he reaches. At this age he glances continuously between the object and his hand as if checking the relationship between them. By five or six months he can grasp the object even if he cannot see his hand before he begins to reach. Initially the infant grasps crudely with his palm. As the shape of the hand develops and control improves, however, he will be able

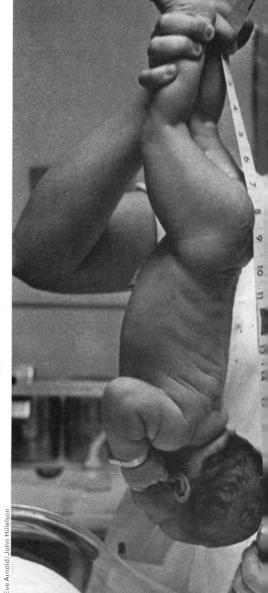

Eve Arnold/John Hillelson

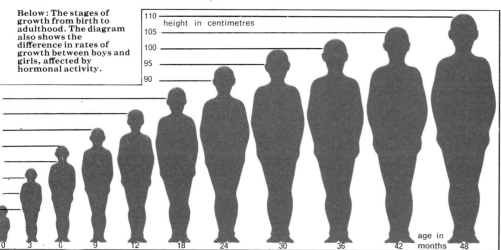

Below: The stages of growth from birth to adulthood. The diagram also shows the difference in rates of growth between boys and girls, affected by hormonal activity.

height in centimetres

Left and below: Malnutrition is still a problem in underdeveloped countries. Poor soil and unpredictable rainfall severely limit the amount and types of fruit and vegetables produced. As well as obvious symptoms of malnutrition, like the West African child's bloated belly, the growth of all these children is probably stunted, preventing them from reaching their full potential. Lack of protein and other minerals also accounts for thin hair, emaciated limbs and poor brain functioning. They also have little resistance to infectious diseases like typhoid and cholera.

Bruce Coleman

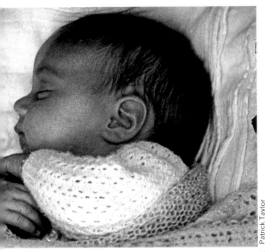

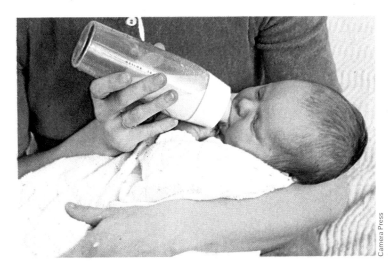

Far left: Babies are weighed and measured at birth to check that development is normal. The average full-term infant is about 51 cm (20 inches) long and weighs 3-4.5 kg (6-10 lb).

Left: Sleep is one of the two most crucial activities in a newborn baby's development. It is necessary for growth and restoration of the cells of the brain and developing tissues.

Right: The period of weaning from breast-feeding to bottle-feeding is slightly hazardous for the mother of the newborn. She must ensure that her baby receives an adequate amount of nutrition without over-feeding.

Patrick Taylor

Camera Press

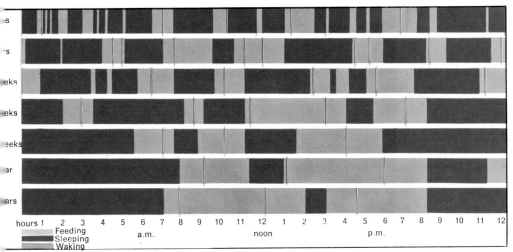

hours	1	2	3	4	5	6	7	8	9	10	11	12	1	2	3	4	5	6	7	8	9	10	11	12
			a.m.										noon								p.m.			

- Feeding
- Sleeping
- Waking

Below: Indian babies, like this young Apache infant, spend a large proportion of their day strapped to boards on their mother's back, except for short periods of play. But there is no evidence that their development is in any way retarded since they learn to crawl and walk at about the same age as babies in other societies, who have more freedom of movement.

Above: Diagram of a baby's pattern of activity—sleeping, waking and feeding—from birth to four years. As daytime waking increases, the nocturnal pattern becomes established.

Unicef

to make use of the opposition of the finger and thumb in complementary movements giving him more sophisticated manual control. When the child is able to guide his reaching movements with his eyes, he is able to expand his repertoire of experiences because of the feedback with which he is provided. This feedback consists of the signals the infant's brain receives from his own body and from changes in external sensory input as he moves. He must learn to 'fit' his body to the world and know where parts of his body are in relation to each other. Feedback information tells him where his hand is without him having to look for it.

Development of the limbs
Most infants can crawl on four limbs and pull themselves to a standing position with the help of furniture by the age of nine months. At birth the lower limbs are poorly developed: they make up only one-third of the length of the body as compared with half the height of an adult. This means that the infant's centre of gravity is very high because he is top-heavy.

In his first attempts at standing he must keep his legs far apart to prevent toppling over. By 10 months the infant may walk with help and by 12-15 months he can walk unaided. He will be bow-legged at first but as the proportions of the limbs alter the centre of gravity moves downwards and posture becomes more stable.

By the age of two years, most children can stand on one foot and run without toppling over. The same kind of feedback is needed to develop walking in just the same way as in reaching, in the form of nerve impulses to the brain informing it of changes in the position of the limbs.

Reaching or walking consumes all of the infant's concentration at first. He must continually concentrate on what he is trying to do. As his actions become more skilled, however, they can be controlled by lower areas of the brain permitting attention to be freed for further activities. This is similar to an adult learning a new skill such as driving a car. At first there seem to be too many things to do simultaneously but it soon becomes more automatic.

The relative importance of maturation and learning is difficult to assess. In activities such as toilet training, learning seems to play no part. In a study carried out with twins, one of them was toilet-trained throughout the first year until completely in control. The untrained twin achieved control at almost precisely the same time. This result suggests that learning is unimportant compared with the normal course of neuromuscular development.

Hopi Indian infants are confined to a cradle board during the first year of life, yet they walk at the same time as infants free to crawl around. Even infants reared in institutions, with free movement and toys to play with, develop reaching and walking normally without adult help. The conditions of a normal home probably provide the experience necessary for motor development.

As the infant begins to explore his world through manipulation and movement his understanding of it becomes increasingly complex. At six months an infant will not reach for a toy if it is covered with a cloth. He acts as if 'out of sight is out of mind'. By nine months he will overcome this and search beneath the cloth. If he finds an object in this way several times he will show an interesting error if it is now hidden in a new place. Even though he sees it hidden he will return to the first hiding-place to search for it. This is because his understanding of space is still limited. He is not very mobile so he remembers the positions of things with reference to his own body and actions.

When the infant begins to crawl and walk this type of memory code is no longer useful since his own position is no longer constant. Consequently, he must develop an understanding of space in terms of the relations between objects themselves. One result of this is that he will now understand his own position in space better. He must realize that he is one more object in a common space, not the key reference point. In this way the infant becomes less egocentric.

227

A child's early speech consists of words uttered one at a time, each of which is intended to convey the meaning of a whole adult sentence. Early language, known as *telegraphic*, omits all small words and word endings which change meaning, such as tenses and plural forms.

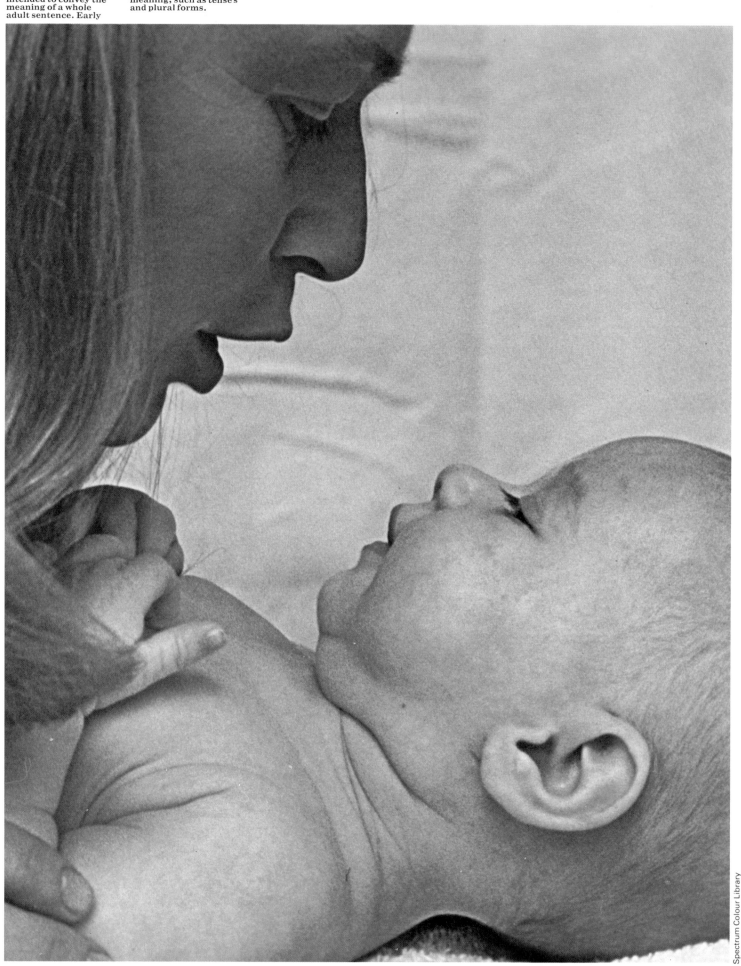

Learning to Speak

Animals show many varied ways of communicating with others of their own kind. Ants send messages to each other in chemical form, certain fishes use electrical discharges. Higher animals, including man, rely mainly on sound and on gestures of the face and body. Those gestures which convey information about inner emotional states or feelings are surprisingly similar in man and his closest evolutionary relative, the chimpanzee. However, the chimpanzee's use of sound to send messages is much more limited than that of man.

The basis of language

Man, unlike animals, is able to form symbols which stand for things he knows about even when they are not actually present. Language is a major kind of symbolism; speech is its spoken form. There are two main parts to every language. The first is a set of symbols which stand for things we know about or understand; these symbols, whether in spoken or written language, are *words*.

The second part of a language is its grammar. This is a set of rules by which words can be combined to express precise relationships between objects and events and to convey new, more complex meanings. The simple sentence, 'John hit Jim' has a different meaning, for example, from, 'Jim hit John'. Although the words are identical the difference in grammatical order changes the way they are understood.

The first sound message

Crying, the baby's first sound message, is much more like animal communication than human speech. Mothers quickly come to distinguish between cries indicating hunger, anger and pain, but they do this largely by considering the conditions surrounding the baby at the time. When a crying baby is hidden behind a screen, mothers and nurses find it hard to determine the 'meaning' of the cry unless they are given clues—such as the time of the baby's last feed, or when his nappy was last changed.

Recent studies have shown that if a mother is sensitive to her baby by responding quickly and regularly to his early cries, he will cry less by the end of the first year than the baby of a mother who is not sensitive in this way. Besides crying less, such babies appear to be better at communicating with gestures and sounds.

By the age of four or five months most babies are making speech-like sounds which are rhythmically repeated in a form of vocal play called babbling. It was once thought that babies, who all over the world initially make the same sounds, continued to use only those which their mothers recognized from their own language and responded to most favourably. This is now thought to be an unlikely basis for speech development.

It seems that babies continue babbling not because they are 'rewarded' but because they enjoy the sounds that they make. Even deaf babies begin to babble at

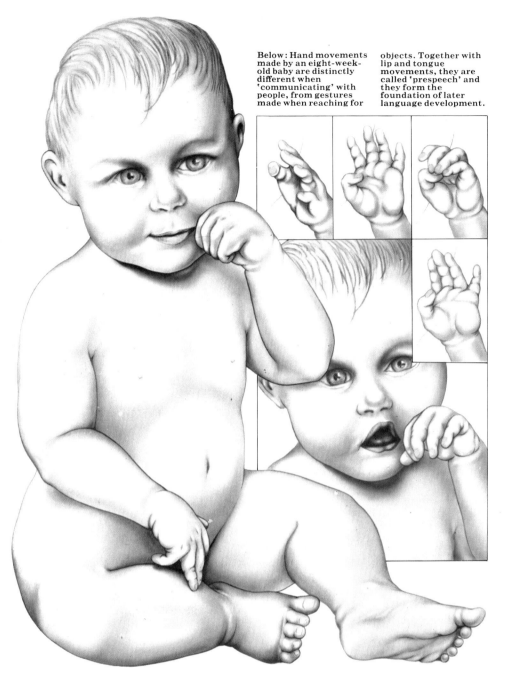

Below: Hand movements made by an eight-week-old baby are distinctly different when 'communicating' with people, from gestures made when reaching for objects. Together with lip and tongue movements, they are called 'prespeech' and they form the foundation of later language development.

the normal age, showing that this is inherited behaviour, although they soon stop unless deafness is diagnosed and a hearing aid provided. Besides enjoyment, babbling gives the baby an opportunity to learn the relationships between the movements of his mouth, tongue and so on and the sounds they produce—experience essential for learning to use speech later.

Very young babies appear to be able to distinguish speech from other types of sound, just as adults do. If a baby of one or two months is taught to suck a dummy to a repeated speech sound—for example, a vowel such as *a*—he will eventually stop sucking as he gets bored with the sound; in other words, when he has built a 'memory model' of it so that it is no longer novel and interesting. When the sound is changed to another vowel, such as *i*, the baby's sucking will increase. He detects the difference and is again interested. But he does not respond in a similar way to, say, musical notes of different pitches.

The way that a baby behaves with physical objects is very different from his behaviour with people. Objects he watches intently, trying to reach for them; but people he tries to 'talk' to from a very early age. In face-to-face contact with his mother a baby will make many facial and bodily gestures similar to those of adults in conversation with each other, and he may move his mouth in what have been called prespeech movements. It is as if the baby wants to talk long before he is able to do so. The expressions and gestures of baby and mother are very similar during such 'conversations'. At first the mother imitates the baby, and it is possible that this is the way in which the mother teaches her baby the social meaning of the gestures which he produces automatically.

Since the 1950s, great advances have been made in understanding the symbolic and grammatical nature of language. These have enabled psychologists and linguists to study children's early speech in great detail and in particular the similarity between children of different countries. Obviously children of different nationalities learn different words. But it is now believed that the meanings expressed by their early words—plus the way the words are placed in an order to convey these meanings, and the way in which sentences gradually become longer and more complex—is the same for every child, regardless of what language he is learning.

At first children use only one word at a time. These words are often nouns referring to people or objects. Studies of the situations in which these words are produced and of the child's accompanying gestures indicate that the child's single word is intended to convey an entire idea which an adult would express in a full sentence. For example, the child may attract his mother's attention while saying 'Milk'; she will understand it in this situation, as 'Give me a drink of milk'.

The number of words a child is able to use in this way increases rapidly, and soon he is using two words together. The child also begins to use words referring to actions (verbs). The role of two-word sentences is the description of relationships between people, objects, actions and events as shown in combinations like 'Daddy hit' and 'Hit ball'. Words are not put together in random order, but in sequences similar to the grammatical order which adults use. While playing a ball game, for example, a child may say, 'Hit ball'; but never, 'Ball hit'. He understands, as an adult does, that this would imply incorrectly that it is the ball rather than himself which is carrying out the action of hitting. He is beginning, in fact, to learn grammar.

The telegraphic period

In this early language, known as 'telegraphic', all small words and word endings which change meaning in subtle ways are missing, as they would be in a telegram. All of the parts of speech which convey number (such as plural forms), time (tenses other than the present) and exact object or place are omitted. Where an adult would say, 'The book is on the table', a small child is likely to describe this relationship by, 'Book table'.

Sentences become longer and more precise in meaning in two ways. Sometimes two thoughts will be put together to form a three-word sentence which expresses them both simultaneously: for example, 'Daddy hit' and, 'Hit ball' may be combined to form, 'Daddy hit ball'. Also, an extra word may be added to describe (more fully) the objects mentioned: for example, 'Sit chair' may now become, 'Sit Mummy chair'. This pattern of development is common to children in all countries so far studied. All extend the length of their sentences in the same way.

Babies do not acquire language just by imitating their parents, for they *say* many things which they have never *heard*. During their first 18 months, it is thought, they gradually learn to 'decode' adult speech. Next they learn the words and ordering rules they can use to express their understanding through speech. The child continues to produce longer sentences as he adds the parts of speech omitted during the 'telegraphic' period and, by the age of four or five, will be able to hold adult-like conversations.

Universal language development

The universal nature of children's language development, and studies of the human brain which show that the left hemisphere is specialized to hear and produce speech, imply that man may be biologically unique in his capacity for language. The vocal systems of other animals are not suited to speech production, but it is possible that the more intelligent might be able to use symbols other than spoken words to express an

Right: Though unable to hold a conversation as such, young children will try out their repertoire of words and phrases on strangers without inhibition.

Below: Visual communication through facial expressions is common to many species. Among primates facial expressions are important—for example, when one ape approaches another to show lack of hostility and gain acceptance. There are many similarities between facial expressions used by chimpanzees and by humans—made possible by the similarity in the muscular set-up of the face. But it is dangerous to 'humanize' expressions used by apes, since these visual signals are the result of an inherited pattern of behaviour influenced by environment: it presents challenges different from those encountered by man.

ZEFA

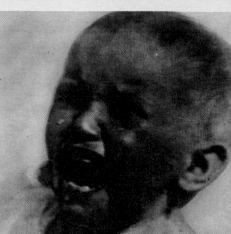

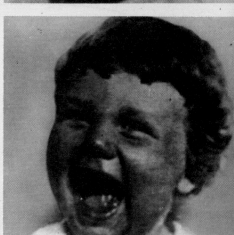

Royal College of Surgeons

Picturepoint

TEACHING LANGUAGE TO A CHIMPANZEE

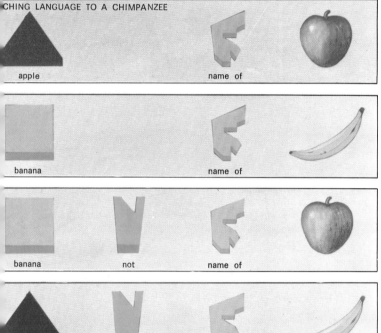

apple		name of	
banana		name of	
banana	not	name of	
apple	not	name of	

Above: By the age of four to five years, most children are able to hold adult-like conversations.

Left and below: Studies conducted with young chimpanzees have yielded surprising information about their skills in using language through symbols and gestures. One chimp called Sarah was taught to use plastic symbols of different shapes and colours, each of which represents a word: noun, adjective or verb— and a concept or condition. These symbols were placed next to the real item (left) and in this way Sarah gradually learned the words for objects. Eventually she was able to use quite complex sentences which required intelligence as well as memory. In other experiments, chimps have been taught American Sign Language (below). Not only can they communicate with both humans and other chimps, but there is evidence to suggest that they may be capable of making up their own signs for words which they have not been taught.

understanding of the world just as sophisticated as that of man.

Attempts have been made to teach American Sign Language (ASL), used by the deaf, to a chimpanzee called Washoe. In many ways Washoe's progress has been similar to that of a young child learning a first language. When taught the sign for a flower Washoe used that sign for all flowers—not just for the one she was first shown. This means that she understands that the sign 'flower' stands for the characteristics which all flowers have in common. Like human symbols, her signs stand for what she knows about objects.

Washoe has even made up her own signs. The first time she saw a duck, she signed 'water-bird' to her human companion. Washoe soon began to put signs together in short sentences, as a young child would, and the meanings she expressed were the same as those of young children. But here a crucial difference emerged for, unlike a child, Washoe does not use order consistently to make her meanings clear. When she asks someone to tickle her, Washoe is as likely to sign 'Tickle you' as she is to sign 'You tickle'. She names the parts of a situation, but does not use a grammatical order to make their relationship clear. This may be because chimpanzees in the wild are not very interested in relations between physical objects: they are social creatures. They do not have the intense curiosity about the way the world works that a human child has. It is also significant that although Washoe is good at answering questions she rarely asks them, unlike a young child who seems to ask, 'Why?' or, 'How?' on a vast number of occasions.

It is possible that only man has needed to evolve a communications system as complicated and sophisticated as language. But this is a possibility, not a proven fact. Washoe, for instance, did not begin to learn ASL until she was over a year old; this may have hindered her development of language. Studies are continuing with baby chimpanzees reared from birth in human homes, and there are already suggestions that they may develop much further than Washoe. The results of these studies are eagerly awaited, for they may show that man is not unique in his ability to communicate.

Paul Fusco/John Hillelson Agency

231

Stages of Learning

Physical growth can be studied directly by measuring and observing changes in the size and form of brain and body, but we cannot see the mind. The processes of *learning*, *memory* and *understanding* are not visible like the growth of a limb, so their existence must be inferred from behaviour. A person's behaviour—the way he reacts to situations and other people—can provide valuable information about the mental skills which he has developed for dealing with the world.

As food provides the material for physical growth, experiences in the world produce changes in behaviour. These changes show that *learning* has occurred and for learning to be possible there must be *memory*, a record of past experiences. Both learning and memory are closely related to the mental structures which we have available for organizing or *understanding* our experiences. We can only remember and learn effectively to the extent that we can understand the information or task involved.

The process of adaptation

Adaptation to the world is a continuous and active process. Initially it is possible only to behave efficiently in a situation if a mental structure exists which is adequate to understand it, that is, if we can *assimilate* the situation. However, as our experiences alter, our mental structures must change to *accommodate* them.

At birth the baby has structures which enable him to make contact with the world through actions such as looking and sucking. It is very noticeable that a baby will try to put even the most improbable objects in his mouth and suck them but this is one of his few ways of understanding or assimilating his world. In the early months the baby can come to recognize objects when they reappear but his memory is not yet good enough for him to recall them when they are not present. This ability emerges between six and 12 months. At this stage the baby can remember that his mother exists even when he cannot see her. He may insist loudly that she stays to play with him whereas a few months earlier he would appear to forget her soon after she had left the room and play happily by himself.

During the first 18 months of life the baby's developing understanding is reflected in an increasing capacity to respond to and search for objects in different situations. He now has the ability to treat an object as if it remains the same even when he sees it from different angles, in different positions and at different times.

Understanding and memory

The next stage of development in the young child involves understanding and memory. These enable the child to encode and understand objects and events in their absence at the level of thought as well as action. Whereas the child under 18 months plays by manipulating objects the child over 18 months will pretend or 'make-believe'. When he lays a cloth on
232 the ground saying 'This is my bed, I'm

going to sleep' he knows that the cloth is not really a bed and he is not really sleeping. What the child is doing is revealing his new ability to show an understanding of the nature of an object or action in the absence of the object or action.

Speech, which is also developing at this time, reflects the formation of a system of social symbols whose meaning is the same for adult and child. These are unlike the symbols of play. They vary markedly from child to child and may be difficult for adults to understand unless accompanied by speech.

The third stage of development involves images of things seen and their locations in space. A child of three or four years can learn to make his way alone from home to a shop or nursery school but if he is asked how he gets there he describes the route in terms of his actions by saying 'I turn like that', 'I go like this' and gesturing or attempting to make the actions as he describes them. But if the child is provided with a model of his neighbourhood and asked to point out his route he finds this impossible. He has no mental map or 'image' of his route of the kind that an adult or older child has.

During this period the child's understanding gradually frees itself from the need for direct sense impressions or actions. But it is still far from adult. For example, if a five-year-old looks at a model of a landscape with animals on it he is easily able to select from a set of pictures showing different views of it the one which shows it from the position he can see it from. However, if he is asked to select a picture of what someone sitting on the

Above, below, right and far right: The drawings of a five-year-old and a nine-year-old demonstrate the child's developing ability to conceptualize. Both children were asked to make two drawings of a scene, one from their own viewpoint and the other from another angle. The five-year-old accurately

described the order in which she saw a number of objects on the table in front of her. She drew them without difficulty, but when asked to draw them from the opposite angle she could describe the reverse order but could not hold on to the concept long enough to capture it on paper.

" The Age of Intellect "

Above: From the age of 11 years, the child goes through a period of rapid intellectual growth, absorbing a great deal of information. As the

cartoon aptly points out, however, information is of little use without experience, the other essential ingredient of maturity.

Left: Jean Piaget, the Swiss psychologist who is regarded as having made the greatest contribution to the study of children. Trained as a biologist, he became fascinated by the behaviour of his own children and began a systematic chronological study of the stages of their development.

Right and far right: Unlike the five-year-old, the nine-year-old child has developed the ability to hold on to abstract concepts. She was asked first to draw her own house from the front. Then, when asked to draw it as if she were looking at it from the back, she did so with meticulous attention to detail.

Keystone

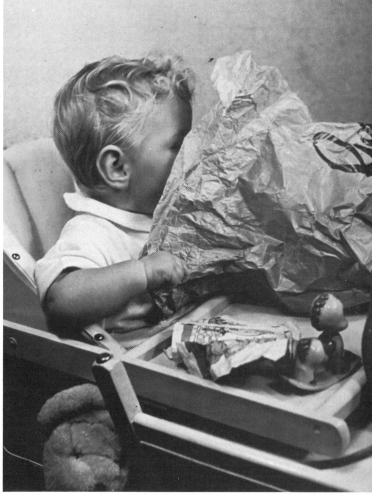

Bruce Coleman

opposite side of the model sees he will again select the same picture. Until the age of about six, the child is still very dependent upon what he sees and is tied to one viewpoint—his own.

The child is unable at this stage to grasp the more abstract characteristics of objects such as number, weight or volume. These concepts involve an understanding which often conflicts strongly with immediate sense impressions. This is evident from the hesitation which even an adult may show when asked the classic riddle: 'Which is heavier, a pound of lead or a pound of feathers?'

At this age the child believes that there is more of something when it goes further. For example, if a row of sweets is placed before him and then spread out he will say 'There are more now'. Similarly, if the child is shown a short, wide beaker full of water and sees it poured into a tall, thin beaker he will also say that there is now more because he believes that the volume changes when the level of the water rises.

However, as the child begins to realize that his intuitive notions are inadequate he will develop mental structures which enable him to co-ordinate several viewpoints. These mental structures or operations develop during the period from six to 11 years. They enable the child to understand that spreading out a row of sweets does not increase their number because not only does the row become longer the sweets are also farther apart and the net result of the two changes is to cancel each other out. Similarly, the child now understands that pouring water into a taller, thinner beaker does not increase its volume because the decrease in width cancels out the increase in height. Before

234

these faculties develop the child can consider height or width but he cannot relate the two.

In the third period of development the child is able to perform mentally the activities which he can act out with objects—he can count them, classify them and order them in a series such as size.

Classification and seriation

The development of classification can be illustrated by the child's behaviour with a bunch of flowers. If a child is shown six primroses and six daisies and asked if there are more flowers or more primroses he will usually answer that there are just as many flowers as there are primroses. He will then be confused if asked whether the primroses are not also flowers. He knows that both primroses and daisies are flowers but he cannot consider the whole class (primroses plus daisies) and part of it (the primroses) at the same time. But when his ability to classify develops, he also begins to understand seriation.

If a child is presented with a set of sticks he will have little difficulty in putting them in order—from the smallest to the largest. He can understand that if the first stick is larger than the second and the second stick is larger than the third then the first stick must also be larger than the third.

In comparison, the younger child who has not developed this ability—known as operational thought—cannot understand this overall relationship and can only form a series by trial and error, comparing every stick with every other stick.

Operational thought forms the basis for logical thought about the world. It is probably no coincidence that schooling

Above left: Children develop skills in many different types of learning situations. This Mexican nine-year-old is learning to weave.

Above: The understanding of the relationship of objects in space is one of the most important developments in the young child. Up to the age of nine months, when an object is hidden —in a paper bag, for example— he will continue to search in the place he first found it, even though he sees it hidden elsewhere. After this age, he will begin to look elsewhere when he fails to find it in the first hiding-place.

Eve Arnold/John Hillelson Agency

M. Cartier-Bresson/John Hillelson Agency

usually begins at the age of five or six years when the child is ready to begin thinking in this way. Just as a child cannot be taught to walk until he has reached an adequate level of neuro-muscular maturity he cannot be taught number concepts until he has been through all the usual stages of development up to this point.

The child is like a scientist with an inadequate theory of the world and to accelerate his mental growth he must be provided with experiences which challenge that theory and force him to modify it until it becomes more like the theories of the adults around him. Language is of great importance in this development. It enables adults to tell the child when his theory conflicts with their own. In this way the child can learn about and benefit from the experiences of others without having to undergo them himself.

The development of logical thought

The final period of mental development does not begin until the age of about 11 years. During this period the young adult develops his ability to think about things and events which are possible although not necessarily present in the world of concrete experience. The young adult can do more than think logically about objects, he can think about his thoughts. This is shown by his ability to work out whether or not an argument is logical.

It is important to realize that mental skills do not develop in isolation. Examinations and intelligence tests can measure a child's ability to understand and think but a poor performance does not necessarily indicate low potential. Mental, emotional and physical development are intricately connected in ways which are not yet fully understood and the reasons why a child may fail to develop his full mental potential, at any given stage, are numerous and complex.

Emotions are intimately linked with the reasons why we do things, and with our motives. As we develop, both change as a result of our experiences. When we are successful at learning we feel good and this supports our motivation to learn further, but the opposite occurs if we fail. We feel so anxious that we are unable to learn effectively—there is a 'mental block'. The very young child shows an innate curiosity and desire to learn but these need adult support if they are to continue. Adults who set unrealistically high goals for children will be placing them continually in situations where failure is inevitable. The goals set for a child must take into consideration his current level of ability for if they exceed it greatly he will learn less. Worse, he will lose the desire to learn.

Personality and behaviour

The developing child learns not only about the world around him but about himself. He learns about the type of person he is largely by observing the reactions of other people to his behaviour. Gestural communication develops before speech and children of a very young age are able to tell when an adult is disappointed with them even though the adult may say that he is pleased with their performance. In this way the child may come to see himself as a failure and will believe that he is incapable of learning, an attitude which may shape the rest of his life and his relationships with others.

Above and right: For the child between five and 11 years, learning and education are almost synonymous. But the methods by which the basic skills of literacy and numeracy are taught have changed considerably since formal schooling became compulsory in many countries. Children were once forced to learn everything by rote and punished if they failed to do so. Educational and technological research have heralded more enlightened teaching methods in which children are encouraged and stimulated into learning.

Below: Six-year-olds having their ability to think logically—which develops around this age—tested.

John Hillelson Agency

235

The Child and the Family

Between birth and going to school, the child undergoes many transformations. He slowly develops from a small, helpless organism into a walking, talking individual. Although his body functions may be well on the way towards maturity and his brain may be virtually complete in its structure, he still has to be protected and nurtured for many more years of his life until he is truly capable of living an independent existence. Most importantly he has to undergo the process of *socialization*—he has to learn the norms, values, behaviour and mannerisms which enable him to relate to other people within his own society.

The universal institution

The only human group which seems to be formally established in most societies to undertake this task is the *family*. Perhaps the universal nature of the family is not so strange when the needs which it fulfils are examined. The family is basically an economic unit which provides a context for the social and emotional needs of two partners, for the reproduction of children and for the care and social training of all its respective members. But the family group may not be restricted to this small unit; it may be extended to include other related family groups, so that the transformation process of the child is influenced by several generations of adults and their children as well as his own parents, brothers and sisters.

Through family relationships, the young child learns to relate to groups outside the family—friends, neighbours and later, schoolfriends and colleagues. The skill that he must develop in order to do this is the use of language. Learning to talk is therefore one of the most important social skills which he develops

within the family group and which the family are primarily responsible for.

Through his developing use of language —which is almost fluent by the age of five or six—the child learns what is expected of him as a member of the family, as a pupil, as a friend and as a member of society. He learns what the limits are in all these roles: what is right, wrong, acceptable, unacceptable, praiseworthy and punishable.

Before he is able to understand what his position is in society and the behaviour appropriate to it, he must learn where he stands within the family group. He is taught that he belongs to a sex or gender, that he is a child as opposed to adult, as his parents are, and that he is the eldest, elder, younger or youngest, depending on how many brothers and sisters are in the hierarchical family structure. He begins to understand who is responsible for what and to whom he is responsible. He learns, for example, that when father tells him to do something, to disobey may mean punishment; but when an elder brother gives the same order, he can sometimes be ignored, insulted or told to go away.

He also begins to understand the relationship between discipline and security and through them to discover his own skills. The young child has no innate experience of what is 'safe' either within physical limits or within social limits through behaviour. He has to be taught where the boundaries are so that he can develop his own judgement and self-control in adhering to them or trying to go beyond them. He rapidly learns about physical boundaries: disobeying an order to climb a tree which results in a cut or grazed knee teaches him the inherent danger in that activity. If he wants to do it again, he must risk physical damage or learn how to do it without hurting himself, which means exercizing better control over his movements and his judgement of height and distance. He also learns in the process why the order not to climb the tree in the first place was given and that discipline—although not always pleasant or agreeable—is generally in the

Above: An Edwardian family group. As head of the household, the father had absolute authority over his children, sometimes even when they were well into adulthood. This strictness of upbringing and discouragement of individuality is reflected in their clothes.

Below: The mid-20th century family group presents a striking contrast to the Edwardian family (above). The affectionate, informal relationship these children have with their mother allows them to explore their environment more freely and to become confident and independent.

Left: An etching by the English humouristic cartoonist, George Cruikshank (1792-1878). His work was noted for its satirical social comments and he enjoyed inventing words to sum up some of the situations he illustrated. This cartoon, called *Philoprogenitiveness* (basically meaning 'a great many children') shows a typically working class family of the Regency era. It was common for entire families of that period to live together communally, so that the children were influenced by grandparents, aunts, uncles and cousins, as well as their own parents, brothers and sisters.

Mansell

John Hillelson Agency

interests of his own safety.

Up to the age of seven or eight, his physical skills develop quite rapidly. His social skills take longer. In most cases, he has no moral judgement, for example. He is unable to apply criteria or standards of behaviour—he judges the 'badness' of an act by how much damage has resulted from it. An older child is able to assess how bad it is in relation to the person who committed it: how much damage was intended and did they know in advance what the result of the act would be? Until he is able to make these assessments for himself, the young child must have standards set for him. Since he cannot understand the reasons underlying particular types of behaviour, he adopts them through imitation. His father and mother, with whom he spends most of his time during his early years are constantly emulated, so that he does what his mother or father do.

Personality development

The development of his own personality is dependent on what his status is within the family. An only or first child is more likely to mature early than second or subsequent children. He has the benefit of having had his parents to himself, for a time at least. Because he is the first, they are intensely involved in his development and he will consequently receive more attention and encouragement in mastering skills. The very fact that all his contact in his most formative years is with adults means that he is more likely to adopt adult attitudes and interests.

His parents will come to expect him to demonstrate this level of relative maturity, particularly when a second

Below: A Tasaday family from the Philippines. This near-extinct group of cave-dwellers live together in complete harmony and while there are distinct male and females roles, both parents are equally responsible for looking after the children, who are constantly learning from adult conversation and behaviour.

Above: Gurkha children from Nepal. There are special roles for some members of the family in many societies, one of the most common being the care of older children for the junior members. This young girl will be well aware of certain adult responsibilities before she is out of childhood herself.

Right: In some societies, children are still taking on the role of breadwinner relatively early. At the age of 12 or 13, these Moroccan children have been sent to work in a carpet factory to supplement the family income, already stretched by too many children and poor social conditions.

Above: Young children often benefit from the relationship with grandparents, who have the experience of having brought up their own children. They may also have the time and patience to enter into the child's world of curiosity and exploration which their parents may be too busy working to enjoy.

Below: In the anxiety to appear as adult as their elders, younger siblings—who learn many skills from imitating older children in the family— are just as likely to adopt bad habits as good ones. Big brother is here seen initiating his junior into the grown-up art of smoking.

child arrives. The first-born is under a certain amount of strain during this time. He not only has to adjust to his altered status and cope with feelings of jealousy or insecurity, but finds that new demands are made of him: he has to be 'grown-up' and help care for his brother or sister who is 'only a baby' and cannot take care of his/herself.

The youngest child in the family may also develop at a reasonable rate. He not only has his parents to attend to him but has the benefit of older brothers or sisters to imitate and from whom he can learn verbal and physical skills.

His relationship with his elder brothers and sisters will alternate between companionship and rivalry: he learns to respect them and turn to them for protection, but he may also resent their privileges such as being allowed to stay up longer. Parents have to exercise tact and firmness in maintaining this privilege on behalf of a first-born in particular, in recognition and as a reward for his attempts at maturity and self-restraint. The youngest child may also reap the benefit from the fact that he is the last— his parents will have had the experience of bringing up his predecessors and will probably have given up trying to produce a model of child-like perfection by the time he arrives, so that he will have fewer restraints imposed on him.

The middle child probably has the most difficult time during his early years. He neither has the attention and privileges of the first-born nor the freedom or advantages of the youngest. He has to struggle for attention and is likely to feel so displaced that he adopts negative means of getting it. While his mother is preoccupied with a new baby, for example, he will attempt dangerous feats of climbing or balancing which are likely to result in him falling and being hurt. Unless his parents are understanding and tolerant of his behaviour, he is likely to grow up with more emotional problems than the other children in the family.

An only child has greater material advantages, quite often, than those who belong to larger families. Like the first-born he will spend a great deal of his time in the company of adults and will be therefore quick to adopt adult behaviour. His parents may be better off economically because they only have one child and he may therefore have more room, greater privacy and access to instruments which may aid in his development like radio or television.

The only child is often equipped with greater inner resources as a result of being on his own much of the time. He learns how to create his own entertainment and cope with his own boredom. If he does not have real friends, he may attempt to enrich his life through fantasy by inventing an imaginary friend or acting out his own stories or those he has read. It has been suggested that only children are more egocentric or possessive than those brought up with other children. So far, there is little evidence that this is the case. They are just as likely to be able to share their possessions.

Most children have contact at some period in their lives with older or elderly relatives in a way that influences their growing up. If grandparents, for example, live in the home, the child will be directly affected by their state of health. An ailing or bed-ridden grandparent can severely restrict the child's activities: he may not be able to give free expression to his exuberance or imagination in his play as he is perpetually told to be quiet. An active and energetic grandparent, on the other hand, can provide the child with an additional source of affection and companionship and through interest in the child's activities, encourage him in his development. It can also mean conflict. The elderly parent can cause extra economic stress and if they have a tendency to interfere with or undermine the parents' authority as well, relationships among all members of the family may be severely affected. The child's behaviour may be affected to the extent that he is brought up to regard this as the norm and may have a tendency to be defensive, argumentative or just difficult in relationships with people outside the family.

The overall influence of all these relationships on the child is hard to determine and even harder to predict. Many of the attitudes adopted from his parents which see him through his early years will be changed or totally discarded when he comes in contact with other social groups. The kind of adult he turns into usually depends on the kind of adults his parents are: if they are confident and assertive, encouraging his efforts and rewarding his successes, he will be at least motivated to become a useful, adequate member of society.

Picturepoint

Camera & Pen Int.

By relating to his parents the child discovers how to relate to the outside world. Before learning behaviour appropriate to his role in society, he first finds out where he stands within the family.

The Child at Play

Play is one of the most important activities in a child's development. Through it he can gradually experience the skills, attitudes and modes of behaviour appropriate to adult life.

Until only a few decades ago, play was not regarded as a serious subject of study. It was felt in scientific circles that it was not a manageable activity for experimental research. 'Cowboys-and-indians' and other fantasy games—with which children are preoccupied during certain phases of their development—could neither be defined nor kept within certain limits necessary to comply with the sober-minded approach with which psychologists generally scrutinized human behaviour. The respected critic, Harold Schlosberg, of Brown University published a paper advising researchers to steer clear of this field of enquiry since he maintained that 'so antic a phenomenon as play' would provide little data of worth and was unlikely to give any insights into early human development.

However, the subject was not closed. Enquiries into behaviour among other primates provided vital clues which furnished experimental psychologists with a new approach to child behaviour. From observation of young monkeys, early investigators such as the Dutch primatologist J. A. R. A. M. van Hooff, observed that there was a distinct difference between activities in which survival skills were practised and play. They were accompanied by very clear forms of signalling to indicate that when play was intended, aggression was not, so that real fighting only occurred when one monkey did not see the signal sent by another. It was gradually noted by later observers—David Hamburg of Stanford and Jane van Lawick-Goodall—that young chimpanzees spend a great deal of their first five years observing adult forms of behaviour and incorporating them into their play. Eventually the resemblances between child and chimpanzee behaviour were recognized and a pattern of child behaviour became apparent.

The purpose of play

It has been established by experiments done by a number of investigators that the central requirement of play is the opportunity to acquire skill in certain specific activities. In fact it has even been postulated that play is a means of neutralizing the effects of the 'push' or force which drives children to complete an act successfully. And, indeed, it would seem that there is a need for children to

Bowling (1378)

Trap-ball (1381)

Club-ball 14th century

Early form of golf

Above: Ball games. Although they probably began as unstructured forms of play requiring only something to kick or hit, most ball games have developed into highly structured games with complex rules. These games (above) popular in the 14th century, are developments of games played by the Romans and the ancient Greeks and may be the precursors of many popular modern games. Games of this nature have a timeless, universal appeal to children. Through them they can develop their judgment and muscular co-ordination and pit themselves against their own last performance as well as against their playmate's.

Above: A 17th century Chinese scroll painting of *wayeng golek*, or puppetry. Puppets can be made in almost any shape to portray information on almost any subject, and as such, provide a valuable tool for the education of children. Apart from improving dexterity, puppetry gives children the opportunity to be creative and organized in the making of the costumes and in the actual performance.

Right: Like many traditional games the meaning of *Oranges and Lemons* is almost forgotten. The 'oranges' and 'lemons' represent bells which pealed along the 16th century London 'traitors' route' to execution.

240

alleviate pressure.

In an experiment done at Harvard University in the early 1970s, three-, four-, and five-year olds—divided equally into groups of 36—were given the task of fishing an object out of a container which was just out of reach. They were all given a number of sticks which, when properly clamped together, provided an effective fishing rod. The 'training' procedures varied among the groups. One was shown how to clamp the sticks together, another was allowed to practise clamping the sticks together, a third was allowed to watch the experimenter carry out the complete task, while a fourth was left to play with the materials and it was implied to the children in this group that the task was part of the play.

The group to which the complete task was demonstrated and the play group had significantly better results than the other groups; their success rate was twice as high as that of the other groups—in other words, twice as many children in each of those two groups successfully completed the task.

But what is perhaps of greater significance is that the experimenters noticed a different approach to the task between the play group and all the other groups. They were less intense about completing the task because they regarded it as a form of play. Consequently, they gave up less easily on failed attempts and were eventually able to solve the problem.

Above: For children in some societies the boundaries between work and play are indistinct, since the periods spent in learning are not restricted to formal schooling. This young member of the Karaja tribe of Brazil has to learn how to make and use weapons and the art of hunting. Learning to use a bow and arrow may be merely a game at the moment but his life will depend on it when he is an adult.

Below: 'Children's Games' by Pieter Breugel, the 16th century Flemish artist.

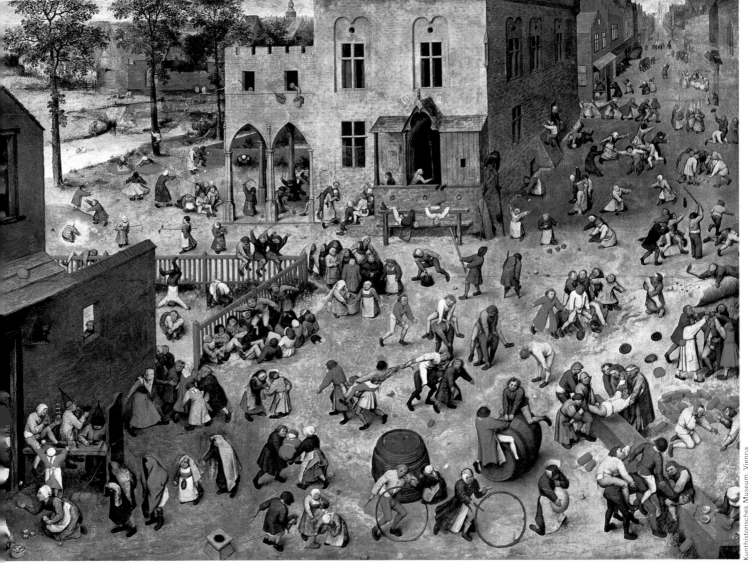

241

The stages of play

At all stages in a child's development play is a means of discovery: the child can be attempting to understand what is happening, how something works or to achieve a new skill. After he has made the discovery he seems to enjoy repeating the action 'just for fun', through which he acquires the skill and which he will go on repeating long after there is any new information to be gained from the action. But it appears to be necessary for children to 'waste' time in this way. It takes them much longer than adults to assimilate a new experience and the younger the child is, the longer it takes.

Children begin to play at a very early age. At four to five months, an infant will enjoy a game of peek-a-boo, and it is common for babies of this age to pull their mother's hair and to chuckle happily when she pretends to be startled.

Playing with sand and water is popular with young children, because the effect of their action upon it is immediately visible. They soon grow out of this, however, as it does not lead to the development of skills and so children eventually become bored with it. Up to the age of ten years, building is a favourite activity with both sexes. Building with bricks offers almost unlimited potential.

The kinds of activities that play involves are many and varied, but they can be roughly divided into *structured* and *unstructured* play. Structured play includes all those types of games which have rules or are organized in a specific way, some of which have been played since the dawn of recorded time—*tug-of-war* and *blind man's buff* are known to be pre-Roman, for example. Unstructured, or 'free', play starts from chance happenings. A child will discover his effect on something—sand, for example—and will follow it up: perhaps making his first sandcastle.

Play and the environment

Play allows the child to explore his environment but it also enables him to experiment with the skills he has acquired in using his own body and in manipulating objects. He needs a certain amount of exercise to promote the development of the co-ordination of his muscles and nervous system. Many traditional games provide this opportunity and also enable him to explore his physical capabilities to his own satisfaction. Games and pastimes such as *follow the leader*, *skating*, *cycling*, and *hopscotch* fall into this category, since they depend on improvement on the child's own last performance as much as the performance of his playmates. Some of his physical limits will also be tested by taunts and dares, and others by direct testing of his strength in fighting.

There is a noticeable difference between the way boys play compared with girls and this difference shows up quite distinctly by the time they are five years old. 'Rough and tumble' play is probably the best illustration of this difference. It involves wrestling, tumbling and jumping up and down. It is much more attractive to boys than to girls, who are inclined to be a little more timid about joining in this kind of boisterous activity. Although 'rough and tumble' play usually only occurs between friends, or in a very

Left: A young Lebanese soldier. Kicking a football alleviates some of the stress of being forced into an adult role before he is fully equipped for it.

Below: No matter how sophisticated toys have become, children are still fascinated by everyday, mundane materials. Discarded cardboard boxes have great potential for their imaginations to work on.

Philippe Ledru/John Hillelson Agency

J. Allan Cash

J. Allan Cash

friendly context, less confident children have difficulty joining in.

Imitation and make-believe

The most important developments in the child's socialization take place through imitation. The child's postures, vocabulary, emotional reactions and mental attitudes have been copied from the behaviour of those around him. He may learn simply by watching an action or game being carried out, or he may insist on acting it out himself. Between the ages of two to eight, for example, he will progress from emulating his parents' activities—making cakes like Mummy does—to imitating generalized social situations like playing 'shop'.

Through this kind of play, both at school and in the home, the child can be taught some basic skills such as counting, understanding weight, quantity and the cost of items. Through games of this nature, the child will also develop his verbal facility. He will become practised in the kinds of interactions he is likely to become involved in later on in life and in this way can store and digest impressions which lessen anxiety and teach him the social rules which govern acceptable behaviour.

A child has his own private world filled with anxieties, aspirations, dreams and fantasies. He has feelings about his environment—that it is safe and friendly or insecure and hostile. Some of the child's outward behaviour reflects his inner feelings, but his inner experience cannot be totally understood using only his behaviour as a basis for interpretation. A child's world of make believe

develops between the ages of 18 months and eight years. It allows the child to bend reality to fit his own intellectual or emotional requirements. For example, children sometimes enact events in the way they would have liked them to happen, rather than the way they actually did happen. They also tend to act out events they have never experienced or are likely to experience just to see what they 'feel' like—being chased by tigers, for example.

The child also learns through the imaginary acting out of various roles what it feels like to be on the receiving end or the giving end of various situations—shopkeeper and customer, doctor and patient, teacher and pupil, employer and employee. Some or all of these he will eventually experience as an adult and through the combination of enacting the fantasy and the reality will gradually make the transition from the child's to the adult world.

But in order to make this transition smoothly, he must be aided by understanding adults. It is easy for adults to forget the contours of the child's world—both inner and outer—and to overlook the fact that play is not merely an activity to while away the time until he is able to take on more responsible adult-like activities. The child who is not allowed to play or to play in a way that is conducive to learning and the development of skills will probably not grow into a responsible adult. Without the opportunity to explore and experiment and to experience what it means to be a child, he will never learn to explore and experience what it really means to be an adult.

Above: A 'glue-in' at a community centre in San Francisco.

Below: Dressing-up. Make-believe is an

essential form of play for two- to eight-year olds. It enables them to explore reality by bending it to fit their own requirements.

Right: Nepalese children learning to count and name things through the universally popular game of 'shop', or 'store'.

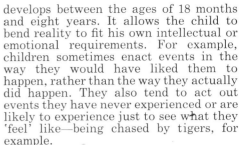

Play is one of the main activities in a child's development. It is a means of acquiring the skills, attitudes, and modes of behaviour in preparation for adult life.

Learning and Intelligence

Everybody knows roughly what intelligence is, but it is hard to define precisely —and even harder to measure. Psychologists themselves cannot agree on it. Over the years, some have called it 'the ability to learn'. Others have called it 'the ability to adapt adequately to the environment'. Still others have thought it 'a general tendency towards achievement'.

One early psychologist, Professor E. L. Thorndike, suggested that intelligence could be broken up into three groups— mechanical, social and abstract. *Mechanical* intelligence meant skill in manipulating tools and gadgets, *social* intelligence covered people's ability to act wisely in human relationships, and *abstract* intelligence was the ability to handle symbols (words and numbers) and scientific principles.

One aspect which Thorndike's classifications certainly undervalued, however, was *creativity*. In the 1950s, J. P. Guildford, dissatisfied with existing methods of testing intelligence, developed his own research along the lines of *divergent* and *convergent* thinking. He defined convergent thinking as a person's ability to produce the 'expected' answer to a problem, and divergent thinking—or creativity—as ability to produce the 'unexpected' answer.

'Unexpected' in this sense does not mean 'wrong'. As one example, in his book *Children Solve Problems* Edward De Bono cites children who were asked to solve the problem of how to build houses more quickly. Most of their drawings showed conventional thinking—more highly mechanized versions of normal building methods. But one highly creative child suggested starting with a huge balloon 'printed on the inside with an attractive wallpaper pattern', inflating it, spraying it with concrete, and then cutting away those areas like doors and windows where concrete was not wanted. This is the exact opposite of normal methods—but a similar system to the child's has in fact been made to work.

R. B. Cattell in 1971 similarly held that there were two types of intelligence, which he called *fluid* and *crystallized*. A child with fluid intelligence, his research showed, could somehow sidestep the learned or expected answer to a problem, producing a creative and unexpected answer. The child with crystallized intelligence, however, would accurately produce an already-formulated answer to a problem, but not attempt to go beyond it.

Intelligence tests

The first, crude attempts to measure people's intelligence were as long ago as the 1890s. Then in 1904 the French Minister for Public Instruction set up a commission to study the problems of 'backward' children. Among its members was a 47-year-old psychologist, Alfred Binet, and his first problem was: who *were* the backward children?

With his assistant, Théophile Simon, Binet set out to devise a series of test

Above and below: Differences in cultural background have an enormous impact on the kind of learning that children acquire, and hence in their performances in traditional IQ tests such as the Stanford-Binet. The young Chinese is learning the philosophy of Chairman Mao—and western algebra—in an attempt to progress in an increasingly industrialized society. The novice Buddhist monk is learning self-denial, meditation and religious belief in an attempt to reach the ultimate purity of the spirit. The Chinese might do better in an IQ test. But is he more intelligent?

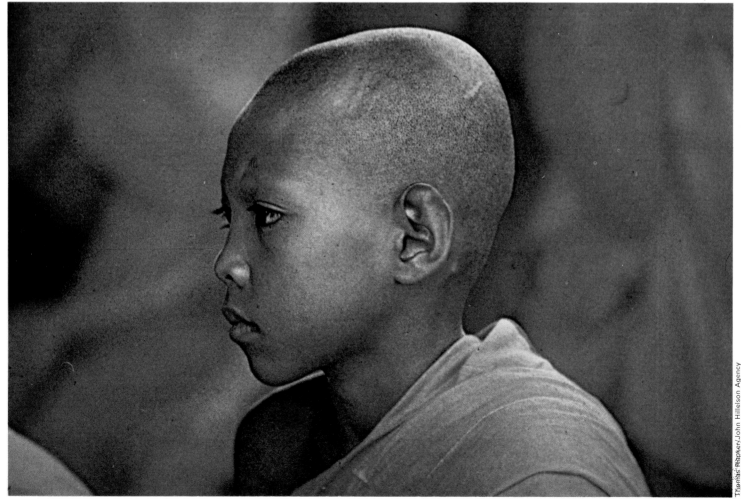

problems—and succeeded, because he had no preconceived ideas of what problems to use. If the average six-year-old could copy a drawing of a square, but the average five-year-old could not, then this test was for Binet a perfectly suitable measure of six-year-old intelligence.

Binet spent the rest of his life revising his tests and, after his death in 1911, the American Lewis Terman carried on the work at Stanford University. Hence tests of this type, still widely used, are called Stanford-Binet tests.

From the results of Binet's work there developed the concept of *mental age*. He supposed that a child's brain increased in intellectual power year by year. So two children shown by the tests to have the same intellectual power had the same mental age—regardless of their actual ages. A 13-year-old whose results matched those of the average 12-year-old was held to be one year retarded, while a 13-year-old whose results matched those of the average 14-year-old was held to be one year advanced.

But one year's 'backwardness' at the age of, say, five, is far more significant than at the age of 13, since it represents a much greater proportion of the child's total development. So it was later suggested that the *ratio* between mental age and true (chronological) age was a better measure than just the *difference* between them. This ratio, when multiplied by 100, is called the *intelligence quotient*, or IQ. (IQ = mental age multiplied by 100, then divided by chronological age). A child whose mental and chronological ages are the same is, by definition, an average child; his IQ is 100 exactly.

However, a person's intellectual capacity does not go on increasing indefinitely; somewhere between the ages of 14 and 18, it begins to level out.

How does IQ vary from person to person? About 50 per cent of people, on a big enough sample, will have an IQ of somewhere between 90 and 110. About 25 per cent are below IQ 90, and another quarter above IQ 110. The numbers with an IQ below 70 (traditionally taken to be 'retarded') or above 130 (the 'brilliant') are small—about 3 per cent in each case.

Testing by this method shows no differences between the IQs of men as a whole and of women as a whole. But tests have shown marked differences between people of different backgrounds—for example, members of an affluent majority and of a deprived minority in the same country.

This is one reason why many psychol-

Above: Imitating his elders is a normal part of a child's learning process, even if what is learned—such as IRA-type 'weapons' training —is out of the ordinary.

Below: Standards of drawing are a measure of 'fluid intelligence' in pre-school children. Circles, for example, are easily visualized —but too hard to draw.

Above and below: Tests with Kaleidoblocs, with which children can make structures of amazing complexity, can tell psychologists much about the intelligence of unusually gifted or retarded children— such as Paul, aged 7, whose IQ is too high to be measured by standard methods. His mental age may be as high as 11.

Right: Modern IQ tests use universally understood symbols, rather than words or numbers, to eliminate 'cultural bias'.

Below right: Chess requires a special kind of intelligence—the ability to analyze in advance the possible outcomes of an infinite number of moves.

ogists today do not regard such traditional tests as adequate. Children from homes where books, toys, records, lively conversation—among themselves, and especially with adults—and other stimuli are present tend to perform better than others in school discussions with both teachers and testers. Since most tests are based on a child's skill with words, it is difficult to measure accurately the intelligence of children whose homes do not provide such advantages. In fact, some children who appear to be slow, or even dim-witted, in the verbal sections of tests can score well in the non-verbal sections.

Conventional tests are also, according to most psychologists, heavily loaded towards 'crystallized intelligence' rather than 'fluid intelligence', and far too concerned with abstract concepts. So they are useful for measuring intelligence of the kind needed by schools in assessing a child's potential for future academic work, but virtually useless in measuring perseverance or creativity—both important aspects of other types of work, and indeed of a well-rounded human being.

Memory

Much easier to define than intelligence, but equally important in the learning

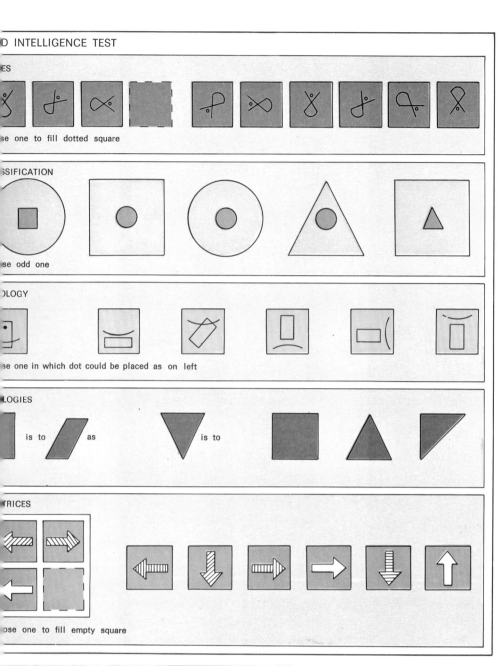

INTELLIGENCE TEST

ES

se one to fill dotted square

SSIFICATION

se odd one

OLOGY

se one in which dot could be placed as on left

LOGIES

is to ___ as ___ is to

TRICES

ose one to fill empty square

ENGLAND JULIAN HODGSON = HOLLAND HELMUT CARDON

Keystone

process, is memory. It is the ability to learn, retain what we have learned, and retrieve what we have retained when we need it.

Doctors do not know by what process, or even in what part of the brain, memory is developed. They do know, however, that failure to memorize can be caused by deterioration of brain cells which are active in the learning process; by certain types of injuries to, or diseases of, the brain; by activities which intervene between the time we learn something and the time we want to recall it; and last but not least, by repression.

In the learning process, our ability to remember is dependent both on the methods used to convey the information and the circumstances in which the learning takes place. Any schoolchild who has done last-minute 'swotting' for a test knows that what is crammed into the brain today can as easily be forgotten by tomorrow night, or whenever the test is over. What is not so well known is that children who take examinations in a room where they have been taught a particular subject score higher marks than when they are tested in less-familiar surroundings.

In general, forgetting is not caused by the fading out of impressions but rather by the crowding out of old material by a constant inflow of new. Sometimes this new material demands that we unlearn, or reorganize, the original material, causing a 'scrambling' of the original material to the point of confusion—not so much a matter of being unable to remember, but of not knowing *what* to remember.

Repression is another matter. Most people are much more likely to forget a dental appointment than an invitation to a party; the human mind rejects the unpleasant much more readily than the pleasant. The early psycho-analyst Sigmund Freud took this concept a stage further: he built a whole theory of adult behaviour on the belief that we repress certain memories because if we retrieved them they would evoke painful emotions, acute feelings of guilt and a loss of self-esteem.

Some modern psychologists say that the same sort of thing holds true of school-type learning. If teaching methods or the atmosphere in a child's home do not allow for the fact that a child can be hurt or painfully embarrassed, they contend, the child's mind may react by 'blocking out' the material that he is supposed to learn. Similarly, parents who do not help their children to learn, but demand that a child passes examinations in spite of their lack of interest, can make the child forget what he has learned out of unconscious spite.

Tiring during the learning process, or simply losing interest in what is being taught, can also cause memory lapses. In 1932 Van Alstyne discovered that a child's *attention span*—that is, the length of time that he can concentrate on a subject—increases systematically with age. For two-year-olds, he found, the average attention span was seven minutes; for three-year-olds, 8.9 minutes; for four-year-olds, 12.4 minutes; and for five-year-olds, 13.6 minutes. So that, as W. Fowler and O. K. Moore have shown, it is perfectly possible to teach an average child to read by the age of three or four—if they are taught in very short lessons.

Puberty

Puberty is the stage of development when the body makes its great leap forward from childhood into adulthood. This is achieved by several metabolic processes in the physiology of boy and girl, and is accompanied by psychological changes in mood, drive and general behaviour.

The average age of onset of puberty is 13 years—although any age between 11 years and 16 years can be regarded as within the normal limits. Signs of physiological maturing of the body before 11 years is described as 'precocious puberty' and invariably requires medical investigation. In both sexes, there has been a trend over the past century for puberty to arrive earlier, even in the range of normal limits, in children of the affluent and developed countries. This is partly related to improved physical health and better nutrition.

But in poorer countries which have a tropical or sub-tropical climate, there was often evidence of earlier puberty than in temperate climates. The reverse trend in the second half of the twentieth century, with earlier puberty in Western Europe and the North American continent, may be due to increased exposure to artificial light in these societies. This is a theory derived from experimental work on young female rats undertaken by N. Jafarey and co-workers at a Karachi medical school in Pakistan.

The pace of growth
Puberty is another of the phases in life when the pace of body growth changes. Clearly and visibly through childhood, boys and girls make a steady and regular increase in height and in weight. The pace or velocity of these growth changes tends to slow down as puberty nears. Then, just before the effects of puberty become apparent in the human organs and tissues, the pace of growth sharply increases.

This growth spurt is first apparent in the girls who show the height and weight changes around 11 years of age. The spurt appears in the boys around 13 years of age. The actual figures for increase in height vary, due to familiar and inherited characteristics and to nutritional factors. Over a two year period, a rise of around 20 cm and a weight gain of around 18 kilograms is the 'typical pattern' that can emerge.

Other physiological measurements and indications of organ changes also alter at puberty. Blood pressure, as measured in the upper arm, is in indication of the force of the output of the human heart and of the resistance in the elastic arteries which carry the blood away from the heart. From infancy and throughout childhood, there is a steady increase in the blood pressure. Again, a spurt in the blood pressure takes place at puberty to accommodate the changes in size and function of other organs. By the age of 15 years, the adolescent blood pressure has reached normal adult levels.

The hormones at work
The physiological maturation process at puberty is organized and set going by hormonal command from the *anterior*

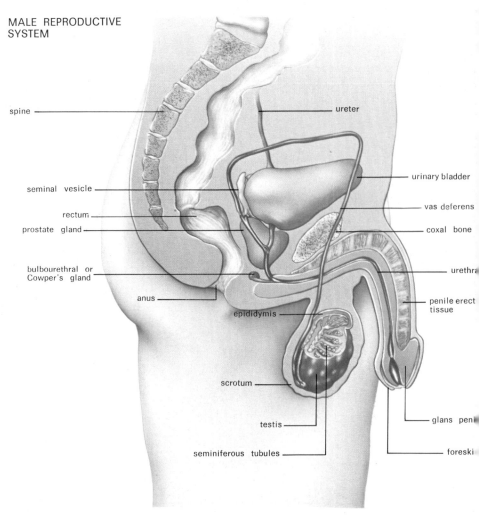

MALE REPRODUCTIVE SYSTEM

spine — ureter — seminal vesicle — urinary bladder — rectum — vas deferens — prostate gland — coxal bone — bulbourethral or Cowper's gland — urethra — anus — penile erect tissue — epididymis — scrotum — testis — glans penis — seminiferous tubules — foreskin

Above: Diagram of the male reproductive organs. They consist of the testes—the gonads or sex glands—which produce sperm and various ducts which store or transport the sperm to the exterior. The gonads also contain male hormones responsible for the physical changes which occur during puberty.

Below: A testis, one of the pair of oval-shaped male sex glands. Each testis measures about 5 cm (2 inches) long and is about 2.5 cm (1 inch) in diameter. They lie in the abdominal cavity during foetal development but descend into the outer sac-like scrotum at birth since coolness is essential for sperm manufacture.

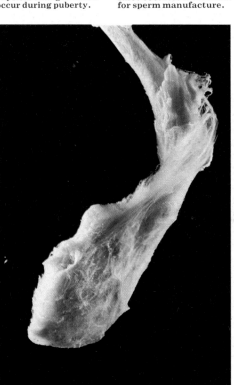

A COMPARISON BETWEEN THE MALE AND FEMALE PELVIS

MALE PELVIS

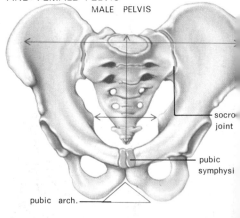

sacro-iliac joint — pubic symphysis — pubic arch

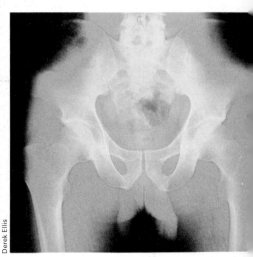

Dave Kelly

Derek Ellis

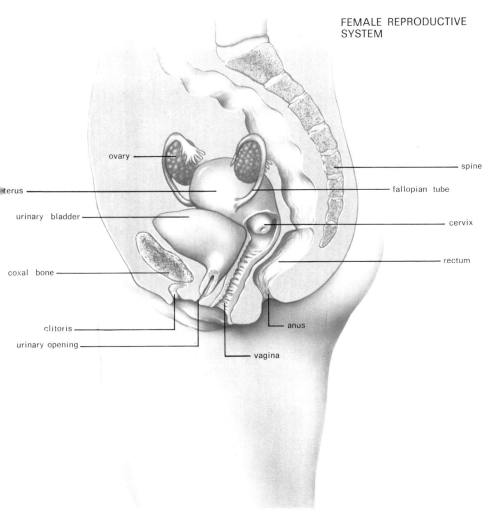

FEMALE REPRODUCTIVE
SYSTEM

ovary

terus

fallopian tube

urinary bladder

cervix

spine

rectum

coxal bone

clitoris

anus

urinary opening

vagina

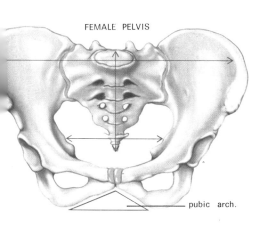

FEMALE PELVIS

pubic arch.

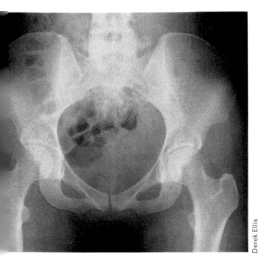

Derek Ellis

Left: The male and female pelvis. The female pelvis enlarges during puberty under the influence of the female hormone oestrogen, in preparation for pregnancy. The pubic bones are also moveable, so that they can be separated to increase the vaginal opening in childbirth.

Above: The female reproductive system. The almond-shaped ovaries release ova (eggs) once a month which are drawn down the uterine tube to the uterus (womb) to await fertilization.

Below left: X-rays of the male and female pelvis in normal adulthood.

pituitary gland of the human brain. The anterior pituitary itself is triggered off by a nerve message supply from the *hypothalamus* which appears to have a built-in genetic regulator that is set to turn on at just the right age in the individual. (Presumably the artificial light effects suggested in some way excite the hypothalamus to a premature turning on.)

The anterior pituitary produces growth hormone, and it is the flow of this chemical which accounts for the increase in height and weight just before the other features of puberty appear. Growth hormone enlarges the bones of the skeleton, increases muscle mass, enlarges individual organs like the heart, and helps build up protein in the human tissue cells. Again, the girls gain from these effects before the boys but after the age of 15, the growth hormone effects on the male body overtakes that of the female body.

Puberty announces the arrival of physical sexual maturation. This is achieved through hormones also produced by the anterior pituitary glands. The main hormones involved are FSH (Follicle Stimulating Hormone) and LH (Luteinising Hormone) in the girls, and ICSH (Interstitial Cell Stimulating Hormone)

in boys. Known as *gonadotrophic hormones*, FSH and LH act on the once dormant ovaries to begin major production of the female sex hormones, *oestrogen* and *progesterone*. ICSH acts on the once dormant testes of the boy to produce the male sex hormone, *testosterone*. At the same time, another hormone from the anterior pituitary, ACTH (Adrenal Corticotrophic Hormone) causes the adrenal glands above the kidneys to increase production of androgens in both sexes.

Secondary sexual characteristics

Androgens from the adrenals in the maturing boy and girl are responsible for the appearance and growth of hair under the arms, axillary hair, and pubic hair, hair above and around the genital area. The pubic hair itself shows a distinctive sexual pattern. In the pubertic girl, the upper border of the hairline is concave upwards. In the pubertic boy, the upper border of the pubic hairline is convex upwards. Because the boy has additional male hormones—testosterone from the testes—the overall hairiness of the body is much greater than in the girl.

Moreover the boy also starts to grow considerable facial hair, in the chin and upper lip areas, from the effect of the male sex hormones. The effect of the androgens on hair growth begins about 11 years of age and is not fully complete until the seventeenth year.

The effects of testosterone and androgen in the pubertic boy are considerable. The voice deepens as the larynx grows, and changes from a high pitch to a lower pitch, when it is said to 'break'. In the genital area, the whole picture changes. Apart from the hair growth, the *penis* enlarges and so do the accessory sexual organs—the *prostate*, the *epididymis* and the *seminal vesicles*—that play a part in full sexual activity. The scrotal skin thickens and inside the testes—the pair of oval-shaped gonads, or sex glands— sperm are manufactured, accompanied by the formation of seminal fluid for their transport.

The development of a masculine physique in terms of build and musculature becomes apparent at this time, as the male sex hormones, like the growth hormone, help to build up protein and muscle. The skin also shows changes— the most obvious (and often troublesome) feature being that it become more oily and greasy. This stems from sebum production by the enlarged sebaceous glands. Too much sebum or too 'rich' a content tends to be associated with the skin complaint of *acne*, which is more common in adolescent boys than in adolescent girls.

With the active production of the male sex hormones, and the maturing of the sexual organs, the hormone and nerve link-up controlling sexual activity is completed in a physical sense. Boys become capable of erection of the penis and subsequently of ejaculation of the sperm in the seminal fluid. The sex drive is established in the maturing boy.

The onset of menstruation

The effects of oestrogen and progesterone in girls are also considerable. There is no real voice change parallel to that of boys, although some girls do have a slight deepening of the voice—presumably due to the androgens produced by the adrenal glands. An adult feminine appear- 249

HEIGHTS OF MATURING BOYS AND GIRLS

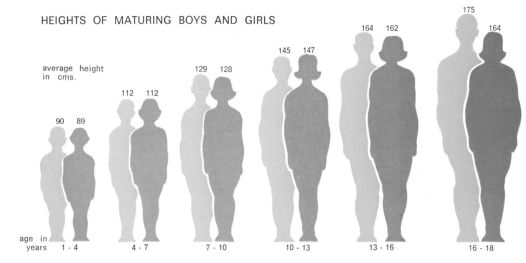

average height in cms.

| 90 | 89 | 112 | 112 | 129 | 128 | 145 | 147 | 164 | 162 | 175 | 164 |

age in years: 1 - 4 | 4 - 7 | 7 - 10 | 10 - 13 | 13 - 16 | 16 - 18

George Rodger / John Hillelson Agency

Above: Diagram showing the comparative rates of growth between males and females. Girls gain a few inches at the onset of puberty with which the boys catch up and surpass by late adolescence.

Left and below: Circumcision ceremonies. Circumcision, which removes all, or part, of the foreskin of the penis takes place in childhood in some societies—in Morocco, for example (below)—and at puberty—as in the Tanzanian group (left). The underlying motive is the same, however, in as much as it is an initiation ceremony. Circumcision may coincide with the biological transition from childhood to adulthood. Many theories have been advanced about its medical efficacy but there is little evidence that it is 'more hygienic' or that it improves the quality of sexual experience in adult life. It must therefore be seen as part of the religious life and rites of the traditional societies where it is still practised, such as in Judaism.

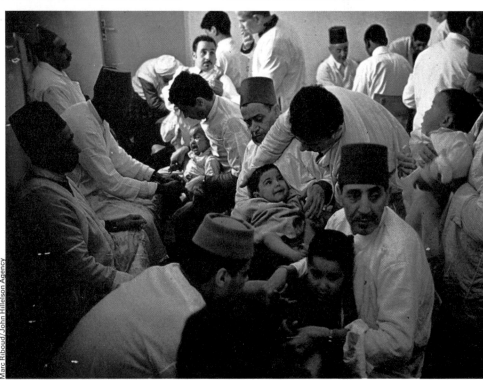

Marc Riboud / John Hillelson Agency

ance begins to take shape. The female shape of the pelvic bones becomes apparent. The breasts begin to grow and develop and the nipples also enlarge. Breast growth is rather uneven at first, giving a slightly assymetrical appearance to the pubertic breast outline, but the growth pattern usually evens out later on in adolescence. The degree of breast enlargement varies a good deal, not only due to the development of new tissue in the interior of each breast but also because of variable quantities of fat deposited in the chest wall.

Increased fat is also laid down in the face, abdomen, thighs and buttocks, helping to create the rounded contours which are seen as distinctively 'feminine' in established medical terms.

The growth of the bones just before puberty is gradually slowed down and usually completed within three years. The rising levels of oestrogen act against the effects of the growth hormone, and the special 'bone ends' or *epiphyses* of the long bones finally close, giving a fixed adult height.

In the genital area, the pubic mound, or *mons veneris*, enlarges beneath the growing pubic hair and the lips of the *vulva* or *labia majora* become much larger. In the inside, the vagina becomes larger and the *uterus*, or womb, also grows in size. The body portion of the uterus becomes functional, being primed by the oestrogen and progesterone hormones in turn. This hormone cycle affecting the quality and lining of the uterus eventually starts off the first *menstruation*, known as the *menarche*. This menarche generally appears in the 13th year, although it can occur as early as the 11th year or as late as the 16th year followed by a normal menstrual pattern. An adolescent who has not yet menstruated after her 16th year should be referred for medical advice. Menstruation is often irregular at the beginning of monthly cycles and no ova may actually be discharged in the early periods.

Oestrogen is responsible for the sheen and bloom of the youthful skin of adolescence and subsequent adulthood. Other hormone-producing glands in the body may be noticeably affected at puberty, although outside the 'sexual gland circle'. The thymus gland starts to wither away, while the thyroid gland in the neck may enlarge.

Once the ovaries start producing ova on a regular basis, and menstruation is properly established, the adolescent is physically mature for human reproduction. For a girl this means that sexual activity with a mature boy and the introduction of semen into the vagina, can result in conception. As with the pubertic boy, the completion of the hormone and nerve link-up to the brain sees the start of the female sex drive and sex interest though this is often more diffuse than in the pubertic boy who has a focal area of sexuality in his new penile function.

Ill-health, for example, anaemia or infection, can sometimes delay the onset of puberty. Disturbances of the endocrine system can also act as delaying factors, and these too may require investigation and treatment. Modern hormone therapy can substitute both male and female hormones where these are absent or insufficient, initiating puberty and helping to ensure subsequent physical and sexual maturation.

The progression from puberty to adolescence is a time of upheaval on many levels, characterised by emotional 'highs' and 'lows'. Society's attitude reflects these confusions – for instance, the British teenager can get a marriage licence before he can get a driving licence.

When Girl Becomes Woman

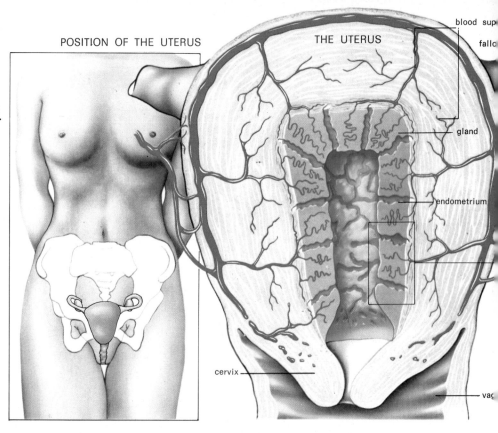

blood sup

fallo

gland

endometrium

cervix

vag

Menstruation generally starts some time after a girl's tenth birthday during the phase of development known as *puberty*. Puberty in the female child is a period of intense hormonal activity during which changes take place in her body, adapting her for the essential biological function of childbearing. By the time she has had her first menstrual period, however, she is not immediately fertile—she is not quite ready to accept and nurture the fertilized *ovum* or egg cell which grows into a new human being.

The first period
The first period is called the *menarche* and a preparatory period of two years follows it without ova being produced. During this time, a monthly cycle is established in which a discharge of mucus, cell fragments and blood is discharged from the *vagina*, the passage from the uterus to the vulva. This discharge is the result of the disintegration of the *endometrium* (endo meaning 'within' and metros, 'mother'), the lining of the *uterus* or womb which has been stimulated by the hormone *progesterone* into forming a thick layer with a special blood supply, ready to receive an embryo if the ovum becomes fertilized. If fertilization does not take place, however, the *corpus luteum*—the small gland which produces the progesterone—withers. Deprived of progesterone, the lining is shed, leaving the surface raw. This bleeds for a few days, flushing out the discarded lining.

This monthly loss of blood, known as the *menstrual period*, occurs roughly every 28 days for the next 30 or 40 years of a girl's life. It coincides with the *ovarian cycle*, in which one of the many thousands of immature ova—already present in the ovaries, the sex glands, before a girl is born—is released. The ova are formed from the cells of the *germinal epithelium*, which pass from the surface of the ovary to the interior, where they acquire a primitive membrane or follicle.

The egg producing function of the ovaries is governed by the *pituitary* gland in the brain, which is controlled in turn by the *hypothalamus* lying above it. The pituitary gland releases chemicals called *hormones* into the bloodstream, and these hormones carry out two distinct tasks: they influence the development, or ripening, of an ovum in one of the ovaries, and stimulate that ovary into producing hormones of its own. These ovarian hormones effect the endometrium directly, and the result is that the lining of the womb is prepared to receive the fully developed egg cell in two stages.

The effects of hormone activity
The hormones produced by the ovary when stimulated by the pituitary are *oestrogen* and *progesterone*. The hormone oestrogen brings about the primary preparation of the womb lining, and its partner progesterone later completes this process. Meanwhile, the ovum has reached full maturity within the ovary, and about 14 days after the commencement of menstruation, bursts from its

Above: Diagram of the female pelvic area. It shows the location of the ovaries, the female sex glands, just above the pubic bone in the middle of the pelvis.

Above right: The uterus or womb showing the arrangement of vessels which supply it with blood. The uterus is a hollow muscle about the size of a duck's egg.

Left: The infundibulum, a group of finger-like projections at the mouth of the Fallopian tubes. They beat the fertilized ovum into the tube along which it travels to the uterus, where it implants itself.

Below: Cervical mucus on the 14th day, the first day of ovulation.

Dave Kelly

John Watney

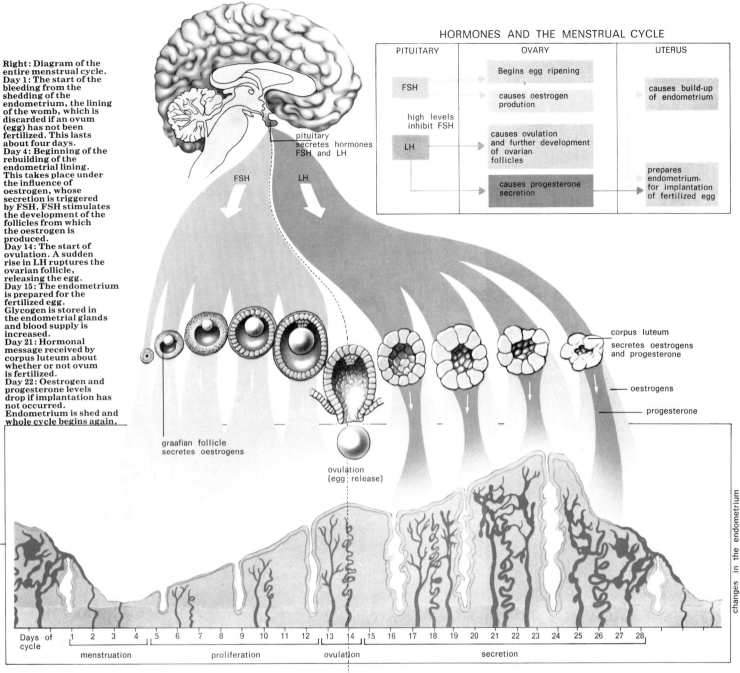

Right: Diagram of the entire menstrual cycle. Day 1: The start of the bleeding from the shedding of the endometrium, the lining of the womb, which is discarded if an ovum (egg) has not been fertilized. This lasts about four days.
Day 4: Beginning of the rebuilding of the endometrial lining. This takes place under the influence of oestrogen, whose secretion is triggered by FSH. FSH stimulates the development of the follicles from which the oestrogen is produced.
Day 14: The start of ovulation. A sudden rise in LH ruptures the ovarian follicle, releasing the egg.
Day 15: The endometrium is prepared for the fertilized egg. Glycogen is stored in the endometrial glands and blood supply is increased.
Day 21: Hormonal message received by corpus luteum about whether or not ovum is fertilized.
Day 22: Oestrogen and progesterone levels drop if implantation has not occurred. Endometrium is shed and whole cycle begins again.

PITUITARY	OVARY	UTERUS
FSH	Begins egg ripening	causes build-up of endometrium
	causes oestrogen prodution	
high levels inhibit FSH		
LH	causes ovulation and further development of ovarian follicles	
	causes progesterone secretion	prepares endometrium for implantation of fertilized egg

pituitary secretes hormones FSH and LH

FSH

LH

graafian follicle secretes oestrogens

ovulation (egg release)

corpus luteum secretes oestrogens and progesterone

oestrogens

progesterone

changes in the endometrium

Days of cycle: 1 2 3 4 5 6 7 8 9 10 11 12 13 14 15 16 17 18 19 20 21 22 23 24 25 26 27 28

menstruation — proliferation — ovulation — secretion

birthplace and starts out on its journey down the Fallopian tube to the womb. This is the part of the process known as *ovulation*.

The manufacture of the hormone progesterone by the ovary, however, is much more complicated than that of producing oestrogen. It is the ovary itself which must signal to the pituitary gland in the brain that progesterone is required, and the form that this signal, or message, takes is the bursting forth of the fully ripened ovum.

When the pituitary gland receives this signal, it immediately releases a return chemical signal to the ovary, which allows the ovary to manufacture progesterone. All of this is done under the guidance of the hypothalamus. So, as the ovum travels toward the womb, the hormone progesterone is released into the bloodstream, and by the time the ovum reaches it, the womb lining has become a moist bed of *endometrial cells* capable of supporting and nourishing it. However, this bed will be used by the ovum only if it is fertilized by a male sex cell.

The effects of hormone production by the ovary can also be seen during menstruation in the behaviour of the Fallopian tubes, which are connected to the upper

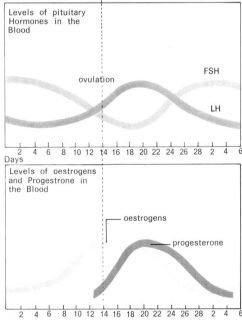

Levels of pituitary Hormones in the Blood

ovulation

FSH

LH

Days: 2 4 6 8 10 12 14 16 18 20 22 24 26 28 2 4 6

Levels of oestrogens and Progestrone in the Blood

oestrogens

progesterone

2 4 6 8 10 12 14 16 18 20 22 24 26 28 2 4 6

Above: Graphs showing pattern of hormonal activity throughout a typical 28-day menstrual cycle. The top diagram shows the levels of FSH, which triggers the production of the ovum, and of LH which completes the process. Oestrogen and progesterone (bottom) prepare the endometrium for the fertilized ovum.

part of the uterus at one end and open into the abdominal cavity at the other. When oestrogen production is at maximum, the Fallopian tubes go through a series of contractions which help to transport the ovum, which cannot move on its own, to the uterus.

The linings of the tubes also become active and begin to secrete materials thought to be helpful in the fertilization and nourishment of the journeying egg. The probable fertilization of the egg is also assisted by the fact that during ovulation the cervical mucus at the neck of the womb becomes more fluid, so allowing easier penetration by the approaching spermatazoa. When the ovulation cycle is complete these activities gradually cease due to the domination of progesterone. The first stages of pregnancy are apparent, whether the ovum has been fertilized or not. So that, in effect, a woman becomes 'pregnant' once every month. However, if the egg cell remains unfertilized, it flows out through the neck of the womb along with the endometrial lining and brings the whole process to a stop. But at that very moment yet another egg cell is ripening in one of the ovaries, and the whole process is on the point of starting up all over again.

253

Left and below: The *menarche*, the first menstrual period, is celebrated in some societies as *initiation* into womanhood, followed by complete acceptance into the rites and traditions of adulthood. Initiation takes many forms, however. For some groups, such as this Nigerian tribe (left) it is a public celebration of feasting with a special initiation dance. Other societies seclude their young women for up to two years, at the end of which they might undergo an initiation ritual. These pubertic Brazilian girls (below) emerge from seclusion with their faces covered by their hair, which is then cut to reveal their transformation into women.

Bottom: The use of internal tampons, which absorb the flow of menstrual blood, has enabled modern women to lead fuller, less restricted lives.

cycle, for the *dysmenorrhoea* from which between five and eight women out of every 10 suffer has been found to be more than 'merely psychological'.

Basically there are two types of dysmenorrhoea, 'spasmodic' and 'congestive'. On the whole they appear in two particular types of women, although there are always exceptions. Spasmodic dysmenorrhoea is related to the first day of menstruation, and is described as acute colicky pains in the lower abdomen. This kind of pain dulls after a few minutes, then flares up again about twenty minutes later. The spasms may be severe enough to cause fainting or vomiting, and in many ways resemble labour pains.

Sufferers from spasmodic dysmenorrhoea have been found to be predominantly of introvert personality and to have small breasts with pale nipples and scanty pubic hair. As it seldom occurs during the first few menstruations at puberty, it is thought to be directly related to the process of ovulation.

Congestive dysmenorrhoea, on the other hand, is composed of pains which erupt prior to menstruation, and constitutes a kind of warning signal. This type of pain is often accompanied by nausea, lack of appetite and constipation, and is closely linked to pre-menstrual tensions in general. Sufferers often have large breasts, dark brown nipples and ample pubic hair. It has been observed that congestive dysmenorrhoea tends to increase with each successive pregnancy.

The pre-menstrual syndrome

Pre-menstrual tension, which comes under the blanket title of the *Pre-menstrual Syndrome*, is still not fully understood. From available research, however, it seems that many of the symptoms are characterized by *water retention*—an accumulation of excess cellular fluid.

A good example of this is the marked rise in pressure which can result in the eye due to minute increases of its natural fluid. Such increases in pressure automatically lead to pain in the form of headaches. Similar rises in pressure due to water retention can cause tenderness of the breasts, aching sinuses, pain in the eyeballs, swollen ankles and a host of other annoying (and sometimes disabling) interruptions of daily life. But water retention does not account for all the symptoms which can occur.

The psychological effects of pre-menstrual tension, such as irritability, depression and lethargy, would seem to be brought about by *sodium retention* and *potassium depletion* in the cells. But the phenomena of fainting, sweating and general weakness which often occur, may very well be due to a drop in the level of blood sugar. The basic reason for this kind of imbalance throughout the system is thought to be the insufficient production of progesterone in the ovary. This insufficiency would cause the same hormone to be drawn from some other source, and as a result, upset the delicate balance of the body's whole metabolism.

When both the biological processes and their effects on female behaviour are understood and put into their proper context, women will be able to ride out the symptoms of menstruation in a wholly reasonable manner, accepting them as part of their feminine nature, or seeking help, rather than 'suffering in silence' as so many of their forebears have had to do.

There is not a day in the life of a woman when she is not subject, in one way or another, to the ebb and flow of hormonal influence directly related to the repetition of the menstrual cycle. During the menstrual period itself, swelling and tenderness of the breasts and abdomen, headaches, irritability and depression, not to mention lack of concentration and poor memory, are likely to occur. Because many women are ignorant about the changes taking place in their bodies, they are apt to accept the charge—common among men in some societies—that women are over-emotional, or worse, illogical. Research has shown that, since hormones and emotions are strongly linked, this sort of attitude can cause *further* imbalance in hormonal secretion. Most women have experienced, at least once in their lives, a menstrual interruption due to great distress or over-excitement.

Biochemists are attempting to assess the exact amount of hormones circulating in the bloodstream during the menstrual

The average age for the arrival of puberty is 13 years, although any age between 11 and 16 is regarded as normal. Improved physical health, better nutrition and greater exposure to artificial light have led to an earlier arrival in children of more affluent countries.

Adolescence

Although *puberty* and *adolescence* are commonly regarded as synonymous, they are, in fact, different things. Both mark the transition from childhood to adulthood but each is a different part of the process. Puberty is the biological event which marks the physiological onset of adulthood. It has definite, observable stages—particularly in girls—and takes place within a particular period of time. Adolescence, on the other hand, is the name given to an indefinite period of development in which psychological and sociological changes take place in the maturing boy and girl. It has no observable beginning or end, and some of the problems arising from the adjustments which have to be made during adolescence may take many years to resolve.

In industrialized western countries especially, adolescence is the period which marks the maturing individual's search for identity. He is no longer a child, but he is not yet an adult. So what is he?

The physiological changes

The adolescent is subject to quite violent changes in his body, due to hormonal activity, which require a great deal of mental adjustment. His body image—his ability to understand the relationship of himself to the space around him—is no longer reliable. He is often clumsy and unco-ordinated; his arms and legs seem to be too long, because in a sense they are—he is going through a period of accelerated growth in height and weight.

Sexual maturity and increased awareness of his own and others' sexuality bring special problems for the adolescent. He must decide how to view his sexual impulses: does he see them as a natural part of growing up or is he shocked and upset at their strength? Almost all adolescents masturbate, but many suffer agonizing guilt because they are taught to believe the practice may harm them. Masturbation is a natural and normal activity which cannot cause any harm.

The adolescent boy or girl must also decide what his or her sexual behaviour with others should be. Should they strive for chastity? What rules should govern their sexual conduct? These are questions which may not be resolved even after a lifetime of questioning; but adolescents are so vulnerable to group pressures that many of them feel pushed into courses of action without having a chance to fully think out the consequences. Much of the talk of daring sexual exploits—a major topic of conversation among groups of adolescents—is the equivalent of the fisherman's 'one that got away'. Some members of the group may react with feelings of shame and inadequacy that they cannot match the reported feats of their friends: others may participate unwillingly in sexual activities, afraid of being the 'odd man out'.

This adolescent confusion is reflected in behaviour. As he reaches so impatiently for adulthood and self determination, the teenager can be assailed by doubts and uncertainties of his abilities to cope with the demands of maturity. He has not yet organized his experiences, thoughts and feelings into a consistent

Ian Berry/John Hillelson Agency

Above: Two English teenagers on holiday in a popular seaside town. The slogan on their hats demonstrates both their new-found sexual awareness and their need to shock their elders into realizing that they are growing up—by being outrageous in their style of dress and in their unpredictable behaviour.

Below: Drum majorettes. A peculiarly American phenomenon approved of by the middle classes, in spite of the fact that, in some ways, it embodies some of the more negative aspects of adolescence—vanity, exhibitionism and extreme competitiveness. However, the drum majorette is also a symbol of patriotism and order, and as such is upheld as a respectable ideal to which the adolescent should aspire.

Right: A Hell's Angel. Despite the fact that he flaunts society's orthodox codes he will adhere to the laws of his own subculture, which are just as rigid.

Raymond Depardon & Marie-Laure De Decker/John Hillelson Agency

Above and right: Every generation of teenagers is fired by some political cause. Since adolescents are only just beginning to exercise their powers of thought and belief, they tend to see things in black and white terms. The Aldermaston marcher (above) was one of thousands protesting against Britain's nuclear defence programme. The fervour of the Red Guards, formed during China's Cultural Revolution, was deliberately employed by Mao to stamp out the traditional values of their parents.

pattern. So his behaviour can fluctuate between childish over-dependence and arrogant rebellion.

He may come to view all adults with the same jaundiced eye as he does the members of his family. He longs for certainty and security and yet is unconvinced of the wisdom of his parents and teachers. Only his peers, those in the same position as himself, offer shelter. Within the group, freed from childhood memories and family pressures, he can find the freedom to become truly himself. But since the other members of the group are likely to be similarly confused as to their status and identity, the group itself becomes all-powerful. It puts on its members even stronger pressures to conform to the group's standards than most family groups do. So to the adult, the adolescent presents a picture of aggressive nonconformity to society's norms of conduct—coupled with rigid adherence to the rules and norms of his own subculture or group.

Examination of these rules may illustrate the relationship of the subgroup to the larger culture within which it occurs. For example, some groups centred around the motorcycle have rituals akin to the marriage ceremony, but in which the bike's handbook takes the place of the Bible. Such a ritual, being a caricature of that of society as a whole, demonstrates the ambivalence of the smaller group toward its parent group. It is not genuinely free-thinking or independent; rather, its rules and rituals are distortions and travesties of those of the parent culture.

The search for autonomy

Along with this search for personal identity and autonomy, the typical western adolescent is striving to understand the nature of the world and of reality. According to the Swiss child-psychologist Jean Piaget, the adolescent is better able to theorize than the child. He is much less restricted by the given data—the concrete reality. He becomes able to suspend judgment and see that many interpretations of data are possible. He becomes aware that his family's way of living, his parent's ideas on morality, his country's policies, are not the only possibilities, and may not even be the best ones in the circumstances. Therefore the adolescent can find himself faced not only with the question 'who am I?' but with the unanswerable questions: 'what is Truth?' and 'what is Reality?' Often he 257

Above: The Hitler Youth Movement, an organization set up by Hitler to further the cause of the Nazi Party and to outlaw all non-Nazi movements for young people. Through the strict, physical, intellectual and moral training which they received, it was hoped to preserve the spirit of national socialism and Germany's future which rested on the shoulders of its young people.

Below right: Some societies have definite rituals marking off the passage from boyhood to manhood. This Jewish boy is undergoing his *Bar Mitzvah*, after which he will officially be recognized as a man.

Above: The annual Queen Charlotte's Birthday Ball, which, until recent years, marked the opening of London's *debutante* season. Young ladies over the age of 18 were said to have 'come out' at this event, that is, they were presented to aristocratic society as eligible for marriage.

Below: Teenagers travel miles and camp out in uncomfortable conditions to hear their idols play at pop festivals.

Right: Schoolboys from the 'King's College of Our Lady of Eton Beside Windsor' founded by Henry VI in 1440. These teenage boys, seen here during a rowing regatta on the river Thames, are educated as 'future leaders' of the British nation and as such are expected to conform to rigid principles and standards. Individuality is strongly discouraged even among the pupils themselves, who adhere to a hierarchical structure set by hundreds of years of tradition.

sees, with fiery and untempered indignation, the injustices of the world. He burns with untried, hence untarnished, desire to put things right.

Because of this urgent search for ideals and truth, adolescence for most is a time of upheaval on many levels, sometimes making the adolescent vulnerable to extraordinary forces. Some observers even see a connection between adolescents and poltergeists—forces, or 'spirits', which perform mysterious acts such as switching lights on and off, moving furniture or locking and unlocking doors. Poltergeists, they claim, nearly always appear in homes where there is a teenager in the family. Some investigators of the phenomenon think that a spirit, or 'force', is attracted by the upheaval of energy—particularly sexual energy—in the adolescent's body. Others think that the upheaval of energy allows the adolescent to perform a kind of *telekinesis*—to project energy into inanimate objects and make them move— and that it has nothing to do with any kind of external 'force'.

Adolescence can also be a time of religious and political fervour. The mob hysteria and individual devotion of pop fans, in some observers' view, are other aspects of the same type of experience. In many ways the 'worship' of pop idols appears to serve the same functions as religious or political ceremonies. There is the same sense of a common aim, a unity of purpose that transcends individualism and creates feelings of safety and security. In each case the adolescent is trying to find meaning and structure in his life through identification with, and participation in, a group. Star-worship, like gang membership, is usually strongest in early adolescence. Religious and political affiliations tend to become more prominent later on, as the individual exercises his developing powers of thought and belief.

However, a young person's ideas and values may crystallize during adolescence in such a way as to map out the course of his whole future life, or at least a significant portion of it. Decisions now about careers, vocations, political or religious commitments may rapidly propel him into a way of life from which it may be difficult for him to disentangle himself. It is therefore at this period that adequate guidance and support from parents, teachers and other adults can be most valuable.

The attitude of society

Most of the typical adolescent's confusion about himself, his identity and his codes of behaviour may be a direct reflection of western society's confused attitude towards him.

Even the ages at which he is considered to be capable of taking on certain responsibilities can be quite inconsistent. At 16, for example, a British teenager may marry and have children. But he cannot drive a car until he is 17, or even join a public library without someone else's sponsorship until he is 18. He may become a professional soldier, and begin learning the techniques of killing people, before he reaches 18, the age at which he can vote. But if he happens to be homosexual, he may not legally engage in sexual activity with another individual until he is 21.

If most western societies cannot decide at what age an individual becomes an adult, and make apparently random decisions about the ages at which he may assume different kinds of responsibility, then social scientists see it as inevitable that he will be confused. He is undergoing change on all levels: hormonal, physiological, sexual, cognitive and spiritual. If a society does not provide him with clear guidelines about his status, they argue, it is hardly surprising if the end result is a moody, changeable, restless and chronically dissatisfied young person.

Of all the factors which exert pressure on the potential adult, his society's attitudes may well play the biggest part. In many of the world's societies there are distinct events, rituals and tasks which differentiate childhood from adulthood. Before an individual goes through such a ceremony, the person is a child, with the expectations and experiences of childhood. Through the ceremony the individual is initiated into adulthood and accorded the full status, duties and rights of adulthood in that society. Among westernized cultures an equivalent function is performed by, for example, the *Bar Mitzvah* of the Jews. This religious ceremony takes place in a boy's 13th year and celebrates his attainment of manhood.

In cultures where there are clear boundaries between childhood and adulthood, it seems the phenomenon of 'adolescence' is almost unknown. A boy becomes a man and joins the men; a girl becomes a woman and joins the women. The concept of the teenager as part of a separate group exists only in cultures where there are anomalies in the various roles he or she is expected to fulfil. In Western Europe and North America, for example, it is possible for a 17-year-old to wield considerable economic power in terms of earnings but to have no political power because he is not entitled to vote.

So not only does teenaged youth find itself questioning the society's values, but it is also constantly exposed to the changes taking place within society as a whole. Traditional values are being challenged and discarded continuously. Broader and more widespread education and the greater availability of the means to travel (not only within one country but all over the world) have made the twentieth century a time more than any before it marked by instability, change and revolution. Given such a global situation, the adolescent faces a formidable task. He has to decide what kind of person he wishes to become, what kind of life he wishes to lead, and what kind of society he wishes to work towards. This is a lifelong task, and adolescence is just the beginning of the journey towards it.

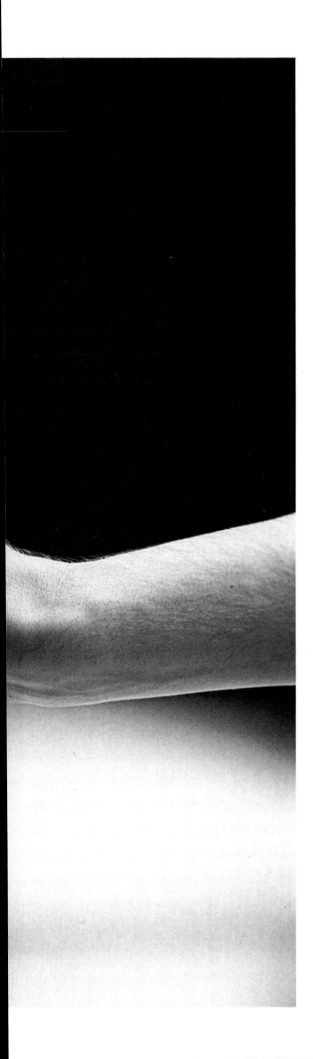

Chapter 3
The Adult

Marriage, like other social institutions,
modifies adult behaviour by requiring
partners to maintain a balance
between individuality and the rights
of others.

Adulthood

An adolescent is generally defined as a young person in the process of passing from childhood to adulthood or maturity. But what is this state known as adulthood to which the child is expected to pass? And what guarantee does she or he, or indeed, society as a whole, have that the person will necessarily be mature when they reach it?

The state of adulthood is difficult to define. The man who runs no risks, who keeps himself out of trouble, who is never upset by changes of fortune or by the attitudes of those around him—is he necessarily a more mature person than the artist who feels so strongly about life that despair tempts him to end it?

An example of the dangers of generalizing on what is, and what is not, maturity is the Russian novelist Dostoevsky. He was a compulsive gambler, arrogant and self-pitying—but is still regarded as a genius by literary critics, historians and even some psychiatrists. His novels show a penetrating insight and understanding of human nature. So how, on the evidence of his private life, can he be called emotionally immature? Similarly, should the sustained and forceful ambition necessary, say, to take an American politician through the rigours of campaigning for the Presidency be considered as a product of emotional maturity—or as neurotic drive?

In most societies, a set of rules governing the behaviour of an adult person exists. But the ages at which the individual is allowed to enter fully into the various rights and duties of adulthood can vary, even within one country, so that even when a society sets out laws to which the individual is expected to adhere, these laws—and this is especially true of, for example, English society—may indicate to the individual only what he *cannot* do, rather than what he *can*. Adulthood, therefore, is not a definitive state, but rather a concept or ideal which exists within a particular society. During the 100 or so years which psychology has been in existence, many psychologists have been interested in this problem of whether there is such a state as adulthood, and, if so, how is it actually defined and by whom?

The individual and society

The complications of human life have always presented great challenges. One of the basic problems is how to maintain a balance between behaviour in an individual level and the effect that it has on society. In other words, certain needs and drives which are distinctly human affect not only the individual's life but also the lives of others. Although behaviour may be both natural and human, it may have to be modified or regulated so that its actual effect on the whole society is beneficial, rather than detrimental, to society's other individuals.

Psychologists have observed throughout many years of study that what is considered 'adult' may vary from society to society. Polygamy, an accepted custom in some parts of the world, is forbidden elsewhere. Practices accepted in one period of history may be challenged in later eras. Caning children as a means of

Above and below: Adults in most societies are expected to adhere to a particular code of conduct. The cult of *machismo*—the belief that a man must behave in a certain fashion in order to be a man—predominates in some Mediterranean countries. The *macho* must defend his family's honour and conduct himself with dignity. Although basically the idea of a macho is one who is 'his own man', the importance of masculinity is exaggerated. The transvestites (below) would be regarded by the macho as a travesty of manhood and an insult to women, whose virtue and purity must be protected.

Sunday Times

Sunday Times

Constantine Manos/John Hillelson Agency

Left and below: In most societies adult behaviour is supposed to be self-regulated, but there are generally laws which keep it within certain limits. Those responsible for enforcing the laws may not necessarily have made them. The English judges (left) are part of the formal legal system typical of most democratically ruled countries, in which power is distributed among different authorities. In societies ruled by dictatorship, on the other hand, absolute power is assumed by the ruler (below). He may not only ignore existing laws and introduce new ones, but may also openly disregard his own laws while expecting everyone else to obey them. In effect he may be behaving in an 'un-adult' way.

Above: The 1976 American Democratic Convention. Adult members of a democracy have the right to participate in the choosing of their leaders.

discipline was widely accepted in England as normal, adult behaviour until very recent years. Yet today it is increasingly condemned both by teachers and psychologists; and in some countries it has always been considered barbaric.

If adolescents growing up in industrialized Western societies have difficulties in coming to grips with what seem to be conflicting ideals and standards, there are many institutions which can attempt to guide and assist them towards adulthood. They include the family, the education system, the church and the state.

Some of these institutions express directly to the potential adult the ways in which his behaviour will be modified by them; others attempt to redirect it into serving the needs of the group through example.

Criteria of adulthood

An attempt to summarize the observations of the many psychologists who have studied the overlap between an individual's behaviour and the expectations of the social group with which he interacts was made in 1967 by the British psychologist Dr Abraham Sperling. Western society, he found, had eight criteria for adulthood: heterosexuality; independence of family; emotional maturity; social maturity; economic independence; intellectual capability; productive use of leisure; and a coherent view or philosophy of life. Dr Sperling suggested that society expects a mature adult to adhere to these requirements throughout his or her life, and that the outcome will be a balanced and objectively sane individual capable of contributing something of worth and importance to society as well as fulfilling their own personal needs.

However, these eight criteria represent an ideal. Few 'adults' can actually measure up to all of them but none can be considered in isolation. People are unlikely to become emotionally mature unless they develop the coherent *overview*, or philosophy of life, which provides them with a frame of reference to which

263

Mark Godfrey/John Hillelson Agency

John Hillelson Agency

Left and above: Modern industrialized societies have become so large and complex that some of its members feel alienated and attempt to provide alternatives. Both the young 'drop-out' (above) and the Ku-Klux-Klan member (left) are attempting to protect certain beliefs or moral values. The KKK member belongs to a secret society which evolved into a political group whose main preoccupation is to prevent the integration of black Americans into a white, mainly middle-class society. The 'drop-out', on the other hand, is part of a movement which feels that individual freedom is being eroded by the 'dehumanizing' effect of technology.

they can relate their behaviour and the behaviour of others. But such a coherent philosophy may not evolve if, for example, the young adult does not become independent of his parents and learn to become financially and emotionally dependable. Again, if his intellectual faculty remains at adolescent level, then it is extremely difficult for him to appreciate the meaning of social maturity or to use his working and leisure time productively and creatively.

The state of adulthood

Many psychologists summarize adulthood as a state of 'good adjustment'. The well-adjusted person, they consider, solves his or her personal problems with the same *objectivity* as that applied to impersonal problems. For example, he will attempt to evaluate an argument with a friend or relative in which he has been emotionally involved as impartially as he would a mathematical problem, in the conclusion of which he has no emotional investment. Then, to ensure that his view of the situation is realistic, he may check it against the opinion of someone who did not participate in the experience. He will then think out the best course of action possible, weigh up the immediate and

long-term results and, finally, act as vigorously and as wholeheartedly as possible.

If, however, his decision proves to be inadequate, he accepts that it was arrived at as honestly as possible from the information available to him at the time and is 'philosophical' about it—that is, he applies an over-view to the situation, accepting it as a lesson from which he can apply knowledge to future encounters of a similar nature.

An individual who is truly adult, therefore, can be said to be one who recognizes that he or she is obliged to conduct themselves in a way that does not hurt anyone else, rob them of human dignity, belittle anyone, or demand participation in actions distasteful to individual conscience. He or she also has the right to expect to be treated similarly by others.

Countless people, in fact, are unable to establish satisfactory relationships with other individuals or with society in general. Many psychologists would consider such people immature; although they never manifest signs of illness, they are unable to fulfil themselves as human beings. To maintain a satisfactory personal relationship in adult life, a person must be able to gratify the needs

of another and to be gratified by the other, to sense the partner's needs and to communicate with him or her. The relationship must include an understanding which is prepared to demand less than perfection and which respects the other's differences. The mature individual, in short, must be able to see another person as a distinct individual—not just as an extension of his own needs and desires, or someone to be exploited in order to fulfill a personal ambition.

'Anti-social' behaviour

Behaviour which varies from what society regards as 'proper conduct', however, may still be regarded as 'adult' by a large number of people. Like all living organisms, a society is made of entities at different stages of growth and development. What one section of a society is only just learning to understand, another has already assimilated and superseded. It has a broader conception, therefore, of the consequences of a given action, event or attitude.

Often, too, extremes of social behaviour, though anti-social in themselves, provide the members of a society with a clearer view of its values and may even provide it with a new sense of direction. Football 'fans' who go on the rampage after a match, beating up rival supporters and wrecking trains and shops, are certainly showing signs of immaturity; but they are also highlighting a weakness, or even illness, in the society which produced them.

An adult person learns how to deal with society's apparently, or actually, conflicting attitudes. He learns how and when to 'toe the line' and behave in a prescribed manner, but he also learns when to 'stick his neck out' and take risks. For a mature person realizes that exploration and discovery are integral ingredients of human nature. They not only require individual expression but also keep society alive and healthy, supplying a mature framework within which its future adults can live a harmonius and productive life.

Adolescents coming to maturity in Western societies are confronted by apparently conflicting standards and ideals.

They may wish to 'drop out' of society, at the same time acquiring supposedly 'adult' habits such as drinking alcohol.

Fertility and Reproduction

For any species to reproduce itself and continue its evolutionary line, some of its members, at least, must be fertile—they must have the ability to reproduce. However, the males of many species father a vast number of offspring compared with a man who, in spite of thousands of ejaculations, may fertilize only one or two eggs in his whole lifetime.

For the human species, the ability to conceive is therefore more than a matter of physiology. In spite of the fact that every man and woman has the basic apparatus for producing children, only 50 per cent of humanity is actually responsible for producing the next generation. This figure was worked out in the 1960s by Professor L. S. Penrose of London University. The other 50 per cent, whom Professor Penrose termed 'unreproductive', include babies who die before birth (15 per cent), stillborn babies (three per cent), babies who die soon after birth (two per cent), and children who do not reach maturity (three per cent). Of those who do reach adulthood, about 20 per cent do not marry, and 10 per cent marry but have no children.

In Britain, about one in six marriages is *sterile*—that is, one of the partners is unable to reproduce. Despite a common belief that this is usually the 'fault' of the woman, statistics show that infertility is just as frequently attributable to a deficiency in the man. To understand the factors involved in infertility, however, we must first understand the processes leading to fertilization.

The sexual act

The fertilization of the ripened egg by a mature sperm, the central event of human reproduction, follows *coitus* or sexual intercourse. The male sperms, produced in the *testes*, are conveyed to the penis through a system of ducts and deposited in the vagina of the female partner. A state of sexual *arousal* is necessary to make this part of the process possible. On the man's part, the penis must become erect and stiff so that it can penetrate the vagina. This is facilitated by the expansion of the blood vessels flowing into, and contraction of the blood vessels flowing out of, the *erectile tissue*. Thus the penis becomes engorged with blood. On the woman's part, sexual arousal results in the secretion of mucus to moisten the walls of the vagina, enabling the penis to enter comfortably and safely. The *clitoris*, which is an embryonic penis, also becomes erect, and muscular contractions of the vagina take place.

Insertion of the penis into the vagina, followed by rhythmical movements, stimulates sensitive nervous receptors. This stimulation results in a sexual climax, an *orgasm*, hopefully in both partners. In the male it is accompanied by ejaculation, which is a two-part nervous reflex controlled by a 'message' to and from the spinal cord. Firstly, a mucus-based secretion called semen is emitted from the *vas deferens* into the urethra, then, during ejaculation proper, the semen is propelled from the uretha

Below right: Diagram of the route taken by the male sperm on its way to fertilize the female ovum. The sperm is manufactured in the *testes* and stored in the *epididymis* until needed. During sexual intercourse, it is first emitted via the *vas deferens* into the *urethra* and then, at the moment of orgasm, ejaculated into the vagina. From there it travels to the *Fallopian tube*, where fertilization takes place. Although sperm are produced by the hundreds of thousands, only one is needed for fertilization.

rectum

seminal vesicle

vas

urinar

anus

prostate

man's pubic bone

epididymis

testis

erect penis

urethra

This page: Oriental art has traditionally been far more frank than European in depicting the sexual act. The sculpture below is from a temple in Khajuraho, India, all of whose walls are covered with such erotic art. Apart from one from Japan (far right), the paintings too are from India.

Bruno Barbey/John Hillelson Agency

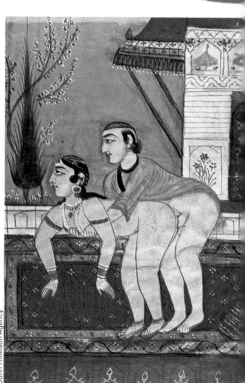

John Hillelson Agency

out of the penis at considerable speed.

The semen, which contains not only sperm but also the secretions of the seminal vesicles and prostate gland, is essential for the fertilization of the female's waiting ovum. Each ejaculation produces an average of 2.5 to 3.5 ml of semen, and there are normally about 100 million sperms per ml of semen even though only one sperm is required for fertilization. Each tadpole-like sperm consists of a 'head', containing the genetic material, and a 'tail' which enables the sperm to 'swim' up the vagina, at an approximate speed of 3 cm per minute, through the cervix, into the uterus and up into the Fallopian tubes where fertilization—union with the ovum, or egg—takes place.

Sperms survive for no more than 48 hours in the female genital tract. The ovum, on the other hand, lives for approximately 72 hours after it has been extruded from the ovarian follicle. So that during a woman's 28-day menstrual cycle the fertile period, in which sexual intercourse can lead to actual conception, is of only 120 hours at the most.

Infertility

Although about one couple in six are unable to have children, they are not usually regarded as infertile or sterile unless pregnancy has not occurred after about a year, during which time coitus has taken place at regular intervals. There are several causes of infertility, in both the male and female. However, careful diagnosis and treatment can restore fertility in many cases.

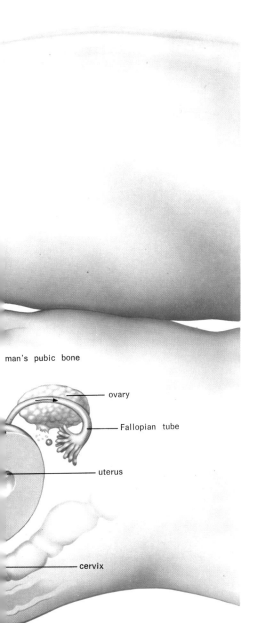

man's pubic bone

ovary

Fallopian tube

uterus

cervix

J. L. Charmet

Barnaby's

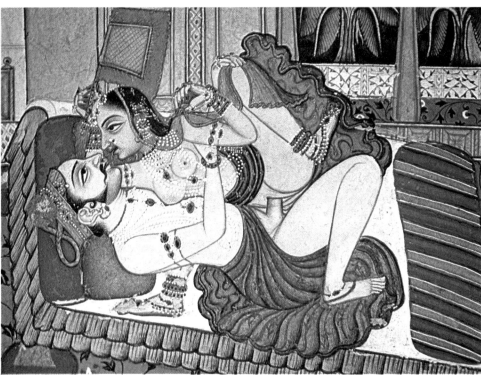

British Museum

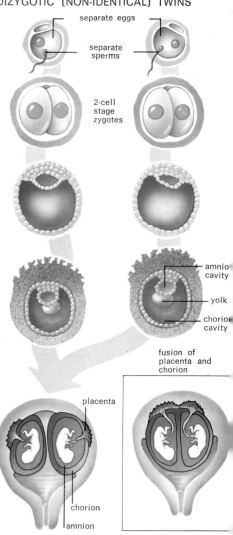

separate eggs

separate sperms

2-cell stage zygotes

amnio cavity

yolk

chorio cavity

fusion of placenta and chorion

placenta

chorion

amnion

J. L. Charmet

Among men, *impotence* (the inability to produce an erection), *premature ejaculation* (before intercourse has actually taken place), and *azoospermia* (deficiency in the number of viable sperm or a complete lack of sperm production) are the most common reasons for sterility.

Among woman, sterility can result from an intact *hymen*—the membrane partly covering the opening of the vagina, which is usually torn at her first experience of intercourse—malformation of the vagina, and a variety of abnormalities of either the ovaries, Fallopian tubes or vagina. These abnormalities may either prevent ovulation occurring, inhibit the movement of the egg down the Fallopian tubes into the uterus, or prevent implantation of the *zygote*—the fertilized ovum—into the endometrium, the lining of the womb.

Other causes of sterility, relating to the partners jointly, include a mechanical difficulty in coitus preventing adequate penetration, or periods when the partners are apart, so that intercourse never takes place at the most fertile time in the woman's cycle. A full investigation of infertility in a particular couple may take up to six months. It may be necessary for them to undergo a variety of tests, and obtain all the available results, before treatment can begin.

Problems directly related to sexual intercourse, such as impotence or premature ejaculation, can usually be treated. Careful counselling of both partners with a therapist, psychiatrist or marriage counsellor can help to change their physical and psychological attitudes towards sex so that they become more compatible.

268

Above: Many ancient festivities—like the maypole dance, here revived by English youngsters—originated as fertility rites. The symbolism of the maypole itself is obvious.

Right: Developing quintuplets, as seen on an ultrasonic display unit. Such advance warning of a multiple birth helps hospitals prepare the intensive care needed for the babies, who are usually premature and seldom survive.

Far right: Quadruplets, three boys and a girl, born to a French couple. Overdoses of fertility drugs have been the most usual cause of such large-scale reproduction.

Derek Ellis/Physics Dept UCH

Diagnoses of other causes of infertility require physical examination and consequent treatment. For example, it may be necessary to find out whether sufficient sperm is being produced, in which case the man's semen is examined either from a seminal specimen or from cervical mucus which is taken from his partner a few hours after coitus. If no sperm is present at all, the doctor will try to find out what is preventing it from being ejaculated. However, if the sperm count is merely below normal and there are no obvious physical abnormalities, the man may be advised on steps he should take to improve his general health, such as losing weight—or, perhaps, simply advised to avoid hot baths and thus keep his genitalia cooler.

There are many physical abnormalities

that can lead to sterility in a woman. Infections of the uterus, or polyps—non-malignant tumours—and fibroids on the endometrium can prevent pregnancy. These can be simply and easily removed. Blockage of the Fallopian tubes can prevent fertilization, but, providing there are no major lesions, the free passage of the tubes can be restored. Women who suffer from this kind of complaint are usually able to ovulate normally.

Fertility drugs
However, there are cases in which a woman may become *anovulatory*, unable to ovulate. This is often the result of lesions or cysts in the ovaries themselves. Apart from the removal of the cysts, treatment with a fertility drug to stimulate the release of *gonadotrophins* (sex hor-

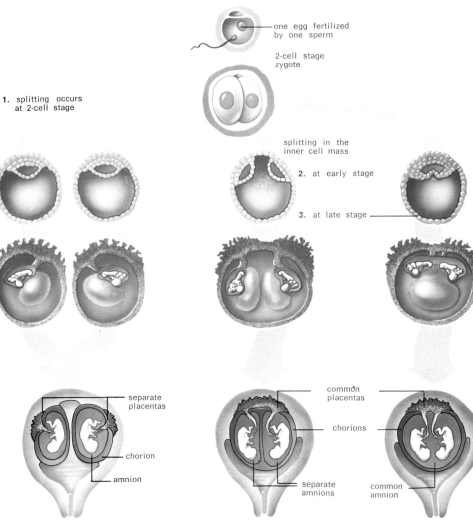

one egg fertilized by one sperm

2-cell stage zygote

1. splitting occurs at 2-cell stage

splitting in the inner cell mass

2. at early stage

3. at late stage

separate placentas

common placentas

chorions

chorion

amnion

separate amnions

common amnion

Above left: Twin births occur about once in every 80 deliveries. This diagram shows how non-identical twins (also called fraternal or *dizygotic*) are produced. Two eggs are released from the ovaries at the same time, and each is fertilized by a different sperm. Sometimes each embryo has its own placenta —the organ that anchors it to the uterine wall and is later discharged as 'afterbirth'—but sometimes one placenta envelopes both twins. Because they begin life as separate eggs and develop separately, fraternal twins may be of different sexes and quite dissimilar in physical appearance.

Above: Identical, or *monozygotic*, twins come from one egg which has been fertilized by the same sperm. Usually this splitting occurs when (1) the *zygote*, the large cell formed by the union of the male and female sex cells, has become two cells in its normal process of 'multiplying by dividing'. Sometimes, however, the whole cell mass can divide (2). If this happens at a late stage (3), 'Siamese' twins, joined together at some part of their bodies, will very occasionally result. Virtually 'two halves of the same person', identical twins are always of the same sex, with the same colouring and blood group.

mones) has been successfully used to promote ovulation. More recently gonadotrophins themselves have been administered to anovulatory women. Such treatments can be given only under specialized medical supervision with biochemical tests, sometimes daily, to estimate the exact dosage of the drug that is needed. The difference between an ineffective dose and one that will over-stimulate the ovaries so that they produce many eggs at once is extremely small.

Even with this exact supervision, excessive doses *have* been given and women have conceived several babies at once. Many of the pregnancies have resulted in miscarriages, and the quadruplets, quintuplets—and on at least one occasion octuplets—who have actually been born have seldom survived for long. Even then, such hormones can be used only when infertility is due to failure of ovulation, and when the woman is perfectly healthy otherwise.

The fertile period
When ovulation does occur, this fact is indicated by certain changes in the body—changes in the cervical secretions, hormones, menstrual cycle, or body temperature. Temperature is one of the means by which a woman can determine her 'fertile' period. Just before ovulation there is a small rise in the basal body temperature which can be recorded before she gets up in the morning. Thus, a carefully-recorded daily temperature chart can usually indicate the time of ovulation in a woman's cycle, and coitus should take place during this fertile period if pregnancy is desired.

In a few cases, infertility is the result of incompatability of the male sperm with cervical secretions from the woman. A woman will produce antibodies against the antigens contained in the seminal fluid, and what should be a normal defensive mechanism will damage the sperm so that it is no longer capable of fertilizing an ovum.

Psychological factors—particularly anxiety and stress—are other causes of infertility. Where a couple do not readily conceive it is common for the woman to suffer feelings of inadequacy and to fear that she is unable to become pregnant at all. This itself can inhibit ovulation and result in sterility, even though there are no physical abnormalities. This syndrome has been found to be especially prevalent in cultures—such as the Masai of Kenya —where the marriage is threatened if the woman is unable to bear her husband's offspring. Other women unconsciously fear pregnancy because they feel they will not be able to cope with bringing up a baby. This can also result in infertility, although in many cases the adoption of a first child alleviates such fears—and the couple find they are able to produce children after all.

Apart from other considerations, perhaps one thing that infertility demonstrates, more than any other malfunction, is that people are more than just a set of functions. The close relationship between the brain, the sex hormones and the control of sperm production or ovulation can be upset by apparently insignificant factors. An obsessive thought can prevent one of the most important events in human evolution—that of reproduction— from taking place.

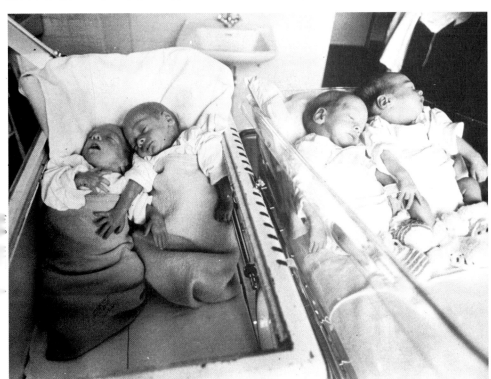

Contraception

Contraception is used by couples who wish to engage in sexual intercourse, but wish to prevent pregnancy. The idea of contraception is not new. As early as the nineteenth century BC Egyptian women were mixing honey, natron (sodium carbonate) and crocodile dung to form a vaginal contraceptive paste as a deterrent to conception. Other early references mention the use of various fruit acids, peppermint juice, rock salt and alum. Since such acidic, alkaline or salt solutions are hostile to sperm, these early 'recipes' probably did have some effect in limiting conception, although their reliability must have been highly suspect.

There are now many ways in which pregnancy can be effectively prevented. These can be broadly categorized into five classes: the natural methods; barrier methods; intra-uterine devices (IUDs); oral contraceptives; and sterilization.

Natural methods

The two natural methods of birth control are the rhythm or 'safe period' method and *coitus interruptus*. The biological basis for the rhythm method was not discovered until the 1930s, when two independent research workers showed that ovulation occurs about 14 days after the beginning of the previous menses. For women who have regular 28-day menstrual cycles, abstinence from intercourse three days before and three days after the predicted time of ovulation may prove a successful method of birth control. However, if a woman's cycles do not occur with complete regularity and vary from say, 26 to 31 days, only 12 to 18 days per cycle (including the period of menstruation) would be safe for intercourse.

The second natural method, *coitus interruptus*, involves interrupting sexual intercourse before the man ejaculates. Although this is still widely practised, it is often difficult to predict the correct time of withdrawal, and some sperms can be released before ejaculation proper. It has a high risk factor.

Barrier methods

Barrier contraceptives are those which prevent the viable sperm either from entering the vagina or from reaching the uterus, leaving them unable to 'swim' up the fallopian tubes and fertilize an ovum. They include the male sheath or *condom*, the female *diaphragm* (or 'Dutch cap') and vaginal *chemical contraceptives*.

The earliest condoms were made of animal intestines, silk and other materials and were used mainly as prophylactics against venereal disease. Their production, however, was minimal until the introduction in the mid-nineteenth century of the rubber condom. Strict quality controls on flaws and strength have been enforced in many countries and nowadays the thin rubber condom has become a reliable contraceptive device. The condom is unrolled over the erect penis before intercourse, and disposed of afterwards.

Whereas the condom prevents sperm entering the vagina, the diaphragm prevents the released sperm from reaching the uterus. It is a rubber cap which fits snugly between the pubic bone and the

Robert Harding

Left: Casanova, the eighteenth-century Italian lover, is known to have used condoms as contraceptives. His procedure for testing for leaks was something of a party piece.

Above: Family planning posters in Pakistan emphasize the heavy economic burden carried by the man with a large family, in an effort to control the country's population 'explosion'.

Right: Marie Stopes was a pioneer in promoting contraceptive methods, especially the use of diaphragms and caps by women, and she set up an advice clinic in London in 1921. Her ideas on contraception and other sexual matters were highly controversial, but her books helped to change society's views on sex and the need for contraceptives.

Below: The campaign to reduce the numbers of unwanted babies being born in the 1960s and 1970s included posters such as this one in Britain, whose target was the male who takes inadequate contraceptive precautions, or none at all. The Family Planning Association estimates that 200,000 unwanted pregnancies occur every year in Britain. Many of these pregnancies are aborted, and some of the unwanted babies born are adopted.

Mansell

Health Education Council

Would you be more careful if it was you that got pregnant?

Anyone married or single can get advice on contraception from the Family Planning Association. Margaret Pyke House, 27-35 Mortimer Street, London W1N 8BQ. Tel. 01-636 9135.

The Health Education Council

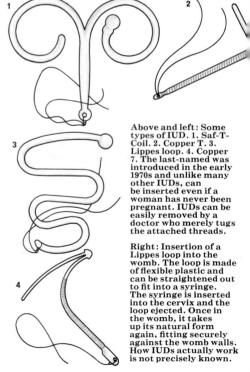

Above and left: Some types of IUD. 1. Saf-T-Coil. 2. Copper T. 3. Lippes loop. 4. Copper 7. The last-named was introduced in the early 1970s and unlike many other IUDs, can be inserted even if a woman has never been pregnant. IUDs can be easily removed by a doctor who merely tugs the attached threads.

Right: Insertion of a Lippes loop into the womb. The loop is made of flexible plastic and can be straightened out to fit into a syringe. The syringe is inserted into the cervix and the loop ejected. Once in the womb, it takes up its natural form again, fitting securely against the womb walls. How IUDs actually work is not precisely known.

270

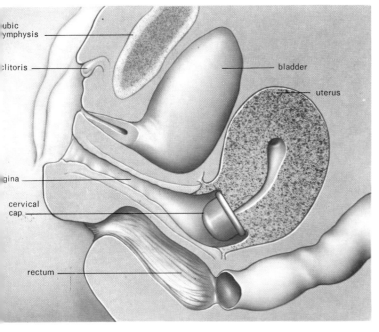

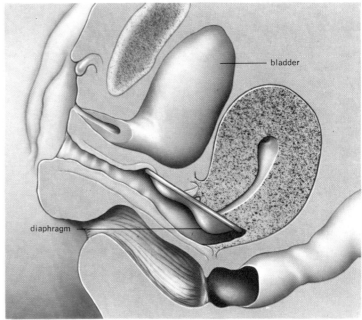

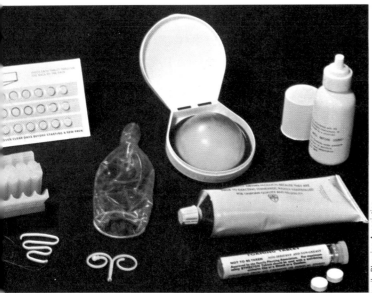

Above left: A cervical cap in place. In order to block sperm from entering the womb, the cap must fit the cervix closely and securely. Thus, the cervix must be long, parallel-sided, healthy and readily accessible, if a cervical cap is to be fitted.

Above right: The Dutch cap or diaphragm is the largest of the caps. It can be obtained in sizes between 50 and 100mm in external diameter. It is made of soft rubber and fits across the vaginal vault, shielding the cervix from direct insemination. The Dutch cap should be used only with a spermicide and must be left inside the vagina for at least six hours after intercourse.

Left: An illustration of the relative sizes of some contraceptives. A couple usually choose the device they find the most comfortable and convenient to use.

Family Planning Association

back of the vagina and covers the cervix (the entrance to the womb).

Before the wide distribution of oral contraceptives and IUDs the diaphragm was the most effective contraceptive for women. Other types of uterine barrier include the *cervical cap* and the *vimule*, although their use is not as widespread.

Vaginal chemical contraceptives or spermicides have been in use for thousands of years. Today's creams, jellies or suppositories are made of a relatively inert base material, which physically blocks sperm, plus an active spermicidal agent which chemically immobilizes or destroys sperm. Their failure rate is relatively high, however, unless they are used in conjunction with either a condom or a diaphragm.

Intra-uterine devices
An almost infinite variety of intra-uterine devices (IUDs) are now available in different parts of the world—rings, loops, spirals, coils, Dalkom Shields, Copper T's, Copper 7's—all shapes and sizes. These small devices, ranging from just under 1 in to 3 in (2-7 cm) in length or diameter, are inserted into the uterine cavity. Some of these devices can be used both by women who have had previous pregnancies and by those who have never conceived. Though they have proved to be effective contraceptives, they do substantially increase menstrual flow and lengthen the time of menses. One of the major problems of IUDs is the relatively high incidence of unpleasant side effects such as bleeding, pain and infection. Another problem is that of involuntary expulsion of the device which, if unnoticed, can lead to pregnancy. But cervical threads, or 'tails' attached to the IUD can be used to check that the IUD is in place.

Oral contraceptives
Oral contraceptives, commonly known as 'the pill', were first marketed in 1960. As early as 1945 the potential of sex steroids in preventing pregnancy had been foreseen but it was not until 1956 that large-scale clinical trials to test their effectiveness and side actions were undertaken in Puerto Rico.

The pill contains the hormones oestro-

INSERTION OF THE I.U.D.

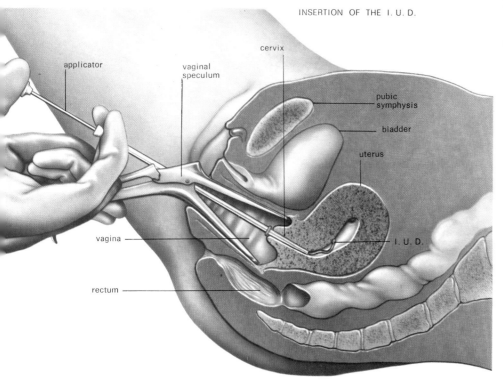

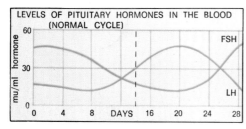

LEVELS OF PITUITARY HORMONES IN THE BLOOD (NORMAL CYCLE)

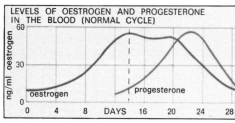

LEVELS OF OESTROGEN AND PROGESTERONE IN THE BLOOD (NORMAL CYCLE)

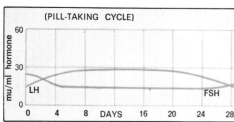

(PILL-TAKING CYCLE)

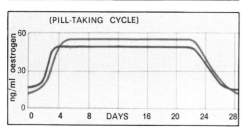

(PILL-TAKING CYCLE)

Syntex Pharmaceutical

Left: Variation in blood hormone levels during normal cycle and pill-taking cycle. Variations during the normal cycle in the levels of oestrogen and progesterone act on the pituitary to change the levels of LH and FSH, and this triggers ovulation. During pill taking, oestrogen and progesterone levels are kept at a constant high level, and this acts on the pituitary to level out the secretion of LH and FSH. Thus ovulation does not occur.

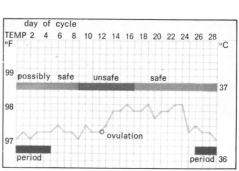

Above: The Mexican yam, *Dioscoreus composita*, a steroid extract of which is used as the basis for the synthesis of potent progesterone analogues, used in the pill.

Left: Some women find that ovulation can be detected by changes in body temperature. A drop in temperature occurs at ovulation and is followed by a rise. This can form the basis of the 'rhythm method', in which intercourse is avoided around the time of ovulation.

gen and progesterone. These are also produced naturally by the ovaries, acting on the pituitary gland to produce a surge of the gonadotrophin hormones LH (luteinizing hormone) and FSH (follicle stimulating hormone), which trigger ovulation. When the pill is taken for 21 days of the menstrual cycle, the oestrogen and progesterone are maintained at a constant high level, and as a result the gonadotrophin surge does not take place. Thus ovulation is not triggered, and without an ovum, pregnancy cannot occur.

The first pills to be marketed contained high doses of oestrogen and progesterone. Today these doses have been dramatically reduced in order to minimize side effects. There is still a relatively high prevalence of nausea, dizziness, headaches and the like in women taking the pill but these may be alleviated simply by changing to another brand of pill with different proportions of oestrogen and progesterone.

More substantial hazards associated with long-term use of the pill, such as blood clots and gall bladder disease, are relatively rare. Other potentially serious changes, such as increased blood pressure or 'steroid' diabetes, are usually temporary and disappear when pill-taking stops. In fact, intensive research and evaluation of the effects of pill-taking show that the advantages of the pill (for example, reduction of menstrual disorders, iron deficiency anaemia and cancer of the breast) can outweigh the disadvantages and the small risk of serious side-effects.

Another form of oral contraceptive is the *minipill* which contains only proges-

terone. It is not widely used because it is less effective than the combined oral contraceptives and produces a high incidence of breakthrough bleeding and other menstrual irregularities. However, minipills can be used by women who require oral contraception but who are lactating or who should avoid oestrogens for other reasons.

Sterilization

Sterilization is an extremely effective method of contraception because it is permanent. It can be performed by a surgeon on either men or women. In men, the sperms are prevented from leaving the testes, where they are formed, by cutting and tying the *vas deferens*, along which they must pass from the testes to the penis. The operation, *vasectomy*, is normally irreversible, although in certain cases the vas deferens may be rejoined. In women, the surgeon closes the Fallopian tubes along which the egg cells must pass in order to reach the uterus. This operation usually requires a few days in hospital. It is also normally irreversible.

Neither operation results in any loss of sexual drive or performance. With vasectomy, a complete absence of sperm in the semen does not occur immediately, because some sperm still linger in the genital tract below the block. These have to be emptied out by repeated ejaculation, which may take several months, during which time other contraceptive precautions are necessary. Female sterilization, on the other hand, takes effect immediately, since a woman normally produces only one egg during each monthly cycle. Because of its irreversible nature, sterilization is normally performed only on

one partner of a couple who have decided they do not want further children.

Abortion

Abortion is not strictly a form of contraception, since it refers to the termination of a pregnancy as opposed to its prevention. An abortion is normally carried out by a gynaecologist after approval by a doctor. The procedure is safer and easier the earlier in pregnancy it is done. If a pregnancy is no more than 12 weeks old, it is usually terminated through the vagina, by one of two main methods. The newest method, *vacuum aspiration*, involves inserting a suction catheter through the cervix and sucking out the womb contents.

If a pregnancy is over 12 weeks old, termination can usually be done only by the abdominal route. In the case of a woman verging on middle age, actual removal of the womb, called *hysterectomy*, may be carried out instead.

Relative effectiveness

The effectiveness of each method of contraception has been evaluated in a variety of studies, but the results do not always agree. Oral contraceptives and sterilization have been found to be the most effective, followed closely by IUDs. Condoms and diaphragms provide reasonably reliable protection. The highest failure rates are among users of spermicides (alone) or natural methods.

There is continuing conflict between religious beliefs on the rights and wrongs of using contraceptives. But today's social and economic pressures are making their use more widespread than ever before.

272

Intrauterine devices
(I.U.D.'s) are made in
a variety of shapes,
ranging in size from
1 to 3 ins (2 to 7 cms).

They are inserted into
the uterine cavity, and
are a generally effective
method of
contraception.

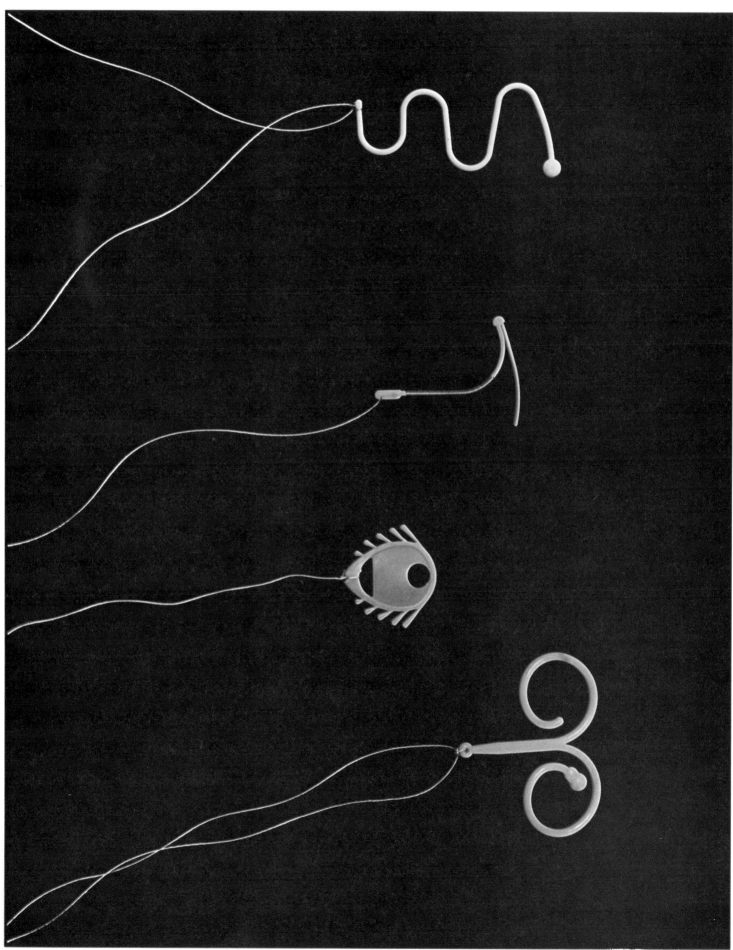

Pregnancy

For a woman, the bearing and delivering of a baby can be a richly satisfying experience. The process, however, involves complex and interrelated bodily changes, some physical and some psychological. They do not end with delivery, and often the woman's physical and psychological balance does not return to normal for a year afterwards, especially if she breastfeeds her baby. It is not precisely known in what way many of these changes are brought about, and they become all the more confusing because some changes are undergone by certain women but not others, and even in the same woman different pregnancies may follow different courses.

The course of pregnancy falls into three periods, called *trimesters*, of about three months each. Broadly, each trimester produces its own group of bodily changes, though some changes may occur during any period. Sometimes a woman will feel sensory and emotional changes long before any overt physical changes have occurred. She may notice an odd metallic taste in her mouth, or suddenly dislike the taste of beverages such as coffee which she had previously enjoyed. Her reflexes may become sluggish, judgement impaired and mood variable between irritability, tears and excitement. The woman may easily become tired and depressed, however pleased she is about being pregnant.

The first trimester

The first physical symptom of pregnancy is usually that the menstrual period fails to occur on the expected date. Marked changes in the breasts also take place very early in pregnancy, involving a rapid increase in size together with feelings of fullness, tenderness and tingling in the nipples. The hormones oestrogen and progesterone, produced first by the mother's body and later by the placenta, and possibly others such as prolactin, cause these breast changes by stimulating growth of the milk sacs and ducts, increasing the flow of blood to the breasts and encouraging the storage of a cushion of fat around the milk apparatus.

Feelings of nausea, and sometimes actual vomiting, occur in about two-thirds of pregnant women. They vary in intensity, and may happen at any time of the day although 'early morning sickness' is most frequent. The cause is obscure but thought to be a reaction to the sudden increase in blood hormone levels. These discomforts usually disappear by the end of the first trimester.

In early pregnancy the kidneys, too, often become over-efficient. The bladder fills with urine more quickly, and the woman frequently needs to pass water. This discomfort disappears by about the twelfth or fourteenth week, only to reappear for different reasons in the last weeks of pregnancy. Constipation is common in early pregnancy, and is due to the action of progesterone which reduces the movements of all smooth muscles such as the gut and the uterus. A similar relaxing effect on the muscles which guard the entrance to the oesophagus from the stomach may allow food and stomach juices to be regurgitated into the oesophagus, especially after a large meal.

274

Above: Diagrams of a pregnant woman. Each stage of pregnancy is accompanied by changes in the mother-to-be's appearance, outward indications of the development of the baby in her uterus. Pregnancy is divided into three periods known as *trimesters*. The first is from the beginning of the last menstrual period to the 14th week, the second from the 15th to the 28th week and the third from the 29th to the 40th week, around which time the baby is delivered.

Top right: The uterus, or womb, must enlarge to accommodate the developing foetus, which grows from an almost invisible cell to a 6-8 lb infant. It increases in capacity by up to 500 times its pre-pregnancy size. The muscle fibres of the uterus may elongate up to 10 times their normal size, and to prevent the walls from becoming too thin, new muscle fibres may develop to give extra strength and support. After delivery, the uterus can 'shrink' back to its original size within six weeks.

Werner Forman Archive

Alphabet & Image

Left and above: Embryology was not established as a science until after 1827. The 19th century drawing from a door in New Guinea (left) and the 16th century woodcut (above) are two earlier attempts to depict the position of the foetus in the womb.

1½ months / 4 months / 5½ months

Since the stomach juices consist mainly of hydrochloric acid, this may result in heartburn and unpleasant indigestion. Since levels of progesterone increase throughout pregnancy, these changes caused directly by the hormone tend to persist.

The second trimester

For the pregnant woman the second trimester is often very pleasant. The expectant mother's condition becomes more obvious to the outside world as the growing foetus swells the uterus and pushes out her abdomen. Most of the discomforts of early pregnancy disappear once the pregnancy is well established. Feelings of extreme vitality and well-being are common and the woman in mid-pregnancy is frequently said to have a

special 'glow'. Her hair may become thicker and glossier, and her skin may seem smoother and healthier because of the increased blood flow. The foetus, via the placenta, requires such a large supply of blood that the mother's blood volume is increased by 40%. Circulation of maternal blood is improved in two ways, by an increase in the number of heartbeats per minute and also by an increase in the amount of blood pumped out by each beat. Darkening of the skin often occurs, especially around the nipples, as a 'butterfly mask' on the face, or as a thin line from the umbilicus down to the pubic hair. All of these pigmentation changes return to normal after delivery, except that the nipples often remain slightly darker than before.

During the second trimester the woman

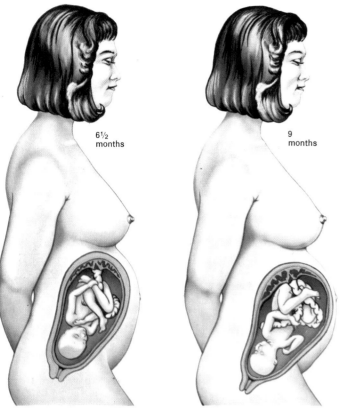

6½ months

9 months

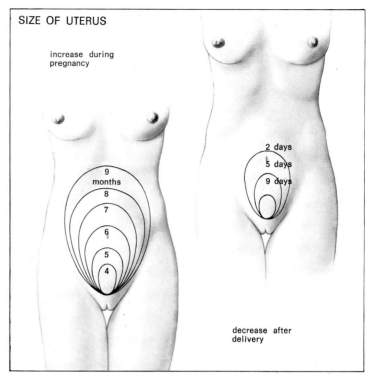

increase during pregnancy

9 months
8
7
6
5
4

2 days
5 days
9 days

decrease after delivery

THE PLACENTA

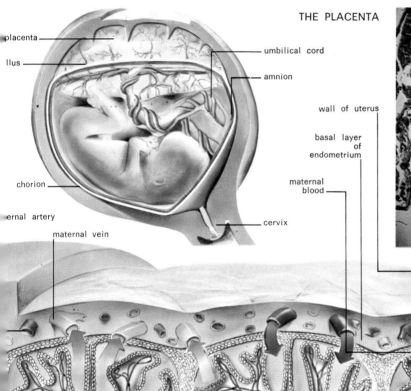

placenta

llus

chorion

ernal artery

maternal vein

umbilical cord

amnion

wall of uterus

basal layer of endometrium

maternal blood

cervix

trophoblast

foetal blood vessels

two foetal arteries

Wharton's jelly

foetal vein

umbilical cord

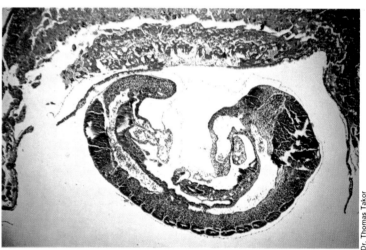

Dr. Thomas Takor

Left: The placenta, the organ of respiration, nutrition and excretion which develops from the embryo's outer layer of cells. Dissolved oxygen and nutrients diffuse from the mother's blood into the infant's bloodstream; carbon dioxide and other waste products pass from the infant to the mother for excretion.

Above: The stage of development which this mouse embryo has reached can be seen from the number of somites present on the placenta. Each of the somites—the bead-like blocks on the outer surface of the placenta (bottom)—is a group of cells which will later be specialized into muscle, bone or nerve.

usually feels her baby's movements for the first time. They are difficult to identify at first since the sensation is similar to that of wind or gas moving in the stomach, but by the twentieth week most women can reliably identify their baby's movements. These first movements are known as 'quickening' and it was once believed that the baby became alive only at this time. Later in the pregnancy, there is no problem in feeling the baby move, and the mother may find it difficult to get to sleep if her baby decides to get some exercise when she has gone to bed.

The third trimester

The third trimester of pregnancy, from the twenty-ninth week until delivery, mainly involves the mother's adjustment to the rapidly increasing maturity of her

275

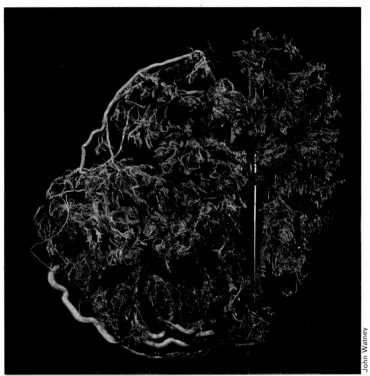

John Watney

corpus luteum

2 months

4 months

8½ months

oestrogen

progesterone

chorionic gonadotrophin

hormone levels in mother's blood

months of pregnancy

0 1 2 3 4 5 6 7 8

baby and her preparation for labour. Some of this preparation is mental. Even the normally alert and intellectually active mother experiences an increased placidity and drowsiness as pregnancy advances. Her clarity of thought and precision diminish. The focus of her interest turns inwards to the contents of her womb. She becomes forgetful of matters unconnected with the coming baby. The action of progesterone on the nervous system is thought to be the cause of these mental changes and after delivery the mother's usual powers of thought will return.

Progesterone also softens up muscles and ligaments throughout the body. This softening effect is directed at the pelvis, uterus and cervix, in order to make them more elastic for the birth. Unfortunately it also affects other ligaments such as those in the feet. During the last ten weeks of pregnancy the lower part of the body of the uterus stretches and gradually enlarges in order to accommodate the baby's head. The cervix, which is firm and hard before pregnancy, rapidly becomes softer and gradually becomes larger as pregnancy advances. The canal of the cervix fills with a tenacious plug of thick mucous material which prevents infection ascending from the vagina into the uterus.

Late pregnancy brings a variety of minor discomforts to the expectant mother. Her increasing bulk makes her feel clumsy and awkward and her feelings of tiredness and lassitude become strong. Pressure of the baby on her lungs, at one end, makes it difficult to breathe, and on her bladder, at the other end, elicits a frequent desire to urinate. A sudden upsurge of energy may be a signal that delivery is near. Many women at this time are seized by the 'nesting instinct' and feel compelled to scrub, clean and tidy everything in preparation for the baby.

Labour

Like pregnancy, labour falls into three stages, each of which has different characteristics. It is difficult to define

Above: This complex circulatory system was taken from the placenta of triplets. The arteries, which carried oxygenated blood to the three embryos, are stained blue, and the veins, carrying the deoxygenated blood, are red.

Top right: Apart from its main function as the foetus's organ of nutrition, excretion and respiration, the placenta also acts as an endocrine gland for the mother. Hormones that maintain the pregnant state are produced by the corpus luteum—the small body which develops from the follicle from which the ovum erupts in the ovary— until the placenta develops.

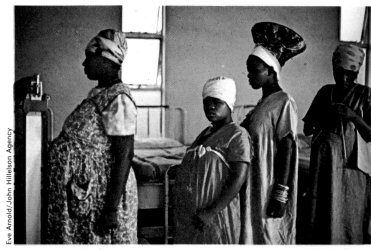

Eve Arnold/John Hillelson Agency

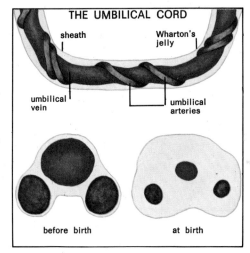

THE UMBILICAL CORD

sheath

Wharton's jelly

umbilical vein

umbilical arteries

before birth

at birth

Above: The umbilical cord connects the unborn child with its placenta. It is made up of two arteries twisted around a vein, surrounded by a clear material known as Wharton's jelly. Before birth the blood vessels are distended by the blood flow which passes through the cord at the rate of four

miles per hour. The speed of the blood flow prevents kinking and knotting in the cord. Immediately after birth, the cells of the jelly-like coating swell up, constricting the blood vessels and stopping the flow. The cord can then be cut near the baby's navel and the remaining stump withers and falls off.

Robert Harding Associates

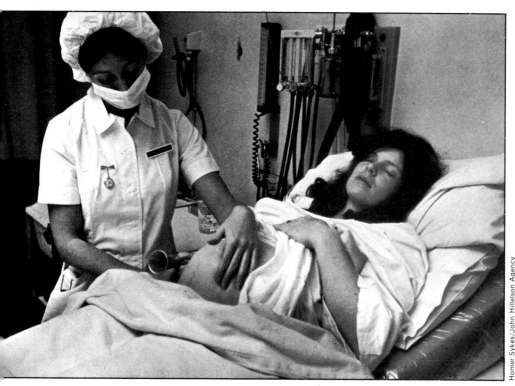

Emotionally, the end of the first stage is often a difficult time for the mother. She may feel drained and exhausted. It is not known what causes these feelings but fortunately they disappear when the second stage is well established.

The second stage of labour lasts from the time of full cervical dilatation until the moment the baby fully emerges. It rarely lasts more than two hours. During this stage, the uterus probably produces stronger contractions than any other human muscle is capable of. The contractions occur once every two to three minutes and last for up to 100 seconds, but some women are able to relax between contractions to summon new energy. The mother feels an overwhelming desire to 'bear down', to actually push the baby out. By taking in a deep breath, tensing her diaphragm and pushing downwards with her abdominal muscles she aids the uterus in its work and significantly speeds up the whole process of birth.

The third stage of labour is the time between delivery of the baby and the expulsion of the placenta from the uterus. Contractions recommence shortly after the baby's delivery and within 20 minutes the placenta is expelled.

Changes after delivery

After childbirth changes continue to occur in the mother's body. Some of these changes are directed towards getting the mother's functions and systems back to their pre-pregnancy state. Some are directed towards the continuing care of the baby. During pregnancy, and for the first three days after delivery, the breasts produce a thick yellowish liquid, *colostrum*. This is rich in protein and antibodies, and provides all the baby's immediate needs. On the third and fourth day of the *puerperium* (time after delivery) the mother begins to produce milk and her breasts may become tender. As the milk supply stabilizes this symptom gradually disappears. Changes in the composition of the milk continue at least until the tenth day when it becomes mature human milk. At each stage the mother's breasts produce exactly what the baby needs.

Breastfeeding speeds up many of the processes by which the mother's body returns to normal, but retards others. For example, milk production delays the occurrence of menstruation so that conception is less likely, although by no means impossible, while a woman is breastfeeding. The baby's suckling also stimulates the release of a pituitary hormone, *oxytocin*, which causes the mother's uterus to contract and hastens its return to a pre-pregnancy size. This *involution* of the uterus is usually complete six weeks after delivery. During this time, the uterus sheds its lining and the blood from the site of placental attachment. This is gradually lost through the vagina rather like a prolonged menstrual period. The loss is known as *lochia*, and generally lasts for about three weeks.

Emotional changes during the puerperium, probably caused by the sudden enormous hormonal changes, may be strong. Nearly all women feel a little shaky and vulnerable, and may easily become weepy and upset. As the mother's hormonal balance gradually readjusts itself, however, her emotional equilibrium will return.

Far left, below left and above: Pre-natal care has improved in many parts of the world but the Brazilian Indian (far left) is still protected more by the supernatural than by antiseptics. The Zulu women (below left) are 'weighing in' at their pre-natal clinic. Most women in industrialized societies are content to give birth in sterile surroundings (above), although an increasing number are opting for 'natural' childbirth.

Left: A 14th century way of coping with the discomfort of pregnancy.

Right: Pregnancy has fascinated many artists. The art nouveau style of Gustav Klimt (1862-1918) gives the subject a romantic aura.

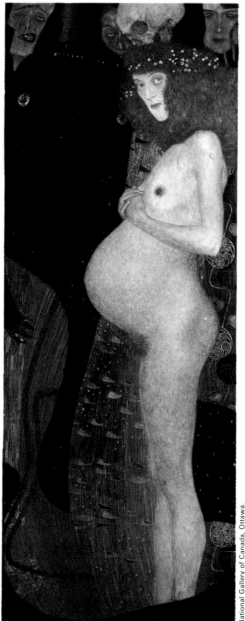

accurately at what point labour begins. Like all involuntary muscles, the uterus contracts regularly throughout life; the change from these mild contractions to the stronger ones of true labour is gradual and subtle. The woman may remain unaware of her contractions until the cervix has opened up enough to release its plug of mucus. This 'show' of thick, jelly-like substance, which may be bloodstained, indicates that labour has begun.

The first stage of labour lasts until the cervix has opened to its full extent. This *dilatation* of the cervix can last about 13 hours for a first birth, and about seven hours in subsequent ones. The contractions grow in regularity from once every 20-30 minutes to once every 3-5 minutes, and in intensity until each may last up to one minute. The mother's main task during this stage is to relax and to avoid tensing other muscles during the contractions. Unnecessary tension not only causes pain but quickly tires the mother. It also interferes with the functioning of the uterus by reducing the efficiency of its contractions, and in this way prolongs labour. Towards the end of the first stage, the amniotic fluid surrounding the baby gushes out through the vagina, and effectively sterilizes the birth canal.

277

The Mother's Role and Status

Procreation is the result of the urge to reproduce. Charles Darwin and several biologists who came after him have observed that this urge to ensure continuation is present in every species but, in the human species, whether or not it is present in every *individual* may be another matter.

Some of these same observers have noted that biological evolution has a modifying effect on all basic drives.

Animals have no influence over the direction their biological drives take—whether it be towards over-production, thereby exposing the group to shortage of food and space, or under-production, thus reducing their overall chances of survival—but human beings do. Regardless of what is necessary or vital for the human species as a whole, humans can choose to produce offspring or remain childless.

This has given rise to an interesting question in sociological terms—one with which some social scientists have been preoccupied for many years. Is there any longer such a thing as the *need* to pro-create? In other words, has it, too, been modified by evolution so that a proportion of the human race no longer has this urge, thereby ensuring that the species will increase at a reasonable rate and not drive itself to extinction through over-population?

Nobody has tried to find an accurate answer to this question in the only way that might be feasible: to interview thousands of people scientifically selected to represent the whole population of the earth.

What most observers have done is to look at particular societies and their attitudes towards related aspects of the problem. For example, what is a society's attitude towards childbearing as a whole and maternity in particular? And does the society regard maternity as synonymous with womanhood, or separate from it?

Childbearing and maternity

In many societies, past and present, the pregnant woman and the mother and her newborn have been powerful symbols in art and religion. They represent eternal themes: the unity of life, the promise of renewal, the never-ending recreation of hope and potential.

In mythology the child is unspoiled and uncorrupted: and somehow this aura of wholeness is transferred to the mother-to-be and the new mother so that together mother and baby form a complete and perfect unit, above the hurly-burly of every-day life.

This fascination with maternity is by no means confined to humans. The work of Harry Harlow with rhesus monkeys—and of other primatologists such as Jane Goodhall van Lawick with chimpanzees and baboons—shows that the response to a newborn infant is common to all of the higher primates. The mother's status in the group grows: both males and females pay her and her offspring a great deal of solicitous attention.

As the baby gets older the other adults lose interest in him, but the mother-child bond continues to grow in strength and endures for many years. Indeed, it is this relationship which forms the core of the animals' society. It is stronger than any other bond formed in the group—and the higher the place on the evolutionary scale, the stronger the mother-infant attachment.

The status of the mother

The earliest recorded religions also show the power of the mother. Early man in many societies worshipped a female deity or goddess who took many forms—Universal Mother, Earth Mother and Mother Goddess among them—all of which symbolized her regenerative or procreative power.

The initiates of these religions—the class which held the knowledge and power

Bulloz

Camera Press

Left and below: Motherhood is regarded as the most essential feminine role in many societies, although attitudes towards mothers have often been ambivalent. The late 16th century painting by Georges de la Tour (below) conveys the simplicity, tenderness and purity he sees as incarnate in all mothers.

The engraving of a peasant woman by Pieter Bruegel, although almost contemporary with the painting, takes a grosser view of the mother's role as a child-rearer.

Above: Preparation for motherhood begins early through toys considered 'feminine' and therefore appropriate for girls.

Cooper-Bridgeman Library

Left: The 'Venus of Willendorf', a neolithic mother goddess figure in sandstone. The fecund, or fertile, aspect of woman is shown in the exaggeration of the breasts and belly. Some contemporary scholars believe— and have uncovered evidence to suggest— that the male priests of some early religious cults helped to tie women to their procreative role by encouraging fertility worship, so rendering women politically powerless.

Below: A wood carving from Northern Yorubaland, Nigeria, part of an altar panel of a fertility shrine.

Erich Lessing/John Hillelson Agency

Werner Forman Archive

of the religion—were female priestesses. It has often been assumed that these priestesses did not engage in sexual activity. In fact, 'vestal virgins' and 'temple prostitutes' were the same things, for the essence of the term which is now translated as 'virgin' (sexually inexperienced) originally meant 'not belonging to any man': the priestesses were nobody's property. Several writers interested in woman's position in society— for example, Dr Esther Harding in her book *Woman's Mysteries*—have noted that confusion over the very word 'virgin' may be responsible for the ambivalent attitude towards women which still persists in some Christian societies.

Inheritance of wealth and goods in these ancient societies was matrilineal (through the mother's line) and hence a person's social standing depended on who his mother was: his father's identity was not important.

Later religions, particularly Judaism and—later still—Christianity, worshipped a male deity and the initiates of the religion were men. The reasons why these societies became male-orientated are complex and difficult to assess. However, it has been suggested by some scholars—the American professor Merlin Stone and Dr Harding (a pupil of Dr C E Jung) among them—that the reasons may have derived from evolving property laws. Restrictions on a woman's sexual activity may have been introduced so that a man

Left: 'Suffragettes', depicted in a late 19th century French journal. Although the movement was sparked off by the publication of Mary Wollstonecraft's book

A Vindication of the Rights of Women in 1792, British women did not succeed in attaining the right to vote on equal terms with men until 1928.

Below: A creche in every commune allows mothers in the People's Republic of China to fulfil an equally valuable role as part of the work force.

Mansell

Bruno Barbey/John Hillelson Agency

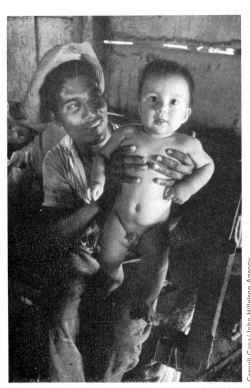

could ensure that the children to whom he was to pass on his wealth and status or power were his own.

It has been argued that, in providing for their children in this way, women in these early societies sacrificed their independence and, consequently, their equal status with men. In some cases, as the laws became more complex and rigid, it even resulted in subjugation to the point where the entire female population was (and still is, in some Moslem societies) reduced to an inferior status with few, or no, political or social rights.

However, even under these conditions the power of the maternal bond is not completely lost. To the Christian, the Madonna and child symbolize love at its strongest and purest.

In a broad evolutionary and social context, attitudes to the process of childbearing appear to be universal and unaltered by time. But does the overall view

Left and below: Not all societies have the kind of problems integrating male and female roles prevalent in industrialized countries. This young father from a Central American agricultural community (left) spends as much time looking after his infant son as his wife does. The Shipibo Indian mother (below) carries her baby around with her as she works, fulfilling her roles as mother and woman in a way that is useful to her society.

put forward by a society necessarily represent the feelings or beliefs of its members—and particularly its female members?

In the individual woman, the urge to bear children is a difficult characteristic to define. However, studies by Helen Singer Kaplan (recorded in her *Manual of Sex Therapy*) and by Masters and Johnson—pioneers of the clinical approach to sexual functioning—have established that the procreative urge is different from the sexual urge: only a small proportion of women regard the two as synonymous. In other words, few women, according to these observations, enjoy sex only when they are trying to conceive. But there is, nevertheless, some biological component in the desire for motherhood, or it would not persist.

One of the longest-standing controversies in scientific circles is that of *heredity* versus *environment*. The argument concerns the effects that each of them has on all aspects of human behaviour, but their effect on the maternal instinct in the early years of a child's life has been one of the main issues in question. Some child psychologists, among them Corinne Hutt in her book *Males and Females*, have noted that among three-year-olds there is a definite tendency for girls to act out mothering roles more frequently than boys do. However, the reasons why this should be so are not yet clear. Some observers attribute it wholly to heredity (that is, because they are *born* girls); others to the learning process and the effects of the environment (that is, that they are encouraged to *behave* as girls). Still other researchers have open minds.

Society and the individual

For many years, in Western industrialized societies anyway, it was believed that a woman who had no maternal instinct was abnormal. But it has since been discovered that a woman's response to the discovery that she is pregnant, and, later, to the birth of her baby, is very individual. She can be affected by a variety of factors: her hormonal activity; her intellectual and social needs; her economic status; and even her reactions to her own childhood. And she is influenced not only by her own needs but also by society's view of them.

In some cases—in certain African tribal communities, for example, and some Mediterranean countries such as Greece where the social structure is built around the family—a woman's *only* viable position is motherhood. Childlessness brings social scorn, as well as the woman's own feelings of failure or disappointment. Even in societies where a choice is apparently available, women may be no better off. Ellen Peck contends in *The Baby Trap* that childless women are often pressurized by their family and friends in ways that are equally destructive to their own self-esteem. In the face of such pressures, how can any woman decide whether or not she should have children?

One possible answer is given by Dr Harding in *The Way of All Women*: that this is, for women, what growing up is all about. When women decide what fulfilment really means—is it to be creativity or *procreativity*?—perhaps the male half of humanity will come to terms with their decision. And the result will be happier—and fewer unwanted—children in the future.

The baby's suckling
during breastfeeding
stimulates the
production of *oxytocin*,
a pituitary hormone
which causes the uterus
to contract and hastens
its return to pre-
pregnancy size.

Ageing

Ageing is a process that actually begins from the moment a human being is born. However, the decline in physical and mental functioning which is the popular concept of ageing does not begin until a person is in his early 20s, and the more overt changes do not occur until middle and old age. There is a wide individual and geographical variation in the rate of ageing, and because of this it is difficult to define at what point middle age and old age begin. In western society, the measurement of age purely by 'years lived' gives a convenient definition of middle age as the years between 45 and 65 and old age as the years after 65. However, in countries with a lower life expectancy, a man of 35 may be considered middle aged and a man of 50 old-aged. Hence it is more accurate to describe the various stages of ageing in terms of the physical, mental, and social changes that occur, rather than by 'years lived' alone.

Changes in middle age
Most cells which make up the body are dying and being replaced throughout life, but before the age of 20 there is a net increase in cells, leading to growth. In the early 20s, the cell turnover begins to have an effect on the body and there is a net cell loss in certain organs, in particular the brain. However, few marked physical changes take place until middle age.

Middle age brings certain characteristic physical and social changes. Some of these are undergone by both sexes, and others are peculiar to one sex. For women, there is a distinctive event which clearly draws attention to middle age. This is the *menopause*, also known as the *climacteric* or 'change of life'. The monthly cycles of ovulation and menstruation finally stop, marking the end of the fertile period of female life. The menopause may occur at any time from the age of 40 onwards, but normally occurs around the age of 45. It may take place gradually, or quite suddenly. With the 'closing down' of the ovaries, there is a decline in the body level of the female sex hormones, oestrogen and progesterone, which the ovaries had previously manufactured.

The decline in oestrogen in particular affects the health and appearance of the woman. Individual variations in the rate of its decline account for the fact that some women pass through the menopause with few mental and physical upsets and little external change; while others suffer sagging and a reduction in the size of the breasts, thinning and drying of the vaginal and vulval tissues, increased wrinkling of the skin, and mental upsets like headache, insomnia and listlessness.

Traditional medical therapy or 'treatment' of female menopausal changes involves hormone replacement of the missing oestrogen for a few months after the menopause arrives. This reverses many of the mental and physical changes, but cannot alter the shutdown of the ovaries nor reverse the loss in fertility. The desirability of long-term hormone replacement therapy is still controversial. It is widely advocated by some members of women's liberation movements and by

Camera Press

Below left: Mother George, an inhabitant of nineteenth century London, described by the artist as being in her 120th year. Such reports of longevity are usually exaggerated. Since the introduction of birth certificates to authenticate age not one person in Britain, for example, has been proved to reach 115.

Below: The process of ageing may be speeded up for those living in countries where poverty, disease and hunger are widespread or where continuous physical labour is required to sustain a living. This mother from Honduras is only in her thirties, but in terms of physical deterioration is 'old' by any country's standards.

Mansell

Cornell Capa/John Hillelson Agency

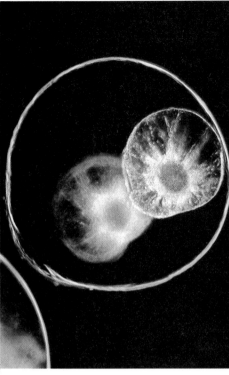

some gynaecologists, but others allege that it promotes malignant changes in the uterus and breast.

The loss in fertility in middle age takes place at a time of considerable self-reassessment—and possibly some problems of adjustment—for a woman. She may still feel in the mainstream of life, having achieved some of her ambitions but still having other goals to strive for. If she has never married, the menopause may accentuate the fact that motherhood is no longer possible. If she already has and enjoys a family, it may emphasize the fact that, with the children already grown and some even flown the coop, her role as a nurturing mother may soon be over. Conversely, a woman who has felt tied down and unable to flower creatively because of her job as a mother may feel that social freedom is at last available.

Before the menopause, the sexual needs and the patterns of sexual behaviour of an individual woman are reasonably stable. At the menopause, physical, mental and hormonal changes may alter her sexual needs. They may increase, due to her new social role as 'woman' rather than 'mother', or because of her freedom from the possibility of becoming pregnant. Or they may decrease, due to depression and anxiety over 'the change'. This can result in tension and arguments between husband and wife, sometimes even leading to separation and break-up of the marriage. This may be avoided, however, if the couple recognize the basic cause of their problems and can discuss possible solutions. Marriage problems or not, many women find that the menopause coincides with a renewed vigour in a new or previously interrupted career, or in

Above: Many rich and famous people seek to cover up their age by surrounding themselves in glamour, or through cosmetic surgery. Film stars such as Mae West, here seen reclining in a limousine, are notorious for this. She may look fifty, but anyone who made films in the 1920s must have been born by around 1900.

Below: Despite the slow decline in some of their physical functions, many old people remain deft with their fingers, possessing skills that have been developed over a lifetime. This Aymara Indian woman from South America is preparing Alpaca wool ready for weaving without even having to use a spinning wheel.

Below right: After the menopause and the departure from home of their children, many women find satisfaction in a new career or in undertaking voluntary activities in which they can employ their experience with children. This hospital 'granny' is amusing a young patient with an injured arm.

Above: The process of ageing is not universal to all forms of life. When the working parts of these unicellular dinoflagellates 'wear out', they merely divide in two. By abandoning the machinery of their cells but duplicating their nuclei, they can start afresh using the instructions held in their nuclear DNA.

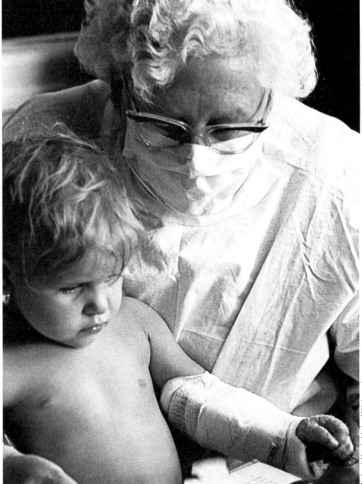

283

Left: An old couple of the minority Chinese Hakka group living in the New Territories of Hong Kong. Marital companionship may compensate for the relative lack of mobility and activity usually experienced by old people and is an important factor in maintaining their health and happiness.

Below: A carving in the Japanese *netsuke* style, called *The Sage with the Toad*. As in most eastern countries, old people are revered in Japan as fountains of wisdom and knowledge. They are often consulted in matters of law, philosophy and religion and appear frequently in Japanese art.

voluntary activities.

For men, there is no physiological change in middle age directly comparable with the female menopause—the true male climacteric, or loss of the ability to father children, does not occur until the 70s at the earliest. The only marked physical change in middle age for men is a gradual thinning of the scalp which may later lead to baldness. This is widely variable in extent, since it is largely determined by genetic factors. The man's sexual needs may alter, especially if he is less interested sexually in his regular partner (whose appearance and attitudes may have altered) or if his career or social activities are changing. As for women, for many men middle age may be a time for reassessment of past successes and future goals and this may bring an anxiety or depressive reaction. But in general it is a less traumatic time for the male than for the female.

Changes in old age

Changes in old age fall into three categories: physical, mental and social. Physical changes result from the decline in the quality and functioning of certain tissues and organs, through the degeneration or loss of individual specialized cells. Loss of scalp hair, which is more obvious in men but also affects some women after the menopause, continues into old age. Muscles become gradually weaker and thinner, causing a general appearance of weight loss and, later, of frailty. Good nutrition and exercise may delay these changes. The bony parts of the skeleton gradually lose their structural protein, leading to a greater liability to fractures. The spongy discs between the spinal vertebrae degenerate and there is a loss of spinal mobility. A real loss in height, from the pressing together of the verte-

bral bones, and an apparent loss, from the tendency to stoop, may lead to a shortening of stature. A protruding abdomen or 'paunch' may be caused by obesity in the abdomen and from a lack of tone in the supporting external muscles of the body frame. A gradual decline and loss of elastic tissue leads to wrinkling and sagging of the skin, notably in the face, neck, and arms.

A loss of elastic tissue in the lens of the eye may lead to *presbyopia* or 'old eye', a decline in the ability to focus on near objects; this requires correction by reading glasses. Degeneration of the cells of the inner ear produces a decline in hearing ability, known as *presbycusis*. Reduced mobility in the muscles and cartilages of the *larynx*, the voice box, can produce either a roughened hoarseness or a high-pitched, piping timbre in the voice. The thin quality of the ageing voice is particularly noticeable in professional singers who, with few exceptions, 'lose their singing voice' after the middle 50s.

Stiffness and slowness of movement in old age stems in part from wear and tear in the major joints of knees, hips and spine, because of the loss of cartilage and lubrication. Poor resistance to extremes of air temperature also occurs because of thinner skin, a slower blood flow and the impairment of the reflexes which make us shiver and our blood vessels contract. All these changes can be speeded up by the presence of *arteriosclerosis*, the narrowing or obstruction of the arteries caused by the degeneration of the arteries' lining. This process diminishes the supply of oxygen and food reaching the body's organs and inevitably affects most people. The degree of its severity varies tremendously from person to person, and is a major factor in deciding

Above left and above right: Queen Victoria was the longest-ruling British monarch, her reign spanning 64 years from 1837 to 1901. Here she is seen (left) at the start and (right) near the end of her reign. At her death she left a large number of living descendants, including thirty-seven great-grandchildren.

Left: In his poem *Father William*, Lewis Carroll expresses his personal views on old age:
'You are old', said the youth, 'as I mentioned before, and have grown most uncommonly fat; yet you turned a back-somersault in at the door—pray, what is the reason of that:'
'In my youth,' said the sage as he shook his grey locks, 'I kept all my limbs very supple by the use of this ointment—one shilling the box— allow me to sell you a couple?'

whether a 75-year-old looks, talks and behaves like a 58-year-old, a 75-year-old or a 90-year-old. Factors which slow arteriosclerosis are mainly of a genetic nature. Factors which accelerate it include obesity, high blood pressure, heavy smoking, sugar diabetes, thyroid hormone shortage, excess animal fats in the diet, and lack of exercise.

The second type of change is mental and intellectual. Mental alertness can be well preserved into old age, but there is a slow and steady decline in reasoning and thinking power. The understanding of new situations and ideas, the ability to co-ordinate actions and functions, and the memory for recent events are all impaired. However, people, places and events from the past are often well recalled.

Emotional changes may also appear.

The elderly person may show a narrowed and restricted emotional reaction to people and events, or may tend to depression and apathy, or may reveal an exaggerated form of previous personality traits—aggression, for example, or bonhomie. In some cases, normal mental processes may be irreversibly damaged by a severe degree of brain arteriosclerosis, or by accelerated ageing of the brain cells. This pathological state, *senile dementia*, is an abnormal form of mental ageing. It is characterized by loss of concentration and drive; confusion about people and time; loss of control over social habits and hygiene; unstable and inappropriate emotions; and a degree of physical and mental dependency that demands constant care.

Several social changes occur in old age. Once a person retires from an active

working life, his goals of ambition and drive towards success may be replaced by a need for personal comforts and satisfaction. He must adjust to the fixed income of retirement, to having a 'non-productive' status, and to having far more leisure time. A decline in physical function and mobility may encroach on the individual independence of a retired person as the years progress. He may have to seek out help from relatives, friends, neighbours and official professional and social services. Hobbies, indoor and outdoor, can be enjoyed and expanded in retirement, and part-time jobs are deservedly popular, too.

The cause of ageing
The ageing process is not well understood, but there are indications that the principal cause of ageing is *cell mutation*. Most cells which die in the body are replaced by the division of other living cells. However, some of these living cells suffer *mutations*, which occur either before or after division. Mutations are caused by exposure over a lifetime to natural radiation from the sun or sometimes by disease or nuclear radiation. They are changes in the structure of a cell's DNA, which controls the functioning of the cell. If a mutation impairs a cell's functioning, it will have an increasing effect as the mutated cells multiply. This will lead to a disorder of the organ of which the cells are the building blocks, and in turn to disorders of the whole body.

Some cells, including nerve and muscle cells, are after a certain age not replaced when they die and this loss can result in a decline in an organ's function. Loss of neurones (nerve cells) from the brain begins in the early 20s and is accelerated in old age by arteriosclerosis.

285

Chapter 4
Food for Health

No one food contains all the vitamins
and minerals essential for a healthy
metabolism, so a varied diet is needed.
Fruit provides vitamins A, B₁, and
C. Niacin, phosphorus and iron are
derived from nuts.

Cheese and fish are *complete* proteins – i.e. they provide a balanced protein diet. Shortage of protein slows down the metabolism, resulting in tiredness and a lowering of barriers to infectious disease.

Paul Kemp

Food for Growth

Man's need for a constant supply of protein to provide for the growth and maintenance of his body has had a profound effect on the course of history. Advanced civilizations become possible only when a steady protein supply has been secured; so long as men have to spend their whole day hunting, or growing low-protein crops, little time is left for creating new tools or new surroundings.

The word 'protein' comes from a Greek word meaning 'of first importance'. This is an apt description. All living cells, animal or plant, contain proteins. Some form the cell's structural components;

Left: Domestication of animals can provide a source of both protein and income. Pigs were evidently an integral part of this rural household in nineteenth century Britain. Once 'fattened', every part of them would be used.

Below: Baron Justus von Liebig, a nineteenth century German chemist and biochemist, made several advances in organic chemistry and the science of nutrition. He was the first to classify foods according to their various uses in the human body and, through analysis of blood, bile and urine, clarified many important biochemical processes. He became famous for his special food for infants and for his nutritive meat extracts.

Left: A Bushman from the Etosha plain of South-West Africa out hunting for antelope. If he is successful he will both eat the flesh and drink the animal's blood. Lacking domesticated animals, such nomadic peoples spend most of their time in the search for proteins—necessarily restricting their creative development.

Below right: Famines occur frequently in parts of the world where farming is not varied enough to offset fluctuations in climate. Inevitably, poor people are the most affected due to rising food costs. Here, sufferers from a famine in India in the nineteenth century ask for help from a better-fed British officer.

others are enzymes, the molecules that catalyze the essential cellular processes such as *anabolism* (energy-consuming synthesis of large molecules) and *catabolism* (energy-releasing breakdown of large molecules). When a living organism is growing, it requires a constant protein supply both for new cellular components and for enzymes. Even when the organism stops growing, such as when a person reaches maturity, the requirement for protein does not stop. This is because living cells are not static, but in a state of *dynamic equilibrium*, in which their components are continuously being broken down and replaced. Components of certain organs, such as the heart, liver and kidneys, have a *half-life* of only ten days—that is, after ten days half of them have been replaced, ten days later half the remainder have also been replaced, and so on. After ten weeks the heart, liver and kidneys are virtually 'new'. Other body components such as those of muscle and bone are more stable, having a half-life of five or six months. A little of the protein which breaks down in the body is reformed into new protein. Some is converted into urea and excreted in the urine, and another part is oxidized and serves as a source of energy. A steady supply of protein is thus required throughout life to maintain the tissues.

Protein in food
Since proteins are found in all living cells, all raw foods, whether animal or vegetable, contain some proteins. Proteins are complicated molecules, consisting of chains of simple substances called *amino acids*, the chains sometimes being

200 or more 'links' long. Twenty-two amino acids commonly occur, but different proteins contain different relative proportions of each amino acid. The sequence in which the amino acids occur in the chain is also variable, and thus an infinite variety of different proteins is theoretically possible. The number used by living organisms is finite, but each type of protein has its own particular properties. Those found in meat and plants are different from those in the human body and may not be suitable for direct use by humans. Thus, the body has to break down the proteins in the diet into their constituent amino acids. This is done by enzymes in the digestive system. The amino acids are then circulated in the blood, from which each organ can select the amino acids required to build the proteins it needs.

Of the amino acids, fourteen, called *non-essential*, can be manufactured by the body, either from other amino acids or from other simple molecules. The other eight, called *essential*, cannot be manufactured by the body and must be directly provided for in the diet. A good diet must therefore contain enough proteins to provide the minimum requirement of these essential amino acids, and also enough extra for the body to be able to manufacture the non-essential amino acids. A protein diet that supplies these needs is called *balanced*. Certain foods, *complete* protein foods, provide this balance and, with the notable exception of the soybean, are mainly of animal origin. Others, called *incomplete*, provide only part of the amino acid requirements, and are mainly of plant origin. This

Left: Combinations in this Z diagram provide a balanced protein diet.

Below: Table of foods containing high protein.

COMPLETE PROTEINS	INCOMPLETE PROTEINS
eggs	powdered skim milk
cheese	wholewheat bread
raw milk	rice
fish	potatoes
meat and poultry	legumes (lentils, beans
brewers yeast	etc)
soybean	corn
wheat germ	

THE ROLE OF PROTEIN IN THE BODY

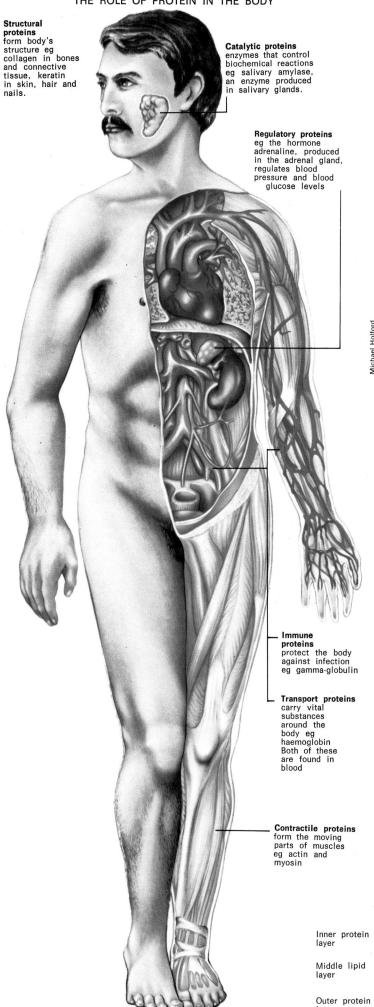

Structural proteins form body's structure eg collagen in bones and connective tissue, keratin in skin, hair and nails.

Catalytic proteins enzymes that control biochemical reactions eg salivary amylase, an enzyme produced in salivary glands.

Regulatory proteins eg the hormone adrenaline, produced in the adrenal gland, regulates blood pressure and blood glucose levels

Immune proteins protect the body against infection eg gamma-globulin

Transport proteins carry vital substances around the body eg haemoglobin Both of these are found in blood

Contractile proteins form the moving parts of muscles eg actin and myosin

Michael Holford

Brian Seed

Above: Ostriches are bred on farms in certain parts of the world for their highly-prized feathers, but their eggs, the largest of any bird's, are also an important product. This woman on a farm at Oudtshoorn in South Africa is cracking open a three-pound egg which contains as much protein as two dozen hens' eggs.

Above: Apart from the cubes of animal fat at centre right, all these foods, including items both of animal and of plant origin, contain appreciable amounts of protein.

Right: Kwashiorkor, a children's disease caused by a deficiency of protein, is clearly marked in these children from Tanzania. It is characterized by a sparseness and lack of colour in the hair, loss of weight, listlessness, and *oedema*, a swelling of parts of the body due to retention of fluid in the tissues.

Left and below: The uses of protein are manifold, both for the whole body (left) and at the level of the individual cell (below).

Dr Maletuloma/London School of Hygiene and Medicine

STRUCTURAL PROTEIN THE CELL

All membranes (orange) contain protein

1 Plasmalemma

2 Mitochondrion

3 Endoplasmic reticulum

4 Ribosomes

5 Lysosome

6 Golgi body

7 Nuclear envelope

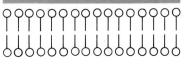

The plasmalemma magnified and stained to show three-layer structure. Outer orange bands represent protein

Inner protein layer

Middle lipid layer

Outer protein layer

Presumed position of protein and lipid in cell membranes

290

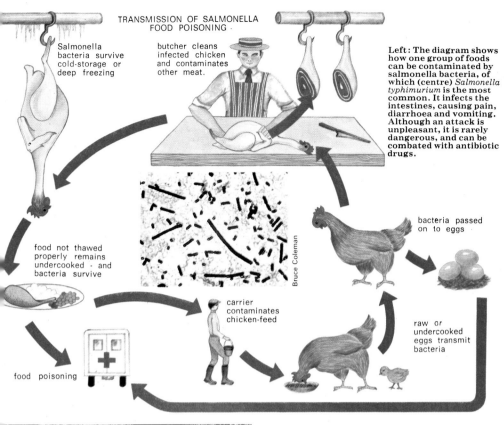

TRANSMISSION OF SALMONELLA FOOD POISONING

Salmonella bacteria survive cold-storage or deep freezing

butcher cleans infected chicken and contaminates other meat.

food not thawed properly remains undercooked - and bacteria survive

food poisoning

carrier contaminates chicken-feed

bacteria passed on to eggs

raw or undercooked eggs transmit bacteria

Bruce Coleman

Left: The diagram shows how one group of foods can be contaminated by salmonella bacteria, of which (centre) *Salmonella typhimurium* **is the most common. It infects the intestines, causing pain, diarrhoea and vomiting. Although an attack is unpleasant, it is rarely dangerous, and can be combated with antibiotic drugs.**

A. Pasieka/ZEFA

Above: Crystals of the amino acid *asparagine*, **photographed using polarized light, which produces colours that vary with the crystal thickness. Amino acids are simple organic compounds containing carbon, oxygen, hydrogen and nitrogen. They combine to form proteins, but are crystalline solids in the pure form.**

Below: Colouring is an important factor in the attractiveness of food. Many people might not find this dyed loaf palatable, although it tastes the same as the white or brown bread they are accustomed to. Similar ideas on what food should look like prompt food processors to dye margarine yellow and peas bright green.

Sunday Times

division is not surprising, since animals, being closer to humans in evolutionary terms than plants are, use similar, but not identical, proteins to those used by humans. Thus meat and dairy products contain a close approximation to the human amino acid requirement.

Balanced protein diets

Quality of protein intake is thus as important as quantity. For example, protein makes up 12% of an egg but 25% of a peanut, yet it is the egg which is regarded as nutritionally superior. In fact egg protein provides such a complete balance of amino acids that all other proteins are measured against its standard. And although the peanut contains plenty of protein, a diet consisting exclusively of peanuts would soon lead to a deficiency in certain amino acids.

Eating meat and dairy products is not the only way to obtain a protein balance, and would prove expensive. If incomplete protein foods are analyzed for their amino acid content, however, certain combinations of foods are found to complement each other. For instance, baked beans and wholewheat bread are both incomplete protein foods, but the amino acids lacking in wholewheat bread are found to excess in baked beans, and vice-versa. Their combination gives a surprisingly complete protein snack—baked beans on toast. The addition of an egg to this produces a highly nutritious dish.

This system for providing a balanced protein diet can be represented on a 'Z' diagram. The four basic types of protein foods—meat and dairy products, cereals, legumes, and seeds—are placed at the corners of a Z. Food combinations joined by any line of the Z will usually provide a balanced protein diet.

This idea is not new. The human race has worked it out on a trial-and-error basis over thousands of years and traditional dishes throughout the world consist of combinations contained in the Z diagram. Many of the well-known dishes of the western world consist of a combination of a dairy product or meat with a

cereal: for instance, the US Thanksgiving dinner of turkey with corn, Italian lasagna with mozzarella cheese, and British roast beef with Yorkshire pudding. Combinations of cereals with legumes, such as beans or peas, (sometimes with a small supplement of animal protein) include Spanish paella, made from beans and rice, Mexican pancakes, made from fried cornmeal and beans, and the typical Chinese meal of fried rice with vegetables and soya bean curd. The typical Indian dish of curried vegetables with boiled rice, dahl (cooked lentils), chapattis (wholegrain pancakes), yogurt and sesame seeds, is a combination of all four protein groups.

Meat is thus not an essential dietary item, and indeed, about half the world's population survives without eating meat. For many this is due to necessity rather than choice, but there are many people who make a conscious decision not to eat meat for ascetic, ethical, religious and sometimes nutritional reasons. These people are of two types. The first are called *lacto-vegetarians*, for although they exclude flesh from their diet, they eat animal products such as milk, eggs and cheese in addition to vegetable foods. This can be an excellent form of diet and is often favoured by top-class athletes. The second type, *vegans*, eat plant food only. It is possible to eat well this way, but since most plant foods are incomplete protein sources, it may require considerable ingenuity and dedication from the vegan to work out a varied yet complete food combination every day.

Protein-deficient diets

Protein deficiency occurs for one of two reasons. It is due either to a lack in quantity of protein, *undernutrition*, or to an unbalance in the proteins eaten, *malnutrition*. Undernutrition often occurs in areas and at times when food is scarce because of famine; malnutrition in communities that eat almost exclusively a single type of low protein crop, such as cassava, without enough supplementary protein to provide a balance.

A shortage of protein produces a slowing down of the whole person, with resultant tiredness, listlessness and susceptibility to infectious illness. In South America, medical teams have successfully treated widespread protein deficiency with a Z mix of cottonseed flour, sorghum and maize, which gives roughly the protein equivalent of milk.

New protein sources

Protein deficiency is widespread in many parts of the world and there is continuing research to find high-quality substitutes for animal protein. A good substitute would alleviate the world protein shortage since animal protein is expensive to produce, in terms of both money and land. Efforts are being made to make edible protein from wool, grass and even coal and petroleum, but these are in the experimental stage. The most successful efforts so far have been in the production of textured vegetable protein, using the soybean as a base. Having little taste of its own, it takes up the taste of whatever it is mixed with—meat, for example. The total world need cannot be met from animal protein alone, so unless artificial protein can be manufactured, the best solution may be to combine various types of plant protein into the most nutritional dishes possible.

The average annual consumption of refined sugar in industrialised countries is an alarming 55 kg per person. The body cannot deal satisfactoryily with concentrated sugar and starch – as they are found in biscuits and cakes – and high sugar diets can lead to obesity and its attendant illnesses.

Food for Energy

The human body needs energy for three purposes. First, it needs energy to maintain its *basal metabolic rate* or BMR; that is, to operate vital services such as running the brain and keeping the heart beating. Second, energy is needed to carry out cell activity involved in growth. Third, it is required for daily activities such as walking, working and playing. The body has created ingenious storage and bio-feedback systems to cope with variations in these needs.

The energy value of the foods from which the body derives its energy is measured in units known as *calories*. The original calorie is so small as to be suitable only for laboratory use. In nutritional work, what is used is the 'Big C' *Calorie*—in fact a kilocalorie, since it equals 1,000 'little c' calories.

Calories are measured in a *calorimeter*, which literally burns food and measures the energy released. This measurement does not correspond exactly to the energy produced inside the body by the same food, but it shows that a low calorie food such as a cabbage produces as little as 8 kcal per 100 grams while a herring, which is a high calorie food, produces over 200 kcal per 100 grams.

Energy requirements

People's energy requirements vary with their size and individual variations in BMR. Some people 'burn' fuel more quickly than others. Calorific needs are related to the amount of lean flesh on the body, not to the total weight, including fat. Average minimal basic calorie requirements are 500 kcal a day for an infant, 1,000 for a child of eight, 1,300 for an

adult woman and 1,500 for an adult man. However, once activity above the minimum is taken into account, the energy consumption varies greatly from 180 kcal per hour with light activity, to 450 kcal per hour with heavy activity such as swimming or mining. Hence a miner doing six hours of actual work would need 2,700 kcal to cover this period alone, to which must be added a further amount to cover the remaining 18 hours of 'normal' living but an office worker might find 2,000 kcal a day sufficient.

Energy can be obtained from almost any sort of food, but foods which contain high percentages of fats and carbohydrates have the highest calorie values. Fat is found in milk, cheese, butter, margarine, egg yolk, oily fish, the fatty part of meat, and in certain legumes such as the peanut and soybean. Carbohydrates are found in cereals such as wheat, rice and maize, root crops such as potatoes, some dried fruits, legumes, nuts, and foods containing sugar, which is pure carbohydrate. A combination of a little of some of these foods will provide a fair part of the daily energy requirement. For instance, a slice of bread will give 80 kcal. When buttered it gives 130 kcal, and if a 50 gram piece of Cheddar cheese is added, the total figure rockets to 350 kcal —15 per cent of many people's needs.

The body can also obtain energy from protein. But protein is used primarily for growth and the body gives this use a priority. Only when there is a surplus of protein, or a calorie deficiency, is it passed to the liver for use as an energy source.

Fats and oils

Fats and oils are highly concentrated energy sources. In addition, since many food flavours are fat-soluble, fats provide much of the palatibility of food.

Fats can be divided into *saturated* or

Top of page: François Magendie, a 19th century French physiologist and the founder of modern pharmacology, was the first man to evaluate the components of foods.

Right: The traditional Christmas pudding is a high energy food. This specimen of about 10 kg would supply the average person's energy needs for over a fortnight.

Below: 'Jack Sprat could eat no fat, his wife could eat no lean. And so between them both, you see, they licked the platter clean.'—a good illustration that 'we are what we eat.' However, neither's diet is well balanced. Jack could have done with some additional calories and his wife's fat diet was deficient in protein.

USES OF FAT-LIKE SUBSTANCES IN THE BODY

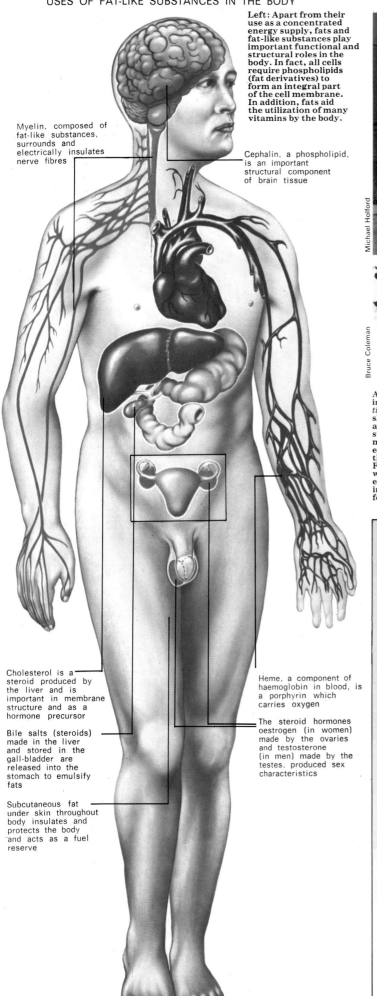

Left: Apart from their use as a concentrated energy supply, fats and fat-like substances play important functional and structural roles in the body. In fact, all cells require phospholipids (fat derivatives) to form an integral part of the cell membrane. In addition, fats aid the utilization of many vitamins by the body.

Myelin, composed of fat-like substances, surrounds and electrically insulates nerve fibres

Cephalin, a phospholipid, is an important structural component of brain tissue

Cholesterol is a steroid produced by the liver and is important in membrane structure and as a hormone precursor

Bile salts (steroids) made in the liver and stored in the gall-bladder are released into the stomach to emulsify fats

Subcutaneous fat under skin throughout body insulates and protects the body and acts as a fuel reserve

Heme, a component of haemoglobin in blood, is a porphyrin which carries oxygen

The steroid hormones oestrogen (in women) made by the ovaries and testosterone (in men) made by the testes, produced sex characteristics

Michael Holford

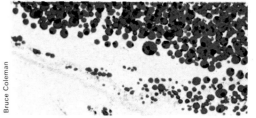

Bruce Coleman

Above: A selection of carbohydrate foods. To provide energy needs, a large proportion of the diet should consist of one of more of these foods, but not so large a proportion that the appetite is satisfied before enough protein and other essential nutrients have been eaten, nor so much as to cause obesity.

Above: Fat stained red in a slice of *adipose tissue* from under the skin, where it acts as an insulator and energy store. One end of a fat molecule, the *hydrophilic* end, attracts water and the other end repels it. Fat molecules cluster with their hydrophilic ends pointing outwards into the watery tissues, forming globular shapes.

Right: A cube of sugar burning and releasing energy. A similar type of process occurs in muscles where glucose is oxidized to water and carbon dioxide, releasing energy for work.

Below: Energy needs vary greatly. Strenuous activity may use up 10 times the energy that is required to sit still.

James Webb

ENERGY EXPENDITURE WITH VARIOUS ACTIVITIES

walking up stairs

skiing

swimming

cycling

dancing

sweeping

gardening

walking slowly

sitting

standing

lying down

kilocalories expended per hour

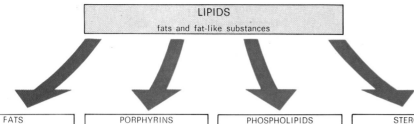

LIPIDS
fats and fat-like substances

FATS	PORPHYRINS	PHOSPHOLIPIDS	STEROIDS
n only carbon, en, oxygen. ts of glycerol tty	Highly complex organic molecules which have a lipid portion in their structure for example haemoglobin, bile pigments	2 fatty acid chains joined to a phosphate group	steroid ring structures from which cholesterol, oestrogen, testosterone are derived

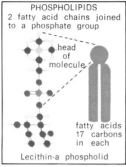

glycerol end of molecule

3 fatty

14 carbons in each

arin-a saturated fat

● carbon
● oxygen
○ hydrogen
○ nitrogen
● phosphorus

head of molecule

fatty acids 17 carbons in each

Lecithin-a phospholid

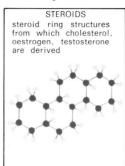

Above: The term *lipids* refers to all the fats and fat-like substances with the common property of being insoluble in water. Fats are composed of a glycerol end and three *fatty acid* chains (of different lengths in different fats). In phospholipids, one fatty acid is replaced by a phosphate group. Other lipids are more complex.

Below: In the developed countries, most people's sugar intake is far too high—partly, as here, because of the many ways of 'dressing it up' to make it sell.

Bottom: For the Xhosa tribe of South Africa, maize is a staple. It provides carbohydrate, but is deficient in certain amino acids.

Brian Seed

Brian Seed

unsaturated types according to their molecular structure. Those containing some double bonds in their carbon chain are unsaturated, those with only single bonds are saturated. Animal fats are mainly saturated. The main sources of unsaturated fats or oils are cereals such as corn, seeds such as linseed or sunflower seed and legumes such as soybeans and peanuts.

Fats in the diet are digested in the small intestine. With the aid of bile salts, an ultra-fine emulsion known as *chyle* is produced. It consists of *chylomicrons*, tiny globules capable of passing into the bloodstream and circulating. About 70 per cent appear to go directly into the blood, from which they may be extracted for use by various tissues.

Other chylomicrons are converted in the liver into glycogen and become a part of the carbohydrate distribution system. Any surplus is deposited in the fatty tissues.

When the body becomes deficient in energy, stored fat is further broken down and enters a cycle of chemical reactions called the *Krebs cycle* which releases energy and furnishes simply molecules from which new cell components needed for growth may be manufactured.

The composition of fats in the blood is naturally influenced by the type of fat ingested in the diet. Excess animal fat can produce high blood levels of *cholesterol* which is undesirable in that it is thought to increase the chances of heart disease. A high cholesterol level can be avoided by replacing animal fat in the diet with unsaturated fats.

Carbohydrates
For most people carbohydrates form the main bulk of the diet, being the chief constituent of the world's staple foods such as rice, wheat, maize and cassava. The simplest carbohydrates are *monosaccharides*, of which glucose is the most important. Glucose occurs in only a few foods such as honey and grapes, together with another monosaccharide called fructose. *Dissaccharides* are formed by the combination of two monosaccharides and include sucrose, better known as sugar, and lactose, which is found in milk. The most important *polysaccharide*, formed by the condensation together of many monosaccharide molecules, is starch, the main carbohydrate component of cereals and root crops. Another important polysaccharide is *glycogen*, the substance built up from monosaccharides by the body to provide an energy store.

Carbohydrates, gram for gram, do not provide as many calories as fats. One gram of carbohydrate provides about 4 kcal while a gram of fat produces about 8 kcal or 9 kcal. However, carbohydrate has the advantage that it can be more readily absorbed and used up by the body.

Starch is broken down in the body into glucose molecules. Some of the glucose is released into the bloodstream, where it plays the crucial role of providing an easily metabolized energy source for the nervous system, and some is rebuilt into glycogen for storage. Any surplus may be converted into fat via the Krebs cycle. A surge of excess glucose into the blood causes fat to be deposited. This subsequently creates a drop in the blood glucose causing a temporary shortage of energy.

Every time mankind has learned to concentrate food the result has been beneficial—until concentrated sugar and starch arrived. The consumption of refined sugar in industrialized countries has risen to a staggering 55 kg per person per year. The results can be gauged from a survey of the health of Africans who lived on a sugar-free diet, compared with members of the same families who had gone to live in mining townships, where they ate a western diet containing upwards of 25 kg of refined sugar every year. Whereas heart trouble, constipation, and varicose veins were virtually unknown in the village communities, the people living in the mining communities contracted these illnesses much as western communities do.

One explanation for this is that the human body can cope with sugar and starch only in a 'dilute' form, that is when it is supplied together with plenty of roughage such as the cellulose in bran. It appears unable to deal satisfactorily with starch and sugar in concentrated form, as in biscuits, cakes or sweet drinks. Too much sugar consumed this way may lead to obesity, from which a whole group of more serious illnesses stem.

Calorie deficiency
If the energy input to the body is insufficient, first weight loss and then starvation occurs. During starvation, top priority goes to supplying energy to the brain, then the heart, the eyes and so on. First, the reserve of glycogen in the liver is released as glucose. Then the tissue fat is broken down and passed through the liver for fuel. Up to this point the whole process is quite harmless. However, eventually the body starts using its protein for energy and literally begins to burn itself up. First to go are the muscles of the limbs, and so on until eventually the vital organs themselves are used and death ensues.

In most countries, high energy foods form the basis of people's diet and are fortunately relatively inexpensive. Only when a very large amount of heavy manual labour is done, or in countries where famine is common, is there any risk of a shortage. In industrialized countries, where manual work has been superseded by machines, there is no shortage at all; if anything, there is a surplus of energy foods. But 'energy' in this sense does not refer to the subjective feeling of energetic well-being. This healthful feeling, in fact, does not appear when the so called 'energy' foods are over-supplied—it appears only when the diet is complete in every respect.

Many people live predominantly on food which has been processed, packaged and stored, with a resultant loss of goodness. The best sources of vitamins and minerals are fresh foods, especially plant foods, milk, fish and liver.

Vitamins and Minerals

Today's concept of the healthy diet dates from the work of Sir Robert McCarrison, who used a whole sub-continent for his laboratory. As the head of British medical services in India at the beginning of the twentieth century, McCarrison observed that certain religious and tribal groups had characteristic health patterns. He saw that the Madrassi tended to be thin, the Sikhs and Pathans to be sturdily built, and so on.

He followed these observations with a scientifically controlled experiment in which the diets of the different groups were fed to rats. The rats developed the same health patterns as the human groups using the corresponding diet. The Madrassi-diet rats tended to be thin, the Sikh-diet rats grew strong, and so on. To extend his findings McCarrison placed some more rats on a diet of typical western refined foods. These rats developed illness patterns identical to those of the poorest of Indian diets.

This discovery that there was a relationship between specific foods and health patterns was an entirely new concept. It had been considered enough that a diet contained protein, fat, and carbohydrate. Now it became essential to examine the tiny fraction of food categorized as 'trace' or 'impurity'. And this fraction turned out to contain the minerals and vitamins without which good health is impossible.

Most vitamins and minerals cannot be manufactured by the body. If they are lacking or undersupplied, one or more of a whole range of deficiency diseases—such as *scurvy*, the scourge of sailors until the eighteenth century—can result. Although treatment can yield spectacular results, a supply of the correct vitamin reducing the symptoms within hours, the after-effects may remain.

Vitamins

Vitamins are a group of organic compounds which are essential for normal metabolism. They appear in various quantities in a variety of foods, but no one food contains all of the vitamins together: hence the need for a varied diet. Vitamins do not appear in large amounts in food, but this is of no consequence since their role is often that of *co-enzymes*. That is, they help trigger chemical reactions, but are often left over for re-use after the reactions are completed.

The vitamins fall into two main groups. The first group, vitamins A, D, E and K, are fat-soluble and so are usually found in the dietary fats. They tend to be stored in the body, making it possible to build up a reserve. The other group are water-soluble and include the vitamin B complex and vitamin C, both of which tend to be excreted in the urine, although the body does retain a small reserve of them.

Minerals

Acting in conjunction with the vitamins are the minerals. A lack of these can produce a similar group of deficiency diseases, which also yield to the simple

Above: A Mexican woman treating a *tortilla* (maize pancake) with limewater. This avoids the danger of niacin deficiency, common when maize is a staple food, since it converts the niacin in maize from a non-absorbable to an absorbable form. Niacin can be manufactured by the body from the amino-acid *tryptophan*, but maize contains little tryptophan and a maize diet must thus supply niacin directly.

Below: A microscope photograph of a crystal of vitamin A (retinol), which is a fine yellow powder in its pure form. Its chemical structure is fairly simple and it can be synthesized for use as a food supplement.

Above: The disease beri-beri is caused by a deficiency of thiamine, a vitamin which occurs in rice husks. This was discovered in 1901 by a Dutch doctor called Eijkman. Chickens to which he fed polished, huskless rice (left) soon showed symptoms of beri-beri, but they recovered rapidly when their diet was changed to include whole, unpolished rice (right).

Below: A table of the more important vitamins, their sources and uses. The vitamins B_1, B_2, B_{12} and niacin form the most important part of the vitamin B complex. They take part in the same metabolic reactions and are commonly found together in food.

VITAMIN	GOOD SOURCES	IMPORTANCE
A Retinol	Fish liver oils, liver, eggs, butter, milk, green leafy vegetables, carrots, tomatoes, yellow fruits. The body can make Vitamin A from carotenes, the yellow pigments in fruits and vegetables.	Essential for normal functioning of the retina. Lack leads to inability to see in dim light, and diseases of the skin and internal body linings. Children with insufficient vitamin A do not grow properly.
B_1 Thiamine	Yeast, meat, wheatgerm, nuts and beans, milk. Milled wheat and polished rice contain only 30% of the thiamine in the whole grain, but white bread is often fortified.	Essential for oxidation of glucose in the body to give steady energy release. Also needed for growth and nerve and muscle functioning. Lack leads to beri-beri, with muscle wasting, partial anaesthesia, loss of appetite, swelling of the limbs.
B_2 Riboflavine	Wheatgerm, liver, meat, milk, green vegetables, eggs.	Essential for food metabolism. Lack has ill effects on eyes, tongue, mouth.
Nicotinic acid (Niacin)	Yeast extracts, meat, poultry, fish, nuts, corn treated with alkali. Also manufactured by intestinal bacteria.	Needed for growth. Deficiency results in pellagra, characterized by inflammation of skin and mouth and mental disorders.
B_{12}	Raw liver, meat, fish, milk.	Essential for red blood cell formation.
C Ascorbic acid	Citrus fruits, currants, fresh vegetables, milk. Much is lost in preparation and cooking.	Essential for healthy condition of bones, teeth, blood vessels. Lack leads to scurvy, characterized by spongy and bleeding gums.
D Calciferol	Cod-liver oil, cream, egg yolk and liver. Also formed from Vitamin D precursor when sunlight falls on the skin.	Concerned with growth of bones and teeth. Can only function with sufficient calcium and phosphorus. Deficiency in children leads to abnormal bone formation called rickets.
E Tocopherol	Wheatgerm oil, soybeans, liver, butter, egg yolk, oatmeal.	Necessary for normal reproduction, and metabolism of muscle tissue. Lack can lead to sterility and muscle wasting.
K	Green leafy vegetables, pig's liver, eggs and milk. Also manufactured by intestinal bacteria	Essential factor in blood coagulation. Rarely lacking in adults, but newborn babies may suffer bleeding since they lack the bacteria which make the vitamins.

treatment of a supply of the correct mineral. But most of the required minerals appear so widely in foods that only three are commonly in short supply —calcium, iron and iodine.

An adult body contains about 1,300 grams of *calcium*, mainly in the bones and teeth. Calcium is also important in the nervous system. A satisfactory daily supply appears to be 400 milligrams and, for this mineral to be deposited, a supply of vitamin D is also necessary. Since one of the main sources of vitamin D is the effect of sunlight on a vitamin D precursor in the skin, the deficiency disease of *rickets* (soft bones) is most prevalent in industrial slums of cold countries where clothes, buildings and pollution block sunlight from reaching the skin.

Iron is an essential component of blood, being necessary for the formation of *haemoglobin*. A minimum daily intake appears to be about 12 milligrams. In its absence, especially during adolescence, pregnancy or the menstrual period, the deficiency disease *anaemia* (lack of haemoglobin) may appear.

Iodine forms part of a substance secreted by the thyroid gland. Its lack in the diet leads to *goitre*, an enlarged condition of the thyroid. Iodine is found in all sea foods, including kelp. Central areas of continents are known as 'goitre belts', because of the lack of iodine in the crops and the scarcity of seafood, but the use of iodized table salt can overcome such shortages.

The best sources of both vitamins and minerals are natural, fresh foods, especially plant foods, milk, fish and liver.

When mankind learned to preserve and store food against winter hunger, a great advance in civilization became possible. However, by the middle of the twentieth century this technique had begun to backfire. During the preserving of food some of its nutrient value is lost, while still more is lost during storage, especially the vitamin content. Now, large sections of the world's population live almost wholly on packaged, stored food—to which the increase in degenerative diseases is thought to be related.

Two major worldwide foods, wheat and rice, are also commonly subjected to processing which is nutritionally disastrous. Wheat grains undergo high-speed milling which removes the husk and the wheat germ in order to produce white flour. The effect of this is to lose the roughage of the husks, some of the protein, and some of the vitamin B complex and vitamin E contained in the wheat germ. Some doctors think removal of the roughage causes *diverticulosis*, a disease of the intestine, which can be treated by the simple administration of two spoonfuls daily of the bran removed from the wheat by the milling. A similar milling process is used for de-husking and 'polishing' rice, a staple in most oriental countries' diets. This removal of the husks can virtually eliminate the B-complex vitamins from the diet, causing the widespread disease *beri-beri*.

Excessive and badly managed home cooking is also a potent destroyer of nutrients. In the case of vitamins C and E, losses can reach as high as 90 per cent. Cooking of foods containing these vitamins should be as gentle and as brief as possible.

The increase in consumption of vitamin-deficient foods has stimulated the

A. F. Kersting

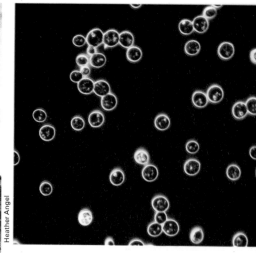

Heather Angel

Victoria & Albert Museum

Above: The Roman baths at Bath, England. Water is discharged from a hot spring at Bath at the rate of half a million gallons every day. The health-giving properties of the minerals in these waters have long been known. The waters are drunk as a medicine as well as being bathed in.

Below: A table of the more important minerals. Some, like cobalt, are required in tiny amounts, but five grams each of sodium and potassium are required daily.

Above right: Yeast cells viewed in polarized light. Yeast and yeast extracts contain plenty of the vitamin B complex and iron. Yeast is also a good protein source and can be grown as a protein supplement for humans and animals.

Right: A dish decorated with flowery symbols in the Chinese *yin* style. Chinese superstition holds that nutrients from the flowers are absorbed by food in the dish and so consumed by whoever eats the food.

MINERAL	SOURCES	IMPORTANCE
Calcium	Milk, egg yolk, shellfish, green leafy vegetables.	Constituent of bones and teeth; required for blood clotting, hormone synthesis, membrane integrity and muscular contraction.
Phosphorus	Dairy products, meat, fish, poultry and nuts.	Needed for normal bone and tooth structure. Plays an important part in muscle contraction and nerve activity, and is a component of many proteins and enzymes, ATP, RNA and DNA.
Iron	Meat, liver, shellfish, egg yolk, legumes, nuts and cereals.	Essential component of haemoglobin (which carries oxygen to cells) and of coenzymes involved in ATP formation.
Iodine	Iodized salt, seafood and cod liver oil.	Required by thyroid gland to synthesize thyroxin, the hormone which regulates metabolic rate.
Copper	Eggs, wholewheat flour, beans, beets, liver, fish, spinach and asparagus.	Required, with iron, for synthesis of haemoglobin. Component of the enzyme needed for melanin pigment formation (skin colour).
Sodium	Widespread in foods. Table salt is sodium chloride.	Necessary for conduction of nerve impulses. Strongly affects the osmotic movement of water, for example in kidney tubules.
Potassium	Contained in most foods.	Functions in transmission of nerve impulses and muscular contraction. Required for growth
Chlorine	Contained in most foods, also table salt.	Important in the acid-base balance of blood, water balance and formation of hydrochloric acid in the stomach.
Magnesium	Contained in most foods.	Required for the normal functioning of muscles and nerves. Participates in bone formation, and is a constituent of many enzymes and coenzymes.
Sulphur	Beef, lamb, liver, fish, poultry, eggs, cheese, beans.	Component of many hormones (eg. insulin) and vitamins (eg. thiamine) so is involved in the regulation of various body activities. Also a component of the contractile protein of muscle.
Zinc	Widespread in foods.	Important component of some enzymes. Needed for normal growth, and insulin formation.
Manganese	Traces present in green plants.	Activates several enzymes. Needed for haemoglobin synthesis. Required for growth, reproduction and lactation.
Cobalt	Traces present in green plants.	As part of vitamin B_{12}, is needed for red blood cell formation.

Left: Lime juice being distributed to prevent scurvy aboard the British ship 'Alert' during an Arctic voyage. Scurvy, caused by a lack of vitamin C, frequently affected whole crews on long voyages, and was fatal for many. The nickname 'limey', applied to the British, came from some British captains' insistence on their crews drinking lime juice as an anti-scorbutic, a measure that was rarely popular.

Right: Although what could be scurvy appears in ancient records, the first definite accounts of it are found in descriptions of the crusades, for instance the crusade to Tunis in 1269 by Louis IX (Saint Louis) of France, which is depicted here.

Ronan

Mary Evans

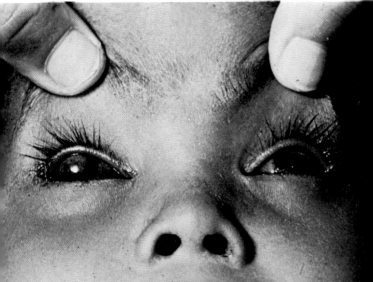

James Webb

Left: A child suffering from serious vitamin A deficiency. The opaque cornea of his right eye indicates blindness. This deficiency also harms skin and teeth, although in mild cases only night blindness is experienced. When rice and cassava, which contain no vitamin A, are staple foods, the deficiency is common.

Below: A Japanese boy suffering from Minamata disease, which affected several hundred people in the fishing community of Minamata in the 1950s. The cause was traced to mercury outflow from a nearby industrial plant into Minamata bay. The mercury was converted into an organic form, became a constituent of marine plants in the bay and was concentrated in fish which ate the plants. When humans ate these fish, the organic mercury built up in them, causing nerve disorders, seizures and death.

production of vitamin and mineral supplements, created synthetically in laboratories or concentrated from extracts of the natural food source. The virtues of the synthetic products are that they are often more stable, more exact in their dosage, and cheaper. However, natural nutrients may be better absorbed by the body. This improved absorption is thought to be due to *intrinsic factors*—substances which accompany a vitamin in its natural source. Vitamin C, for example, is always found accompanied by the intrinsic factors *rutin* and the *bioflavonoids*. Reliable manufacturers recommend that supplements such as vitamin C pills should be taken only at mealtimes so that there is a better chance of the correct intrinsic factors being available to improve the vitamin absorption.

Food contamination

Since the human body can be so beneficially affected by chemicals in the small amounts that are provided by vitamins and minerals, it follows that the reverse effect can take place if even small amounts of unwanted chemicals are absorbed from foodstuffs.

The first source of food contamination is from additives used in the food industry to preserve or improve the appearance of products. Each country has its own regulations to control food additives since, in the past, some have been proved to be *carcinogenic* (linked to cancer).

The second source of contamination arises from industrial pollution, particularly from the contamination of the environment with organochlorine pesticides such as DDT. Pesticides used on fields drain into estuaries and lakes where some fish have their breeding grounds. For instance, the salmon in Lake Michigan became uneatable after organochlorine sprays had drained into the lake. The average daily human consumption of DDT is estimated at 0.10 micrograms. The amount considered harmful is upward of 10 micrograms daily per kilogram of body weight, since the human body is better able to rid itself of these chemicals than are fish.

Modern food processing means that man has simply substituted one set of problems for another. But certain basic rules can still produce healthy eating. As far as possible, fresh food, plenty of mixed vegetables and fruit, and a supply of complete protein should be eaten. Also, the diet should include a plentiful supply of roughage, and excess sugar and starch consumption should be avoided.

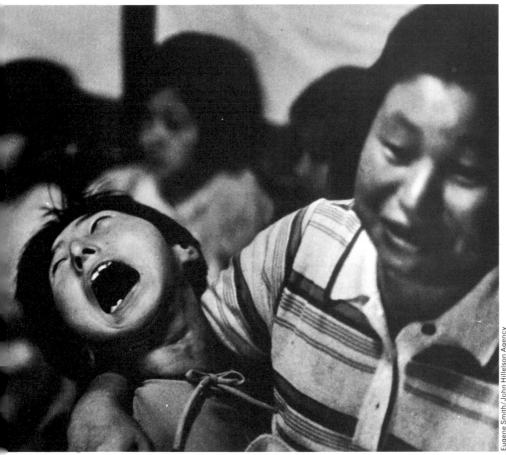

Eugene Smith/John Hillelson Agency

Fitness

Fitness, in its most general sense, is the ability to cope with one's environment. For primitive man, fitness was essential for survival since it was required to escape predators, obtain food, combat illness and endure adverse climatic conditions. Primitive man remained fit for two reasons. First, unfit individuals died young and did not reproduce; hence, only 'fit' genes passed on to the next generation—'the survival of the fittest'. Second, the necessity to hunt prey for food required a great deal of physical activity, which promoted fitness.

By contrast, among people living in the industrialized world, physical fitness is the exception rather than the rule. Food, transport, shelter and treatment for illness are all easily bought as long as one has a source of income from a job, from one's family or in some cases from the state. Most jobs neither require nor promote physical fitness. Only for those individuals whose occupations involve strenuous physical activity, such as miners or professional footballers, is fitness essential.

However, in the long run, fitness is a valuable asset. The fit person is better able to resist illness, cope with stress, and enjoy activity than the unfit person, and is likely to achieve a greater sense of well-being. Fitness is indeed admired, as can be judged by the enthusiasm with which the Olympic Games and other exhibitions of physical ability are watched, and the adulation that is poured upon sporting champions. Many people regard fitness as attainable only by a dedicated minority through gruelling exercise, but this is a misconception. Fitness can be achieved without the need for several hours of training daily—for many, a reasonable level of fitness could be obtained merely by giving up detrimental habits such as smoking.

Components of fitness

Fitness is not a single attribute, but a complex combination of various factors. These factors are developed to various extents in different types of athlete. For instance, a weightlifter has well-developed muscular strength, a gymnast rates highly on joint flexibility and agility, while a marathon runner relies on efficient respiration and muscular endurance. These various factors are interdependent: no one factor can reach its optimum unless the other factors are also at an efficient level.

The central component of fitness is the performance of the muscles and joints. In the human body there are more than 600 muscles, groups of which work together to enable us to walk, stand, sit, run, look around, chew food and carry out all other types of physical activity. The performance of a muscle depends on two factors, *strength* and *endurance*. Strength is a measure of the maximum force a muscle can apply in one action, and there are two types: *isometric* strength, the force applied against a fixed resistance, and *isotonic* strength, the force applied through the full range of movement of the muscle. Both kinds can be seen in arm-wrestling. To begin with, as the opponents' arms lock

Above: Two peppered moths, *Biston betularia*, resting on lichen-covered bark. In this particular environment, the darker, *melanic*, moth is the less fit, since a predator could spot and catch it more easily than its camouflaged companion. However, on a darker background, the melanic moth might be considered the fitter of the two.

Right: Russian athlete Juriy Zurin receiving oxygen after a 5000 m race in Mexico City, where oxygen in the air is eight per cent less than at sea level. In this situation, athletes cannot obtain enough oxygen during a long race, with the result that a severe oxygen debt occurs, requiring immediate treatment.

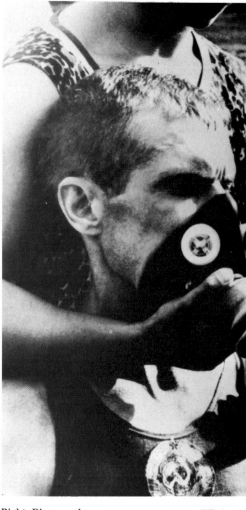

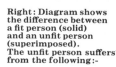

motionless against each other, isometric strength is being applied. When one person starts to force his opponent's arm to move downwards, isotonic strength is being applied. The two factors are partly independent. Isometric strength is directly proportional to the number of fibres in the muscle, while isotonic strength, since it involves movement, is also dependent on the efficiency of the relevant joint or joints.

Muscular endurance is the ability of a muscle to go on working over a period of time. It relies on the efficiency with which the muscle uses its energy reserves as much as on sheer muscle size, but strength and endurance are closely interrelated. A muscle capable of a maximum force of 50 kg will go on working longer against a resistance of 10 kg than will a muscle that has a maximum force of 20 kg.

In most joints of the human frame, the bone ends are prevented from rubbing against each other by a lubricant-filled sac, the *synovium*, and also by a gristly material called cartilage on the bone ends. Stability of the joints is achieved by means of *ligaments*, strong bands of fibrous tissue binding the bones together, as well as by the muscles and tendons. In a fit person, the synovium and cartilage are in good condition and function efficiently to lubricate the joint, and the ligaments are strong and elastic enough to allow a full range of movement of the joint without the risk of undue strain or injury.

As well as the muscles that work the joints of the skeleton, the internal muscles must also be in good condition. The heart, for example, which is regularly

Right: Diagram shows the difference between a fit person (solid) and an unfit person (superimposed). The unfit person suffers from the following:-

1 Effects of ageing, such as balding, are speeded up.

2 Drooping head due to bad posture and reduced feeling of well-being.

3 Weak back and shoulder muscles lead to rounded shoulders and back pain.

4 Bad posture reduces chest capacity, and internal muscle weakness prevents lungs being fully emptied, so that they cannot work at full capacity. Respiratory efficiency is thus reduced.

5 Weak heart muscle has to work harder to provide the same blood flow as a fit person's heart. Clotting time of blood is increased, adding to the chances of arteriosclerosis.

6 Sagging abdomen due to weak muscles and poorly balanced diet.

7 Excess fat results in the body carrying an extra burden, which can strain the hip and knee joints.

8 Reduced joint flexibility through lack of exercise and weakness of associated muscles.

9 Atrophied leg muscles.

10 Flat feet, caused by obesity overstretching the ligaments in the foot.

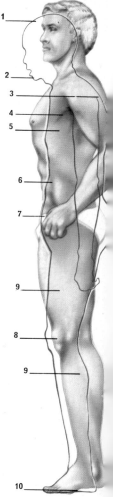

Left: *Satan Rousing the Rebel Angels*, by the 19th century English artist William Blake. Satan is here depicted as the epitome of fitness with his ideal male form—a perfectly proportioned structure, well-defined muscular development and a fine sense of balance.

Right and below: A Polish athlete having his fitness tested at the Institute of Sports Medicine in Warsaw. Three electrodes are taped to his chest which pick up electrical changes in his heart and monitor his heart beat. He then does a standard amount of exercise, such as a 400 metre run. After a pause, the electrodes are connected via a lead to a machine (below) that records the small electrical currents from the electrodes on a graph, called an electro-cardiogram. This shows the rate of his heart beat. The speed at which this rate decreases is a measure of his circulo-respiratory fitness. Any abnormality in heart functioning is easily recognizable on the electrocardiogram, so it can also be used as a diagnostic tool.

Left: An eighty-year-old Hungarian gymnast gives a display of strength and agility. Although the ageing process leads to a gradual decrease in muscular, respiratory and nervous performance, regular exercise can delay or slow down the changes, allowing an octogenarian to perform feats of which many teenagers are incapable.

contracting throughout life, must remain strong to keep the blood flowing round the body. If the heart stops, even for a few minutes, death can result. It therefore needs exercising, normally best done by exercising the rest of the muscular system. Similarly, the smooth intestinal muscle acts to move liquified food along the intestinal tract, while the bowel muscles act to excrete waste. 'Fitness' implies the correct action of these muscles too.

Energy supply

Muscles cannot work without an efficient supply of energy. This is supplied by *glycogen*, a carbohydrate like starch which is stored in the muscle and acts as a fuel. As the glycogen is broken down, first to glucose and ultimately to carbon dioxide and water, considerable amounts of energy are released. Under normal conditions glucose is broken down in many small steps and through many intermediate compounds, notably *pyruvic acid*, to release the energy needed to work the muscles. The process (respiration) requires oxygen and this is supplied by the blood which picks it up in the lungs

At times of extreme exertion, however, the bloodstream may not be able to supply oxygen fast enough for normal respiration to supply all the muscles' energy requirements. When this happens, pyruvic acid is converted to *lactic acid*, a reaction which does not require oxygen, and this allows the breakdown of glucose to continue, with release of energy. This process, known as *anaerobic respiration*, can last for only a limited period, for the lactic acid must eventually be broken down by oxidation in the normal way.

Anaerobic respiration can be seen in a sprinter, who may not take a breath during a 100-metre dash. He quickly builds up an *oxygen debt*—an excess of lactic acid in his muscles and blood-stream. The lactic acid in the blood acts on brain centres to increase respiration and heart rate, thus supplying oxygen at a faster rate to oxidize the acid. Hence the sprinter will find, after his dash, that his heart rate and depth of breathing are greatly increased.

The amount of work and the length of time for which the muscles can perform depends on the efficiency of the heart and lungs in supplying oxygen. This is called *circulo-respiratory efficiency*. A fit person has a greater lung capacity and a stronger heart than an unfit person, and his energy reserves are more efficiently metabolized—that is, his work output for a set amount of energy input is greater because of improved function-ing of his metabolic systems. It has been calculated that the average person is only about 20 per cent efficient. The other 80 per cent of his energy input is not turned into useful work, but is lost as heat. On the other hand, very fit people may achieve 50 per cent efficiency —a better performance than that of many man-made machines.

Another important component of fitness is the performance of the nervous system. Nervous impulses initiate muscle activity. Co-ordinated movement, agility and quick reactions all depend on the correct and integrated functioning of the nervous system.

The fit and the unfit

Variations in fitness are due either to variations in potential fitness or to impairment of its components. Even if all people were as fit as possible, their physical abilities would not be equal since potential fitness is limited by factors such as age and sex. The ageing process decreases the efficiency of the whole body, but different aspects of fitness reach peak potential at different ages. Speed is greatest in the early twenties, strength in the late twenties, and endurance improves up to middle age. The different distribution of muscle and fat on men and women imparts different types of fitness to the two sexes.

Below: The siege of the castle of Mortaigne, in the French province of Poitou, which was held by the English during Richard II's reign. In medieval times, fitness often meant 'fighting fitness', the ability to survive such a battle.

Right: An 'Apparatus designed to afford the advantages of mountain climbing without leaving one's apartment.' Exercise on this type of machine probably improved the heart, lungs and leg muscles, despite its tediousness.

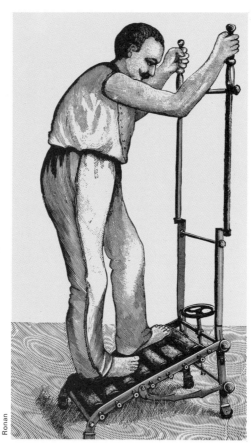

Ronan

SPORT AND FITNESS

● considerable effect
◗ some effect

■ cardiovascular and respiratory performance
■ muscular endurance
□ strength
■ power
□ agility

SOLO ACTIVITIES	cardiovascular and respiratory performance	muscular endurance	strength	power	agility
archery		●	◗		
bicycling	●	◗	◗		
canoeing	●	◗	●		
gymnastics			●	●	
hiking	●	◗			
running	●	◗			
sculling	●	●	◗		
skipping	●	●			
skiing	●	●	◗		
swimming	●	●	◗		●
TEAM SPORTS					
basketball	●	●			●
hockey	●	●	◗		●
rowing	●	●	●		●
soccer	●	●	●		●
volleyball		◗			●
OPPONENT SPORTS					
badminton	●	◗			●
bowling		◗			
golf	◗				●
tennis	●	◗			●
skating	●	●	◗		●
skiing	●	●	◗		

British Museum

Women are constitutionally fitter—they are better at withstanding extremes of environment, and have a longer life expectancy. Men are specifically fitter in terms of muscular power and speed.

Fitness depends on so many components that it may be impaired by a wide variety of causes. Muscles, like many other organs, become less efficient if not frequently used. They tend to atrophy; that is, they become smaller and weaker and respond less rapidly to nervous stimulation. Weak muscles 'complain' and become stiff after exercise has been taken by someone normally inactive.

Like muscles, joints must be used regularly to remain functional and strong and to prevent injury to the lubricating system. This may occur with increasing age in the weight-bearing joints of hips and knees, when the cartilage may be damaged, and the synovium may degenerate, leading to painful and restrictive arthritis.

Anything which reduces the reserve capacity of the lungs or heart impairs fitness. This may occur as a result of a lung disease, such as bronchitis, an inflammation of the air tubes. Smoking helps to cause and worsen bronchitis. Tobacco smoke also produces carbon monoxide, which is a potential poison, weakens the heart, and is taken up by blood haemoglobin in preference to oxygen, thereby reducing the quantity of oxygen available to the tissues. No-one who smokes is completely fit.

An unbalanced or inadequate diet can also impair fitness. Malnutrition produces weak muscles, though this is not often seen in developed countries, where an excess intake of food, leading to fat deposition, is the main problem. Excess fat affects the action of muscles and throws a greater strain on certain joints. The liver, which controls the metabolism of glucose and glycogen, may be impaired by fat deposits or by excessive alcohol intake, resulting in reduced efficiency of the glucose supply to the muscles. An unbalanced diet combined with too much alcohol may also lead to inadequate nerve functioning.

Finally, fitness or the lack of it affects the way the individual feels in himself. An unfit body produces many aches and pains and this may lead to an unfit state of mind—often displayed in irritability, anxiety and introspection about health. This in turn may lead to excessive indulgence in food, tobacco or alcohol—and possibly to the development of physical and psychological illness which could have been avoided by keeping fit.

Left: A chart showing the effect of different activities on components of fitness. *Power* is a measure of the amount of work the muscles can do in a certain time, while *strength* is the instantaneous force the muscles can produce.

Above, below and below right: Three varieties of fitness. Mr Paul Grant (above) prepared himself for the 1972 Mr Universe contest by lifting weights for three hours every day for several years. He also swallowed a daily total of 624 pills. During a bath in the Ganges river, a Brahmin yogi (below) performs *pranayama*, a conscious control of the breathing which improves the economy of respiration and other bodily systems. At the 1976 Olympics, Nadia Comaneci (below) was the first gymnast ever to be given a perfect score by the judges for her performance on the assymetric bars. Here we see a display of her agility on the floor.

Daily Telegraph Colour Library

Paolo Koch

Don Morley/Allsport

303

Exercise

The importance of exercise in the maintenance of both physical and mental efficiency has been recognized throughout history, and has often been encouraged by states, often to keep their citizens in a state of military readiness. In the Greek state of Sparta for instance, children from the age of seven would undergo an education that consisted largely of physical exercise, with the arts and literature taking a subordinate role. In medieval England, regular archery practice was obligatory for the male population, in order to preserve England's military monopoly with the longbow.

In the twentieth century, regular exercise is still encouraged, and sometimes enforced, in schools, since it is seen as being beneficial to health and providing an enjoyable release of energy. For many people, however, leaving school provides a welcome relief from the 'P.E. teacher', and as this often coincides with the beginning of a sedentary job, regular exercise is often discontinued or severely curtailed. The prevalence of inactive use of leisure time, exemplified by the popularity of spectator sports and television, may contribute to a vicious circle in which lack of exercise leads to reduced fitness, which in turn leads to a reduced desire to take exercise. This tendency can be counteracted only through regular exercise.

Types of exercise

The type of exercise a person takes in order to improve or maintain his fitness can vary with age, sex, time and facilities available, and personality—he may prefer to take exercise by himself, or with other people. The two main types of exercise are sports, which usually involve a competitive aspect and exercise the whole body, and 'keep-fit' schedules, which involve no competitive aspect and usually develop only particular components of fitness.

The main advantages of sports are that they are more sociable, and provide the competitor with the satisfaction of seeing his efforts rewarded with an improvement in skill. Sports can be divided into team sports, such as football, hockey and cricket, which involve some team cooperation, and individual sports, such as tennis, squash and golf. The individual variety is often favoured by competitive personalities who prefer to depend on their own skill and effort to decide the outcome of a contest rather than relying partly on the efforts of others.

The degree of activity that a sport requires varies and is related to the amount of time the sport takes up. For instance, squash, ice hockey, and rowing are highly strenuous and take place in short bursts of from a few minutes to half an hour. Slightly less strenuous are sports such as tennis and badminton, which last for an hour or more, while cricket, in which games may last for several hours or days, and golf are considerably less strenuous, although requiring an occasional burst of effort. The most suitable sport for the individual depends on the time he has available, and the degree of activity he requires and can withstand. A very busy, but fit,

Left: A dish from the Agora museum in Athens, depicting a wrestling bout. The ancient Greeks encouraged exercise through the Olympic games, traditionally founded in 776 BC. In those days, the games lasted for up to seven days, and included track and field events, boxing, wrestling, and chariot racing. Winners of the games became heroes, and their feats are recorded in art and poetry. The Greek preoccupation with physical fitness contributed to their military successes against the Persians and other invaders.

Right: The southern Nuba of the Sudan believe in a dynamic life-force which can be tapped for the community's benefit through ritual sports. In two villages, this takes the form of fights between young men, who strike at each other with heavy brass wrist bracelets, as can be seen here. Fight rules prevent serious injury.

Right: Workers at the Mitsubishi shipbuilding yard at Nagasaki in Japan doing their daily 'keep fit' exercises. Companies in Japan tend to exert more control than those of western states over the welfare, including the fitness, of their employees. As can be seen from the picture, not everyone is enthusiastic about this. But by increasing physical and mental efficiency the group exercise may contribute to the high productivity generally found in Japanese industry compared with that in other industrial nations.

Below: Joe Bugner, who became British and European heavyweight champion in the 1970s, is seen here improving his strength and aim with a punch-bag. Many regard boxing as a barbaric sport, but it can provide a controlled release for those with aggressive tendencies, as well as a means of getting fit.

individual will favour a sport such as squash, a retired person with plenty of time but reduced fitness may favour golf, while a partially fit person with limited time available may have to find a compromise such as tennis.

'Keep fit' exercises suffer from the drawback that they are somewhat repetitious or boring, and provide little immediate reward for the individual since they develop only pure physical ability and have no skill component. However, they may be the only type of exercise available for the person with very limited time, such as only a quarter of an hour a day, or for people who have just started getting fit after a long period of inactivity and for whom any sport would be too strenuous. 'Keep fit' classes, where a group of people go through a schedule of exercises in unison, are of psychological benefit to individuals who might give up regular exercise at home after a few days. They also add a degree of sociability to this type of exercise. 'Keep fit' exercises are of two types. *Isotonic* exercises involve contraction of the muscles through their full range, and can be used to develop particular groups of muscles. They are useful for increasing joint flexibility and stretching the ligaments, and also improve circulo-respiratory efficiency. For instance, press-ups develop the arm and shoulder muscles, improve respiration and exercise the elbow and shoulder joints. Sitting up to touch one's knees from a lying position is good for the muscles of the back and abdomen and the flexibility of the backbone. Stepping up and down on a bench improves the leg muscles and their associated joints and ligaments.

Isometric exercises, on the other hand, involve the application of force by a muscle against a fixed resistance. An example is an attempt to lift an immovable object, or holding the arms out sideways and stationary. Various types of machine have been devised to provide a means of performing isometric exercises. They are particularly suitable for increasing strength in the shoulder, arm and chest muscles, but do little to increase circulo-respiratory efficiency or joint flexibility.

Exercises are best combined in a schedule in which each exercise develops a particular component of fitness or muscle group. One type of training which does this is weight training, in which bars with weights on either end are used in a series of graded exercises, starting with light weights and gradually building up. Schedules have been devised to exercise all the major muscle regions.

Another type of schedule that systematically stimulates the whole body is part of the physical system of yoga, called *hatha* yoga. Here the emphasis is on gentle physical and mental relaxation, as opposed to exertion, through a series of postural exercises. Some of these postures, called *asanas*, are static and are held for a certain length of time, while others are dynamic, requiring movement of either the whole body or parts of it. Breathing is also important in yoga, the aim being to use the respiratory system to its full extent, with a resultant increase in efficiency and respiratory control. Through the practice of quiet meditation in conjunction with the physical aspects of the system, the experienced yoga practitioner acquires both mental and physical fitness, and

Above: This Indian's balancing ability is his source of livelihood. The development of such ability involves years of practice and much suffering, but the doctrine of *asceticism*, requiring strict self-discipline, may have helped him overcome these difficulties.

Left: 4000 participants set out on the Engadine ski marathon, which takes place yearly at St Moritz in the Swiss Alps. Skiing is a most strenuous sport. When going downhill at speed, the legs have to work like pistons to control the skis on an uneven surface, while pushing oneself uphill is even more tiring.

Below: A good cyclist requires exceptional strength and endurance in the legs. In order to get rid of the excess heat being produced by the calf muscles, the leg veins enlarge to such an extent that they stand out from the legs.

305

1

2　　　　3

3

5

3

6　　　　4

5

5

1. Heat is lost from the skin by radiation and sweat production.

2. Blood capillaries near the skin surface enlarge to enhance heat loss from the blood. This accounts for the reddening of the face.

3. Lungs respond to the greater demand for oxygen and build-up of carbon dioxide by increasing depth of breathing. Ventilation may rise up to 12 times the resting rate.

4. Rate and volume of heartbeat increase to hasten the transport of oxygen, nutrients and waste products by the blood.

5. Muscles require more oxygen. If the supply is not great enough, they can function anaerobically (without oxygen) for a time, but this leads to accumulation of lactic acid (oxygen debt).

6. Liver works harder to convert waste lactic acid to glucose. This maintains blood glucose levels and slows the build-up of oxygen debt.

John Hillelson Agency

Left: Changes that occur in the body during exercise, many of which are brought about by the release of the hormone *adrenaline* into the bloodstream from the adrenal glands. During an emergency, when the body must move fast to escape danger, this occurs automatically as a response to signals from the brain.

Above and below: Cross-country running, or jogging, can provide a chance of seeing the countryside while getting fit. Some (above) find that doing this in a group is more sociable and hurries along the less fit individuals, while British athlete Alan Rushmer (below) prefers to set his own pace during training.

Right: Many people's idea of a holiday is to move from a sedentary existence at their jobs to a sedentary existence on a beach. These German holidaymakers, however, have been jerked out of their inactivity by an enthusiastic beach entertainer, and are taking their partners for a dance around the sandcastles.

Gerry Cranham

indicates a poor level of fitness. People with an index this low who wish to get fit should start off with light exercise in the home and build up gradually to more strenuous forms.

A good way to start exercising is by doing standing press-ups against a chest of drawers at chest height. When about 30 of these can be performed without difficulty, an object 18 inches lower is used, such as a table or a sideboard, and the exercises repeated. Continuing in this fashion the muscles will become strong enough in a few days to start press-ups on the floor. Other types of exercise, such as sitting up to touch the knees, first from lying on a board at an angle of 45 degrees to the floor and then from progressively lower angles, should be performed together in a daily schedule. In this way the hardest of exercises, which appear impossible at first, are within the reach of anyone with determination.

To quantify progress, the pulse recovery index and resting pulse should be measured at regular intervals. These will improve encouragingly. Once the resting pulse is down to 80, and the recovery index up to 25 per cent, one is well on the road back to full fitness and can begin strenuous sports and exercises.

Above: Pupils at the North London Collegiate School for Girls taking some mild gymnastic exercise in 1882. Great physical ability was thought 'unladylike' in those days, but women have since taken an increasing role in sport. Top women gymnasts, for instance, especially those from the USSR and Eastern Europe, became famous sporting figures in the 1970s.

Below: A summary of the factors that promote the occurrence of cardiovascular disease, which accounts for 50 per cent of deaths in developed countries. Regular exercise and a good diet radically reduce the chances of incurring the two main factors, high blood pressure and high cholesterol levels. Exercise can also help relieve other factors such as mental stress.

— mental stress

— high cholesterol levels and high blood pressure

— effect of smoking on lungs and arteries

— overeating and overdrinking

— obesity

CAUSES OF CARDIOVASCULAR DISORDERS

Dangers of exercise

Although sport and exercises are on the whole harmless, certain injuries do occasionally occur. Apart from the risk of cardiovascular strain, specific sports and exercises carry with them the chance of various types of injury. Knee and ankle injuries are common in ball games and cycling, head and neck injuries are common in rugby football and wrestling, while tendon and muscle injuries are common in athletics, tennis (*tennis elbow*), and squash. The simplest kind is a strain, affecting the muscle, tendon or joint, which responds to rest for 48 hours and a gradual return to the sport. This type of injury can be avoided by 'warming up' the muscles and ligaments through a few moderately strenuous exercises before the game commences.

A more serious type of injury is tendon or muscle rupture, or cartilage damage, which may require sophisticated treatment and a more delayed return to the game.

Certain types of exercise also carry with them an environmental danger. Hill climbing, mountaineering, skiing and scuba diving can all be dangerous unless a high degree of training is first acquired. *Hypothermia*, or *exposure*, is not uncommon in these activities, occurring when an accident exposes the individual to bad weather and the body temperature falls to dangerous levels. Anyone suffering from hypothermia, which is characterized by shivering, giddiness, and reduced mental awareness, must be warmed up as quickly as possible. This can be done by immersing the victim in a hot bath, wrapping him in warm clothing, or if nothing else is at hand, by cuddling him.

Most types of exercise, however, can only be beneficial. Much of the benefit is in the increased strength of the lungs and heart. Since these are the organs which most often fail in middle and old age, keeping them in good shape makes sense. A new world of enjoyment, exhilaration and relaxation opens up to the fit person, producing a healthy mental and physical balance.

develops slender muscles, good posture, a supple, efficient body, and a sense of well-being. Yoga is an excellent form of exercise for those who wish to develop all-round fitness, rather than just brute strength.

Exercise for the unfit

For the unfit person, sudden strenuous activity after a long period of inactivity may be dangerous, since it may overburden the heart. Anyone with a history of heart or lung disease should have a medical check-up before recommencing strenuous exercise, and for others a simple test of one's own fitness is a good idea before deciding on a schedule for getting fit. This can be done by measuring one's pulse rate and its recovery after exercise. At rest the heart normally beats between 60 and 100 times per minute, (the lower this *resting pulse* the fitter the person), but with exercise it rises to between 140 and 160 times per minute.

The speed with which it returns to the resting level, called the *recovery index*, and usually expressed as the drop in pulse after 90 seconds as a fraction of the maximum pulse, is an index of fitness. For instance, if the pulse immediately after exercise is 160, and this drops by 40 after 90 seconds, then the fractional drop is 40/160, or 25 per cent. Someone with this index is fairly fit and can begin moderately strenuous exercise without fear of strain or damage. Someone with an index of 30 per cent or more is in very good condition and could undertake the most strenuous of activities. On the other hand an index of 15 per cent or less

307

Obesity

Many citizens of all ages in many countries are obese. A person can be defined as obese if his weight is 10 per cent or more above the ideal weight for his height, sex, age and frame size. This 'ideal weight' is the weight which, statistically, gives the individual his longest life expectancy. The best known tables of these ideal weights are those published by the Metropolitan Life Insurance Company of the United States. Anyone who claims his obesity is due to big bones may find that such an excuse is not valid if he consults these tables, for they take into account frame size—small, medium, or large—as well as age, sex and height. However, most obese individuals do not have to consult tables to know that they are overweight. Their main problem is to discover the cause of their obesity and ways of counteracting it.

Causes of obesity

There are at least five approaches to the problem of why obesity develops in some people but not in others. These different approaches consider different factors: mechanism of fat metabolism; family influences; personality influences; glandular disorders; and social factors.

The first approach involves examination of the nature of fat itself, its production, storage, and movement in and out of the tissues. Fat is not fixed or inert material. Its chemical content of *triglycerides* is constantly being moved in and out of the body cells. This movement and deposition is controlled chemically by a range of hormones, such as *growth hormone*, *noradrenaline* and *thyroxine*, and also by unknown factors. Fat is stored in the body in fat cells called *adipocytes* which are present both in the layers of fatty tissue under the skin and in deeper body tissues and organs.

The number of adipocytes increases steadily in the normal individual from the first year of life up until sexual maturation at puberty. However, constant overfeeding of an infant in the first year of life may increase the number of adipocytes at a more rapid rate, and a similar increase may occur with excess food intake at puberty. This leaves a permanently enlarged number of fat cells for the rest of the individual's life. Obese children and adolescents are hard to treat for obesity in later life as a result of the excess adipocytes. One way to avoid obesity is thus to prevent overfeeding in the first year of life and subsequently through childhood to puberty.

The body lays down more fat if there is plenty of sugar, starch and other carbohydrates available to provide body energy. Conversely, restriction of carbohydrates in the diet reduces the amount of fat laid down. Hence, an unbalanced or high carbohydrate diet, rather than a high fat diet, is the main dietary cause of obesity.

A second way to consider how obesity arises looks at the influence of the family, in both genetic and environmental terms. Obesity often appears to run through a family, down the generations and across brothers and sisters. Research has been undertaken to look for a genetic influence on metabolism which might lead to

Left: Brazilian Agnaldo Galdino weighed a normal 3.5 kg at birth, but more than doubled his weight in each of his first three years of life. He weighed over 35 kg at age three, when most children weigh about 15 kg. Such children's greatly increased number of fat cells, due to overfeeding, may make weight reduction very difficult in later life.

Right: An American housewife preparing a vast quantity of meat pies for her family. The tendency for obesity to run in families is caused mainly by common patterns of diet within the family rather than by any genetic influence. Children become used to the types of food that are provided by their mothers, and if these include excessive amounts of carbohydrate food, obesity will commonly result.

Below: Some people, such as these Japanese *sumo* wrestlers, cultivate obesity for professional reasons. Champion sumo wrestlers weigh up to 170 kg and rely as much on their vast bulk as on strength to push their opponents out of the ring.

obesity, but the only type of altered metabolism that has been found with a possible genetic cause is one which predisposes some individuals to the opposite of obesity—thinness. People under this influence tend to be 'fast burners' in that, however much they eat, the body metabolizes it so quickly that fat storage is barely affected and they remain the same light weight.

The majority of people are not 'fast burners', and as no 'obesity gene' has been identified, it seems that among these people, obesity is mainly caused by overeating, and not by genetically altered fat metabolism. Obesity which runs in families can thus be explained as being a result of social habits and customs within the family—an environmental, rather than genetic, cause. Examples of habits that run in families which may lead to obesity are: heavily sugared tea or coffee drinks; a regular intake of sweets, candies and chocolates between meals; the enlarging of meals with plenty of bread, pie crusts, biscuits, puddings and other high carbohydrate foods; and the custom of eating, or drinking alcohol, on a regular basis to provide hospitality.

Alongside this, a family's income level may influence the tendency of its members to obesity. Sugar and starch foods have long been cheaper than protein foods. People on low or fixed incomes may therefore become obese because carbohydrate food is all they can afford.

A third approach is a consideration of the mood, personality, and mental state of obese individuals. The idea of the 'jolly, fat person', perpetuated by fat

Constantine Manos/John Hillelson Agency

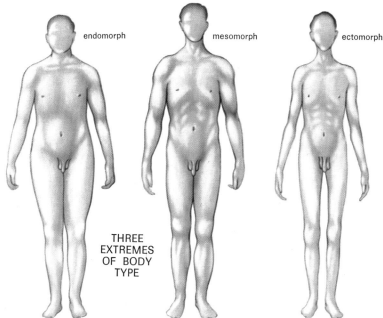

endomorph   mesomorph   ectomorph

THREE
EXTREMES
OF BODY
TYPE

Right: Susceptibility to obesity is thought to be determined partly by body type. American psychologist W. Sheldon classified body types according to their relative content of three variables, called *ectomorphy*, *mesomorphy*, and *endomorphy*, the main characteristics of which are seen here. A person's body type stays constant throughout life and a predominantly endomorphic person, with a rounded and stocky body, is more susceptible to obesity than the muscular and athletic mesomorph or the thin, angular ectomorph. This is thought to be due to differences in the rates of food metabolism by the different types.

Below right: Daniel Lambert, an 18th century jail-keeper of Leicester, led an active life but died aged 39 weighing 336 kg and wearing a waistcoat measuring over 255 cm at the waist. His name became a synonym for immensity in 19th century England, but his British weight record was overtaken in 1878 by a Scotsman weighing 341 kg.

Below: Widespread obesity is not unique to the 20th century. Many people in 19th century England were fat, as seen in this cartoon of 1831. Improvements in road surfacing at this time, and the resulting popularity of stagecoach riding instead of more active means of travel, may have initiated the obesity problem.

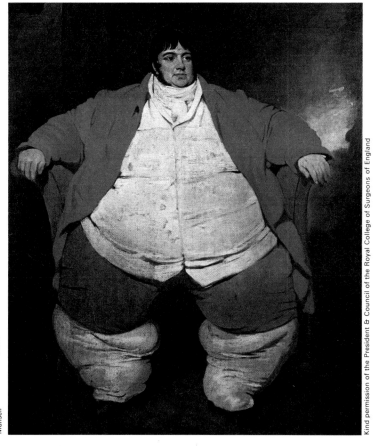

Kind permission of the President & Council of the Royal College of Surgeons of England

"Just room for three insides sir"

Mansell

figures of fun such as Santa Claus, is often inaccurate. Anxiety and depression is common in obese individuals and for such people, food and drink—especially sweet food and alcohol—provide a warm and pleasurable feeling and help to soothe the anxious mind and soften the depressed mood. Food and alcohol may also be used as a substitute (however ineffective) for the stimulus and excitement of life's experiences which may not be available in a boring job or in a monotonous home life. Excess intake of food and alcohol is also seen in emotional problems of puberty and adolescence, and in sexual disturbance in marriage. The risk of obesity is increased when a depressed mood leads to apathy, lethargy, and a reduction in physical activity and energy output.

Many fat individuals claim that the cause of their obesity is their 'glands'. A variety of glandular hormones are known to play a role in weight changes and fat deposition, but glandular disorders, such as Cushing's syndrome (due to excess cortisol production), Stein-Leventhal syndrome (in association with ovarian cysts), or male sex hormone deficiency, are very rare. Their existence in an individual can be readily excluded or confirmed by a careful medical examination, and anyone who claims that his obesity is due to 'glands', without medical confirmation, may simply be not facing up to the truth.

The fifth approach to the cause of obesity is to consider it as a symptom of certain countries and social groups, rather than as a symptom of particular individuals. Different races, societies and occupational groups vary in their susceptibility to obesity, but since there is no genetic influence at work, it must be the differences in life styles of these groups which leads to the differing extents of their obesity problem. For instance, affluent societies of Europe and North America have a major problem with obesity—the result of the exercise-reducing habits of the affluent: driving rather than walking; taking lifts rather than walking upstairs; watching television rather than playing active games. Within the affluent society, particular occupational groups are particularly vulnerable to weight gain, often because their work patterns do not allow a correct balance of food intake over energy output. Business executives are one such group. Business lunches, official dinners, a 309

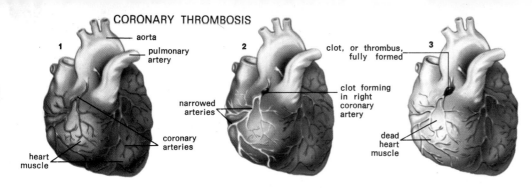

CORONARY THROMBOSIS

1 — aorta
— pulmonary artery

narrowed arteries

coronary arteries

heart muscle

2 — clot forming in right coronary artery

3 — clot, or thrombus, fully formed

dead heart muscle

Above: The course of coronary thrombosis, caused by *atherosclerosis*, which is common in obese people. (1) In normal hearts the arteries are clear. (2) Deposition of plaques, consisting largely of cholesterol and other lipids, narrows the arteries. (3) This leads to formation of a clot, which closes off the blood supply to part of the heart muscle. This then ceases to function, resulting in a heart attack.

Right: A Chinese businessman riding to his office in Hong Kong in a rickshaw, rather than walking. He is tending towards obesity, while the rickshaw operator, whose work involves physical activity, manages to remain slim.

Bryn Campbell/John Hillelson Agency

Popperfoto

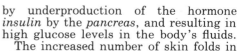

Thomas Hopker/John Hillelson Agency

Left: A Bavarian sits down to a traditional feast of roast pig, pretzels, sausages, and *knodel* (potato dumplings flavoured with liver and bacon). In addition to their immense appetite, Bavarians average 50 gallons a year in their beer consumption. It is not surprising that many of them are obese.

Above: Danish politician Per Haekerrup drinking a beer while on holiday. Alcohol is broken down in the liver to carbon dioxide and water and can provide significant amounts of energy. If a heavy or moderate beer drinker does not expend this energy in active work, he may develop obesity, often as an abdominal 'paunch'.

sedentary pattern of work and excess consumption of high-calorie beverages such as wines and spirits, all combine to make weight maintenance difficult.

Disadvantages of obesity

The adverse influence of obesity on the life, health and welfare of twentieth century men and women has led some doctors to describe obesity as a disease rather than a weight problem. In men, obesity can shorten the normal expectation of life (about 68 years in industrialized countries) by up to 25 per cent in a given individual. The effect on the life expectancy of women is much less significant—but this is counterbalanced by a greater preponderance of obesity-associated illnesses in women.

Direct ill-effects of the increased weight load carried by an obese person, and of his altered shape, include varicose veins, in which the one-way valves in the return blood flow from the legs become incompetent, and osteoarthritis, in which the weight-bearing joints of spine, shoulders, hips and knees show increasing stiffness and discomfort due to wear and tear of the cartilages. Poor balance, with the risk of falling and breaking bones, reduced chest expansion, and increased risk of chronic bronchitis developing are other effects.

Fatty deposits in the blood vessels account for the association of obesity with heart attacks, *angina pectoris* (chest pain), and high blood pressure. There is also an association between obesity and the occurrence of *diabetes mellitus*, a disease involving impairment of the ability of muscles to use glucose, caused by underproduction of the hormone *insulin* by the *pancreas*, and resulting in high glucose levels in the body's fluids.

The increased number of skin folds in obese people can also create problems of hygiene. Excessive sweating in hot weather, and resultant skin irritations under the breasts in women and in the genital area in both sexes, are common.

Social concern over obesity is mainly a matter of fashion. Admiration of the rotund and grossly curvaceous figure beloved of classical painters has given way to fashions in both outerwear and undergarments which are designed for the slimmer individual. Slimness also tends now to be considered sexually more appealing, at least in the West. Emotional aspects of obesity are tied in with this social unacceptability of being too fat. In particular, the obese adolescent may suffer from psychological doubts, and even social rejection by members of his own age group. Older obese individuals may fall into a vicious circle in which obesity leads to anxiety, often relieved by eating, and leading to further obesity.

The understanding of the medical dangers of obesity and the changed attitude of society to fitness has led to a greater interest in weight reduction and control in the affluent countries. The main approach to 'curing' obesity is still a dietary one, but psychological treatment to strike at the causes, rather than the results of obesity may be more effective in the long run. In particular, medical attention to the problems of anxiety or depression and 'weight watchers' groups in which the obese individual can share the resolution of his problems with others, are most beneficial.

Slimming

Perhaps the first person to appreciate the consequences of over-eating and the benefits of slimming was the Greek scientist Hippocrates. In about 400 BC he observed, correctly, that 'those naturally very fat are more liable to sudden demise than the thin'. Slimness, however, is a matter of fashion as much as of health, and therefore it has not always been considered a desirable attribute. For instance, plump women were considered more attractive in sixteenth and seventeenth century Europe.

Twentieth century interest in slimming has grown in parallel with the affluence of developed societies and the sharp rise in the percentage of people in these societies who are overweight. There are two important reasons why people are encouraged to slim, namely to conform to society's concept of the beautiful body shape and to improve health. The dictates of fashion in clothes have placed increasing emphasis on the slimmer figure. This began in styles for teenagers and later spread to adult clothes, crossing both class and national boundaries. Slimming is now also seen to be of increasing importance for health reasons, and people professionally concerned with health and health education have supported this trend.

Effective means of slimming
A person who sets out to slim may be grossly overweight, only mildly above

the ideal weight, or even a normal weight, but in all cases, weight reduction can only be achieved when energy output exceeds energy input in the form of food. This goal is beset with difficulties. For example, if an individual is eating too much because of an anxiety state or depression, then medical help will be required in addition to an effective diet. The person with a 'sweet tooth' may be asked to eliminate sugar and sweets from his diet and must replace these with non-sugar artificial sweeteners. The individual who claims not to eat anything all day until the evening meal, yet cannot lose weight, may not realize that the small nibbles of food taken during the day constitute a definite energy intake.

Any diet which reduces carbohydrate intake or reduces the total calorie intake, including carbohydrate, fat and protein, is an effective means of slimming. The principle of the low carbohydrate diet is that restriction of carbohydrates causes the body to convert fats to energy instead of storing them.

The low calorie diet simply alters the energy balance towards excess energy output instead of intake.

The low carbohydrate diet is most suitable as a mild way of slimming for

those who are not more than 15 per cent overweight. Sheets describing a diet of this type usually stipulate that no more than 120 grams of carbohydrate should be taken daily. Those who do not wish to weigh their food can simply eliminate sugar-containing foods, potatoes, alcohol and flour-containing foods. This diet is often hard to keep to strictly, since the sweetness of sugary foods is missed by those with a sweet tooth as is the 'well-filled' effect of eating starch foods—bread, potatoes, cake, puddings and biscuits. Similarly, alcohol restriction may be difficult for a regular social drinker.

For those who have to eat out as part of their work, a low carbohydrate diet can be observed by avoiding potatoes in any form but welcoming unbuttered vegetables and salads, ordering grills but ignoring fried food, and drinking clear rather than thick soup. Instead of wine, low-calorie long drinks can be taken; if wine is considered mandatory, dry wine is preferable to sweet wine. Extras such as rolls and butter should also be avoided.

For those who do not find a low carbohydrate diet effective, or for those more than 15 per cent over their ideal weight, the alternative diet is a low total intake

Right and below left: Changes in society's concept of the beautiful female body shape are reflected in variations in the style of outer clothing in different eras. The representation (right) of the Roman lady Lucretia, who was considered a beauty in her time, reveals the fashionable body shape prevalent at the time of the artist, the 16th century Venetian Lorenzo Lotto. The model's plumpness is emphasized by the voluminosity of her dress at the arms and hips. In contrast, the tall slim figure of one 20th century symbol of beauty, the model Verushka (left), is emphasized by the skin-tight blue jeans and shirt she is wearing. The desire to attain a body shape like this motivates many 20th century women to slim.

Below: These French ladies are participating in a dietetic cruise. Isolated at sea, they can only eat the closely controlled diet provided by the ship, and are made to exercise to aid slimming. However, the lady on the left appears to be putting rather less than her full effort into this.

National Gallery

Raymond Depardon/John Hillelson Agency

311

ENERGY VALUE OF SOME COMMONLY EATEN FOODS	Kilo-calories in 100 g of food
Bread and flour	
White bread	253
Wholemeal bread	241
Wheatgerm bread	237
White flour	348
Toast	299
Other cereal foods	
Rye crispbreads	318
Cream crackers	557
Cornflakes	365
Boiled rice	122
Sweet foods	
Mixed sweet biscuits	496
Boiled sweets	327
Plain chocolate	544
Milk chocolate	578
Honey	288
Jam	262
Marmalade	261
Sugar—white demerara	394
Ice cream	192
Black treacle	257
Fats and oils	
Butter	793
Margarine	793
Lard	894
Olive oil	899
Suet	894
Dairy produce	
Cheddar cheese	412
Cream cheese	813
Milk	65
Sweetened condensed whole milk	322
Egg	158
Double cream	449
Single cream	189
Meat and fish	
Fried back bacon	597
Grilled beef steak	304
Grilled lamb chop—lean and fat	500
Fried pork sausage	369
Fried sheep's kidney	199
Fried calf's liver	262
Roast beef—lean and fat	385
Roast lamb—lean and fat	292
Roast pork—lean and fat	455
Steamed cod	82
Fried cod	140
Soused herring	189
Grilled kipper	108
Salmon, canned	133
Fruit and vegetables	
Eating apples	45
Bananas	76
Grapes	60
Pears	41
Oranges	35
Dates	248
Dried sultanas, raisins, currants	248
Baked beans	92
Fresh peas—boiled	49
Dried peas—boiled	100
Boiled cabbage	8
Boiled old potatoes	79
Potato crisps	559
Potato chips	236
Miscellaneous	
Peanuts	586
Cocoa	446
Spirits, 70° proof	222
Red wine	67

Note: Figures are based on edible portions.

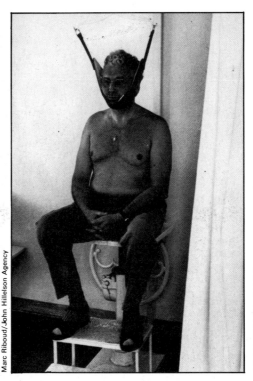

Marc Riboud/John Hillelson Agency

Left: A middle-aged Czechoslovakian having his chin massaged by a vibrating apparatus in an effort to remove his facial fat. There is little evidence that machines like this are of real use in slimming.

Far left: Slimming involves avoidance of high energy foods.

Above: A Spanish mother taking mild exercise with her daughter in an effort to slim her waist. Mild exercise alone is ineffective in weight reduction as it burns off only about 15 grams of fat per hour, but is useful as a supplement to dieting and tones the muscles, producing an attractive appearance.

Right and below: Control over feeding is thought to be exerted by a brain mechanism called an *appestat*, centred around the *hypothalamus*. If an area called the *lateral nucleus* of a cat's hypothalamus is cut, the cat will stop eating, while if another area, the *ventromedial nucleus* is cut, the cat will overeat. This indicates that in a normal cat, the lateral nucleus exerts a stimulatory effect on the appetite, and the ventromedial nucleus an inhibitory effect, the two effects acting as a balance. Overeating may inhibit the effect of the lateral nucleus, causing feeding to stop, while reduced feeding inhibits the effect of the ventromedial nucleus, and stimulates eating. A similar mechanism exists in humans and must be overcome if weight reduction is to be achieved by the slimmer.

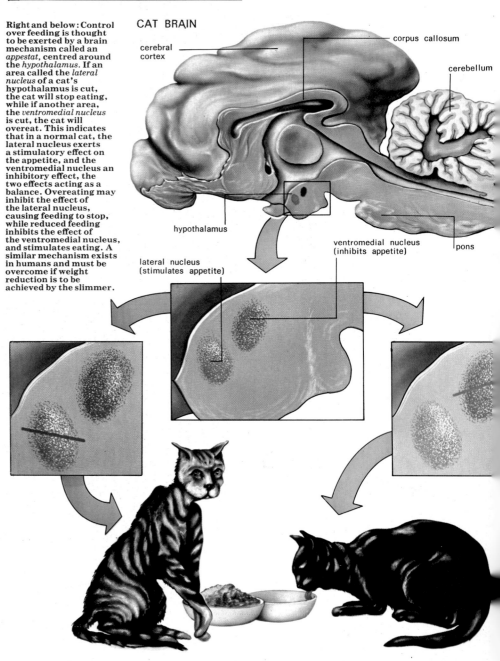

CAT BRAIN

corpus callosum

cerebral cortex

cerebellum

hypothalamus

ventromedial nucleus (inhibits appetite)

pons

lateral nucleus (stimulates appetite)

A CORRECT VIEW OF THE NEW MACHINE FOR WINDING UP THE LADIES

Mansell

Above: The fashion for extremely slim waists, brought about by wearing increasingly tight-fitting corsets, reached its peak of popularity in Britain around the 1880s. This humorous cartoon of the period only mildly exaggerated the situation, since waist measurements down to 33 cm (13 in) have been recorded in women of normal height.

Right: A selection of health foods. There is a common misapprehension that these foods provide a short-cut to weight reduction. They are good sources of vitamins and other nutrients, but slimming requires a reduction in quantity of food intake more than improvement in quality. Only health foods which are low in calories are of use to the slimmer.

Picturepoint

of daily kilocalories—no more than 1000 kcal in a day. This allows a better balance of liked and less-enjoyed foods, but requires periodic adjustment by a dietary adviser, both to avoid monotony and to ensure there is no deficiency of vitamins or an imbalance of protein. For either diet, the slimmer should weigh himself no more than once a week, since daily fluctuations in weight are normal and frequent weighing may give a false picture. Consistent and gradual weight reduction is more effective than rapid reduction in the long run. The aim is to lose half to one kilogram each week.

Grossly obese individuals with a persistent inability to slim with any diet can undergo treatment of a medical or surgical variety. One treatment involves total starvation as a hospital in-patient, with only vital salts, fluids and vitamins permitted. Surgical methods include cosmetic fat removal from the abdomen, splint wiring of the teeth to allow only fluid intake, and operations on the digestive system designed to 'by-pass' parts of the intestinal tract responsible for digesting food products. Each of these approaches has its risks and can be carried out only under strict medical supervision.

Effective slimming is difficult to undertake alone and group support can prove helpful. National and local slimming clubs can help in keeping and adjusting diets. For the well-to-do, temporary success in weight reduction can be achieved at health farms.

Slimming myths

Because of the difficulties inherent in slimming, people are constantly looking for short cuts to fast weight reduction. For example *thyroxine*, a hormone which is known to exert some control over metabolism, has been tried as a weight reducing drug. In a healthy person with a normally functioning thyroid gland, this hormone is ineffective and may produce dangerous side-effects. *Amphetamine* drugs, which act to increase energy expenditure, have also been tried, but have been discredited since they are highly addictive and have not been found to produce weight loss. However three drugs, which can help, on a short term basis only, to support a slimmer are *fenfluramine*, *phenmetrazine* and *diethylpropion*. These do not cause weight reduction directly, but indirectly by acting on brain centres to reduce appetite. The slimmer who depends on drug support

is liable to relapse and gain weight when he stops taking the drugs.

Another alleged short-cut to weight reduction is the so-called 'crash diet'. This involves eating only one or two items each day. Common combinations are bread and butter, banana and milk, grapefruit and coffee, and eggs only. Such diets do produce a quick temporary weight loss because the food, and therefore energy, intake is very low. However, diets of this kind are monotonous, fail to produce proper attitudes to long-term weight reduction, and are often nutritionally unbalanced, producing vitamin lack, excess cholesterol or protein deficiency over long periods. The same holds true for patent formula foods which are not recommended over long periods.

Neither is there any scientific evidence for the use of such substances as cider vinegar, acetic acid vinegar, herbal extracts, vegetable extracts or lemon juice to 'slim a person down'. There is no such thing as a slimming food since every food has some energy content.

Water loss to reduce weight can be induced by tablets or injections, or by sweat loss in Turkish or sauna baths but this is not an effective way to slim since the water is quickly replaced once the individual starts drinking.

Another disappointing approach is the use of hypnosis. The idea of this is that the slimmer is put into a hypnotic trance and given suggestions on subsequent diet. Once out of the trance, the post-hypnotic suggestion is supposed to reduce food intake. Relapse is common even in those subjects who can be hypnotized.

Exercise alone is normally insufficient to produce a steady weight loss, since a great deal of activity is required even to lose a few grams a day. However it can be useful to supplement weight loss through dieting. There is no scientific evidence that passive exercise applied by massage or machines of an automatic nature can help weight reduction.

Contemporary interest in slimming has highlighted a disorder which appears to be a result of 'slimming excess'. The disorder is known as *anorexia nervosa*, and involves persistent aversion to food intake on the part of the sufferer. It usually occurs only in teenage or young adult girls. Over weeks and months, the individual starves herself in the most severe fashion. She insists that she feels quite well but becomes increasingly emaciated, despite the inevitable encouragement to eat given by worried parents, relatives and friends. For those not brought under medical and psychiatric care for treatment, death due to starvation or lack of resistance to infection is a serious risk.

At least half of the sufferers say that the illness began when they started dieting but the condition appears to be caused by personality and psychological factors rather than as an effect of diet. Three out of four individuals with this condition have personality disorders characterized by a need to draw attention to themselves, and a few suffer from serious mental disorders such as obsessional illness, in which the individual feels unable to free herself from abnormal behaviour, or schizoid illness in which, among other symptoms, thought is disordered. All need medical help, psychological support and often hospital care, to help their return to normal weight.

Chapter 5

Thought
and Behaviour

A sports crowd whose thoughts are concentrated on a single event are capable of acting in unison to a considerable degree. The individual may submerge his personality in the atmosphere created by the occasion and the crowd around him.

Human Adaptation

Man is the most adaptable of all animals, being able to live in a great variety of environments. This is not because he has a particularly adaptable body. It is because he has a vast learning capacity, allowing him to protect himself against nature's extremes by using both natural materials from the environment and objects which he himself creates.

The successful exploration of such alien environments as the depths of the ocean and outer space has necessitated subjecting volunteers to conditions of unprecedented severity. But there are limits to the extent that technological innovation can compensate for man's physiological limitations. Beyond them, technological 'success' might spell human disaster.

Heat and cold
The range of man's tolerance to extremes of the environment can be judged from the temperatures of some of the places he inhabits. At one extreme, people live in polar regions where temperatures drop as low as —40°C. These people cannot survive direct exposure to such temperatures, for below —15°C more heat is lost from the surface of the body than the heat produced by the tissues. To survive, man either has to insulate his body by wearing heavy protective clothing or raise the temperature of his environment through the use of shelter and fuel. Eskimos, the most permanent inhabitants of northern polar regions, do both. In addition to their unusual amount of body fat, they protect themselves in seal skins, and have devised an ingenious type of shelter, the igloo, for use where normal building materials such as wood are usually absent. In addition, eskimos have genetically adapted to their environment in that their body shapes tend to be short and rounded. This means that the surface areas of their bodies, compared with their mass, is relatively small, reducing the rate at which their skin surface loses heat.

At the other extreme, people live in tropical or desert climates where temperatures can reach 50°C. In such environments, the body's main problem is to lose enough heat to keep its temperature at the normal level of 37°C, but even people tested at 50°C on a treadmill have managed to prevent overheating. This is achieved by the exudation of sweat, the subsequent evaporation of which from the surface of the skin removes considerable amounts of heat from the body. The rate at which the body can lose heat through sweating depends to some extent on the amount of water vapour already in the air. In humid climates sweat evaporation is far more difficult than in desert climates where the water content of the air is low.

Water lost by sweating, which may be up to 10 litres per day in extreme conditions, has to be replaced, since the loss of more than five litres of water leads to dehydration and damage to the tissues, and the loss of more than 10 litres causes death. Loss of salt from the body in sweat similarly, can cause heatstroke, in which cramps and sometimes collapse are

experienced. A further problem in hot climates is protection from ultra-violet radiation from the sun, which can damage the skin. In the wet tropics, vegetation and cloud cover provide protection, but in desert regions light clothing must be worn.

High altitudes
Climbing high above sea-level exposes man to cold, wind, increased ultra-violet radiation and oxygen deficiency. For every 5,500 m (18,000 ft) rise in altitude, the air pressure, and hence the pressure of oxygen, decreases by half. There comes a point when it is impossible to breathe in enough oxygen for the cells to carry out their normal metabolic functions and an oxygen supply must then be carried.

Above, above right and left: Two groups of people who were forced to adapt to highly adverse conditions. The efforts to survive of the 1912 South Polar exploration party (above) led by Captain Robert Scott were in vain. Having been the second to reach the pole, their return was halted just a few miles from a food depot by severe blizzards. Scott and his companions died soon after Scott wrote the last entry in his diary, seen here. In contrast, many of the Uruguayan rugby team that crashed in the Chilean Andes in 1972 (left) did manage to survive—but only by eating flesh from the corpses of companions killed in the crash.

More than 10 million people live permanently above 3,500 m (11,500 ft) mostly in the Andes and Tibet. It is possible to ascend to higher altitudes for short periods, and most healthy young people should be able to survive at 8,000 m (26,000 ft) for a short time. Complex changes in respiration occur as a sea-level dweller ascends to high altitudes. The rate and depth of breathing increases and is maintained until return to sea-level. This is accompanied by an increase in the amount of haemoglobin in the blood to increase the blood's oxygen-carrying capacity.

Anybody who ascends rapidly to above 4,250 m (14,000 ft) from sea-level without slowly acclimatizing will suffer from acute *mountain sickness* within a few hours. The most prominent symptoms are

Popperfoto

Right: A diver explores a reef near the Canary Islands off the West African coast. One of the greatest problems involved in *free* diving —that is, without an air supply from the surface— was in providing divers with air at pressures that varied with depth. This was solved by the French diving pioneer Jacques Cousteau, who invented the aqualung. This consists of a valve which delivers air from a tank strapped to the diver's back at a pressure equal to the external water pressure.

Below: At the Ames research laboratory in the US, an astronaut acclimatizes to the effect of very high acceleration forces. By enclosing him in a capsule and swinging this round in circles, it is possible to subject the astronaut to high centripetal forces, very similar to the acceleration forces experienced during rocket take-off. In this way, the astronaut's heart, lungs and blood supply can adapt to the conditions expected at take-off and scientists are able to observe the effect on the human body of high accelerations.

ZEFA

Below: British climber Nick Estcourt nearing the summit of a mountain in the Kashmir region of the Himalayas, which contain numerous peaks over 8,000 metres high. At these heights, the air pressure is reduced to about one third the pressure at sea level, making it necessary to use oxygen tanks when climbing for long periods.

Photri

severe headache, nausea, dizziness, weakness and lack of judgement. These begin to subside after two days and usually disappear within a week. By ascending slowly and spending days or weeks at intermediate altitudes, mountain sickness can be avoided. No drugs, hormones or other chemical treatments overcome the need for slow adaptation, or improve performance at high altitudes.

In space

Modern jets and spacecraft have pressurized cabins to protect the occupants from the low pressures outside, and are provided with an oxygen supply. Should the window or door of a modern jet blow out at 15,000 m (50,000 ft), it would take several minutes for the cabin to depressurize completely, probably causing little harm to the occupants as long as oxygen was provided and the plane descended. In a spacecraft, however, the pressure outside the cabin is zero, and sudden depressurization gives the astronaut only five or six seconds to take any corrective action. After this time he will lose consciousness, his lungs will burst, and his blood will begin to boil. This is because the gases inside the lungs will expand very rapidly, and those which are normally dissolved in the blood will bubble out.

Another problem with spaceflight is the effect of accelerational forces on the body. For a rocket to escape the gravitational force of a planet as large as the Earth, the accelerational forces are so high that the astronauts are subjected to ten times the normal gravitational force for short periods of time. This means that the astronaut's body, including his blood, will be ten times heavier than usual, causing a severe strain on the pumping mechanism of the heart. If the astronauts were upright as the rocket accelerated, the increased weight of the blood would cause it to 'pool' around their feet. Their brains would not receive enough blood and they would become unconscious. To overcome this, astronauts lie transversely to the direction of the rocket, but even so, distortion occurs to loosely-attached body organs such as the eyes and heart.

A similar problem will arise if man ever lands on any of the larger planets of the solar system. Planets and satellites within relatively easy access such as the Moon, Venus and Mars all have a lower gravity than Earth's, but Jupiter and Saturn, for

317

Burst lung

lung rupture

air bubbles

venous drainage

alveoli

Bends

patella

femur

nitrogen bubbles around joint

Above: Some hazards associated with diving. *Burst eardrum* results from descending without equalizing the pressure in the inner ear with external pressure. *Burst lung* results if a diver does not breathe out when he ascends. *Bends* occurs if the ascent is too fast. An *embolism* can result from either burst lung or bends.

Photri

Above: These astronauts are being flown by plane along a flight path called a *parabolic arc*, which produces a short period of weightlessness. This trains astronauts to adapt to conditions to be expected in space. Effects of prolonged weightlessness are much milder than was predicted before the advent of lengthy space flights.

Right: Man has been able to work at successively greater depths by the use of different gas mixtures to avoid hazards like nitrogen narcosis and oxygen poisoning. Dives of long duration below 10 metres require decompression stops on the way up, and dives below 50 metres may require several hours in a decompression chamber.

instance, have much greater gravitational fields. Our muscles and bone structures are evolved for Earth gravity, and even at three times this, most people cannot stand. On Jupiter and Saturn man's muscles would not be strong enough, and the bones would break. A possible way to overcome this problem would be by travelling around on the surface of these planets immersed in some fluid of about the same density as the human body. The buoyancy of the fluid would then counteract the effect of gravity. The heart would need to be cushioned by the introduction of fluid into the chest cavity or lungs. Scientists are trying to develop a liquid which could dissolve large amounts of oxygen and be 'breathed' by the lungs.

The opposite to high gravitational force is weightlessness, which occurs during orbital flights and interplanetary journeys. Man adapts quite well to these conditions, the main immediate problems being those of movement and co-ordination when objects move around freely, and motion sickness due to the uncontrolled movement of the inner ear fluid which imparts the sense of balance. Both of these problems can be overcome by training and by taking anti-motion-sickness drugs.

EXPLORATION OF THE OCEAN

1. Diver clears ears on descent by holding nose and breathing out. This equalizes the pressure across his eardrums.

2. Diver can use air down to 60m. Nitrogen narcosis is debilitating below this, so nitrogen is replaced by helium.

3. High concentrations of oxygen can cause convulsions, so oxygen is diluted with helium.

4. Diver can use pure oxygen/helium mixtures down to 160m. Below this he may suffer from high pressure nervous syndrome (HPNS).

5. Addition of small amounts of nitrogen to gas supply reduces the effect of HPNS allowing dives to 200m and below.

6. Decompression chamber, used for dives below 50m.

7. Diver free-ascends from short or shallow dives, breathing out to avoid burst lung.

8. Diver decompresses at 15,10 and 5 metres after long or deep dives.

9. Diver risks several hazards if he does not observe correct diving procedures

components of gas mixtures used in diving

nitrogen

oxygen

helium

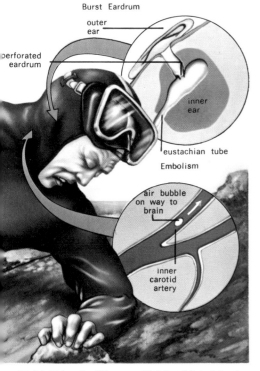

Burst Eardrum
outer ear
perforated eardrum
inner ear
eustachian tube
Embolism
air bubble on way to brain
inner carotid artery

Right: This scientific balloon flight in 1862 by two high-altitude experimenters, Glaisher and Coxwell, nearly ended in disaster. At a height of 11,000 metres

Glaisher fainted due to oxygen lack but Coxwell summoned the strength to pull the release valve, thus saving their lives. Later flights carried their own oxygen supply.

Left: A Tuareg camp in the Sahara. The Tuareg live constantly in areas where temperatures often reach 50°C. They survive by hiding from the sun during the day, by their domestication of desert-adapted animals such as goats and camels and by their intimate knowledge of the location of water sources in the desert.

Below: Eskimos from the north-west territories of Canada crossing sea ice with their dogs. Living in areas where winters last for nine months and are extremely cold, the Eskimos have adapted by making full use of the only resources available to them—seals and polar bears for food, clothing and fuel, snow houses for shelter, and their husky dogs as a means of transport.

The most worrying problem of weightlessness is the loss of calcium from the bones. In normal conditions calcium is constantly being removed and laid down on the bones in response to the stresses placed on them by movement and gravity. When these stresses are removed, the bones lose calcium but do not replace it. They therefore become weak, and when the astronaut returns to normal Earth gravity his bones are liable to break under the strain. The answer to this problem seems to be to simulate during the flight the normal stresses placed on the body on Earth. If spacecraft could be made large enough and rotated during flight, the astronauts would experience a centripetal force from the walls of the spacecraft, simulating gravity.

Undersea environments

The undersea continental shelf comprises an area about the size of Africa, and is full of mineral and biological resources but has, as yet, been only sparsely explored. Man's main problem in working there is with pressure, which increases by one atmosphere for every 10 m (33 ft) increase in depth. Hence at 30 m (100 ft) the pressure is four atmospheres. To prevent the chest being crushed by this pressure, the lungs must contain air at the same pressure.

The high pressure of air in the lungs causes large amounts of gases (oxygen, nitrogen and any other gases present) to dissolve in the blood. This is quite harmless as long as the diver stays at the same depth, but when he begins to come to the surface after extended periods below 10 metres, the pressure decrease causes gas to come out of the blood at a faster rate than it can be exhaled through the lungs. The blood begins to fill with gas bubbles which interrupt the blood flow, causing agonizing pains, and in bad cases paralysis or death. This decompression sickness is sometimes called the *bends*, since the pain caused by bubbles in the knee, shoulder and elbow joints can be eased only by contorting these joints. To avoid decompression sickness, divers must ascend to the surface slowly, stopping at intervals to allow the gases in the bloodstream to be exhaled through the lungs. Dives to depths greater than 50 m (160 ft) require several hours, or even days, of decompression, and for this purpose *decompression chambers* are provided. The diver seals himself into the chamber, is hauled to the surface, and is decompressed by gradual decrease of the pressure through external control.

Another diving problem is that, below 30 metres, increased concentrations of nitrogen in the bloodstream act on the central nervous system as an intoxicant causing lack of concentration and confusion. This *nitrogen narcosis* becomes debilitating below 60 m (200 ft)—at which depth some divers have been known to offer their air supply to passing fish. The problem is overcome by replacing nitrogen in the air supply by helium, a gas that does not produce the same intoxicating effect. The use of oxygen/helium mixtures allows dives to depths of 100 m (330 ft) and deeper.

As man continues to adapt himself to ever more hostile environments, further problems are bound to arise, but judging from past experience, he should be able to overcome these with his ingenuity and uniquely adaptable brain.

319

Biorhythms

Human life is constantly influenced by the rhythms of the universe. The Earth rotates on its axis once every day, subjecting its inhabitants to cyclical changes of light and darkness. The seasons change as the Earth orbits the Sun; the tides ebb and flow in time to the phases of the Moon. People are surrounded by rhythmical changes in light, temperature, gravity, electromagnetic radiation, and air pressure. Life on Earth has grown attuned to these rhythms of nature. Together with plants and animals, man has adapted to a 24-hour cycle of activity. This biological rhythm is called the *circadian rhythm*, the name coming from the Latin *circa dies* meaning 'around the day'.

People are often aware only of the most conspicuous of their circadian cycles—those of sleep and wakefulness. Yet people's temperature, pulse, blood pressure, respiration and indeed most of their other life processes also fluctuate regularly in time with an invisible clock. The health of the body depends on the co-ordination of these rhythmical timekeepers which direct periods of activity and rest and influence moods and dreams. The rhythms vary from person to person, and manifest themselves in individual preferences for early or late mornings, work and rest routines, and the way people order their lives within the cycle of light and darkness.

Circadian rhythms

One of the most easily observed fluctuations in the daily cycle is that of body temperature. Each day a person's temperature systematically rises and falls by one and a half to two degrees, following an internal clock unaffected by activity or by long periods of isolation. The high point in the temperature cycle usually occurs in the afternoon or evening for a person who sleeps at night, and this often coincides with a person's favourite time of day. The low point occurs during sleep, with temperature generally rising towards awakening. People who are very bright and active when they get up tend to have a temperature rise that occurs earlier than normal. Those who wake slowly and get up unwillingly have a temperature cycle which is only just beginning to rise when they get up.

Along with the peak in the body temperature goes the peak in pulse rate, which also follows a circadian rhythm. It rises to a maximum during the afternoon, and drops along with the temperature during the night. The activity of the adrenal glands also fluctuates over a 24-hour period. The level of the adrenal hormones, which regulate blood-sugar levels and energy production, drops at night and rises to a peak in the morning. When the level is high a person feels alert and active and is able to deal with stressful situations. When it is low he feels tired and lazy.

The body's rate of urine production also varies over the day, although most people only notice this when the rhythm is disturbed and they are annoyed to be awakened from sleep in order to urinate. People usually do not have to urinate at night even if they drink more during the

Heather Angel

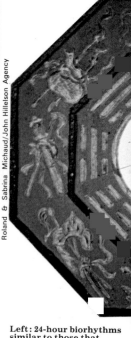

Roland & Sabrina Michaud/John Hillelson Agency

Left: 24-hour biorhythms similar to those that affect humans can be seen to striking effect in plants. Petals of this chamomile flower fold down (above) at night and open (below) by day. Even in constant laboratory light, the rhythm persists for several days, showing that it is controlled internally. However, in the absence of changes in light intensity to 'set' the internal clock, the rhythm's period may alter slightly from 24 hours and the rhythm eventually fades away.

Heather Angel

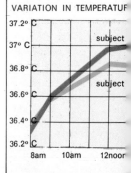

VARIATION IN TEMPERATUF

37.2° C		subject
37° C		
36.8° C		
36.6° C		subject
36.4° C		
36.2° C		
8am	10am	12noor

Above and below: People show variations in the pattern of their daily rhythms according to their temperament. In the chart above, subject A showed a temperature peak (averaged over 20 days) at noon, but subject B showed his peak at 6 p.m. In the chart below, the hand steadiness of the subjects is shown. This was tested by asking

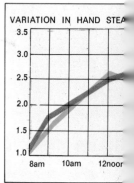

VARIATION IN HAND STEA

3.5		
3.0		
2.5		
2.0		
1.5		
1.0		
8am	10am	12noor

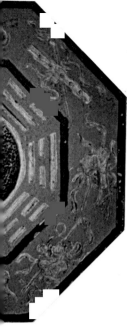

Above: Ancient Chinese philosophers recognized the influence of the rhythms of the universe on the behaviour of man. Part of this belief is encapsulated in the Chinese symbol of yin and yang, seen in the centre of this design. Yin, the black part, symbolizes Mother Earth and her inhabitants, and yang, the white part, symbolizes the ruler, or father of the heavens. The cyclical interaction of the two was seen as the basis of harmonious human existence.

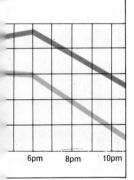

6pm   8pm   10pm

the subjects to place a stylus in a tiny hole— if the stylus touched the sides of the hole, they failed the test. The scale on the left is a measure of their success rate. Again, subject A reached peak performance at noon and subject B at 6 p.m. Subject A appeared to be a 'morning type' of person while subject B preferred the evening.

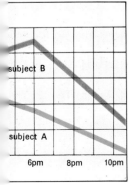

subject B

subject A

6pm   8pm   10pm

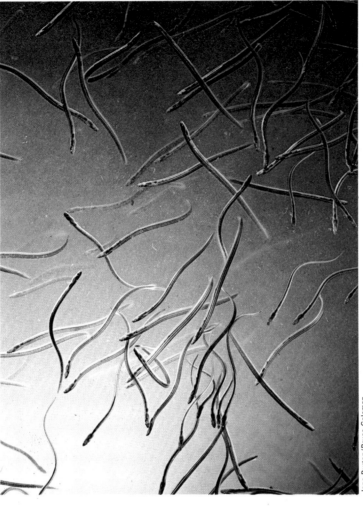

Jane Burton/Bruce Coleman

Above and below: Young eels (above) migrating up a river and flamingos (below) migrating to warm African climates are examples of animals that rely on their own biological clocks to navigate. Ocean voyagers are able to navigate with precision from one continent to another by reference to the position and movement of the Sun, provided they have a clock and a sextant. Animals are also able to fix their position by observing the arc of the Sun across the sky and its position above the horizon at a certain time of the day. But not having mechanical clocks, they have to tell the time by reference to their own internal state. Knowing their position, they can then navigate by moving in a certain direction relative to the Sun's position. In this way birds migrate thousands of miles to their winter residences, and all eels find their way back to the Sargasso sea to breed. The accuracy of these migrations is an indication of the precision of the clocks.

Bruce Coleman

evening than during the day. The kidneys are responsible for producing urine, and do this under the control of a hormone secreted by the pituitary gland, situated underneath the brain. The level of this hormone fluctuates in a pronounced circadian cycle, cutting down the flow of urine during sleep.

The urine itself undergoes cyclical fluctuations in its chemical components which act as a mirror of the body's chemical processes. Each chemical has its own daily rhythm to follow, yet they are all in tune together giving an overall feeling of steadiness in bodily functions.

The senses are not immune from daily cycles. Their sensitivity varies during the day, rising to a peak of awareness usually between five and seven in the evening. This is the time of day when most people's sense of taste, smell and hearing are at their best, so good food, drink and music are more appealing then than earlier in the day. On the other hand, unpleasant noises and bright lights some-times become more irritating as a person becomes more sensitive in the evening.

The effects of the circadian rhythms dramatically change the body's reactions to physical or chemical disturbance at different times of the day. Experiments on animals have shown that a dose of a particular drug, virus or exposure to X-rays which might kill an animal at one time during its circadian cycle only annoys or makes it sick at another time. Similarly, a high-flying aeroplane pilot who might become unconscious due to lack of oxygen at 4 p.m. would be much less affected under the same conditions at 4 a.m. Understanding the circadian rhythms may solve such problems as determining the best time for administration of a particular drug or deciding whether a surgical operation should be performed early or late in the day.

The constancy of circadian rhythms has been shown by volunteers who have lived for up to six months in deep caves or simulated space capsules. In these isolated conditions of constant light and temperature, the body still maintains its circadian rhythms, although in the absence of any cue to 'set' the internal clock, the length of the average person's cycle tends to increase to about 25 hours.

Some conditions do upset the circadian cycles temporarily. Changing from a day to a night shift at work, for example, means that the body's hormones and temperature cycles are completely out of phase. The person in this situation is attempting to work with his body tem-perature and hormones at the normal sleeping levels. While asleep he will have high blood-sugar levels and may have to periodically get up and urinate since the cycles take some time to adjust to the newly imposed schedule.

Similarly, international jet travel causes gross disturbances in the internal clock. A businessman arriving in central Europe from New York might attempt to conduct his business affairs at 10 a.m. central European time, but his body would be functioning as though it were 4 a.m., the time in New York. He would be sleepy, wide awake or hungry at the wrong time of day since his systems would be totally out of synchronization with local conditions. Travellers adjust to a new circadian cycle at the rate of about one hour per day, so a New York business-man might take six days to adapt to Euro-

Heather Angel

Bruce Coleman

air conditioner
and heater
maintain constant
temperature

soundproof walls
reduce auditory
stimuli

Left: Biorhythms with different periods are sometimes combined. This is illustrated by limpets, which actively feed every 12.5 hours whenever the tide covers their part of the shore, and also every night—even at low tide—since then the rocks are not dried out by the heat of the sun. These activity cycles are maintained even if the animals are kept in constant conditions.

Above: Female grunions show precise biorhythms in spawning activity. They bury eggs in the sand every two weeks, just after the high point of a spring tide. The eggs stay buried for two weeks until washed out by the next spring tide in time for hatching.

pean time—sometimes just in time for his return trip to New York, there to find himself waking up six hours too early.

Symptoms of fatigue often accompany these phase shifts. It has been noticed that rodents which have been subjected to phase-shift experiments are more vulnerable to various poisons and stresses. Inversion of their light-dark cycle once a week results in a small, but significant, reduction in their life span. It is possible that people may suffer similar ill-effects from disturbance of their biorhythms.

Monthly, annual and seasonal rhythms

Circadian cycles are only one of the rhythms of life. Underlying the circadian rhythms are cycles of electrical activity in the brain and nerve cells which last for mere microseconds. At the other extreme there are monthly, seasonal and annual cycles. The most noticeable monthly cycle is the female menstrual cycle which involves dramatic monthly hormonal changes affecting a woman's emotional and physical state. An estimated 60 per cent of women suffer from some form of pre-menstrual stress which can affect their sight, respiration, susceptibility to infection and behaviour.

Men are also susceptible to monthly rhythms. Although these are not quite as conspicuous as the menstrual cycle, they are nevertheless measurable. Monthly episodes of psychosis have been discerned among adolescent boys, and have their counterparts in men who undergo emotional cycles in which their mood rises and falls in a regular cycle. The cycle varies from person to person, from

David Hurn/John Hillelson Agency

Left: British miners emerging from a coal pit after working the night shift. After a few days on a night shift their biorhythms settle down to a 12-hour *phase reversal*—they relax in the morning and sleep in the afternoon. However, continual disturbance of biorhythms because of frequent changes in work shift can cause stress.

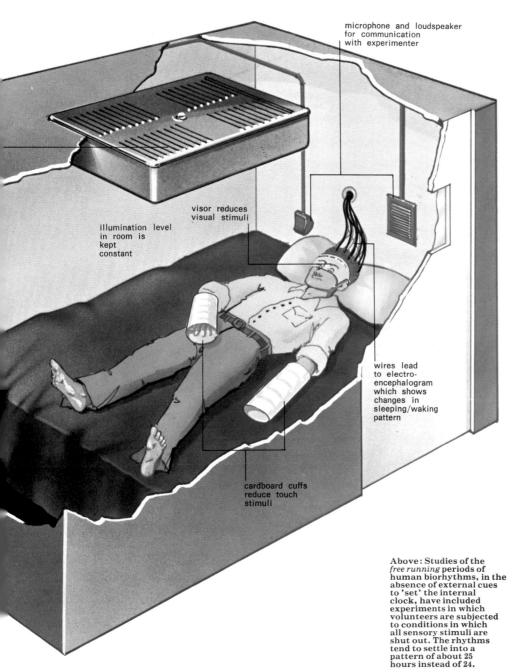

microphone and loudspeaker for communication with experimenter

illumination level in room is kept constant

visor reduces visual stimuli

wires lead to electro-encephalogram which shows changes in sleeping/waking pattern

cardboard cuffs reduce touch stimuli

Above: Studies of the *free running* periods of human biorhythms, in the absence of external cues to 'set' the internal clock, have included experiments in which volunteers are subjected to conditions in which all sensory stimuli are shut out. The rhythms tend to settle into a pattern of about 25 hours instead of 24.

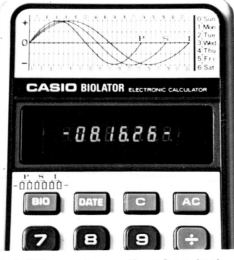

CASIO BIOLATOR ELECTRONIC CALCULATOR

-08.16.26.3.

BIO DATE C AC

7 8 9 ÷

Dave Hoskings

Popperfoto

Left: With no watch or radio, David Lafferty begins an attempt to beat a stay-down record in a cave in Somerset. His only contacts with the outside world were occasional phone calls in which he stated his estimations of the time. His estimates soon became inaccurate as the span of his biorhythms began to deviate from normal.

Above: One make of electronic calculator is claimed to compute a person's intellectual, physical and emotional state on any day of his life, on the assumption that these are biorhythms with fixed periods. The method also assumes that at a fixed reference point, the date of birth, the value of each state is equal for all people.

four weeks to as long as 13 weeks in duration. Diseases which often occur periodically are well-known by doctors, common ones being manic depression, epilepsy, migraine and some illnesses characterized by fevers or swellings.

Seasonal and annual rhythms are more difficult to study, and hence there is much less data available about them than about the shorter cycles. Nevertheless it is now known that the thyroid gland secretes something known as a 'summer hormone' which helps to reduce body heat. The hormone's release is somehow triggered in anticipation of hot summer months. Another seasonal rhythm is a strange winter madness called 'arctic hysteria' which affects some Eskimos. This is a hallucinatory type of experience which lasts for a few hours or days. It is thought to be related to fluctuations in the Eskimos' bodily content of calcium, which is known to affect the nervous system. During the summer months there is continuous sunlight in the high latitudes where Eskimos live, and this stimulates the formation in the skin of vitamin D which enhances the absorption of calcium from food. This results in an excess of calcium during the summer but a rapid loss of calcium in winter, when sunlight is absent for several months.

In tune with the universe

Various reasons have been suggested for the occurrence of biological rhythms. Studies of the development of children have indicated that the evolution of many rhythms might be brought about by the physical and social environment. Infants develop rhythms of sleeping, waking and urination only slowly, being unpredictable for the first weeks of life. It seems that to some extent the 24-hour clock is learned rather than inherited; an infant might learn a completely different routine of sleeping and waking if taught differently early in life.

Some scientists believe that people are sensitive to rhythmical changes in the universe far removed from their immediate vicinity, including changes in electrical fields, cosmic radiation, magnetism and gravity. Evidence for this theory comes from the study of some mental patients who become excitable, hostile and sometimes violent whenever there is solar flare activity (sunspots) on the Sun. Solar flares change the magnetic field on Earth, and can occasionally move a compass needle. There are indications that the brain is at least as sensitive to magnetism as a compass, and may respond to these changes in the magnetic fields of the Earth.

The study of time and the cycles of nature has helped to mould the history and culture of many civilizations. Chinese astronomers and philosophers saw relationships between the cycles of the Sun, the Moon and human behaviour: 'The Sun at noon is the Sun declining; the creature born is the creature dying'. Ancient doctors usually took into account the cyclical events of the Sun and Moon, both when prescribing cures and when diagnosing illnesses. Yet it is only since the early 1960s that western science has begun to investigate the importance of biological rhythms in man, and it seems likely that the findings of this research will increasingly influence medical practice and the organization of society in the future.

Sleep and Dreams

A baby born in an industrialized country can expect to spend 23 years of its life fast asleep. At first, babies follow a one-hourly pattern of sleep which continues irrespective of night or day, and a larger portion of the 24 hours is spent asleep than awake. Gradually the sleep periods lengthen and fuse together and eventually the sleep takes place at night and waking activity during the day. A minority of people break this pattern—there are a few who can survive on as little as two hours of sleep a day. But for the vast majority of people just under eight hours of sleep at night is the average.

Until well into the twentieth century, the descriptions of poets and philosophers were the only guides to the nature of sleep. However, all early sleep research foundered on one simple problem: the lack of an objective test of whether someone was fast asleep or not—without actually waking them up and involuntarily ending the experiment. Only after World War II did sleep researchers gain the tool they needed. This was the *electro-encephalograph*, or 'eeg' machine.

The importance of 'brain-waves'
As far back as 1875, an Englishman named Richard Caton had discovered that animal brains show continuous changes in electric potential. The eeg machine picks up these tiny changes in potential and magnifies them sufficiently to cause them to operate a series of pens on a continuously running belt of paper so that the brain quite literally writes its own characteristic pattern as a series of 'brain-waves' of various shapes.

Recordings on the eeg reveal that there are several different patterns of electrical activity during sleep. As the sleeper closes his eyes, fairly regular electrical waves with a frequency of about 10 cycles per second appear. These are called *alpha* waves. As the subject becomes drowsy, these disappear. They are replaced by more irregular waves which eventually slow down to about 1-3 cycles per second and are intermittently interrupted by short, sharp busts of faster waves called sleep 'spindles'. The subject is now in the *slow-wave* type of sleep. After a while the eeg changes again, the slow waves being replaced by much faster waves, similar to those recorded during drowsiness. At the same time, the eyes begin to execute rapid movements. This type of sleep is called *rem* (rapid eye movement) sleep.

The exact function of these two phases of sleep is not clearly understood but some clues have been provided by waking subjects during sleep. This has shown that if a person is continuously wakened at the start of periods of rem sleep, so that over the night he is getting only the slow-wave type of sleep, then on the first undisturbed night he experiences longer periods of rem sleep than normally, as though to compensate for the rem sleep that he missed on the previous nights.

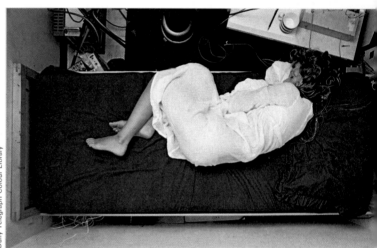

Right and below right: In a sleep experiment, a subject is connected to an *electroencephalograph* (eeg) by wires leading from metal cups attached to her face and scalp (below right). Some of these pick up changes in electrical potential in her brain. Others detect electrical changes caused by eye movement. These electrical changes are magnified by the machine and traced by pens on a moving sheet of paper as 'brain-waves' or as changes in eye-movement frequency. The subject goes to sleep on a couch (right) and is observed simultaneously with the eeg tracings. During sleep, people move every six minutes on average. Movements are most frequent during *rem* sleep, when the eyes make rapid movements.

Daily Telegraph Colour Library

Left: *Flaming June* by the 19th century English painter Baron Frederic Leighton. Outwardly, sleep appears a serene and relatively uneventful experience, as this painting well expresses. But within the mind, the unconscious third of people's lives is a time of great activity, full of bizarre and dramatic surprises.

Right: Eeg recordings from a subject during different sleep phases. As a person drops off, his eeg changes from the regular alpha-rhythm to irregular waves during drowsiness, and then to slow-waves interrupted by short fast bursts called sleep *spindles*. The eeg traces during rem sleep are similar to those during drowsiness.

Cooper Bridgeman

Daily Telegraph Colour Library

Similarly if the subject is deprived of slow-wave sleep, this occurs for longer periods on subsequent nights. It has been surmised from this that both types of sleep are essential, but that their functions in maintaining health are different.

Studies of this type have also shown that if people are asked to report whether they were dreaming when wakened, dreams are reported more often during rem sleep than during slow-wave sleep. For some time rem sleep became known as 'dream' sleep—and the rapid eye movements were thought to be the result of the dreamer scanning the events occurring in his mind. However, current opinion is that dreaming occurs during any period of sleep, but that the most vivid and well-remembered dreams occur during periods of rem sleep.

The sleep mechanism

As a whole, sleep mechanisms seem to be adjusted to the survival needs of a particular animal; sleep is triggered only when the necessity for vigilance is reduced. Thus ruminants, which are prone to attack by predators, sleep very little, whereas gorillas, which are subject to virtually no such attacks, can apparently sleep indefinitely. Man has to seek a protected place to sleep, free from sensory stimuli such as loud noises and bright lights. Nevertheless, although people can normally exert conscious control over when they sleep, they may, in cases of extreme sleep deprivation, fall asleep even in bright, noisy or dangerous situations. There thus appear to be two systems that influence when we sleep. One, the *sleep-triggering* mechanism, exerts a positive influence which increases in strength the longer we stay awake. The other, the *alertness* system, inhibits sleep and is stimulated by sensory inputs from the environment.

Studies have shown that the 'alertness' system is centred around an area in the *brainstem* called the *reticular formation*. When this area is in an 'excited' state, it passes nerve impulses up to the cerebral cortex, the area of the brain responsible for thought and consciousness, and thus keeps the brain in an alert state. Various factors act to keep the reticular formation excited. Nerve pathways from the sense organs have direct connections to the reticular formation, so that sensory stimuli such as noises and lights directly excite it. Nerve pathways also lead directly from the sense organs to the

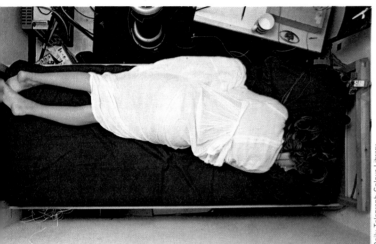

Daily Telegraph Colour Library

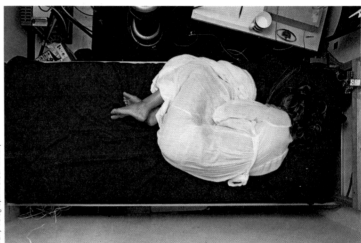

Daily Telegraph Colour Library

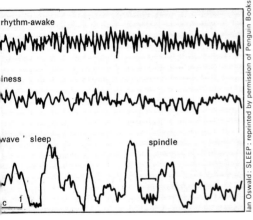

rhythm-awake

iness

wave ' sleep   spindle

c f

Ian Oswald: SLEEP: reprinted by permission of Penguin Books

Below: Sleep deprivation or boredom is often accompanied by yawning. A slight increase in heart-rate occurs during the yawn, which seems to be an attempt to raise blood-flow to the brain.

Right: The mechanism which causes people to sleep seems to be triggered by security and a lack of sensory stimuli such as noise. This Nigerian has apparently found such conditions.

Mansell

Mark Edwards

cerebral cortex, where they are analyzed. Signals from the environment of special significance stimulate the cerebral cortex to send messages down to the reticular formation, thus exciting the alertness system. In this way, if a person is asleep, he may be wakened by signals of particular significance to him.

The sleep-triggering system appears to function mainly through chemical means. That most people start feeling sleepy at certain times of day indicates that the mechanism is affected by changes in the body's chemical and hormonal levels, which fluctuate rhythmically in a 24-hour cycle. Also, since the sleep-triggering mechanism increases in strength the longer a person is kept awake, it seems probable that there is a build-up of some chemical during wakefulness that stimulates the sleeping mechanism.

Two chemicals that have been postulated to be sleep inducers in this way are *serotonin* and *noradrenaline*. Serotonin is located in a group of nerve cells called the *nuclei of raphe* in the brainstem. In one experiment, the administration of a drug that inhibits the manufacture of serotonin led to several days of insomnia in cats. However, the administration of the same drug, called PCPA, to humans did not induce insomnia, so that serotonin has not been firmly established as a sleep inducer.

Noradrenaline is concentrated in an area of the brainstem called the *pons*, and is known to be important in the transmission of nerve impulses. During rem sleep in cats the pons fires off electrical messages to the cerebral cortex, but this does not occur during wakefulness or slow-wave sleep. The pons is thus thought to exert primary control over rem sleep, the phase of sleep in which vivid dreams are most common. The pons also exerts an inhibitory influence on the muscles of the body, to prevent them acting out the content of dreams. When the French sleep-researcher Jouvet destroyed a tiny part of the pons in cats, they began to act out their dreams—lapping nonexistent milk off the floor, for example.

Sleep deprivation

Insomnia, lack of sleep, appears to be almost as much a state of mind as an actual condition. When sleep deprivation approaches 100 hours cortical control begins to break down, accompanied by hallucinations, impaired judgement and burning eyeballs. Yet even with this extreme deprivation of sleep, early tests showed that the brain retained an extraordinary ability to deal with problems. It was only when the subjects were given continuous work tests that their performance dropped dramatically.

Eventually it was realized that so highly does the human mechanism prize sleep that sleep-deprived subjects indulge in 'micro-sleeps'—tiny emergency bursts of sleep during which their eyes remain open. During these micro-sleeps the immediately preceding mental activity is forgotten and concentration is impossible, so that a continuous task cannot be performed.

It is not only acute sleep deprivation that can induce these micro-sleeps. Experiments have shown that one of the most effective methods of inducing microsleeps, or putting people to sleep altogether, is to feed in a continuous pattern of similar and boring signals. The dangers

Right: Sleep takes place in cycles during which *slow-wave* ('deep') sleep alternates with *rapid eye movement* (*rem* or 'light') sleep, with intermediary phases similar to the state of drowsiness. The slow-wave phases, characterized by reduced movement, heart rate and blood pressure are longer during the first few hours of sleep, while rem phases are longer during the last hours. Dreams may occur during any phase but are most vivid during the rem phases, and most dreams that are remembered occur during the final extended period of rem sleep. Several dreams with widely different themes may be experienced during a single night's sleep.

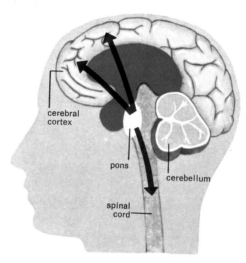

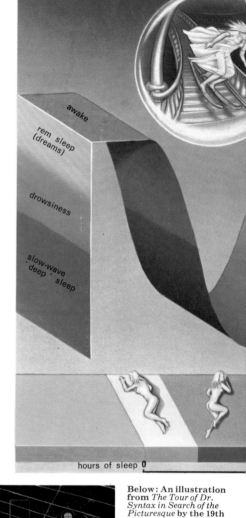

awake

rem sleep (dreams)

drowsiness

slow-wave deep sleep

hours of sleep 0

Above: The *pons*, located in the brainstem, is thought to exert control over dreaming. It sends excitatory messages to the cortex to start dreams and inhibitory messages to the muscles to prevent physical enactment of the dream.

Below: *Chrysis*, a dream painting by the French surrealist Delvaux. Some people dream frequently of walking around naked without reaction from onlookers. Psychologists say such people often suffer inhibitions due to being scolded as children for their exhibitionism. The dreams reveal the cause of their inhibitions and indicate that their behaviour could be less reserved without fear of social disapproval.

Below: An illustration from *The Tour of Dr. Syntax in Search of the Picturesque* by the 19th century writer William Combe. The doctor, having spent an evening reading in a library, dreams he is walking the banks of the River Thames, with humanoid books flying all around him. Especially in the first few hours of sleep, dream content tends to be moulded around prominent events or objects from the day, in this case the books. Many psychologists see this as evidence that dreaming is a procedure for sorting out and filing the day's events.

Left: A 15th century woodcut depicting, in a medieval setting, the biblical figure Joseph interpreting Pharaoh's dream. In ancient times dreams were thought to be prophecies of future events rather than manifestations of past or present circumstances. Pharaoh's dream of seven fat cattle devoured by seven thin cattle was correctly interpreted by Joseph as indicating seven years of plenty followed by seven years of famine. The famine was avoided by storing grain, and as a result Joseph was made second in command over Egypt.

of this for tired motorists, who may start indulging in micro-sleeps while driving along a featureless motorway, have been recognized.

Millions of people take sleeping pills each night to combat insomnia but their effect can actually appear to be the same as sleep deprivation, since they reduce or even eliminate rem sleep. Often these tablets are combined with the use of amphetamines, which also eliminate rem sleep, in combating depression. When either or both types of pill are stopped an enormous increase in rem sleep can result, often accompanied by nightmares.

The function of dreams

There have been several approaches to the question of the function and meaning of dreams. The first approach, the mystic or occult, maintained that man may have access to different times and places during dreams. Hence the importance given in the past to 'prophetic' dreams.

The second approach maintains that dreams are generated out of an individual's daily experience and are manifestations of attempts by the unconscious mind to express repressed thoughts and wishes. The main proponent of this line of thought was the psychoanalyst Sigmund Freud, who maintained that dreams consisted of a universal 'language', consisting mainly of sexual symbols. Although dreams are still seen to have a 'language', this is thought to be an individual, rather than a universal language, and is not necessarily sexual in nature. Thus a dream about a stallion is no longer interpreted as a sexual symbol—it may just be a dream about a horse. Nevertheless, there is a connection between rem sleep, in which dreams are most vivid, and sexual activity. Dreams of a sexual nature are common in both sexes, and in men, erection of the penis often occurs during rem sleep, sometimes resulting in orgasm and sperm emission—the 'wet dream'.

The third approach maintains that dreaming is a means of removing tension from the brain and 'sorting out' information collected during wakefulness, primarily on an unconscious level. The conscious dream (one that can be remembered) may be a method of bringing to the mind a situation or difficulty which needs urgent attention because it might disturb the body's balance or endanger survival. If people are continuously deprived of vivid dreams by being wakened during rem sleep, disintegration of their personalities and impairment of their mental functioning soon follows. Thus, as with sleep generally, dreams play an essential role in health and indeed in survival.

Sensory Coding

The world beyond the immediate vicinity of the human body is perceived predominantly by means of the pattern of light entering the eyes and the pattern of sound pressure entering the ears. Before the brain can make sense of these patterns, they must be transformed into electrical signals in the nerve cells that connect the sense organ (eye or ear) to the brain. These signals can be thought of as a coded message, describing the pattern in a way the brain understands.

Signals from the eye are understood by the brain as indicating light, however they are caused. By pressing gently on the corner of one's eyelid, it is possible to produce artificially nerve signals from the *retina*, the part of the eye that is responsible for converting visual stimuli into electrical messages. These are interpreted by the brain as being caused by light, and a spot of colour is seen in the opposite corner of the eye. 'Seeing stars' from a blow on the head has a similar cause. In these cases the brain is deceived into interpreting mechanical stimuli as visual stimuli.

The realization that the world is perceived by means of coded messages from the sense organs can solve some old problems. For instance, the image on the retina of the eye is upside down, and people used to wonder why the world is not seen upside down. The explanation is that signals to the brain from nerve cells near the *bottom* of the retina are the code for a patch of light at the *top* of the field of view. Provided the brain holds the key to the code, the signals are correctly decoded and the field of view is seen the right way up.

Breaking the code

Scientists can work in two different ways to investigate the way in which the sensory codes operate. By inserting very fine electrodes into the nerve cells of

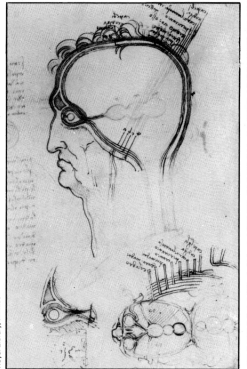

Left: A drawing by the 15th century Florentine artist and scientist Leonardo da Vinci. Leonardo seems to have recognized that the eyes send information to the brain, and his drawing of the visual pathway from eye to brain is remarkably accurate. He wrote all his notes in reverse script, possibly to keep his ideas to himself. Other people could read his notes only by using a mirror.

Right: An Egyptian mummy. The Egyptians did not know that the brain is the control centre and information processor of the body. When a corpse was being mummified, the brain was not considered necessary for survival in the after-life. It was surgically removed through the nostrils.

Below: Light from the visual field passes through the *cornea, lens* and *vitreous humour* and impinges on the *retina*, which forms a layer over the entire back surface of the eye and contains the light-sensitive *rod* and *cone* receptor cells. These are most closely packed around a region of the retina called the *fovea*.

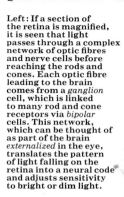

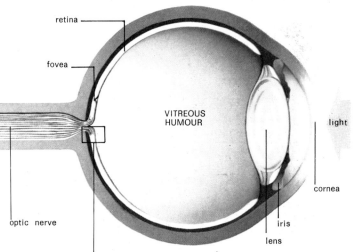

retina

fovea

VITREOUS HUMOUR

light

cornea

iris

lens

optic nerve

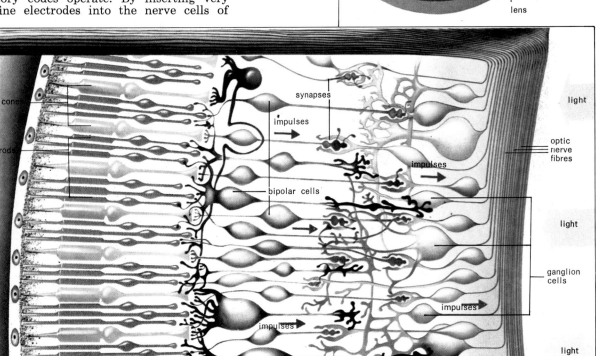

cones

rods

synapses

impulses

impulses

bipolar cells

impulses

impulses

light

optic nerve fibres

light

ganglion cells

light

Left: If a section of the retina is magnified, it is seen that light passes through a complex network of optic fibres and nerve cells before reaching the rods and cones. Each optic fibre leading to the brain comes from a *ganglion* cell, which is linked to many rod and cone receptors via *bipolar* cells. This network, which can be thought of as part of the brain *externalized* in the eye, translates the pattern of light falling on the retina into a neural code and adjusts sensitivity to bright or dim light.

Right: Each ganglion cell is linked to a circular *field* of receptor cells. The rate at which the ganglion cell sends nerve messages to the brain (far right) entirely depends on what area of the receptor field light is falling on. If it falls on the central receptors, an *excitatory* synapse stimulates a volley of impulses in the ganglion. If it falls on surrounding receptors, an *inhibitory* synapse damps the background firing normally present in the ganglion. Overall, the cell responds best to contrasts of light between the centre and surround regions.

animals, they can actually pick up electrical signals, both in the sensory pathways leading to the brain and in the brain itself. In experiments on human beings, they can ask a person what he sees or hears when a particular pattern is delivered to his sense organs.

In the eye, electrical signals are first generated when light hits the sensitive receptor cells, called *rods* and *cones*, of the retina. These cells do not communicate directly with the brain, but send signals via *bipolar cells*, across gaps called *synapses* to *ganglion cells*, forming the optic nerve leading to the brain. Each ganglion cell is activated by a cluster of rods and cones in a particular patch of the retina. Light falling on this patch causes a rapid volley of nerve impulses in the ganglion cell. Surrounding this patch is a group of rods and cones which do not activate, or *excite*, the ganglion cell, but damp down its activity, or *inhibit* it. These centre and surround regions are together called the ganglion cell's *receptive field*, and form a roughly circular area within the retina.

The ganglion cell fires off signals most rapidly when light falls only on the central, excitatory, patch of its receptive field. If light falls on the surround as well, the excitatory and inhibitory effects cancel out, and the ganglion cell emits infrequent signals or none at all. This means that uniform areas of bright or dark are not signalled to the brain, but strong signals are sent if there are edges or spots where there is *contrast* between bright and dark regions. Thus, sharp edges with contrast between dark and light are very conspicuous, but if the light intensity varies gradually across a surface, it is not so conspicuous, even if the total change in intensity is large. This is because once we have information about edges, we can locate surfaces with no further information.

The brain receives very little information about the overall brightness or darkness of a scene. Instead, the eye *adapts* to the light level. This allows the eye to be extremely sensitive in the dark,

and yet still work well in bright sunlight which may be a hundred million times more intense. Part of this adaptation is achieved through the opening and closing of the pupil, which can change the intensity of incoming light by a factor of about 16, but the greatest adaptation occurs through automatic adjustment by the nerve network of the retina.

As well as signalling differences of light intensity within a static scene, the coding system also concentrates on signalling rapid changes in light intensity over time. In normal vision, these changes are occurring all the time because the eyes are continually making small movements, called *saccades*, even when a fixed point in space is being stared at. Thus any point in the retina receives a rapid succession of images of different intensities—a constant stream of information for the brain to use.

The signals from ganglion cells do not themselves tell the brain anything about the shape of the object to whose edges they may be responding. The analysis of shape begins when these signals arrive in a region at the back of the brain called the *visual cortex*. The nerve connexions are arranged so that a number of ganglion cells with a line of adjacent receptive fields all send their impulses to a single *cortical cell*. The total receptive field of a cortical cell is thus not circular but elongated, and a cortical cell responds best to elongated bars of light or edges of contrast. Each cell is highly selective in the pattern of light that will activate it, responding only to edges or bars at a certain angle (whether horizontal, vertical or oblique) and of a certain width, length and sharpness. Many millions of cortical cells are needed to signal all the possible sizes and angles of edges. At this level, the code is far more elaborate than in the ganglion cells: the messages in the brain begin to describe the sizes and whole outlines of objects.

The coded message from the eye is not concerned only with shape and size: variations in the wavelength of the light falling on the retina are also signalled.

Above and below: The information entering the sensory coding system can vary between species. This primrose has been photographed normally (above) and in ultra-violet light (below). Humans see the flower as above but the coding system of bees, whose receptors are sensitive to UV light, signals only the contrast between the UV-reflecting petals of the flower and the UV-absorbing centre, as below. This may help the bee to home in on the centre of the flower, which contains the nectar or pollen it needs.

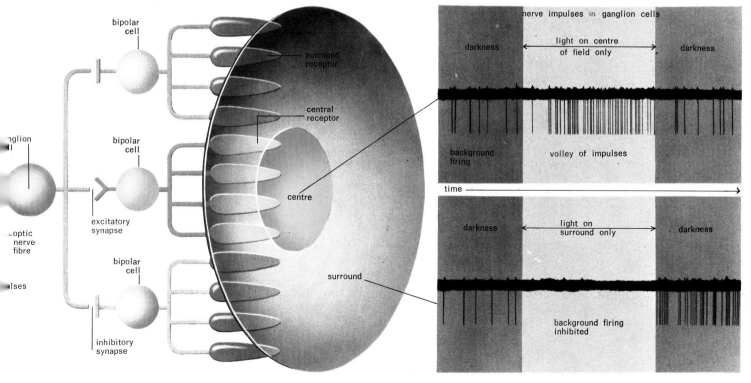

bipolar cell

surround receptor

central receptor

ganglion cell

bipolar cell

centre

optic nerve fibre

excitatory synapse

bipolar cell

impulses

surround

inhibitory synapse

nerve impulses in ganglion cells

darkness | light on centre of field only | darkness

background firing | volley of impulses

time

darkness | light on surround only | darkness

background firing inhibited

Left and above: The cause of geometrical illusions, like the apparent bending of the dark straight lines (left) is contested. They may result from interactions between orientation-sensitive *cortical* cells or from the brain interpreting patterns as images of rectangular objects. The second theory may explain why some illusions do not deceive people who live in environments with no right angles, like the African village (above).

Right: The brightness of an area is determined by contrast with nearby areas. Both greys are the same, but the grey next to a dark surface looks lighter. Information about light contrast, rather than intensity, is signalled to the brain.

These are perceived by the brain as variations in colour. Light of any colour can be matched by mixing light of three primary colours (red, green and blue). This occurs because the colour of the light is signalled by three types of cone receptor, each most sensitive at a different point in the light spectrum. However, as the signals pass along the visual pathway, the code is changed. Ganglion cells do not signal colour simply by responding best to red, green, or blue light. Instead they show an *opponent response*: for example, some ganglion cells are excited by red light but inhibited by green light, while others are excited by yellow light (a mixture of red and green light) but inhibited by blue light. This explains why some mixed colours are seen, but not others. If the red-excited and yellow-excited ganglion cells are active at the same time, reddish-yellow— orange—is seen. But a 'reddish-green' cannot be seen since red and green are signalled by opposite responses in the same ganglion cells.

The code also describes *movement*. Many cells in the visual cortex signal when an edge is moving left-to-right but not right-to-left, or vice versa. If a continuously moving object such as a waterfall is stared at for a minute and the gaze is then transferred to a stationary object, the stationary object appears to start moving upwards. This *motion after-effect* occurs because the cells signalling the downward motion of the waterfall are fatigued by being strongly active for a minute. This fatigue causes an imbalance: after fatigue the upward-sensitive cells are more active than the downward-sensitive cells, and so upwards motion is signalled and seen.

Auditory coding

In hearing, the message to the brain from the ear must signal the pattern of sound frequency, which is perceived as pitch. Two codes, the *place* code and the *periodicity* code, appear to work together.

The place code originates in the structure of the inner ear. Sound causes vibration of the *basilar membrane*, which stretches the length of the spiral cochlea. High pitched sounds (a scream for example) cause maximum vibration at the base of the spiral while lower pitches (a rumble of thunder, for example) cause vibration further along the membrane. The vibration stimulates sensitive *hair cells* on the membrane, which send signals to the brain along particular

Above and right: As someone looks at Queen Nefertiti's head, their eye movements trace out its main features, and project on the sensitive *fovea* of the eye those points in the image that carry most information— usually edges or spots of high contrast.

330

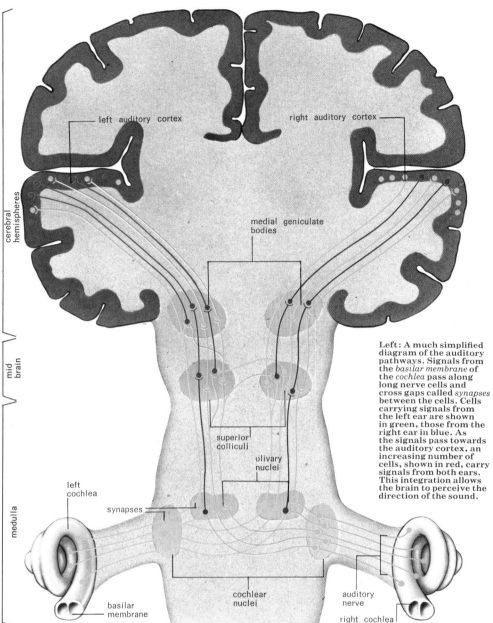

left auditory cortex

right auditory cortex

cerebral hemispheres

medial geniculate bodies

mid brain

superior colliculi

olivary nuclei

left cochlea

medulla

synapses

cochlear nuclei

auditory nerve

right cochlea

basilar membrane

Left: A much simplified diagram of the auditory pathways. Signals from the *basilar membrane* of the *cochlea* pass along long nerve cells and cross gaps called *synapses* between the cells. Cells carrying signals from the left ear are shown in green, those from the right ear in blue. As the signals pass towards the auditory cortex, an increasing number of cells, shown in red, carry signals from both ears. This integration allows the brain to perceive the direction of the sound.

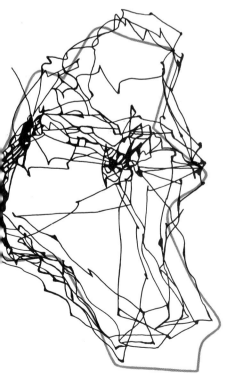

fibres of the auditory nerve. Thus, pitch is signalled by which particular fibres in the auditory nerve are active.

The other coding system, the periodicity code, is quite different. It codes the sound frequency directly through the frequency of nerve impulses. For a sound with a frequency of 400 cycles per second, the basilar membrane vibrates and causes impulses in the hair cells 400 times each second. The auditory nerve will signal repetitively or 'periodically' at this rate, and so the brain can discover the pitch of the sound from this repetition rate.

It seems that the place code is not very useful for coding low frequency sounds, because these are not well separated in their position on the basilar membrane. At these frequencies the periodicity code works best. But at high frequencies the periodicity code cannot work, because there is a limit to how fast the auditory nerve can send repetitive impulses. At these high frequencies, the place code is used. In between, both codes are available to the brain.

The most important sounds to be analyzed are the sounds of human speech. The vibration of a speaker's larynx determines whether his voice sounds low or high pitched. The shape of his mouth produces sound frequencies called *formants* which are much higher than the fundamental larynx vibration. The vowel sounds *a e i o u* are characterized by combinations of these formants. It is probable that the low frequency larynx vibration is signalled to the brain of the listener by the periodicity code, while the high frequency formants are signalled by the place code.

As well as the frequency of sounds, the *direction* from which they originate can also be heard. This depends on the brain decoding together the messages from the two ears. If a source of sound is to one side, the shadowing effect of the head will make it more intense at one ear than the other. It will also reach one ear about a thousandth of a second earlier. The brain can interpret the sound direction either by the intensity difference or by the time difference. Interpretation of the time difference requires the use of the periodicity code, since this allows the brain to directly analyze the time delay between volleys of signals from the two basilar membranes, and thus works best for low frequency sounds. Conversely, interpretation of the intensity difference is more effective at high frequencies. The methods thus complement each other.

331

Perception and Deception

The patterns of light and sound which arrive at the sense organs, and are transmitted as coded signals to the brain, are of little use in themselves. We need a system of interpreting the signals so that we can react to them correctly. The means by which we do this, deriving our knowledge of the world about us from the information collected by the eyes and ears, is known as *perception*.

Perceptual constancy

The human brain immediately recognizes any familiar object, however it is viewed and from whatever distance. A book, for example, looks like a book whether we see it laid flat, upright or on edge. Yet the shape and size of the image that the book produces on the retina of the eye varies a great deal. For instance, if we hold a book flat, and up close to the eyes, the image it produces is of a greatly foreshortened trapezoid, much narrower at the back than at the front. But we still 'see' it as rectangular, because the brain adjusts automatically to the varied image the book produces. This phenomenon is called *perceptual constancy*.

Our mechanisms for producing perceptual constancy can most easily be demonstrated by situations that produce a *non-constant* effect. For example, if we stare at a bright light for a few seconds, our retinas retain an *after-image* when we look away. This after-image, caused by fatigue and recovery in certain retina cells, has a fixed size, shape and position on the retina. But if we then look first at nearby and then at more distant surfaces, the after-image seems to shrink and swell, seeming largest when we are looking at the most distant object. This is because a real object casts a smaller image on the retina when it is further

Alphabet & Image

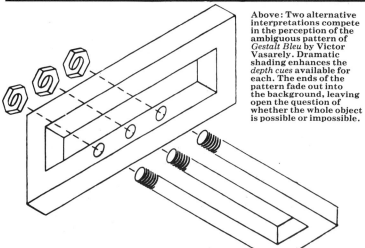

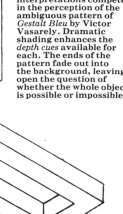

Above: Two alternative interpretations compete in the perception of the ambiguous pattern of *Gestalt Bleu* by Victor Vasarely. Dramatic shading enhances the *depth cues* available for each. The ends of the pattern fade out into the background, leaving open the question of whether the whole object is possible or impossible.

Mary Evans

Above: Perception is a form of problem-solving. Sometimes, as with this 'impossible' object, the problem has no solution. *Perceptual hypotheses* can be made to interpret different local parts of the object, but as the lines of the drawing are followed along it is found that the different perceptual hypotheses are incompatible.

Left: In this ambiguous illustration, *Blossom and Decay*, two perceptual hypotheses of equal validity can be formed. The illustration is perceived either as a skull or as two people seated in front of an arched gateway. The two interpretations rival each other and are hard to perceive simultaneously.

Right: Perception is a personal phenomenon. People may perceive sensory stimuli such as colour, music or pain in quite different ways, due to modification of their perception by experience. For instance this Balinese dancer's perception of the 'feel' of fire on his foot is quite different from the painful feeling most people would perceive, because of his experience at fire-walking.

John Hillelson Agency

away, and to maintain perceptual constancy the image is 'scaled up' by the brain in a process called *constancy scaling*. The same scaling effect is applied to after-images, producing changes in their apparent size.

The mental processes that perform this 'scaling' are unconscious and effortless; we automatically perceive the real, or *veridical*, shape and size of objects. In fact, to consciously perceive objects exactly as they are presented on the retina requires mental effort and training. This can be seen from the drawings of small children, which are 'flat' and lack *perspective*; the small child draws not what he sees, but what he knows is there. The same lack of perspective can be seen in the art of such otherwise advanced people as the ancient Egyptians (who drew people with their heads in profile, but their bodies face-on) and Chinese (in whose paintings nearby and more distant objects were all the same size, with no attempt at scaling down).

To carry out constancy scaling, the brain requires information about the distance of objects. This three-dimensional information is extracted from the two-dimensional image on the retina by a variety of means, called *cues*. One of the most important is *binocular disparity*—that is, the difference between the views seen by the two eyes, which produces slightly different signals from the two retinas. This cannot be the only cue to distance and depth, however, since if one eye is closed the world does not appear 'flat'.

Motion parallax is another effective depth cue; if the head is moved from side to side, nearby objects move further across the retinal image than do more distant ones. Another powerful factor is *interposition*; if one object is partly obscuring another one, we know instantly that it is nearer.

Further information comes from *perspective* cues. In man-made environments, the convergence of parallel lines as they become more distant (railway lines, for example) gives us an immediate sense of depth. Perspective works in natural environments, too. Since most natural surfaces—grasslands, pebble beaches, arrays of tree trunks—are textured, *gradients of texture*, such as the steadily shrinking size of beach pebbles as they get further away, provide a 'frame of reference' within which we can perceive the distance of any object in the outdoor scene.

Ambiguous figures

Perceptual cues are normally effective even when they are fundamentally ambiguous. If railway lines make a converging pattern on our retinal image, we 'read' them as converging parallel lines. But we interpret quite differently the same retinal pattern when it is produced by genuinely converging lines viewed head on—the outline of a church steeple, for example. We are rarely aware of such alternative interpretations; instead, the brain's perceptual mechanisms take the evidence provided by the eyes and interpret it in a way that makes sense.

The interpretations chosen most often by the brain's perceptual mechanism are those having right angles and straight lines. And this is where illusions can be created. The experimental 'Ames room', for example, is so constructed that, although its walls and corners are bizarrely angled, they produce from a fixed viewing point the same perspective image as a normal, rectangular room. A person viewing the room from this point cannot help but perceive it as rectangular.

In some special cases, we can draw two —apparently equally valid—deductions from the same sensory pattern. Such patterns are called *ambiguous figures*.

Left and below: Two examples of *mimicry*. The well-known French mime Marcel Marceau (left) interacts with imaginary objects on an empty stage, creating a context in which the spectator virtually perceives real objects. The hairstreak butterfly *Spindaris ella* (below) mimics a slightly larger insect through the false head incorporated in its rear wings—its real head is here facing to the left. This illusion confers a survival advantage on the insect. If a predator approaches the insect from behind, it may be scared off when it perceives the insect as larger than it really is. If the predator attacks, it may only damage the insect's wings instead of fatally wounding it in the head.

B.B.C.

NHPA

Left: An example of the importance of *context* in perception. Identical shapes are perceived as the letters 'H' and 'A' in different words. The brain selects the most probable of the possible letter combinations this particular pattern is intended to convey. It rejects the improbable combinations 'The cht', 'Tae cat' and 'Tae cht'.

Below: An experiment in *perceptual learning*. The movements of the passive kitten are controlled by the other, active kitten. They experience the same visual input, but only for the active kitten is this associated with its own actions. The passive kitten's co-ordination and visual development are retarded compared with the active one's.

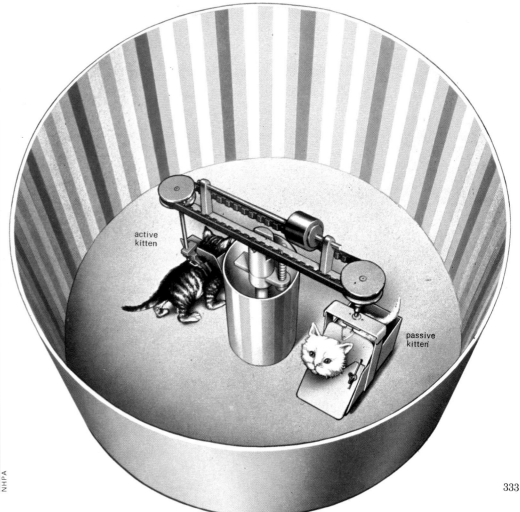

active kitten

passive kitten

Two different scenes seem to alternate in our perception, in a way over which there is no conscious control, even though the 'input' via the eyes does not vary.

Still other patterns have been drawn which fit no possible interpretation. In these 'impossible objects' each segment of the pattern provides cues to our perception of form and distance—but the deductions we make are immediately contradicted by the cues coming from other segments of the pattern. Here, too, perceptual alternation may occur, as first one part of the drawing, then another is scrutinized. But in this case the alternation occurs not because there are two possible interpretations but because the interpretations conflict.

Once the brain has formed a *perceptual hypothesis*—that is, a preliminary interpretation of the information the senses are feeding to it—this determines how the whole sensory pattern is interpreted. In this way, once the Ames room is perceived as rectangular, then the two corners of the rear wall must appear to be the same distance from the viewer.

This is one example of the importance of *context* in perception. We do not perceive, or interpret, an object merely from the information provided by its own sensory pattern. We also take into account the information provided by the object's surroundings. And what we perceive is the object (or event) that, experience has taught us, is most likely in a particular context.

Thus, when a spoken word is transmitted against a background of interfering noise, it is heard correctly more often if it is a common word rather than a rare word, or if it is a word that fits the rest of the sentence rather than one that is out of place.

This illustrates the fact that the brain can produce correct perception even when its 'inputs' from the senses are fragmentary or indistinct; but it also means that improbable events are sometimes not picked up. An example is the misprint that goes unnoticed; the misprinted word is an improbable combination of letters—such as the someti*n*es in the last sentence—which is perceived as the probable, correct, word.

Visual artists through the ages have exploited the properties of perception to achieve their effects. Skilful use of the depth cues of perspective and texture gradient can create, from a flat canvas, the illusion of depth. What is most striking about representational art is how powerfully the artist can create the impression of real objects with simple and even sketchy patterns. The effectiveness of many cartoon drawings with an extreme economy of line, or of the scenes hinted at in patterns of light and colour by the Impressionists or by Turner in his watercolours, demonstrates how perceptual mechanisms can derive hypotheses of the outside world from the most fragmentary input.

Perception and experience

How we manage to interpret sensory information so effectively has been the cause of much argument among philosophers and psychologists. Traditionally, *nativists* believed that perceptual ability is inborn; *empiricists* that all human knowledge is acquired through the senses, and hence that our perception of the world around us comes solely from

Alphabet & Image

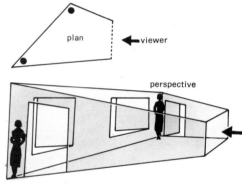

Above and right: The bizarrely angled shape of the Ames room, a plan and perspective drawing of which are given at right, produces the same perspective pattern at the viewing position as a normal rectangular room. Perceptually, the rectangular interpretation is preferred and as a result the two women are misperceived as being the same distance from the viewer. The size of the woman on the left is thus not 'scaled up' by the brain, and as a result she is misperceived as smaller than the other woman.

Below: The 'real' ex-US President Nixon in this picture is perceived normally since the brain scales up the perspective foreshortening produced by the camera. But in the background Nixon looks distorted because the poster is itself a foreshortened perspective. The brain cannot correct for this double effect.

Below right: *Dynamism of a Dog on a Leash* by Giacomo Balla. The illusion of movement is created by superimposing successive images—a technique borrowed from photography.

AP

National Gallery, London

Above: In *An Autumn Landscape with a View of Het Steen* **by the Flemish painter Peter Rubens, the artist has created the feeling of depth on a flat canvas by the use of a** *texture gradient.* **The foreground is roughly textured while the background is given a smooth texture.**

Right: Our perception is conditioned to interpret a round, white object in the night sky as the moon. But as this cartoon by Mordillo illustrates, human (and giraffe) perception can sometimes be misled.

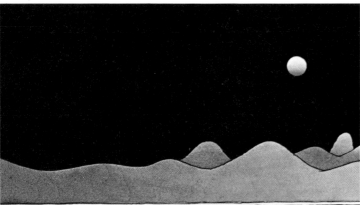

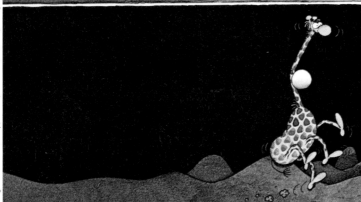

Albright-Knox Art Gallery, Buffalo, New York, Courtesy George F. Goodyear and the Buffalo Fine Arts Academy.

Camera Press

our experience of that world.

Some research has favoured the empirical approach. It has shown that perceptual learning is possible—that long experience in making subtle perceptual distinctions allows the expert to use cues in the sensory input which are not recognized by the novice. Examples are naturalists who can identify the species of a bird from just a fleeting glimpse; and wine tasters who can recognize the vineyard and vintage of a wine from one sip.

Experience can also modify the relationship of one sense to another—for example the connection between vision and the sense of touch. Volunteers made to wear special goggles that turn the visual image upside down are unable at first to coordinate their inverted visual world with their movements and sense of touch. However, as they continue to wear the goggles for days or weeks, co-ordination develops until they can perform tasks as delicate as riding a bicycle. When the goggles are removed, they are again disoriented, and have to re-learn how to use normal vision.

These experiments have shown how experience can affect perception in an adult. Presumably similar processes occur in a baby as he learns how to use sensory information for the first time. However, babies do not come into the world completely without perceptual abilities—it is difficult to see how a baby could learn anything if his sensory input was not initially organized in some way. Studies of babies only a few weeks or few months old show that they already have the capacity to recognize certain patterns and to make some response to the way objects are arranged in space. Thus, neither pure nativism nor pure empiricism seems to fit the facts: human beings have some inborn perceptual abilities, but these can be developed to fit the visual world to which they are exposed.

Much of this perceptual development is in the co-ordination of vision, touch and movement. In particular a person must learn to form mental links between changing visual patterns and the body movements that cause these changes.

A special example of the co-ordination of vision and movement occurs in eye-movements. The eyes make movements several times a second, making an image of the exterior world sweep across our retinas. But no motion is perceived when this happens; the perceptual apparatus, in interpreting the sweeping of the image across the retina, takes account of the commands the brain has sent to move the eyes.

The relationship between vision and movement is two-way. On the one hand, knowledge of his own movements allows a person to see the outside world correctly. On the other hand, vision is vital in controlling those movements. Even the most basic example of motor control—keeping our balance when we are standing upright—involves the use of visual information. Experiments in which the visual surroundings are artificially moved show that such movements cause body sway and even loss of balance, even though the floor underfoot remains stationary. The much greater demands placed on perception in high-speed driving or flying, or fast-moving ball games, show how rapid and exact the complex processes of interpreting the sensory pattern must be.

Basic
Mental Skills

Once information about the outside world has been obtained through the senses and interpreted by perception, this information can be used, through a variety of *mental skills*, to determine a person's reaction to events or circumstances in the future. Through *attention*, the brain can select the most important pieces of information to be retained; through *memory*, information can be stored in the brain; through *learning*, mental links are formed between specific memories; through *recall*, memories can be brought back to consciousness, and through the use of *language*, information can be communicated to other people.

Although these skills are largely taken for granted, they operate by means of electrical messages circulating in the most complex wiring system imaginable. There are approximately 10 thousand million nerve cells in an adult human brain, and the connections between the cells number 40 million per cubic centimetre. As yet an exact understanding of the function of even one cell in one person's brain has never been achieved. The processes that underlie these skills are beginning to be understood, however.

Attention

If a person is at a crowded, noisy party, he can decide which of several conversations he is going to listen to. But once he starts listening to one conversation, he cannot listen to any of the others simultaneously, although information about these conversations is continuously entering his brain. This is the selectivity of *attention*. To some extent, attention works through the brain 'latching on' to the physical characteristics of the voice that is being listened to—for instance its tone or pitch—but there is more to attention than this.

If a person listens to a tape recording of two voices, one speaking a meaningful sentence and the other talking gibberish, and suddenly the 'meaningful' voice starts talking gibberish and the 'gibberish' voice finishes off the meaningful sentence, the listener immediately switches from one voice to the other to attend to the meaningful sentence. In this case the brain is attending to which of the two messages is most significant, not to a particular voice. The brain must make some analysis of the 'gibberish' voice, in order to switch attention so rapidly when this voice began to make sense. It is important that the brain makes some analysis of all the information reaching it, since concentrating on just one 'channel' of information is useful only as long as we are interrupted immediately something more important occurs.

Psychologists have suggested that each information channel has an *attenuator*, a mechanism which allows only the most important parts of the information through. The brain can affect how rigorously each attenuator is operating. If a succession of important or significant messages comes through one 'channel', the brain will relax this channel's attenuator to allow an increased amount of

336

Above: Cocktail parties call for several mental skills. Names have to be *memorized* or *recalled* as the participants engage in a *learned programme* of language and social skills—the 'polite conversation'. *Attention* is used to focus on a particular conversation.

Left: Computers fill certain gaps in man's abilities, particularly in recalling information with perfect accuracy and performing complex analyses without 'losing' relevant information.

Below: The rows of beads on an *abacus* provide a greater storage capacity than the brain's short-term memory, allowing calculations to be performed on it that are too difficult to be done 'in the head'.

information to come through and be attended to.

Memory

Memory is considered a three-part system: *sensory information store* (SIS), *short-term memory* (STM) and *long-term memory*. The SIS forms an instant, but very temporary, storage of every piece of information that comes in. Information can last for only about three-tenths of a second in the SIS. If it has not been selected and transferred to short-term memory within this time, it fades away.

Short-term memory is used for carrying information a person needs for a few seconds, but can afford to forget later, for instance a telephone number about to be dialled. Two characteristics of short-term memory prevent its use as a permanent information store. First, concentration is required to maintain a particular piece of information in it. Switching concentration to something else or performing another mental task completely wipe out the information previously held in the STM. Second, it is able to store only six or seven items. A seven-figure telephone number is easily stored, but few people can rapidly memorize a ten-digit number.

For any information to be permanently

Left and below: Various animals tabulated according to learning ability, measured by how many actions they can memorize and perform in sequence to obtain a reward. The numbers indicate the relative abilities of the animals in each group. Man, and other primates, can learn complex action sequences but animals further down the table are less capable of associating present actions with future rewards. Man's discovery of the rewards to be gained from the use of tools was a key factor in his ascendancy.

primates

1

2

3

vores

1

2

ungulates

1

2

3

es

ibians

s

Mansell

Above: The Rev. W. A. Spooner was famous for his *spoonerisms* —his occasional transposition of the initial letters in adjacent words—for instance, 'I have just received a blushing crow.' Studying defects such as this has contributed to an understanding of mental skills.

Below: A prediction of how learning may take place in the future. Animal experiments have suggested that specific memories may be transferred by injecting brain *homogenate* from one animal into the brain of another animal, presumably because memories are to some extent coded chemically. There is no evidence that memories can be induced in the brain through artificial stimulation with specific electrical patterns. However, since this is the basis by which natural memory processes are thought to operate, it is a theoretical possibility.

stored, it has to be passed from short-term to long-term memory by the mechanism of *rehearsal*. The more often an item is rehearsed or occurs repetitively in short-term memory, the more likely it is to get transferred to long-term memory. Much of this rehearsal takes place automatically and unconsciously, but it can also take place consciously, as when a person is learning his lines for a play.

The third part of the system, long-term memory, has a virtually unlimited capacity. It allows a person to remember events that have happened years before, and also stores the memory 'links' formed through learning. Long-term memory probably takes place through permanent chemical or structural changes in nerve cells, caused by patterns of electrical activity in these cells. The longer an electrical pattern relating to a particular memory has been taking place, the stronger the chemical or structural basis of this memory.

It has been suggested that each memory is stored in a *unique cell* in the brain. One objection to this theory is that the number of events a person memorizes in a lifetime exceeds the number of nerve cells in the brain. However, if each memory was stored by a unique *pattern* of cells, linked in a characteristic electrical circuit, it would be quite possible for the number of cell patterns to exceed the number of events to be memorized.

Another objection to the unique cell theory is that specific memories are not stored in specific places in the brain. This was discovered by a psychologist called Lashley in the 1930s. He taught various tasks to an animal and then surgically destroyed parts of the animal's brain, hoping to find that memories for specific tasks could be erased. Instead he found that although the animal's ability for a particular task decreased as more of the brain was destroyed, no specific memory could ever be completely erased. The fact that memory is so diffuse has suggested to psychologists the idea of a memory *hologram*, similar to the technique of storing a three-dimensional

EN L'AN 2000

Mary Evans

337

Roland & Sabrina Michaud/John Hillelson Agency

National Theatre

Left: British actor Albert Finney playing the leading role in Shakespeare's *Hamlet*. This requires committing about 1,500 lines of Shakespeare to *long-term memory* and recalling them again (in the right order) night after night on stage. The only way to do this is by frequent rehearsal of the lines in *short-term memory*. Retaining information in long-term memory is easy compared with the difficulties in getting the information there in the first place.

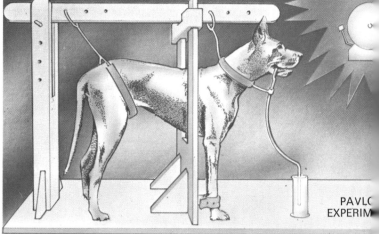

PAVLO
EXPERIM

Above: How the Russian physiologist Pavlov demonstrated *classically conditioned* learning. Normally, a dog salivates only when presented with food. By ringing a bell whenever he fed the dog Pavlov *conditioned* it to salivate whenever a bell was rung, whether food had been presented or **not**. The dog had formed an association between food and bell-ringing.

Right: Gulls demonstrate classical conditioning in associating the sight and sound of a tractor with increased chances of food on the ground. But they also show instrumental learning— by trial and error they have learned that looking for food behind the tractor is the most rewarding behaviour.

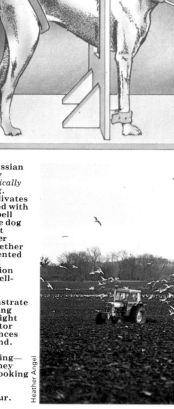

Heather Angel

machine in order to obtain a banana, it will soon learn to do this by trial and error. Being able to press the button becomes a desirable reward in itself, and if the chimp has to pull a rope in order for the button to appear, it will soon learn to do this as well. Similarly, it can learn to operate a switch in order to get at the rope, and so on. The chimp memorizes a series of *chained actions* in order to obtain the eventual reward of a banana.

Human learning is essentially similar. Through modification of the memory store by the addition of new links, whole programmes of actions can be formed to obtain a reward. These programmes range from simple ones such as the series of three or four chained actions required to make a cup of tea, to highly complex programmes which may take years to form such as those required to play a musical instrument well or make a beautiful pottery vase.

Recall
Storing information is of little use unless it can be readily retrieved for dealing with the situation at hand. When a person loses his memory, a condition called *retrograde amnesia*, the recall system has been impaired. Information is recalled through a search mechanism in the same way that data might be retrieved from an enormous cross-indexed filing system. A mental 'probe'—an image with the basic characteristics of whatever is trying to be recalled—is formed. The brain searches through the memory system for a pattern that matches this probe. If this procedure does not find the memory, additional information may be added to the probe. For example, if a person is trying to recall on which date a certain event occurred, information about what happened just before, or after, the event may be added to the probe to help in the retrieval, since when the event was memorized, links will have been formed between the event and other events closely associated in time.

Language
Once memories have been recalled they can be transmitted to other people through language. Language is the ability to form links between the physical action of producing a sound in the vocal chords and the mental image of what this sound means—for instance, the link between the sound 'dog' and the mental image of a dog. Like any other ability, language has to be learned and the language 'links' are themselves laid down in the memory.

One result of language experiments was the discovery that language ability was developed almost entirely in just one of the two *cerebral hemispheres* of the brain, usually the left hemisphere. This is most clearly seen in people who have *split brains*, in which the bundle of nerve fibres, called the *corpus callosum*, connecting the two hemispheres has been cut. Split-brain patients display abnormalities when presented with an object in the left hand side of their field of view. All the visual information about this object goes to the *right* hand hemisphere, which recognizes the object by comparing information about it with memorized information. But since the right hemisphere does not have any language ability, the split-brain person—although he *knows* what the object is—is unable to *say* what it is.

Above left and above: Most skills consist of series of chained actions leading to an eventual reward. The reward can take a variety of forms, from writing ability for the Tibetan taking a handwriting lesson (above left) to physical protection for the Ethiopian roofing his hut (above). In developing a skill, new links in the series of chained actions are formed mentally by *instrumental learning*, in which actions with desirable outcomes are repeated.

Right: The basis of the *Struwwelpeter* stories is that actions resulting in, or just threatening, punishment should be avoided. Here Conrad Suck-a-thumb is being chastized by the red-legged scissor man.

Dr. Georg Gerster/John Hillelson Agency

picture of an object on a photographic plate by superimposing laser images of the object. Superimposed memories might mean that each brain cell takes part in hundreds of memories.

Learning
There are two basic types of learning. *Classically conditioned learning* was first recognized by the Russian physiologist Pavlov, who showed that animals form memory links between events in the external world. A dog will salivate when given food, but if a bell is rung whenever food is given, the dog forms a link between food and bell ringing, and eventually salivates whenever a bell is rung, whether food is presented or not.

In *instrumental learning*, a memory link is formed between an action and the outcome of this action, together with a classification of whether the outcome was desirable or undesirable. This is summarized by the *Law of Effect*, which states that 'an action leading to a desirable outcome is likely to be repeated in similar circumstances'. Similarly, an action leading to an undesirable outcome is less likely to be repeated—we learn from our mistakes as well as our successes.

In most animals, actions and outcomes have to be closely associated in time for links to be formed between them. Thus, a seal will keep balancing balls on its nose only if it is given instant rewards of fish.

Humans, and to some extent apes, can go further than this and form links between present actions and rewards in the future, by the mechanism of *chaining*. If a chimpanzee must press a button on a

Thought and Creativity

Rationality, the capacity to think, has often been described as man's defining attribute. Yet although history has produced many great thinkers—Plato, Aristotle, Leonardo da Vinci, Newton and Einstein among them—none of these has ever produced a convincing explanation of the nature of thought and creativity. This is partly because the word 'thought' is so ill-defined, being applied to several different mental activities. Studying thought is also difficult because it is the ultimate case of 'diamond cut diamond'—when a man thinks about thinking he can only examine thought by his own thoughts.

The Greek philosopher Plato wrote that the creative thinker loses himself at the moment of creation and becomes the agent of higher powers: 'God takes away the minds of these men and uses them as his ministers'. Albert Einstein, one of the 20th century's greatest scientists, was unable to produce a scientific explanation of the nature of thought. He claimed that there is no logical path to a great scientific discovery: 'the mind has to make a jump, much like that of a poet or a painter.'

These men were only considering the more advanced forms of creative thought leading to great scientific discoveries or original works of art. Only exceptionally gifted individuals are able to engage consistently in these forms of thought. Yet thought is continually required in everyday life and no study of psychology would be complete without a scientific analysis of how everyday thought processes operate.

In one type of thinking, called *concept attainment*, the goal is to produce a satisfactory explanation of a number of observed facts. Examples of this type of

Dr. Georg Gerster/John Hillelson Agency

Royal Library, Windsor Castle

Above: A Los Angeles wall painting by Kent Twitchell. As well as the inspiration required in conceptualizing an idea such as this, considerable motivation and artistic ability is needed to carry it out.

Left: Some sketches by Leonardo da Vinci, one of history's greatest creative thinkers. It is not known whether the sketch at left is a self-portrait. Those at right, comparing water eddies with human hair, remained a unique record of the behaviour of flowing water until the advent of slow-motion photography. In addition to his ability to make penetrating scientific observations, Leonardo was a famous artist, military engineer and medical researcher.

SP

Ronan

Left: Sherlock Holmes gives his associate Dr. Watson a summary of a case he is handling. In Holmes's thinking style, various *concepts* would be formed to explain the different, and seemingly unrelated, aspects of a case and these would be combined into a *hypothesis* to fit all the facts. The validity of a hypothesis would be ascertained by testing it against any new facts that might emerge or could be uncovered as the case was investigated. Once a hypothesis proved valid within reasonable doubt, Holmes would present it as the correct solution— usually to Dr. Watson's utter astonishment.

Right: Considerable thought is required in both the compilation and comprehension of this story about a man and his unruly pig. To translate it, the concept that each picture is intended to convey must be found. The correct concept is the one whose associated language sound best fits the context of the story. As a clue, the correct concepts for the last two pictures in the second line of the story are 'hen' and 'sum'.

Mary Evans

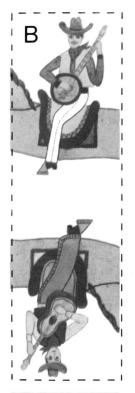

B

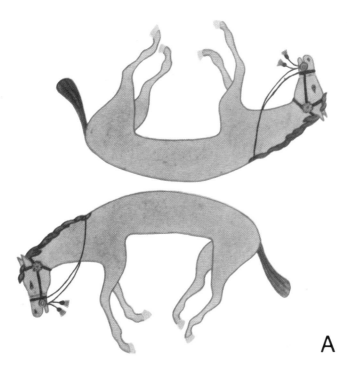

A

Left and above right: Two puzzles that can be solved by a straightforward approach. In the mosaic (above right) is hidden a regular five-pointed star which has to be found. In the maze (left) a path must be found between the centre and the cul-de-sac in the left bottom quarter. Either puzzle can be solved by a trial-and-error approach based on fixed assumptions.

Above and right: In contrast, two puzzles that require some *insight* to solve. The strip with the cowboys drawn on it (above left) has to be placed on top of the horses in such a way that both cowboys are riding a horse. The six matches (right) have to be assembled in such a way that they form four equilateral (equal sided) triangles, in which the sides of each triangle are equal to the length of a match. The solution to these puzzles will come in a 'flash' rather than by a step-by-step logical approach. Making fixed assumptions about the method of solution must be avoided, since these may be misleading.

thinking are a scientist's efforts to find a theory to fit a set of experimental facts or the detective work of Sherlock Holmes and other sleuths.

Another type of thought is required in making *decisions*, whether in a work or a social context. This requires projecting the outcomes of one's own and others' actions, and evaluating their consequence. In resolving *problems*, evaluation of the causes or structure of the problem must be made and a solution found either through the step-by-step method of *logical analysis* or through *insight*, requiring a less conventional approach to the problem. Finally, most people engage in *imaginative* thinking in which new juxtapositions of old experiences or concepts may produce useful, aesthetic or entertaining ideas.

The use of concepts

Psychologists recognize that *concepts* are an important tool in human thinking. The use of concepts in thought is an extension of their use in perception and the way in which concepts operate is best explained by first seeing how they work at the perceptual level.

The concept of a flower is formed from a person's experience of objects he has been told are flowers. If the only flower a person has seen is a buttercup, his concept of a flower will include only the attributes of a buttercup. This concept would be of little use in identifying a poppy as a flower, since poppies have different attributes from buttercups, but by *modifying* the concept so that it includes only the attributes of both poppies and buttercups—green stalks

with attached coloured petals—the concept becomes generalized to be of use in identifying other flowers in the future.

This process of *concept formation* occurs all the time in a developing child as he learns to classify objects he encounters. With experience, a whole range of generalized concepts are developed. When entirely new objects or situations are encountered, several concepts may have to be sifted around and combined to form a satisfactory explanation of a set of observations or facts. This is the process that occurs in thought. The new combination of concepts formed, the solution to the problem, becomes a generalized concept in itself and can be used for dealing with similar situations in the future.

An example of the use of concepts in thought comes from a case presented by Scotland Yard to Sir Arthur Conan Doyle, the inventor of Sherlock Holmes. A man had vanished after withdrawing all his money from the bank and foul play was feared. He had left a music hall at 11 p.m. and after changing his clothes at a hotel had departed in a hurry. To a man of Conan Doyle's experience, the withdrawal of the money indicated that the disappearance was premeditated. His changing clothes near midnight indicated 341

Above: Man's capacity to think relies to a great extent on the brain's ability to pattern the jumble of events occurring in the external world into a meaningful whole. This patterning behaviour is reflected in the symmetry of many of the objects man creates, such as the pattern of this printed fabric.

Above: In Shakespeare's *The Merchant of Venice*, Bassanio chooses between caskets of gold, silver and lead to win Portia's hand in marriage, the inscriptions on the caskets being his only clues to the correct choice of the lead casket. Decisions often involve a choice between several actions, with little information about their consequences.

Above: Creative ideas are often derided if they are contrary to established beliefs or methods. Jonas Hanway, who pioneered the use of the umbrella in Britain, was criticized for 'defying the heavenly purpose of rain'. He had difficulty in displacing the less effective, but established, use of a basket for protection.

a journey of some sort, and his hurried departure indicated an appointment. Juggling the concepts of premeditation, a journey, and an appointment suggested an overall solution to fit the facts. After ascertaining that the only trains leaving London after 11 o'clock were the expresses to Scotland, Conan Doyle announced that the man could be found alive and well in Edinburgh or Glasgow. The man was found in Edinburgh. It was a case worthy of Holmes himself.

Decision making

People are making decisions all the time. The decisions range from the trivial, as when deciding what to eat in a restaurant, to the more taxing, as when choosing moves during a game of chess or making life decisions such as choosing a career or marriage partner.

Logical decisions require an evaluation of all the possible outcomes of possible courses of action and an assessment of which action would result in the most advantageous outcome. The more far-reaching a decision is, the more unknown factors there are which might influence the outcome, and thus the more difficult it is to decide which action to take. In addition, evaluating the relative advan-

Above and right: The urge to express oneself by creating artistic patterns out of a few basic raw materials is a common factor among people throughout the world. The Brazilian Indians (above) are decorating themselves in preparation for a tribal ceremony, while the Panamanian woman of the Cuna tribe (right) is making herself a *mola*, a colourful type of embroidered blouse, in preparation for the Cuna Indians' yearly feast. In addition to providing personal satisfaction, creativity has the advantage of attracting social approval, particularly if the artistic patterns created are of an aesthetically pleasing or original nature. In common with other types of thinking, the thought required in creative art involves the combination of ideas or concepts into a satisfactory product. But unlike the type of thought involved in logical analysis or problem solving, creative art has no fixed rules applied to either its practice or its products, and thus allows great freedom for personal expression.

Right: Puzzle solutions.
Thinking that the match
puzzle can be solved in
2 dimensions, or that the
cowboys can be placed on
the original horses, are
misleading assumptions.

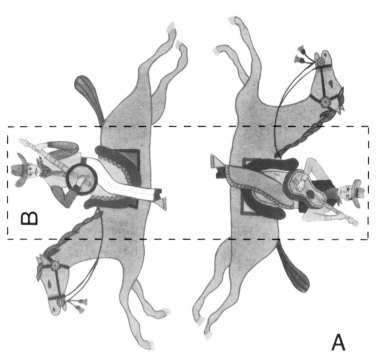

B

A

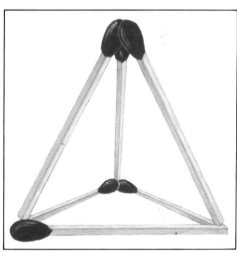

tages of different outcomes may be difficult if the outcomes are of quite different natures—for instance many people might find it difficult to decide whether they would prefer a million dollars or an extra ten years of life, if they could choose.

Several insights into the way logical decisions are made have come from man's attempts to program computers to 'play' games such as chess which require a series of decisions. Man's own thinking processes have been used as a model for these programs. The computer is usually programmed to select seven or eight possible moves for analysis whenever it is its turn to 'play'. It then selects seven or eight of the most likely counter-moves its opponent might reply to each of the computer's moves, and in turn, seven or eight possible replies it could make to each of its opponent's counter-moves. This projection of the course of the game may extend for four or five moves ahead, depending on the capacity of the computer. The computer makes an evaluation of the outcome of each projected series of moves by assessing the strategic advantage of each, and then works back again to find the initial move which would lead to the most advantageous outcome. Finally, it makes this move.

Human decision-making is essentially similar, although in most situations it is the world, rather than a human opponent, that is being 'played' against. Man's capacity to evaluate all the possible outcomes of his actions are rather more limited than a computer's. A person can usually only perform a complete analysis for three or four moves ahead. The sheer effort and time required to make rigorous logical decisions often encourages people to abandon this approach completely and rely instead on habit, intuition, or pure guesswork. On the other hand, through *insight*, people sometimes see useful combinations of actions that might not be picked up by a purely logical approach. This explains why champion chess computers are still unable consistently to beat chess grandmasters.

In some situations where decisions are needed, none of the possible courses of action appears to hold an advantage over the others. These are often the most difficult decisions to make. The mathematical study of decision-making and strategy, called *game theory*, has sometimes proved useful in helping people to decide on the most appropriate course of action.

Similarly, decisions that may at first seem overpoweringly difficult may be simplified by writing down the possible outcomes of various courses of action and assigning values, whether positive or negative, to these outcomes—in fact to help thought processes by examining on paper the 'pros and cons' of various courses of action.

Creative thinking

Thinking logically has long been regarded as the only way to arrive at the solution to a problem. But many modern philosophers regard this approach, requiring the processing of inflexible concepts, certainties and absolutes, as inadequate in dealing with the types of problem encountered in the modern world. In many cases, the data about the causes of a problem is insufficient to form a base from which a solution can be worked out by a logical approach.

Edward de Bono, a philosopher and leading exponent of *lateral thinking*, feels that because life does not fit neat logical equations, people have come to prefer feeling to thinking. Comparing the progress made in technology with the lack of progress in the human sphere (exemplified by the wide range of social and economic problems man has brought upon himself), he suggests that our thinking methods require a radical revision since the present system confuses information with thinking.

Dr de Bono's *lateral thinking* tool is designed to unlock peoples' creative reserve and enable them to make more effective use of the patterning behaviour of the brain. Lateral thinking has already been used to solve industrial problems and make education more meaningful.

The company whose office lifts were inefficient provides an example of lateral thinking. Its employees kept injuring themselves hurrying down the slippery office stairs. The firm's directors saw two alternative solutions: to speed up the lifts, or to install a new lift, both costly and lengthy operations. The lateral thinkers suggested a simple and more effective solution: install mirrors on the stairs. The employees became so preoccupied with their reflections that they descended the stairs slowly, and thus did not risk injury.

It appears that there are no rigid rules by which thought processes operate in finding satisfactory solutions to problems. Much of the effort involved in finding a solution goes on quite unconsciously. Many people report that after several hours of concentrating on the structure of a problem, the eventual solution only arrives after the problem has been allowed to incubate in the unconscious for hours or even days. The solution may arrive in a 'flash' or in symbolic form through dreams. How the unconscious sifts through the facts of a problem or synthesizes creative ideas is quite unknown. As Einstein observed: the mind has to make a 'jump'.

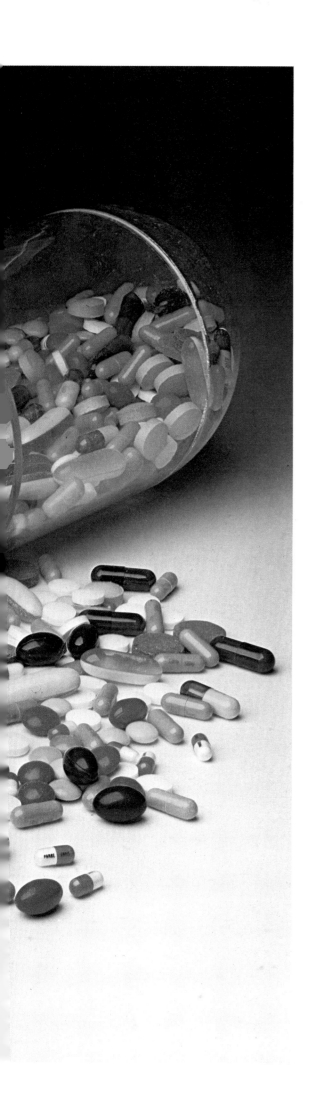

Chapter 6
Medicine

At the beginning of the 20th century
the most effective remedies were still
derived from plants. Now they are
mass produced according to
prescriptions worked out in laboratories.
Some natural products can be
manufactured synthetically.

Some sources of drugs before technology came to the chemist's aid. A drug may be described as any substance which alters the way a living organism works. Coffee and tea may be regarded as plant derived stimulant 'drugs'.

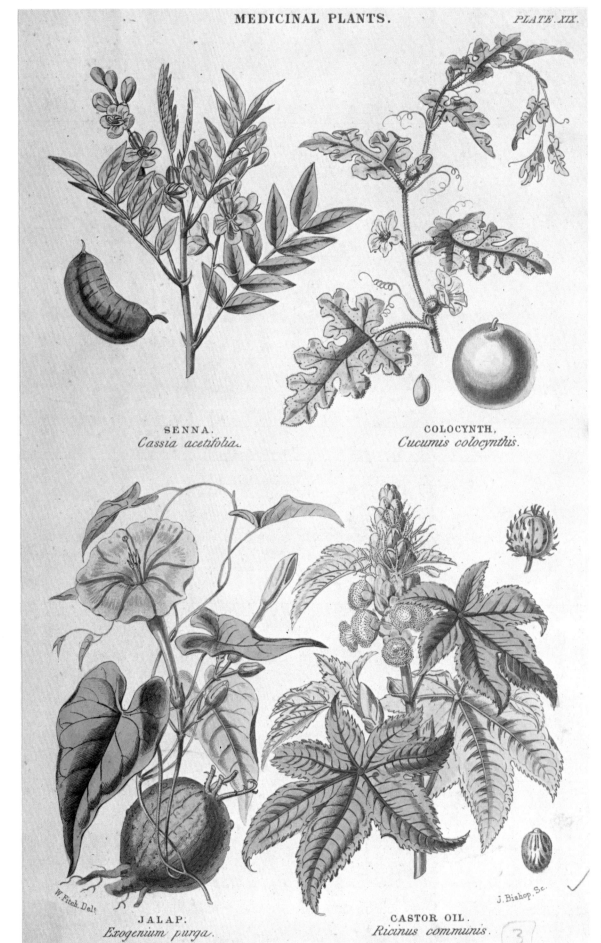

MEDICINAL PLANTS.

PLATE XIX.

SENNA.
Cassia acetifolia.

COLOCYNTH,
Cucumis colocynthis.

JALAP.
Exogenium purga.

CASTOR OIL.
Ricinus communis.

W. Fitch. Del.

J. Bishop. Sc.

Medicinal Drugs

People have been using plant extracts for thousands of years to combat illness and disease. The inhabitants of ancient India, for instance, used a vegetable oil called *chaulmoogra* to treat leprosy and a root, *rauwolfia*, as a tranquillizer in cases of mental illness. But it is only in the twentieth century that the use and manufacture of drugs has taken off. Technological progress has allowed the extraction of an enormous variety of chemicals from plant and mineral sources and effective testing of these substances for therapeutic properties. At the same time, advances in biology have led to a better understanding of how drugs work, and the development of synthetic drugs designed for specific therapeutic tasks.

Modern drugs are powerful agents produced after considerable research and testing, often taking several years and costing millions of pounds. Laboratory testing involves checking the effects and side-effects and lethal dosage levels of the drug on a wide range of experimental animals. Human trials follow and are carefully monitored by official safety bodies who permit commercial release of the drug only when fully satisfied.

Antibiotics
Paul Ehrlich, the nineteenth century German chemist, originated the idea of using chemicals to kill or inactivate specific bacteria without harming the body itself. He called this treatment chemotherapy. The first effective chemotherapeutic agent was developed by G. Domagk in 1935 using a dye, *prontosil red*, and from it was developed the family of drugs called *sulphonamides*. Their action depends on the similarity of their chemical structure to *para aminobenzoic*

acid, a chemical which is used normally by bacteria for growth. The bacteria mistakenly absorb the sulphonamide, which blocks rather than promotes their growth. This blocking effect halts the multiplication of the bacteria and allows the body's defences to overcome them.

The sulphonamides were found very useful against one particular class of bacteria, the *cocci*, which are responsible for several complaints and diseases including sore throats, tonsillitis, and gonorrhea. Some bacteria, however, were found to develop *resistance* to the drugs: mutations in individual bacteria rendered these insensitive to the inhibitory effects of sulphonamides, and these bacteria were thus allowed to multiply, producing new generations unaffected by the drug.

Chemotherapeutic agents derived from micro-organisms are called *antibiotics*, and the first of these was *penicillin*, discovered by Sir Alexander Fleming in 1928. He noted that the mould *Penicillium notatum* stopped the growth of cocci bacteria on a bacterial culture plate. Sir Howard Florey and Ernst Chain developed penicillin from the mould in the early 1940's. The drug was found effective against a wide range of cocci as well as the organisms causing tetanus, gas gangrene, anthrax and syphilis. It kills bacteria by causing them to swell up and disintegrate.

Given originally by injection, penicillin was later produced in a tablet form. It is remarkably non-poisonous to humans, but has some side-effects. The main problem is allergic response to the drug, but this can usually be relieved with other drugs called *antihistamines*. Resistance to the original penicillin occurred when some bacteria developed an enzyme that was able to destroy the drug. This snag was initially overcome by developing alternative antibiotics from other moulds or fungi. These included *chloramphenicol* and *streptomycin*, the

Above: Prior to the discoveries that led to the development of effective drug therapies, many illnesses were fatal. Religious exhortations sought (as here) to drive away the 'evil spirits' causing the illness. They were usually unsuccessful.

Below: A 19th century medical chest containing a selection of drugs, many of them simple metallic salts still used medicinally. Bicarbonate of soda is an *antacid*, used to treat indigestion since it neutralizes

acid secretions in the stomach. Chlorate of potash can be used for treating sore throats, since it has a soothing action on inflamed mucus membranes.

Below right: The British bacteriologist Sir Alexander Fleming, who in 1928 discovered the antibacterial action of the mould *Penicillium notatum*. He was awarded a Nobel prize in 1945, together with Sir Howard Florey and Ernst Chain, who succeeded in isolating the active constituent of the mould, *penicillin*.

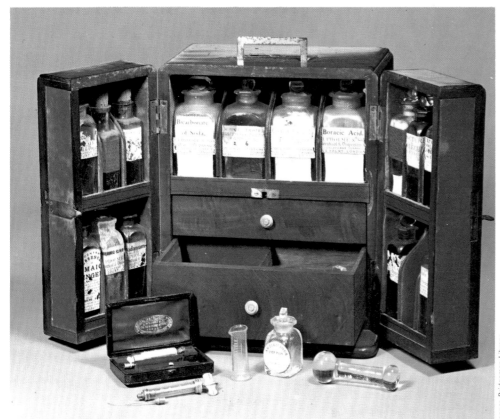

first drug active against the tuberculosis bacillus. Later, semi-synthetic pencillin analogues such as *Ampicillin* were developed which can be used against bacteria resistant to the original penicillin. Other modern antibiotics include the *tetracycline* group and the *cephalosporins*.

Analgesics

The pain killers, or *analgesics*, do not cure diseases, but can suppress their symptoms. There are two main groups. Those which act on pain associated with muscle and bone and their related structures are known as the *peripherally acting* analgesics. The best known of these is *aspirin*, first synthesized in 1899, and produced in huge commercial quantities ever since. Its active constituent is *acetylsalicylic acid*.

The second group of pain-killers are the *centrally acting* analgesics, originally derived from opium, an extract of the poppy plant. *Morphine*, the most important of these drugs, *methadone* and *diamorphine* (heroin) depress the brain activity of the cortex and thalamus, in the parts which receive messages from the body's pain receptors. They act most quickly and effectively when injected into a muscle or vein and they are especially useful for the relief of pain associated with medical shock, as in heart attacks, and for injuries involving broken bones or wounds.

Both types of pain killer have a number of side-effects which partially limit their use. Aspirin can irritate the stomach producing dyspepsia and indigestion or, more seriously, may cause an ulcer. If used habitually, aspirin can also lead to *anaemia*, due to loss of blood in small amounts from the inner surface of the stomach.

Morphine drugs may cause nausea and vomiting, but this unpleasant side-effect can be blocked by giving the drug *cyclizine* at the same time. More seriously, morphine and its allied drugs can become physically addictive when used for a prolonged period, so their prescription and use is carefully controlled.

Cough and cold preparations

Among the most traditional of drug therapies are those for the common cold and troublesome cough. For colds, the most effective drugs are *antipyretic*, in other words they lower the feverish body temperature associated with the cold. Salicylates are antipyretic as well as being analgesic, and aspirin is thus an effective treatment for colds and influenza. *Quinine*, from the Peruvian bark *cinchona*, was a regular constituent of prescriptions for the common cold until the middle of the nineteenth century. But because in large doses it is poisonous to the cells of the central nervous system, producing severe headaches and difficulty in seeing, its use is now largely limited to the treatment of malaria.

'Cough mixtures' have always been popular and are of two types: the *expectorants* and the *suppressants*. Expectorant cough mixtures increase mucus production and liquefy the phlegm in the bronchi, making the cough less painful and more effective in clearing the lungs.

The suppressant cough mixtures reduce the response to irritation by damping down the cough reflex centrally in the brain's control centre. The most effective suppressants are *codeine* and *pholcodine*.

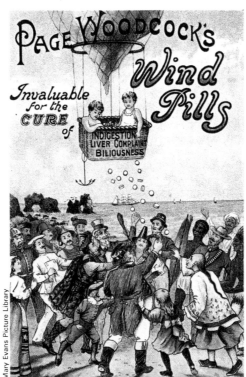

Pleasure Boat.

Left: Advertisements may help to cure people by convincing them that they will get better, even if the pills they extol are of limited therapeutic value.

Above: Even people who claim never to require medication sometimes rely on travel sickness pills. *Antinauseants* suppress the nausea

and vomiting set off when the balance organ of the inner ear is disturbed. Evidently the seafarers seen here did not have a supply.

Right: Many drugs are extracted from plant sources. The roots of this autumn crocus provide *colchicine*, a drug effective against gout and rheumatism.

DRUGS ACTING ON SPECIFIC SYSTEMS

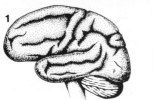

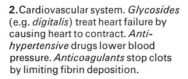

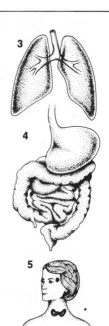

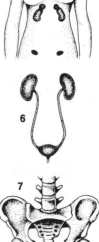

1. Nervous system. *Analgesics* relieve pain, acting either at its source (e.g. *aspirin*) or on the brain itself (e.g. *morphine*). *Tranquillizers* relieve anxiety. *Barbiturates* promote sleep.

2. Cardiovascular system. *Glycosides* (e.g. *digitalis*) treat heart failure by causing heart to contract. *Antihypertensive* drugs lower blood pressure. *Anticoagulants* stop clots by limiting fibrin deposition.

3. Respiratory system. *Expectorants* (e.g. *potassium iodide*), loosen phlegm to make coughing easier. *Suppressants* reduce coughing. *Adrenaline* relaxes air passages in treating asthma.

4. Digestive system. *Antacids* neutralize secretions that cause stomach ulcers. *Antinauseants* prevent nausea e.g. in travel sickness. *Kaolin* treats diarrhoea by absorbing water.

5. Endocrine system. Hormone deficiency treated by replacing missing hormone, e.g. *cortisone* for adrenal deficiency. Overactivity of a gland treated with an inhibitor, e.g. *carbimazole* inhibits thyroid manufacture.

6. Excretory system. *Diuretics* promote flow of urine, e.g. *thiadiazine* promotes sodium, and hence water, elimination.

7. Skeletal system. Gout, caused by deposition of *uric acid* in joints, treated with *probenecid* which promotes elimination of uric acid from the kidneys.

Above: Drugs may be administered in a variety of ways. Drops (1) are used for treating the eyes, ears and nose. Gas inhalation (2) administers respiratory drugs and anaesthetics. Injections can apply drugs *subcutaneously* just under the skin (3), *intravenously* into the bloodstream (4) or *intramuscularly* into a muscle, often a buttock (5). The site of an injection depends on how quickly an effect is desired. Intravenous injections have the quickest effect. Orally administered drugs (6), usually solid pills or capsules, or liquid syrups or linctuses, enter the digestive system. Ointments, creams and lotions (7) are applied to the skin

Left: A variety of ways in which drugs are administered orally. Capsules (1) contain drugs which are liberated when the capsule wall, made of gelatine, is digested in the stomach. Lozenges (2) are medicated sweets which slowly release drugs for mouth and throat complaints. Tablets (3) are made by mixing drugs with a base which binds them together. A cachet (4) is a small wafer impregnated with a drug and swallowed whole. Mixtures (5) contain a suspension of drugs in a liquid. Syrups (6) are strong sugar solutions containing a drug. Pastilles (7) are similar to lozenges, but sugar coated. Pills (8) are similar to tablets.

Right: One of these bottles contains a selection of sweets, the other a selection of drugs, some of them fatal if taken in large doses. Keeping pills and tablets out of the reach of children is an essential precaution.

Below: Between January 1960 and August 1962, 349 children with limb deformities were born in England and Wales to mothers who had taken the sedative drug *thalidomide*. This girl was one of the victims. The tragedy occurred because at that time the screening of new drugs for side-effects did not include tests during pregnancy. Since then, greater controls on the testing of new products have been introduced.

Heather Angel

Pharmaceutical Society of Great Britain

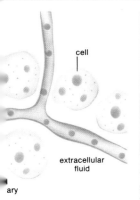

cell

extracellular fluid

ary

dug molecule

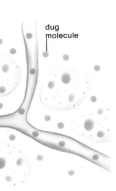

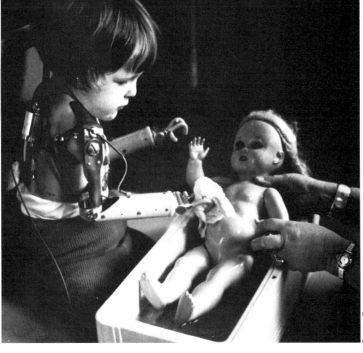

Camera Press

Left, top to bottom:
1. However they are administered, drugs eventually find their way to the bloodstream (except for ointments, creams and drops which act on the surface). The blood carries the drug to all parts of the body.
2. Molecules of the drug diffuse into the extracellular fluid.
3. Some drugs act by penetrating body cells and interfering with the cell's biochemical machinery. Others work by replacing chemical deficiencies, either in the extracellular fluid or in the cell itself, allowing the normal processes to resume. *Antibiotics* interfere with the chemical processes of bacteria, and are most useful if they do not at the same time harm the body cells.

Tranquillizers and antidepressants

An important advance in drug therapy has been the development of drugs to treat mental disturbance. These include the tranquillizer drugs for people suffering from anxiety and the anti-depressants drugs for treating depression.

The first member of the tranquillizer drug family was *phenothiazine*. This was first synthesized in the 1880's but its potential remained unrecognized for nearly 70 years. In 1950, French researchers synthesized the first widely-used tranquillizer, *chlorpromazine*. Chlorpromazine and allied drugs lower activity in areas of the brain concerned with emotion, such as the cortex, thalamus and hypothalamus and also have a sedative effect. A rather lighter tranquillizing action is produced by the *benzodiazepine* drugs, which include *Valium* and *Librium*. Some tranquillizers are used in the treatment of the psychotic mental illness, *schizophrenia*.

The tranquillizer drugs are taken by mouth and enter all the body tissues. Side-effects are not uncommon and include drowsiness, made worse by alcohol, and a tendency to low blood pressure. They may also affect the liver, producing jaundice, and by sensitizing the skin to light, may cause skin rashes.

The initial member of the anti-depressant drugs was *imipramine*, and further members of the group include *amitriptyline*, *nortriptyline*, and *protriptyline*, known as the *tricyclic* anti-depressants. The drugs are taken by mouth and act on the brain to produce a mood-elevating effect, helping to relieve the gloom and apathy experienced by the depressed person. Antidepressants are used with caution in sufferers from heart disease for they can raise the blood pressure.

Antihistamines

In 1927, the brilliant pharmacologist Lewis suggested that a substance called *histamine* was released by the body cells when an allergic reaction took place, causing itching, swelling and rashes. Scientists realized the value of a drug which would interfere with the action of histamine. The first therapeutically effective *antihistamine* drug was *pyrilamine maleate* and today there are a wide range of similarly acting drugs. They block the action of histamine through their chemical structure, which always contains an *ethylamine* group. This group competes with a similar group on the histamine molecules to fill receptor sites on cells where histamine creates its undesirable effects.

Antihistamines can be used to combat hay fever, asthma, drug rashes, reactions to stings, reactions to vaccines or any more serious allergy-based response. When taken by mouth, a major side-effect is drowsiness. Alcohol increases the drowsiness effect and should never be taken with antihistamines.

Psychiatry

In modern industrial societies, mental disorders have become a serious and widespread problem. In Britain, at least one third of the complaints that bring people to their general practitioner involve mental disturbance. In other industrial societies the situation is similar.

A number of factors can cause mental disorder. Some of these, such as a person's genetic make-up, personality and the experiences of his childhood, are *predisposing* factors. They may cause a disorder in themselves, or may make a person more vulnerable to develop a disorder later in life in reaction to a *precipitating* factor. Probably the most important precipitating factor in industrialized countries is mental *stress*.

Stress can occur whenever the demands placed on an individual by society are more than he can cope with. This situation is commonplace in modern industrial societies: financial worries, overwork, unrealistic or frustrated ambitions and loss of social 'face' can all precipitate mental illness, particularly when their effects are cumulative. Stress can also occur when an individual is placed in a conflict situation. Religious repression, for instance, may conflict with an individual's need to express his sex drive. Stress can become debilitating when, as is common in large urbanized communities, it is compounded by loneliness.

The treatment of mental disorder is the realm of *psychiatry*. An important role of the psychiatrist is just to listen to the problems of his patients. But, in addition, he can employ a variety of therapeutic techniques. The rapid advance in these techniques in the last 100 years has meant that many mental patients can now be restored to health.

Classification

Mental *illness* implies previous mental health and primarily involves emotional or behavioural disturbance, sometimes, though not necessarily, accompanied by intellectual deterioration. It is quite distinct from mental *deficiency*, or limited intelligence, which when it occurs, is present from birth. Up to 5% of people have an IQ below 70, and are regarded as mentally deficient.

A distinction is made between the *organic* and the *functional* mental illnesses. Organic illnesses arise from damage or disease in the brain. In the functional illnesses, the brain's machinery remains intact, but the way in which it works has become disordered.

Another distinction is between the *neuroses* and the *psychoses*. The neurotic suffers impairment of his mental functioning that may make his life difficult, but maintains contact with reality and is fully aware of his difficulties. The *psychotic* on the other hand is 'living in another world'.

An additional class of disorders are the *personality disorders*, suffered by people with immature or extreme personalities, who as a result may find it difficult to 'fit in' to society. The *psychopathic* personality, for instance, appears incapable of learning the values of the society he is living in, and as a result may engage in anti-social behaviour.

Right: In 1793, Dr Phillippe Pinel decided to unchain the mental patients at the Bicêtre hospital in Paris. Pinel's gesture led the way towards a more humane concern for the mental patient as an individual, an attitude that is indispensable to both the theory and practice of modern psychiatry. Prior to this unprecedented step, the mentally ill were treated so brutally that their chances of recovery were remote. An example of the totally unsympathetic attitude prevailing in Elizabethan society towards mental illness comes from this line in Shakespeare's *As You Like It* '... Love is merely a madness. And I tell you deserves as well a whip and a dark cell as madmen do.'

Left: The incidence of the psychotic illness *schizophrenia* is highest in the dilapidated inner areas of large cities. There are two possible explanations for this and both are probably important. One is that victims of the illness tend to drift towards the poorer areas of the city. Alternatively, the depressing atmosphere and social isolation of the inner city, where a person may have only a pet to share his problems with, may themselves precipitate the illness. To distinguish the cause of a mental illness from its effects is often hard, but it is important because treatment of an illness is rarely fully effective unless its underlying cause is known.

1. TOUCHES SOFT TOY SPIDER

2. SHOWN PICTURE OF SPIDER

4. HOLDS SMALL LIVE SPIDER

5. APPROACHES OPEN TANK OF LARGE LIVE SPIDERS

Right: *Behaviour therapy* is based on the idea that behavioural or emotional disturbances, such as compulsions or phobias, are acquired as *conditioned responses*, provoked automatically by particular objects or situations. It aims to *decondition* these responses. Here it is being used to treat spider phobia. The boy is gradually exposed to the situation he fears. Once he is used to toys or pictures of spiders, he can move on to real ones and is eventually able to hold a large spider without fear.

Left: This woman was described by the artist as a hysteric, but her apparent elation is more often a symptom of *mania*. *Hysteria* involves the expression of symptoms of illness in an unconscious attempt by the victim to gain some advantage from their expression. It rarely takes the form of wild laughing or crying.

Above and above right: A schizophrenic artist's paintings of a cat, as it appeared to him (above) at the start of his illness and (above right) when the illness had progressed, show the radical distortion of perception that occurs in schizophrenia. In a further painting the cat completely disappears into the background.

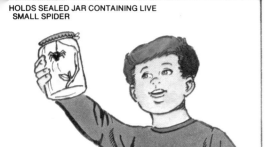

HOLDS SEALED JAR CONTAINING LIVE SMALL SPIDER

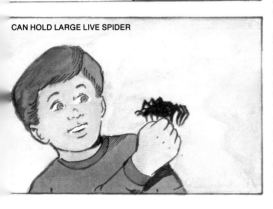

CAN HOLD LARGE LIVE SPIDER

Organic illnesses

Organic illnesses involve damage to, disease, or loss of the brain's nerve tissues. Certain of these illnesses are together called *dementia*. In *primary* dementia (sometimes called *senile* dementia), the reason why the nerve tissues degenerate is not well understood, but it may be due to metabolic disturbances in the brain's chemistry. *Secondary* dementia is caused by specific factors such as brain tumours, injury, degeneration of the brain's blood supply or infectious disease.

Dementias have certain common symptoms. Characteristically there is a gradual decrease in memory and logical thinking ability, a lack of insight, emotional disturbances such as undue suspiciousness or bursts of depression or elation, and degeneration in the sufferer's personal habits. Particular illnesses may produce more specific symptoms. For instance, the mental deterioration that accompanies the final stages of the venereal disease syphilis often involves grandiose delusions.

Epilepsy may be an accompanying symptom of a diseased or damaged brain, but it is also suffered by otherwise perfectly normal people, in which cases it is called *idiopathic epilepsy*, and may be due to a microscopic scar in the brain tissue. Epileptic attacks occur in one of two main forms: *petit mal* normally involves only a momentary loss of consciousness and attention. *Grand mal* is the full-blown fit brought about by a temporary excessive discharge of electrical activity in the brain. The victim falls down with a cry, usually loses consciousness, and his muscles first stiffen and then jerk violently for up to two minutes. Through the use of drugs such as the *anticonvulsant* drug *phenytoin*, the attacks may be controlled.

Psychoneuroses

Psychoneuroses are functional illnesses and among the most likely to be precipitated by environmental stress. They include *anxiety* states, *hysterical reactions* and *obsessive-compulsive* disorders. Anxiety state is the most common of all psychiatric disorders and simply involves unwarranted anxiety and apprehension. This is usually accompanied by restlessness, headaches and sleep disturbance.

Phobias are a special type of anxiety state, characterized by specific irrational fears of certain objects or situations. The most common is *agoraphobia*, the fear of going out alone into an open space. The main problem with phobias is that the victim may go to ridiculous lengths to avoid the feared object or situation, thus severely cutting down his activities.

An example of a *hysterical reaction* is the person who becomes paralyzed, not due to disease, but because of an intolerably stressful situation at work. The unconscious mind's 'solution' to the problem is to remove the stress by preventing the person from going to work.

Obsessive-compulsive disorders involve repetitive ideas or patterns of behaviour that carry on despite the conscious resistance of the sufferer. For instance, a person may be *obsessed* with the idea that their hands are contaminated, and as a result exhibit the *compulsion* of washing their hands every few minutes, although they realize that this behaviour is irrational.

351

Left: *Sketch of an Idea for Crazy Jane* by Richard Dadd. It was painted in 1855, 12 years after the artist had murdered his father in a fit of madness, since diagnosed as paranoid schizophrenia.

Below left: This crude treatment used in 1804, in which an electric current from a voltaic pile was used to produce an epileptic convulsion in the mental patient, was reported to be of therapeutic value. The principle of modern ECT is the same, except that nowadays the patient is first anaesthetized and given relaxant drugs, so he feels nothing. Modern ECT was originally based on the belief, now known to be incorrect, that epileptic fits prevent schizophrenia. It was,

however, found to be an effective treatment for depressive illness.

Right: The rhyme of Little Miss Muffet was based on a true story about a little girl with a phobia of spiders. This type of phobia is fortunately less debilitating than most.

Below: In diagnosing a patient's illness, the psychiatrist may use psychological tests such as the *Rorschach* test in which the patient is asked to describe what he sees in ink-blot patterns similar to these. This may provide the psychiatrist with an insight into the mental preoccupations of the patient, or alternatively may provide a talking point if the patient is inhibited.

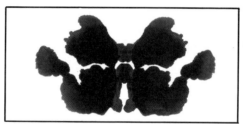

Affective disorders

Disturbances of *affect*, or mood, include *depressive illness* and *mania*. Depressive illness occurs in one of two main forms. *Exogenous* depression is a combination of misery and malaise that may occur in reaction to a disaster or the loss of a personal friend or relative, but exceeds in duration and intensity the normal reaction to such events. *Endogenous* depression occurs without any obvious external cause. Recent research has shown that a metabolic disturbance in brain chemistry, involving a deficit of a chemical called *noradrenaline* may precipitate it.

In both types the sufferer is unhappy, lacks vitality and interest in life and experiences guilt, reduced appetite for food and sex, and disturbed sleep rhythms. Endogenous depression may become psychotic in nature. Suicide is a real danger in severe cases of depression.

Mania is virtually the opposite of depression, since it involves excessive elation, energy and excitement. A person suffering from mania dashes about relentlessly and launches innumerable projects, completing none. In some individuals, mania and a psychotic form of depression alternate in bouts, in a condition called *manic-depressive* psychosis.

Schizophrenic psychoses

The term *schizophrenia* is applied to a number of disorders which exhibit one or more common symptoms. It literally means 'splitting of mind'. This does not refer to an individual having two personalities, but to a split between his thoughts and his emotional reaction to these thoughts so that he may, for instance, react to news of a disaster by

giggling. The schizophrenic is often unable to maintain a line of thought or carry on a simple conversation. His mental experiences may be so novel that he may have to invent new words or *neologisms* to describe them. Hallucinations may also occur, often in the form of 'inner voices'.

In some cases, the predisposing factor in schizophrenia appears to be hereditary. In other cases, abnormal family relationships are found, suggesting that the illness may arise from a family atmosphere which blocks the normal development of the personality. Recent studies have suggested that schizophrenia may be precipitated by a metabolic error in the brain's chemistry.

Therapies

Therapies are divided into treatments that are based on communication between the psychiatrist and the patient, which include *psychotherapy*, and *group* and *behaviour* therapy, and the physical treatments that include *drug therapy* and *electro-convulsive therapy*.

Psychotherapy is of particular value in treating psychoneuroses. There are two main kinds: *supportive psychotherapy* includes sympathetic advice combined with direct intervention in the particular problem that is causing the illness. The more ambitious *interpretative psychotherapy* is based on the principles that the roots of mental disturbance reside in the unconscious areas of the mind; and that bringing these to the conscious attention of the patient can bring about increased mental stability and emotional control. The three best known 'schools' of interpretative psychotherapy are *psycho-*

analysis, *analytical psychology* and *individual psychology*, developed by Sigmund Freud, Carl Jung and Alfred Adler respectively, though there are many other schools. These therapies are rigorous and exhaustive, and a full scale analysis usually requires several sessions every week for several years.

Group therapy is based on group communication between a number of patients with similar complaints, with the psychiatrist acting as an observer and occasional interpreter. New insights into the behaviour and problems of the patients may be revealed, prompting them to tackle their difficulties in a logical manner. Another form of group therapy is used in the treatment of schizophrenia, where a current approach is to regard the disorder as one of the schizophrenic's whole family.

Drugs are increasingly used in therapy. *Tranquillizers* are of particular importance in treating anxiety states, mania and schizophrenia, and act by reducing tension and agitation. *Anti-depressants* are of greatest use in treating endogenous depression, where they probably work by restoring the metabolic imbalance in brain chemistry that is thought to precipitate the illness.

Electro-convulsive therapy (ECT) involves the passage of an electric current through the forehead of the patient. ECT appears to be beneficial in the relief of severe endogenous depression and some forms of schizophrenia, but how it achieves its effects is unknown. Very careful diagnosis should be made by the psychiatrist before ECT is administered, for in some disorders it has no effect or makes matters worse.

352

The Structure of the Mind

During the nineteenth century it was already recognized in medical circles that mental activity takes place on two levels —the conscious and the unconscious. Of these only the most accessible area—the conscious—was at all well understood. It fell to a Viennese doctor, Sigmund Freud, to map the unconscious areas.

Freud, born in 1856, originally wanted to concentrate on pure medical research but the needs of a growing family forced him into private practice. Many of his patients suffered from *neuroses*. These are mental aberrations that can cause anxiety, depression and in some cases apparent physical illness, and prevent full development of the personality. It was from the clinical observations of his patients that he developed his *model*, or overall explanation, of the mind.

Freud postulated the hitherto unheard-of idea that sexual behaviour began not at puberty, but in earliest infancy, and that these early sexual drives affected the entire subsequent development of an individual's personality. The implications of this were shattering to a largely Christian western world, which for centuries had equated spiritual purity with sexual ignorance. As a result, Sigmund Freud became simultaneously the most renowned and the most reviled psychotherapist in medical history.

Below: Sigmund Freud, the founder of psycho-analysis, photographed at the age of 29 with his fiancée Martha, just before their marriage.

Mary Evans

Freud's theories

Freud's model was not based on a single theory but on a number of overlapping theories developed over the 40 years up to his death in 1939. One of the most important was that the mind had a three-tier structure, consisting of the *id*, *ego* and *superego*, of which only the ego impinged upon conscious mental activity.

The *id* contained everything that was present at birth and was a reservoir of instinctive drives and impulses, many of which were of an aggressive or sexual nature. The *ego* developed out of the id during childhood. Its function was to satisfy the instinctive drives of the id through contact with the outside world, partly through conscious mental activity. In doing this, the ego was modified by events and experiences. The *superego* developed in reaction to the id and dominated the ego on an unconscious level. Its function was to damp down the ego's activity in seeking satisfaction of the id; it could, in fact, be thought of as an internal 'monitor', exercising the same sort of control as would a parent. It observed the ego and threatened it with punishment, just like the parents whose place it had taken. Freud considered that all feelings of guilt and anxiety resulted

Below: Freud's study at his flat in Vienna. After listening to neurotics for most of the day, he would retire to his study and spend several hours writing about his day's discoveries. As Freud's reputation for treating neuroses grew, poets, philosophers and princesses came to lie on his couch and reveal their fears and fantasies.

Right: Freud's theory of the *Oedipus complex* was that all boys pass through a stage in which they unconsciously fall in love with their mother. The phrase was derived from the story of Oedipus, whose reward for solving the riddle of the sphinx, seen here, was to marry the widowed Queen of Thebes who, unknown to Oedipus, was his mother.

Erich Lessing/John Hillelson Agency

Giraudon

353

Mary Evans

Eve Arnold/John Hillelson Agency

Above: Carl Jung, a Swiss psychologist, was originally a disciple of Freud's, but their ideas eventually diverged. He added the idea of the 'collective unconscious' to Freud's conscious and unconscious areas of the mind. Jung saw this as a memory reservoir from man's past which holds the roots of all the psychological functions.

Right: Obsessional money hoarding, as practised by the Dickens character Scrooge, seen here, was regarded by Freud as a *sublimation* of the desire to retain the faeces, a desire which arose from the *anal retentive* stage of infantile sexuality. If this argument were true, the whole of Western capitalism could be seen as anally orientated.

Above: To Freud, thumb-sucking was a classic example of *oral erotism*, one of the stages of infantile sexuality.

Below: Megalomania, as manifest in individuals such as Adolf Hitler, was considered by Alfred Adler to result from a neurotic individual over-compensating for his inferiority feelings.

Right: A simplified representation of Freud's tri-partite structure of the mind. The *id* is a reservoir of instincts and drives. The *ego* deals with the external world in order to satisfy the demands of the id, and mediates between the id and the controlling influence of the *superego*, which is an internalized version of the parents.

from the ego disobeying the superego.

Freud realized that this structure contained a number of conflicting influences which caused a degree of inner stress to be built up and to manifest itself as anxiety. In searching for mechanisms by which normally adjusted people reduced this anxiety, Freud identified several *defence mechanisms*, which the ego employed in its role of mediating between the often conflicting influences of id and superego. Of these defence mechanisms, he considered some to be successful since, in an indirect way, they allowed the instincts of the id to be expressed. Others, considered unsuccessful, simply prevented the id's expression. These had to be used over and over again as the id persisted in seeking satisfaction.

The most important of the successful defences, according to Freud's theories, was that of *sublimation*. This involved the deflection of instinctual drives in a manner acceptable to the superego.

A common unsuccessful defence was that of *repression*, in which unacceptable impulses whose expression might prove painful were pushed back into the unconscious. But, although the pain was no longer felt, the repressed impulse still retained its ability to hurt the individual. Another defence was *reaction formation*, in which a reaction was formed in the conscious to oppose the unacceptable impulse in the unconscious. For instance, people who fainted at the sight of blood might be reacting to their own aggressive impulses.

All these defences, Freud held, took place unconsciously and were beyond the control of the individual, but exerted considerable influence on an individual's

Mary Evans

behaviour. If an individual adopted only unsuccessful defences, conflict, anxiety and eventually mental illness might arise. The technique Freud founded, called *psychoanalysis*, seeks to elucidate the particular defences neurotic individuals have been adopting in order to understand and treat their neuroses.

Infantile sexuality

Alongside Freud's theories on the tripartite structure of the mind were his *psychosexual* theories. He considered that as a result of the instinctive drive towards pleasure infants sought stimulation of their bodies and that this infantile sexuality went through several stages. Early on in life during the *oral* stage, the sexual drive manifested itself in stimulation of the mouth area. At about two years of age during the *anal* stage, the

Mary Evans

anus became the most important zone. After this, the *phallic* stage was reached in which for the boy, the penis became the most important zone, and for girls, the clitoris. At puberty, all the stages were reorganized and subordinated to the adult sexual aim of reproduction.

A further important Freudian theory of infantile sexuality was that all male children passed through a stage in development called the *Oedipus complex*, and girls the *Electra complex*. It was, he held, a part of normal development that, at an unconscious level, a boy should fall in love with his mother and seek to exclude the rival for his mother's love—his father. The complex was resolved when the boy, in fear of castration from his father, had instead to identify with his father. In girls, during the Electra complex, a similar type of process occurred

Mansell

MICHELET, SC.

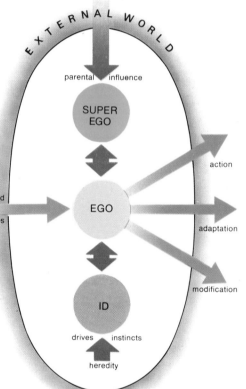

Mary Evans

Above and right: How behavioural differences between boys and girls are brought about is contested. Freud's view was that they developed sex roles by identifying with their same-sex parent after resolution of their Oedipus or Electra complexes. Some biologists believe that behavioural differences are inborn. Others consider that they are brought about by the different methods of socializing boys and girls—for instance, giving boys guns to play with, but giving girls dolls' houses.

Diagram labels:

EXTERNAL WORLD

parental influence

SUPER EGO

action

EGO

adaptation

modification

ID

drives   instincts

heredity

with the parental roles reversed.

The great task of the individual, Freud considered, was to resolve these complexes and thus to free himself from his parents. Since most of the processes by which they were resolved took place during the first five years of life, these years were of utmost importance in the development of the personality.

At first, Freud used the technique of *hypnosis* to reach the unconscious content of his patients' minds, but he discarded the method when he realized that it did not allow him to observe directly his patients' unconscious defence mechanisms. Consequently he relied on interpreting his patients' dreams in conjunction with the technique of *free association*. Free association makes use of the fact that any thought or memory has a 'halo' or complex of other thoughts and mem-

ories related to it. During a psychoanalytic session, a patient would be asked, starting with the content of a recent dream, to say whatever came into his head. Freud often found that this free association from the content of the dream would lead the patient to the source of his anxiety—a repressed impulse.

Modifications to Freud's theories

Freud's theories came into almost as much conflict with the medical profession as with the church. Since the first congress of psychoanalysis in 1908, there have been continual variations and modifications of Freud's theories. Several completely opposing theories have also emerged. Among these are the theories of the behavioural school of psychology, who do not consider the mind to have an inner structure like that described by Freud; but rather that the mind is organized to respond to external events, and that the driving forces behind behaviour are these external events.

Among those who originally adhered to Freud's theories, but later diverged, was the Swiss psychiatrist C. G. Jung, who set up his own school of psychoanalysis called *analytical psychology*. Jung's structure of the unconscious was somewhat different from Freud's and involved, among other ideas, the concept of the *collective unconscious*. Jung regarded this as a memory reservoir from the whole of man's past, which formed the foundation of the personality.

The other famous name associated with Freud was another Austrian, Alfred Adler. Adler's psychology was based on the concept that man's behaviour was motivated chiefly by social urges, whose

main driving force was an innate desire for superiority. This conflicted with Freud's view that the chief driving force was sexual gratification. Adler considered that for each individual, a lifestyle was formed early in childhood with the goal of achieving superiority. The particular lifestyle chosen by an individual depended on which aspects of his personality the individual felt to be inferior. Out of this was born the concept of the *inferiority complex*, an unconscious construction which each individual seeks to *compensate* for by striving for superiority.

Further modifications to Freud's theories took place in the 1930s and 1940s, through the work of the American psychologists Karen Horney, Erich Fromm and Harry Sullivan. Horney recognized that Freud's insistence on sexual repression as the source of most neuroses was due to the type of patients Freud had been dealing with—mainly young women living in the sexually-repressed atmosphere of Vienna at the turn of the century. She believed that the concealment of any impulse or desire was as important a factor as repressed sex in causing neuroses. By placing less importance on sex, she helped to make Freudian analysis more acceptable to the public.

Some of Freud's theories are now discredited by the majority of psychologists, partly because it is impossible to validate them in a rigorous scientific manner. Freud's critics have also pointed out that the curative value of psychoanalysis is unproven. Many of his ideas about the development of the personality structure are still accepted, however, especially the strong effects of early experiences.

Dental Care

In a modern civilized society one can manage without teeth. False teeth are so common and acceptable these days that they are taken for granted—and about half of the population of Britain over the age of 30 have them. But a healthy natural dentition makes a notable difference to eating and enjoying a normal healthy diet; it plays an important part in the formation of sounds when we talk, and it also makes a major contribution to the attractiveness of our appearance. Dental disease is the commonest ailment of civilization; dental decay and gum disease affect over 99 per cent of the adult population in developed countries. But the prevalence of dental disease, especially decay (*dental caries*), is very much less in communities which have had little or no contact with civilization, and this is as true for the predominantly meat-eating Eskimos as for some largely vegetarian tribes living in the tropics. All the evidence seems to indicate that one of the main causes of dental decay is the sugar and other refined carbohydrates

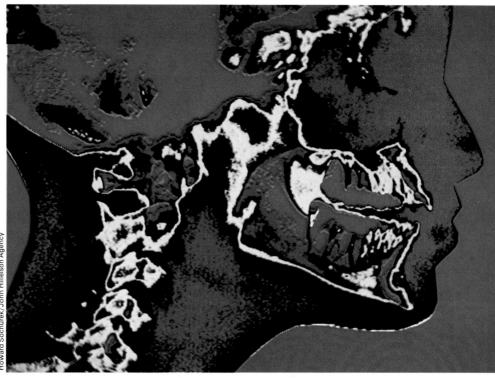

Howard Sochurek/John Hillelson Agency

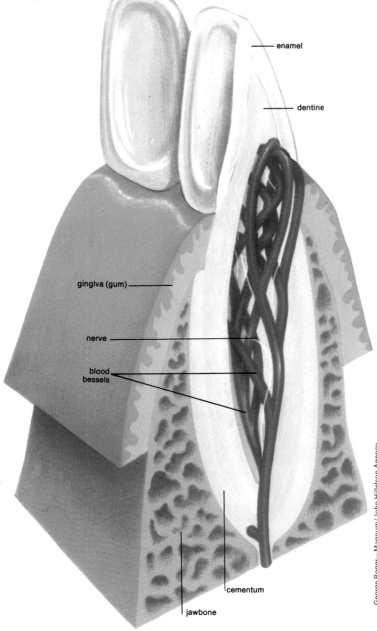

— enamel

— dentine

gingiva (gum) —

nerve —

blood bessels —

cementum

jawbone

Left: This cross section shows the components of a healthy incisor tooth, one of the four in each jaw at the front of the mouth. These are used for biting into food, while the molars and premolars, at the side and back, are used for grinding it up. The enamel which covers a tooth is the body's hardest substance.

Above: The technique of sonography uses a beam of ultrasonic sound, above the range of human hearing. The colour of this display varies with the density of the material through which the beam has passed, showing up the jaw and spinal column (yellow). This technique is used for illustration purposes only.

Below: A perfect set of teeth is common among people with a low-sugar diet, as the smile of this Nuba girl from Sudan shows. There was a great reduction in the occurrence of dental caries in Europe during World War II when sugar became hard to obtain, particularly in Norway where it was almost non-existent.

George Roger—Magnum/John Hillelson Agency

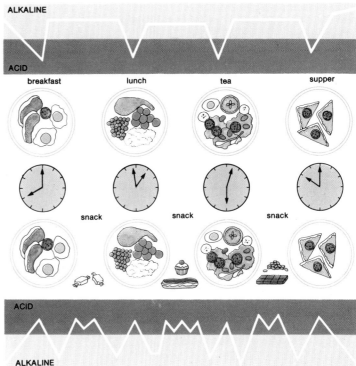

Above: Once a rare treat, sugar-rich meals and drinks are now common for many children, putting their teeth at high risk at an early age.

Right: The mouth's natural defence against acid produced by sugar is the saliva, which is alkaline. These graphs show the effect of sugary snacks between meals: each food intake produces excess acid which is neutralized quickly by the saliva. But snacks result in a much greater risk of acid attack.

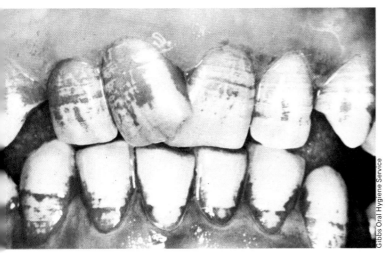

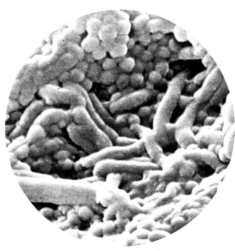

Left and far left: Plaque is normally hard to see, but it can be made visible by using a 'disclosing solution' which stains it red, as shown at far left. The magnified view shows a sample of plaque as seen with a scanning electron microscope: the area shown is just 8 microns (8 millionths of a metre) across. The growth starts with the globules, which are accumulations of bacteria. The time taken for them to appear probably depends on the health of the *gingiva* (gum). If the gums are inflamed, bacteria appear within 30 minutes of cleaning. This sample is 2 days old, and some long filamentary structures have begun to gather as well as globules.

which form such a large part of our modern diet.

From the Middle Ages up until relatively recently the only dental care available to most people was in a booth at the local fairground. Itinerant tooth drawers moved around the country with travelling fairs and extracted aching teeth while an assistant banged a large drum to drown the cries. Fortunately, the last 150 years has seen the evolution of the skilled dental surgeon who is trained both to repair the ravages of dental disease and, increasingly in recent years, to initiate public health programmes which try to prevent it.

Tooth structure
We have two sets of teeth during our lifetime. The initial 20 deciduous or milk teeth are replaced by 32 permanent teeth. Each tooth consists of a crown and from one to three roots depending on its type and position. The crown is that portion which appears above the surface of the gum, while the root is contained in the socket in the jaws. The bulk of the tooth consists of a hard yellow material known as *dentine*. The exposed surfaces of the crown are covered by the dense white *enamel* which is the hardest substance in

the body. The surface of the root is covered with a thin layer of another dense tissue known as the *cementum* which anchors the fibres of the *periodontal ligament*—this can be thought of as a sling joining the tooth to the bone of the socket wall. Each tooth has a *pulp* chamber with blood vessels and nerves connected to the blood and nerve supply of the jaw bone by the narrow root canal. The gums are made of *epithelial* tissue which is tightly bound by fibres to the jaw bones forming a protective cuff around the teeth to prevent infection spreading from the mouth into the jaw bones via the sockets of the teeth.

The mechanisms by which teeth decay are still not completely understood, but the most commonly accepted explanation is that the teeth become covered with a thin film of mucus-like material which contains bacteria. This film is called *dental plaque* and when sugar in the food diffuses into the plaque certain bacteria metabolize the sugar with the formation of acid. This free acid then attacks the tooth substance and the decay gets under way.

The decay process usually starts on the more vulnerable surfaces of the enamel cap, either between the teeth where the

plaque is hard to remove, or at the bottom of fissures in the crowns of the cheek teeth. The process can be likened to a tunnelling process as it penetrates the relatively hard enamel, but once into the softer tissue it undermines the overlying enamel. If untreated the decay will involved the soft tissues of the pulp which will become inflamed and eventually *necrotic*—that is, dead. The necrosis will spread down the root canal and into the surrounding bone, and the ensuing inflammation is known as a dental *abscess*.

Filling a tooth
Once decay is present in a tooth it is not yet possible to reverse the process and to effect a 'cure' (although experiments with fluoride contact solutions have shown that some remineralization of eroded enamel can occur). The treatment is to remove the decayed tissue using rotary drilling instruments. In the modern air turbine the drill or *bur* rotates at speeds of up to 400,000 rpm and generates so much heat that it has to be water cooled when in use. The tooth is then restored with one of a variety of filling materials. It is usual to extend the cavity to include any areas of the tooth that are especially susceptible to decay. To protect the pulp a 357

cavity is usually lined with a bland material which insulates the tooth interior from temperature changes; the amalgam which is used for filling conducts heat easily.

The silver amalgam (finely ground silver, tin, copper and zinc, bound with a small amount of mercury) used for filling back teeth is soft and plastic during insertion but soon sets hard. With this type of material the cavity is prepared in such a way that the filling can be keyed into position. In the front of the mouth the material has to be more aesthetically acceptable, so a tooth coloured filling is used. There are several varieties but all suffer from the disadvantage of not being as strong as silver amalgam.

Once a tooth has become so broken down that a cavity which will give retention for a moulded filling cannot be prepared then a more complex restoration using either gold or porcelain becomes necessary. This usually means removing the remains of the enamel cap and replacing it with a gold or porcelain crown. Modern developments include porcelain crowns which are fused on to a gold backing: these have the tooth-like appearance of porcelain while the metal gives added strength.

If the decay has reached the pulp then it is sometimes possible to remove the dead tissue that remains in the pulp chamber and root canal, mechanically clean out the space left using reamers and then to stop it up with a filling, so preventing infection reaching the core.

Extraction
Despite all that can be done to restore teeth, they still often have to be extracted, either to relieve the pain of a dental abscess or because gum disease has progressed so far that there is not enough support left for the tooth to function properly. Usually teeth can be removed with special forceps which are designed to grip the root just below the crown of the tooth, which is then moved from side to side to break it out of its socket.

Dental work would be painful if it were not for the use of anaesthetics. Most restorative work and the majority of extractions are now done under *local analgesia*, the pain impulses being prevented from travelling along the nerve by the injection of suitable local anaesthetics—nowadays synthetic compounds resembling cocaine. At other times a general anaesthetic is used, either because the patient prefers it or because the dentist thinks it more suitable, and here the patient is put to sleep, often by means of intravenous drugs.

Periodontal or gum disease is an insidious process which leads to the destruction of the tissues supporting the teeth and so to eventual loss of the teeth themselves. If it is not removed, the dental plaque will eventually irritate the surrounding *gingival epithelium*, which then becomes soggy and enlarged. Unless it is treated, this process leads to a painless destruction of the fibres of the periodontal ligament and of the bone in the vicinity. Eventually the patient's teeth become loose, but by this time the damage is often very considerable and treatment can be very prolonged and time consuming.

Gum disease is treated by a meticulous removal of all the plaque, together with a thorough cleaning of the teeth, which is followed in many cases by surgical recon-

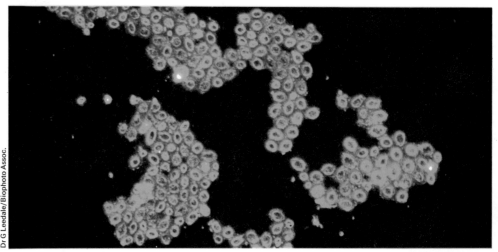

Dr G Leedale/Biophoto Assoc.

1. crown
2. roots
3. cusp
4. enamel
5. dentine
6. pulp
7. gingiva (gum)
8. jawbone
9. pulp canal
10. cementum
11. decay
12. necrotic tissue
13. abscess

Left: A cutaway view of a molar (back tooth). Molars have either two or three roots: in this example, one root has become infected while the other remains healthy. Decay has broken through the enamel and dentine to the pulp, so that the nerves in the root are exposed, causing toothache. The pulp in the diseased root has become necrotic all the way down to the root end where it has caused a painful abscess.

Right: Dental experts these days place great importance on getting people to visit their dentist regularly so that dental decay and gum disease can be spotted in their early stages.

Below: This colony of yeast-like cells is *Candida albicans*, the fungus which causes 'thrush', a gum infection particularly common among babies and young children. In this view the cells have been made to fluoresce; the magnification is 1,850 times.

touring of the gum margins. For treatment to be successful the patient must cooperate by maintaining a high standard of oral hygiene.

False teeth
Unfortunately, despite all that the dentist is able to achieve, far too many people lose some or all of their teeth and need artificial replacements or dentures. If only a few teeth are lost a small plastic or metal plate can be made which is attached to one or more of the remaining teeth by clasps. When all the teeth have gone the plates are retained by a mixture of suction and unconscious control using the muscles of the cheeks and tongue.

All types of dentures are made in the same way. First, impressions of the jaws are taken in a non-toxic, elastic material which sets soon after it is put into the mouth. A positive replica of the jaws can be obtained by making a cast of the impression with plaster of Paris. A wax model of the dentures then forms a pattern for the mould which is used in the preparation of the completed denture.

Irregularities in the shape of the dental arches and similar *malocclusions*—crooked teeth—are another major reason why people go to the dentist. It is probable that the genetic mechanisms which govern jaw growth are separate from those that control tooth size and in populations of mixed racial stock, such as exist in most of the developed world, the genes for these characteristics are often ill assorted. The consequences can be gross discrepancies in both jaw and tooth size which lead to malocclusion.

when did YOU last have your MOUTH SERVICED?

VISIT YOUR DENTIST REGULARLY

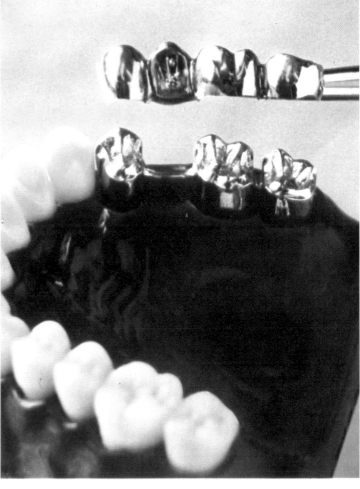

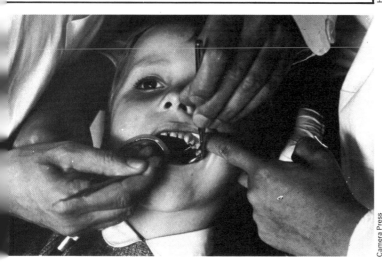

Above: The problem of restoring a single missing tooth is solved by making a double gold bridge. One part is cemented into the mouth, while the other fits precisely over it. The fit is so good that the bridge will not come adrift in the mouth though the patient can remove it for cleaning.

Left: A dentist uses a mirror to examine the tooth while he works on it with mechanical and powered devices.

Right: Brushing the teeth is not by itself sufficient: they should be brushed in the proper way, as shown here. The use of dental floss (a waxed thread) is also recommended to remove plaque and particles of food.

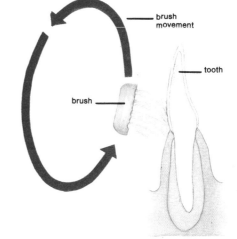

Orthodontics is the name given to the work of straightening the teeth and preventing and treating malocclusion. Special appliances which move the teeth are used. There are two main types—the removable and the fixed. The removable brace usually has springs or expansion screws which exert a continuous gentle pressure on the teeth to be moved, attached to a plate which can be removed from the mouth for cleaning. In recent years there has been a tendency to use fixed appliances with stainless steel bands which are cemented to the tooth to form the anchorage for the springs.

More and more research is going into dentistry. New and better materials are being produced, and the latest filling materials are almost indistinguishable from the natural tooth in appearance and will adhere to the tooth as well. At the same time there is now a greater understanding of the mechanisms which underlie the process of decay and the role of bacteria. This has led scientists to investigate the possibility of producing a vaccine against dental decay.

Nowadays more attention is going into the prevention of dental disease, especially by better education. A diet that avoids excess sugar, particularly between meals, will cut down the likelihood of decay very much. Oral hygiene plays an important part, and if the dental plaque is removed properly at least once a day the development of tooth decay and gum disease is arrested. This can be done by using a toothbrush in the proper manner, linked with the use of dental floss (a waxed thread) to thoroughly clean out the spaces between the teeth. Brushing the teeth is not by itself sufficient: they should be brushed in the correct way, getting at those parts of the teeth which are least accessible.

One of the most important ways to prevent decay has been shown to be the addition of a fluoride to the water in one part per million. The fluoride is incorporated into the developing enamel and dentine which then become harder and more resistant to acid attack. This reduces the incidence of decay by up to 50% and seems to be safe and economical.

A sensible low sugar diet, the fluoridation of water supplies, careful oral hygiene and regular visits to the dentist for the early treatment of disease or malocclusion should result in a healthy mouth with teeth that will last a lifetime.

Non-infectious Diseases

Disease literally means 'lack of ease' or discomfort, but this definition is far from comprehensive: some diseases may be present long before any discomfort is felt, while others may be 'carried' genetically throughout a person's life without that person ever exhibiting symptoms of illness. One of the greatest tasks of medicine has been to pinpoint the underlying causes of particular diseases to make treatment of the 'discomfort' possible.

Diseases and disorders that are present from birth are called *congenital* disorders. They are of two main types. *Hereditary* disorders are caused by a specific genetic defect passed down from previous generations—one or both of the sufferer's parents either exhibit the defect or carry the defective gene in a *recessive* form. More commonly, however, congenital defects are the result of an 'accident' which has occurred either during the formation of the ovum or sperm or during the development from fertilized ovum to embryo in the womb.

The accident may be purely genetic in nature, as when the ovum accidentally acquires an extra piece of *chromosome* (genetic material) during its formation. Even when the disorder is precipitated by external factors such as injury to the embryo as it is developing, genetic make-up may determine whether an abnormality results, since it affects the embryo's reaction to external factors.

Diseases that appear or develop during a person's lifetime are termed *acquired* diseases. These include such diverse disorders as nutritional defects (such as scurvy), *degenerative* diseases (such as multiple sclerosis), *neoplastic* disorders (new growths including cancer) and the *infectious* diseases. A person's genetic make-up again may *predispose* the development of an acquired disorder in reaction to a *precipitating* factor such as nutritional deficiency, invading organisms, or unhealthy habits such as smoking. For instance, the metabolic disease *diabetes mellitus* may be precipitated by faulty nutrition, but at the same time appears to have a genetic predisposing factor since it tends to run in families.

Congenital disorders

Hereditary diseases are uncommon since people who exhibit disadvantageous genetic defects are less likely to reproduce and thus pass on the defect to their children. Those hereditary diseases which do occur are usually the result of recessive, rather than dominant, genetic defects: in other words far more people 'carry' the defect than suffer from the disease.

The way in which hereditary diseases take their effect is, in many cases, well understood. For instance, *phenylketonuria*, caused by a simple recessive genetic defect, can be treated quite simply. The defect leads to the absence of a certain enzyme in the liver of afflicted babies, and as a result they are unable to break down (to harmless products) the amino acid *phenylalanine* which thus accumulates in the brain causing mental retardation. All babies are now screened for the presence of this disease at birth and if found to be affected are given a diet deficient in phenylalanine and thus do not develop an illness.

In some parts of the world, *sickle-cell anaemia* is a very common disease, with up to 40 per cent of the population being carriers of the recessive gene that causes

National Gallery

Robert Harding/Leimbach

Michael Holford

Above: *A Grotesque Old Woman* by **Quinten Massys.** The painting is closely related to a Leonardo drawing, believed to be of a real person. The subject's ugliness may have been exaggerated, but her ambiguous appearance suggests she had a congenital disorder caused by a wrong number of sex chromosomes. This type of defect may give rise to both male and female features.

Left: Dwarfism is often caused by the hereditary defect *achondroplasia.* The defect is dominant, so one would expect at least one parent to be also affected. Achondroplastics may, however, be born to normal parents as a result of mutation in a parent's egg or sperm cell. The defect is, however, passed on (on average) to half the victim's children.

Above right and right: Congenital disorders may only develop fully in reaction to external factors. Although some children are predisposed to congenital hip dislocation, they are more likely to develop it if carried on a board (right) than if carried in a sling (above right).

Robert Harding

STROKE

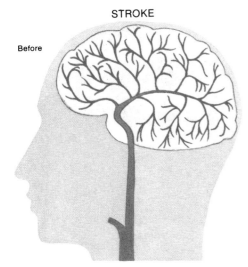

Before

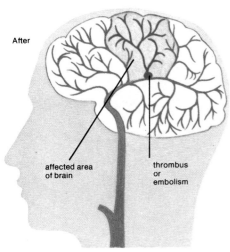

After

affected area
of brain

thrombus
or
embolism

Left: *Stroke* is usually
caused by a degenerative
disease of the arteries
involving both *atheroma*,
the deposition of fatty
material in the arteries,
and *arteriosclerosis*, a
thickening of the
arterial walls. These
can lead to a *thrombus*,
or clot, forming and
blocking the blood flow
in a brain artery; or
blockage may result from
an *embolism*, a flake of
material carried to the
brain from a diseased
artery in another part
of the body. In either
case, the part of the
brain normally served by
the blocked artery does
not receive sufficient
oxygen and its cells soon
die. This can result in
sudden death for the
victim, or paralysis of
those parts of the body
controlled by the damaged
area of the brain.

Above right: *Gout* is
caused by excess blood
levels of *uric acid*, which
is deposited as urate
crystals in the joints
resulting in a painful
inflammation. Factors
such as diet sometimes
precipitate the excess
uric acid, but in some
people the disease may
result from a hereditary
defect, either causing
over-synthesis of uric
acid or impairing the
excretion of the chemical
from the body. A classic
attack of gout appears
suddenly, proverbially
at the base of the big
toe. Several drugs can
relieve the affliction.

Right: Many degenerative
diseases are the
inevitable result of
the ageing process. This
women is being treated
for *osteoarthritis*, a
degenerative disease of
the joints.

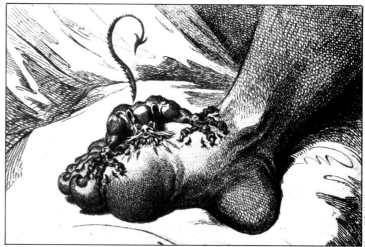

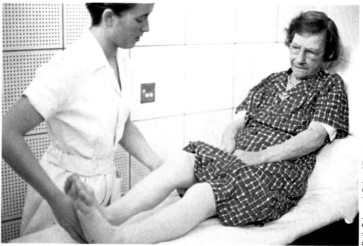

it. The reason for its preponderance is that, although the disease is usually fatal to children who suffer from it, carriers are conferred with an increased resistance to malaria, which is common in these areas. Carriers are thus marginally more likely to survive and reproduce than people who do not carry the defective gene at all, and so the defect retains a hold on the genetic 'pool' of the population.

Congenital disorders caused by chromosomal abnormalities are of particular interest. These occur if, during cell division, a parent's egg or sperm acquires an extra piece of chromosome accidentally. This is the case in *Down's syndrome* (mongolism), caused by the acquisition of an entire extra chromosome in the formation of the ovum. Some disorders are the result of abnormalities in the sex chromosomes. A normal female has two 'X' sex chromosomes whereas the male has one 'X' chromosome and one 'Y'. *Klinefelter's syndrome* occurs in men with a normal Y chromosome but two X chromosomes. The Y chromosome gives the individual a male appearance and psychology but the additional X chromosome affects testicular development and renders him infertile, though not impotent.

There are a wide range of congenital defects caused by abnormal development of the embryo. They are often the result of injury, with the abnormality generally occuring in the organ that is being formed at the time. An injury during the period of spinal column development may lead to *spina bifida*, in which one of the spinal vertebrae does not develop fully and as a result part of the spinal cord is exposed. Congenital heart defects include the 'hole in the heart', where the *septum* that

divides the two sides of the heart fails to develop. Fortunately, many defects such as these can now be corrected by surgery.

Degenerative diseases

Degenerative diseases involve a gradual breakdown of certain tissues or organs of the body. In Western countries they are among the most widespread of diseases, and are often associated with the processes of ageing. *Arteriosclerosis*, thickening of the walls of the arteries, together with *atheroma*, the deposition of fatty substances on the arterial walls, are included in this category, and since they often lead on to a heart attack or 'stroke' (the result of failed blood supply to the brain) they are the most common cause of death in Western countries.

Some degenerative diseases may appear long before old age is reached. Such is the case with *multiple sclerosis*, in which small, scattered areas of nerve fibre in the spinal cord and the brain lose the insulating myelin sheath that normally covers them. This impairs their ability to conduct electrical impulses and may lead to paralysis and loss of feeling in the limbs and other parts of the body.

Neoplastic diseases

Neoplasms, or new growths, involve an abnormal multiplication of cells. They are of two types. *Benign* neoplasms include such aberrations as warts, moles and the common fatty swelling called *lipoma*, and do not harm neighbouring tissues or spread to other parts of the body. *Malignant* neoplasms, better known as *cancers*, invade and harm neighbouring tissues, can migrate around the body and are usually fatal unless treated.

Despite intensive research on the causes of cancer, the alteration in cellular biochemistry that causes some cells to start suddenly multiplying in an abnormal fashion is imperfectly understood. However, research has revealed a number of factors that appear to set the process off.

Viruses have been shown to precipitate some cancers in animals. The link between virus and cancer is less certain in humans, but some human cancers, such as those of the cervix and of the lymphoid tissue, are linked to virus infection. Certain chemicals are *carcinogenic*, that is liable to precipitate cancer in tissues with which they come into contact. When, in the eighteenth century, large numbers of chimney sweeps were found to be suffering from cancer of the scrotum, it was correctly suggested that the coal tar found in soot was a carcinogenic agent.

The most likely, and most widely accepted, explanation of the higher incidence of lung cancer in smokers than in non-smokers is that certain chemicals in tobacco smoke are carcinogenic. Other carcinogenic agents include asbestos, which precipitates a cancer of the pleural covering of the lungs called *mesothelioma*, and *aniline dyes*, which are associated with the bladder cancer.

Some diseases appear to predispose the development of cancer. *Ulcerative colitis*, an inflammatory disease of the large bowel, may become cancerous. Various skin diseases such as *lupus vulgaris* and the strangely named *lichen planus* often precede cancer of the skin.

All forms of radiation can give rise to cancer. Sunlight may be a factor in skin cancer, particularly for people whose natural protection against harmful radiation, the skin pigment *melanin*, is not present in levels sufficient to be effective. Thus light-skinned Europeans who emigrate to the tropics increase their chances of developing skin cancer. As regards other forms of radiation, there is a higher rate of cancer among people who operate X-ray equipment in hospitals, and exposure to excessive doses of X-rays while in the womb increases a baby's chances of developing *leukaemia*, a cancer of the white blood eclls.

Cancer can also result from atomic radiation, whether this comes from the radioactive materials to which some people are exposed during their work, or from the fall-out of an atomic explosion.

In some cases, genetic make-up appears to be a predisposing factor. Some cancers occur in families, such as cancer of the

WHERE CANCER OCCURS

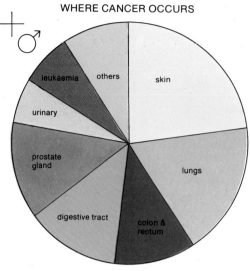
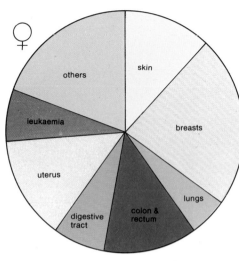

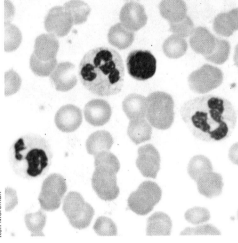

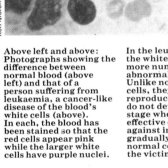

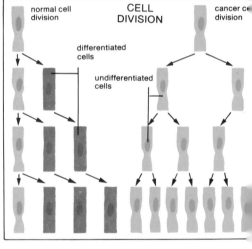

Above: Pie charts showing the relative incidence of cancer in the sites where it occurs in men (left) and women (right), combining information from all countries. Individual countries may show a marked variation on this pattern. For example, in Britain in 1966, 36 per cent of all cancers in men were lung cancers.

Below: The main characteristic of cancer cells is that they are *undifferentiated*. In normal cell division (left) differentiated cells are formed to perform a specific useful function in the body. In cancerous growth (right) the cells do not develop any useful function. Their only activity seems to be self-reproduction.

Below: Stages in the development of lung cancer over time. 1: The lining of an air passage consists of a layer of *epithelial* and mucus-producing *goblet* cells, underlain by a mosaic of *basal* cells, which multiply at an early stage of cancer. 2: When irritated, the top layer of cells is not replaced when it dies but flat

squamous cells form instead. The basal cells revert to their former growth rate. 3: Basal cells multiply again, some transforming into cancer cells. 4: These replace normal basal cells and the overlying squamous cells, and break through the *basilar membrane*. 5: The cancer cells invade underlying connective tissue.

Above left and above: Photographs showing the difference between normal blood (above left) and that of a person suffering from leukaemia, a cancer-like disease of the blood's white cells (above). In each, the blood has been stained so that the red cells appear pink while the larger white cells have purple nuclei.

In the leukaemic blood, the white cells are far more numerous and have abnormally shaped nuclei. Unlike normal white cells, they are able to reproduce themselves but do not develop to a stage where they are an effective defence against infection. They gradually replace the normal cells, weakening the victim's defences.

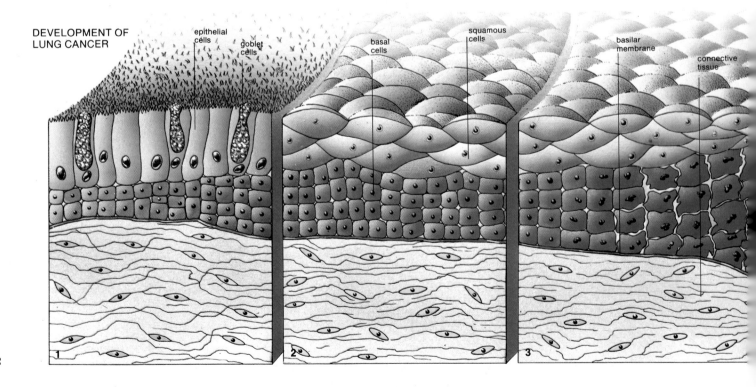

DEVELOPMENT OF LUNG CANCER

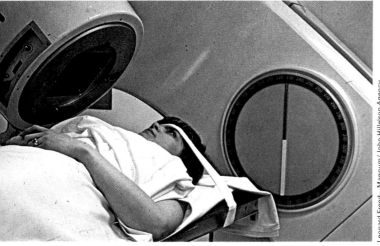

Left: Radiotherapy is one of three main forms of treatment for cancer. Taking into account the site and extent of the cancer, a radiologist calculates a dose and wavelength of radiation that will be absorbed by, and damage, the cancerous tissue, but will pass through, and not harm, intervening tissues. This is then delivered to the patient. X-rays and *gamma* rays from radium are the main types of radiation used.

Below: An excess dose of radiation, as suffered by these victims of the Hiroshima atom bomb, may kill, or failing that, may precipitate cancer or *radiation sickness*, an often fatal disease. The effects of the Hiroshima bomb are still being found today.

Leonard Freed—Magnum/John Hillelson Agency

Below: Probably the greatest danger of a cancerous growth is if it *metastasizes*, or spreads to other parts of the body. Here we see how a cancer can spread from a primary tumour in the lung. Cancer cells find their way into the bloodstream either directly into the pulmonary vein, or via the lymphatic vessels.

They are then carried to the heart where they may establish a new growth, or may be carried by an artery to other vital organs such as the liver or brain. While a cancer is still localized and not directly harming a vital organ it may be curable, but once cancer cells have metastized, it is very difficult to treat.

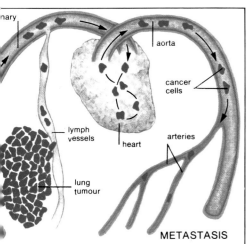

METASTASIS

Bilderdienst Süddeutscher Verlag

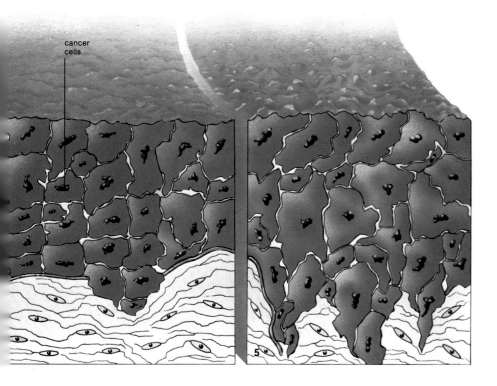

colon in families who suffer from the hereditary disease *polyposis coli*. Genetic or chromosomal abnormalities are often found in cancer cells. But it is difficult to decide whether these are a cause or a result of the disease.

Whatever causes cells to become cancerous, and probably more than one factor is at work, it is now believed that a breakdown in the body's normal defence mechanisms for controlling cell-growth must occur before the abnormal cells can multiply. Finding out why this breakdown happens is one of the most important aims of modern cancer research.

Effects and treatment of cancer

The effects of cancer are more obvious than the causes. Because of their invasive nature, cancer cells may damage nearby vital organs and cause death by direct action. This is especially true of brain tumours. Furthermore, the ability of cancer cells to migrate to other parts of the body, a process called *metastasis*, may lead to fatal secondary cancers developing in vital organs such as the lungs, liver and brain. Cancer cells are also 'greedy'. They grow faster than normal cells and thus extract undue amounts of nutrients from the body, leaving the sufferer more susceptible to infection, or even 'starving' him to death.

The treatment of cancer varies according to its type, site and degree of development. Early diagnosis of the disease is particularly important if treatment is to be successful. People can help themselves in an early diagnosis through being aware of the symptoms of early cancer, and for women through regular inspection of the breasts for any abnormal swelling. Medical checkups, such as routine cervical smears for women at risk of developing cervical cancer, are also important.

The main types of treatment for cancer are surgery, drug therapy and radiotherapy. In many cases a combination of these treatments is used. Surgery is the most drastic treatment, and aims to remove all the cancerous cells. The main disadvantages of surgery are that it may involve destruction of nearby healthy tissue, and it runs the risk of releasing cancer cells into the bloodstream. Some cancers, such as certain bowel cancers, are nevertheless curable by surgery alone.

Both drug therapy and radiotherapy depend on the fact that cancer cells are more active than normal cells and are thus more susceptible to interference, whether by drugs or through bombardment by short wave radiation. The most common type of childhood leukaemia now appears to be curable by drugs alone, although some radiotherapy may also be necessary. Radiotherapy alone cures some skin cancers and is also of use in the control of cancers in less accessible organs.

Unfortunately, many cancers are incurable either, as in many lung cancers, because of their site, or because of a late diagnosis. Much, however, can be done to alleviate the symptoms of the disease and prolong life by using the three available forms of treatment, together with special techniques such as selective nerve destruction to alleviate pain.

Although cancer, next to arteriosclerosis, is the most common cause of death in Western countries, better techniques for early diagnosis and further advances in treatment improve the chance that one day all cancers may be curable.

Infectious Diseases

For as long as man has been on Earth he has suffered from infectious diseases. Throughout history, epidemics have periodically decimated human populations: in 1664-5 the Great Plague of London killed 70,000 of the city's 460,000 inhabitants, and the influenza pandemic which followed World War I was responsible for many millions of deaths.

In the twentieth century, great steps forward have been made in the control of infectious disease. Most disease caused by bacteria and parasites can now be effectively treated, mainly as a result of the development of modern drugs, particularly antibiotics. But several problems remain to be solved. Firstly, treatment of virus diseases is still, in general, unsatisfactory. Because of the unique biology of viruses, which only come to life once they have invaded a living cell, no effective method has yet been devised to destroy them once they have invaded the body. The outbreak of Ebola disease (also known as Marburg or 'green monkey' disease) in the Sudan and Zaire in 1976, serves as an impressive reminder that virus disease can still be lethal. At present, the main weapons against virus diseases are preventative, especially vaccination.

Secondly, although infectious diseases are now rarely a cause of death in developed countries, in the less developed countries they still account for most of the disease-related deaths. Next to malnutrition, the two greatest killing ailments in the world as a whole are malaria and tuberculosis, both infectious diseases of the less developed countries. They remain common not because effective treatment is unavailable, but because public health and preventative medical facilities are poor. Some infectious diseases, such as the worm infection bilharzia (*schistosomiasis*), are actually on the increase in many of the less developed countries.

A third major problem has been the development of drug resistance in some infectious organisms. This has occurred, for instance, in the bacterium which causes tuberculosis and in some areas in the parasite responsible for malaria. Haphazard use of antibiotics is leading to the appearance of increasing numbers of antibiotic-resistant strains of bacteria.

Infecting agents

The agents, or 'germs', responsible for infectious disease are practically all viruses, bacteria or protozoa. Viruses are the smallest of these, and consist of nucleic acid, usually enclosed in a protein sheath. They are invariably parasitic, being unable to multiply independently outside a plant or animal cell.

Bacteria are considerably larger than viruses and consist of small rods or spheres made up of *protoplasm* (in which nucleic acid is dispersed) within a cell-wall made of *lipo-polysaccharides*. They require amino acids and vitamins for survival; free-living bacteria can synthesize these essential components, but most pathogenic bacteria have lost this ability and have to live within a host.

Bacteria live everywhere, in soil, air

Above: A sufferer from the Great Plague that broke out in Britain in 1665. This was one of a series of *bubonic* plague epidemics that swept Europe in medieval times. The disease mainly affects rats but can be transmitted to man by rat fleas. At present plague is a rare disease.

Right: A centre for the rehabilitation of poliomyelitis victims in Rwanda. The virus that causes polio is fairly common. A sore throat is usually the most serious symptom of the disease, but in one out of every hundred or so cases infection spreads to the spinal cord which can result in paralysis to some muscle groups.

Below: The long threads in this blood sample are *Borrelia* bacteria, which cause relapsing fever. Louse-borne, the disease often occurs following a breakdown of hygienic services. The disease subsides and recurs in cycles, hence its name.

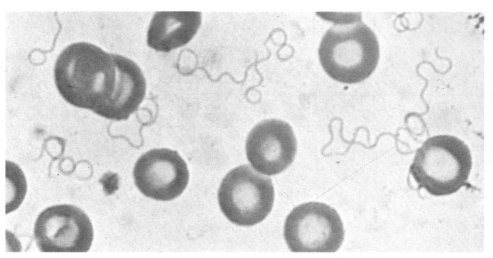

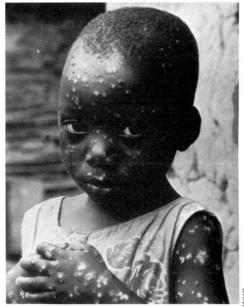

and water and especially in dead organic material. Some, such as the bacteria responsible for tetanus, exert their effects in man by releasing a toxin rather than by invading the tissues themselves. Two groups of micro-organisms that look like small bacteria but which can only be grown inside living cells (or in very special laboratory conditions) are *myco-plasmas* and *rickettsiae*. Such organisms produce a certain type of pneumonia and typhus fever respectively.

Pathogenic protozoa are single-celled organisms, larger than bacteria but still not visible to the naked eye. Examples are the malarial parasite and the organisms which produce amoebic dysentery, sleeping sickness (*trypanosomiasis*) and black fever (*leishmaniasis*).

In addition, various worms and fungi are responsible for disease in many parts of the world. Worm infections include bilharzia, *filariasis* (which produces elephantiasis and river blindness in many parts of the tropics) and *hookworm* (which produces severe anaemia throughout the less developed world.) Of the fungal infections, *ringworm* in the hair and fungal rashes in the groin are the best known.

Many protozoa and worms have a complicated life cycle which involves another organism as well as man. Thus, the malarial parasite multiplies in the *Anopheles* mosquito, while the worm responsible for bilharzia uses fresh water snails as its intermediate host.

Left: A cattle herd in East Africa. Throughout tropical Africa, sleeping sickness, suffered by both man and cattle, is a continuous menace. It is transmitted by species of tsetse fly. Some of these bite man by choice; others prefer animals.

Below: Table of a few of the better-known infectious diseases.

Above: This Congolese child has smallpox, a highly infectious disease, of which over 100,000 cases were recorded throughout the world in 1963. By 1977, due to vaccination programmes by the World Health Organization, the disease was confined to a few individuals living in remote border areas of Ethiopia and Somalia.

SE	HOW TRANSMITTED	INCUBATION PERIOD	SYMPTOMS AND EFFECTS	TREATMENT	PREVENTATIVE MEASURES
fections					
	Air-borne	1-2 days	Fever, cough, appetite loss, headache	Rest, liquid food	Vaccination or an attack immunizes against one viral strain but not against new strains
	Air-borne	10-14 days	Fever, running nose and eyes, sore throat, white spots in mouth, rash on face and trunk	Rest, liquid food, antibiotics to combat secondary bacterial infections	Vaccine or a childhood attack gives lifelong immunity
ox	Air-borne	10-20 days	Fever, itchy rash of spots, then blisters	Rest, good diet, avoidance of scratching	Childhood attack gives lifelong immunity
	Carried to mouth from contaminated faeces	1-3 weeks	Fever, sore throat; in serious cases, partial paralysis due to infection of nerve cells	Bed rest in isolation	*Salk* vaccine (injected) or *Sabin* vaccine (oral) gives virtual total immunity
	Air-borne	7-16 days	Severe fever, backache, followed by spots and blisters on face and body	Artificial airway if infection blocks throat; *penicillin* to combat secondary infections	Vaccine gives 3 years' immunity
ver	Bite of *Aedes* mosquito	3-10 days	Fever, failed liver, jaundice, failed kidneys	Bed rest; no specific treatment	Vaccine gives 10 years' immunity
obia)	Bite of infected dog or other mammal	Variable	Muscle spasms fits, delirium, difficulty in breathing, inability to drink	None effective yet: sedation makes death (a few days after symptoms appear) less painful	Effective quarantine regulations; killing of infected animals; rabies vaccine if bitten
er	Unknown	3-17 days	Severe fever, influenza-like symptoms	Injection of serum from convalescent patient	Eradication of rodents which harbour virus
ease	Unknown	3-9 days	Fever, headache, rash, bleeding	Injection of serum from convalescent patient	None at present
l infections					
	By entry into a wound, releasing a toxin	2 days to many weeks	Fever, pain, muscle spasms in jaw and neck	Sedation, muscle relaxants to ease pain, antitoxin to prevent disease getting worse	Vaccine gives 5 years' immunity; anti-toxin injections after any penetrating wound
	Contaminated food or drinking water	7-14 days	Fever, headache, constipation or diarrhoea	Antibiotics (*ampicillin* or *chloramphenicol*)	Sanitation and hygienic food-handling; vaccine gives 1 year's immunity
	Water contaminated with human faeces	1-7 days	Violent diarrhoea, dehydration, disturbed fluid balance due to loss of salts and water	Replacement of water and salt losses	Sanitation; vaccine gives 6 months' immunity
	Rat fleas; or air-borne	2-10 days	Fever, swollen lymph nodes, blotches on skin	Antibiotics (usually *streptomycin*)	Rat control; vaccine gives 1 year's immunity
	Sexual intercourse	3-12 weeks (first stage)	3 stages: 1. Hard lump at site of infection. 2. Mild illness and rash. 3. Many years later, widespread damage in any tissue of the body	*Penicillin* effective in first stage; later stages require intensive antibiotic treatment	Avoidance of sexual intercourse with known or probable carriers; if infected, immediate treatment, abstention from sexual intercourse until cured and notification of recent sexual contacts that they should be medically checked or treated
a	Sexual intercourse	About 3 days	Men: pain in urinating and pus discharge from penis. Women: possible vaginal discharge	Antibiotics (usually *penicillin*)	
y sis	Air-borne; or in milk from infected cattle	Variable	Continued ill-health due to pockets of infection in lungs; sometimes fever, cough	Rest, fresh air, good diet, antituberculous drugs	BCG vaccine reduces risk of attack; milk pasteurization prevents bovine tuberculosis
	Prolonged contact with infected person	Several years	Blotches and lumps on the skin, deformed limbs, loss of sensation in the skin	Prolonged drug therapy cures or renders non-infectious; reconstructive surgery	Population surveys for early diagnosis
fections					
	Rickettsiae transmitted by body lice or ticks	2-23 days	Severe fever, skin rashes	Rest, liquids, antibiotics	DDT to control lice; control on rats which harbour the rickettsiae
	Protozoa injected by bite of *Anopheles* mosquito	10 days to many months	Attacks of fever, violent shivering, headache, sometimes at regular intervals	Quinine-like drugs alleviate attacks; *Primaquine* actually eliminates the protozoa	Mosquito control in infectious areas; anti-malarial drugs provide protection
	Protozoa injected by bite of tsetse fly	10 days to many years	Fever, lump on skin, swollen lymph nodes, drowsiness, apathy	Drugs such as *pentamadine* are effective in the early stages	Eradication of tsetse fly in infectious areas
	Worm penetrates skin, while victim is bathing in contaminated water	Several weeks or months	Inflammation of liver, bladder, intestine, and lungs; anaemia, discomfort, general ill-health.	Drugs such as *lucanthone*	Eradication of water snails which harbour the worm from lakes and rivers where they breed; avoidance of bathing in such places

Susceptibility and transmission

An individual's suceptibility to infectious disease depends on many factors. Some ethnic groups seem particularly prone to certain infections such as measles and tuberculosis, and these two diseases are also more severe in badly nourished populations. Age is another factor: some of the virus fevers of childhood produce a more severe illness if they are encountered in adult life. Most importantly, having had the disease in the past confers some degree of immunity. In some diseases, such as measles, the immunity is complete.

In a given community, a particular disease is either present in an *endemic* form or an *epidemic* form. In the endemic form, the disease is present at a low level, with most of the population immune. Epidemics involve an explosive outbreak, due to the introduction of an infectious agent into a highly susceptible population.

Pathogenic organisms can be transmitted to man in a variety of ways. It has been estimated that at least one half of all episodes of human disease are caused by organisms entering the respiratory tract (nose, windpipe and lungs). Such infections are called *droplet infections* because minute droplets of mucus from coughs or sneezes transmit the infectious organisms. Most, such as the common cold, are trivial, but a few, such as *lobar pneumonia* and *pulmonary tuberculosis*, are potentially lethal. Many diseases are introduced into the digestive tract by food or water contaminated with the infecting agent. Examples are typhoid fever, cholera and bacillary dysentery. *Venereal* diseases, of which syphilis and gonorrhoea are the best known, are transmitted by direct contact, usually during sexual intercourse, because the organisms causing these diseases are unable to survive outside the body.

Apart from certain worms (such as the worm responsible for bilharzia) infectious agents are unable to penetrate intact skin. They may, however, be transmitted by the bite of an insect or other animal. Thus the bite of the *Anopheles* mosquito transmits malaria and that of the *tsetse* fly transmits sleeping sickness. Rabies is the best known virus disease transmitted by the bite of animals other than insects.

Infectious agents may also gain access to the body through cuts or wounds when they would otherwise have no route of entry. The bacteria which cause tetanus are frequently present in soil, but only gain access to a human host through a wound.

Some agents can infect unborn babies by way of the mother's placenta: syphilis and *rubella* (German measles) are examples of these. In some African virus infections, such as Lassa fever and Ebola disease, the route of entry is not yet clear, but all seem to originate from a reservoir of infection in animal species: the reservoir for Ebola disease, for instance, might be the green monkey.

Defences

Man's natural defences against infectious disease fall into three main groups. First there are mechanisms which prevent entry of infectious agents into the body. The skin and mucus membranes form mechanical barriers. Hydrochloric acid in the stomach combats entry of organisms into the intestinal tract. Mucus production by the upper respiratory tract en-

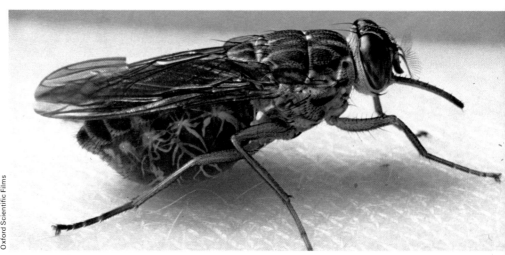

Oxford Scientific Films

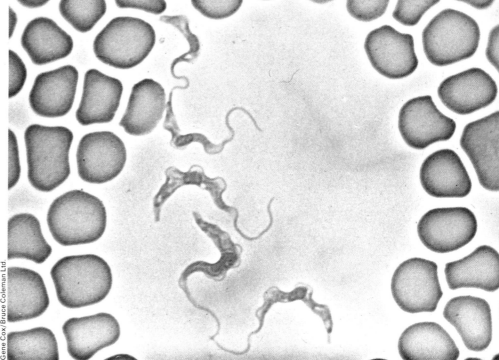

Gene Cox/Bruce Coleman Ltd.

Top and above: *Trypanosomal* infections, like sleeping sickness, are confined to the tropics and are caused by various species of trypanosome protozoa. *Glossina palpalis* (top) is a tsetse fly that transmits the form of sleeping sickness found in West Africa. When it bites man, it injects *Trypanosoma gambiense.* Five of these protozoa are photographed (above) in human tissue, showing they are uni-cellular organisms with long flagella. They cause fever and swellings in the victim, and later may invade his nervous system, making him drowsy and apathetic.

Right: Chagas' disease, trypanosomiasis from S. America, is transmitted by bugs such as *Rhodnius prolixus*, the assassin bug. They come out at night and first bite the victim, often near the eyes, and then defecate on the wound. Trypanosomes in the faeces then penetrate the body and may invade and weaken muscle tissue. If this happens to the heart it can be fatal. When bugs bite an infected person they re-ingest trypansomes, starting the cycle again.

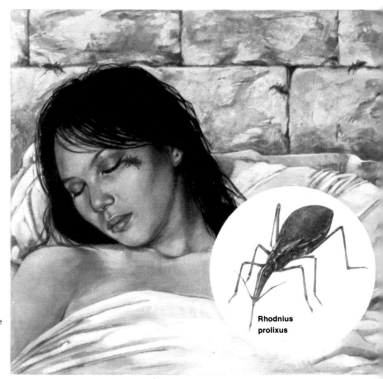

Rhodnius prolixus

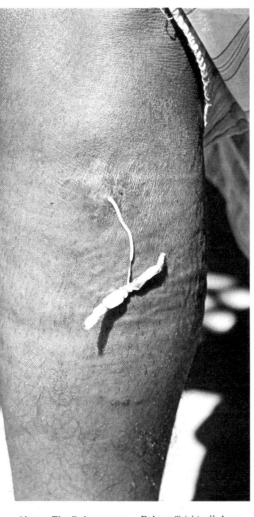

meshes inhaled viruses and bacteria. Recent work has shown that a protein known as *IgA* (immunoglobulin type A), which also forms part of blood serum proteins, is present in many of the body's secretions and exerts a protective action.

Secondly, white blood cells form an important line of defence by engulfing bacteria. And thirdly, there is a further and far more subtle system of defence that involves *antibody* production. Specific antibodies are produced by the body in reaction to specific *antigens*, or foreign particles such as viruses. They coat the antigens, thus nullifying them, and the antibody-antigen complex is then engulfed by a white blood cell. *Immunoglobulins* are large protein molecules that form an important component of antibodies. Although there are at least five immunoglobulins, it is type G (*IgG*), a protein of molecular weight 155,000 which is quantitatively the most important in the defence mechanism.

Course of an infection

In general, infectious diseases fall into *acute* and *chronic* groups. Acute infections are of fairly sudden onset and are over in a short time. If the host has plenty of antibodies and reacts favourably, he recovers; but if his defence mechanisms are deficient he dies in the absence of effective treatment. Examples are pneumonia, influenza and typhus fever. Chronic diseases are usually of insidious onset and take a protracted course before either recovery or death occurs. Examples are tuberculosis and leprosy.

With the majority of diseases, the course of the illness has certain well-defined characteristics. Following infection, there is an *incubation period*, while the agent is finding its way to the tissues where it exerts its effects. This is followed by a *prodromal phase* (often consisting of an influenza-like illness) during which the agent is multiplying. Following this, the specific symptoms of the illness appear. In the case of lobar pneumonia, for instance, this consists of fever, a severe pain in the chest, and a cough with blood-stained sputum. At this point, antibiotics (in the case of bacterial infections) may be administered to help the body's defence systems.

In untreated lobar pneumonia, after some ten days, a sudden drop in body temperature, signifying a successful response of the defence mechanism, usually heralds recovery. If an antibiotic is given early in the illness, the temperature soon falls and recovery is more rapid.

Incidence

Nowadays, most of the common viral diseases of childhood present few problems in the developing countries, although many of them, especially measles, are still a menace in less developed countries. Poliomyelitis is also an enormous problem in these countries. With some other viral diseases, such as smallpox and yellow fever, sustained preventative measures have reduced the incidence to manageable proportions.

Venereal diseases remain a colossal problem throughout the world. Treatment, once diagnosis has been made, is fairly satisfactory and sex education to remove the guilt once associated with these diseases and to encourage immedi-

Above: The Guinea worm enters man in infected water and settles just under the skin, often in the leg, causing fever and a painful local swelling. When it emerges to lay eggs in water, the traditional remedy is to pull it out by winding it round a stick, as here. Female worms may attain a length of 1 m (3 ft).

Below: *Trichinella* larva embedded in a muscle. Parasites of pigs, the trichinella worms, just 3 mm long as adults, enter the body in undercooked pork and inhabit the intestines. Their larvae penetrate the wall of the intestine, sometimes causing diarrhoea and fever, and settle in a muscle, where they cause mild aches and pains.

Right: Parasites can live in virtually any organ or tissue in man, but individual species are only found in certain parts of the body. Shown here are the usual sites of some of the best known parasites, and their incidence throughout the world. Most parasites are more common in the less developed countries.

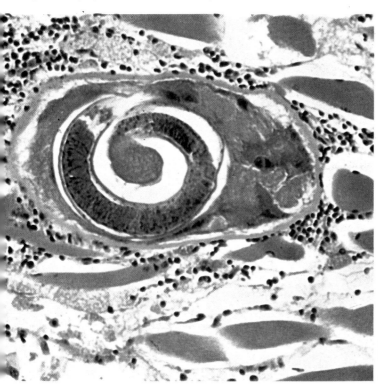

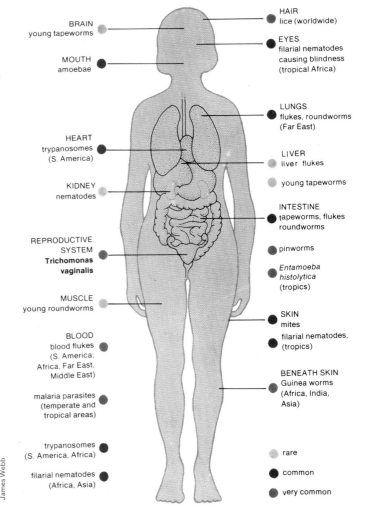

HAIR
lice (worldwide)

BRAIN
young tapeworms

EYES
filarial nematodes
causing blindness
(tropical Africa)

MOUTH
amoebae

LUNGS
flukes, roundworms
(Far East)

HEART
trypanosomes
(S. America)

LIVER
liver flukes

young tapeworms

KIDNEY
nematodes

INTESTINE
tapeworms, flukes
roundworms

pinworms

REPRODUCTIVE
SYSTEM
**Trichomonas
vaginalis**

*Entamoeba
histolytica*
(tropics)

MUSCLE
young roundworms

SKIN
mites

filarial nematodes.
(tropics)

BLOOD
blood flukes
(S. America;
Africa, Far East,
Middle East)

BENEATH SKIN
Guinea worms
(Africa, India,
Asia)

malaria parasites
(temperate and
tropical areas)

trypanosomes
(S. America, Africa)

rare

common

filarial nematodes
(Africa, Asia)

very common

L'ESPAIGNOL
AFFLIGE
DV MAL
DE NAPLES.

ate treatment, together with the availability of special treatment clinics, will hopefully reduce their incidence.

Diseases associated with rickettsiae, protozoa, worms and fungi are now largely confined to the less developed countries. However, with the increasing mobility of people brought about by air travel, these are by no means unknown in Europe and North America.

Immunization

In the developed countries, public health facilities are well advanced and food and water are largely free of infection. This is in many ways a satisfactory state of affairs, but it does prevent individuals from developing natural immunity to certain diseases. Poliomyelitis only became a major problem in the developed

Above left: Louis Pasteur, the French 19th century chemist and biologist, used samples of wine to show that fermentation was caused by yeast microbes. If air to which the wine was exposed was filtered free of microbes, or if the microbes were killed by heat, no fermentation occurred. He then showed that infection too was caused by microbes. His method of heating milk to stop the transmission of tuberculosis by infected milk is known as pasteurization. His findings marked a major turning point in medicine.

Below left: About half of all episodes of human infection are caused by microbes carried in droplet form, usually the result of coughs or sneezes.

Above: The venereal disease syphilis was once called the disease of Naples due to its high incidence there. Placing victims in a barrel and fumigating them was then considered a suitable cure, but was presumably ineffective. The origin of syphilis is obscure: some believe Columbus and his crew imported it from America; others that the biblical 'leprosy' was actually syphilis. The disease is still widespread. It can be cured with antibiotics in its early stages but treatment is difficult in the final stages.

Below: A Pakistani smallpox vaccinator preparing her kit. The easy use of the freeze-dried vaccine contributed much to the eradication of this disease.

countries when public health facilities arrived. Previously virtually every child contracted a mild form of the illness, and by thus developing immunity did not suffer from it in adulthood, when the disease is more severe. Nowadays, however, immunization provides an alternative defence.

Immunization started with Edward Jenner's discovery in 1798 that an injection of cowpox virus, which causes only a mild illness in man, could protect an individual against smallpox. The virus was so closely related to smallpox that it triggered off the same immune mechanism in the body. In the latter half of the nineteenth century, work on killed bacterial vaccines led to advances in anthrax, diptheria and tetanus immunization. Now, immunization is available against a wide range of bacterial and virus diseases.

Many antibacterial vaccines contain the bacteria of the disease killed with heat, formalin or alcohol. An inactivated virus is used in the *Salk* polio vaccine but most modern virus vaccines rely on the injection of attenuated (altered) live viruses, which provoke the same antibody production as the normal viruses but do not harm the body.

Injecting live viruses may not sound very safe, but recent trials, for instance with the *Sabin* vaccine against poliomyelitis, which uses an attenuated virus, have removed such fears. Other modern vaccines using attenuated bacteria or viruses include the *BCG* (bacille Calmette-Guérin) vaccine for tuberculosis, and the vaccines for smallpox, yellow fever, measles, mumps and rubella. For infections whose effects are caused by a toxin, killed vaccines remain the most effective treatment and this applies to cholera, tetanus and diphtheria.

In a very small percentage of cases immunization can give rise to undesirable side-effects, such as *encephalitis*, an infection of the brain by injected live viruses. Such effects are extremely rare and the risk is far outweighed by the colossal benefits of immunization to the individual and the community.

MINISTRY OF HEALTH SAYS—

COUGHS AND SNEEZES SPREAD DISEASES—

trap the germs in your handkerchief

HELP TO KEEP THE NATION FIGHTING FIT

Water smails harbour *bilharzia* worms. The worm penetrates the skin whilst the victim is bathing in infected water, and incubates for several weeks. Eventually, inflammation of the bladder, intestine, liver and lungs occurs.

Skin Disorders

The skin is the largest organ of the human body. Apart from its obvious structural importance, skin fulfils a number of vital protective roles; for example, it is remarkably efficient at resisting bacteria. Although tens of millions of bacteria normally live on healthy skin, few of these are capable of causing disease and even fewer ever penetrate the skin surface. Another important function of the skin is in controlling the body temperature, and for this purpose it is equipped with numerous sweat glands. Evaporation of moisture produced by the sweat glands cools the skin surface in hot weather.

Skin disorders, although fairly common, are rarely serious: they range from chilblains to acne and dermatitis. Even when the skin becomes cancerous, a cure is almost certain provided the malignancy has not progressed too far.

Chilblains and frostbite

In cold weather chilblains, *erythema pernio*, are a relatively common skin complaint. They usually appear as itchy, bluish-red eruptions on one or more toes; and occasionally they affect the fingers as well. In cold weather, the vessels beneath the skin close up to restrict the flow of blood and thereby conserve body heat. It is thought that chilblains occur as a result of fluid leaking into the tissue under the skin when the capillaries open wide as the foot is rewarmed. Chilblains are commonest among adults who work out or doors and children, and the complaint seems to run in families, suggesting an inherited tendency.

Frostbite is caused by severe narrowing of the skin blood vessels in very cold weather conditions, and leads to blackening and death of the affected tissue. The loss of fingers or toes as a result of frostbite is not uncommon among polar explorers and mountain climbers. To avoid frostbite travellers in extremely cold climates must wear thick insulating clothing, especially over the extremities. Modern treatment includes administration of oxygen in a pressure chamber and injection of the sympathetic nerve plexus to open the blood vessels.

Heating for long periods is no better for the skin than exposure to cold. Heat leads to a build up of the skin pigment *melanin* and this is seen as a dark, patchy discolouration on the skin surface. The commonest condition is known as *erythema ab igne*, a mottling of the skin at the front of the shins which results from constantly 'toasting' the legs in front of an open fire or central heating radiators.

Sunlight both heats the skin and subjects it to radiant energy. The melanin in the skin normally protects against both of these, but in white-skinned people it is inadequate if exposure is prolonged. In such circumstances the ultraviolet light (a component of sunlight) leads first to reddening, then to blistering and finally to weeping and peeling—second degree burns, in fact. Protective oil can be used to screen some of the harmful ultraviolet light. Constant exposure to sunlight over many years tends to break up the elastic tissue in the skin, and this can lead to premature wrinkling.

Right: A cartoon (1800) by the well known British caricaturist James Gillray depicting a somewhat drastic treatment for corns. Corns are caused by badly fitting footwear: a layer of thick, dead epidermal tissue forms and this irritates the inner layer of the skin (*corium*) which contains blood vessels, nerves and sweat glands.

Bottom: Skin protects itself against the harmful effects of the ultraviolet component of sunlight by increasing the amount of the brown pigment *melanin*. The result is a suntan. As many holidaymakers know to their cost, overexposure before the level of melanin has had time to build up leads to sunburn—the skin blisters and peels. Suntan lotions filter out some of the ultraviolet rays and so protect the skin. Some people, through a recessive genetic defect, lack the enzyme responsible for synthesizing melanin. Known as *albinos*, their skin is very fair and highly sensitive to sunlight.

Below: Antarctica during a 60 knot gale. Frostbite is a very real danger in polar climates, and thick, thermally insulating clothing is vital. The hands and feet are particularly at risk. A related complaint is *trench foot* which occurs when the feet are exposed to cold, wet conditions for prolonged periods. The waterlogged skin is susceptible to the slightest infection.

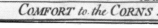

COMFORT to the CORNS.

Mansell Collection

Picturepoint

Thomas Hopker—Magnum/John Hillelson Agency

Below: Dermatitis is an inherited or acquired sensitivity of the skin to some normally harmless agent. In this case the dermatitis shows as an allergic reaction to gold. Possibly the gold changes one of the skin proteins into an antigen which then triggers the body's immune response.

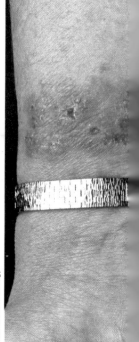

Institute of Dermatology

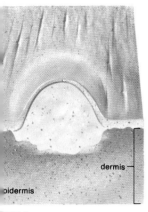

STULE
mall pus-filled cavity between
epidermis and the dermis

CER
area of complete loss of the
dermal layer of skin

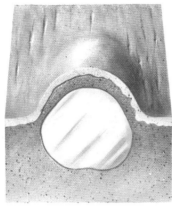

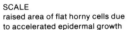

CYST
a fluid filled cavity deeply
situated in the dermis

SCALE
raised area of flat horny cells due
to accelerated epidermal growth

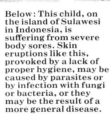

BLISTER
clear fluid between the top and
underlying epidermal layers

LICHENIFICATION
thickening of epidermis gives skin
a leathery appearance

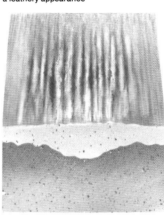

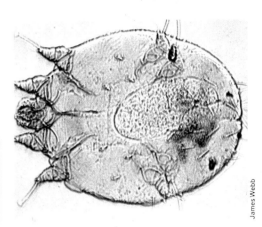

James Webb

Below: A severe case of
dermatitis causes
extensive reddening and
peeling of the skin.
Dermatitis invariably
causes itching, and if
the affected part is
scratched the
inflammation will get
worse. For this reason
it is often hard to say
just how serious a
particular attack is.

Above: Some common
sores. Pus forms when
white blood cells are
mobilized by the body
to attack invading
bacteria. Most skin
disorders cause changes
in the epidermis—in
ulcers it is lost
altogether while in
scale and lichen it
becomes thicker
and discoloured.

Below: This child, on
the island of Sulawesi
in Indonesia, is
suffering from severe
body sores. Skin
eruptions like this,
provoked by a lack of
proper hygiene, may be
caused by parasites or
by infection with fungi
or bacteria, or they
may be the result of a
more general disease.

Top right: A scabies
mite, *Sarcoptes scabei*.
These tiny parasites
burrow under the skin
surfaces to lay their
eggs. The chief symptom
of scabies is itching,
but the disease also
increases the risk of
infection from bacteria
or fungi. It is easily
cured by applying benzyl
benzoate emulsion.

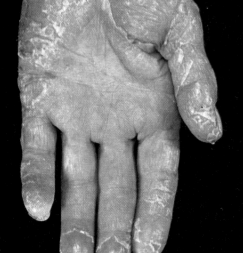

Institute of Dermatology

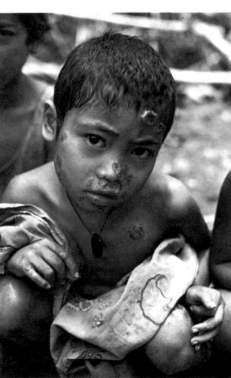

Robert Harding Associates

Sometimes patients who are being
treated with certain drugs (notably sulphonamides, tranquilizers, tetracyclines
and fungicides) develop an unusual
sensitivity to sunlight. The reaction,
known as *photo-sensitivity*, is hard to
predict in advance and is caused by that
small proportion of the drug which
reaches the skin reacting photochemically
to produce a toxic chemical. Patients on
such drugs should keep out of direct sunlight while being treated: the irritation
disappears once the drugs are withdrawn.

Skin infections

Human skin normally resists bacteria,
viruses and fungi that land on it, but
minor scratches, cuts, pulled hairs or a
poor state of health may permit their
entry and result in a skin complaint.
Regular washing with water and soap
reduces the risk of skin infection and is
still the prime preventive measure.

Staphylococcal bacteria infecting a
follicle produce that most familiar of skin
complaints, a boil or *furuncle*, which first
appears as a red cone or pimple. Some
people seem to have a naturally low
immunity which is not fully understood.
When more than one follicle is involved
the infection is called a *carbuncle*.

The usual method of treating a boil is
to cover it with an adhesive plaster
dressing whose centre has been cut out so
as to expose the boil head. This protects
the boil until it is ready to discharge.
Locally applied magnesium sulphate
(Epsom salts) gives some relief, but with
severe or persistent boils antibiotics may
be required to combat the infection.

Another staphylococcal infection, commonly seen in children, is *impetigo con-
tagiosa*. The normal site is on the face,
particularly around the mouth and the
cheeks. The bacteria enter the outermost
layer of skin, producing a pink *papule* or
raised area. This is followed by a blister
or vesicle which is not painful. Eventually
white cells enter the blister to form a
pustule which ruptures producing an
oozing, weeping rash. Impetigo is cured
in a few days by applying an ointment
containing an antibiotic such as neo-
mycin or more often with an antibiotic
taken internally such as penicillin.

The commonest skin disorder among
teenagers is *acne vulgaris*, usually just
called acne. It occurs in both sexes but is
more often encountered in boys than
girls, and the usual sites are the face, the
front and back of the upper chest and
sometimes over the shoulders. It is caused
by overactivity during puberty of the
sebaceous glands which feed oily *sebum*
into the hair root follicles. The follicle
eventually becomes blocked with skin

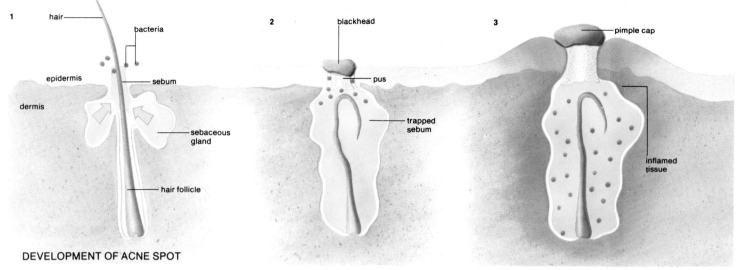

1 hair
bacteria
epidermis — sebum
dermis
sebaceous gland
hair follicle

2 blackhead
pus
trapped sebum

3 pimple cap
inflamed tissue

DEVELOPMENT OF ACNE SPOT

debris, thickened sebum and skin scales, and a blackhead or *comedo* forms. The blocked follicle is particularly prone to infection with the bacterium *Propionibacterium acnes* which acts on the sebum to produce irritant substances such as propionic acid, and a pustule then forms.

Among the best known virus diseases of the skin are warts or *verrucae*. They come in all shapes and sizes and may appear on any part of the body, even under the nails. A variety of treatments are available, including freezing with solid carbon dioxide, the application of chemical 'paints' and burning away by *electrocautery* under local anaesthetic.

The most familiar fungal infection of the skin is ringworm or *tinea*, which attacks the scalp, the groin and the feet (athlete's foot). The infection is usually picked up from a moist surface, for example in a swimming bath, and it causes cracks or fissures in the spaces between the toes. The skin in the cracks becomes white, soggy and unpleasant; on the sole of the foot the fungus causes scaling of the skin; and blisters or vesicles may form. Treatment involves twice daily foot baths, a daily change of socks and avoidance of damp places. Tablets of *griseofulvin* (an antibiotic) may be prescribed and an anti-fungal talc or ointment applied to the site of the infection.

Dermatitis

Some skin disorders are caused neither by extremes of temperature nor by infection. They are the result of an inherited or acquired oversensitivity of the skin and are lumped together under the term *dermatitis*. In dermatitis the skin becomes inflamed as an allergic response to some normally harmless substance such as penicillin, aspirin, shellfish or strawberries. Inherited dermatitis is recognized by the presence of other allergic disorders, such as hay fever, bronchial asthma or the skin complaint *urticaria*, in members of the close family.

Dermatitis is caused by an over-reaction of the *immune response* mechanism, the body's defence against disease. Under normal circumstances, when a foreign substance, an *antigen*, usually a protein, enters the body it stimulates the production of white blood cells which release *antibodies*. The antibodies are formed of proteins called *immunoglobulins* (Ig) and their function is to neutralize the foreign protein, which may be part of an invading bacterium or virus.

In dermatitis it is the immunoglobulin IgE which is responsible for the immune response. Its reaction with the antigen causes *mast cells* in the skin to release

Above: These three diagrams show how an acne spot develops. First of all a hair follicle becomes blocked (1), either as a result of infrequent washing or from overproduction of grease (*sebum*) by the sebaceous gland. Under these conditions bacteria thrive, and as sebum continues to be produced the blocked follicle swells. Pus forms as white blood cells attack the invading bacteria, and the blocked entrance of the follicle attracts dirt which gives it the familiar appearance of a blackhead (2). As the process continues, a typical acne pimple forms (3). Degreasing lotions, sulphur creams, sunlight or antibiotics may help to clear up acne, but the spots should not be squeezed with unclean fingers.

Above right: As this advertisement suggests the best way to avoid skin infection is regular washing with soap and water. Washing prevents dead skin and hardened sebum—prime breeding grounds for bacteria—from building up on the skin surface.

Right: Sometimes a person's skin becomes sensitive to a substance such as soap, a cosmetic (for example lipstick), a detergent or even a metal. The condition is known as *contact dermatitis* and its symptoms are similar to those of eczema. Treatment involves identifying the compound which is causing the allergic reaction—it might be a particular oil in a lipstick formulation—and avoiding it. The itching can be relieved with a cortisone cream.

Mary Evans Picture Library

histamine which in turn produces itching reddish areas and raised weals on the skin surface. The itching can be relieved by taking antihistamine tablets. The original antigen may be generated by all sorts of things—primula plants, chrysanthemum flowers, insect bites, sleeping tablets and particular items of food are common triggers for antigen production.

Eczema is a kind of dermatitis found in children. The skin becomes itchy and red, and scaling, weeping and crusting may occur. The rash usually starts on the face and spreads from there to the rest of the body. Locally applied cortisone cream and antihistamine liquid relieve the itching, and a diet free of antigens (for example, egg protein and some milk proteins) may be prescribed.

One of the commonest skin disorders

(two per cent of the British population suffer from it) is *psoriasis*. An inherited disorder, it can appear at any age and results in raised red areas on the skin. The red areas are covered with marked scaling giving a 'frosted' appearance to the inflammation. Psoriasis most often affects the elbows and knees but may appear on the scalp, trunk and even the fingernails. Tar and cortisone skin preparations relieve the complaint.

Occasionally the skin undergoes a malignant or cancerous change in the epidermis or dermis. This is usually a localized condition, such as a *basal cell tumour* or a *squamous cell tumour*, and it can generally be cured by surgery or radiotherapy. Pigmented moles which darken or increase in size are sometimes an indication of such cancerous changes.

Public Health and Safety

The massive outbreaks of infectious diseases—plague, cholera, typhoid and smallpox—in the seventeenth, eighteenth and nineteenth centuries spread rapidly across countries and continents. These migrating infections killed many thousands of people and created a recurring reservoir of sickness and disability around the globe. Such mass epidemics, however, acted as a major stimulus for the development of national and international measures to improve public health.

Quarantining

Even before the causative germs were isolated and understood, and the possibility of environmental preventive measures appreciated, public health officials tackled the problem by isolating sufferers from those who were free of the disease.

Quarantine survives to the present day in the form of public health regulations for both ships and aircraft, but nowadays these are based on international agreement. They are administered by local health authorities and port health authorities. Sufferers from the illness or contacts from the infected areas are medically inspected then transferred for hospital isolation.

Passengers not affected may be allowed to disembark, but in most countries must give their addresses so that the local area medical officer can keep a check for symptoms for a specified period of time. In a case of suspected smallpox, for example, the observation time is two weeks. Where appropriate, passengers may be offered vaccinations against the illness or *gammaglobulin* may be prescribed to raise immunity.

At international borders travellers may be asked to show valid certificates of vaccination for certain infectious illnesses, most commonly for cholera and smallpox. This ensures that people coming from a country where the disease is prevalent have at least been immunized; a vital precaution in an era of jet travel. The vigilance of the World Health Organization spotlights new outbreaks of infectious diseases, such as influenza or yellow fever, and alerts member countries to the risks from travellers from the outbreak areas.

Environmental hygiene

To preserve sound sanitation every community needs an efficient system of refuse removal, reliable sewage disposal, clean and unpolluted food and a regular supply of pure and uncontaminated water for drinking and washing.

Each local authority arranges for dry refuse disposal by collecting it from individual homes, stores and factories in specially designed vehicles, or by mobile collection 'dustcarts' in the streets. The refuse is then brought to a depot for burning in an incinerator, or dumped in a suitable pit or quarry which is earth-sealed when full.

Underground sewer systems collect toilet and sink sewage from individual homes and buildings into main sewerage pipes. Streets and roads also have drains from road guttering systems which lead off into the sewers. The sewage is led first to separation and filtration plants and then to aeration tanks where it is 'digested' by bacteria and blue-green algae. The purified sewage liquid is ultimately discharged into a river or stream which must be periodically

F. Jackson/Robert Harding Associates

Left: Desert travellers in the Republic of Niger and their camels using the same water hole. An important aspect of public health is to prevent transmission of germs which may be relatively harmless to animals but dangerous to man, a precaution that is evidently not being adopted in this case.

Sepp Seitz—Magnum/John Hillelson Agency

Below left: Regular refuse disposal is essential in preventing the proliferation of rats, which are common carriers of disease. The New York refuse collectors' strike in 1975 endangered the city's health. Burning refuse was one way of reducing the hazard but firemen came to douse the fires nonetheless.

Below: Despite the spread of the disease across Europe in the 20th century, rabies outbreaks have been prevented in Britain by strict quarantine regulations. Dogs and other animals may be isolated for periods of up to 6 months when they arrive from overseas and are destroyed if found to be infected.

The British Isles are free of rabies and wish to remain so. No animal may be landed there without having an import licence and undergoing quarantine, even if it has been vaccinated.
If you are visiting Britain, it is recommended that you do not take your animals with you. (If you come in your own boat, the pet would have to be strictly confined on board throughout your visit.)
To prevent the introduction of this fatal and expensive disease, severe penalties (heavy fines and up to a year's imprisonment) are imposed on anyone attempting to smuggle animals. Any illegally imported animal is liable to be destroyed.

DON'T SPOIL YOUR VISIT. KNOW THE REGULATIONS

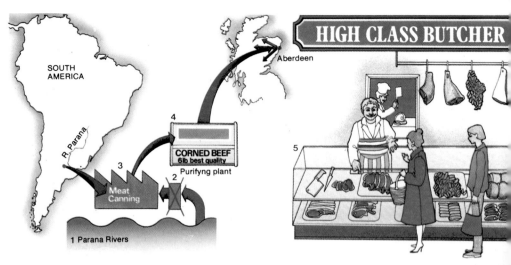

sampled to ensure that there is no accidental pollution.

In all developed countries, a piped supply of clean water is available. Water sources include underground and river waters and natural or man-made reservoirs. From such storage points, the water is led through sand and chemical filters and then purified by adding very small amounts of chlorine. Sometimes water supplies are sterilized by using ultraviolet light or ozone rather than chlorine.

Pest control is another important aspect of environmental sanitation. Rats remain a dangerous source of bacterial infection and are kept under control by such precautions as the proper disposal of dry refuse and de-ratting and fumigation of ships. Rats invading drains and sewers are routinely destroyed by poisons. Food stores should be properly protected and proofed against rat invasion: this is particularly important below street level.

Food hygiene

Developed countries have a wide range of published regulations on food processing, food additives and food sales. Milk, for example, must be pasteurized, sterilized or ultra-heat-treated to destroy pathogenic bacteria before retail sale is permitted. Meat intended for sale must be inspected following the slaughter of animals, and standards are laid down for every abattoir. Slaughtermen must usually also be licensed.

In Western communities, the addition of colouring and preservatives to food is strictly controlled and periodic sampling by health inspectors prevents any lowering of standards in food processing. Inspectors pay particular attention to shops, canteens and restaurants and to factories involved in the handling of food and food preparation equipment. Prevention of food contamination is the keynote of this area of public health.

Pollution

The Industrial Revolution added new impurities to the atmosphere. Carbon and soot from domestic and industrial fires and furnaces mixed with chemical impurities such as sulphur dioxide and ammonia gases from the industrial processes. Smoke, fog and smog, particularly in winter and on still days, caused major chest illnesses such as chronic bronchitis and recurring asthma. In Britain, successive Clean Air Acts have produced regulations that limit industrial smoke production to fixed periods of the day and

Above: A breakdown in health precautions can lead to outbreaks of infection far removed from the original site of contamination.

Right and below: Occupational medicine is largely concerned with protecting people who face hazards in their work. It is as yet underdeveloped in some countries like Pakistan where this worker at a power plant (right) is inadequately protected against dust which can cause lung disease. In contrast, workers (below) exposed to radioactive materials at a nuclear plant in Britain must wear a protective 'frog-suit' and take a shower after work to remove traces of radioactivity.

UKAEA

Robert Harding Associates

Popperfoto

Above right: A child living in a village in Iran being dusted with BHC, an organochlorine insecticide that kills the lice which transmit typhus fever. All the villagers, and their clothes and bedding, received this treatment regularly as part of a public health programme carried out by the World Health Organization. Since the late 1950's, programmes such as this have greatly reduced the incidence of many infectious diseases.

Right: In many parts of the world, automobiles pose a continual threat to health and safety. In Britain, an important role of adventure playgrounds such as this is to allow children to play in safety well away from the roads.

Rex Features Ltd

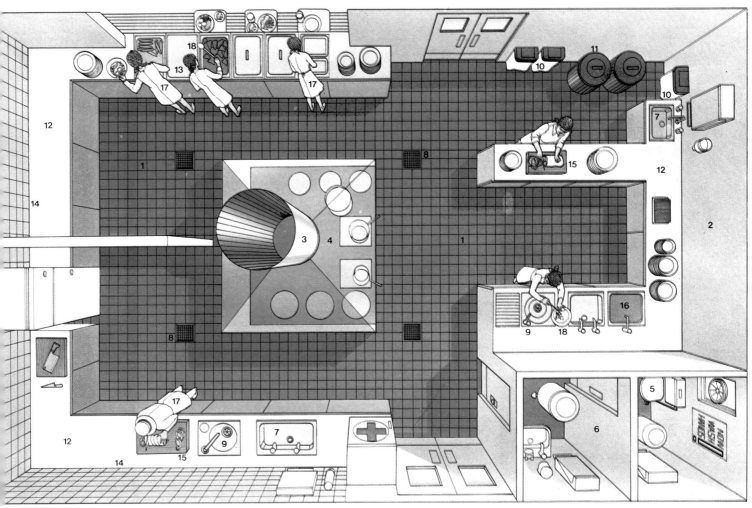

they have created so called 'smokeless zones' where domestic smoke production is prohibited.

Dusty occupations are known to produce a variety of illnesses, particularly affecting the lungs. Coal dust causes *pneumoconiosis* among miners, stone dust causes *silicosis*, cotton mill dust causes *byssinosis* and asbestos dust causes tumours of the lung lining. Inhalation of mouldy hay dust causes 'farmer's lung' in farm workers. Unless proper precautions are taken, chemical workers are also at risk in some jobs. Workers with naphthylamine are subject to tumours of the urinary bladder while workers with mercury or cadmium may suffer blood or kidney poisoning. Employees handling wool, hair and hides may contract anthrax (a bacterial infection) while those involved in the handling of tar, pitch and bitumen may suffer tumours of the skin.

Safety

In Britain the Factory Acts of the nineteenth and twentieth centuries control the age for starting work, the hours of work put in by young people, the shielding of potentially dangerous machinery, sanitation, first aid, the reporting of accidents and the appointment of factory inspectors to ensure the application of such provisions for the health and safety of workers. Doctors with a special interest in industrial medicine and occupational health problems are appointed as factory doctors. Their duties include the monitoring of possible occupational diseases and accidents, periodic examinations of employees and notification to the chief inspector of factories of employees suffering from known occupational diseases.

The health and welfare provisions of the 1961 Factories Act are comprehensive and wide, embracing such work conditions as ventilation, overcrowding and temperature. The Act also draws attention to potential fire hazards in industrial premises; fire prevention precautions are now mandatory in all buildings and premises used by the public—stores, hotels and offices, as well as hospitals and institutions. Fire control doors, escape route exits, automatic sprinkler systems, fire extinguishers at strategic points and fire alarm points are among the precautions covered, as well as the regular teaching of fire drill to employees by the fire prevention officer of the local authority.

National bodies in the developed countries also encourage the teaching and informing of citizens on risks and dangers in the home and on the street. Road safety has become particularly important with the mass usage of cars, lorries and public transport. Typical legislation designed to raise safety levels includes a minimum age for licensing drivers, the provision of tests for would be drivers, the imposition of speed limits, enforced wearing of crash helmets for motor cyclists, the provision of controlled pedestrian crossings and an upper limit to the blood alcohol level for drivers.

The vehicle itself has also come under scrutiny, with the use of safety belts and head restrainers, the provision of safety glass windscreens and generally improved crash resistance. Several countries require periodic tests of braking, lighting, steering and other safety elements of the vehicle before a roadworthiness certificate is issued to allow renewal of the road licence.

First Aid

In Britain alone more than half a million industrial and road accidents are reported annually. Because trained doctors and nurses are rarely present when accidents occur, it is left to the non-professional to provide an accident victim with encouragement, reassurance and medical attention until skilled help arrives. But anyone undertaking *first aid* of this sort needs to have learned certain basic principles in order to be sure of helping rather than hindering the injured person's recovery.

Proper treatment of an accident victim follows a standard pattern. First of all, the helper will check that the victim is still breathing and that his supply of oxygen is not restricted by any blockage in the airway to his lungs. Next, he will make sure that there is no bleeding and, if there is, he will take immediate steps to control it. And finally he will do whatever he can to ease discomfort and control shock, and he will call an ambulance and sometimes a doctor.

Breathing

Normal breathing takes place at a rate of between 12 and 14 breaths every minute: oxygen is absorbed into the blood through the lung walls and carbon dioxide is expelled. Abnormal breathing is recognized by a blue or purple skin coloration around the lips and earlobes—a sign that insufficient oxygen is reaching the blood —or by noisy breathing, gasping or frothing at the mouth and nose, which indicates a blocked air passage.

Obstructed breathing is commonly encountered in cases of coma and semi-consciousness, and especially when the victim has had a solid object in his mouth or in cases of head or chest injury, windpipe compression or an epileptic fit. If breathing is obstructed the patient is placed face down, head turned to one side, and his mouth checked for any solid objects (including dentures). Sometimes vomit can block the airways, in which case the patient is placed on his front with his head below the rest of his body. His mouth contents are then mopped out.

If breathing is absent or virtually absent, resuscitation is urgently needed. This is carried out by artificial respiration. The patient is turned on his back with his head pushed back. The rescuer supports the patient's chin, applies his open mouth around that of the patient and then breathes out, exhaling his own air into the patient's lungs. He then removes his mouth and allows the air to be exhaled from the patient. The cycle is repeated about 10 times per minute and is continued until the patient starts breathing naturally. If the patient is an adult, his nostrils are pinched during artificial respiration. In the case of a child, both mouth and nose are covered by the rescuer's mouth and about 30 puffs of air given per minute. If the patient's heart has stopped, the rescuer may also have to carry out external cardiac massage, or enlist another helper to carry this out simultaneously.

Cardiac arrest

The shock of an accident or injury may cause the heart to stop beating, especially if the victim has a history of heart dis-

Cooper-Bridgeman Library

Above: *Awaiting admission to the Casualty Ward* by the nineteenth century British artist Sir Luke Fildes. The painting was a social comment on the general lack of efficiency in first aid and treatment facilities for the sick and injured at that time. Modern hospitals generally give the patient more prompt attention.

Below: *The Dreadful Story of Harriet and the Matches* illustrates the dire consequences of playing with fire. If clothing catches fire, the victim's immediate action should be to roll on the floor, smothering the flames with the nearest available wrap. Rescuers should quench the flames, then flood any burns with water.

ease. Symptoms include absence of breathing, no pulse at the wrists or neck and dilated pupils. If the heart has stopped the rescuer has just four minutes to restart it and get the blood circulating before lack of oxygen causes irreversible brain damage.

The victim is laid flat on a hard surface, face upwards. He is given one thump with the closed fist, or three violent slaps, slightly to the left of the lower third of the breastbone. The blow is quite severe, though moderated for children, and the rescuer may even break one of the victim's ribs in his efforts to get the heart beating again. As soon as a heartbeat is detected, artificial respiration begins.

If this treatment fails to restart the heart, external *cardiac massage* is applied. Kneeling to one side of the victim, the rescuer places the heel of one hand firmly over the lower third of the breastbone and over this hand he places the other. He then raises himself over the victim and allows his weight to apply full pressure once every second. After each pressure the hands are lifted to permit full expansion of the chest. When artificial respiration is proceeding at the same time, five chest pressures are applied for each mouth blowing. This is continued until a pulse, heartbeat and regular breathing are apparent.

Bleeding

Bleeding may be internal or external, and if it is severe symptoms of shock are usually apparent. These include a pale face and skin, rapid breathing and pulse, and cold, clammy sweating. Unless the bleeding is from the head, the victim is laid with the head lower than the body to help maintain the blood supply to the brain.

Assuming no bones are broken, the arms or legs are raised above the level of the heart to reduce blood flow. If a blood clot has actually formed, it is left undisturbed. Using a pad of clean cloth, firm pressure is applied with fingers or thumbs over any obvious bleeding area. If blood oozes through, the original pad is left in position and another pad is placed on top

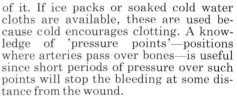

Left: Red cross workers must be prepared for furious activity when disasters occur. Here a victim of an air crash in Nairobi is being rushed to hospital.

Below: If an accident victim's heart has stopped beating, he is laid on his back and one attempt is made to restart it by thumping the lower third of the breastbone (sternum), slightly to the left. If this does not work, *external heart massage*, shown here, is started. Diagram 1 shows where the rescuer's hands are placed, on the lower third of the sternum. Diagram 2 shows a cross-section of the chest. The rescuer bears down over the victim to apply full pressure once a second, releasing his hands after each to allow the chest to rise. Artificial respiration is carried out at the same time by another rescuer at the rate of one lung inflation for five heart compressions.

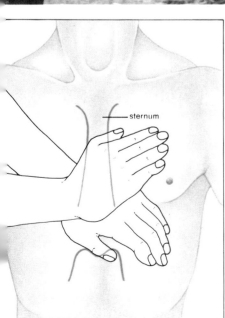

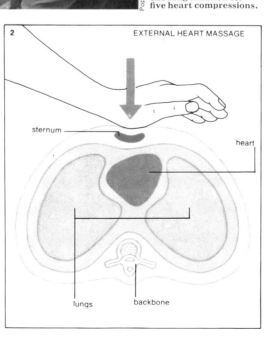

sternum

2

EXTERNAL HEART MASSAGE

sternum

heart

lungs

backbone

of it. If ice packs or soaked cold water cloths are available, these are used because cold encourages clotting. A knowledge of 'pressure points'—positions where arteries pass over bones—is useful since short periods of pressure over such points will stop the bleeding at some distance from the wound.

For nose bleeds the patient sits upright and his nostrils are pinched for a full ten minutes. Cold compresses or ice packs are placed over the upper part of the nose and mid-forehead. In cases of internal bleeding, recognized by signs of medical shock, there is little that can be done by way of first aid—the condition requires urgent hospital attention.

Broken bones

Bone fractures are not easy to recognize unless they are compound fractures in which a portion of broken bone juts through the skin. They are to be suspected after heavy blows or falls, and can be recognized by swelling and bruising, pain, signs of shock, tenderness over the injured area, inability to move a limb, obvious deformity or a grating sound at any attempt at movement. If there is the slightest suspicion of any of these when treating an accident victim it is assumed that a bone is broken.

All broken bones need hospital treatment so an ambulance is summoned as soon as possible. Since the victim may require an anaesthetic, nothing is given to him to eat or drink. No attempt is made to put the bones back in a normal position because movement encourages the bone ends to move apart and results in more pain and shock. To prevent movement a temporary splint is fixed—this can be made from a broom handle, an umbrella, or even thickly folded newspapers. It should be long enough to cover the joints above and below the break and is padded with cloth or soft material before being gently bound along the limb with broad bandages or cloth strips. If the pain gets worse or more swelling appears, the bandages are loosened.

Apart from limb bone fractures, special   377

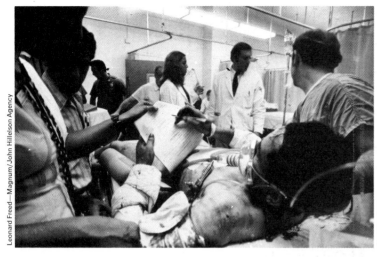

Leonard Freed—Magnum/John Hillelson Agency

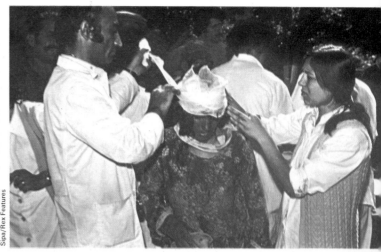

Sipa/Rex Features

Above: Accident victim signing forms in a New York hospital. Patients sometimes have to give signed permission for surgery to go ahead.

Above right: Bandaging the head of a Turkish earthquake victim.

Right: A consignment of human blood on its way to a military hospital in China. Large amounts of blood are required in war areas or at disaster sites. The British Red Cross organized the first blood transfusion service in London after World War I, and this is still an important part of the Red Cross's work. Blood donation, either voluntary or for a small payment, is encouraged in many countries.

League of Red Cross

first aid is necessary for certain other bones. For example, a broken collar bone needs support by an arm sling and a broken jaw bone by a bandage or scarf passed under the chin and round the top of the head. Where the skin is broken over the area of a fracture, it is covered with a light sterile dressing. If spinal or pelvic injury is suspected, the patient must not be moved until skilled medical help is available, and he should be told to keep still.

Shock, burns and poisons

Shock may occur in any accident or injury, and involves a dangerous reduction in the victim's blood pressure. This may be due to bleeding, dilation of the blood vessels caused by pain and anxiety, or reduced efficiency of the heart muscle. Shock requires urgent hospital therapy and all the helper can do is to reassure the victim and keep him warm with coats or blankets, though he should not be warmed with hot water bottles. The patient's clothing should be loosened. He should not be given alcohol, but can be given sweet tea, unless it is anticipated that he will require an anaesthetic in hospital.

Burns may result from fire, heated metal and the sun, as well as from contact with electricity, caustic chemicals, and hot water, oil or fat (which cause scalds). Burns and scalds vary in severity from mild skin reddening, to severe loss of skin and underlying muscle tissue.

Immediate first aid of burns and scalds is by flooding the burnt area with cold water for 10 minutes. Burnt clothing is not removed. The burnt area is covered with a clean and preferably sterile dressing, loosely secured, and in mouth burns, if the sufferer is conscious, he is given sips of cold water. In electric burns, the first thing to do is to make sure the current has been switched off. The rescuer also watches for any signs of heart failure or abnormal breathing.

Poisons may be inhaled as gases or fumes, swallowed as liquids or solids, or injected by needle, by the bite of an insect or by a snake. The rescuer should send for

Syndication International

Left: An air-sea rescue. Radio communication, and the use of helicopters equipped with hydraulic hoists, has enabled rescue forces to reach and help those in danger on the sea with great speed and efficiency.

Below: The chin tow is an important method of saving a drowning person. The lifesaver places himself behind the subject, passing an arm over his shoulder and round his chin, thus securing a firm grip on the subject and keeping his mouth and nose above water. The lifesaver uses his free arm and legs to swim backwards. If the subject struggles, he can be restrained with the lifesaver's free arm.

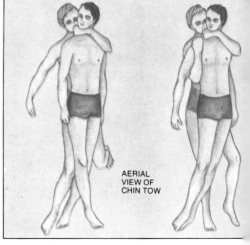

AERIAL VIEW OF CHIN TOW

Below: Mouth-to-mouth method of artificial respiration. 1: The victim is placed on his back with head pushed back and chin up. In this position the tongue does not obstruct the air flow. 2: Pinching the victim's nose, the rescuer exhales into the victim, watching for his chest to rise. 3: He then removes his mouth and watches for the victim's chest to fall, then repeats the process. The first four breaths are given as quickly as possible and subsequent inflations at the normal breathing rate.

Right: Artificial respiration saved this electrician's life in Jacksonville, Florida. He stopped breathing and was turning blue from lack of oxygen after an electric shock ten metres up a pole. A colleague ran 50 metres, climbed the pole and began the first aid he had learnt on a course.

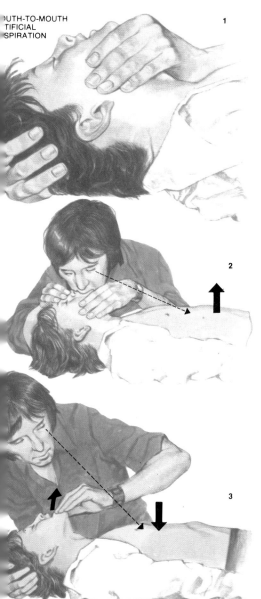

MOUTH-TO-MOUTH ARTIFICIAL RESPIRATION

1

2

3

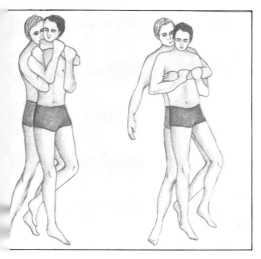

WHO/Red Cross

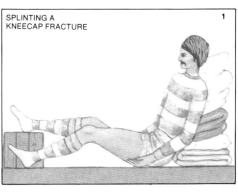

SPLINTING A KNEECAP FRACTURE

1

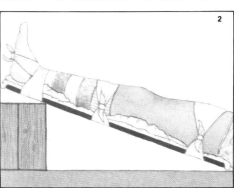

2

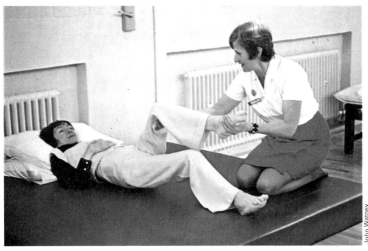

John Watney

Above: Splinting the leg in the case of a broken kneecap. 1: The victim is laid down with his back supported and his injured leg raised to a comfortable position. 2: The splint, which can be improvized from a walking stick, broom handle, umbrella or even rolled up newspapers or magazines, is placed along the back of the leg, reaching from the buttock to beyond the heel. Soft padding is placed between the splint and the leg, and the splint secured by three wide bandages, placed as shown.

Left: Physiotherapy is an important part of hospital accident treatment. Its aim is to restore to the patient full use of the injured part of his body.

medical help urgently. Any pills, liquids, plants or killed insects or snakes suspected of the poisoning, as well as any vomited material, should be kept for later identification.

If the victim is unconscious, he is placed in a semi-prone position and his air flow checked. If he is conscious, and the poison has been swallowed, vomiting is encouraged by tickling the back of his throat. This is not done, however, if the patient is in a coma or if there is any evidence of mouth burns suggesting caustic or corrosive poisons. If a known antidote to the poison is available, it is administered.

Insect stings and bites are not usually dangerous unless they are near the mouth where swelling can block the air flow, in which case medical help may be needed. No attempt should be made to suck the venom from an insect bite, but stings can be removed with sterilized forceps or a needle and the wound washed with a solution of bicarbonate of soda or, in the case of wasp stings, vinegar. When treating snake bite, the bitten part is kept low relative to the heart, and a tight bandage applied on the heart side of the bite to restrict circulation of the poison in the bloodstream. This is maintained until an antidote can be administered.

Hospital treatment

The need to provide prompt, skilled and effective attention to injured people and accident victims has meant a steady development of specialized accident hospitals as well as accident and emergency departments in general hospitals. These are sited strategically in relation to major roads and motorways as the likely source of major multiple accidents.

Such departments require specialist teams which include a radiologist, to assess X-ray photographs of suspected fractures; an anaesthetist, who can give mechanical respiration and provide general anaesthetics to carry out operations; an orthopaedic surgeon to treat dislocations and bone damage, and to re-set bone fractures using plaster of Paris or metal plates and pins to hold the bones together; a general surgeon to treat wounds, lacerations, cut tendons and nerves, and to correct internal bleeding; a specialist burn surgeon who may also be a plastic surgeon; expert nurses, to assist in operations and attend to dressings, stitches and plasters; and finally physiotherapists, to teach re-education of stiff and weak muscles following recovery from accidents or injury, and to instruct in the use of artificial aids.

Diagnosis

Whereas treating the sick and injured can be quite straightforward, finding out what is wrong with them in the first place is often much more difficult. This process of *diagnosis* is both a skilled art and an exact science, and it has much in common with the unravelling of a mystery by an expert detective.

The first clues to help in diagnosis are the patient's *symptoms*—the information that the patient himself reports about the illness—and his *signs*, valuable fragments of evidence that the doctor may discover on physical examination. Nowadays a variety of instruments and machines help in the diagnosis which is also aided by laboratory examination of tissue specimens, blood and waste products.

A chronological report by the patient of all the symptoms and events that led up to his illness is of prime importance. The patient is encouraged to describe this *case history* in his own words. Often a carefully elicited case history will provide enough evidence to permit a full diagnosis without recourse to more complex diagnostic tools.

Physical examination

After the case history, the next step is a physical examination, which is carried out using a programme of techniques known as *inspection*, *palpation*, *percussion* and *auscultation*.

Inspection consists of a visual assessment of the patient's external appearance. Significant abnormalities that may help in diagnosis include asymmetry of the two sides of the body, pallor, blue tinges, lumps and rashes on the skin, disturbances of hair growth, alteration in limb or muscle thickness, twitches and tics.

The doctor then checks the size and consistency of any obvious lumps or bruises, feels for any abnormal vibrations in the chest due to heart or arterial disease, assesses the tenderness of inflamed or painful areas, and tests the tone of the muscles. This is the process of palpation. Moving on to percussion, the doctor taps the body over organs that should be partially or totally hollow such as the lungs or bladder. The presence of fluid or insufficient air produces an abnormal resonance in the percussion note.

For the auscultation, or listening process, a *stethoscope* is used. The first stethoscope was made by the French physician Laennec and consisted of no more than a straight tube. Nowadays a binaural, or two earpiece instrument is most commonly used.

When the stethoscope is placed on the chest, it can be used to check that air is entering various parts of the lungs, and will pick up a crackling sound if there is fluid in the lungs, indicating bronchitis or pneumonia. It also picks up the beating of the heart and detects any abnormal heart sounds or *murmurs* which might indicate damaged heart valves. When applied to the abdomen, the sound of air moving through the intestines can be heard, together with any murmurs arising from kinked or narrowed arteries.

To examine the lens and retina of the eye, a multi-lensed battery-lit instrument called an *ophthalmoscope* is used. With this, it is possible to observe the thick-

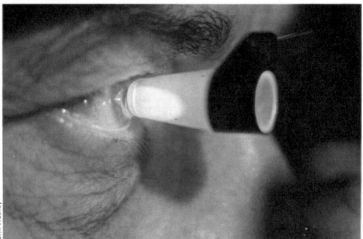

Above: *The Doctor*, a painting by Sir Luke Fildes. Diagnosis can be a puzzling business for only a small minority of illnesses (chickenpox for example) are immediately recognizable from their symptoms.

Left: Using a *fluoroscope* to examine damage to the eye surface. A dye called fluorescein is dropped into the eye and then washed out. The eye is then inspected through a lens. Any accumulation of the dye in cuts or abrasions on the cornea shows up as a brilliant green.

Below: The *stethoscope* is among the most familiar items in a doctor's arsenal of diagnostic tools. Its greatest value is in diagnosing heart and lung disorders.

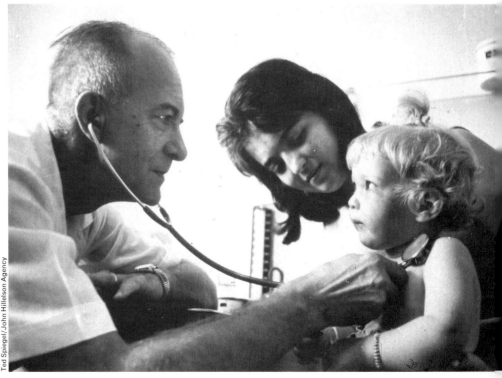

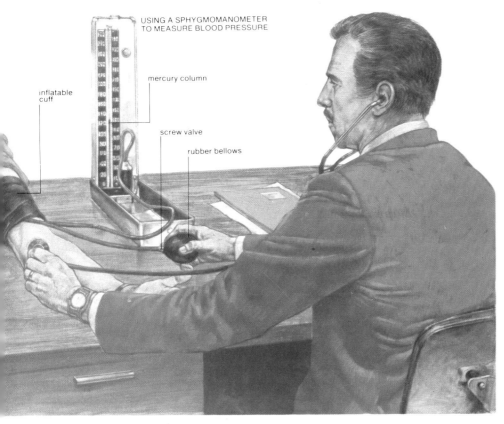

USING A SPHYGMOMANOMETER
TO MEASURE BLOOD PRESSURE

mercury column

inflatable cuff

screw valve

rubber bellows

Above: Measuring blood pressure using a *sphygmomanometer*. An inflatable cuff is wound round the patient's upper arm and is pumped up by a rubber bellows until the wrist pulse stops. The pressure in the cuff is then measured by means of a calibrated mercury column. Placing his stethoscope as shown, the doctor slowly releases the cuff pressure by means of a screw valve. The mercury column then begins to drop. The first sounds heard in the stethoscope indicate the *systolic* pressure. At this point the doctor notes the mercury column reading. When the cuff pressure is further reduced, a characteristic slapping sound indicates the *diastolic* pressure, which is measured in similar fashion.

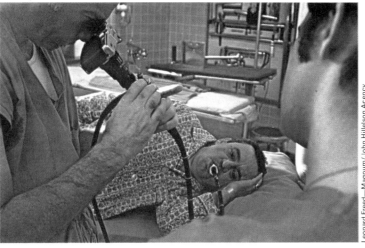

Leonard Freed—Magnum/John Hillelson Agency

Colin Davey/Camera Press

Left: Testing a girl's ability to recognize a letter in the left hand side of her visual field. This test is used to diagnose cases of 'split brain' in which the brain's language centre is separated from the right visual cortex. These people recognize, but cannot name objects at the extreme left of their visual fields.

Above: Photographing the inside of a patient's stomach with a type of *endoscope* called a *fibre-gastroscope*. This is a bundle of flexible glass fibres that can be used both to illuminate the stomach and to return a visual image. By viewing stomach ulcers directly, doctors are better able to decide on appropriate therapy.

ening of the lens known as cataract, or changes in the retina that may indicate high blood pressure, arteriosclerosis, or diabetes mellitus.

The outer ear canal and eardrum can be observed with a battery-lit instrument called an *auriscope*, which consists of a lens inside a cone-shaped probe. With this it is possible to diagnose an infected eardrum or an inflamed ear canal.

Physiological functions

Two important diagnostic measurements are the *systolic* and *diastolic* blood pressures. The systolic blood pressure is a measure of the force with which the left ventricle of the heart contracts to expel blood into the arteries. The diastolic blood pressure is a measure of the resistance of the arteries to this outflow.

Abnormalities in the two blood pressure readings may indicate such conditions as shock, heart disease and arteriosclerosis.

Apart from blood pressure, the three basic observations of body functioning are the body temperature, the pulse rate and the respiratory (breathing) rate. The body temperature is measured with a clinical thermometer placed under the tongue, under the arm or in the rectum. The normal temperature is 37°C (98.4°F). An above-normal temperature usually indicates bacterial or viral infection, while a low temperature, known as *hypothermia*, may result from exposure to intense cold or may indicate some malfunctioning of the thyroid gland.

The pulse is generally measured as beats per minute in the radial artery of the wrist. Normally, the rate is about 70 beats per minute, and the pulse rhythm is regular. An increase in pulse rate may indicate an infectious illness or anaemia, but also occurs with emotional arousal and exercise, so is significant only if measured when the patient is relaxed. A slowed pulse rate may indicate thyroid deficiency disease or abnormal heart functioning. An irregular pulse rhythm is also a probable sign of heart disease.

Respiration normally takes place at a rate of 12 to 14 breaths per minute. An above-normal respiratory rate can indicate a variety of illnesses such as anaemia and acute bronchitis.

Testing the nervous system

Examination of the brain and spinal cord is carried out in several ways. Assessment of memory and intellect can be made by direct questioning and by psychological tests. Assessment of neuromuscular control is made by checking muscle and limb movements, both passively and against a resistance. The possible site of a disturbance in nerve functioning is tested indirectly by tapping certain points on the body with a light hammer to produce an involuntary neuromuscular jerk, or *reflex*. The usual points tapped are the biceps, triceps and supinator muscles in the arm, and the knee and ankle muscles. The perception of pain can be tested by pricking parts of the body with pins, touch sensitivity tested with cotton wool, and the patient's ability to sense vibration tested with a tuning fork applied over a bone.

The absence of nervous reflexes or an impaired ability to perceive different sensations may provide important clues to the location of a damaged area in the brain or spinal cord but do not show the cause of the damage. To find this out, a procedure called *lumbar puncture* may be carried out. With the lower part of the spine under a local anaesthetic, a needle is passed through the skin and through the gap between the lumbar vertebrae of the spinal column. A small amount of *cerebro-spinal fluid*, a substance which bathes the brain and spinal cord, is then withdrawn. The cellular and chemical composition of this fluid may show whether the damage has been caused by bleeding, infection, tissue degeneration or by a tumour and is thus a help in deciding on suitable treatment.

Specimens and samples

Laboratory examination of specimens derived from body organs and tissues is of considerable value in diagnosis. Urine specimens can reveal the presence of kidney or bladder disease, diabetes 381 mellitus, liver disease or internal bleeding. Examination of the sputum can distinguish various types of lung infection such as bronchitis or pneumonia. Faecal specimens can reveal evidence of bleeding from ulcers or tumours in the stomach or gut, or may show the presence of harmful bacteria or parasites.

Samples removed from diseased tissues may on examination reveal the nature of the tissue disorder. This method is used in diagnosing the nature of skin tumours and liver disease. For women, a cervical smear may be taken as a routine precaution, since this may reveal signs of cancer of the cervix at an early stage, when remedial therapy is most effective.

Examination of the blood is a major method of diagnosis. Simple tests can be done in a doctor's clinic, but modern pathology laboratories have large auto-analysers which can run off a whole series of blood tests while a computer prints out the results for interpretation. Diagnoses that can be made using modern blood analysers include: anaemia through examination of the blood's red cells; infectious illnesses through examination of the white cells; and liver disease through analysis of bile and enzyme levels in the blood.

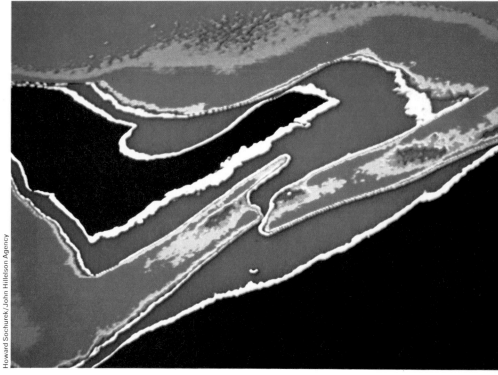

Howard Sochurek/John Hillelson Agency

Diagnostic machines
Produced by a beam of high energy electrons striking a metallic target, X-rays can penetrate the softer body tissues but are absorbed by denser tissues, the degree of absorption increasing with the density of the tissue. Thus, a sensitized photographic plate placed behind the body when X-rays are passed through it shows up

Below: Barium sulphate is opaque to X-rays, and since it cannot be absorbed by the intestines can be safely taken as a 'meal' to reveal the digestive tract on X-ray plates. In this photograph, the large blank area at the bottom is caused by an accumulation of barium around a stomach cancer. The tube leading off at

the top of the picture is the oesophagus.

Above: A fracture of the upper arm as revealed by *ultra-sonography*. Sound waves are transmitted through the arm and picked up by the sonograph. The sound intensity indicates the density of the tissue through which the sound has passed,

and the signals are converted into a colour display by a process called *colour slicing*. This sometimes gives a better picture of bone damage than the more conventional use of X-rays, and is also a completely safe method.

Below: A small boy from a village in Basutoland having his chest X-rayed

by a World Health Organisation mobile X-ray unit. The WHO team was screening the village for tuberculosis in order to detect and treat this disease, one of the most common and serious in Africa, at an early stage. Tuberculosis is revealed on X-ray plates by characteristic blotches on the apices of the lungs.

John Watney

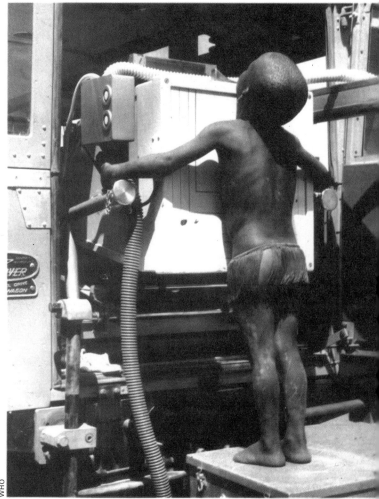

WHO

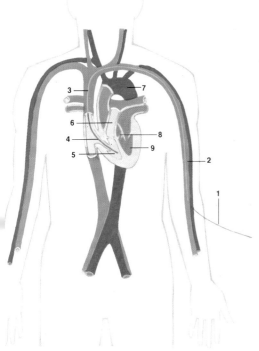

CARDIAC
CATHETERIZATION

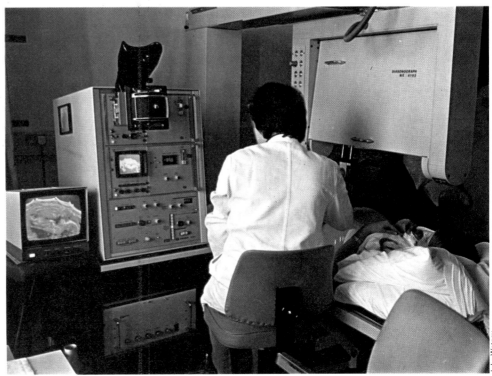

John Watney

Above: *Cardiac catheterization* is a technique used to study diseases and congenital defects of the heart. The catheter (1), a flexible nylon tube filled with saline to prevent air entering the blood, is inserted into an arm vein (2) and pushed up to the *superior vena cava* (3). From there it is moved into the *right auricle*

(4) and through to the *right ventricle* (5) or even into the *pulmonary artery* (6). Blood oxygen levels in these areas of the heart can be found by analyzing blood samples withdrawn through the catheter, and blood pressure readings can be taken by linking the catheter to a pressure recorder. Variations in these readings from the

normal, due for example to oxygenated blood leaking through a hole from the left side of the heart, can indicate a variety of defects. With difficulty, the left side of the heart can also be catheterized by pushing a catheter up an artery to the *aorta* (7) and through the *aortic valve* (8) into the *left ventricle* (9).

Above: Using a *diasonograph* to examine the size and growth of an unborn foetus. A probe placed above the abdomen transmits sound waves and picks up the echoes. These signals are electronically converted into a picture on a television monitor. This can be used to check that the foetus is developing normally.

dense materials, such as bone, contrasted against less dense surrounding tissues. X-rays can be used to show up bone fractures and to locate 'foreign bodies' such as swallowed coins. If the patient swallows a dense fluid containing barium, the so-called *barium meal*, its presence in the digestive tract will reveal on the X-ray plate such abnormalities as gastric ulcers in the stomach, or polyps in the bowel. Patients can also be injected with a dye that is opaque to X-rays. The dye finds its way to the kidneys and bladder and may reveal kidney stones and bladder tumours.

Electrodes placed on the head or body can pick up changes in electric potential associated with nerve and muscle activity. The electrodes can be linked to an instrument which records these electrical changes as a graph on a continuously moving sheet of paper. The pattern of electrical activity from the heart is known as an *electrocardiogram* or ECG. This is an accurate record of the heart rate and rhythms, including any irregular rhythms. On interpretation, these may reveal the presence of high blood pressure or diseased heart valves.

The pattern of electrical activity from the brain is known as an *electroencephalogram* or EEG. An EEG shows up normal brain rhythms such as *alpha waves*, and the various patterns of electrical brain activity associated with sleep. Abnormal patterns may help to diagnose disorders such as epilepsy, or the sites of brain tumours or abscesses.

Radioactive isotopes are sometimes used in diagnosis. For example, if radioactive iodine is injected into the bloodstream, a geiger counter can be used to measure how much of it is being taken up by the thyroid gland. This shows how well the thyroid gland is working to produce *thyroxine*, a hormone that contains iodine.

Many tumours concentrate injected radioactive elements such as strontium and technetium. The tumours may be revealed by searching for local increases in radioactivity and displaying these pictorially as 'hot spots' using a scanning system known as a *scintiscan*.

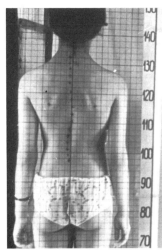

Camera Press

Above: Diagnosing a spinal disorder at a research institute in Moscow. The patient is suffering from sideways curvature of the spine called *scoliosis*. The extent of the curvature is being assessed with reference to a grid, using a scanning machine.

Left: Using radioisotopes to diagnose a kidney disorder. The woman has been injected with a dose of the isotope iodine 131, which concentrates in the kidneys. The two tubes placed against her back are scintillation counters which detect radioactivity. By linking these to a recorder, the readings from the counters are converted into graphs which show the build up of iodine in the two kidneys, and its rate of excretion.

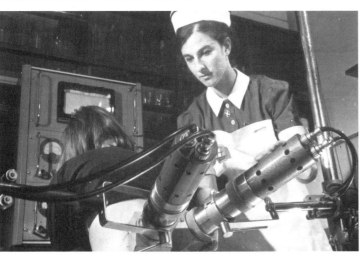

UKAEA

383

Surgery and Anaesthetics

Skeletal remains show that the first major surgery, *trepanning*, was performed in prehistoric times. This consisted of drilling a hole in the skull, probably to let out the devils that were thought to cause madness. Hippocrates, the 'father of medicine', laid down some of the principles of surgery in the fourth century BC, while another Greek physician, Galen, held an appointment as surgeon to the gladiators at Pergamum in the second century AD.

After Galen, few significant advances in surgery were made until the sixteenth century, and by that time surgery had become separated from medicine and was regarded as an inferior craft. Surgery was performed mainly by itinerants who specialized in a single operation, such as removing stones from the bladder—'cutting for stone'. Not until the eighteenth century did surgery start to become respectable again.

Royal College of Surgeons

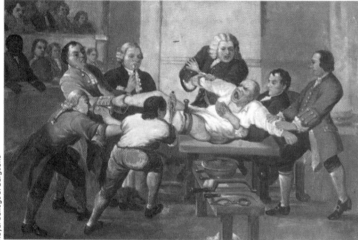

Royal College of Surgeons

Above: Henry VIII with the barber surgeons, the only surgeons to gain any status in medieval Britain. They were given a charter in 1540. They probably rose to fame because monks liked to have their hair cut, their teeth pulled and their gallstones removed by the same person.

Left: Before anaesthesia, surgery was extremely painful. Many mixtures, usually based on alcohol or opium, were used to allay the pain, but were largely ineffective and the patient had to be physically restrained.

Right: The first public display of anaesthetic surgery in Massachusetts in 1846. W. T. G. Morton administered ether while J. C. Warren performed a painless operation.

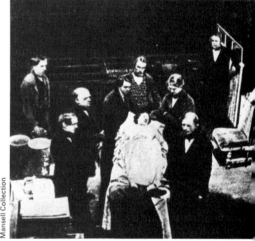

Mansell Collection

At this time, most surgical operations were restricted by two severe limitations: firstly, surgery was extremely painful for the patient—the definition of a 'good' surgeon was one who worked quickly—and secondly, any operation on the body cavities, such as abdomen, chest or skull, was almost bound to introduce infection which could well prove fatal.

Anaesthesia and antisepsis
In 1797, the British chemist Sir Humphry Davy inhaled some 'laughing gas', nitrous oxide, and found that one of its effects was to banish pain. Davy reported this, and in 1844 the first dental operation using nitrous oxide as an anaesthetic was carried out in the US. Two years previously, the first painless operation had been carried out using *ether* as an anaesthetic, and in 1847 *chloroform* was reported to have similar anaesthetic effects. At last surgeons had found the tool they needed: a method of overcoming pain, allowing them to carry out lengthy operations without undue haste.

Two types of anaesthetic are in use today. *Local anaesthetics* are used to abolish sensation in a restricted part of the body. They act by blocking the transmission of electrical impulses along nerve cells, and are usually injected around the nerves that normally carry impulses from the area to be operated on. The first of these anaesthetics was *cocaine*. This was superseded by a synthetic drug *procaine* in 1905. Numerous drugs related to procaine are now used, such as *lignocaine*.

General anaesthetics remove sensation from the whole body, acting on the brain to induce a sleep-like state. Nitrous oxide, ether and chloroform are included in this category, together with more recently developed, and less flammable drugs such as *halothane*. Once inhaled, they act within seconds, but recovery starts immediately the drug is withdrawn.

Under general anaesthesia, the patient's respiration may be controlled externally. There are two reasons for this. First, general anaesthetics depress the area of the brain that controls respiration. Second, for many operations the patient's muscles need to be relaxed, and although this could be achieved with large doses of the anaesthetic, it is safer to administer a muscle-relaxing drug called *curare*. However, curare paralyzes the respiratory muscles in the chest, making controlled respiration necessary, The anaesthetist inserts a tube into the patient's wind-pipe via nose or mouth and connects the other end to a ventilator. This machine pumps controlled volumes of oxygen into the lungs, together with the anaesthetic.

The second obstacle was overcome in 1867 by Lister, who showed how infection could be avoided during surgery by using an antiseptic carbolic spray and hygienic surgical techniques. Lister's ideas laid the basis for precautions that are taken for granted in modern surgery. These include the sterilization of surgical instruments and the thorough washing of hands before operations.

Surgery today
In addition to the traditional scalpels, clamps, forceps and retractors, the modern surgeon may also use *diathermy* (electrical cutting or coagulation of tissue), *cryoprobes* to freeze tissue, air powered tools for cutting through bone, *fibre-endoscopes* for looking into body cavities and laser beams for eye surgery.

During an operation, the patient's heart rate and blood pressure are monitored to ensure that the vital organs are receiving enough oxygen. Any loss of blood may lead to a drop in blood pressure, so the amount of blood lost during the operation is accurately assessed and re-

Left: Surgical repair of a hole in the heart or *foramen ovale* between left and right auricles.
A: Oxygenated blood from the left auricle (1) is forced through the hole (2) into the right auricle (3) and mixes with venous blood from the vena cava (4). As a result, mixed blood (purple) is pumped to the lungs from the right ventricle (5) via the pulmonary artery (6), putting an overload on the pulmonary circulation. The heart also has to work harder to maintain pressure in the aorta (7).
B: The hole can be repaired by opening the vena cava and *suturing*, or stitching together, the sides of the hole.
C: Alternatively, a tissue graft or a piece of shaped plastic can be stitched over the hole.
D: The vena cava is then closed and normal circulation resumes in the heart. The whole operation is performed using a heart-lung machine to bypass the blood circulation from the heart and lungs.

Right: Modern surgery is carried out by a skilled team consisting of the surgeon, the anaesthetist, assistant surgeons, nurses and theatre technicians, each of them performing an important role. Before the operation, the patient is given a drug to calm him. This prevents any violent reaction when the anaesthetic is first administered, and obviates any strain on the heart due to anxiety.

Below right: How blood vessels are joined after surgery or injury, or during transplants.
1: Arteries are joined by introducing three threads to close the ends together, then the ends are sewn together by overstitching.
2: Veins are joined by *suspended suture*. The vessel is sutured to a metal ring which prevents collapse due to low blood pressure in the vein.

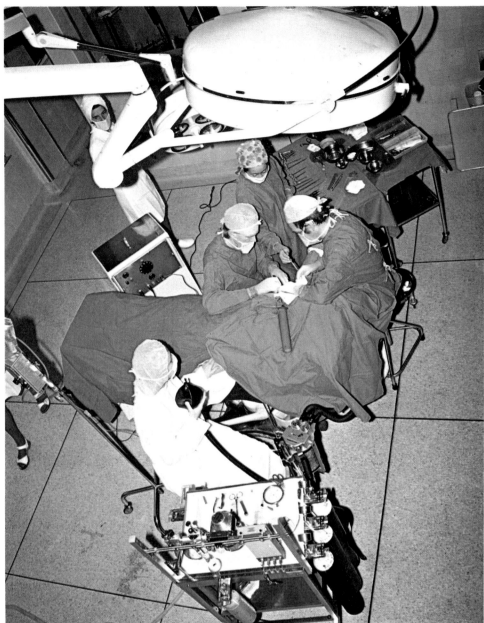

John Watney

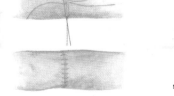

1   2

suturing an artery   suturing a vein

Royal College of Surgeons

Left: The great English surgeon Joseph, Lord Lister. His first paper on antisepsis appeared in 1867. It extolled the use of carbolic acid as a method of combating infection when treating compound fractures. He later introduced the carbolic spray and encouraged the practice of hygiene in surgery. Carbolic acid was soon replaced by less toxic antiseptics, but Lister transformed surgery from a craft hardly less dangerous than the disorders it attempted to cure into a relatively safe form of treatment.

Right: By enclosing the operating site in a sterile plastic bubble, and by wearing sterile gloves, modern surgeons can work in an *aseptic* or germ-free environment.

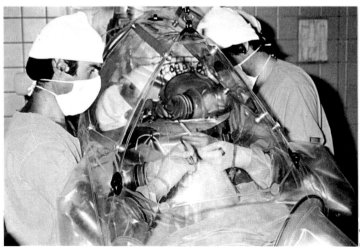

Rex Features

385

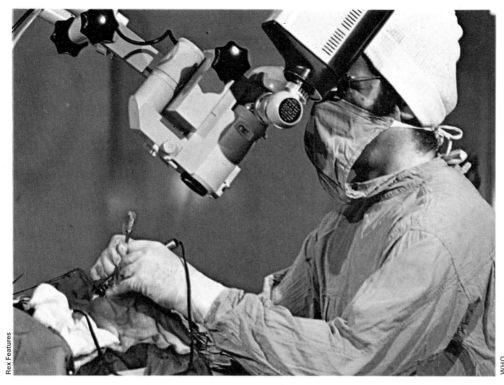

Rex Features

WHO

placed by transfusions.

Surgery is often undertaken to remove something. This may be a foreign body such as a bullet or a swallowed coin, a stone which has formed in the urinary tract or gall bladder, infected or dead tissue, or a tumour. Many of these *ablative* operations are performed on abdominal organs. The surgeon has to take great care not to spill the contents of the organs, since fluid or bacteria from the organs can cause a dangerous chemical inflammation or infection of the *peritoneum* (the membranous lining of the abdomen). As a precaution, the digestive tract is usually 'sterilized' before the operation by giving the patient a course of antibiotics.

When excising cancerous tumours, care is taken to prevent cancer cells from entering the bloodstream, where they may *metastasize* and start a new tumour in another part of the body. For this reason veins leading away from the tumour may be tied before it is removed.

Where there is doubt as to its nature, a small piece of the tumour may be taken for examination, a procedure known as a *biopsy*. This may help the surgeon to decide whether the surgery is going to be *simple*, in which case the tumour only is removed, or *radical*, in which considerable amounts of tissue surrounding or associated with the tumour are also removed to prevent any regrowth.

Sometimes the surgeon has to decide whether it is wise to operate at all—it may be as dangerous to remove the offending tissue as to leave it. The surgeon has to weigh the chance of success against the quality and length of the patient's life if the operation is not done.

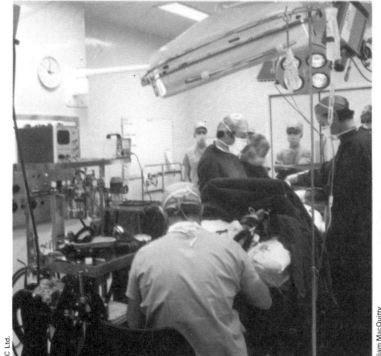

BOC Ltd.

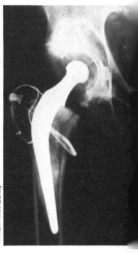

William MacQuitty

Heart surgery

The scope of heart surgery has vastly increased since the introduction of the 'heart-lung machine' in the 1950s. This machine pumps blood from the veins to the arteries without it passing through the heart. Most machines oxygenate the blood, thus completely bypassing the lungs as well. Using the heart-lung machine, the heart can be stopped and opened for up to four hours.

Deep hypothermia, cooling of the body, is sometimes artificially induced for heart surgery. It causes a decrease in the metabolic rate, and therefore the oxygen requirements, of the body's tissues, and allows the heart to be opened and operated on for a few minutes without the use of a heart-lung machine. But often deep hypothermia and the heart-lung machine are used in conjunction.

For children, heart surgery is generally performed to correct a congenital defect of the heart or its major blood vessels. Some of these can be repaired without opening the heart. An example is *patent ductus arteriosus*, in which a duct between the aorta and the pulmonary artery, which allows blood to by-pass the lungs in the foetus, fails to close at birth. This defect is usually treated when the child is about five by ligaturing the duct.

For adults, the usual reason for heart surgery is a diseased heart valve. If, say, the *mitral valve* between the left atrium and left ventricle is constricted, blood does not flow through it properly, and the heart is overworked. Usually, the heart is opened and the defective valve replaced with a human valve or an artificial one.

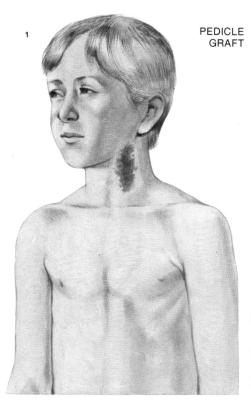

PEDICLE
GRAFT

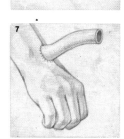

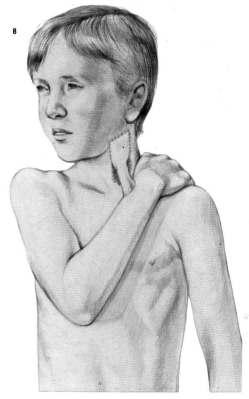

Right: One of the most commonly performed techniques of plastic surgery is the facelift. A strip of skin is removed from the face or neck and the remaining skin is stretched to close the gap. This photograph, taken after half the subject's face had been treated, demonstrates the effect on facial wrinkles.

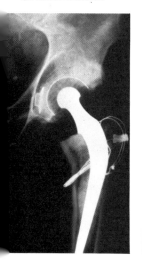

Above: A *pedicle* graft is a full skin graft used to convey skin over long distances. The main priority is to maintain a good blood supply to the graft. 1: In this case, an extensive burn on the patient's neck is to be covered with a graft taken from his belly. 2: A broad flap of skin is freed. 3: The flap is formed into a tube. 4: The exposed area is closed up. 5: When a good blood supply is established through the tube, one end is cut. 6: This is sewn on to a wrist. 7: Once blood flow is re-established, the other end is freed. 8: This is then stitched to healthy skin next to the burn and the tube is finally unrolled and stitched over the burn.

Tumours near the surface may be cut out, but in some cases, removal is not possible because too much healthy tissue would be damaged. In cases of haemorrhage, the bleeding point is blocked.

Some brain diseases, such as *Parkinson's disease*, are caused by a disorder in a known area of the brain. In these cases, *stereotactic* operations may be performed. The head is fixed in a carefully calibrated frame and a small probe is inserted through a hole in the skull. It is then guided accurately to the site of the lesion, which is destroyed, usually by diathermy.

Plastic surgery

Plastic surgery is concerned with the prevention and treatment of deformities, either because these are interfering with the body's functioning, or purely to improve the patient's appearance.

Skin grafts are the ideal treatment for serious burns. Where possible the graft is taken from the patient himself, since this avoids any problems of rejection. *Split-skin grafts* are used in most situations. The graft is removed from the donor site using a *Humby knife*, which regulates the thickness so that only the outer layer of the skin, the epidermis, is removed. Minute blood vessels nourish the graft at the receptor site, and new skin soon grows at the donor site. *Full-thickness* grafts do not 'take' as well as split-skin grafts, and require a good blood supply of their own.

Bone grafts may be used to replace bone loss, or sometimes to encourage the healing of a fracture, by providing a framework over which new bone can grow. A common donor site for bone grafts is the *ilium*, the largest of the pelvic bones.

Blood vessel surgery

Atherosclerotic plaque which constricts the blood flow can be treated surgically if the constriction is limited to just one part of the artery. The artery is cut open, and the plaque, together with the inner layers of the artery and any clot that has formed, is carefully scraped out. The artery is then stitched up again.

Arterial *embolisms* (free-moving flakes of clotted blood or air bubbles) must be removed within a few hours, or blood circulation may be damaged to such an extent that amputation is necessary. The embolism may be removed by suction, or with a *Fogarty catheter*. This is a slim tube which is pushed along the artery past the block. A small balloon at its tip is inflated and the catheter is withdrawn, bringing the embolism with it.

Brain surgery

The most common reasons for brain surgery are brain tumours, haemorrhage (bleeding), injury due to skull fractures, and clots in brain arteries. As the brain is enclosed in a rigid box, the skull, any swelling of the brain's tissues and fluids results in compression and possible damage. This poses special problems for the anaesthetist. He has to keep a good blood circulation going in the brain, but too high a blood pressure can lead to swelling. To overcome this the anaesthetist may give the drug *chlorpromazine* to cool the body and lower the oxygen demand, so that he can lower the blood pressure.

To get to the brain, the surgeon uses a drill to bore holes in the skull. If necessary, a wire saw may be used to cut between these holes and raise a flap of skull.

Rex Features

387

Alternative Medicine

The origins of alternative or 'fringe' medicine can be traced to two historical sources. One of these was the belief that disease was an affliction of the soul of the sufferer. In tribal communities, illness was attributed to divine displeasure or sorcery; and as early civilizations rose and fell, the assumption lingered on that magic, or faith, was the cure. But after the Renaissance in sixteenth century Europe, this *vitalist* creed was confronted by the *mechanist* theory that disease was caused and spread by physical factors.

In the nineteenth century, the discovery of bacteria and viruses as the agents of infectious disease provided apparent confirmation of the mechanist theory. This led to the appearance of a new mechanistic form of medicine, based on the *allopathic* principle of treating illness with substances that produced effects opposite to that of the disease. As a result, healers in the newly industrialized societies of Europe and North America became increasingly polarized into those who jumped on to the mechanist bandwagon and those who stayed with the old vitalist creeds.

In the less industrialized countries of Asia, Africa, and South America, allopathic medicine had little impact at first. Facilities to teach and practice the mechanist theories were lacking, while countries such as China and India had elaborate forms of medicine based on vitalist creeds, which, being intricately related to the philosophies and religions of these countries, were resistant to change. Thus, while allopathy emerged as a new orthodox medicine in the industrialized societies, vitalist creeds lingered on elsewhere.

The practitioners of the new medicine had soon formed themselves into a profession, and this was the second reason for the split into orthodox and alternative camps. Previously, physicians, surgeons and apothecaries had gone their separate and often mutually hostile ways, running their own affairs and learning their own crafts, usually by apprenticeship. But with the establishment of medical schools, all medical students were taught mechanistic theories and practice. Alternative theories and practice were either derided or ignored. Among these were *nature cure* including herbalism, *homeopathic* medicine, *bone-setting* and the manipulative treatments of *osteopathy* and *chiropractic* that grew out of it, and *faith healing*.

Nature cure

Nature cure, now more commonly described by its practitioners as *naturopathy* is derived from the Hippocratic idea of the *Vis Vindicatrix Naturae* or *life force*. When we cut ourselves the body gets to work on our behalf to staunch the blood flow; on the same principle, the naturopath claims, we can rely on our bodies to heal themselves in other ways, if we treat them well. Most naturopaths look on drug treatment with disfavour, particularly if the drug is designed to do the body's work for it. But many, and especially those practitioners of the

Roland & Sabrina Michaud/John Hillelson Agency

Roland & Sabrina Michaud/John Hillelson Agency

Above: Dioscorides, the first century AD Greek physician whose *Materia Medica* was the greatest compendium of drugs in antiquity, donating a *mandragora*, or mandrake plant, to one of his disciples. The origin of some modern 'fringe' medicines can be traced to the use of plants imbued with magical properties in ancient times. Superstition surrounded the mandrake in the Middle Ages: its

forked root resembled a man and was believed to imprison a lost soul which shrieked when the mandrake was uprooted. Although poisonous, in small doses the plant acts as an anaesthetic and anti-spasmodic, and is still used as such in the East, where it is also believed to facilitate pregnancy and to have aphrodisiac properties. Orthodox Western medicine has no use for the mandrake.

Right and below: Perhaps the most widespread and well-accepted form of alternative medicine in Britain is *osteopathy*, founded by an American, Andrew Taylor Still (right). It is based on the idea that misaligned spinal vertebrae are the cause of most illness. The modern osteopath (below) is instructing a pupil in a manipulative technique used to reposition displaced thoracic vertebrae.

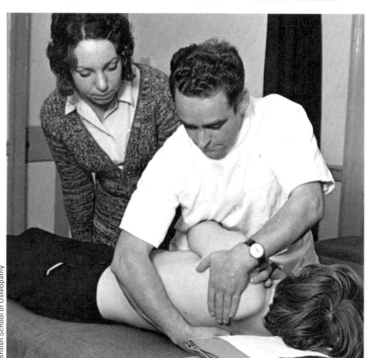

British School of Osteopathy

British School of Osteopathy

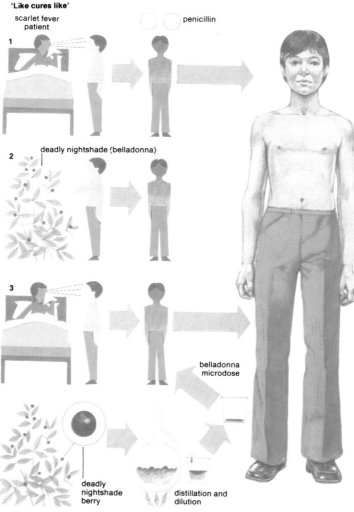

'Like cures like'

scarlet fever patient — penicillin

1

2 deadly nightshade (belladonna)

3

belladonna microdose

deadly nightshade berry — distillation and dilution

Above left and below: Although little known in the West before 1960, *acupuncture* has been practised in the East for 5,000 years. This 15th century bronze head from Korea (above left) shows the approximate locations of some of the acupuncture points. Needles placed in these points are believed to help the life force flow along channels called meridians. The points are little larger than pin-pricks, and their exact locations are not easy to find. Some acupuncturists feel for 'nodules' at the correct sites, others measure variations on the skin's electrical resistance, and yet others rely on sixth sense. For some people acupuncture is an effective anaesthetic during major surgery (below), but in the East it is mainly used to maintain health rather than to cure illness.

Above: Illustrating the homeopathic principle of 'like cures like'. 1: If a person gets scarlet fever, he develops a red flush. Orthodox medicine fights the infection with penicillin. 2: Belladonna poisoning produces a similar flush. 3: Homeopaths see the flush of scarlet fever as a sign that the body's defences are at work and try to aid the defences by administering a tiny dose of belladonna.

branch of naturopathy called *herbalism*, make an exception in the case of certain herbs which are felt to be natural aids to the healing process.

Herbalism lost ground during the 'wonder drug' era between the 1930s and the 1960s. But recently the euphoria stimulated by the discovery of drugs such as the antibiotics and cortisone has been replaced by a degree of disillusionment with drug treatment, and herbalism has staged a recovery.

Homeopathy

Homeopathy was originally a development out of herbalism. Towards the end of the eighteenth century, a German doctor named Samuel Hahnemann decided that what were thought to be the symptoms of illness were really symptoms of the body's resistance to disease—fever for instance was a sign that the body's defences were going into action. It followed, he felt, that to treat a disorder like malaria which involved bouts of delirious fever, what was needed was a herb or drug which would produce a fever by itself, thus aiding the body's healing powers.

Given this principle of like curing like, Hahnemann found it unnecessary to prescribe the drug in strength. In fact, he postulated that the drug's potency was actually increased by diluting it. Thus, for the drug to be most effective, the patient received an infinitesimal dose. Although homeopathy was savagely attacked by orthodox physicians as being unscientific, and its practitioners often labelled as quacks, it managed to establish itself as an alternative treatment.

With their infinitesimal microdoses, homeopaths could never be accused of harming their patients. Orthodox physicians were quick to point out that homeopathic cures might just be placebo effects, but even if this were true, it did not detract from the fact that homeopathic treatment has had some remarkable successes: during cholera outbreaks in Vienna in 1836 and London in 1854, for instance, the death rate among cholera victims in homeopathic hospitals was significantly lower than the general death rate from cholera.

Perhaps the most positive aspect of homeopathic treatment is its insistence on attending thoroughly to the patient's symptoms, and tailoring the treatment accordingly, with a concern that is sometimes lacking in orthodox medicine. Homeopaths were also among the first to recognize that the appearance of an illness was not simply the result of microbial invasion, but also depended on the individual's susceptibility to infection.

Osteopathy and chiropractic

Historically, bone setting was practised as a sort of hobby by individuals with a knack of being able to reposition dislocated joints with minimal discomfort to the patient. Bone setters were excluded from the medical profession not so much because what they did was unorthodox, but because they could not afford the fees for medical education, even if they could achieve the scholastic qualifications. By the time they had formed themselves into a profession, a new kind of bone setter had emerged: the osteopath.

Osteopathy was derived from the teachings of an American, Andrew Still, who believed that the cause of any illness was an impaired blood flow. The flow, he claimed, was impaired by misalignment of the spinal vertebrae, which could be put back in place by manipulation. A few years later an American named D. D. Palmer introduced chiropractic, based on much the same principle—although Palmer believed it was the effect of misaligned vertebrae on the condition of the nerves, rather than the blood, which was crucial, and advocated somewhat different manipulative methods.

Osteopaths and chiropractors now flourish in most countries. Increasingly they have come to use the paraphernalia of orthodox medicine, such as X-rays and drug injections; but spinal manipulation remains their chief form of treatment. The general consensus of opinion, even among orthodox doctors, is that manipulative therapy is an effective form of treatment for many cases of backache.

The status of osteopaths and chiropractors varies from country to country. In the US, osteopaths have become barely distinguishable from qualified doctors: in France, they can still be (and often are) prosecuted as quacks, the practice being illegal. In Britain, it is now possible for a general practitioner to recommend osteopathy provided that he retains the responsibility for the patient.

Faith healing
Nowadays British doctors can even, if they wish, refer patients to faith healers, or as they now prefer to describe themselves, spiritual healers. In Britain, the National Federation of Spiritual Healers has more than 2,000 members, and there are perhaps three times that number who, though not members, are in practise, most of them using the 'laying on of hands'.

The most famous of spiritualist healers, Harry Edwards, frequently allowed himself to be tested, sometimes in front of television cameras, with striking results. And his obvious integrity did much to reassure doctors, deeply suspicious though most of them remain, of spiritualist notions.

Imports from the East
The form of alternative medicine which has done most to upset preconceived orthodox opinions has been *acupuncture*. Until the 1960s it was usually dismissed as a primitive superstition which had happened to linger on in rural China. But teams of doctors from the West, originally invited by Mao Tse-tung to come and investigate it for themselves, have been forced to conclude that it works.

How it works remains a mystery. The Chinese explanation involves the life force—in this case believed to flow along channels called 'meridians'. The flow can be encouraged by pricking certain points on the surface of the body through which the meridians pass. Chinese charts show where to stick the needles, but these are only a rough guide, and Western acupuncturists have sometimes disagreed over the correct method of finding the exact location of the acupuncture points. In Western countries, acupuncture is most commonly used to treat disorders such as rheumatism, backache and headache, in cases where orthodox methods have had little success.

Acupuncture is not the only recent import from the East. Since the 1960s people have increasingly been turning to techniques of meditation, such as Yoga

Right: Where Western medicine remains largely unknown, the belief that spiritual or magical forces cause illness still lingers on. This witchdoctor from the Indonesian island of Bali is displaying a variety of herbal medicines. Some of the herbs are used because sick animals are seen to eat them and are thus thought to have natural healing powers. But to the islanders, the value of a medicine generally derives from its magical powers rather than from any physical effects it may have. In small communities, the witchdoctor may act as a social psychotherapist, mustering the goodwill of the community in aid of afflicted individuals. Since many illnesses are recognized to have a significant psychological component, the power of the witchdoctor to ease the mind of the sufferer has undoubted therapeutic value.

Below: In Western countries, herbalists have abandoned the idea that herbs are magical, but concentrate on accurately observing their effects. Here a herbal extract is to be examined for purity under a microscope. In contrast to orthodox medicine which tends to fight the symptoms of illness with the refined 'active' constituents of plants, herbalists stress the value of whole plant extracts as an aid to health generally.

Below right: Preventing illness, rather than curing it, is the aim in many Eastern countries This figure from the Bay of Bengal is believed to ward off the evil spirits that cause sickness.

ZEFA

Nursing Times

Alan Hutchison

Left: King Charles II touching a victim of 'King's Evil', a form of tuberculosis now called *scrofula*. British Kings descended from Louis IX of France (St Louis), via his great-great-grandson Edward III, were deemed capable of curing scrofula by a method similar to the Christian healing technique of the 'laying on of hands'. The Stuart kings were the last to practise this remarkable gift.

Right: A modern spiritual healer, the Irishman Finbarr Nolan. Born the seventh son of a seventh son, Nolan was virtually born to heal, according to Irish tradition. Some of his patients describe a tingling sensation when touched by him, and many spiritual healers report a 'vital force' that flows out of them during the healing process, which may be an as yet unexplained physical phenomenum. Doctors believe that many of the illnesses which spiritual healers claim to cure are *hysterical reactions*—disorders of the mind rather than the body—which are quite liable to disappear in a flash anyway. But most people who go to spiritual healers care little how or why they are cured as long as they are cured—and doctors do not deny that spiritual healers can be effective.

Below: These Sierra flowers are believed in Bolivia to be of use as abortificeants. Herbs used for this purpose are usually either ineffective, or highly dangerous, since they act by poisoning the embryo and may poison the mother at the same time. So folk medicines cannot always be trusted.

Mansell Collection

Les Wilson/Camera Press

Tony Morrison

and Zen, to provide a degree of mental control over the body which is thought to enable the individual to resist disease.

Here, too, orthodoxy's scepticism has been shaken by the discovery of the technique of *bio-feedback*. It has long been known that blood pressure rises with emotional tension, and falls with relaxation. The discovery that it is possible for a patient to monitor his own blood-pressure with the help of a machine, and thereby to work out suitable techniques of relaxation to keep his blood pressure down to acceptable levels, has given the esoteric cults a new clinical significance.

Prospects

If alternative medicine is to survive, much will depend on whether the medical profession introduces more flexible policies. Already, certain forms of treatment which might be otherwise regarded as 'alternative' have in fact been accorded recognition. Chiropodists and physiotherapists, for example, are recognized as para-medical allies. There is no reason why osteopaths, and acupuncturists should not acquire similar status.

There is increasing recognition that, for all its success in the recent past, allopathy has its drawbacks—the development of drug resistance in bacteria, for example, and the unwanted side effects, both short and long term, that sometimes arise from prolonged drug treatment. If orthodox medicine is eroded much further, the vitalist theories of alternative medicine may have to be re-examined, and some of them re-instated.

Index

cephalosporins 348
cerebellum *29, 37*, 38, *43*
cerebral cortex *37*
  fissures *37*
  hemispheres *43*, 339
cerebrum *29, 37*, 38
cervical cap contraceptive 271
  dilatation 277
  nerves 33
cervix, uterine 192
Chagas disease *366*
Chain, Ernest 347
chained actions learning 339
Charnley, John 386
chilblains 370
childbirth 207-11, 276
chiropractic 390
chloramphenicol 347
chloroform 384
chlorophyll 169
chlorpromazine 349
cholecystokinin 118, 122
cholera 368
cholesterol *61*, 118, 295
chorda tympani 112
chorion 200
chromatids 181
chromatin 180
chromosomes 173, 178, 187
  abnormal 216
  crossing over 215
  human 188, *189*
  sex determining 188, 212
  spermatogonia 191
  X 188, 212
  Y 188, 212
chyle 74, 295
chylomicrons 164, 295
chyme 116, 118
cilia, cellular 173
  Fallopian 197
  nasal 98
ciliary muscles, eye 13
cinchona bark 348
circadian rhythms 320
circulation of blood *58*, 63-5
circulo-respiratory efficiency 301
circumcision *250*
cirrhosis of liver 121
cisternae 177
classically conditioned learning 339
clavicle *51*
cleavage 197
climacteric 282
clitoris 266
clotting, blood, *61*, 62
cocaine 384
cocci 347
coccyx *51*
cochlea 20, *22*
codeine 348
coeliac plexus *35*
coenzyme *160*, 161, 175, 297
coitus interruptus 266
cold tolerance 316
collagen 50, 148, 167
collateral circulation 65
collective unconscious 355
colloid 92
colon 126
colostrum 210, 277
colour blindness 15, *215*
  vision 15
communication development 229-31
computer, brain analogy 39
concept 343

attainment 342
conception 191-5
condom 270
cones, light sensitive 14, 329
  development 221
congenital disorders 360
conjugated protein 169
constancy scaling, perceptual 333
constipation 129
contraception 270-3
contractile protein *290*
contractions, uterine 208, 277
convergent thinking 245
co-ordination *44*, 54-7
cornea 12
  grafting 13
corpus callosum *37, 43*, 339
  luteum 252
corpuscles, Meissner 24, *25*
  Pacinian 24, *25*
  red 60
  Ruffini 24, *25*
  white 60
cortex, adrenal 207
  cerebral 40
  kidney 131
  visual 329
Corti, organ of 22, 23
corticosteroids 207
cortisol 92
cosmetic surgery 387
cough reflex 101
  suppressants 348
cranium *50, 51*
crawling reflex *223*
creative thinking 343
cristae 174
crossing over chromosomes 215
crying behaviour 222
  communication 229
cryoprobes 384
crystallized intelligence 245
curare 49, 384
Cushing's syndrome 309
cyanosis 103
cyclizine 348
cyst *371*
cytochromes 169
cytoplasm 172, *178*
cytosine 178

D

Davey, Humphry 384
Da Vinci, Leonardo *328*
deafness 22-3
De Bono, Edward 343
decompression sickness 69, 319
decibels *21*
decision making 341, 342
defaecation 129
defence mechanisms 353
degenerative diseases 361
dehydration 141
dehydrogenases 161
dementia 351
denatured protein 159, 169
dendrites 28, 38
dental caries 356
  plaque 357
dentine 357
Denys, Jean-Baptiste *72*
deoxyribonucleic acid 173, 175, 178, 187
depressive illness 352

depth perception 221
dermatitis 372
dermis 148
development, infant 220-7
diabetes 94
  insipidus 135
diagnosis 380-3
  infertility 268
  respiratory disorders 104
dialysis 137
diaphragm 100
  contraceptive 270
diarrhoea 129
diasonograph *383*
diastole 80
diastolic blood pressure 65, 381
diathermy 384
diet, balanced 291
  low calorie 311
diffusion process 67
digestion 110-117
  drugs affecting 348
digestive juices 122
digits *51*
dilatation, cervix 277
diphtheria 368
diplopia *14*
disaccharide 163, 295
distal convoluted tubule 132
diuretics 135, 141, 348
divergent thinking 245
diverticulosis 298
dizygotic twins *268*
DNA *see* deoxyribonucleic acid 173
dominant genes 212
double helix 178
  vision *14*
Domagk, G. 347
Down's syndrome 216, 361
dreams 327
  psychoanalysis 355
droplet infections 366
drugs, addictive 348
  analgesic 348
  anticonvulsant 351
  antipyretic 348
  medicinal *344, 346*, 347-9
  resistance 347
ductus arteriosus 203, 210, 386
  venosus 203, 210
duodenum 117, 118
dust deseases 102
Dutch cap 270
dysmenorrhoea 254
dyspepsia *114*, 116
  aspirin-caused 348
dyspnoea 103

E

ear canal 20
  structure 20, *21*
Ebola disease 364, 366
eccrine glands 151
ECG *see* electrocardiograph
ECT *see* electroconvulsive therapy
ectoderm, embyonic 200
ectomorph *309*
eczema *372*
Edwards, Harry 390
EEG *see* electroencephalograph
efferent nerve fibres 28
Ehrlich, Paul 79, 347
Einstein, Albert 340

elastin 148
electrical brain activity 37
electrocardiograph *84*, 383
electro-convulsive therapy 352
electrodes, diagnostic 383
  insertion in cortex 40
electroencephalograph *41*, 324, 383
electron transport chain 176
eleidin 148
embolism, arterial 387
embryo development *198*, 200
enamel, dental 357
encephalitis 368
endemic diseases 366
endocrine glands 88
  drugs affecting 348
endoderm, embryonic 200
endogenous depression 352
endometrium 197, 252
endomorph *309*
endoplasmic reticulum 171
endothelium 67
energy 159
  dietary 293
  expenditure *294*
  flow *170*
  release 175
  requirement 293
  supply 301
environmental hygiene 373
enzymes 60, 160, 166
epidemic diseases 366
epidermis 148
epididymus 249, *266*
epiglottis 98, *105*
epilepsy 43, 351
epiphyseal plate *50*
epiphyses 250
erectile tissue 266
eructation 115
erythrocytes 169
erythema aboigne 370
  pernio 370
essential amino acids 289
Estcourt, Nick 317
ether 384
Eustachian tube 20
excretory system, drugs affecting 348
exercise 304-7
exocrine glands 88
exogenous depression 352
expectorants 348
exposure 307
extension, muscular *47*
extracellular fluid 30, 139
eye, foetal formation 205
  structure 12, *13*

F

Factor VIII 62
faeces 126
fainting 69
faith healing 390
Fallopian tubes 192, 253
false teeth 358
family relationships 236
farmer's lung 103
fatigue 57
fats 162
  digestion 164
  dietary 295
  structure 164
femur 50, *51*
fertility drugs 268